JOHN WILLIS

SCREEN

WORLD

1988

Volume 39

CROWN PUBLISHERS, INC.

NEW YORK

with Rod LaRocque
in "The Locked Door"
1929

with Ralph Graves
in "Ladies of Leisure"
1930

The "Miracle Woman"
1931

with Adolphe Menjou
in "Forbidden"
1932

"So Big"
1932

with Joel McCrea
in "Gambling Lady"
1934

"Annie Oakley"
1935

"Stella Dallas"
1937

with William Holden
in "Golden Boy"
1939

with Gary Cooper
in "Ball of Fire"
1942

with Fred MacMurray
in "Double Indemnity"
1944

with Van Heflin
in "The Strange Love of
Martha Ivers" 1946

"Sorry Wrong Number"
1948

with Walter Huston
in "The Furies"
1950

with Clark Gable
in "To Please a Lady"
1950

2

| Ruby Stevens 1908 | 1929 | 1932 | 1955 | 1962 |

TO

BARBARA STANWYCK

whose appearance, in either comic or tragic roles, has been thoroughly professional, emotionally honest, skillfully and realistically portrayed, critically praised, and gratefully enshrined in the memories of her millions of adoring fans.

FILMS: Broadway Nights (1927), The Locked Door, Mexicali Rose, Ladies of Leisure, Illicit, Ten Cents a Dance, Night Nurse, The Miracle Woman, Forbidden, Shopworn, So Big, The Purchase Price, The Bitter Tea of General Yen, Ladies They Talk About, Baby Face, Ever in My Heart, Gambling Lady, A Lost Lady, The Secret Bride, The Woman in Red, Red Salute, Annie Oakley, A Message to Garcia, The Bride Walks Out, His Brother's Wife, Banjo on My Knee, The Plough and the Stars, Interns Can't Take Money, This Is My Affair, Stella Dallas, Breakfast for Two, Always Goodbye, The Mad Miss Manton, Union Pacific, Golden Boy, Remember the Night, The Lady Eve, Meet John Doe, You Belong to Me, Ball of Fire, The Great Man's Lady, The Gay Sisters, Lady of Burlesque, Flesh and Fantasy, Double Indemnity, Hollywood Canteen, Christmas in Connecticut, My Reputation, The Bride Wore Boots, The Strange Love of Martha Ivers, California, The Two Mrs. Carrolls, The Other Love, Cry Wolf, B. F.'s Daughter, Sorry Wrong Number, The Lady Gambles, East Side West Side, Thelma Jordan, No Man of Her Own, The Furies, To Please a Lady, The Man with a Cloak, Clash by Night, Jeopardy, Titanic, All I Desire, The Moonlighter, Blowing Wild, Witness to Murder, Executive Suite, Cattle Queen of Montana, The Violent Men, Escape to Burma, There's Always Tomorrow, The Maverick Queen, These Wilder Years, Crime of Passion, Trooper Hook, Forty Guns, Walk on the Wild Side, Roustabout, The Night Walker (1965)

| 1987 | with Robert Ryan in "Clash by Night" 1952 | with Ronald Reagan in "Cattle Queen of Montana" 1954 | with Elvis Presley in "Roustabout" 1964 |

(standing) Ann Sothern, Vincent Price, (seated) Lillian Gish, Bette Davis
in "Whales of August"
© *Alive Films*

CONTENTS

EDITOR: JOHN WILLIS

Assistant Editors: Barry Monush, Stanley Reeves, Walter Willison

Staff: Marco Starr Boyajian, William Camp, Mark Cohen, Mark Gladstone,
Miles Kreuger, Jerry Lacker, Tom Lynch, Giovanni Romero, John Sala, Van Williams
Designer: Peggy Goddard

Acknowledgments: This volume would not be possible without the cooperation of Ian Abrams, Stacy Adams, Marlene Adelstein, Gary Aldeman, Tom Allen, Jane Alsobrook, Eden Ashley, David Badagliacca, Fred Baker, Nina Baron, David Bass, Karen Basto, Mike Berman, Jim Bertges, Marion Billings, Seymour Borde, Michael Brady, Joseph Brenner, Susan Brockman, Michael Broidy, Donette Brown, Don Buckley, Ken Burns, John Calhoun, Fabiano Canosa, Philip Castanza, Helen Cavanaugh, Rita Chambers, Howard Cherman, Phyllis Ciccone, Anne Cochran, Ben Commack, Robert Conkling, Bill Connelly, Karen Cooper, Gary Croudus, Lynne Dahlgren, Alberta D'Angelo, James Darbinian, Ira Deutchman, Donna Dickman, Anne Dillon, Michael Donnelly, Bob Dorfman, Dennis Dorph, Betty Einbinder, Allison Enelio, Catherine Ericson, Steve Fagan, Suzanne Fedak, Al Finley, Mary Lou Finnin, Elliott Fishoff, Rodman Flender, Peter Flynn, Dom Frascella, Renee Furst, Glennis Gold, Ted Goldberg, Thomas Grane, Joseph Green, Loritta Green, Christina Haller, Lisa Halliday, Mark Halpern, Allison Hanau, Peter Haas, Richard Hassanein, Ted Hatfield, Stan Hayes, Amy Heller, Gary Hertz, Lauren Hyman, Lloyd Ibert, Sam Irvin, Jeffrey Jacobs, Michael Jeck, Jim Jeneji, Terry Johnson, Stephen Jones, Andy Kaplan, Mike Kaplan, Steve Kasloff, Helen Kavanaugh, Michael Kelly, Bill Kenly, Ken Kenyon, Thomas Keough, Allison Kossow, Ziggy Kozlowski, Don Krim, Richard Kronberg, Jack Kurnes, Ann Lander, Maryanne Lataif, Lori Long, Wynn Lowenthal, Peter Lowry, Arlene Ludwig, Jeff Mackler, Steve Mackler, Cathy Magill, Howard Mahler, Craig Marks, Barbara Marshall, Ed Martin, Jane Martin, Pricilla McDonald, Jeff McKay, Blanca Merced, Lou Morino, Paul Mowry, Robert Newcombe, Bill O'Connell, Kevan Olesen, Ivy Orfa, Mario Ortiz, Sue Oscar, Cynthia Parsons, Chris Paton, Janet Perlberg, Brenda Perry, John Pierson, Jim Poling, Heather Probert, Gerald Rappoport, Jackie Rayanal, David Restivo, David Rice, Ruth Robbins, Reid Rosefelt, Melisa Rosen, Richard Rosenberg, Kelly Ross, Mary Runsen, Ed Russell, Cindy Ryfle, Suzanne Salter, Carl Samrock, Jeff Saxon, Les Schecter, Barbara Schwei, George Schrul, Russell Schwartz, Mike Scrimenti, Eve Segal, Ron Sherwin, Jacqueline Sigmund, Marcia Silen, Michael Silverman, Stephen Soba, Fran Speelman, Barbara Sperry, Alicia Springer, John Springer, Anne Marie Stein, Larry Steinfeld, Moira Stokes, Stuart Strutin, Ken Stutz, Sarah Talbot, John Tilley, Maureen Tolsdorf, Bruce Trinz, Mary Vole, Debbie von Aherns, Marc Weiss, Cara White, David Whitten, Christopher Wood, David Wright, Jane Wright, Stuart Zakim, Michael Zuker

1. Eddie Murphy

2. Michael Douglas

3. Michael J. Fox

4. Arnold Schwarzenegger

5. Paul Hogan

6. Tom Cruise

7. Glenn Close

8. Sylvester Stallone

9. Cher

10. Mel Gibson

11. Patrick Swayze

12. Kathleen Turner

13. Clint Eastwood

14. Tom Selleck

15. Bette Midler

16. Danny DeVito

TOP BOX OFFICE STARS OF 1987

(Tabulated by Quigley Publications)

17. Steve Martin

18. John Candy

19. Meryl Streep

20. Kevin Costner

1987 RELEASES

January 1 through December 31, 1987

21. Jack Nicholson

22. Dan Aykroyd

23. Richard Dreyfuss

24. William Hurt

25. Harrison Ford

Whoopi Goldberg

Paul Newman

Sigourney Weaver

CRITICAL CONDITION

(PARAMOUNT) Producers, Ted Field, Robert Cort; Director, Michael Apted; Story, Denis Hamill, John Hamill, Alan Swyer; Screenplay, Denis Hamill, John Hamill; Executive Producer, Bob Larson; Photography, Ralf D. Bode; Designer, John Lloyd; Editor, Robert K. Lambert; Music, Alan Silvestri; Costumes, Colleen Atwood; Casting, Margery Simkin, Shari Rhodes; Associate Producer, Eric Lerner; Production Manager, Robert E. Larson; Assistant Directors, Robert V. Girolami, Louis D'Esposito, Jane Paul; Production Associate, Ann Pollack; Stunts, David Ellis; Sound, Willie Burton; Set Decorator, George Robert Nelson; Special Effects, Joe Unsinn, Stan Amborn, John Bruce Robels, Jim Fredberg: Orchestrations, James B. Campbell; Set Designer, Steven Schwartz; Song, Rick James; Technicolor; Rated R; 100 minutes; January release

CAST

Eddie/Kevin	Richard Pryor
Rachel	Rachel Ticotin
Louis	Ruben Blades
Chambers	Joe Mantegna
Dr. Foster	Bob Dishy
Maggie	Sylvia Miles
Stucky	Joe Dallesandro
Box	Randall "Tex" Cobb
Dr. Joffe	Bob Saget
Palazzi	Joseph Ragno
Kline	Jon Polito
Helicopter Junkie	Garrett Morris
Tommy Pinto	Brian Tarantina
Jack Kinney	Jude Ciccolella
Dr. Hoffman	Cigdem Onat
Fido	Lucius Houghton
Prosecutor	Joe Aufiery
Nurse Mary	Kate McGregor-Stewart
Jackson	Randell Haynes
Reggie	Al White

and Marquerita Wallace, Manera Smith, Verna Hampton, Lou Walker, Doris Dworsky, Denis Hamill, John Hamill, Ralf D. Bode, Ann Pollack, Miriam Cruz, Teresa Yenque, Wesley Snipes, Mike Silver, Kevin Campbell, Mel Shrawder, Larry Graves, Jack Hallett, Michael Medeiros, Keith Roberts, Karen Jones-Meadows, Feiga Martinez, Elizabeth Arlen, Peg Banesse, Joe Rivers, Clifford Jackson, Lara Marshall, Leroy Staples, Johnny Howie, Steve Boles, John Woodson, Ben Moore, Jeffrey Pillars, Joseph Coscia, Del Roy, Laura Bastianelli, Lee Lawrence, Geoff Gordon, Ron Amari, Raymond Rosario, Larry Kirsc, Steve Davison, Tim A. Davison, Richard Miller Ellis, Robert V. Girolami, Diane Hetfield, Buddy Joe Hooker, Rashon Khan, John Larson, Alan Oliney, Ron Oliney, Jackie Resch, John Sherrod, David Welch

Right: Rachel Ticotin, Richard Pryor, Randall "Tex" Cobb, Above: Richard Pryor, Ruben Blades Top: Feiga Martinez, Sylvia Miles, Rachel Ticotin, Bob Dishy
© Paramount/Bob Fletcher

Bob Dishy, Richard Pryor, Bob Saget

Roger Pryor, Lucius Houghton

ASSASSINATION

(CANNON GROUP) Producer, Pancho Kohner; Director, Peter Hunt; Screenplay, Richard Sale; Executive Producers, Menahem Golan, Yoram Globus; Photography, Hanania Baer; Designer, William Cruise; Music, Robert Ragland, Valentine McCallum; Editor, James Heckert; Production Managers, George Van Hoy, Barbara Michaels; Assistant Directors, Craig Huston, Terence D. Buchinsky, Robert C. Ortwin Jr.; Production Executive, Ronny Yacov; Casting, Perry Bullington; Art Director, Joshua S. Culp; Sound, Thomas Brandau; Set Decorator, Patricia Hall; Costumes, Shelley Komarov; Production Coordinator, Jeanne M. O'Brien; Special Effects, Pioneer FX, Inc, Melbourne A. Arnold, John Hixson, Jr., Daniel H. Lott, Jr.; Musical Supervisor, Paula Erickson; Stunts, Jack Gill; TVC Color; Rated PG-13; 88 minutes; January release

CAST

Jay Killian	Charles Bronson
Lara Royce Craig	Jill Ireland
Fitzroy	Stephen Elliott
Charlotte Chang	Jan Gan Boyd
Tyler Loudermilk	Randy Brooks
Reno Bracken	Erik Stern
Senator Bunsen	Michael Ansara
Briggs	James Staley
Polly Sims	Kathryn Leigh Scott
Osborne Weems	James Acheson
"The Zipper"	Jim McMullan
Pritchard Young	H. H. Royce
President Calvin Craig	Charles Howerton
Chief Justice	Chris Alcaide
Kerry Fane	Jack Gill
Danzig	Mischa Hausserman
Finney	Robert Axelrod
TV Announcer	Peter Lupus
Female TV Reporter	Lori Stephens
June Merkel	Beverly Thompson
Claire Thompson	Natalie Alexander
Sally Moore	Linda Harwood
Reporter	Mihoko Tokoro
Journalist	Susan J. Thompson
Barstow	Arthur Hansel
Platt	John Salvi

and Frank Zagarino, Tony Borgia, Paul McCallum, Robert Dowdell, Vivian Tyus, Jason Scura, David L. Bilson, Larry Sellers, Elizabeth Lauren, Lucille Bliss, John Hawker, J. Michael Patterson, James Clark, Ed Levitt, Michael Welden, Jack Gill, Clayton D. Wright

Top: Jill Ireland Right: Jan Gan Boyd, James Acheson, Charles Bronson, Jim McMullan, Randy Brooks, James Staley Below: Ireland, Bronson © Cannon

Charles Bronson, Jan Gan Boyd
Above: Bronson, Jill Ireland

9

THE BEDROOM WINDOW

(DE LAURENTIIS ENTERTAINMENT GROUP) Producer, Martha Schumacher; Director/Screenplay, Curtis Hanson; Based on the novel *The Witnesses* by Anne Holden; Executive Producer, Robert Towne; Photography, Gil Taylor; Editor, Scott Conrad; Music, Michael Shrieve, Patrick Gleeson; Costumes, Clifford Capone; Designer, Ron Foreman; Casting, Mary Colquhoun; Production Managers, Richard Prince, Marilyn Stonehouse; Assistant Directors, Jose Lopez Rodero, Katy Emde, Leigh Webb, Barbara Bruno; Art Director, Rafael Caro; Set Decorator, Hilton Rosemarin; Sound, Billy Daly; Assistant Set Decorator, Michael Anderson; Production Coordinator, Angela Heald; Stunts, Thomas Rosales; Special Effects, Ray Massara, Marty Bresin, Greg Hull, Lynn Dodson, Special Effects Unlimited, Inc.: Songs, Raun & Jon Butcher, and various other artists; Technicolor; Panavision; Rated R; 112 minutes; January release

CAST

Terry Lambert	Steve Guttenberg
Denise	Elizabeth McGovern
Sylvia	Isabelle Huppert
Collin	Paul Shenar
Quirke	Carl Lumbly
Henderson's Attorney	Wallace Shawn
Jessup	Frederick Coffin
Henderson	Brad Greenquist
State Attorney Peters	Robert Schenkkan
Pool Player	Maury Chaykin
Dancing Girl	Sara Carlson
Man in phone booth	Mark Margolis
Blowsy Neighbor	Kate McGregor-Stewart
Judge	Penelope Allen
Maid	Myvanwy Jenn
Bartender at Edgar's	Francis V. Guinan, Jr.
Policemen	Kevin O'Rourke, Richard McGough
First Victim	Sydney Conrad
Receptionist	Wendy Womble
Secretary	Libba Marrian
Usher	Scott Colson
Man in theatre	Carl Whitney
Cocktail Waitress	Jodi Long
Late Night Shopper	Richard Olsen
Seedy Bartender	Leon Rippy

and John Patrick Maloney, Kerry Lang, J. Michael Hunter, Joyce Flick Wendl, Joyce Greer, Winston Hemingway, Michael Lynn Burgess, J. Rich Leonard, Craig Jahelka, Tobi Marsh

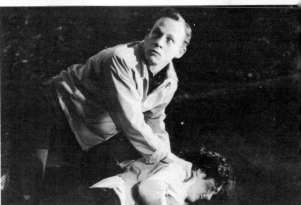

Steve Guttenberg, Elizabeth McGovern Above: Brad Greenquist, Elizabeth McGovern
Top Right: Isabelle Huppert, Steve Guttenberg © *DEG*

ALLAN QUATERMAIN AND THE LOST CITY OF GOLD

(CANNON) Producers, Menahem Golan, Yoram Globus; Director, Gary Nelson; Screenplay, Gene Quintano; Based on the classic novel by H. Rider Haggard; Executive Producer, Avi Lerner; Line Producer, Michael Greenburg; Editor, Alain Jakubowicz; Music, Michael Linn; Designer, Trevor Williams; Photography, Alex Phillips, Fred Elmes; Costumes, Marianne Fassler; Supervisor, John Stodel; Additional Scenes Director, Newt Arnold; Assistant Directors, Tony Tarruella, Nicholas Batchelor, Steve Fillis, Steve Chigorimbo, Douglas G. Gardner; Set Decorators, Patrick Willis, Portia Iversen; Special Effects Make-up, Colin Arthur; Flying Effects, Kevin Mathews; Sound, Mark Ulano; Special Effects, Eric Allard, Rick Hill, Al Brousard, Scott Forbes, Tom Pahk, Stuart Ziff, Germano Natali; Color; Ultrastereo; Rated PG; 103 minutes; January release

CAST

Allan Quatermain	Richard Chamberlain
Jesse Huston	Sharon Stone
Umslopogaas	James Earl Jones
Agon	Henry Silva
Swarma	Robert Donner
Nasta	Doghmi Larbi
Nyleptha	Aileen Marson
Sorais	Cassandra Peterson
Robeson Quatermain	Martin Rabbett
Dumont	Rory Kilalea
Dutchman	Alex Heyns
Nurse	Themsi Times
Bartender	Philip Boucher
Trader	Stuart Goakes
Eshowe Warrior Chief	Fidelis Cheza
Toothless Arab	Nic Lesley
George	George Chiota

Right: Sharon Stone, Richard Chamberlain
Top: James Earl Jones, Sharon Stone, Richard
Chamberlain © *Cannon*

James Earl Jones, Martin Rabbett, Richard Chamberlain, Sharon Stone

RADIO DAYS

(ORION) Producer, Robert Greenhut; Director/Screenplay, Woody Allen; Executive Producers, Jack Rollins, Charles H. Joffe; Photography, Carlo Di Palma; Designer, Santo Loquasto; Editor, Susan E. Morse; Costumes, Jeffrey Kurland; Casting, Juliet Taylor; Musical Supervision, Dick Hyman; Associate Producers, Ezra Swerdlow, Gail Sicilia; Production Manager, Thomas Reilly; Assistant Directors, Ezra Swerdlow, Ken Ornstein; Production Coordinator, Helen Robin; Production Associate, Joseph Hartwick; Assistant Art Directors, W. Steven Graham, Dan Davis, Tom Warren, Michael Smith, Randall Drake, Steve Saklad; Set Decorators, Carol Joffe, Les Bloom; Sound, James Sabat, Louis Sabat, Frank Graziadei, Lee Dichter; Assistant Costume Designer, Judiana Makovsky; Assistant Editors, Martin Levenstein, Jon Newburger; Casting Associate, Ellen Lewis; Additional Casting, Todd M. Thaler; DuArt Color; Rated PG; 90 minutes; January release

CAST

(in order of appearance)

Woody Allen (Narrator), Mike Starr, Paul Herman (Burglars), Don Pardo ("Guess That Tune" Host), Martin Rosenblatt (Needleman), Helen Miller (Mrs. Needleman), Danielle Ferland (Child Star), Julie Kavner (Mother), Julie Kurnitz (Irene), David Warrilow (Roger), Wallace Shawn (Masked Avenger), Michael Murray (Avenger Crook), William Flanagan (Avenger Announcer), Seth Green (Joe), Michael Tucker (Father), Josh Mostel (Abe), Renee Lippin (Ceil), William Magerman (Grandpa), Leah Carrey (Grandma), Joy Newman (Ruthie), Hy Anzell (Waldbaum), Judith Malina (Mrs. Waldbaum), Dianne Wiest (Bea), Fletcher Farrow Previn (Andrew), Oliver Block (Nick), Maurice Toueg (Dave), Sal Tuminello (Burt), Rebecca Nickels (Evelyn Goorwitz), Mindy Morgenstern ("Show & Tell" Teacher), David Mosberg (Arnold), Ross Morgenstern (Ross), Kenneth Mars (Rabbi Baumel), Andrew Clark (Sidney Manulis), Mia Farrow (Sally White), Lee Erwin (Roller Rink Organist), Roger Hammer (Richard), Terry Lee Swarts, Margaret Thomson (Nightclub Customers), Tito Puente (Bandleader), Denise Dummont (Latin Singer), Dimitri Vassilopoulos (Portirio), Larry David (Communist Neighbor), Rebecca Schaeffer (Communist's Daughter), Belle Berger (Mrs. Silverman), Guy LeBow (Bill Kern), Brian Mannain (Kirby Kyle), Stan Burns (Ventriloquist), Todd Field (Crooner), Peter Lombard (Abercrombie Host), Martin Sherman (Mr. Abercrombie), Crystal Field, Maurice Shrog (Abercrombie Couple), Marc Colner (Whiz Kid), Roberta Bennett (Teacher with carrot), Joel Eidelsberg (Zipsky), Danny Aiello (Rocco), Peter Castellotti (Davis), Gina DeAngelis (Rocco's Mother), Shelley Delaney (Chekhov Actress), Dwight Weiss (Pearl Harbor Announcer), Ken Levinsky, Ray Marchica (USO Musicians), Jeff Daniels (Biff Baxter), J. R. Horne (Biff Announcer), Kuno Spunholz (German), Henry Yuk (Japanese), Sydney A. Blake (Miss Gordon), Kitty Carlisle Hart (Radio Singer), Robert Joy (Fred), Henry Cowen (Principal), Philip Shultz (Whistler), Mercedes Ruehl, Bruce Jarchow (Ad Men), Greg Gerard (Songwriter), David Cale (Director), Ira Wheeler (Sponsor), Hannah Rabinowitz (Sponsor's Wife), Edward S. Kotkin (Diction Teacher), Ruby Payne, Jaqui Safra (Diction Students), Paul Berman (Gay White Way Announcer), Richard Portnow (Sy), Tony Roberts ("Silver Dollar" M.C.), Barbara Gallo, Jane Jarvis, Liz Vochecowizc (Dance Palace Musicians), Ivan Kronenfeld (On-the-Spot-Newsman), Frank O'Brien (Fireman), Yolanda Childress (Polly's Mother), Atie Butler (New Year's Bandleader), Diane Keaton (New Year's Singer), and Greg Almquist, Jackson Beck, Wendell Craig, W. H. Macy, Ken Roberts, Norman Rose, Kenneth Welsh

Top Left: Dianne Wiest, Robert Joy Below: Julie Kavner, Seth Green, Michael Tucker © *Orion/Brian Hamill*

Dianne Wiest Above: David Warrilow, Mia Farrow

Front: William Magerman, Seth Green, Leah Carrey Rear: Michael Tucker, Julie Kavner, Dianne Wiest, Joy Newman, Renee Lippin, Josh Mostel Above: (L) Michael Tucker, Julie Kavner (R) Josh Mostel Top: (L) Diane Keaton (R) Tony Roberts, Dianne Wiest © *Orion/Brian Hamill*

OUTRAGEOUS FORTUNE

(TOUCHSTONE) Producers, Ted Field, Robert W. Cort; Director, Arthur Hiller; Screenplay, Leslie Dixon; Co-Producers, Peter V. Herald, Scott Kroopf, Martin Mickelson; Photography, David M. Walsh; Designer, James D. Vance; Editor, Tom Rolf; Costumes, Gloria Gresham; Music, Alan Silvestri; Casting, Lynn Stalmaster & Associates, Mally Finn; Production Manager, Peter V. Herald; Assistant Directors, Jim Van Wyck, Bruce Allen Humphrey, Princess McLean, Robert Roda; Set Decorator, Rick T. Gentz; Art Director, Sandy Veneziano; Set Designer, Daniel Maltese; Assistant Editors, Mellissa Bretherton, Jean Caperonis; Sound, Gerald Jost; Production Coordinator, Chip Fowler; Special Effects, Dennis Dion; Visual Effects, Michael Lloyd, Bob Scifo, Phill Huff, Steve Rundell; Stunts, Glenn R. Wilder; Dolby Stereo; Color; Rated R; 100 minutes; January release

CAST

Sandy	Bette Midler
Lauren	Shelley Long
Michael	Peter Coyote
Stanislov Korzenowski	Robert Prosky
Atkins	John Schuck
Frank	George Carlin
Weldon	Anthony Heald
Cab Driver	Ji-Tu Cumbuka
Ticket Agent	Florence Stanley
Tobacco Clerk	Jerry Zaks
Police Lieutenant	John Di Santi
Madam	Diana Bellamy
Panansky	Gary Morgan
George	Chris McDonald
Dealer	J. W. Smith, Robert Pastorelli
Russell	Tony Epper
Boyd	Bill Hart
Actress	Sally R. Brown
Receptionist	Carol Ann Susi
Coroner	R. G. Clayton
Helicopter Pilot	Donald Ambabo
Airport Attendant	Paul Brooks
Airport Woman	Barbara De Kins
Security Officer Brown	Thomas Dillon
Newswoman	Sandra Eng
Vasily	Tom Lillard
Eddie	Steven Rotblatt

and Debra A. Deliso, Roger Engstrom, James Espinoza, Barney Garcia, Jose G. Garcia, Mike Henry, Neil Hunt, Coral Kassek, James McIntire, Joan McMurtrey, Greg Mace, Tammy Manville, Bill Marcus, Phil Mead, J. Clell Miller, Lonna Montrose, Bob O'Connell, Johnny Sanchez, Pat Santino,, Ade Small, Ebbe Roe Smith, Bunny Summers, Anna Marie Wieder, Eyan Williams

Top: Bette Midler (R) Shelley Long, Peter Coyote
Below: Shelley Long, Bette Midler
© *Touchstone/Laurel Moore*

George Carlin, Bette Midler, and
above with Shelley Long

THE STEPFATHER

(NEW CENTURY/VISTA) Producer, Jay Benson; Director, Joseph Ruben; Screenplay, Donald E. Westlake; Story, Donald E. Westlake, Carolyn Lefcourt, Brian Garfield; Photography, John W. Lindley; Editor, George Bowers; Music, Patrick Moraz; Sound, Larry Sutton; Designer, James Newton Westport; Art Director, David Wilson; Set Decorator, Kimberly Richardson; Assistant Director, Michael Steele; Production Manager, Warren Carr; Casting, Mike Fenton, Jane Feinberg, Judy Taylor, Sid Kozak; An ITC Production; Color; Ultra-Stereo; Rated R; 98 minutes; January release

CAST

Jerry Blake	Terry O'Quinn
Stephanie Maine	Jill Schoelen
Susan Blake	Shelley Hack
Jim Ogilvie	Stephen Shellen
Dr. Bondurant	Charles Lanyer

Jeff Schulz, Jill Schoelen, Shelley Hack, Terry O'Quinn
Top Right: Charles Lanyer, Jill Schoelen
© *ITC Productions*

TOUCH AND GO

(TRI-STAR) Producer, Stephen Friedman; Director, Robert Mandel; Screenplay, Alan Ormsby, Bob Sand, Harry Colomby; Executive Producer, Harry Colomby; Photography, Richard H. Kline; Designer, Charles Rosen; Production Executive/Production Manager, Jack Grossberg; Casting, Penny Perry, Deborah Brown; Music, Sylvester Levay; Editor, Walt Mulconery; Assistant Directors, Paul Deason, Gary Daigler, Katterli Frauenfelder; Sound, Arthur Rochester, Glenn Williams; Set Decorators, James Payne, Jean Alan; Costumes, Bernie Pollack; Additional Editors, Jere Huggins, Anne Goursaud; Assistant Editors, Michael Mulconery, Richard Alderete; Production Coordinators, Barbara Spitz, Nancy Rae Stone, Linda Toner; Stunts, Bill Couch; Songs, Richard Page, Steve George, John Lang, Greg Phillinganes, Nathan East, and other artists; Technicolor; Rated R; 111 minutes; January release

CAST

Bobby Barbato	Michael Keaton
Denise DeLeon	Maria Conchita Alonso
Louis DeLeon	Ajay Naidu
Jerry Pepper	John Reilly
Dee Dee	Maria Tucci
Gower	Richard Venture
Lester	Max Wright
McDonald	Michael Zelniker
Levesque	Jere Burns
Lupo	D. V. deVincentis
Lynch	Denis Duffy
Green	Steve Pink
Courtney	Lara Jill Miller

and Clair Dolan, Carri Lynn Levinson, Charlotte Ross, Jean Bates, Lynda Weisneir, Cynthia Cypert, Earl Boen, Ed Meekin, Nick DeMauro, Ron Stokes, Richard McNally, Marc Jacobs, Ford Lile, Ron Presson, Drake Collier, Alex Ross, Jean Larette, Bill Morrison, Ron Pace, Kristin Collins York, Jack White, Michael F. Kelly, Steve Giannelli, Scott Berg, Kevin Boike, Luc Boileau, Vincent Carter, Bob Clasby, Claude Cohen, Craig Daniger, John Blom, Dan Miller, Mark Nahan, Louis Nicholai, Jon Scott Rayfield, Eric Repas, J. Paul Timmons, Victor Venasky, Mike Wehrman, Robert Udell, Adam Peck, Eric Troy Adams, Robert Bayer, Steve Cameron, Allan Cleland, Dan Coburn, Craig Cullen, Robert Destocki, Dennis Gilbert, Jay Green, Ian Hendry, Blair Hughes, Tim Jarvi, Stephen Kelly, Michael Koble, Mike McGee, Edward Mertz, Douglas Newsham, Rico Roth, Steve Zavislak, Wayne McGinnis, Joseph Miazowics, Tim O'Donnell

Top Right: Michael Keaton, Ajay Naidu
Below: Maria Conchita Alonso, Michael Keaton
© Tri-Star Pictures

Tawny Kitaen

WITCHBOARD

(CINEMA GROUP) Producer, Gerald Geoffray; Director/Screenplay, Kevin S. Tenney; Executive Producer, Walter Josten; Associate Producer, Roland Carroll; Supervising Producer, Ron Mitchell; Photography, Roy H. Wagner; Art Director, Sarah Burdick; Costumes, Merrill Greene; Casting, Rebecca Boss; Editors, Daniel Duncan, Stephen J. Waller; Sound, Lee Haxall; Music, Dennis Michael Tenney; Theme performed by Steel Breeze; Theme, Dennis Michael Tenney; Assistant Directors, Robin Jones, Chris Medak, Terry Edwards; Production Coordinator, Lesli J. Lehr; Production Manager, William R. Wright, Jr.; Special Effects, Tassilo Baur, Lewis Abernathy, John Cork, Bruce Scivally, Mick Strawn; Stunts, Chuck Couch, Buck McDancer; Assistant Art Director, Pola Shrieber; Associate Producers, Patricia Bando-Josten, Donna Reynolds, Bolton Sullivan; Color; Rated R; 98 minutes; January release

CAST

Jim Morar	Todd Allen
Linda Brester	Tawny Kitaen
Brandon Sinclair	Steven Nichols
Zarabeth	Kathleen Wilhoite
Lt. Dewhurst	Burke Byrnes
Mrs. Moses	Rose Marie
Lloyd	James W. Quinn
Dr. Gelineau	Judy Tatum
Wanda	Gloria Hayes
Malfeitor	J. P. Luebsen
Chris	Susan Nickerson
Roger	Ryan Carroll
Mike	Kenny Rhodes
Anchorman	Clare Bristol

BLACK WIDOW

(20th CENTURY FOX) Producer, Harold Schneider; Director, Bob Rafelson; Screenplay, Ronald Bass; Executive Producer, Laurence Mark; Photography, Conrad L. Hall; Designer, Gene Callahan; Editor, John Bloom; Costumes, Patricia Norris; Casting, Terry Liebling; Music, Michael Small; Production Manager, Harold Schneider; Assistant Directors, Tommy Thompson, Nilo Otero; Makeup Design, Dorothy Pearl; Set Decorators, Jim Duffy, Buck Henshaw, Rick Simpson; Additional Music, Peter Rafelson; Sound, David MacMillan; Special Effects, Allen Hall, Jerry Williams; Production Coordinator, Patty Raya; Casting Assistant, Lora Kennedy; In association with Amercent Films and American Entertainment Partners L.P.; Dolby Stereo; De-Luxe Color; Rated R; 103 minutes; February release

CAST

Alexandra	Debra Winger
Catharine	Theresa Russell
Paul	Sami Frey
Ben	Dennis Hopper
William Macauley	Nicol Williamson
Bruce	Terry O'Quinn
Sara	Lois Smith
Michael	D. W. Moffett
Ricci	Leo Rossi
Shelley	Mary Woronov
Irene	Rutanya Alda
Shin	James Hong
Etta	Diane Ladd
Etta's Husband	Wayne Heffley
Martin (Houston Attorney)	Raleigh Bond
Reporter	Donegan Smith
Detective	Danny Kamekona
Artie	Christian Clemenson
Tran	Arsenio "Sonny" Trinidad
Attorney	Thomas Hill
Dawn	Darrah Meeley
James	Johnny "Sugarbear" Willis
Young Girl	Kathleen Hall
Italian Man	George Ricord
Doctor	Richard E. Arnold
Clerk	Bea Kiyohara
Poker Player	Chris S. Ducey
Sid	Tee Dennard
Herb	David Mamet
Mr. Foster	Gene Callahan
Priest	John L. Sostrich
Attendant	Juleen Murray
Clerk	Allen Nause
Stewardess	Denise Dennison
Steward	Robert J. Peters
Helicopter Pilots	Rick Shuster, Al Cerullo
Limo Driver	David Kasparian
Doorman	Mick Muldoon
Underwater Diving Doubles	Marcia Holley, Julie Robinson

Top Right: Theresa Russell, Dennis Hopper; Nicol Williamson, Theresa Russell Below: Russell, Sami Frey
© *20th Century Fox/Elliott Marks*

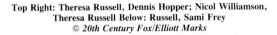

Debra Winger, Theresa Russell

**Nicol Williamson, Debra Winger
Above: Debra Winger, Terry O'Quinn**

DEAD OF WINTER

(MGM/UA) Producers, John Bloomgarden, Marc Shmuger; Director, Arthur Penn; Screenplay, Marc Shmuger, Mark Malone; Photography, Jan Weincke; Designer, Bill Brodie; Editor, Rick Shaine; Music, Richard Einhorn; Associate Producer/Production Manager, Michael MacDonald; Casting, Maria Armstrong, Ross Clydesdale; Assistant Directors, Tony Thatcher, David Till, David Vaughn; Production Coordinators, Deborah Zwicker, Shelley Boylen, Lori Greenberg; Sound, D. Bruce Carwardine, Glen Gauthier; Lighting, Rae Thurston; Art Director, Alicia Keywan; Makeup Design, Ann Brodie; Costumes, Arthur Rowsell; Set Decorator, Mark S. Freeborn; Special Effects, Neil N. Trifunovich; Stunts, Dwayne McLean; Assistant Editors, Lori Kornspun, Mark Livolsi; Orchestrations, Larry Hochman; Production Associates, Daniel Bernheim, Barbara Glazer, Chip Phillips, Sabra Van Dolsen; Color; Rated R; 100 minutes; February release

CAST

Julie Rose	
Katie McGovern	
Evelyn	Mary Steenburgen
Mr. Murray	Roddy McDowall
Dr. Joseph Lewis	Jan Rubes
Rob Sweeney	William Russ
Officer Mullavy	Ken Pogue
Officer Huntley	Wayne Robson
Roland McGovern	Mark Malone
Highway Patrolman	Michael Copeman
Gas Jock	Sam Malkin
Woman at audition	Pamela Moller
Killer	Dwayne McLean
New Year's Eve Reveler	Paul Welsh

and Denise Lute, Rick Forsayeth, Leslie Munroe, Anton Tyukodi

Left: Mary Steenburgen
© *M-G-M*

Jan Rubes, Roddy McDowall, Mary Steenburgen

84 CHARING CROSS ROAD

(COLUMBIA) Producer, Geoffrey Helman; Director, David Jones; Screenplay, Hugh Whitemore; Based on the book by Helene Hanff; Originally Adapted for the Stage by James Roose-Evans; Executive Producer, Mel Brooks; Photography, Brian West; Editor, Chris Wimble; Music, George Fenton; Designers, Eileen Diss, Edward Pisoni; Costumes, Jane Greenwood, Lindy Hemming; Associate Producers, Randy Auerbach, Jo Lustig; Casting, Judy Courtney, D. L. Newton; Marilyn Johnson; Production Managers, Ken Golden, Gerry Levy; Assistant Directors, Mark McGann, Jake Wright, Johanna Jensen, Paul Frift, Julia E. Cort, Carol Brock; Production Coordinators, Eileen Eixhenstein, Bi Benton; Sound, Gary Alper, David John; Assistant Art Directors, Charles Beal, Judith Lang; Set Decorator, Gretchen Rau; A Brooksfilms Production; Color; Rated PG; 97 minutes; February release

CAST

Helene Hanff	Anne Bancroft
Frank Doel	Anthony Hopkins
Nora Doel	Judi Dench
Maxine Bellamy	Jean DeBaer
George Martin	Maurice Denham
Cecily Farr	Eleanor David
Kay	Mercedes Ruehl
Brian	Daniel Gerroll
Megan Wells	Wendy Morgan
Bill Humphries	Ian McNeice
Ginny	J. Smith-Cameron
Ed	Tom Isbell
Mrs. Boulton	Anne Dyson
The Lady from Delaware	Connie Booth
Businessman on plane	Ronn Carroll
New York Bookseller	Sam Stoneburner
The Print Buyer	Charles Lewsen
Willie, the Deli Owner	Bernie Passeltiner
Maxine's Stage Manager	MichaelJohn McGann
Bill's Great Aunt	Gwen Nelson
Stately Home Butler	Roger Ostime
Labour Party Canvasser	John Bardon
Maxine's Mom	Betty Low
Joey, the dentist	James Eckhouse
Coronation Party Friends	David Davenport, Max Harvey, Rupert Holliday-Evans, Freda Rogers
Baseball Commentator	Marty Glickman
Demolition Workman	Tony Todd
Arresting Cop at Columbia	Kevin McClarnon
Joan Todd (Mrs.) Secretary	Janet Dale
Mary Doel-Aged 4	Zoe Hodges
Mary Doel-Aged 21	Kate Napier Brown
Sheila Doel-Aged 12	Rebecca Bradley
Sheila Doel-Aged 29	Barbara Thorn
Cecily Farr's Children	Danielle Burns, Lee Burns

Top: Ian McNeice, Anthony Hopkins, Eleanor David, Maurice Denham, Wendy Morgan © *Columbia Pictures*

Anne Bancroft Above: Anthony Hopkins

FROM THE HIP

(DE LAURENTIIS) Producers, Rene Dupont, Bob Clark; Director, Bob Clark; Screenplay, David E. Kelley, Bob Clark; Story, David E. Kelley; Executive Producers, Howard Baldwin, Bill Minot, Brian Russell; Editor, Stan Cole; Music, Paul Zaza; Photography, Dante Spinotti; Designer, Michael Stringer; Associate Producer, Ken Heeley-Ray; Costumes, Clifford Capone; Casting, Mike Fenton, Jane Feinberg; Production Manager, Marilyn Stonehouse; Assistant Directors, Ken Goch, Jay Tobias; Additional Casting, Marcia Shulman, Fincannon & Assoc.; Sound, David Stephenson; Art Director, Dennis Bradford; Set Decorator, Edward "Tantar" LeViseur; Production Coordinator, Angela Heald; Assistant Art Director, Timothy Galvin; Assistant Editors, Scott Summersgill, Neil Grieve, Sydney Conrad; Songs by various artists; Panavision; Technicolor; Rated PG; 111 minutes; February release

CAST

Robin Weathers	Judd Nelson
Jo Ann	Elizabeth Perkins
Douglas Benoit	John Hurt
Craig Duncan	Darren McGavin
Larry	Dan Monahan
Steve Hadley	David Alan Grier
Roberta Winnaker	Nancy Marchand
Phil Ames	Allan Arbus
Raymond Torkenson	Edward Winter
Matt Cowens	Richard Zobel
1st Judge	Ray Walston
Scott Murray	Robert Irvin Elliott
2nd Judge	Beatrice Winde
Lt. Matt Sosha	Art Hindle
Mrs. Martha Williams	Priscilla Pointer
Mr. Wilby	Royce D. Applegate
TV Reporter	Robert Inman
Bailiff	Jack Riel
Foreman	Pearl Jones
Reporter	David Fitzsimmons
Biggs	William Alspaugh
Malcolm	Terry Loughlin
Rampart	Jon Thompson
McAlbee	Lou Criscuolo
Wilson	H. Richard Greene
Baxter	Ed L. Grady
Warren	Everett Quinton
Bailiff-Benoit Trial	Arthur J. Fasciani
Dr. Charles Peckham	Robert Dickman
Harvey Beals	George Hall
TV Anchorman	Harvey Kirck
Charlie	Eric Tilley
Security Guard	Will Knickerbocker

Top Right: Ray Walston, Darren McGavin,
Judd Nelson Below: Nelson, John Hurt
© *DeLaurentiis Entertainment Group*

FIRE AND ICE

(CONCORDE) Director/Photography, Willy Bogner; Director's Assistant, Petra Von Oelffen; Additional Photography, Peter Rohe, Yuri Farrant, Gerd Huber, Georg Ostler, Detlev Ponke, Christina Troschke; Editors, Petra Von Oelffen, Claudia Travnecek; Production Managers, Jochen Richter, Stefan Zurcher, Sylvia Benedikt; Location Managers, Dede Brinkman, Pat Parrish, Cornelia Kiss, Richard Bolz; Sound, Manfred Maier; Wardrobe, Gabi Ortega; Special Effects, Richard Richtsfeld; Songs, Harold Faltermaier, Gary Wright, Gavin Sutherland, Alan Parsons; Project, Hermann Weindorf, Curtis Briggs, Willy Bogner, John Denver; Ski Suit Design, Jutta Jaeger, Gotthardin Thylmann, At Bogner, Munich; Dolby Stereo; Color; Rated PG; 80 minutes; February release

CAST

John	John Eaves
Suzy	Suzy Chaffee
Snowboarders	Tom Sims, Steve Link
Windsurfers	Kelby Anno, Matt Schweitzer, Mike Waltze
Hangglider	Philippe Bernard
In the Bobrun	Bob Salerno, Wolfgang Junginer
Ballet in the glacier	Jan Bucher
Ribbon Dancer	Jennifer Wilson
Breakdancers	Kevin Wright, Richard Pineiro
Photographer	Tony Corapi
Waitress	Kathy Pelowski
Cowboys	Masayoshi Hija, Wong Kong
Texas Stinger	Alan Trafford
Hell's Angel	Joey Stevens
John's Voice	John Cooper

and Mike Nemesvary, Sandro Wirth, Rudi Zangerl, Thomas Uberall, Michael Teichmann, Manfred Gschaider, Ann McIntire, Suzy Kay, Kay Kucera, Janet Liefer, Jan Schwartz, Scott Brooksbank, Robert Young, Mike Chew, Bob Salerno, Phil Boehne, Bobby Chambers, Jerry Douglas, Jeff Evans, John Tavers, Fuzzy Garhammer, Ernst Garhammer, Manfred Kastner, Peter Lindecke, Rudi Kirmaier, Henri Authie, Willy Birk, Pio Stecher, Lissi Lambsdorff, Angelica Walch, Georges Pequigont, Georg Jauss, Federico Vincenti, Kurt Starz, Hubert Pollinger, Klaus Steiner, Stefan Heigenhauser,

Suzy Chaffee, John Eaves
in "Fire and Ice"

LIGHT OF DAY

(TRI-STAR) Producers, Rob Cohen, Keith Barish; Director/Screenplay, Paul Schrader; Executive Producer, Doug Claybourne; Photography, John Bailey; Designer, Jeannine Claudia Oppewall; Editor, Jacqueline Cambas; Music, Thomas Newman; Music Supervisor, Danny Goldberg; Associate Producer, Alan Mark Poul; Costumes, Jodie Tillen; Casting, Bonnie Timmermann; Production Manager, Graham Place; Assistant Directors, Mark Radcliff, James R. Giovannetti, Stefanie A. Moore; Set Decorator, Lisa Fischer; Sound, J. Paul Oddo, Bill Pellak; Special Effects, Dieter Sturm; Stunts, Rick LeFevour; Production Coordinator, Erika Pearsall; Taft/Barish Productions; Title Song, Bruce Springsteen; Songs by various artists; Soundtrack on CBS Associated/Black Heart Records; Dolby Stereo; Color; Rated PG-13; 107 minutes; February release

CAST

Joe Rasnick	Michael J. Fox
Jeanette Rasnick	Gena Rowlands
Patti Rasnick	Joan Jett
Bu Montgomery	Michael McKean
Smittie	Thomas G. Waites
Cindy Montgomery	Cherry Jones
Gene Bodine	Michael Dolan
Billy Tettore	Paul J. Harkins
Benji Rasnick	Billy Sullivan
Benjamin Rasnick	Jason Miller
Reverend Ansley	Tom Irwin
Sean	Jerry Gideon
Crystal	Cherise Vonae Haugen
Oogie	Michael Rocker
Laurie	Yvette Heyden
Dr. Natterson	Del Close
Dr. Gould	Ray Bradford
Club Manager	Jolly Roger
Roger	Clarence L. Chavers III

and Kathleen Caffrey, Ann Whitney, Maureen Mueller, Jason Shepley, Sharon Kay Hodgson, John Rubano, Barbara E. Robertson, Mark Herzog, Erick Leeper, David Pasquesi, Bryan Stillman, Erwin Martin, Dan Shriver, Marleen Paulette, Camilla Hawk, Laura A. Holzheimer, Ron Dean, P. K. Doyle, Barbara Sullivan, Karel King, Kim Vander Bie, Clyde L. Morse, Maris Sodetz, Alan Mark Poul, Linda Reisman, Lisa Fischer, Ray Krawczyk, Pam Majeski, James H. Saft, Mars Frehley, Sandi Dublo, Lisa Ann Barney, Amy R. Delorean, Jeff Dieter, Scott Catino, Brian Troch, Mark Diamond, Mark Franco, Joe Aparo, Jimi Bell, Kimberly A. Rittwage, J. Howard Calvin, Ted Peplowski, Craig E. Norman, Norman F. Tischler, Dennis D. Bunkley, John E. Sferra, Mark Addison, Frank Vale, Trent Raznor, Jimmie L. Vaughan, Kim Wilson, Fran Christina, Preston Hubbard

Top Right: Michael Dolan, Michael McKean, Joan Jett, Michael J. Fox, Paul J. Harkins Below: Gena Rowlands, Michael J. Fox Right Center: Fox, Jett
© *Taft Entertainment Pictures*

Michael J. Fox

Billy Sullivan, Michael J. Fox

Robert Englund

John Saxon, Craig Wasson, Heather Langenkamp
Top: Patricia Arquette

A NIGHTMARE ON ELM STREET 3: DREAM WARRIORS

(NEW LINE CINEMA) Producer, Robert Shaye; Director, Chuck Russell; Screenplay, Wes Craven, Bruce Wagner;; Co-Producer, Sara Risher; Executive Producers, Wes Craven, Stephen Diener; Line Producer, Rachel Talalay; Production Executive, Gerald T. Olson; Photography, Roy Wagner; Casting, Annette Benson; Freddy Krueger; Makeup, Kevin Yagher; Makeup Effects, Peter Chesney; Editor, Terry Stokes; Art Directors, Mick Strawn, C. J. Strawn; Assistant to Director, Susan Graham; Music, Angelo Badalamenti; Song, Dokken; Color; Rated R; 97 minutes; February release

CAST

Nancy Thompson	Heather Langenkamp
Kristen Parker	Patricia Arquette
Max	Larry Fishburne
Dr. Elizabeth Simms	Priscilla Pointer
Dr. Neil Goldman	Craig Wasson
Elaine Parker	Brooke Bundy
Joey	Rodney Eastman
Phillip	Bradley Gregg
Will	Ira Heiden
Kincaid	Ken Sagoes
Jennifer	Penelope Sudrow
Taryn	Jennifer Rubin
Lorenzo (Orderly)	Clayton Landey
Nun	Nan Martin
Marcie	Stacey Alden
Little Girl	Kristin Clayton
Freddy Krueger	Robert Englund

and Sally Piper, Rozlyn Sorrell, James Carroll, Jack Shea, Michael Rougas, John Saxon, Dick Cavett, Zsa Zsa Gabor

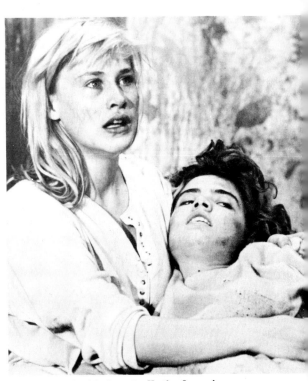

Patricia Arquette, Heather Langenkamp

NUMBER ONE WITH A BULLET

(CANNON GROUP) Producers, Menahem Golan, Yoram Globus; Director, Jack Smight; Story, Gail Morgan Hickman; Screenplay, Gail Morgan Hickman, Andrew Kurtzman, Rob Riley, James Belushi; Photography, Alex Phillips; Editor, Michael J. Duthie; Designer, Norm Baron; Music, Alf Clausen; Associate Producer, Gail Morgan Hickman; Production Manager, Leonard Bram; Assistant Directors, Gerald Walsh, John Whittle, Michael Charles Kennedy, Bob Del Valle; Production Supervisor, Rony Yacov; Casting, Robert MacDonald, Perry Bullington; Stunts, Fred Lerner; Sound, Russell Williams, II; Set Decorator, Linda Allen; Set Designer, Eva Bohn; Special Effects, John Hartigan, Paul Hickerson, Frank Pope; Costumes, Rosalie Wallace; Production Coordinator, Claire Baker; Music Supervisor, Paula Erickson; Orchestrations, Hummie Mann, Brad Dechter, Alf Clausen; Songs, Martin Bram, Steve Winwood, Muff Winwood, Spencer Davis, Jim Capaldi, Chris Wood, and others; Ultrastereo; TVC Color; Rated R; 101 minutes; February release

CAST

Berzak	Robert Carradine
Hazeltine	Billy Dee Williams
Teresa Berzak	Valerie Bertinelli
Captain Ferris	Peter Graves
Mrs. Berzak	Doris Roberts
Malcolm	Bobby Di Cicco
Lt. Kaminski	Ray Girardin
DaCosta	Barry Sattels
Casey	Mykel T. Williamson
Bobby Sweet	Jonathan Gries
Pogue	Michael Goodwin
Blonde	Lagena Hart
Boudreau	Alex Rebar
Rotweiler	Artie Ripp
Carlo	Daniel Demorest

and Vanessa Bell, Valerie McIntosh, Eddie Frescas, John Durbin, Tony Pierce, Joyce Cunning, Larry Poindexter, Christopher Derose, Ken Gibbel, Jerome Chambers, Venice Kong, Stacey Binn, David Sargent, Gene LeBell, Nick Cinardo, Angela Gibbs, Bill Gazzarri, Manuel Marquez, Jose Gonzalez, Jeff Jensen, Dave Efron, Spice Williams, Jean Malahni, Casey Griffen, Timothy Noyes, Patricia L. Desmond, Ancel Cook, Shari Shattuck, John Hazelwood, Chris Brown, Willy Reaves, Yvette Cruise, Jason Scurra, Dan Halleck, Bill Ryusaki, Carl Ciarfalio, Manuel Perry, Dyee Dysart, Virgil Wilson, Stanley Tanney, Kim Marriner, Prince Hughes, Jim Wilkey, Bob Apisa, Michael Yama, Faith Minton, Jimmy Halty, Lorrie Marlow, Natalie Alexander, George Vasilios Choulos, Gerald Walsh, Ted Mehous, Claude A. Wyle, Michael Porter

Top Right: Robert Carradine, Billy Dee Williams
Below: Carradine, Valerie Bertinelli
© *Cannon Films*

Billy Dee Williams, Robert Carradine

Robert Carradine

SOME KIND OF WONDERFUL

(PARAMOUNT) Producer/Screenplay, John Hughes; Director, Howard Deutch; Executive Producers, Michael Chinich, Ronald Colby; Photography, Jan Kiesser; Designer, Josan Russo; Editors, Bud Smith, Scott Smith; Costumes, Marilyn Vance-Straker; Music, Stephen Hague, John Musser; Casting, Judith Weiner, Steven Jacobs, Ruth Lamvert; Music Supervisor, Tarquin Gotch; Production Managers, Ronald Colby, Jerry Baerwitz; Assistant Directors, Jerry Ziesmer, Bryan Denegal, Vicki LeMay; Production Associates, Elena Spiotta, David Gonzales; Art Director, Greg Pickrell; Set Decorator, Linda Spheeris; Sound, David MacMillan; Production Coordinator, Nanette Siegert; Special Effects, Louis Cooper; Songs by various artists; Soundtrack on Hughes Music/MCA; Dolby Stereo; Technicolor; 93 minutes; Rated PG-13; February release

CAST

Keith Nelson	Eric Stoltz
Watts	Mary Stuart Masterson
Amanda Jones	Lea Thompson
Hardy Jenns	Craig Sheffer
Cliff Nelson	John Ashton
Skinhead	Elias Koteas
Shayne	Molly Hagan
Laura Nelson	Maddie Corman
Carol Nelson	Jane Elliot
Cindy Nelson	Candace Cameron
Mia	Chynna Phillips
Ray	Scott Coffey
Museum Guard	Carmine Caridi
Gym Instructor	Lee Garlington
Holly	Laura Leigh Hughes
Laura's Friends	Laura Tubelle, Amy Lynne
Skinhead's Friends	Michel Bergman, Megan Daniels, Dale L. Evans
Maitre'd	Peter Elbling
Mrs. Gale	Patricia Gaul
Detention Teacher	Kenneth Kimmins
Hardy's Friend	James G. MacDonald
Fight Teacher	J. Patrick McNamara
Carparkers	Jonathon Schmock, James Vallely
Amanda's Friend	Lita Stevens
Waitress	Christine Spiotta
The March Violets	Tom Ashton, Laurence Elliott, Cleo Murray, Andy Tolson

Left: Mary Stuart Masterson Above: Lea Thompson, Eric Stoltz Top: Mary Stuart Masterson, Scott Coffey, Eric Stoltz
© *Paramount Pictures/Joyce Rudolph*

Lea Thompson, Craig Sheffer

Elias Koteas, Mary Stuart Masterson, Eric Stoltz

SQUARE DANCE

(ISLAND PICTURES) Producer/Director, Daniel Petrie; Screenplay, Alan Hines; Executive Producers, Charles Haid, Jane Alexander; Associate Producers, P'nenah Goldstein, Cyrus Yavneh; Photography, Jacek Laskus; Designer, Jan Scott; Editor, Bruce Green; Music, Bruce Broughton; Production Manager, Dwight Chooluck; Assistant Directors, Katterli Fraunfelder, Gregg Chooluck; Production Executive, Ester Greif; Casting, Shari Rhodes, Liz Keigley, Phalia Blassingame; Costumes, Elizabeth McBride; Set Decorator, Erica Rogalla; Sound, Bob Wald; Special Effects, Jack Bennett; Production Coordinators, Marisa Alcarez, Dee Whitehurst; Sound, Dane A. Davis; Production Supervisor, Leon Chooluck; Stunts, Randy "Fife", Tim Butler, Jackie Resch; Produced in association with NBC Productions; Allied Lab Color; Rated PG-13; 110 minutes; February release

CAST

Dillard	Jason Robards
Juanelle	Jane Alexander
Gemma	Winona Ryder
Rory	Rob Lowe
Gwen	Deborah Richter
Frank	Guich Koock
Beecham	Elbert Lewis
Aggie	Charlotte Stanton
Dub Mosley	J. David Moeller
Dolores	Dixie Taylor
Preacher Dixon	Irma P. Hall
Miss Lawson	Barbara Britt
Drunk Cowboy	Brad Leland
May Tompkins	Dee Pyland
Doreen Hadley	Gwen Little
Jack Springer	Jim Bynum
Eunice Tanner	Linda Nye
Bubba Springer	Newt Davis
Ray Ferrys	Harlan Jordan
Bob Hadley	Dennis Letts
Mrs. Weeks	Annabelle Weenick
Miss Harley	Liz Williams
Bayou Band	Tracey D. Adkins, E. J. Bodin, III, Steven Grisaffe, Benny Sonnier, Kip Sonnier
School Girls	Stephanie Binford, Barbara McCauley

**Top: Winona Ryder, Rob Lowe Right: Jason
Robards Below: Winona Ryder, Rob Lowe**
© Island Pictures

Deborah Richter, Jane Alexander

OVER THE TOP

(WARNER BROS.) Producers, Menahem Golan, Yoram Globus; Director, Menahem Golan; Screenplay, Stirling Silliphant, Sylvester Stallone; Story, Gary Conway, David C. Engelbach; Executive Producer, James D. Brubaker; Photography, David Gurfinkel; Designer, James Schoppe; Editors, Don Zimmerman, James Symons; Associate Producer, Tony Munafo; Music, Giorgio Moroder; Casting, Ron Surma; Production Manager, Duncan Henderson; Assistant Directors, Tom Davies, Josh McLaglen; Music Coordinator, Robin Garb; Production Executives, Christopher Pearce, Rony Yacov; Art Director, William Skinner; Assistant Art Director, David Klassen; Set Designers, Rolan E. Hill, Jr., Ross Galliochotte; Set Decorator, Cloudia; Sound, Charles M. Wilborn; Production Coordinator, Mauri Syd Gayton; Stunts, Gary McLarty; Special Effects, Dennis Peterson; Songs by various artists; Soundtrack on Columbia Records; Dolby Stereo; Panavision; Metrocolor; Rated PG; 93 minutes; February release

CAST

Lincoln Hawk	Sylvester Stallone
Jason Cutler	Robert Loggia
Christina Hawk	Susan Blakely
Bob "Bull" Hurley	Rick Zumwalt
Michael Cutler	David Mendenhall
Tim Salanger	Chris McCarty
Ruker	Terry Funk
Announcer	Bob Beattie
Collins	Alan Graf
Smasher	Magic Schwarz
Grizzly	Bruce Way
Big Boy (Richie)	Jimmy Keegan
Colonel Davis	John Braden
Tony	Tony Munafo
Mad Dog Madison	Randy Raney
Carl Adams	Paul Sullivan
Big Bill Larson	Jack Wright
Bosco	Sam Scarber
Landis	Richie Giachetti
Jim Olson	Michael Fox
McBroom	Ross St. Phillip

and Seth Mitchell, Dale Benson, Joe Kiel, Dean Abston, Flo Gerrish, David Van Gorder, Kelly Sahnger, Charles M. Wilborn, Terry Burns, William Nichols Buck, Bob Eazor, Ed Levitt, Andrew Rhodes, Bob Rogers, Reggie Bennett, Joshua Lee Patton, James Mendenhall, Danny Capri, Gregory Braendel, Sly Ali Smith, Rose Dursey, Marion Mickens, II, Dave Patton, Alexa Lambert, Ronnie Rondell, Jr., James H. Shana, Norman Howell, Rex Pierson

Sylvester Stallone, David Mendenhall

Page Moseley, Hilary Shepard, Melanie Vincz,
Doug Shanklin, John Allen Nelson

HUNK

(CROWN INTERNATIONAL) Producer, Marilyn J. Tenser; Associate Producer, Steven J. Wolfe; Director/Screenplay, Lawrence Bassoff; Photography, Bryan England; Editor, Richard E. Westover; Casting, Paul Bengston, David Cohn; Music, David Kurtz; Production Manager, Merry Tigar; Production Coordinator, Alan Z. McCurdy; Assistant Directors, R. B. Braham, Coni Lancaster Smith, John Keefer; Sound, Bernie Kriegel; Costumes, Bernadette O'Brien; Special Make-up Effects, Thomas Wayne Swartz; Art Director, Catherine Hardwicke; Assistant Art Director, Hoagie K. Hill; Set Decorator, Beau Petersen; Stunts, John Barrett, Alan Marcus; Music, Coordinator, Suzie Katayama; Songs, David Kutz, Monday, John Baer, Robbie Baer; Dolby Stereo; Panavision; Foto-Kem Color; Rated PG; 102 minutes; March release

CAST

Hunk Golden	John Allen Nelson
Bradley Brinkman	Steve Levitt
O'Brien	Deborah Shelton
Sunny	Rebeccah Bush
Dr. D.	James Coco
Garrison Gaylord	Robert Morse
Constantine Constapopolis	Avery Schreiber
Chacka	Cynthia Szigeti
Laurel Springs	Melanie Vincz
Skeet Mecklenburger	Doug Shanklin
Coaster Royce	Page Moseley
Alexis Cash	Hilary Shepard
Director	J. Jay Saunders
Camerman	Charles Dougherty
Lifeguard	John Barrett
Dragon Lady	Jacqueline Jacobs

Left Center: James Coco, Deborah Shelton
© Crown International Pictures

ANGEL HEART

(TRI-STAR) Producers, Alan Marshall, Elliott Kastner; Director/Screenplay, Alan Parker; Based on the Novel *"Falling Angel"* by William Hjortsberg; Executive Producers, Mario Kassar, Andrew Vajna; Photography, Michael Seresin; Designer, Brian Morris; Editor, Gerry Hambling; Music, Trevor Jones; Casting, Risa Bramon, Billy Hopkins; Production Manager, Michael Nozik; Assistant Directors, Ric Kidney, Sarah M. Brim, Nina Kostroff; Production Supervisor, Simon Bosanquet; Sound, Danny Michael; Costumes, Aude Bronson-Howard; Choreographer, Louis Falco; Art Directors, Kristi Zea, Armin Ganz; Production Executive, Dan Mark; Assistant Art Directors, Maher Ahmad, Jeremy Conway; Set Decorators, Robert J. Franco, Leslie Pope; Assistant Costume Designers, Alvin Perry, Dana-Jean Cicerchi; Production Co-Ordinator, Ingrid Johanson; Stunts, Harry Madsen; Special Effects, J. C. Brotherhood, Russell Berg; Songs by various artists; Soundtrack on Antilles Records/Island Records; Dolby Stereo; Technicolor; Panavision; Rated R; 113 minutes; March release

CAST

Harry Angel	Mickey Rourke
Louis Cyphre	Robert DeNiro
Epiphany Proudfoot	Lisa Bonet
Margaret Krusemark	Charlotte Rampling
Ethan Krusemark	Stocker Fontelie
Toots Sweet	Brownie McGhee
Doctor Fowler	Michael Higgins
Connie	Elizabeth Whitcraft
Sterne	Eliott Keener
Spider Simpson	Charles Gordone
Winesap	Diann Florek
Nurse	Kathleen Whihoite
Izzy	George Buck
Izzy's Wife	Judith Drake
Pastor John	Gerald L. Orange
Mammy Carter	Peggy Severe
Deimos	Pruitt Taylor Vince
Baptism Preacher	David Petitjean
Cajun Heavys	Rick Washburn, Neil Newlon
Big Jacket	Oakley Dalton
Margaret's Maid	Yvonne Bywaters
Mike	Loys T. Bergeron
Toothless	Joshua Frank
Harlem Mourner	Karmen Harris
Ellie	Nicole Burdette
Oyster Cajuns	Kendell Lupe, Percy Martin
Concierge	Viola Dunbar
Bartender	Murray Bandel
Epiphany's Child	Jarrett Narcisse

and Ernest Watson, Rickie Monie, Sugar Blue, Pinetop Perkins, Deacon Johnmoore, Richard Payne, W. Alonzo Stewart, Lillian Boutte, Joel Adam, Darrel Beasley, Stephen Beasley, Jerome Reddick, Louis Freddie Kohlman, Stephen Kenyatta Simon, Curtis Pierre, Kufaru Aaron Mouton, Roselyn Lionheart, Marilyn Banks, Lula Elzy, Francesca J. Ridge, Hope Clarke, Oscar Best, Sarita Allen, Noel Jones, Valerie Jackson, Greer Goff, Arlena Rolant, Karen Davis, Shirleta Jones, Mark Taylor

Right: Lisa Bonet, Mickey Rourke
Top: Charlotte Rampling, Mickey Rourke
© *Tri-Star Pictures/George Kontaxis*

Robert DeNiro
© *Tri-Star Pictures/Alan Parker*

Lisa Bonet © *Tri-Star/Alan Parker*

LETHAL WEAPON

(WARNER BROS.) Producers, Richard Donner, Joel Silver; Director, Richard Donner; Screenplay, Shane Black; Photography, Stephen Goldblatt; Designer, J. Michael Riva; Editor, Stuart Baird; Costumes, Mary Malin; Casting, Marion Dougherty; Associate Producer, Jennie Lew; Music, Michael Kamen, Eric Clapton; Music Performances, Eric Clapton, Michael Kamen, David Sanborn; Production Manager, Steve Perry; Assistant Directors, Benjamin Rosenberg, Terry Miller, Jr., Willie E. Simmons, Jr.; Producer's Associate, Michael Benjamin Thau; Set Decorator, Marvin March; Assistant Art Directors, Eva Bohn, Virginia L. Randolph; Sound, Bill Nelson; Stunts, Bobby Bass; Special Effects, Chuck Gaspar, Joe Day; Arrangements/Conductor, Michael Kamen; Assistant Editors, Billy Meshover, Michael Greenfeld; Songs by various artists; Dolby Stereo; Technicolor; Rated R; 110 minutes; March release

CAST

Martin Riggs	Mel Gibson
Roger Murtaugh	Danny Glover
Joshua	Gary Busey
The General	Mitchell Ryan
Michael Hunsaker	Tom Atkins
Trish Murtaugh	Darlene Love
Rianne Murtaugh	Traci Wolfe
Amanda Hunsaker	Jackie Swanson
Nick Murtaugh	Damon Hines
Carrie Murtaugh	Ebonie Smith
Beat Cop	Bill Kalmenson
Dixie	Lycia Naff
Policewoman	Selma Archerd
Police Officer	Richard B. Whitaker
Psychologist	Mary Ellen Trainor
Capt. Ed Murphy	Steve Kahan
McCaskey	Jack Thibeau
Boyette	Grand Bush
Mendez	Ed O'Ross
Gustaf	Gustav Vintas
Endo	Al Leong
McCleary	Michael Shaner
Alfred	Donald Gooden
Patrol Cop	Lenny Juliano
Plainclothes Cop	Henry Brown
Hooker	Teresa Kadotani
Beat Cop	Frank Reinhard

and Patrick Cameron, Don Gordon, Jimmie F. Skaggs, Jason Ronard, Blackie Dammett, Gail Bowman, Robert Fol, Paul Tuerpe, Chad Hayes, Chris D. Jardins, Sven Thorsen, Peter DuPont, Gilles Kholer Cedric Adams, James Poslof, Natalie Zimmerman, Deborah Dismukes, Cheryl Baker, Terri Lynn Doss, Sharon K. Brecke, Alphonse Philippe Mouzon, Shaun Hunter, Everitt Wayne Collins Jr., Lenny Juliano, John O'Neill, Tom Noga, Dar Robinson, Burbank the Cat, Sam the Dog

Left: Darlene Love, Ebonie Smith, Traci Wolfe, Damon Hines, Danny Glover Top: Danny Glover, Mel Gibson © *Warner Bros. Inc.*

Gary Busey (center)

Mel Gibson, Michael Shaner

BLIND DATE

(TRI-STAR) Producer, Tony Adams; Director, Blake Edwards; Screenplay, Dale Launer; Executive Producers, Gary Hendler, Jonathan D. Krane; Co-Executive Producer, David Permut; Photography, Harry Stradling; Designer, Rodger Maus; Editor, Robert Pergament; Costumes, Tracy Tynan; Music, Henry Mancini; Associate Producer, Trish Caroselli; Casting, Nancy Klopper; Production Manager, Alan Levine; Assistant Directors, Mickey McCardle, David Kelley, Margaret Nelson; Production Executive, Elton MacPherson; Music Supervision, Al Bunetta, Tom Bocci; Art Director, Peter Lansdown Smith; Set Decorator, Carl Biddiscombe; Sound, William M. Randall, David Pettijohn; Special Effects, Roy Downey; Stunts, Joe Dunne; Songs, Henry Mancini, George Merrill, Shannon Rubicam, and various other artists; Panavision; Metrocolor; Dolby Stereo; Rated PG-13; 93 minutes; March release

CAST

Nadia Gates	Kim Basinger
Walter Davis	Bruce Willis
David Bedford	John Larroquette
Judge Harold Bedford	William Daniels
Harry Gruen	George Coe
Denny Gordon	Mark Blum
Ted Davis	Phil Hartman
Susie Davis	Stephanie Faracy
Muriel Bedford	Alice Hirson
Jordan the butler	Graham Stark
Nadia's Mother	Joyce Van Patten
Walter's Secretary	Jeannie Elias
Minister	Sacerdo Tanney
Mrs. Gruen	Georgann Johnson
Mr. Yakamoto	Sab Shimono
Mrs. Yakamoto	Momo Yashima
French Waiter	Armin Shimerman
Maitre D'	Brian George
Japanese Gardener	Ernest Harada

and Emma Walton, Elaine Wilkes, Susan Lentini, Barry Sobel, Arlene Lorre, Timothy Stack, Jack Gwillim, Diana Bellamy, Seth Isler, Paul Carafotes, Bob Ari, Don Sparks, Bill Marcus, Michael Genovese, Randall Bowers, John Demy, Jon Smet, Noele de Saint Gall, Julia Jennings, Dick Durock, Stanley Jordan, Billy Vera, Peter Bunetta, Ricky Hirsch, Darrell Leonard, David Miner, Mike Murphy, Jerry Peterson, Lon Price, Ron Viola, Keith Robertson

Left: John Larroquette, William Daniels Above: Timothy Stack, Kim Basinger, Bruce Willis Top: Bruce Willis, Kim Basinger, George Coe © *Tri-Star Pictures*

Kim Basinger, Bruce Willis, John Larroquette

John Larroquette, Bruce Willis

STREET SMART

(CANNON GROUP) Producers, Menahem Golan, Yoram Globus; Director, Jerry Schatzberg; Screenplay, David Freeman; Associate Producer, Evzen W. Kolar; Photography, Adam Holender; Editor, Priscilla Nedd; Designer, Dan Leigh; Costumes, Jo Ynocenio; Music, Robert Irving III; Casting, Joy Todd; Production Manager, Mychele Boudrias; Production Executive, Rony Yacov; Art Director, Serge Jacques; Sound, Patrick Rousseay; Set Designers, Raymond Larose, Katherine Matthewson; Assistant Directors, Jacques Methe, Jacques LaBerge, Herb Gains, Nathalie Vadim; Production Coordinators, Daniele Rohrback, Polly Chung; Technical Coordinator, Bill Allen; Music Supervisor, Paula Erickson; Additional Music, Adam Holzman; Songs by various artists; Dolby Stereo; TVC Color; 97 minutes; Rated R; March release

CAST

Jonathan Fisher	Christopher Reeve
Punchy	Kathy Baker
Alison Parker	Mimi Rogers
Leonard Pike	Jay Patterson
Ted Avery	Andre Gregory
Fast Black	Morgan Freeman
Harriet	Anna Maria Horsford
Joel Davis	Frederick Rolf
Reggie	Erik King
Art Sheffield	Michael J. Reynolds
Darlene	Shari Hilton
Yvonne	Donna Bailey
Judge Bevis	Ed VanNuys
Ben Singer	Daniel Nalbach
Solo	Rick Aviles
Marty	Les Carlson
Hotel Clerk	Bill Torrie
Suburban John	Richard Mullaly
Hispanic Prostitute	Marie Barrientos
Flashy Man	Eddie Earl Hatch
Transvestite	Joe Dorian Clark
Black Prostitute	Grace Garland
Lowlife	Wally Martin
Undercover Cop	Robert Morelli
Bartender	Shawn Laurence
Woman Magistrate	Kelly Ricard
Jay	David Glen
Ted's Wife	Ulla Moreland
Pablo	Francisco Gonzales

and Lynne Adams, Claudette Roach, Rudi Adler, Melba Archer, Ian Beaton, Victor Bowen, Lois Dellar, Chui-Lin Mark, Manon Vallee, Carole Zelles, Danny Brainin, Ernest Deveaux, Walter Allen Bennett, Jr., Steve Michaels, Margarita Stocker, Eve Napier, Ruth Dahan, Vera Miller, Nadia Rona, Linda Lee Tracey, Terry Haig, Donald Lamoureux, Carol Ann Francis, Ann Pearl Gary, Emmanuelle Lasalle

Top Right: Mimi Rogers, Rick Aviles
Below: Christopher Reeve, Mimi Rogers
© *Cannon Films*

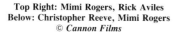

Christopher Reeve, Kathy Baker

Christopher Reeve, Morgan Freeman

30

RAISING ARIZONA

(20th CENTURY FOX) Producer, Ethan Coen; Director, Joel Coen; Screenplay, Fthan Coen, Joel Coen; Co-Producer, Mark Silverman; Executive Producer, James Jacks; Associate Producer, Deborah Reinisch; Photography, Barry Sonnenfeld; Designer, Jane Musky; Editor, Michael R. Miller; Music, Carther Burwell; Costumes, Richard Hornung; Sound Editor, Skip Livesay; Associate Editor, Arnold Glassman; Casting, Donn Isaacson, John Lyons; Stunts, Jery Hewitt; Production Manager, Kevin Dowd; Production Supervisor, Alma Kutruff; Assistant Directors, Deborah Reinisch, Kelly Van Horn, Jon Kilik, Patricia Doherty, Chitra Mojtabai; Sound, Allan Byer; Art Director, Harold Thrasher; Set Decorator, Robert Kracik; Special Effects, Peter Chesney/Image Engineering, Inc., Guy Louthan; Additional Casting, Sunny Seibel, Yvonne Van Orden, Josef Schneider, Inc.; Songs by various artists; Circle Films presents a Ted and Jim Pedas/Ben Barenholtz Production; Dolby Stereo; DuArt Color; Rated PG-13; 94 minutes; March release

CAST

H. I.	Nicolas Cage
Ed	Holly Hunter
Nathan Arizona, Sr.	Trey Wilson
Gale	John Goodman
Evelle	William Forsythe
Glen	Sam McMurray
Dot	Frances McDormand
Leonard Smalls	Randall "Tex" Cobb
Nathan Junior	T. J. Kuhn
Florence Arizona	Lynne Dumin Kitei
Prison Counselor	Peter Benedek
Nice Old Grocery Man	Charles "Lew" Smith
Younger FBI Agent	Warren Keith
Older FBI Agent	Henry Kendrick
Ear-Bending Cellmate	Sidney Dawson
Parole Board Chairman	Richard Blake
Parole Board Members	Troy Nabors, Mary Seibel
Hayseed in the pickup	John O'Donnal
Whitey	Keith Jandacek
Minister	Warren Forsythe
"Trapped" Convict	Ruben Young
Policemen	Dennis Sullivan, Dick Alexander
Feisty Hayseed	Rusty Lee
Fingerprint Technician	James Yeater
Reporters	Bill Andres, Carver Barnes
Unpainted Secretary	Margaret H. McCormack
Newscaster	Bill Rocz
Payroll Cashier	Mary F. Glenn
Scamp with squirt gun	Jeremy Babendure
Adoption Agent	Bill Dobbins
Gynecologist	Ralph Norton
Mopping Convict	Henry Tank
Supermarket Manager,	Frank Outlaw
Varsity Nathan Jr.	Todd Michael Rogers
Machine Shop Earbender	M. Emmet Walsh
The Amazing Voice	William Preston Robertson

and Robert Gray, Katie Thrasher, Derek Russell, Nicole Russell, Zachary Sanders, Noell Sanders, Cody Ranger, Jeremy Arendt, Ashley Hammon, Crystal Hiller, Olivia Hughes, Emily Malin, Melanie Malin, Craig McLaughlin, Adam Savageau, Benjamin Savageau, David Schneider, Michael Stewart

Right: Holly Hunter, Nicolas Cage, T. J. Kuhn
Above: Trey Wilson Top: Nicolas Cage, T. J. Kuhn
© 20th Century Fox/Melinda Sue Gordon

Holly Hunter, Nicolas Cage

John Goodman, T. J. Kuhn, William Forsythe

31

TIN MEN

(TOUCHSTONE) Producer, Mark Johnson; Director/Screenplay, Barry Levinson; Photography, Peter Sova; Designer, Peter Jamison; Editor, Stu Linder; Music, David Steele, Andy Cox; Associate Producer/Production Manager, Kim Kurumada; Costumes Gloria Gresham; Casting, Louis DiGiaimo, Lisa Clarkson; Assistant Directors, Albert Shapiro, Robert Roda; Set Decorator, Philip Abramson; Sound, Jeff Wexler, Don Coufal, James Stuebe; Music Coordinators, Tony Meilandt, G. Mark Roswell; Distributed by Buena Vista; Panavision; DeLuxe Color; Dolby Stereo; Rated R; 112 minutes; March release

CAST

BB	Richard Dreyfuss
Tilley	Danny DeVito
Nora	Barbara Hershey
Moe	John Mahoney
Sam	Jackie Gayle
Gil	Stanley Brock
Cheese	Seymour Cassel
Mouse	Bruno Kirby
Wing	J. T. Walsh
Carly	Richard Portnow
Looney	Matt Craven
Stanley	Alan Blumenfeld
Masters	Brad Sullivan
Bagel	Michael Tucker
Nellie	Deirdre O'Connell
Ada	Sheila McCauley
Mr. Shubner	Michael S. Willis
Mrs. Shubner	Penny Nichols
Diner Waitress	Florence Moody
Murray	Myron Citrenbaum
Mr. Hudson	Ralph Tabakin
Mrs. Hudson	Norma Posner
Cadillac Salesman	Walt MacPherson
Ruthie	Katherine Ellis

and Susan Duvall, David DeBoy, William C. Godsey, Sharon Ziman, Lois Raymond Munchel, Kathy Jones, Cindy Geppi, Ellen Sills, Mary Morgan, Marcia Herr, Karen Barth, Sharon Crofoot, Geri Lynn Kelbaugh, Lisa Ford, Rebecca Lucia Weidner, Patricia Pohlman, Shirley Ann Wilson, Josh Billings, Jeffrey Moser, Freddie Stevens, Bill Danoff, Eva Jean Berg, Todd Jackson, Barbara Rappaport, Theodore Goldman, Kathleen Goldpaugh, Brian Costantini

Left: Danny DeVito Above: Barbara Hershey, Richard Dreyfuss Top: J. T. Walsh, Jackie Gayle, Danny DeVito, Stanley Brock, Bruno Kirby © Touchstone Pictures

Richard Dreyfuss

Matt Craven, Richard Portnow, Alan Blumenfeld, Richard Dreyfuss, John Mahoney, Seymour Cassel

STRIPPED TO KILL

(CONCORDE) Executive Producer, Roger Corman; Director, Katt Shea Ruben; Screenplay, Andy Ruben, Katt Shea Ruben; Producers, Mark Byers, Andy Ruben, Matt Leipzig; Production Manager, Clif Gordon; Production Coordinator, Steve Lustgarten; Assistant Directors, Mark Byers, Richard Hench, Jon Lee Freels; Special Effects Make-up, Michael Westmore; Sound, Ann Krupa, Jan Brodin; Costumes, Beverly Klein; Costume Associate, Amy Gilbert; Art Director/Sculptor, Jan Ferris; Set Decorator, Greg Maher; Assistant Art Director, Miranda Amador; Stage Lighting Design, Michael L. Ross; Special Effects, Roger George; Special Effects Coordinator, Lise Romanoff; Editor, Bruce Stubblefield; Assistant Editors, Tammis Chandler, John Travers; Songs, Andy Ruben, John O'Kennedy, David Russ, Ed Martel, Gail Lennon, Clyde Leiberman, Ken Fake, Mark McKinnis, Larry Brown, Steve Sykes; Vocals, Larry Streicher, Joan E. Jones, Gail Lennon, Darryl Phinnessee, Anita Sherman, Mark McKinnis, Anne-Marie Brown; Color; Rated R; 83 minutes; March release

CAST

Cody	Kay Lenz
Heineman	Greg Evigan
Ray	Norman Fell
Eric/Roxanne	Pia Kamakahi
Fanny	Tracy Crowder
Dazzle	Debbie Nassar
Brandy	Lucia Lexington
Cinammon	Carlye Byron
Zeena	Athena Worthey
Angel	Michelle Foreman
Shirl	Diana Bellamy
Mr. Pocket	Peter Scranton
Derek	Brad David
Mobile Entrepeneur	Tom Ruben
Margolin	J. Bartell
Punk	Jon Lee Freels
Amateur Dancer	Debra Lamb

Top: Kay Lenz, and below with Greg Evigan
Right: Kay Lenz and Top with Greg Evigan
© Concorde

Greg Evigan

WAITING FOR THE MOON

(SKOURAS) Producer, Sandra Schulberg; Director, Jill Godmilow; Executive Producer, Lindsay Law; Screenplay, Mark Magill; Story, Jill Godmilow, Mark Magill; Line Producer/Production Manager, Frederic Bourboulon; Associate Producer, Barbara Lucey; Photography, Andre Neau; Designer, Patrice Mercier; Costumes, Elisabeth Tavernier; Sound, Scott Breindel; Music, Michael Sahl; Editor, George Klotz; Associate Editor, Adeline Yoyotte-Husson; In association with American Playhouse Theatrical Films; A production of New Front Films, A. B. Films, The Laboratory for Icon & Idion; Co-Producer, La Societe Francaise de Production; In association with ARD/Degeto, Channel 4; Best Picture/Joint Best Actress Award, Houston Film Festival, 1987; Rated PG; 88 minutes; March release

CAST

Alice B. Toklas	Linda Hunt
Gertrude Stein	Linda Bassett
Fernande Olivier	Bernadette Lafont
Ernest Hemingway	Bruce McGill
Guillaume Appollinaire	Jacques Boudet
Henry Hopper	Andrew McCarthy

**Top: Linda Hunt Below: Linda Bassett, Andrew
McCarthy Above: Bruce McGill, Linda Hunt**
© Skouras Films/Maryse Alberti

Linda Hunt, Linda Bassett
(also top)

SWIMMING TO CAMBODIA

(CINECOM) Producer, R. A. Shafransky; Director, Jonathan Demme; Screenplay, Spalding Gray; Executive Producers, Lewis Allen, Peter Newman; Co-Executive Producers, Amir Malin, Ira Deutchman; Associate Producers, Edward Sacon; Photography, John Bailey; Editor, Carol Littleton; Designer, Sandy McLeod; Music, Laurie Anderson; Color; Not rated; 87 minutes; March release CAST: Spalding Gray, Sam Waterston, Ira Wheeler

Left and Below: Spalding Gray

MY DEMON LOVER

(NEW LINE CINEMA) Producer, Robert Shaye; Director, Charles Loventhal; Screenplay, Leslie Ray; Co-Producer, Sara Risher; Executive Producers, Pierre David, Larry Thompson; Line Producer, Pieter Jan Brugge; Production Executive, Gerald T. Olson; Photography, Jacques Haitkin; Casting, Annette Benson; Special Makeup Effects, Carl Fullerton, John Caglione, Jr., Neal Martz, Doug Drexler; Editor, Ronald Roose; Designer, Brent Swift; Art Director, Douglas Dick; Costumes, Tom McKinley; Production Manager, Lisa Hollingshed; Assistant Director, Mike Topoozian; Music Supervisor, Kevin Benson; Color; Rated PG-13; 86 minutes; April release

CAST

Kaz	Scott Valentine
Denny	Michelle Little
Fixer	Arnold Johnson
Charles	Robert Trebor
Captain Phil Janus	Alan Fudge
Sonia	Gina Gallego
Man in Healthfood Store	Calvert DeForest

Above: Michelle Little, Gina Gallego
Top Right: Gina Gallego, Alan Fudge
© *New Line Cinema Corp.*

Scott Valentine, Michelle Little

EXTREME PREJUDICE

(TRI-STAR) Producer, Buzz Feitshans; Director, Walter Hill; Screenplay, Deric Washburn, Harry Kleiner; Story, John Milius, Fred Rexer; Executive Producers, Mario Kassar, Andrew Vajna; Photography, Matthew F. Leonetti; Designer, Albert Heschong; Editor, Freeman Davies; Music, Jerry Goldsmith; Associate Producer, Mae Woods; Casting, Judith Holstra, Marcia Ross; Production Manager, Jo Ann May-Pavey; Assistant Directors, Dick Petersmann, Bob Simon, Barry Thomas; Source Music Producer, Ry Cooder; Sound, Richard Bryce Goodman; Stunts, Bennie Dobbins; Art Director, Joseph C. Nemec, III; Assistant Art Director, Craig Edgar; Set Decorator, Ernie Bishop; Special Effects, Tom Fisher, Jay King, Dave Domeyer, Greg Curtis; Set Designer, Beverli Eagan; Costumes, Dan Moore; Production Coordinator, Chriss Strauss; Songs by various artists; Soundtrack on Intrada Records; Dolby Stereo; Technicolor; Rated R; 104 minutes; April release

CAST

Jack Benteen	Nick Nolte
Cash Bailey	Powers Boothe
Major Paul Hackett	Michael Ironside
Sarita Cisneros	Maria Conchita Alonso
Sheriff Hank Pearson	Rip Torn
Sgt. Larry McRose	Clancy Brown
Sgt. Buck Atwater	William Forsythe
Sgt. Declan Patrick Coker	Matt Mulhern
Sgt. Charles Biddle	Larry B. Scott
Sgt. Luther Fry	Dan Tullis, Jr.
Merv	John Dennis Johnston
Lupo	Luis Contreras
Hector	Carlos Cervantes
Monday	Tom "Tiny" Lister, Jr.
Deputy Cortez	Marco Rodriguez
Deputy Purvis	James Lashly
Clarence King	Tony Frank
Chub Luke	Mickey Jones
T. C. Luke	Kent Lipham
Pearly Grips	Sam Gauny
Rincon Norte Bartender	Gil Reyes
Arturo	Rick Garcia
Jesus	Larry Duran
Andy	Humberto De La Torre
Donna Lee	Erin Bowden

and Richard Duran, Christina Garcia, Charles Lewis, Fred Eisenlohr, Anthony Galvan III, Frank Lugo, Jimmy Ortega, Lin Shaye, Anthony Lattanzio, Ken Medlock, Michelle Lynn Rosen

Top Left: Powers Boothe, Nick Nolte
Below: Larry B. Scott, Michael Ironside
© *Tri-Star Pictures*

Nick Nolte, Maria Conchita Alonso

Rip Torn, Nick Nolte

MAKING MR. RIGHT

(ORION) Producer, Mike Wise, Joel Tuber; Director, Susan Seidelman; Screenplay, Floyd Byars, Laurie Frank; Executive Producers, Susan Seidelman, Dan Enright; Photography, Edward Lachman; Casting, Risa Bramon, Billy Hopkins; Editor/Associate Producer, Andrew Mondshein; Designer, Barbara Ling; Music, Chaz Jankel; Music Assistant, Philip Bagenall; Production Manager, Jon Landau; Assistant Directors, Joel Tuber, David Dreyfuss; Visual Effects, Bran Ferren; Costumes, Rudy Dillon, Adelle Lutz; Art Director, Jack Blackman; Set Decorators, Scott Jacobson. Jimmy Robinson, II; Assistant Art Director, Mark Harrington; Sound, Howard Warren; Production Coordinator, Cynthia Streit; Associate Producer, Lynn Hendee; Stunts, Jeff Moldovan, Paul Nuckles; Associate Editor, Richard Nord; Assistant Editors, Kris Cole, James Flatto; Special Effects, Topher Dow; Songs by various artists; DeLuxe Color; Rated PG-13; 100 minutes; April release

CAST

Jeff Peters/Ulysses	John Malkovich
Frankie Stone	Ann Magnuson
Trish	Glenne Headly
Steve Marcus	Ben Masters
Sandy	Laurie Metcalf
Estelle Stone	Polly Bergen
Dr. Ramdas	Harsh Nayyar
Don	Hart Bochner
Ivy Stone	Susan Berman
Suzy Duncan	Polly Draper
Bruce	Christian Clemenson
Moe Glickstein	Merwin Goldsmith
Manny	Sid Raymond
Jeweler	Sidney Armus
Tux Salesman	Robert Trebor
TV Anchorman	John Hambrick
Newscaster	Susan Lichtman, Steve Rondinaro
Receptionist	Sherry Diamont
Chemtec Receptionist	Ruthe Geier
Skippy	Mike Hanly
Kitchen Maid	Donna Rosae
Station Wagon Driver	P. B. Floyd
Photo Double	Trip Hamilton
Hector	Ronnie Rosado
Hector's Uncle	Roy Datz
Lupe Rodriguez	Frank Sangineto
"Snowball"	"Penny"

and Jill Mallorie, Eve Marsh, Stephen McFarland, Tom Schwartz, Ruth Mullen, Michael Seidelman, James F. Murtaugh, Ralph Gunderman, Bob Cruz, Harry Chase, Ken Ceresne, Janice Frank, Stanley Kirk, Garitt Kono, Kevin Williams, Clayton Ludovitch, Alan B. Minor, Jose Ramirez, Luisa Rodriguez, Guy Trusty, Gerald Owens, Julie Lamm, Syndi Robin Tracton, Chick Bernhardt, Mr. Mike

**Top: Glenne Headly, John Malkovich Left: Malkovich,
Ann Magnuson Below: Laurie Metcalf, Malkovich
© Orion Pictures/John Clifford**

Ann Magnuson, John Malkovich Above: John Shackford,
Ann Magnuson, Robert deStolfe

POLICE ACADEMY 4: CITIZENS ON PATROL

(WARNER BROS.) Producer, Paul Maslansky; Director, Jim Drake; Screenplay, Gene Quintano; Based on characters created by Neal Israel, Pat Proft; Photography, Robert Saad; Designer, Trevor Williams; Editor, David Rawlins; Music, Robert Folk; Associate Producer, Donald West; Casting, Fern Champion, Pamela Basker; Production Manager, Suzanne Lore; Assistant Directors, Michael Zenon, Bill Bannerman; Art Director, Rhiley Fuller; Set Decorator, Steve Shewchuk; Musical Supervisor, David Chackler; Orchestrations, Don Davis; Sound, Ingrid M. Cusiel; Assistant Art Director, Rebekah Williams; Costumes, Aleida MacDonald; Production Coordinator, Wendie Siford; Stunts, Michael DeLuna; Special Effects, Gene Grigg; "Citizens on Patrol," Mike Stuart, Arthur Funaro; Songs by various artists; Soundtrack on Motown; Technicolor; Rated PG; 87 minutes; April release

CAST

Mahoney	Steve Guttenberg
Hightower	Bubba Smith
Jones	Michael Winslow
Tackleberry	David Graf
Sweetchuck	Tim Kazurinsky
Claire Mattson	Sharon Stone
Callahan	Leslie Easterbrook
Hooks	Marion Ramsey
Proctor	Lance Kinsey
Captain Harris	G. W. Bailey
Zed	Bobcat Goldthwait
Commandant Lassard	George Gaynes
Butterworth	Derek McGrath
Copeland	Scott Thomson
Mrs. Feldman	Billie Bird
Commissioner Hurst	George R. Robertson
Nogata	Brian Tochi
Arnie	Brian Backer
Kyle	David Spade
House	Tab Thacker
Laura	Corinne Bohrer
Zack	Randall "Tex" Cobb
Todd	Michael McManus
Mrs. Kirkland-Tackleberry	Colleen Camp
Bud Kirkland	Andrew Paris
Mr. Kirkland	Arthur Batanides
Mrs. Kirkland	Jackie Joseph

and Arnie Hardt, Frank Canino, Bob Lem, Francois Klanfer, Denis de Laviolette, Joey Pomanti, Harvey Chao, Michele Duquet, Jack Creley, Ted Simonett, Kay Hartrey, Sid Gould, Megan Smith, Don Ritchie, Rummy Bishop, Carolyn Scott, Marc Leger, Larry Schwartz, James Carroll, Brent Myers, Michael Rhoades, Diane Fabian, Glenn Preston, Steve Caballero, Tommy Guerrero, Tony Hawk, Mike McGill, Chris Miller, Lance Mountain, Wayne Charbrol, Jean Frenette, Ed Hsing, Marc Kubota, Wilson Khoa, Harold Kojima, Glenn Kwan, Brian Sakamoto, Jim Wong

Right: Steve Guttenberg, Bubba Smith, Tim Kazurinsky (glasses), David Graf, Leslie Easterbrook Above: Michael Winslow, Steve Guttenberg, Top: Steve Guttenberg, Michael Winslow, G. W. Bailey
© *Warner Bros. Inc.*

G. W. Bailey, Bob Goldthwait

George Gaynes (R)

PROJECT X

(**20th CENTURY FOX**) Producers, Walter F. Parkes, Lawrence Lasker; Director, Jonathan Kaplan; Screenplay, Stanley Weiser; Story, Stanley Weiser, Lawrence Lasker; Photography, Dean Cundey; Designer, Lawrence G. Paull; Editor, O. Nicholas Brown; Casting, Jackie Burch; Music, James Horner; Executive Producer, C. O. Erickson; Production Manager, Don Roberts; Assistant Directors, Albert Shapiro, Russell Harling; Visual Effects, Michael Fink; Set Decorator, Rick Simpson; Assistant Art Director, Dianne Wager; Set Designers, Joseph Pacelli, Lynn Christopher; Additional Editor, Brent Schoenfeld; Assistant Editors, Gregory Gerlich, Sherrie Sanet; Sound, Petur Hliddal; Animal Coordinator, Hubert Wells; Trainers, Fernando Celis, Tom Collord, Mark Harden, Wallace Ross, Cheryl Shawver, Julian Sylvester, Ron Oxley; Costumes, Mary Vogt; Special Makeup, Michael G. Westmore; Special Effects, Robert Willard, Richard Hill, Richard Thompson; Production Coordinator, Dani Regal O'Connell; Stunts, Victor Paul; Casting Assistant, William Damota; Visual Effects, Norman B. Schwartz; Orchestrations, Greig McRitchie; Chimp Vocalization, Keith Critchlow; Song, *"You Baby You"* by Chris McCarty, Gary Mallaber; Vocals, Billy Burnette; Produced in association with Amercent Films and American Entertainment Partners L.P.; Dolby Stereo; DeLuxe Color; Rated PG; 108 minutes; April release

CAST

Jimmy	Matthew Broderick
Teri	Helen Hunt
Dr. Carroll	Bill Sadler
Robertson	Johnny Ray McGhee
Sgt. Krieger	Jonathan Stark
Col. Niles	Robin Gammell
Watts	Stephen Lang
Dr. Criswell	Jean Smart
General Claybourne	Chuck Bennett
Hadfield	Daniel Roebuck
Airman Lewis	Mark Harden
Major Duncan	Duncan Wilmore
Cellmate	Marvin J. McIntyre
Senator	Swede Johnson
Congressman	Harry E. Northup
Lt. Voeks	Michael Eric Kramer
Lt. Frohman	Reed R. McCants
Price	Ward Costello
Tavel	Jackson Sleet
Cochran	Lance August
Daniels	Stan Foster
M. Perks	Gil Mandelik
Mr. Verrous	Shelly Desai
Max King	Dick Miller
Melvin	Michael Milgrom
Miss Decker	Catherine Paolone
Dr. Hutchins	John Chilton
Airman Curtis	David Raynr
Sgt. Huntley	Lynn Eastman
Airman	Julian Sylvester
Lt. Rainey	Kim Robillard
Lt. Durschlag	David Stenstrom
Lt. Hayes	Richard Cummings, Jr.
Mackler	Randal Patrick
Sgt. Ridley	Sonny Davis
Air Policemen	Bob Minor, Raymond Elmendorf
M. P. Rodriguez	Robert Covarrubias
M. P. Jones	Dino Shorte
Finley	Ken Lerner
Fanara	Travis Swords
Warden	William Snider
Reeves	Philip A. Roberson
Wilson	Michael McGrady
Dryer	Rob Fitzgerald
Lenore	Pamela Ludwig
Carol Lee	Deborah Offner
Hamer	Lance Nichols

and Tee Rodgers, Jackie Kinner, Mady Kaplan, Chevis Cooper, Kenneth Sagoes, Louis A. Perez, Sam Laws, Hal Rayle, Arthur Burghardt, Anne Lockhart, Charles Adler, Patrick Pinney, Randy Gardner, Leo Rossi, Bobby Porter, Willie, Okko, Karanja, Luke, Harry, Arthur, Ciafu, Lucy, Lulu, Mousie, Mucho.

Top Right: Matthew Broderick, Virgil
Below: Matthew Broderick, Virgil, Helen Hunt
© 20th Century Fox/Ralph Nelson

Matthew Broderick, Virgil, Helen Hunt

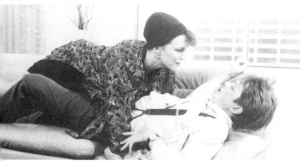

THE SECRET OF MY SUCCESS

(UNIVERSAL) Producer/Director, Herbert Ross; Screenplay, Jim Cash, Jack Epps, Jr., A. J. Carothers; Story, A. J. Carothers; Executive Producer, David Chasman; Associate Producer, Nora Kaye; Photography, Carlo di Palma; Editor, Paul Hirsch; Designers, Edward Pisoni, Peter Larkin; Costumes, Joseph G. Aulisi; Music, David Foster; Line Producer/Production Manager, Joseph M. Caracciolo; Casting, Mary Colquhoun, Hank McCann; Assistant Directors, Robert V. Girolami, Louis D'Esposito, Jane Paul; Musical Supervision, Tommy Mottola, Jeb Brien; Assistant Editors, Peck Prior, Adam Bernardi, John Murray; Sound, Jim Sabat; Set Decorator, Susan Bode; Stunts, Vic Magnotta; Production Coordinator, Jane Raab; Color; Dolby Stereo; Rated PG-13; 110 minutes; April release

CAST

Brantley Foster	Michael J. Fox
Christy Wills	Helen Slater
Howard Prescott	Richard Jordan
Vera Prescott	Margaret Whitton
Fred Melrose	John Pankow
Barney Rattigan	Christopher Murney
Art Thomas	Gerry Bamman
Donald Davenport	Fred Gwynne
Jean	Carol-Ann Susi
Grace Foster	Elizabeth Franz
Burt Foster	Drew Snyder
Maureen	Susan Kellermann
Arnold Forbush	Barton Heyman
Sheila	Mercedes Ruehl
Owens	Ira B. Wheeler
Fletcher	Ashley J. Laurence
McMasters	Rex Robbins
Davis	Christopher Durang
Ferguson	MacIntyre Dixon
Ron	Bill Fagerbakke
Davidson	Jack Davidson
Proctor	John Bowman
Executives	Jeff Brooks, Ascanio Sharpe, Don Amendolia
Mrs. Meachum	Judith Malina
Research Department Clerk	Mary Catherine Wright
Shipping Executive	Joseph Ragno
Fired Executive	Burke Pearson
Liquor Store Owner	Ray Ramirez
Wife of Liquor Store Owner	Gloria Irizarry

and Mark Margolis, Rick Aviles, John C. Capodice, Sally-Jane Heit, Richard Arthur Gallo, Luis Ramos

Top: Michael J. Fox Left: Helen Slater, Fox
Below: Richard Jordan, Michael J. Fox
© *Universal City Studios*

Helen Slater, Michael J. Fox
Above: Margaret Whitton, Michael J. Fox

WILL VINTON'S FESTIVAL OF CLAYMATION

(EXPANDED ENTERTAINMENT) Producer, Will Vinton; Presented by International Tournee of Animation. Includes "*Calaveras County*" sequence from "*The Adventures of Mark Twain*," "*A Christmas Gift*", "*Claymation*", "*Beneficial Finance*", "*Cap'n Crunch*", "*Domino's 'Noid*" "*Intro*", "*Domino's Pizza Puncher*", "*Kentucky Fried Chicken ('Party-Time Experts')*", "*Kraft Rockers 'n' Rollers (Back-Up)*", "*Nickelodeon (Back-Up)*", "*Nike*", "*Raisins I*', "*Raisins II*", "*Scotsman*", "*Creation*" from "The Creation" from "God's Trombones" by James Weldon Johnson, "*Dinosaur*", "*Freak Previews*", "*The Great Cognito*", "*Legacy*", "*Vanz Kant Danz*". Producers, Will Vinton, Susan Shadburne, David Altschul; Directors, Will Vinton, Barry Bruce, David Altschul; Screenplays, Susan Shadburne, Doug Aberle, John Morrison; Executive Producers, Hugh Tirrell, Frank Moynihan, Derek W. Muirden, David Adams, Jerry Kramer; Animators, Tom Gasek, Barry Bruce, Joan Gratz, Will Vinton, Matt Wuerker, Bill Fiesterman, Joanne Radmilovich, Elizabeth Butler, Mark Gustafson, Craig Bartlett, Lorah Cusick Conheim, Doug Aberle, Gairy Bialke, Jim McAllister, Don Merkt, Bruce McKean; Set Design, Bruce McKean, Don Merkt, Joan Gratz; Character Design, Barry Bruce, Bill Fiersterman, Mark Gustafson, Joan Gratz, Don Merkt; Concept, Derek W. Muirden, Barry Bruce, Don Merkt; Editors, George Hood, Dan Hoffman, Skeets McGrew, Michael Gall, Paul Diener, Steve Scott, John T. Peterson; Song, "*Christmas Dinner*" by Paul Stookey; Music, David Friesen, Billy Scream, John Fogerty; Sound, Ron Walker, Glenn Micallef, Gary McRobert, Wayne Woods, Bill Scream; Unit Managers, Ruth Wood, Dianne Drachenbeg, Maureen Mullen; Live Action Photography, Reagan Ramsey, David Altschul, John W. Mincey; Lighting, Robin Willis; Art Direction, Steve Karatzas; Assistant Producer, Marilyn Zornado; Models, Lorah Cusick Conheim, Hillary Van Austin, Gairy Bialke, Tony Merrithew; Musical Arrangements/Production, David Friesen, Billy Scream; Music Performances, David Friesen, John Stowell, Billy Scream; Production Assistance, Ed Geis; Production Manager, Rick Cooper; Story Consultant, Don Roberts; Production Supervisor, Paul Diener; Photography, Gus Van Sant; Production Coordinator, Marilyn Zornado; Color; Not Rated; 90 minutes; April release. WITH: Dallas McKennon, Herb Smith, Scott Constantine, Fred Newman, Daws Butler, Craig Brodley, Larry Mirano, Pons Maar, Andre Stojka, Chick Hearn, Jefferson Dancers, Buddy Miles, J. R. Friday, Tim Conner, Michele Mariana, Jimmy Counterfit, John Morrison, Brian Bressler, Frank Jeffords, Russ Fast, Holly Weikel, Claretta Mariana, James Earl Jones

California Raisins

SUMMER HEAT

(ATLANTIC) Executive Producers, Thomas Coleman, Michael Rosenblatt; Director/Screenplay, Michie Gleason; Producer, William Tennant; Photography, Elliot Davis; Music, Richard Stone; Theme "*The Heart Must Have a Home,*" Will Jennings, Barry Mann, Georges Delerus; Vocals, Kim Carnes; Music Supervisor, Steve Tyrell; Designer, Marsha Hinds; Editor, Mary Bauer; Casting, Junie Lowry; Line Producer/Production Manager, Patricia A. Stallone; Assistant Directors, Elliot Lewis Rosenblatt, Larry Litton, Rebekah E. Wright; Sound, E. Lee Haxall; Costumes, Anthony Marando; Art Director, Bo Johnson; Set Decorator, Jan K. Bergstrom; Assistant Set Decorator, Dudley Leigh Johnson; CFI Color; Rated R; 90 minutes; May release

CAST

Roxy	Lori Singer
Aaron	Anthony Edwards
Jack	Bruce Abbott
Ruth	Kathy Bates
Will	Clu Gulager
Baby	Jessie Kent
Strother	Noble Willingham
Bass	Nesbitt Blaisdell
Neb	Matt Lamond
Georgeanna	Jane Cecil
Aunt Patty	Miriam Byrd-Nethery
Callie	Jessica Leigh Mann
Raider	Michael Mattick
Mr. Tatie	Conrad McLaren
Old Mama	Julia Beals Williams
Gyp	Charmaine Mancil
Estelle	Chris Bass Randolph
Tarboro Sheriff	Robert Albertia
Tarboro Deputy	Pat Miller
Georgia Sheriff	Charlie Baxter
Cabin Owner	Lynne Anchors Hurder
Dr. Best	Laurens Moore
Dr. A	Richard Emery
Mr. Martin	Mert Hatfield
Mr. Hodges	Joe Inscoe
Mr. Riley	Phil Uhler
Bailiff	E. Pat Hall
Reporters	Duke Ernsberger, Robin Dale Robertson, Tony Marando
Court Clerk	Rachel M. Joyner
Judge	Charles H. Gleason

Bruce Abbott, Lori Singer
© *Atlantic Releasing Corp.*

BEVERLY HILLS COP II

(PARAMOUNT) Producers, Don Simpson, Jerry Bruckheimer; Director, Tony Scott; Screenplay, Larry Ferguson, Warren Skaaren; Story, Eddie Murphy, Robert D. Wachs; Based on characters created by Danilo Bach & Daniel Petrie, Jr.; Executive Producers, Robert D. Wachs, Richard Tienken; Photography, Jeffrey L. Kimball; Designer, Ken Davis; Editors, Billy Weber, Chris Lebenzon, Michael Tronick; Music, Harold Faltermeyer; Casting, Bonnie Timmermann, Vickie Thomas; Production Managers, Fred Caruso, Arthur Seidel; Assistant Directors, Peter Bogart, Hope Goodwin, Michael Amundson; Art Director, James J. Murakami; Set Decorator, John Anderson; Sound, William B. Kaplan; Assistant Editors, Claudia Finkle, Peter N. Lonsdale; Assistant Art Director, Cate Bangs; Stunts, Gary McLarty, Alan Oliney; Special Effects, Tom Ryba, Dave Blitstein, Tom Tokunaga, Johnny Borgese; "Shakedown" by Harold Faltermeyer, Keith Forsey, Bob Seger/"Hold On" by James Wirrick/and Songs by various other artists; Dolby Stereo; Technicolor; Rated R; 120 minutes; May release

CAST

Axel Foley	Eddie Murphy
Billy Rosewood	Judge Reinhold
Maxwell Dent	Jurgen Prochnow
Andrew Bogomil	Ronny Cox
John Taggart	John Ashton
Karla Fry	Brigitte Nielsen
Harold Lutz	Allen Garfield
Chip Cain	Dean Stockwell
Jeffrey Friedman	Paul Reiser
Inspector Todd	Gil Hill
Nikos Thomopolis	Paul Guilfoyle
Mayor Egan	Robert Ridgley
Biddle	Brian O'Connor
Jan Bogomil	Alice Adair
May	Eugene Butler
Willie	Glenn Withrow
Chauffeur	Stephen Liska
Sidney Bernstein	Gilbert Gottfried
Russ Fielding	Tom Bower

and Valerie Wildman, Hugh M. Hefner, Carrie Leigh, Frank J. Pesce, Vic Manni, Sheri Levinsky, Ray Murphy, Sr. Todd Susman, Chris Rock, Susan Lentini, Anthony D'Andrea, Robert Pastorelli, Kopi Sotiropulos, Richard Tienken, Teal Roberts, Peggy Sands, Larry Carroll, Carlos Cervantes, Michael DeMarlo, Dana Gladstone, Richmond Harrison, Darryl Henriques, John Hostetter, Tom "Tiny" Lister, Jr., Ed Pansullo, Rudy Ramos, Ritch Shydner, John Lisbon Wood, Carl Bringas, Joe Duquette, Michael F. Kelly, William Lamar, Christopher R. Adams, Danny Nero, Devin Bartlett, Dayna O'Brien, Eugene Mounts, Everett Sherman Jr., Catrin Cole, Ola Ray, Alana Soares, Venice Kong, Luann Lee, Rebecca Ferratti, Kymberly Paige, Kymberly Herrin, Leilani Soares, Anne Lammot, Pamela Santini, Sarah Quick, Marlenne Kingsland, Monet Swann, Natalie Smith, Kari Whitman

Top: Eddie Murphy, Dean Stockwell, Brigitte Nielsen Right: Robert Ridgley, Allen Garfield, Eddie Murphy, Judge Reinhold, Brian O'Connor
© *Paramount Pictures/Bruce Talamon*

Judge Reinhold, Eddie Murphy (also above), John Ashton

AMAZING GRACE AND CHUCK

(TRI-STAR) Producer/Screenplay, David Field; Director, Mike Newell; Executive Producer/Production Manager, Roger M. Rothstein; Photography, Robert Elswit; Editor, Peter Hollywood; Executive Consultant, Ted Turner; Designer, Dena Roth; Music, Elmer Bernstein; Casting, Lynn Stalmaster & Associates, Mali Finn; Assistant Directors, John T. Kretchmer, Carole Keligian; Costumes, Jack Buehler; Art Director, John Myhre; Set Decorator, Michael J. Taylor; Set Designer, Dawn Snyder; Stunts, Orwin Harvey; Production Coordinators, Susan Vanderbeek, Eileen McCahill; Sound, Jonathan Stein; Special Effects, Rick Kerrigan; Visual Effects, Fantasy II Film Effects/Camera Effects LTD.; From Tri-Star-ML Delphi Premier Productions; Dolby Stereo; Metrocolor; Rated PG; 115 minutes; May release

CAST

Sports Broadcaster	Dean Alexander
Strickland	Jim Antonio
Himself	Red Auerbach
George	Alan Autry
Hot Dog	Michael Bowen
Pamela	Frances Conroy
Third Baseman	James Cotterell
Lynn Taylor	Jamie Lee Curtis
Amazing Grace Smith	Alex English
Dick Ferguson	Clarence Felder
Network Anchor	Lynne Turner Fitzgerald
First Baseman	Brian R. Hager
Bowman	Robert Harper
Jerome	James Lindley Hathaway
Shortstop	Matt Kerns
Carolyn	Cortney Kutner
Johnny B. Goode	Dennis Lipscomb
Mad Dog	Harvey Martin
Himself	Johnny Most
Boston Reporter	Natalie Oliver
Tommy	Kurt Olsson
President	Gregory Peck
Russell	William L. Petersen
Jeffries	Lee Richardson
Stuart Shipley	John Russell
Soviet Premier	Vasek C. Simek
Russian Translator	Rudolf Svehla
Johann	Manfred Sypold
Laura	Cara Wilder
Chuck Murdock	Joshua Zuehlke

and Jim Allen, Michael Bond, Steven Bothun, A. J. Kallan, Gwen Petersen, Maite Petersen, Joe Sabatini, Robert Schenkkan, Harris Smithe, Robert Tilson, James Tuomey

Right: Frances Conroy, William Petersen, Cortney Kutner, Joshua Zuehlke, Alan Autry, Jamie Lee Curtis
Above: Alex English, Joshua Zuehlke Top: Robert Harper, Gregory Peck © *Tri-Star Pictures*

Michael Bowen, Alex English, Joshua Zuehlke, Alan Autry

Joshua Zuehlke, William L. Petersen

RIVER'S EDGE

(ISLAND FILMS) Producers, Sarah Pillsbury, Midge Sanford; Director, Tim Hunter; Screenplay, Neal Jimenez; Executive Producers, John Daly, Derek Gibson; Co-producer/Production Manager, David Streit; Photography, Frederick Elmes; Designer, John Muto; Editors, Howard Smith, Sonya Sones; Music, Jurgen Knieper; Costumes, Claudia Brown; Casting, Carrie Frazier-Reinhold, Shani Ginsberg; Assistant Directors, Richard Hawley, Nancy King; Production Executive, Graham Henderson; Production Associate, Kathy Budas; Set Decorator, Anne Huntley; Sound, David Brownlow; Production Coordinator, Liz Galloway; Music Supervisor, Budd Carr; Soundtrack on Enigma/Metal Blade Records; Metrocolor; Rated R; 99 minutes; May release

CAST

Layne	Crispin Glover
Matt	Keanu Reeves
Clarissa	Ione Skye Leitch
Samson	Daniel Roebuck
Feck	Dennis Hopper
Tim	Joshua Miller
Maggie	Roxana Zal
Tony	Josh Richman
Mike	Phil Brock
Bennett	Tom Bower
Madeleine	Constance Forslund
Jim	Leo Rossi
Burkewaite	Jim Metzler
Kim	Tammy Smith
Jamie	Danyi Deats
Moko	Yuzo Nishihara
Checker	Taylor Negron
Tom	Chris Peters
Kevin	Richard Richcreek
Student	Maeve Odum
Aunto	Frances De L'Etanche Du Bois
Tony's Father	Mike Hungerford
Cop	James Terry

© *Island Pictures/Jane O'Neal*

Keanu Reeves, Crispin Glover, Roxana Zal, Phil Brock, Josh Richman, Daniel Roebuck, Ione Sky Leitch Top Left: Dennis Hopper
Below: Ione Skye Leitch, Keanu Reeves

GARDENS OF STONE

(TRI-STAR) Producers, Michael I. Levy, Francis Coppola; Director, Francis Coppola; Screenplay, Ronald Bass; Based on the novel by Nicholas Proffitt; Executive Producers, Stan Weston, Jay Emmett, Fred Roos; Co-Executive Producer, David Valdes; Photography, Jordan Cronenweth; Designer, Dean Tavoularis; Editor, Barry Malkin; Costumes, Willa Kim, Judianna Makovsky; Music, Carmine Coppola; Production Manager, David V. Lester; Assistant Directors, David Valdes, Tena Yatroussis, Dan Suhart; Casting, Janet Hirshenson, Jane Jenkins, Bonnie Timmermann, Aleta Wood-Chappelle; Art Director, Alex Tavoularis; Set Decorator, Gary Fettis; Production Coordinator, Teri Fettis; Stunts, Buddy Joe Hooker; Assistant Editors, Debra Bard, John Gilroy; Sound Designer, Richard Beggs; Sound, Thomas Causey; Special Effects, Robin Hauser; From Zoetrope Studios; DeLuxe Color; Dolby Stereo; 112 minutes; Rated R; May release

CAST

Clell Hazard	James Caan
Samantha Davis	Anjelica Huston
"Goody" Nelson	James Earl Jones
Jackie Willow	D. B. Sweeney
Homer Thomas	Dean Stockwell
Rachel Feld	Mary Stuart Masterson
Slasher Williams	Dick Anthony Williams
Betty Raie	Lonette McKee
Lt. Webber	Sam Bottoms
Pete Deveber	Elias Koteas
Flanagan	Larry Fishburne
Wildman	Casey Siemaszko
Col. Feld	Peter Masterson
Mrs. Feld	Carlin Glynn
Col. Godwin	Erik Holland
Don Brubaker	Bill Graham
Editor	Terrence Currier
Navy Captain	Terry Hinz
Daughter	Lisa-Marie Felter
Lt. Colonel	William Williamson
General	Joseph A. Ross, Jr.
Lt. Atkins	Matthew Litchfield
Lt. Horton	Nick Mathwick
Private	Robert Frerichs
Blue Lieutenant	Grant Lee Douglass

and Mark Frazer, Terry Foster, Marshall Sizemore, Steve Barcanic, Hajna O. Moss, Arthur V. Gorman, Jr., Louis Rangel, Buddy Joe Hooker

Left: Angelica Huston, James Caan, Bill Graham
Above: James Caan, Angelica Huston Top: Mary Stuart Masterson, D. B. Sweeney © *Tri-Star Pictures*

James Caan, D. B. Sweeney, James Earl Jones

James Caan (center)

45

SWEET LORRAINE

(**ANGELIKA FILMS**) Producer/Director, Steve Gomer; Screenplay, Michael Zettler, Shelly Altman; Story, Michael Zettler, Shelly Altman, George Malko; Photography, Rene Ohashi; Editor, Laurence Solomon; Music, Robbins; Designer, David Gropman; Color; Rated PG-13; 91 minutes; May release; No other credits provided

CAST

Lillian	Maureen Stapleton
Molly	Trini Alvarado
Sam	Lee Richardson
Jack	John Bedford-Lloyd
Phil Allen	Freddie Roman
Howie	Giancarlo Esposito
Karen	Edith Falco
Leonard	Todd Graff
Bobby	Evan Handler
Julie	Tamara Tunie

Right: Freddie Roman Top: Lee Richardson, Maureen Stapleton
© *Angelika Films*

(sitting) Mindy Morgenstern, Edith Falco, John Bedford-Lloyd, Trini Alvarado, Maureen Stapleton, (standing) Giancarlo Esposito, Evan Handler, Lee Richardson, Tamara Tunie, Todd Graff

THE BELIEVERS

(ORION) Producers, John Schlesinger, Michael Childers, Beverly Camhe; Director, John Schlesinger; Screenplay, Mark Frost; Based on book *"The Religion"* by Nicholas Conde; Executive Producer/Production Manager, Edward Teets; Photography, Robby Muller; Designer, Simon Holland; Editor, Peter Honess; Designer, Shay Cunliffe; Music, J. Peter Robinson; Associate Producer, Mark Frost; Casting, Donna Isaacson, John Lyons; Assistant Director, Patrick Crowley; Production Coordinator, Patt McCurdy; Special Effects Makeup, Kevin Hayney; Choreography, Wilhelmina Taylor; Stunts, Dean Jeffries; Second Unit Directors, Michael Childers, Patrick Crowley; Production Supervisor, David Middlemas; Assistant Editors, Jeremy Gibbs, Richard Fettes, Mick Monks, Andrew Glen, Jonathan Lucas, Cindy Kalan; Production Manager, Monty Diamond; Art Director, John Kasarda; Set Decorator, Susan Bode; Sound, Todd Maitland, Kim Maitland; Special Effects, Connie Brink; Dolby Stereo; DeLuxe Color; Rated R; 114 minutes; June release

CAST

Cal Jamison	Martin Sheen
Jessica Halliday	Helen Shaver
Chris Jamison	Harley Cross
Lieutenant Sean McTaggert	Robert Loggia
Kate Maslow	Elizabeth Wilson
Donald Calder	Harris Yulin
Dennis Maslow	Lee Richardson
Marty Wertheimer	Richard Masur
Mrs. Ruiz	Carla Pinza
Tom Lopez	Jimmy Smits
Sezine	Raul Davila
Palo	Malick Bowens
Lisa	Janet-Laine Green

and Larry Ramos, Philip Corey, Jennifer Lee, Nonnie Griffin, Bob Clout, Harvey Chao, Christine Pak, Joan Kaye, Eddie Jones, John Bendel, Joseph Pentangelo, Joseph Wilkens, Robert Clohessy, Dick Martinsen, Robert Connelly, Tony DeSantis, Frank Rivers, Ana Maria Quintana, Ray Paisley, Dick Calahan, Christopher Brown, Gary Farmer, Ramsey Fadiman, Juan Manuel Aguero, Maria Magdaleno, Shirley Anthony, Elizabeth Hanna, Micki Moore, Richard Spiegelman, Fernando Queija, Maria Lebb, Khali Keyi, Leroy Radcliffe, Wilhelmina Taylor

Right: Lee Richardson, Martin Sheen, Harris Yulin Above: Robert Loggia, Martin Sheen Top: Helen Shaver, Harley Cross, Martin Sheen
© *Orion Pictures/Takashi Seida*

BENJI THE HUNTED

(BUENA VISTA) Producer, Ben Vaughn; Director/Screenplay, Joe Camp; Supervising Producer/Production Manager/Assistant Director, Carolyn H. Camp; Executive Producer, Ed Vanston; Associate Producer, Erwin Hearne; Sound, C.M.S. Productions, Inc; Benji's Trainers, Bryan L. Renfro, Frank and Juanita Inn; Special Cougar Work, Sled Reynolds, Gideon; Wild Animals Furnished and Trained by Steve Martin's Working Wildlife; Editor, Karen Thorndike; Photography, Don Reddy; Music, Euel Box, Betty Box; Wild Animal Trainers, Steve Martin, Bobi Gaddy, Madeleine Cowie Klein, Sled Reynolds; Cub Mom, Maureen T. Hughes; Bear Trainer, Mark Wiener; Eagle Trainers, Neil R. Egland, Mark Woener; Assistant Director, Dannielle J. Weiss; Director of Arts, Props and Special Effects, Bob Riggs; Assistant-Art, Props, FX, Ray Brown; Assistant Editors, Adrienne "Dee" Chappell, Jeffrey January; Production Coordinators, Maureen Osborne-Beall, Carol Kravetz; Stunt Animals, Cosmekinetics; Music Supervisor, Betty Box; Presented by Walt Disney Pictures; An Embark Production in association with Mulberry Square Productions; Presented in association with Silver Screen Partners III; CFI Color; Dolby Stereo; Rated G; 88 minutes; June release

CAST

TV Director's Voice	Joe Camp
Producer's Voice	Steve Zanolini
Countdown Voice	Karen Thorndike
Newscaster	Nancy Francis
Engineer's Hand	Ben Vaughn
TV Cameraman	Mike Francis
Frank Inn	As Himself
Benji	As Himself
Hunter	Red Steagall

Benji and a cub

DRAGNET

(UNIVERSAL) Producers, David Permut, Robert K. Weiss; Director, Tom Mankiewicz; Screenplay, Dan Aykroyd, Alan Zweibel, Tom Mankiewicz; Executive Producer, Bernie Brillstein; Photography, Matthew F. Leonetti; Designer, Robert F. Boyle; Editors, Richard Halsey, William D. Gordean; Music, Ira Newborn; Associate Producer/Production Manager, Don Zepfel; Casting, Lynn Stalmaster & Assoc., David Rubin; Costumes, Taryn DeChellis; Assistant Directors, David Sosna, Vicki Rhodes; Stunts, Terry Leonard; Production Associate, Kevin M. Marcy; Art Director, Frank Richwood; Set Decorator, Arthur Jeph Parker; Sound, Willie Burton; Special Effects, Cliff Wenger, Whitey Krumm, Roger Hansen, Jim Thomson, Jeff Frink; Special Visual Effects, Syd Dutton, Bill Taylor; Snake Design, David B. Miller; Songs by various artists; "Dragnet" Themes, Walter Schumann, Miklos Roza; Soundtrack on MCA; Dolby Stereo; DeLuxe Color; Rated PG-13; 110 minutes; June release

CAST

Friday	Dan Aykroyd
Streebek	Tom Hanks
Whirley	Christopher Plummer
Gannon	Harry Morgan
Connie Swail	Alexandra Paul
Emil Muzz	Jack O'Halloran
Jane Kirkpatrick	Elizabeth Ashley
Jerry Caesar	Dabney Coleman
Enid Borden	Kathleen Freeman
Mayor Parvin	Bruce Gray
Granny Mundy	Lenka Peterson
Sylvia Wiss	Julia Jennings
April	Lisa Aliff
Tito Provencal	Fred Asparagus
Betsy Blees	Kimberly Foster
Officer Robin Gilbert	D. D. Howard
Roy Grest	Peter Leeds
Mo Sarkus	Chuck Thornton
Narrator	Bill Wittman
Mrs. Gannon	Meg Wyllie

and Joe Altmark, Nina Arvesen, Peter Aykroyd, Larry Bilzarian, Jim Boeke, Sandra Canning, William Chalmers, Donald Craig, Karen Criswell, Josh Cruze, Jenniffer Curry, Gray Daniels, Gary Lee Davis, Susan Deemer, Juli Donald, Sandra Eng, Ava Fabian, Ruben Garfias, Sharon Gilchrist, Chester Grimes, Bert Hinchman, Margaret Lenzey, Lori Leonelli, Lisa London, Kent MacLachlan, Christopher Mankiewicz, Maurice Marsac, Marshall Maurice Mitchell, Stuart Quan, Ingrid M. Rhoades, Casey Sander, Billy Ray Sharkey, Jimmie F. Skaggs, John Walton Smith, Jr., Dona Speir

Top: Dan Aykroyd, Tom Hanks Right:
Dan Aykroyd, Alexandra Paul Below:
Christopher Plummer, Elizabeth Ashley
© *Universal City Studios*

Dan Aykroyd, Tom Hanks, Harry Morgan
Above: (C) Dabney Coleman

48

FULL METAL JACKET

(WARNER BROS.) Producer/Director, Stanley Kubrick; Screenplay, Stanley Kubrick, Michael Herr, Gustav Hasford; Based on novel *"The Short Timers"* by Gustav Hasford; Executive Producer, Jan Harlan; Co-Producer, Philip Hobbs; Associate Producer, Michael Herr; Assistant to Director, Leon Vitali; Lighting, Douglas Milsome; Designer, Anton Furst; Editor, Martin Hunter; Music, Abigail Mead; Sound, Edward Tise; Costumes, Keith Denny; Assistant Directors, Terry Needham, Christopher Thompson; Production Managers, Phil Kohler, Bill Shepherd; Production Coordinators, Margaret Adams; Special Effects, John Evans; Casting, Leon Vitali, Mike Fenton, Jane Feinberg, Marion Dougherty, Dan Tran, Nguyen Thi My Chau; Art Directors, Rod Stratford, Les Tomkins, Keith Pain; Assistant Art Directors, Nigel Phelps, Andrew Rothschild; Songs by various artists; Color; Rated R; 118 minutes; June release

CAST

Pvt. Joker .... Matthew Modine
Animal Mother .... Adam Baldwin
Pvt. Pyle .... Vincent D'Onofrio
Gny. Sgt. Hartman .... Lee Ermey
Eightball .... Dorian Harewood
Cowboy .... Arliss Howard
Rafterman .... Kevyn Major Howard
Lt. Touchdown .... Ed O'Ross
and John Terry, Kierson Jecchinis, Bruce Boa, Kirk Taylor, John Stafford, Tim Colceri, Ian Tyler, Gary Landon Mills, Sal Lopez, Pappillon Soo Soo, Ngoc Le, Peter Edmund, Tan Hung Francione, Leanne Hong, Marcus D'Amico, Costas Dino Chimino, Gil Kopel, Keith Hodiak, Peter Merrill, Herbert Norville, Nguyen Hye Phong

Right: Vincent D'Onofrio, Matthew Modine, Lee Ermey
Top: Matthew Modine © *Warner Bros.*

Arliss Howard, Matthew Modine
Above: Adam Baldwin, Matthew Modine

Dorian Harewood Above: Kevyn Howard,
Sal Lopez, Adam Baldwin

49

PREDATOR

(20th CENTURY FOX) Producers, Lawrence Gordon, Joel Silver, John Davis; Director, John McTiernan; Screenplay, Jim Thomas, John Thomas; Photography, Donald McAlpine; Designer, John Vallone; Editors, John F. Link, Mark Helfrich; Casting, Jackie Burch; Special Visual Effects, R/Greenberg; Creature created by Stan Winston; Music, Alan Silvestri; Executive Producers, Laurence P. Pereira, Jim Thomas; Associate Producers, Beau E. L. Marks, John Vallone; Production Managers, Art Seidel, Beau E. L. Marks; Assistant Directors, Beau E. L. Marks, J. Tom Archuleta, K. C. Colwell, Jose Luis Ortega; Production Associate, Elaine K. Thompson; Art Directors, Frank Richwood, Jorge Saenz, John K. Reinhart, Jr.; Set Decorator, Enrique Estevez; Assistant Art Directors, Theresa Wachter, Carlos Echeverria; Sound, Manuel Topete; Makeup Design, Scott Eddo; Costumes, Marilyn Vance-Straker; Stunts, Craig R. Baxley; Special Effects, Al Di Sarro, Laurencio "Choby" Cordero; Casting Assistant, Billy Damota; Production Coordinators, Emily Gamboa, Dana Taylor, Patti Calhoun; Vocalizations, Peter Cullen; Orchestrations, James Campbell; "*Long Tall Sally*" by R. Penniman, E. Johnson, R. Blackwell; Dolby Stereo; DeLuxe Color; Rated R; 107 minutes; June release

CAST

Dutch	Arnold Schwarzenegger
Dillon	Carl Weathers
Anna	Elpidia Carrillo
Mac	Bill Duke
Blain	Jesse Ventura
Billy	Sonny Landham
Poncho	Richard Chaves
General Phillips	R. G. Armstrong
Hawkins	Shane Black
The Predator	Kevin Peter Hall

Left: Arnold Schwarzenegger, Elpidia Carrillo, Carl Weathers, Bill Duke Top: Carl Weathers, Arnold Schwarzenegger © *20th Century Fox/Zade Rosenthal*

Shane Black, Sonny Landham, Arnold Schwarzenegger, Richard Chaves (kneeling), Carl Weathers, Bill Duke, Jesse Ventura

ROXANNE

(COLUMBIA) Producers, Michael Rachmil, Daniel Melnick; Director, Fred Schepisi; Screenplay/Executive Producer, Steve Martin; From the play *Cyrano de Bergerac* by Edmond Rostand; Photography, Ian Baker; Designer, Jack DeGovia; Editor, John Scott; Casting, Pennie du Pont; Music, Bruce Smeaton; Special thanks to Don Zimmerman; Production Manager, Warren Carr; Assistant Directors, Michael Steele, Casey Grant, Wendy Chesal; Art Director, David Fischer; Set Decorator, Kimberly Richardson; Sound, Rob Young; Costumes, Richard Bruno, Tish Monaghan; Make-Up Design, Michael Westmore; Production Coordinator, Patti Allen; Special Effects, Bill Orr; Stunts, Joe Dunne, V. John Wardlow, Bob Jauregui, Roy Pichette; Produced with LA Films; Songs, Bruce Smeaton, Peter R. Melnick, Joe Curiale, Terry Cox, Jeff Kent, Paul Pesco, Jeff "Skunk" Baxter, Rick Boston, Janet Minto, Pamela Barlow; Vocals, Babi Floyd, Dan Navarro, Pamela Barlow, Janet Minto; Dolby Stereo; DeLuxe Color; Panavision; Rated PG; 107 minutes; June release

CAST

C. D. Bales	Steve Martin
Roxanne	Daryl Hannah
Chris	Rick Rossovich
Dixie	Shelley Duvall
Chuck	John Kapelos
Mayor Deebs	Fred Willard
Dean	Max Alexander
Andy	Michael J. Pollard
Ralston	Steve Mittleman
Jerry	Damon Wayans
Trent	Matt Lattanzi
Sandy	Shandra Beri
Sophie	Blanche Rubin
Dottie	Jane Campbell
Nina	Jean Sincere
Lydia	Claire Caplan
Jim	Thom Curley
Drunks	Ritch Shydner, Kevin Nealon
Cosmetic Surgeon	Brian George
Cosmetics Clerk	Maureen Murphy
Stationery Clerk	Jeffrey Joseph
Peter Quinn	Make Glavas
Mrs. Quinn	Merrilyn Gann
Berni	Bernadette Sabath
Girl in street	Caroline Barclay
Trudy	Heidi Sorenson

Above: Daryl Hannah, Steve Martin Top: Michael J. Pollard, Max Alexander, John Kapelos, Steve Mittleman, Fred Willard Top Right: Steve Martin, Rick Rossovich Below: Daryl Hannah, Shelley Duvall © *Columbia Pictures*

Daryl Hannah, Rick Rossovich, Steve Martin
Above: Hannah, Rossovich

51

SPACEBALLS

(MGM/UA) Producer/Director, Mel Brooks; Screenplay, Mel Brooks, Thomas Meehan, Ronny Graham; Co-Producer, Ezra Swerdlow; Photography, Nick McLean; Designer, Terence Marsh; Editor, Conrad Buff IV; Music, John Morris; Costumes, Donfeld; Casting, Lynn Stalmaster & Associates, David Rubin, Bill Shepard; Production Manager, Robert Latham Brown; Assistant Directors, Dan Kolsrud, Mitchell Bock, Carol D. Donnefil; Visual Effects, Peter Donen; Additional Editor, Nicholas C. Smith; Art Director, Harold Michelson; Assistant Art Director, Diane Wager; Set Decorator, John Franco, Jr.; Set Designers, Peter Kelly, Richard McKenzie, Jacques Valin; Sound, Jeff Wexler, Don Coufal, Jim Steubel; Associate Editor, Jay Ignaszewski; Assistant Editors, Clarinda Wong, Debra Goldfield; Orchestrations, Jack Hayes; Production Coordinator, Mary Courtney; Make-up, Ben Nye, Jr.; Special Effects, Peter Albiez, Richard Ratliff; Visual Effects, Craig Boyajian; Stunts, Richard Warlock; Sound Designers, Randy Thom, Gary Rydstrom; A Brooks Film presentation; Songs, "Spaceballs," Jeff Pescetto, Clyde Lieberman, Mel Brooks, "My Heart Has a Mind of Its Own," Gloria Sklerov, Lenny Macaluso, and songs by various other artists; Dolby Stereo; Metrocolor; Rated PG; 96 minutes; June release

CAST

President Skroob/Yogurt	Mel Brooks
Barf	John Candy
Dark Helmut	Rick Moranis
Lone Starr	Bill Pullman
Princess Vespa	Daphne Zuniga
King Roland	Dick Van Patten
Colonel Sandurz	George Wyner
Radar Technician	Michael Winslow
The Voice of Dot Matrix	Joan Rivers
Dot Matrix	Lorene Yarnell
John Hurt	John Hurt
Radio Operator	Sal Viscuso
Minister	Ronny Graham
Prince Valium	Jim J. Bullock
Commanderette Zircon	Leslie Bevis
Major Asshole	Jim Jackman
Laser Gunner	Michael Pniewski
Dr. Schlotkin	Sandy Helberg
Captain of the Guard	Stephen Tobolowsky
Snotty	Jeff MacGregor
Magnetic Beam Operator	Henry Kaiser
Charlene	Denise Gallup
Marlene	Dian Gallup
The Voice of Pizza the Hutt	Dom DeLuise

and Gail Barle, Dey Young, Rhonda Shear, Robert Prescott, Jack Riley, Tom Dreesen, Rudy DeLuca, Tony Griffin, Rick Ducommun, Ken Olfson, Bryan O'Byrne, Wayne Wilson, Ira Miller, Earl Finn, Mitchell Bock, Tommy Swerdlow, Tim Russ, Ed Gale, Antonio Hoyos, Felix Silla, Arturo Gil, Tony Gox, John Kennedy Hayden, Deanna Booher, Johnny Silver, Brenda Strong

Left: Bill Pullman, Mel Brooks Above: Daphne Zuniga, Lorene Yarnell, Bill Pullman, John Candy Top: Rick Moranis, Mel Brooks
© M-G-M/Peter Sorel

George Wyner, Rick Moranis

John Candy, Lorene Yarnell, Daphne Zuniga, Bill Pullman

THE UNTOUCHABLES

(PARAMOUNT) Producer, Art Linson; Director, Brian DePalma; Screenplay, David Mamet; Photography, Stephen H. Burum; Art Director, William A. Elliott; Editors, Jerry Greenberg, Bill Pankow; Production Manager, Ray Hartwick; Assistant Directors, Joe Napolitano, James W. Skotchdopole, Richard Patrick, Glenn Trotiner; Music, Ennio Morricone; Associate Producer, Ray Hartwick; Visual Consultant, Patrizia Von Brandenstein; Wardrobe, Giorgio Armani; Costumes, Marilyn Vance-Straker; Casting, Lynn Stalmaster & Associates, Mali Finn; Set Decorator, Hal Gausman; Set Designers, E. C. Chen, Steven P. Sardanis, Gill Clayton, Nicholas Laborczy; Technical Advisor, Douglas Kraner; Sound, Jim Tanenbaum; Production Coordinator, Shari Leibowitz; Associate Editor, Ray Hubley; Assistant Editors, Tara Timpone, Deborah Peretz; Special Effects, Albert Delgado, Allen Hall, Charles E. Stewart; Stunts, Gary Hymes; Songs by various artists; Soundtrack on A&M Records; Dolby Stereo; Technicolor; Panavision; Rated R; 120 minutes; June release

CAST

Eliot Ness	Kevin Costner
Jim Malone	Sean Connery
Oscar Wallace	Charles Martin Smith
George Stone	Andy Garcia
Al Capone	Robert DeNiro
Mike	Richard Bradford
Payne	Jack Kehoe
George	Brad Sullivan
Nitti	Bill Drago
Ness' Wife	Patricia Clarkson
Bowtie Driver	Vito D'Ambrosio
Scoop	Steven Goldstein
Lt. Anderson	Peter Aylward
Preseuski	Don Harvey
Mountie Captain	Robert Swan
Bartender	John J. Walsh
Alderman	Del Close
Mrs. Blackmer	Colleen Bade
Rangemaster	Greg Noonan
Cop Cousin	Sean Grennan
Italian Waiter	Larry Viverito, Sr.
Williamson	Kevin Michael Doyle
Overcoat Hood	Mike Bacarella
Ness' Clerk	Michael P. Byrne
Ness' Daughter	Kaitlin Montgomery
Blackmer Girl	Aditra Kohl

and Charles Keller Watson, Larry Brandenburg, Chelcie Ross, Tim Gamble, Sam Smiley, Pat Billingsley, John Bracci, Jennifer Anglin, Eddie Minasian, Tony Mockus, Sr., Will Zahrn, Louis Lanciloti, Vince Viverito, Valentino Cimo, Joe Greco, Clem Caserta, Bob Martana, Joseph Scianablo, George S. Spataro, Melody Rae, Robert Miranda, James Guthrie, Basil Reale, Gary Hymes

Left: Billy Drago, Robert DeNiro Above: Kevin Costner Top: Sean Connery, Kevin Costner
© *Paramount Pictures/Zade Rosenthal*

Academy Award for Best Supporting Actor of 1987 (Sean Connery)

Andy Garcia, Sean Connery, Kevin Costner

Andy Garcia, Sean Connery, Kevin Costner,
Charles Martin Smith

Cher, Susan Sarandon, Michelle Pfeiffer
Right: Sarandon, Jack Nicholson **Below:**
Jack Nicholson

THE WITCHES OF EASTWICK

(WARNER BROS.) Producers, Neil Canton, Peter Guber, Jon Peters; Director, George Miller; Screenplay, Michael Cristofer; Based on the book by John Updike; Executive Producers, Rob Cohen, Don Devlin; Photography, Vilmos Zsigmond; Designer, Polly Platt; Editor, Hubert C. De La Bouillerie; Editor, Richard Francis-Bruce; Music, John Williams; Costumes, Aggie Guerard Rodgers; Casting, Wally Nicita; Production Manager, Michael Glick; Assistant Directors, Chris Soldo, Bob Yannetti; Visual Effects, Michael Owens; Special Make-Up Effects, Rob Bottin; Art Director, Mark Mansbridge; Set Decorator, Joe D. Mitchell; Set Designers, Robert Sessa, Stan Tropp; Sound, Art Rochester; Special Effects, Mike Lanteri, Clay Pinney, Tom Ryba, Robert Spurlock, Don Elliot, Louis Lanteri; Music Supervisor, Keith Holzman; Assistant Editors, Ann Martin, Erica Flaum; Stunts, Alan Gibbs; Orchestration, Herbert Spencer; Dolby Stereo; Soundtrack on Warner Bros.; Panavision; Technicolor; Rated R; 118 minutes; June release

CAST

Daryl Van Horne	Jack Nicholson
Alexandra Medford	Cher
Jane Spofford	Susan Sarandon
Sukie Ridgemont	Michelle Pfeiffer
Felicia Alden	Veronica Cartwright
Clyde Alden	Richard Jenkins
Walter Neff	Keith Jochim
Fidel	Carel Struycken
Mrs. Biddle	Helen Lloyd Breed
Carol Medford	Caroline Struzik
Mrs. Neff	Becca Lish
Mrs. Biddle's Friend	Ruth Maynard
Doctor #1	Lansdale Chatfield
Cashier	Carole Ita White
Nurse	Margot Dionne
Doctor #2	James T. Boyle
Deli-Counterman	John Blood
Ice Cream Counterman	Ron Campbell
Minister	Eugene Boles

and Michele Sincavage, Nicol Sincavage, Heather Coleman, Carolyn Ditmars, Cynthia Ditmars, Christine Ditmars, Craig Burket, Abraham Mishkind, Christopher Verette, Babbie Green, Jane A. Johnston, Merrily Horowitz, Harriet Medin, Corey Carrier, Kate Barret, Dan Edson, Anthony Falco, Kevin Goodwin, Tara Halfpenny, David Hazel, Melanie Hewitt, Matt Kane, Anne Lindgren, Jessica MacDonald, Corinna Minnar, Scott Nickerson, Stephen Oakes, Ann Senechal, James Staunton, Amy Warner, Paula Moody, Spike Silver, Donna Evans, Christine A. Baur

© *Warner Bros.*

Jack Nicholson, Cher Above: Susan Sarandon,
Michelle Pfeiffer, Cher

HARRY AND THE HENDERSONS

(UNIVERSAL) Producers, Richard Vane, William Dear; Director, William Dear; Screenplay, William Dear, William E. Martin, Ezra D. Rappaport; Photography, Allen Daviau; Designer, James Bissell; Editor, Donn Cambern; 'Harry' Designed by Rick Baker; Song: *Love Lives On:* Music: Barry Mann, Bruce Broughton, Lyrics: Cynthia Weil, Will Jennings; Music, Bruce Broughton; Casting, Mike Fenton, Jane Feinberg, Judy Taylor; Production Manager, Frank Baur; Assistant Directors, L. Andrew Stone, Steve Southard, Lynda Gilman; Costumes, Peter V. Saldutti, Marla Denise Schlom; Art Director, Don Woodruff; Set Designer, William James Teegarden; Set Decorator, Linda DeScenna; Make-up, Dan Striepeke, Greg Nelson; Hair, Chris Lee; Sound, Willie Burton; Special Effects, Henry Millar, Michael J. Millar, Eugene D. Hubbard, Curt Dickson, Bob Burns, Robert Henderson, Conrad Krumm; Orchestrations, Mark McKenzie; Band Arrangements, Chris Boardman; Visual Effects, Industrial Light & Magic; Stunts, Mickey Gilbert, Bill Couch; Puppeteers, Rick Baker, Tom Hester, Tim Lawrence; Animation Sequence, John Beug, Cameron Striewski, Darrell Rooney; Songs, Ada Benson, Fred Fisher, Randy Newman, Eubie Blake, Noble Sissle; Soundtrack on MCA; Dolby Stereo; DeLuxe Color; 105 minutes; Rated PG; June release

CAST

George Henderson	John Lithgow
Nancy Henderson	Melinda Dillon
Sarah Henderson	Margaret Langrick
Ernie Henderson	Joshua Rudoy
Harry	Kevin Peter Hall
Jacques Lafleur	David Suchet
Irene Moffitt	Lainie Kazan
Dr. Wallace Wrightwood	Don Ameche
George Henderson, Sr.	M. Emmet Walsh
Sgt. Mancini	Bill Ontiverous
Dirty Harry Officer	David Richardt
DMV Clerk	Jacqueline Moscou
"Mouse" Woman	Laura Kenny
"Mouse" Spouse	Richard E. Arnold
Jerry Seville	Sean Morgan
Stuart	Nick Flynn
Billers	David MacIntyre
Librarian	Peggy Platt
Jerome	Vern Taylor
Police Clerk	Stan Sturing
Kim Lee	Robert Isaac Lee
Little Bigfoot	Debbie Carrington
Feet	John F. Bloom
Little Bob	Britches
Voice/Vocal Effects	Fred Newman
Schwarz	William Frankfather

and Orene Anderson, William Dear, Laurie O'Brien, Michael Loggins, James King, Nathaniel Ellis, Juleen Murray, Mark Mitchell, Connie Craig, Dana Middleton, Richard Foley, Larry Wansley, Steve Sheppard-Brodie, Mickey Gilbert, Tom Hammond, Stuart Schwarz, Justin Mastro, Michael Goodell, Chuck McCollum

Right: Margaret Langrick, John Lithgow, Melinda Dillon, Joshua Rudoy, Don Ameche Above: Dillon, Lainie Kazan, Lithgow, Langrick Top: John Lithgow, Melinda Dillon © *Universal City Studios*

Academy Award for Best Make-Up of 1987

Ally Sheedy, Beverly D'Angelo

MAID TO ORDER

(NEW CENTURY/VISTA) Producers, Herb Jaffe, Mort Engelberg; Director, Amy Jones; Screenplay, Amy Jones, Perry and Randy Howze; Photography, Shelly Johnson; Editor, Sidney Wolinsky; Music, Georges Delerus; Color; Rated PG; 95 minutes; July release; No other credits provided

CAST

Jessie Montgomery	Ally Sheedy
Stella	Beverly D'Angelo
Nick McGuire	Michael Ontkean
Georgette Starkey	Valerie Perrine
Stan Starkey	Dick Shawn
Charles Montgomery	Tom Skerritt
Audrey James	Merry Clayton

ADVENTURES IN BABYSITTING

(TOUCHSTONE) Producers, Debra Hill, Lynda Obst; Director, Chris Columbus; Screenplay, David Simkins; Photography, Ric Waite; Designer, Todd Hallowell; Editors, Fredric Steinkamp, William Steinkamp; Music, Michael Kamen; Casting, Janet Hirshenson, Jane Jenkins; Production Manager, David Coatsworth; Assistant Directors, Tony Lucibello, Madeleine Henrie, Anne-Marie Ferney; Set Decorator, Dan May; Art Director, Barbara Dunphy; Assistant Art Director, Gregory Keen; Additional Orchestrations, Bruce Babcock; Choreographer, Monica Devereaux; Production Coordinator, Mara McSweeny; Sound, David Lee; Costumes, Judith R. Gellman; Special Effects, Neil Trifunovich; Stunts, Branko Racki; Scenic Artist, Matthew Lammerich; Visual Effects, Introvision; Presented in association with Silver Screen Partners III; Buena Vista Pictures Distribution; Dolby Stereo; DeLuxe Color; Rated PG-13; 99 minutes; July release

CAST

Chris	Elisabeth Shue
Sara	Maia Brewton
Brad	Keith Coogan
Daryl	Anthony Rapp
Joe Gipp	Calvin Levels
Dawson	Vincent Phillip D'Onofrio
Brenda	Penelope Ann Miller
Dan	George Newbern
Pruitt	John Ford Noonan
Mike	Bradley Whitford
Graydon	Ron Canada
Bleak	John Chandler
Mr. Anderson	Dan Ziskie
Cleminski	David Blacker
Dr. Nuhkbane	Sam Moses
Mrs. Pruitt	Charlene Shipp
Mrs. Parker	Sandra Shuman
Mrs. Anderson	Linda Sorensen

and Allan Aarons, Marcia Bennett, Rummy Bishop, Lolita David, John Dee, Monica Devereux, Clarke Devereux, Rick Goldman, Deryck Hazel, John Hemphill, Frank Hill, Philip Honey, Clark Johnson, Maryann Kelman, Kirsten Kieferle, Peter Lavender, Kevin Lund, Southside Johnny, Allan Merovitz, Les Nirenberg, Juan Ramirez, Richard Rebiere, Diane Robin, Sandi Ross, Walt Woodson, Branko Racki

Elizabeth Shue, George Newbern
Above: Penelope Ann Miller

Top: Maia Brewton, Anthony Rapp,
Elizabeth Shue, Keith Coogan
© *Touchstone Pictures*

INNERSPACE

(WARNER BROS.) Producer, Michael Finnell; Director, Joe Dante; Screenplay, Jeffrey Boam, Chip Proser; Story/Co-Producer, Chip Proser; Executive Producers, Steven Spielberg, Peter Guber, Jon Peters; Co-Executive Producers, Frank Marshall, Kathleen Kennedy; Music, Jerry Goldsmith; Editor, Kent Beyda; Designer, James H. Spencer; Photography, Andrew Laszlo; Casting, Mike Fenton, Jane Feinberg, Judy Taylor; Production Manager, John Broderick; Assistant Directors, Pat Kehoe, Carol Green; Visual Effects, Dennis Muren; Special Make-Up Effects, Rob Bottin; Art Director, William Matthews; Set Decorator, Richard C. Goddard; Costumes, Rosanna Norton; Orchestrations, Arthur Morton; Sound, Ken King; Special Effects, Michael Wood, Michael Edmonson, James Fredburg, Alfred Broussard, Mike Paris, Joe Sasgen, David Wood; Stunts, Glenn Randall, Jr., Set Designers, Judy Cammer, Gene Nollman; Visual Effects, Caren Marinoff-Montante; Martin Short's Interiors Produced at Industrial Light & Magic; Visual Effects Art Director, Harley Jessup; Songs, Sam Cooke, Narada Michael Walden, Wang Chung, John Crawford, Johnny Mercer; Soundtrack on Geffen Records; Dolby Stereo; Technicolor; Rated PG; 118 minutes; July release

CAST

Lt. Tuck Pendelton	Dennis Quaid
Jack Putter	Martin Short
Lydia Maxwell	Meg Ryan
Victor Scrimshaw	Kevin McCarthy
Dr. Margaret Canker	Fiona Lewis
Mr. Igoe	Vernon Wells
The Cowboy	Robert Picardo
Wendy	Wendy Schaal
Pete Blanchard	Harold Sylvester
Dr. Greenbush	William Schallert
Mr. Wormwood	Henry Gibson
Ozzie Wezler	John Hora
Dr. Niles	Mark L. Taylor
Lydia's Editor	Orson Bean
Duane	Kevin Hooks
Dream Lady	Kathleen Freeman
Messenger	Archie Hahn
Cab Driver	Dick Miller
Man in restroom	Ken Tobey
Waiting Room Patients	Joe Flaherty, Andrea Martin
Scrimshaw's Henchmen	Jason Laskey, Frank Miller
Wendell	Shawn Nelson
Lab Technicians	Christine Avila, Alexandra Borrie, Jenny Cago, Robert Gounley
Rusty	Grainger Hines

and Mike Garibaldi, Richard McGonagle, Terence McGovern, Robert Neches, Rance Howard, Chuck Jones, Laura Waterbury, Kurty Braunreiter, Robert Gray, Brewster Sears, Alan Blumenfeld, Jeffrey Boam, Sydne Squire, Paul Barselou, John Miranda, Jordan Benjamin, Roberto Ramirez, Virginia Boyle, Herb Mitchell, John Harwood, Neil Ross, Charles Aidman

Right: Dennis Quaid, Meg Ryan, Dick Miller
Above: Kevin McCarthy, Robert Picardo, Vernon Wells
Top: Meg Ryan, Fiona Lewis, Kevin McCarthy,
Martin Short © *Warner Bros. Inc.*

1988 Academy Award for Best Visual Effects

Martin Short, Meg Ryan, Dennis Quaid

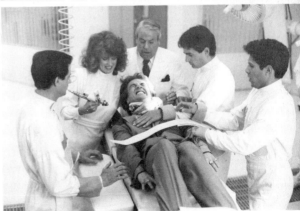

Fiona Lewis, Kevin McCarthy hold Martin Short

LA BAMBA

(COLUMBIA) Producers, Taylor Hackford, Bill Borden; Director/ Screenplay, Luis Valdez; Executive Producer, Stuart Benjamin; Photography, Adam Greenberg; Designer, Vince Cresciman; Editors, Sheldon Kahn, Don Brochu; Casting, Junie Lowry; Associate Producer, Daniel Valdez; Executive Music Producer, Joel Sill; Original Music, Carlos Santana, Miles Goodman; Ritchie Valens' Music performed by Los Lobos; Production Manager, Alan C. Blomquist; Assistant Directors, Stephen J. Fisher, Michael Katleman; Music Editor, Curt Sobel; Sound, Susumu Tokunow; Assistant Editor, Jeffrey Bell; Set Decorator, Rosemary Brandenburg; Assistant Art Director, Terry Weldon; Costumes, Sylvia Vega-Vasquez; Production Coordinator, Misty Carey; Production Associate, Phil Esparza; Casting Associate, Marcy Carriker; Stunts, Steve Davison, Ronnie Rondell; Choreography, Miguel Delgado; Special Effects, Filmtrix, Inc.; A New Visions Production; Songs by Ritchie Valens and various other artists; Soundtrack on Slash/Warner Bros. Records and London Records; Dolby Stereo; DeLuxe Color; Rated PG-13; 108 minutes; July release

CAST

Ritchie Valens	Lou Diamond Phillips
Bob Morales	Esai Morales
Connie Valenzuela	Rosana De Soto
Rosie Morales	Elizabeth Pena
Donna Ludwig	Danielle von Zerneck
Bob Keene	Joe Pantoliano
Ted Quillin	Rick Des
Buddy Holly	Marshall Crenshaw
Jackie Wilson	Howard Huntsberry
Eddie Cochran	Brian Setzer
Lelo	Daniel Valdez
Curandero	Felipe Cantu
Chino	Eddie Frias
Mexican Ed	Mike Moroff
Rudy	Geoffrey Rivas
Mr. Ludwig	Sam Anderson
Mrs. Ludwig	Maggie Gwinn
Alan Freed	Jeffrey Alan Chandler
Big Bopper	Stephen Lee
Bartender	John Quade
Vera	Lettie Ibarra
Ernestine	Diane Rodriguez
Connie Jr.	Kati Valdez
Irma	Gloria Balcorta
Garbage Man	Ernesto Hernandez
Howard	Noble Willingham
Sound Engineer	Thom Pintello
Tommy Allsup	Stephen Schmidt
Sharon Sheeley	Rosanna Locke
Donna's Girlfriend	Kim Sebastian
Rosalinda	Dyana Ortelli
Mr. House	Andy Griggs
Trucker	Art Koustik
Mr. Caballero	Tony Genaro
Girl at party	Allison Robinson
Baseball Announcer	Hunter Payne
Students	Joe Miller, Maryann Tanedo, Barb Jittner, Brian Russell

Left Center: Rosana DeSoto, Elizabeth Pena
Above: Danielle Von Zerneck, Lou Diamond Phillips
Top: Lou Diamond Phillips © Columbia Pictures

Joe Pantoliano, Lou Diamond Phillips

Esai Morales, Rosana DeSoto

Brooke McCarter, Chance Michael Corbitt, Billy Worth,
Kiefer Sutherland, Jami Gertz, Alexander Winter
Above: Corey Haim, Jason Patric

THE LOST BOYS

(WARNER BROS.) Producer, Harvey Bernhard; Director, Joel Schumacher; Screenplay, Janice Fischer, James Jeremias, Jeffrey Boam; Story, Janice Fischer, James Jeremias; Executive Producer, Richard Donner; Photography, Michael Chapman; Designer, Bo Welch; Editor, Robert Brown; Music, Thomas Newman; Costumes, Susan Becker; Co-Executive Producers, Mark Damon, John Hyde; Casting, Marion Dougherty; Production Manager, William L. Young; Assistant Directors, William S. Beasley, Eric Jewett; Art Director, Tom Duffield; Set Decorator, Chris Westlunc; Sound, David Ronne; Vampire Prosthetics & Effects, Greg Cannom; Set Designer, John Warnke; Songs, Lou Gramm, Michael Mainieri, Gerard McMann, and various other artists; Original Soundtrack on Atlantic; Dolby Stereo; Color; Panavision; Rated R; 98 minutes; July release

CAST

Michael	Jason Patric
Sam	Corey Haim
Lucy	Dianne Wiest
Grandpa	Barnard Hughes
Max	Edward Herrmann
David	Kiefer Sutherland
Star	Jami Gertz
Edgar Frog	Corey Feldman
Alan Frog	Jamison Newlander
Paul	Brooke McCarter
Dwayne	Billy Wirth
Marko	Alexander Winter
Laddie	Chance Michael Corbitt
Greg	Alexander Bacon Chapman
Shelly	Nori Morgan
Surf Nazis	Todd Feder, Christopher Peters, Keith Butterfield, Gerald Younggren, Eric Graves
Security Guard	J. Dinan Myrtetus
Maria	Kelly Jo Minter
Beach Concert Star	Timmy Cappello
Gas Station Owner	Jim Turner
Lost Child	Tony Cain
Child's Mother	Melanie Bishop
Runaways	Sandra E. Garcia, Ian Guindon
Frog Mother	Jane Bare
Frog Father	B. Lowenberg
Tattoo Man	Captain Colourz
Security Guard's Wife	Inez Pandalfi
Nanook	Cody
Thorn	Folsom

Top: Jami Gertz, Jason Patric Left: Dianne Wiest
Below: Jamison Newlander, Corey Feldman, Corey Haim
© Warner Bros.

59

Peter Weller, Nancy Allen Right: Miguel Ferrer,
Peter Weller Below: Nancy Allen, Peter Weller

ROBOCOP

(ORION) Producer, Arne Schmidt; Director, Paul Verhoeven; Screenplay, Edward Neumeier, Michael Miner; Executive Producer, Jon Davison; Editor, Frank J. Urioste; Photography, Jost Vacano; Designer, William Sandell; Music, Basil Poledouris; Robocop Design/Creation, Rob Bottin; Casting, Sally Dennison, Julie Selzer; Co-Producer, Edward Neumeier; Associate Producers, Stephen Lim, Phil Tippett; ED-209 Sequences, Phil Tippett; Special Photographic Effects, Peter Kuran, Visual Concept Engineering; Costumes, Erica Edell Phillips; Production Manager, Charles Newirth; Special Effects, Dale Martin; Assistant Directors, Michele A. Panelli, David Householter; Production Coordinator, Allegra Clegg; Art Director, Gayle Simon; Set Decorator, Robert Gould; Set Designer, James Tocci; Stunts, Gary Combs; Robomovement, Moni Yakim; Special Effects, Bill Purcell, Keith Richins, Lawrence Aeschlimann; Sound, Robert Wald; ED-209 Design/Creation, Craig Davies, Peter Ronzana; Visual Effects, Harry Walton; Animation, Randy Dutra; Orchestrations, Steven Scott Smalley; "Show Me Your Spine," P.T.P.; Dolby Stereo Surround Sound; DeLuxe Color; Rated R; 103 minutes; July release

CAST

Murphy/Robocop	Peter Weller
Lewis	Nancy Allen
The Old Man	Daniel O'Herlihy
Jones	Ronny Cox
Clarence	Kurtwood Smith
Morton	Miguel Ferrer
Sgt. Reed	Robert DoQui
Leon	Ray Wise
Johnson	Felton Perry
Emil	Paul McCrane
Joe	Jesse Goins
Kaplan	Del Zamora
Minh	Calvin Jung
Walker	Rick Lieberman
Sal	Lee DeBroux
Miller	Mark Carlton
Manson	Edward Edwards
Lt. Hedgecock	Michael Gregory
Bobby	Fred Hice
Dougy	Neil Summers
Prisoner	Gene Wolande
Slimey Lawyer	Gregory Poudevigne
Bail Bondsman	Charles Carroll
Kinney	Ken Page
Ramirez	Yolanda Williams
Starkweather	Tyress Allen
Chessman	John Davies
Cecil the Clerk	Laird Stuart

and Stephen Berrier, Sage Parker, Karen Radcliffe, Darryl Cox, Jerry Haynes, Bill Schockley, Donna Keegan, Mike Moroff, Marjorie Rynearson, Jo Livingston, Joan Pirkle, Diane Robin, Adrianne Sachs, Maarten Goslins, Angie Bolling, Jason Levine, S. D. Nemeth, Bill Farmer, Michael Hunter, Spencer Prokop, Debra Zach, L. J. King, David Packer, Leeza Gibbons, Mario Machado

© *Orion Pictures/S. Karin Epstein*

Ronny Cox Above: Peter Weller as Robocop

Tommy Hinkley, Lori Loughlin,
Annette Funicello, Frankie Avalon
© Paramount Pictures

SUPERMAN IV: THE QUEST FOR PEACE

(WARNER BROS.) Producers, Menahem Golan, Yoram Globus; Director, Sidney J. Furie; Story, Christopher Reeve, Lawrence Konner, Mark Rosenthal; Screenplay, Lawrence Konner, Mark Rosenthal; Associate Producer, Graham Easton; Executive Producer, Michael J. Kagan; *Superman* created by Jerry Siegel, Joe Shuster; *Superman* appearing in comic books published by DC Comics, Inc.; Music, John Williams; Music Adaptation/Conductor, Alexander Courage; Designer, John Graysmark; Photography, Ernest Day; Editor, John Shirley; Visual Effects, Harrison Ellenshaw; Costumes, John Bloomfield; Stunts, Alf Joint, John Lees; Flying Stunts, Mark Stewart; Flying Director, David Lane; Model Effects, Richard Conway; Special Effects, John Evans; Production Supervisor, Ray Frift; Production Managers, Malcolm Christopher, Graham Ford; Assistant Directors, Gino Marotta, Paul Lowin; Production Coordinators, Christine Fenton, Marilyse Morgan; Sound, Danny Daniel; Casting, Noel Davis, Jeremy Zimmermann, Wendy Murray; Art Directors, Leslie Tomkins, John Fenner; Assistant Art Directors, Reg Bream, Steve Cooper; Set Decorator, Peter Young; Orchestrations, Frank Barber, Harry Roberts; Additional Source Music, Paul Fishman; Song, *"A Whole Lotta Shakin' Goin' On"* by Jerry Lee Lewis; Color; Rated PG; 90 minutes; July release

CAST

Superman/Clark Kent	Christopher Reeve
Lex Luthor	Gene Hackman
Perry White	Jackie Cooper
Jimmy Olsen	Marc McClure
Lenny	Jon Cryer
David Warfield	Sam Wanamaker
Nuclear Man #2	Mark Pillow
Lacy Warfield	Mariel Hemingway
Lois Lane	Margot Kidder
Jeremy	Damian McLawhorn
Harry Howler	William Hootkins
Jean Pierre Dubois	Jim Broadbent
General Romoff	Stanley Lebor
Levon Hornsby	Don Fellows
U.S. President	Robert Beatty

and Bradley Lavelle, Mac McDonald, Czeslaw Grocholski, Steve Plytas, John Hollis, Bob Sherman, Eiji Kusuhara, Yuri Borienko, Boris Isarov, Dorota Zienska, Jiri Stanislav, Jayne Brook, Ron Travis, Matthew Freeman, Indira Joshi, Douglas W. Iles, Ted Maynard, Raymond Marlowe, John Cagan, Malcom Bullivant, Mark Caven, Diana Hunter, Nicholas Colicos, Keith Edwards, David Garth, Esmond Knight, Eugene Lipinski, Dennis Creaghan, Philip Fox, Jimmy Fung, Guinevere John, Petter Penry-Jones, Witold Scheybal, Rex Robinson, Kerry Shale, and the voice of Susannah York

BACK TO THE BEACH

(PARAMOUNT) Producer, Frank Mancuso, Jr.; Director, Lyndall Hobbs; Co-Executive Producers, Frankie Avalon, Annette Funicello; Screenplay, Peter Krikes, Steve Meerson, Christopher Thompson; Story, James Komack, B. W. L. Norton, Bruce Kirschbaum; Based on characters created by Lou Rusoff; Photography, Bruce Surtees; Designer, Michael Helmy; Editor, David Finfer; Music, Steve Dorff; Music Supervisor, Becky Mancuso; Casting, Janet Hirshenson, Jane Jenkins, Denise Chamian; Costumes, Marlene Stewart; Production Manager, Martin Hornstein; Assistant Directors, Michael Pariser, James Lansbury; Set Decorator, Don Remacle; Sound, Kim Ornitz; Assistant Editors, Spencer Gross, Kathryn Camp; Orchestrations, Larry Herbstritt; Surfing Photography, Yuri Farrant; Production Coordinator, William Chapman; Choreographer, Lori Eastside; Stunts, Gary Pike; Surfing Consultant, Geoffrey Hales; Special Effects, Reel EFX, Inc.; "Going Back to the Beach" by Tay Uhler, Scott Lipsker, and songs by various other artists; Ultra-Stereo; Technicolor; Rated PG; 92 minutes; August release

CAST

Annette's Husband	Frankie Avalon
Annette	Annette Funicello
Sandi	Lori Loughlin
Michael	Tommy Hinkley
Bobby	Demian Slade
Connie	Connie Stevens
Zed	Joe Holland
Troy	John Calvin
Mountain	David Bowe
Robin	Laura Urstein
Bridgette	Linda Carol
Airline Hostess	Marjorie Gross
Fleishman	Hartly Silver
Salesmen	Alan Barry, Thomas David Parker
Webby	Todd Bryant
Ernie	Floyd Foster, Jr.
Odie	Emil McKown
Punk	Jon Paul Jones
Surf Dude	Eddie Vail
Surfer	Drew Steele
Punk Baby	Lola Rose Thompson
Baby's Mother	Honey Lea
Autograph Hound	Nicholas Hales
Rodney Bingenheimer	Himself
Dick Dale	Himself
Stevie Ray Vaughan	Himself
"Harbor Master"	Don Adams
"Announcer"	Barbara Billingsley
"Valet"	Edd Byrnes
"Bartender"	Bob Denver
"Judge #1"	Tony Dow
"Bartender's Buddy"	Alan Hale
"Judge #2"	Jerry Mathers
"Himself"	Pee-Wee Herman

and Angelo Moore, Norwood Fisher, Christopher Dowd, Kendall Jones, Walter Kibby II, Phillip Fisher, Steve Aschoff, Ron Eglit, Frankie Avalon, Jr., Gary Usher, Jr., Tony Avalon, Drew Steele, Emil McKown, Rick Avery, Pat Banta, Geof Brewer, Jamie R. Brisick, Bob Brown, Steve Cooper, Jay Currin, Gregory Joe Gault, Robert Keller, Bruce G. Magee, Dwayne McGee, A. J. Nay, Mark B. Orrison, Noon Orsatti, Victor Quintero, William Charles Skeen, Randell Dennis Widner

Mariel Hemingway, Christopher Reeve, Margot Kidder
© Cannon Films

THE BIG EASY

(COLUMBIA) Producer, Stephen Friedman; Director, Jim McBride; Screenplay, Daniel Petrie, Jr.; Photography, Affonso Beato; Designer, Jeannine Claudia Oppewall; Editor, Mia Goldman; Costumes, Tracy Tynan; Music, Brad Fiedel; Associate Producers, Tony Tagliere, Jack Baran; Executive Producer, Mort Engelberg; Casting, Lynn Stalmaster & Associates, David Rubin; Production Manager, John Broderick; Assistant Directors, Michael Schroeder, Daniel Dugan; Production Supervisor, Ann Frisbee; Music Supervision, Peter Afterman; Sound, Mark Ulano; Production Coordinator, Kool Lusby; Set Decorator, Lisa Fischer; Special Effects, William Purcell, Gregory C. Landerer; Stunts, Richard Diamond Farnsworth; Choreography, Tina Girouard; Songs, *"Closer to You"* by Dennis Quaid & Terrance Simien, *"For Your Love I Would Pay Any Price"* by Terrance Simien, and songs by various other artists; from Kings Road Entertainment; DeLuxe Color; Rated R; 108 minutes; August release

CAST

Remy McSwain	Dennis Quaid
Anne Osborne	Ellen Barkin
Jack Kellom	Ned Beatty
Andre De Soto	John Goodman
McCabe	Lisa Jane Persky
Ed Dodge	Ebbe Roe Smith
Bobby McSwain	Tom O'Brien
Lamar Parmentel	Charles Ludlam
Mama	Grace Zabriskie
Vinnie "The Cannon" Di Moti	Marc Lawrence
Daddy Mention	Solomon Burke
Chef Paul	Gailard Sartain
Freddie Angelo	Jim Chimento
Patrolman	Edward St. Pe
"Silky" Foster	Robert Lesser
Hostess	Cheryl Starbuck
Mugging Victim	Margie O'Dair
Sergeant Duvivier	Jeff Hollis
Sergeant Guerra	Joy N. Houck, Jr.
Dewey Piersall	Steve Broussard
George Joel	Elliott Keener
Hugh Dowling	Nik Hagler
Judge	Carole Sutton
Uncle Sos	Dave Petitjean
Justin	Buddy Quaid
Cousin Terry	Dennis Curren
Rodney	Rico Wheat
Desk Sergeant	Robert Kearney
Garage Dispatcher	Joseph Catalanotto

and Terrance Simien, The Mallet Playboys, Arden Lo, Rickey Pierre, Nick Krieger, Gary Sturgis, Byron Nora, Archie Sampier, August Krinke, John Schluter, Zephirin Hymel IV, Jack Harris, George Dureau, Patrick Frederic, Lane Trippe, Don K. Lutenbacher, Peter Gabb, Judge Jim Garrison, The Dewey Balfa Band, St. Augustine's Marching Hundred

Left: Dennis Quaid, Charles Ludlum Above: Ned Beatty, Ellen Barkin Top: Barkin, Quaid
© Columbia Pictures

Dennis Quaid, Ellen Barkin

Lisa Jane Persky, Dennis Quaid, Ned Beatty, Ellen Barkin

Kamala Lopez, Cheech Marin

BORN IN EAST L.A.

(UNIVERSAL) Producer, Peter MacGregor-Scott; Director/ Screenplay, Cheech Marin; Executive Producer, Stan Coleman; Photography, Alex Phillips; Editor, Don Brochu; Music, Lee Holdridge; Casting, Junie Lowry; Production Supervisor, James Cranston; Assistant Directors, Javier Carreno, Sebastian Silvan, David Schrager; Art Directors, J. Rae Fox, Lynda Burbank; Costumes, Isabella Van Soest; Sound, William B. Kaplan; Set Decorators, Steven Karatzas, Enrique Estevez; Art Director, Hector Rodriguez; Production Coordinators, Jacqueline George, Laura Aguilar; Special Effects, Jesus Duran; Editors, David Newhouse, Mike Sheridan, Steve Lovejoy; *Main Title/ What's Happening Boys Theme,* Peter Kaye; Songs, Cheech Marin, Bruce Springsteen, Bernard Edwards, Nile Rodgers; CFI Color; Rated R; 98 minutes; August release

CAST

Rudy	Cheech Marin
Javier	Paul Rodriguez
Jimmy	Daniel Stern
Dolores	Kamala Lopez
McCalister	Jan Michael Vincent
Rudy's Mother	Lupe Ontiveros
Rudy's Sister	Urbanie Lucero
Rudy's Niece	Chastity Ayala
Rudy's Nephew	David Perez
Marcie	Neith Hunter
Oscar	Tito Larriva
Lester	Eddie Barth
Jose	Miguel Delgado
Feo	Tony Plana
Gloria	Alma Martinez
Miguel	Ruben Guevara
Customs Officer	Sam Allen
Harry	Bob McClurg
Harry's Wife	Diana Bellamy
TV Evangelist	Mark L. Taylor
Fernando	Ernesto Hernandez
Father Sanchez	Sam Vlahos

and Larry Blackmon, Geoff Rivas, David Yanez, Bret Chafe, McKeiver Jones III, Terrence Evans, Eloy Casados, Mike Moroff, Alex Garza, George Galvan, Jim Perine, John Villella, Doug Ingold, Mark Istratoff, Robert Masseria, Ronald G. Joseph, Josh Cruze, Noble Willingham, Randal Patrick, Ernest Harden, Jr., Vic Trevino, Sal Lopez, Del Zamora, Ted Lin, Jason Scott Lee, Jee Teo, Dyana Ortelli, Humberto Ortiz, Daniel Valdez, David Silva, Steve Jordan, Austin Cortez Tobar, Cesar Dominguez, R. D. Kennedy, Lilyan Chauvin, Angela Moya, Jorge Andres Fernandez, David Selburg, Dick Hancock

Top: Cheech Marin Left: Paul Rodriguez
Below: Daniel Stern, Cheech Marin
© *Universal City Studios*

DIRTY DANCING

(VESTRON) Producer, Linda Gottlieb; Director, Emile Ardolino; Screenplay/Co-Producer, Eleanor Bergstein; Executive Producers, Mitchell Cannold, Steven Reuther; Editor, Peter C. Frank; Photography, Jeff Jur; Choreography, Kenny Ortega; Music, John Morris; Musical Supervision, Danny Goldberg, Michael Lloyd; Music Consultants, Jimmy Lenner, "Cousin Brucie" Morrow; Costumes, Hilary Rosenfeld; Designer, David Chapman; Associate Producer, Doro Bachrach; Casting, Bonnie Timmermann; Production Manager, Jeffrey Hayes; Assistant Directors, Herb Gains, Nathalie Vadim; Art Directors, Mark Haack, Stephen Lineweaver; Assistant Art Directors, Kevin Allen, Tom Allen; Assistant Choreographer, Miranda Garrison; Sound, John Pritchett, George Baetz, Doug Axtell; Set Decorator, Clay Griffith; Production Supervisors, Tammy J. Green, Eileen Eichenstein; Associate Editor, Farrel Levy Duffy; Assistant Editors, Andrew Marcus, Guy Barresi; Stunts, James Lovelett; Dance Casting, Greg Smith; "She's Like the Wind" by Patrick Swayze and Stacey Widelitz/"(I've Had) The Time of My Life" by Franke Previte, Donald Markowitz, John DeNicola/and songs by various artists; Dolby Stereo; Soundtrack on RCA; In association with Great American Films Limited Partnership; Color; Rated PG-13; 97 minutes; August release

CAST

Baby Houseman	Jennifer Grey
Johnny Castle	Patrick Swayze
Jake Houseman	Jerry Orbach
Penny Johnson	Cynthia Rhodes
Max Kellerman	Jack Weston
Lisa Houseman	Jane Brucker
Marjorie Houseman	Kelly Bishop
Neil Kellerman	Lonny Price
Robbie Gould	Max Cantor
Tito Suarez	Charles "Honi" Coles
Billy Kostecki	Neal Jones
Magician	"Cousin Brucie" Morrow
Stan	Wayne Knight
Mrs. Schumacher	Paula Trueman
Mr. Schumacher	Alvin Myerovich
Vivian Pressman	Miranda Garrison
Moe Pressman	Gary Goodrow
Staff Kid	Antone Pagan
Bus Boy	Tom Cannold

and M. R. Fletcher, Jesus Fuentes, Heather Lea Gerdes, Karen Getz, Andrew Charles Koch, D. A. Pauley, Dorian Sanchez, Jennifer Stahl, Jonathan Barnes, Dwyght Bryan, Tom Drake, John Gotz, Dwayne Malphus, Dr. Clifford Watkins, Denise Amirante, Bill Anagnos, Norman Douglass

Right: Cynthia Rhodes, Jennifer Grey, Patrick Swayze Above: Charles Honi Coles, Jack Weston Top: Kelly Bishop, Jerry Orbach © *Vestron Pictures*

Academy Award for Best Original Song ("I've Had the Time of My Life")

Patrick Swayze, Jennifer Grey

Cynthia Rhodes, Patrick Swayze

CAN'T BUY ME LOVE

(TOUCHSTONE) Producer, Thom Mount; Director, Steve Rash; Screenplay/Associate Producer, Michael Swerdlick; Executive Producers, Jere Henshaw, Ron Beckman; Co-Producer, Mark Burg; Photography, Peter Lyons Collister; Designer, Donald L. Harris; Editor, Jeff Gourson; Music, Robert Folk; Choreographer, Paula Abdul; Casting, Caro Jones; Production Executive, Russell Chesley; Production Manager, Donald C. Klune; Assistant Directors, Jerram Swartz, Warren Glen Chidester; Set Decorators, Christian W. Russhon, Andrew Bernard; Sound, Peter Bentley; Production Coordinator, Gillian P. Glen; Costumes, Gregory Poe; Assistant Editors, Maria Lee Silver, Bill Turro; Assistant Choreographer, Carlton Jones; Casting-Tucson, Holly Hire & Assoc.; Production Supervisor, Rex Stewart III; Presented in association with Silver Screen Partners III; From Apollo Pictures; A Mount Company Production; Buena Vista Pictures Distribution; De-Luxe Color; Rated PG-13; 94 minutes; August release

CAST

Ronald Miller	Patrick Dempsey
Cindy Mancini	Amanda Peterson
Kenneth Wurman	Courtney Gains
Barbara	Tina Caspary
Chuckie Miller	Seth Green
Mrs. Mancini	Sharon Farrell
Patty	Darcy DeMoss
David Miller	Dennis Dugan
Judy Miller	Cloyce Morrow
Iris	Devin Devasquez
Big John	Eric Bruskotter
Ricky	Gerardo Mejia
Quint	Cort McCown
Fran	Ami Dolenz
Lester	Max Perlich
Albert	David Schermerhorn
Moda Clerk	Steve Franken
Rock	Phil Simms
Brent	Tudor Sherrard
Bobby Hilton	George Gray, III
Mr. Webbly	Jimmie Lee Mitchell
Mrs. Hagmar	Jan Rooney
Mr. Wurman	James Gooden
Jr. Wurman	Erin O'Flaherty
Duane	Ty Gray
Camera Salesman	Will Hannah
Stocky Jones	Todd Walsh
African Host	Wayne Chandler
Freshmen	Meredith Wagelie, Jennifer Nelson
Transfer Girl	Corissa Miller
Bambi La Brock	Lisa Givens

Top: Patrick Dempsey, Amanda Peterson Right: Amanda Peterson Below: Patrick Dempsey, Amanda Peterson
© *Apollo Pictures*

Patrick Dempsey, Amanda Peterson

HAMBURGER HILL

(PARAMOUNT) Producers, Marcia Nasatir, Jim Carabatsos; Director, John Irvin; Screenplay, Jim Carabatsos; Co-Producer, Larry De Waay; Executive Producers, David Korda, Jerry Offsay; Photography, Peter MacDonald; Special Effects, Joe Lombardi; Casting, Mary Colquhoun; Casting, Austen Spriggs; Designer, Peter Tanner; Editor, Peter Tanner; Music, Philip Glass; Military Advisor, Command Sergeant Major Al Neal; Production Coordinator, Sallie Beechinor; Assistants to Director, Robin Matthews, Jill James; Assistant Directors, Steve Harding, David W. Rose, Nik Korda; Sound, David Hildyard, John Pitt; Stunts, Tip Tipping; "*I Second That Emotion*" by Alfred Cleveland, William Robinson, Jr./"*Subterranean Homesick Blues*" by Bob Dylan, and Songs by various other artists; An RKO Picture; Dolby Stereo; Technicolor; Rated R; 110 minutes; August release

CAST

Languilli	Anthony Barrile
Motown	Michael Patrick Boatman
Washburn	Don Cheadle
Murphy	Michael Dolan
McDaniel	Don James
Frantz	Dylan McDermott
Galvin	M. A. Nickles
Duffy	Harry O'Reilly
Gaigin	Daniel O'Shea
Beletsky	Tim Quill
Bienstock	Tommy Swerdlow
Doc	Courtney Vance
Worcester	Steven Weber
Lt. Eden	Tegan West
Mama San	Kieu Chinh
Lagunas	Doug Goodman
Healy	J. C. Palmore
Newsman	J. D. Van Sickle

Tim Quill, M. A. Nickles, Anthony Barrile

Top: (R) Don Cheadle, Tim Quill, Daniel O'Shea
(L) Courtney B. Vance, Michael Patrick Boatman,
Don James, Dylan McDermott Below: Squad
(R) Don Cheadle, Tim Quill, Dylan McDermott
© *RKO Pictures/Roger Robles/Don McCullin*

HAPPY NEW YEAR

(COLUMBIA) Producer, Jerry Weintraub; Director, John G. Avildsen; Screenplay, Warren Lane; Based on Claude Lelouch's *"La Bonne Annee"*; Photography, James Crabe; Executive Producer, Allan Ruban; Designer, William J. Cassidy; Editor, Jane Kuson; Music, Bill Conti; Casting, Bonnie Timmermann; Jewels, Harry Winston; Associate Producer, William J. Cassidy; Production Manager, Allan Ruban; Assistant Directors, Clifford C. Coleman, James Chory; Production Associate, Carol Lees; Production Coordinator, Cyndy Streit; Art Director, William F. Matthews; Wardrobe, Mary Lou Byrd; Special Make-up, Robert Laden; Sound, James Sabat; Set Decorator, Don K. Ivey; Special Effects, J. B. Jones; Assistant Editors, Penelope Shaw, Jonathan Shaw; Orchestrations, Jack Eskew; Casting Assistant, Deborah Aquila; *"I Only Have Eyes for You"* by Al Dubin, Harry Warren/ Performed by The Temptations; From Columbia-Delphi IV Productions; DeLuxe Color; Rated PG; 86 minutes; August release

CAST

Nick	Peter Falk
Charlie	Charles Durning
Man on train	Claude Lelouch
Fence	Gary Maas
Bellboy	Jack Hrkach
Jewelry Store Manager	Tom Courtenay
Doorman	Ted Bartsch
Carolyn	Wendy Hughes
Nina	Tracy Brooks Swope
Sunny Felix	Joan Copeland
Curator	Daniel Gerroll
Police Lieutenant	Bruce Malmuth
Sergeant	Gary Richardson
Guard	D. L. Blakely
Warden	Clarence Thomas
Joe	Pinky Pincus
Young Con	Gary Cox
Oriental Housekeeper	Yoshiko Minami
Julie	Dian Piccolo
Young Con's Father	Ray Jason
Cabbie #1	Jackie Davis
Steve	Fritz Bronner
Maitre'D	Reuben Rabasa
Frankie G.	Sal Carollo
Bartender	Don Kalpakis
Taxi Driver	Bruce Kirby
Proprietress	Ellen Simmons
Airline Ticket Clerk	Dan Fitzgerald

and Earleen Carey, Debbi Garrett, Karina Etchevery, Cloyce Morrow, Anthony Heald, Peter Sellars, Richard Street, Ron Tyson, Otis Williams, Ali Woodson, David English

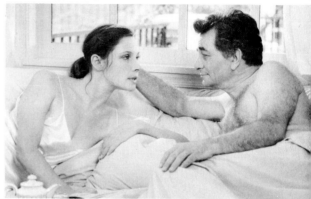

Right: Wendy Hughes, Peter Falk Above: Wendy Hughes, Peter Falk Top: Charles Durning, Peter Falk
© *Columbia Pictures*

Tom Courtenay, Peter Falk

Peter Falk, Tom Courtenay

67

Courteney Cox, Dolph Lundgren
© Cannon Films

MASTERS OF THE UNIVERSE

(CANNON GROUP) Producers, Menahem Golan, Yoram Globus; Director, Gary Goddard; Screenplay, David Odell; Co-Producer/Production Manager, Elliot Schick; Executive Producer, Edward R. Pressman; Photography, Havania Baer; Designer, William Stout; Visual Effects, Richard Edlund; Editor, Anne V. Coates; Associate Producers, Evzen Kolar; Costumes, Julie Weiss; Music, Bill Conti; Assistant Directors, Fredrick Blankfein, John Eyler; Concept Designers, Claudio Mazzoli, Edward E. Eyth; Concept Artist, Joe Griffith; Special Designs, Jean "Moebius" Giraud; Art Director, Robert Howland; Effects Illustrator, George Jenson; Make-up Designer, Michael Westmore; Production Executive, Ronny Yacov; Casting, Vicki Thomas; Stunts, Walter Scott, Loren Janes; Sound, Ed Novick; Assistant Art Director, Lynn Christopher; Set Designers, Daniel Gluck, Michael Johnson; Assistant Costume Designers, Isabella Van Soest, Mira Zabadowski; Production Coordinators, Alan Gershenfeld, Gretchen Iversen; Special Effects, Arthur Brewer, Leo Solis; Based on the toy line by Mattel, Inc.; Dolby Stereo; Panavision; Color; Rated PG; 106 minutes; August release

CAST

He-Man	Dolph Lundgren
Skeletor	Frank Langella
Evil-Lyn	Meg Foster
Gwildor	Billy Barty
Julie Winston	Courteney Cox
Detective Lubic	James Tolkan
Sorceress	Christina Pickles
Kevin	Robert Duncan McNeill
Man-at-Arms	Jon Cypher
Teela	Chelsea Field
Beastman	Tony Carroll
Saurod	Pons Maar
Blade	Anthony DeLongis
Karg	Robert Towers
Charlie	Barry Livingston
Monica	Jessica Nelson
Mrs. Winston	Gwynne Gilford
Mr. Winston	Walter Scott
Carl the Janitor	Walt P. Robles
Gloria	Cindy Eyman

DISORDERLIES

(WARNER BROS.) Producers, Michael Schultz, George A. Jackson, Michael Jaffe; Director, Michael Schultz; Screenplay, Mark Feldberg, Mitchell Klebanoff; Executive Producers, Charles Stettler, Joseph E. Zynczak; Photography, Rolf Kesterman; Editor, Ned Humphreys; Designer, George Costello; Art Director, Maria Caso; Music, Anne Dudley, J. J. Jeczalik; Music Performance, The Art of Noise; Associate Producers, Gloria Schultz, Coral Hawthorne; Co-Producer/Production Manager, Donna Smith; Casting, Melissa Skoff; Assistant Directors, Anthony Brand, Don Wilkerson; Costumes, Susie DeSanto; Consultants, Lynda West, James N. Glenn; Associate Editor, Brian Chambers; Assistant Editor, Brent Schaefer; Production Coordinator, Keith Baumgartner; Sound, Lawrence Loewinger; Assistant Decorator, Damon Medlen; Assistant Costume Designer, Meg Mayer; Special Effects, John Carter, Richard Scott, Greg Blocker; Stunts, Hubie Kerns, Jr.; Casting Assistant, Edie Cornell; Songs, G. Rottger, D. Wimbley, D. Robinson, M. Morales, J. Glenn, Cabera, Moran and Zarr and other artists; Soundtrack on Tin Pan Apple/Polydor Records; Color; Rated PG; 96 minutes; August release

CAST

Markie	Mark Morales
Buffy	Darren Robinson
Kool	Damon Wimbley
Winslow Lowry	Anthony Geary
Miguel	Tony Plana
Happy Socialite	Helen Reddy
Dealer	Lisa Kingston
Luis Montana	Marco Rodriguez
Albert Dennison	Ralph Bellamy
Orderlys	Jim Jackman, Don Woodard
	Charles Green
Nursing Home Owner	Joseph R. Sicari
Kool's Mother	Jo Marie Payton-France
Buffy's Mother	Linda Hopkins
Stewardess	Julie Cook
Lady on plane	Arline Mocerie
Chauffeur	Brian Moore
Sgt. Bledsoe	Don Hood
George, the butler	Garth Wilton
Carla	Troy Beyer
Lily	Tetchie Agbayani
Roller Rink Singer	Laura Hunter
Roller Rink DJ	Donnie Simpson
Funeral Home Director	Robert V. Barron
Pizza Deliveryman	Ray Parker, Jr.
Doctor	Sam Chew, Jr.
Electrician	Brant Von Hoffman
Hijacked Car Driver	Rick Nielsen

and The Beach Boys, Yvette Holland Vasquez, Sara La Porte, Lisa Gallo, Julie Smith, Carlos Cervantes, Joseph Whipp, Terry Bruns, Rick Zumwalt, Ron Doyle

Damon Wimbley, Ralph Bellamy, Mark Morales,
Darren Robinson © Warner Bros.

MATEWAN

(CINECOM) Producers, Peggy Rajski, Maggie Renzi; Director/Screenplay, John Sayles; Executive Producers, Amir Jacob Malin, Mark Balsam, Jerry Silva; Associate Producers, Ira Deutchman, James Dudelson, Ned Kandel; Photography, Haskell Wexler; Editor, Sonya Polonsky; Casting, Barbara Shapiro; Music, Mason Daring; Costumes, Cynthia Flynt; Designer, Nora Chavooshian; Production Manager, Peggy Rajski; Art Director, Dan Bishop; Assistant Production Manager, Sarah Green; Assistant Directors, Matia Karrell, Benita Allen; Additional Casting, Avy Kaufman; Sound, John Sutton; Assistant Editor, Geraldine Peroni; A Red Dog Films Production; Presented by Cinecom Entertainment Group and Film Gallery; Color; Rated PG-13; 132 minutes; August release

CAST

Joe	Chris Cooper
Danny	Will Oldham
Hillard	Jace Alexander
Sephus	Ken Jenkins
C. E. Lively	Bob Gunton
Ludie	Gary McCleery
Hickey	Kevin Tighe
Griggs	Gordon Clapp
Elma	Mary McDonnell
Few Clothes	James Earl Jones
Tolbert	James Kizer
Ellix	Michael Preston
Mrs. Elkins	Jo Henderson
Bridey Mae	Nancy Mette
Fausto	Joe Grifasi
Stennis	Ronnie Stapleton
Sid	David Strathairn
Mrs. Knightes	Ida Williams
Rosaria	Maggie Renzi
Turley	Thomas A. Carlin
Tom	Tom Wright
Cabell	Josh Mostel
Gianni	Davide Ferrario
Old Miner	Frank Pane Jr.
Redneck Miner	Stephen C. Hal
Bass	Bill Morris
Doolin	Michael A. Mantel
Sheb	Charles Haywood
Isaac	Neale Clark
James	Fred Decker
Al Felts	Frank Taylor
Lee Felts	Michael Frasher
Hardshell	John Sayles
Luann	Jennie Cline
Conductor	Delmas Lawhorn
MT Singer	Hazel Dickens

and Thomas Poore, Hazel Pearl, Hal Phillips, Mitch Scott, Percy Fruit, Gerald Milnes, William Dean, P. Michael Nunsey, Mason Daring, Tara Williams

Right Center: Will Oldham Above: James Earl Jones
Top: Chris Cooper © *Cinecom*

Mary McDonnell, Chris Cooper

THE MONSTER SQUAD

(TRI-STAR) Producer, Jonathan A. Zimbert; Director, Fred Dekker; Screenplay, Shane Black, Fred Dekker; Executive Producers, Peter Hyams, Rob Cohen, Keith Barish; Photography, Bradford May; Designer, Albert Brenner; Co-Producer, Neil A. Machlis; Editor, James Mitchell; Visual Effects, Richard Edlund; Monsters, Stan Winston; Music, Bruce Broughton; Casting, Penny Perry; Production Manager, Neil A. Machlis; Assistant Directors, Richard Luke Rothschild, Joan D. Ehrlich; Art Director, David M. Haber; Assistant Art Director, David F. Klassen; Set Decorator, Garrett Lewis; Set Designers, Roland Hill, Harold Fuhrman; Sound, Richard Church; Orchestrator, Mark McKenzie; Special Effects, Phil Cory, Ray Svedin, Hans Metz; Costumes, Michael Hoffman, Aggie Lyon; Stunts, John Moio; Dolby Stereo; Metrocolor; Panavision; Rated PG-13; 82 minutes; August release

CAST

Sean	Andre Gower
Patrick	Robby Kiger
Del	Stephen Macht
Count Dracula	Duncan Regehr
Frankenstein	Tom Noonan
Horace	Brent Chalem
Rudy	Ryan Lambert
Phoebe	Ashley Bank
Eugene	Michael Faustino
Emily	Mary Ellen Trainor
Scary German Guy	Leonardo Cimino
Desperate Man	Jonathan Gries
Detective Sapir	Stan Shaw
Patrick's Sister	Lisa Fuller
E. J.	Jason Hervey
Derek	Adam Carl
Wolfman	Carl Thibault
Gill-Man	Tom Woodruff, Jr.
Mummy	Michael MacKay
Van Helsing	Jack Gwillim
Pilot	David Proval
Co-Pilot	Daryl Anderson
Eugene's Dad	Robert Lesser
Mr. Metzger	Gweill Richards
Night Watchman	Ernie Brown
Peasant Girl	Sonia Curtis

and Paul Barringer, Julius LeFlore, Jim Stephen, Brian Kestner, Denver Mattson, Diana Lewis, Gary Rebstock, David Wendel, Charly Morgan, Phil Culotta, Mary Albee, Joan-Carroll Baron, Marianne DeCamp

(Back) Tom Woodruff, Jr., Tom Noonan, Duncan Regehr, Michael Mackay, Carl Thibault (front) Michael Faustino, Brent Chalem, Andre Gower, Robby Kiger, Ryan Lambert
© *Taft Entertainment Pictures*

END OF THE LINE

(ORION CLASSICS) Executive Producer, Mary Steenburgen; Producers, Lewis Allen, Peter Newman; Director, Jay Russell; Co-Producer, Walker Stuart; Screenplay, Jay Russell, John Wohlbruck; Photography, George Tirl; Designer, Neil Spisak; Editor, Nena Danevic; Costumes, Van Ramsey; Casting, Pat McCorkle; Casting Assistant, Jory Weitz; Additional Casting, Sandy Roberts; Production Manager, Laura Medina; Assistant Directors, Allan Harmon, Jack Kney, Janis Cantwell; Production Coordinator, Anne Nevin; Sound, Gary Alper; Art Director, Vaughan Edwards; Set Decorator, Paul Kelly; Stunts, Randy "Fife", Tim Butler; Assistant Editor, Jim Nau; Presented by Imagine Entertainment; Color; Rated PG; 105 minutes; August release

CAST

Haney	Wilford Brimley
Leo	Levon Helm
Rose	Mary Steenburgen
Jean	Barbara Barrie
Clinton	Henderson Forsythe
Gerber	Bob Balaban
Everett	Kevin Bacon
Alvin	Michael Beach
Charlotte	Holly Hunter
Jeanie	Missy Platt
Chester	Carroll Dee Bland
Maxie Howell	Trey Wilson
Benny Spears	Don Hood
Les Sullivan	Clint Howard
Sharon	Rita Jenrette
Lucy	Lillian Grimes
Travers	Dan DeMott
Billy	Bruce McGill
Gonzales	Armando Garza
Hobo	Howard Morris
Bartender	Velva Walthall
Mrs. Benny Spears	Leone James
Young Photographer	B. J. Hardin
Gas Attendant	Clay Crosby
Tommy	Trey Fancher
Toby	Keith James
Kids	Allison Choate, Jenny Fancher, Zach Hinkle
State Troopers	Steve Wilkerson, Robert Ginnaven
Diner Waitress	Sarah G. Vowell
Bag Lady	Debra Stillwell
Black Guy	John Williams

Levon Helm, Mary Steenburgen
© *Orion Classics*

NADINE

(TRI-STAR) Producer, Arlene Donovan; Director/Screenplay, Robert Benton; Executive Producer/Production Manager, Wolfgang Glattes; Photography, Nestor Almendros; Designer, Paul Sylbert; Editor, Sam O'Steen; Costumes, Albert Wolsky; Music, Howard Shore; Casting, Howard Feuer; Assistant Directors, Ron Bozman, Kyle McCarthy; Art Directors, Peter Lansdown Smith, Cary White; Annie Spiegelman; Set Decorator, Lee Poll; Assistant Editors, Richard Nord, Kris Cole; Sound, David Ronne; Special Visual Effects, Mark Sullivan; Special Effects, Ron Downey, Jack Monroe; Assistant Costume Designer, Harry Curtis; Stunts, Diamond Farnsworth; Casting, Rody Kent, Ellen Locy, Sam Broomall; Production Coordinator, Steven McAfee; from Tri-Star-ML Delphi Premier Productions; Songs by various artists; Metrocolor/Technicolor; Rated PG; 88 minutes; August release

CAST

Vernon Hightower	Jeff Bridges
Nadine Hightower	Kim Basinger
Buford Pope	Rip Torn
Vera	Gwen Verdon
Renee	Glenne Headly
Raymond Escobar	Jerry Stiller
Dwight Estes	Jay Patterson
Boyd	William Youmans
Cecil	Gary Grubbs
Floyd	Mickey Jones
Mountain	Blue Deckert
Sheriff Rusk	Harlan Jordan
Reverend	Norman Bennett
Deacon	James Harrell
Officer Lloyd	John Galt
Reporter	Joe Berryman
Janitor	Linwood P. Walker, III
T.V. Announcer	Ray Walker
Michelle	Shelby Brammer
Charley Draper	Loyd Catlett
Este's Girlfriend	Sidney Brammer

Left: Kim Basinger, Glenne Headly, Jeff Bridges
Below: Kim Basinger, Gwen Verdon, Jeff Bridges
Top: Jeff Bridges, Kim Basinger
© *Tri-Star Pictures*

Rip Torn, Jay Patterson

Jeff Bridges, Kim Basinger

STAKEOUT

(TOUCHSTONE) Producers, Jim Kouf, Cathleen Summers; Director, John Badham; Screenplay, Jim Kouf; Executive Producer, John Badham; Supervising Producer, Gregg Champion; Associate Producer, Dana Satler; Photography, John Seale; Designer, Philip Harrison; Costumes, Mary Vogt; Editors, Tom Rolf, Michael Ripps; Music, Arthur B. Rubinstein; Casting, Mike Fenton, Jane Feinberg, Judy Taylor, Sidney Kozak; Production Manager, Fitch Cady; Assistant Directors, Rob Cowan, Peter Daskewytch, Richard Cowan; Art Director, Richard Hudolin; Assistant Art Director, Michael Ritter; Set Decorator, Rose Marie McSherry; Assistant Set Decorator, Lesley Beale; Sound, Larry Sutton; Assistant Editors, Jean Caperonis, Sandra J. Davis, Michael Smith, Bruce Giesbrecht, Steve Roberts; Stunts, Conrad Palmisano, Jacob Rupp; Special Effects, John Thomas, Dean Lockwood, Rory Cutler, Corbin H. Fox, Lars Lenander, Don B. Leask; Orchestrations, Mark J. Hoder; Buena Vista Distribution; DeLuxe Color; Dolby Stereo; Rated R; 115 minutes; August release

CAST

Chris Lecce	Richard Dreyfuss
Bil Reimers	Emilio Estevez
Maria McGuire	Madeleine Stowe
Richard "Stick" Montgomery	Aidan Quinn
Phil Goldshank	Dan Lauria
Jack Pismo	Forest Whitaker
Caylor Reese	Ian Tracey
Captain Giles	Early Billings
FBI Agent Lusk	Jackson Davies
B. C.	J. J. Makaro
Reynaldo McGuire	Scott Andersen
Tony Harmon	Tony Pantages
Carol Reimers	Beatrice Boepple
Jeffrey Reimers	Kyle Woida
Kelly McDonald	Jan Speck
Billy Steeks	Kim Kondrashoff
Prison Doctor	Gary Heatherington
Prison Officer	Don MacKay
Prison Gate Guard	Don S. Davis
Prison First Guard	Roger Dean
Cafe Waiter	David Brass
Bar Waitress	Elizabeth Bracco
Farol Bernie	Denny Williams
Paramedics	Norma Matheson, Blu Mankuma
Supermarket Cashier	Lossen Chambers
Gas Station Attendant	Lloyd Berry
Winston	Himself

**Right: Richard Dreyfuss, Madeleine Stowe, Emilio Estevez
Above: Richard Dreyfuss, Madeleine Stowe Top: Richard
Dreyfuss, Emilio Estevez**
© *Touchstone Pictures/Richard Corman/Bob Akester*

Madeleine Stowe, Aidan Quinn

Emilio Estevez, Richard Dreyfuss

NO WAY OUT

(ORION) Producers, Laura Ziskin, Robert Garland; Director, Roger Donaldson; Screen Story/Screenplay, Robert Garland; Based on the novel *The Big Clock* by Kenneth Fearing; Executive Producer, Mace Neufeld; Associate Producer, Glenn Neufeld; Photography, John Alcott; Designer, Dennis Washington; Editor, Neil Travis; Music, Maurice Jarre; Casting, Ilene Starger; Production Manager, Mel Dellar; Assistant Directors, Herb Adelman, Jim Charleston, Brad Yacobian; Art Director, Anthony Brockliss; Set Designers, Dick McKenzie, Henry Alberti, Gerald Sigmon; Set Decorator, Bruce Gibeson; Sound, Jack Solomon; Stunts, Richard Diamond Farnsworth; Special Effects, Jack Monroe, Terry Frazee; Production Coordinator, Richard Liebegott; Title Song, Paul Anka, Michael McDonald; Vocals, Julia Migenes, Paul Anka; Songs by various artists; Metrocolor; Rated R; 114 minutes; August release

CAST

Tom Farrell	Kevin Costner
David Brice	Gene Hackman
Susan Atwell	Sean Young
Scott Pritchard	Will Patton
Senator Duvall	Howard Duff
Sam Hesselman	George Dzundza
Major Donovan	Jason Bernard
Nina Beka	Iman
Marshall	Fred Dalton Thompson
Kevin O'Brien	Leon Russom
Mate	Dennis Burkley
Schiller	Michael Shillo
Ensign Fox	Leo Geter
Bellboy	Matthew Barry
Lt. John Chadway	John DiAquino
Seaman Dufor	Peter Bell
Helmsman	Tony Webster
J. O. D.	Matthew Evans
Quartermaster	Gregory Le Noel
Programmer	Joan McMurtrey
Lorraine	Edith Fields
Margaret Brice	June Chandler
Limo Driver	Gordon Needham

and Marshall Bell, Chris D., Nicholas Worth, Gregory Avellone, Jeremy Glenn, David Paymer, Charles Walker, Bob Courts, Bruce Dobus, Eugene Robert Glazer, Darryl Henriques, John Hostetter, Michael Hungerford, Robert Herman, Jay Arlen Jones, Rob Sullivan, Frederick Allen, Scott Freeman, Noel Manchan, Lee Schael, Jeffrey Sudzin, Austin Kelly, Charles Middleton, Stephen R. Asinas, Terrance Cooper, Dorothy Parke, Jill Clark, Cindy Keung, Steve Keung, Lorna Martyn, Arona McDonald

Top: Sean Young, Kevin Costner Right: Iman, Young
Below: Gene Hackman, Sean Young
© *Orion Pictures/Gemma Lamana-Wills*

Sean Young, Kevin Costner
Above: Costner, Gene Hackman, Will Patton

73

WHO'S THAT GIRL

(WARNER BROS.) Producers, Rosilyn Heller, Bernard Williams; Director, James Foley; Story, Andrew Smith; Screenplay, Andrew Smith, Ken Finkleman; Executive Producers, Peter Guber, Jon Peters, Roger Birnbaum; Photography, Jan deBont; Designer, Ida Random; Editor, Pembroke Herring; Music, Stephen Bray; Costumes, Deborah Lynn Scott; Production Manager, Sheridan Reid; Assistant Directors, Ric Kidney, Tena Yatroussis, Dan Suhart; Casting, Glenn Daniels; Additional Music, Patrick Leonard; Associate Producer, Andrew Smith; Art Director, Don Woodruff; Set Decorator, Cloudia; Sound, Ed White; Stunts, Bud Davis; Special Effects, Richard O. Helmer, Jim Schwalm, Richard Hill; Visual Effects, Apogee Inc./Peter Donen; Songs by Madonna, Patrick Leonard and various other artists; Soundtrack on Sire Records; Dolby Stereo; Technicolor; Rated PG; 94 minutes; August release

CAST

Nikki Finn	Madonna
Loudon Troff	Griffin Dunne
Wendy Worthington	Haviland Morris
Simon Worthington	John McMartin
Mrs. Worthington	Bibi Besch
Montgomery Bell	Sir John Mills
Detective Bellson	Robert Swan
Detective Doyle	Drew Pillsbury
Raoul	Coati Mundi
Benny	Dennis Burkley
Buck	Jim Dietz
Sandy	Cecile Callan
Heather	Karen Baldwin
Rachel	Kimerlin Brown
Denise	Crystal Carson
Holly	Elaine Wilkes

and Tony La Fortezza, Thomas Pinnock, Alvin Hammer, Sean Sullivan, Helen Lloyd Breed, Dalton Dearborn, Robert E. Weil, Robert Cornthwaite, Albert Popwell, Alice Nunn, Gary Basaraba, Ron Taylor, Stanley Tucci, Mike Starr, Dwight Crawford, Laura Drake, Efrat Lavie, Mary Gillis, Roy Brocksmith, Ted Hayden, Deryl Carroll, Beatrice Colen, Susan Bugg, Robert Clotworthy, Lexie Shine, Faith Minton, Judy Kerr, Darwyn Carson, Andre Rosey Brown, Brad Rearden, Bert Rosario, Patrick McCord, Liz Sheridan, Shari Summers, Glen Plummer, Lance Slaughter, Alon Williams, Mario Gardner, Dennis Brown, Carmen Filpi, Robert Benjamin Pope, Gerlad Orange, Shelly Lipkin, Ellen Crawford, Pat Romano, Gary Tacon, Jinaki, Glen Chin, Lloyd Kino, Clive Rosengren, Scott Harms, Cristian Letelier, Sanders Cupac, Meilani Figalan, Phil Romano, Lea Lashaway, Michael Scott Henderson, Marilyn Ammons, Murray

Top: Madonna, and Right and Below with Griffin Dunne
© *Warner Bros.*

Madonna, John Mills, Griffin Dunne
Above: Madonna

THE BIG TOWN

(COLUMBIA) Producer, Martin Ransohoff; Director, Ben Bolt; Screenplay, Robert Roy Pool; Based on the novel *"The Arm"* by Clark Howard; Co-Producer, Don Carmody; Photography, Ralph D. Bode; Designer, Bill Kenney; Editor, Stuart Pappe; Music, Michael Melvoin; Executive Producer, Gene Kraft; Casting, Nancy Klopper; Production Manager, Joyce Kozy King; Assistant Directors, Don French, Howard Rothschild, Andrew Shea, Terry Gould; Music Supervision, John Beug; Associate Producer, Jon Turtle; Associate Editor, Kim Secrist; Assistant Editors, Anita Brandt-Burgoyne, Peter Ransohoff, Robin Russell, Michael Pacek; Sound, Owen Langevin; Art Director, Dan Yarhi; Assistant Art Director, Dennis Davenport; Set Decorators, Rose Marie McSherry, Mark Freeborn; Assistant Set Decorator, Daniel Bradette; Production Coordinator, Deborah Zwicker; Costumes, Wendy Partridge; Assistant Costume Designer, Gail Filman; Special Effects, Neil Trifunovich; Stunts, Stuntco International; Choreography, Kelly Robinson; Set Decorator, Raymond Fleischman; Songs by various artists; Soundtrack on Atlantic Records; Color; Rated R; 110 minutes; September release

CAST

J. C. Cullen	Matt Dillon
Lorry Dane	Diane Lane
George Cole	Tommy Lee Jones
Mr. Edwards	Bruce Dern
Ferguson Edwards	Lee Grant
Phil Carpenter	Tom Skerritt
Aggie Donaldson	Suzy Amis
Sonny Binkley	David Marshall Grant
Carl Hooker	Don Francks
Deacon Daniels	Del Close
Dorothy Cullen	Meg Hogarth
Ginger McDonald	Cherry Jones
Prager	Mark Danton
Cool Guy	David Elliott
Roy McMullin	Sean McCann
Boss' Son	Kevin Fox
Madigan	Marc Strange
Patsy Fuqua	Don Lake
Harold	Angelo Rizacos
Shooter	Chris Benson
Duke	Gary Farmer
Sid	Diego Matamoros
Christy Donaldson	Sarah Polley
Adele	Kirsten Bishop
Bartender	Ken McGregor
Doorman	Alar Aedma
Bernstein	Sam Malkin
Sideburns	Robert Morelli
Murphy	Layne Coleman
Black Lace Stripper	Lolita David
Friendly Guy	Errol Slue
Baptist Preacher	Gerry Pearson
Elmo	Hugo Dann
Marvin Brown	John Evans
Detective	J. W. Carroll
Mrs. Rogers	Diane Gordon

and Steve Yorke, Chris Owens, Viki Matthews, Cherie McGroarty, Sandy Czapiewski, Marie Siebert, Julie Conte, Bill Colgate, William Forrest MacDonald, Len Doncheff, Michael Caruana, Richard Comar, Lubomir Mykytiuk, Robert Ramsay Collins

Matt Dillon, Diane Lane
© *Columbia Pictures*

AMAZON WOMEN ON THE MOON (Universal) Producer, Robert K. Weiss; Directors, Joe Dante, Carl Gottlieb, Peter Horton, John Landis, Robert K. Weiss; Screenplay, Michael Barrie, Jim Mulholland; Executive Producers, John Landis, George Folsey, Jr.; Associate Producer, Robb Idels; Photography, Daniel Pearl; Editors, Bert Lovitt, Marshall Harvey, Malcolm Campbell; Casting, Sally Dennison, Julie Selzer; Production Manager, Roger Lapage; Assistant Directors, Deborah Love, Daniel Schneider, David Sosna, Robin Holding, Robin R. Oliver; Designer, Ivo Cristante; Costumes, Taryn DeChellis; Art Director, Alex Hajdu; Set Decorator, Julie Kaye Towery; Production Coordinator, Patricia A. Whitcher; Assistant Producer, Kevin Marcy; Sound, Susumu Tokunow; Assistant Costume Designer, Margaret C. Mayer; Stunts, Rick Barker; Special Visual & Photographic Effects, The LA Effects Group, Inc.; Technicolor; Rated R; 85 minutes; September release

CAST

"Mondo Condo": Arsenio Hall (Apartment Victim); *"Penthouse Video"*: Donald Muhich (Easterbrook), Monique Gabrielle (Taryn Steele); *"Murray in Videoland"*: Lou Jacobi (Murray), Erica Yohn (Selma), Debbie Davison (Weather Person), Rob Krausz (Floor Manager), Phil Hartman (Baseball Announcer), Corey Burton (Anchorman); *"Hospital"*: Michelle Pfeiffer (Brenda), Peter Horton (Harry), Griffin Dunne (Doctor), Brian Ann Zoccola (Nurse); *"Hairlooming"*: Joe Pantoliano (Sy Swerdlow), Stanley Brock (Customer); *"Amazon Women on the Moon"*: Steve Forrest (Capt. Nelson), Robert Colbert (Blackie), Joey Travolta (Butch), Forrest J. Ackerman (U.S President), Sybil Danning (Queen Lara), Lana Clarkson (Alpha Beta), Corey Burton (TV Announcer); *"Blacks Without Soul"*; David Alan Grier (Don Simmons), B. B. King, Bill Bryant, Roxie Roker (Republicans), Le Tari (Pimp), Christopher Broughton (Fan Club President); *"Two I.D.'S"*: Rosanna Arquette (Karen), Steven Guttenberg (Jerry); *"Bullshit or Not"*: Henry Silva, Sarah Lilly (Prostitute); *"Critics Corner"*: Archie Hahn (Harvey Pitnik), Belinda Balaski (Bernice Pitnik), Justin Benham (Pitnik Boy), Erica Gayle (Pitnik Girl), Lohman and Barkley (Frankel and Herbert): *"Silly Pate"*: T. K. Carter (Host), Philip Proctor (Mike), Ira Newborn (Fred), Karen Montgomery (Karen), Corey Burton (Announcer): *"Roast Your Loved One"*: Belinda Balaski (Bernice Pitnik), Robert Picardo (Rick Raddnitz), Justin Benham (Pitnik Boy), Erica Gayle (Pitnik Girl), Rip Taylor, Slappy White, Jackie Vernon, Henny Youngman, Charlie Callas, Steve Allen, Archie Hahn (Harvey Pitnik); *"Don 'No Soul' Simmons"*: David Alan Grier (Don Simmons); *"Video Pirates"*: William Marshall (Pirate Capt.), Tino Insana (Mr. Sylvio), Donald Gibb (Graceless), Frank Collison (Grizzled), Bill Taylor (Gruesome); *"Son of the Invisible Man"*: Ed Begley, Jr. (Griffin), Chuck LaFont (Trent), Pamla Vale (Woman), Larry Hankin (Man), Garry Goodrow (Checker Player), Roger LaPage (London Bobby); *"Art Sale"*: John Ingle (Felix Van Dam); *"First Lady of the Evening"*: Angel Tompkins (First Lady), Terence McGovern (Salesman), Michael Hanks (Announcer); *"Titan Man"*: Matt Adler (George), Kelly Preston (Violet), Ralph Bellamy (Mr. Gower), Howard Hesseman (Rupert King), Steve Cropper (Customer); *"Video Date"*: Marc McClure (Ray), Russ Meyer (Video Salesman), Corinne Wahl (Sherrie), Andrew Dice Clay (Frankie), Willard Pugh (Cop); *"Reckless Youth"*: Carrie Fisher (Mary Brown), Paul Bartel (Doctor), Herb Vigran (Agent), Tracy Hutchinson (Floozie), Mike Mazurki (Dutch), Frank Beddor (Ken)

Carrie Fisher, Paul Bartel
© *Universal City Studios*

FATAL ATTRACTION

(PARAMOUNT) Producers, Stanley R. Jaffe, Sherry Lansing; Director, Adrian Lyne; Screenplay, James Dearden, Based on his Original Screenplay; Photography, Howard Atherton; Designer, Mel Bourne; Editors, Michael Kahn, Peter E. Berger; Costumes, Ellen Mirojnick; Music/Orchestrations, Maurice Jarre; Casting, Risa Bramon, Billy Hopkins; Production Manager, Christopher Cronyn; Assistant Directors, Robert Girolami, Jane Paul, Christopher Stoia; Art Director, Jack Blackman; Set Decorator, George DeTitta; Sound, Les Lazarowitz, Vito Ilardi; Assistant Editors, George C. Villasenor, Tom Bryant, Martha Huntley, Richard Rossi, Diane Asnes Ruggeri; Casting Assistants, Heidi Levitt, Paul Adler; Stunts, David R. Ellis; Songs by various artists; Dolby Stereo; Technicolor; Rated R; 121 minutes; September release

CAST

Dan Gallagher	Michael Douglas
Alex Forrest	Glenn Close
Beth Gallagher	Anne Archer
Ellen Gallagher	Ellen Hamilton Latzen
Jimmy	Stuart Pankin
Hildy	Ellen Foley
Arthur	Fred Gwynne
Joan Rogerson	Meg Mundy
Howard Rogerson	Tom Brennan
Martha	Lois Smith
Bob Drimmer	Mike Nussbaum
O'Rourke	J. J. Johnston
Lieutenant	Michael Arkin
Fuselli	Sam J. Coppola
Receptionist	Eunice Prewitt
Babysitter	Jane Krakowski
Real Estate Agent	Justine Johnston
Teachers	Mary Joy, Christine Farrell
Chuck	Marc McQue
Man in Japanese restaurant	James Eckhouse
Nurse	Faith Geer
Waitress	Carol Schneider
Executive	David Bates
Secretary	Anna Levine
Ellen's Friend	Alicia Perusse
Lawyer	Christopher Rubin
Bartender	Thomas Saccio
Bar Patron	Greg Scott
Doorman	Chris Manor

and Jonathan Brandis, Joe Chapman, Judi M. Durand, Lillian Garrett, J. D. Hall, Barbara Harris, Barbara Iley, Angelo Bruno Krakoff, Carlo Steven Krakoff, Amy Lyne, David McCharen, Larry Moss, Mio Polo, Jan Rabson, Marilyn Schreffler, Vladimir Skomarovsky, Dennis Tufano, Lynnanne Zager

© *Paramount/Andy Schwartz*

Glenn Close, Michael Douglas, Anne Archer Above: Michael Douglas, Ellen Hamilton Latzen
Top: Ellen Foley, Michael Douglas, Stuart Pankin, Anne Archer Below: Archer, Douglas

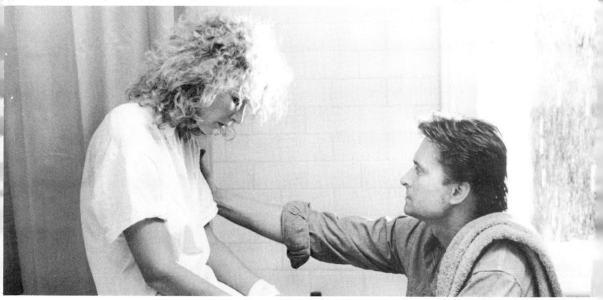

Glenn Close, Michael Douglas (also above)

IN THE MOOD

(LORIMAR) Producers, Gary Adelson, Karen Mack; Director/Screenplay, Phil Alden Robinson; Story, Bob Kosberg, David Simon, Phil Alden Robinson; Photography, John Lindley; Designer, Dennis Gassner; Costumes, Linda Bass; Music, Ralph Burns; Editor, Patrick Kennedy; Associate Producer/Production Manager, Brian Frankish; Casting, Penny Perry, Megan Branman; Assistant Directors, Craig Beaudine, Randall Badger, Dustin Bernard; Sound, Russell Williams II; Assistant Costume Designer, Mary Schuba Stutz; Art Director, Dins Danielsen; Assistant Art Director, Nancy Haigh; Set Decorator, Richard Hoover; Assistant Set Decorator, Suzette Sheets; Choreography, Miguel Delgado; Special Effects, Robby Knott; Production Coordinator, Ronnie Kramer; Songs by various artists; *"Baby Blues,"* Music by Ralph Burns, Lyrics by Phil Alden Robinson; Arranger/Conductor, Ralph Burns; Soundtrack on Atlantic Records; Dolby Stereo; CFI Color; Rated PG-13; 98 minutes; September release

CAST

Ellsworth "Sonny" Wisecarver	Patrick Dempsey
Judy Cusimano	Talia Balsam
Francine Glatt	Beverly D'Angelo
Mr. Wisecarver	Michael Constantine
Mrs. Wisecarver	Betty Jinnette
Mrs. Marver	Kathleen Freeman
The Judge	Peter Hobbs
Carlo	Tony Longo
Uncle Clete	Douglas Rowe
Chief Kelsey (Papa Bear)	Ernie Brown
Wendy	Kim Myers
George	Brian McNamara
Alberta	Dana Short
Tony	Josh Cadman
Madeline	Nan Woods
Gary	Tom Breznahan
Karen	Gillian Grant
Jamie	Lisanne Falk
Mrs. Long	Edith Fellows
Rosie the Riveter	Joycee Katz
Maria, the Tuna Lady	Ana Helena Berenguer
Her Husband, the Tuna Foreman	Jay Varela
Mrs. Kelsey (Mama Bear)	Sheila Rogers

and Barbara Wint, Burr Middleton, Jared Chandler, Tom Tarpey, Crane Jackson, Neil Elliot, Mae Williams, Janet Rotblatt, Harvey J. Goldenberg, Tom Maier, Putter Smith, Lenore Woodward, Lee Garlington, Charles Stevenson, Carl Parker, Wayne Grace, Jeffrey Alan Chandler, Robert Gould, Jordan Myers, Rick Salassi, Walter G. Zeri, Nitche Vo Miller, Laura Bastianelli, Thomas Ryan, Ted Noose, Charlie Holliday, Valerie Reynolds, Rocky Giordani, Darwin Swalve, W. T. Zacha, Kitty Swink, Sarah Partridge, Steve Whittaker, Thomas Albert Clay, Tony Monaco, Terry Camilleri, Mike Darrell, David Schermerhorn, John Zarchen, Cletus Young, Guy Christopher, Paul Keith, Neal Jano, Bert Conway, Michael Bandoni, Heath Jobes, S. A. Griffin, Tom Patten, Ellsworth "Sonny" Wisecarver, Randy Peters, Marilyn Cohen, Niles Brewster, Bess Meyer, Max Perlich, Andrew Roperto, Tom Ashworth, Rocky Parker, Kazan, Steve the Rabbitt

Left: Beverly D'Angelo, Patrick Dempsey, Kathleen Freeman Above: Patrick Dempsey, Talia Balsam Top: Patrick Dempsey, Beverly D'Angelo © *Lorimar Pictures*

Patrick Dempsey

Patrick Dempsey

THE PRINCESS BRIDE

(20th CENTURY FOX) Producers, Andrew Scheinmann, Rob Reiner; Director, Rob Reiner; Screenplay, William Goldman; Based on book by William Goldman; Executive Producer, Norman Lear; Music, Mark Knopfler; Photography, Adrian Biddle; Designer, Norman Garwood; Editor, Robert Leighton; Associate Producers, Jeffrey Stott, Steve Nicolaides; Casting, Jane Jenkins, Janet Hirshenson; Costumes, Phyllis Dalton; Production Executive, Mark E. Pollack; U.K. Production Manager, David Barron; Assistant Directors, Ken Baker, Peter Bennett, Paul Taylor; Sound, David John; Art Directors, Keith Pain, Richard Holland; Assistant Costume Designer, Jane Hamilton; Set Decorator, Maggie Gray; Associate Editor, Adam Weiss; Assistant Editors, Paul Hodgson, Steve Nevius, Adam MacRitchie; Special Effects, Nick Allder, Terry Schubert, Neil Swan, Philip Knowles, John Hatt, Ronald Hone; Special Make-Up, Peter Montagna; Stunts, Peter Diamond; Swordmaster, Bob Anderson; Cliff Climbing Effects, Bob Harmon; Music Performance, Mark Knopfler, Guy Fletcher; Song/Vocals, *"Storybook Love"* by Willy De Ville; Soundtrack on Warner Bros. Records in U.S.A./Polygram Records throughout the world; A Buttercup Films Limited Picture; Presented by Act III Communications; DeLuxe Color; Rated PG; 98 minutes; September release

CAST

Westley	Cary Elwes
Inigo Montoya	Mandy Patinkin
Prince Humperdinck	Chris Sarandon
Count Rugen	Christopher Guest
Vizzini	Wallace Shawn
Fezzik	Andre the Giant
The Grandson	Fred Savage
The Princess Bride	Robin Wright
The Grandfather	Peter Falk
The Impressive Clergyman	Peter Cook
The Albino	Mel Smith
Valerie	Carol Kane
Miracle Max	Billy Crystal
The Queen	Anne Dyson
The Ancient Booer	Margery Mason
Yellin	Malcolm Storry
The King	Willoughby Gray
The Mother	Betsy Brantley
The Assistant Brute	Paul Badger

Left: Mandy Patinkin, Andre the Giant, Cary Elwes, Carol Kane, Billy Crystal Above: Robin Wright, Cary Elwes, Top: Fred Savage, Peter Falk
© *20th Century Fox/Clive Coote*

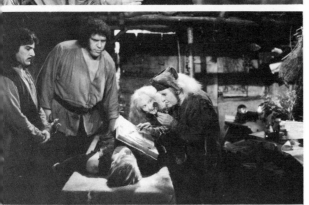

Andre the Giant, Billy Crystal, Mandy Patinkin

Cary Elwes, Robin Wright

ORPHANS

(LORIMAR) Producer/Director, Alan J. Pakula; Screenplay, Lyle Kessler; Based on the play by Lyle Kessler; Co-Producer, Susan Solt; Photography, Donald McAlpine; Designer, George Jenkins; Editor, Evan Lottman; Music, Michael Small; Costumes, John Boxer; Associate Producer/Production Manager, John H. Starke; Assistant Directors, Alex Hapsas, Joseph Ray; Art Director, John Jay Moore; Special Consultant, Richard Ericson; Set Decorator, Carol Joffe; Sound, James J. Sabat, Frank J. Graziadel; Production Coordinator, Gail Geibel; Producers' Coordinator, Catherine Hall; Magic Consultant, Teller; Choreographer, Lynnette Barkley; Stunts, Vic Magnota, Frank Ferrara; Songs by various artists; Originally produced for the New York Stage by Wolf Gang Productions, Inc., Dasha Epstein, Joan Cullman & Steppenwolf Production Company; Technicolor; Rated R; 115 minutes; September release

CAST

Harold	Albert Finney
Treat	Matthew Modine
Phillip	Kevin Anderson
Barney	John Kellogg
Man in park	Anthony Heald
Mattie	Novella Nelson
Rich Woman	Elizabeth Parrish
Lady in crosswalk	B. Constance Barry
Cab Driver	Frank Ferrara
Doorman	Clifford Fearl

**Above: Matthew Modine Top: Modine, Albert Finney,
Kevin Anderson Left: Finney, Modine
© Lorimar Motion Pictures**

Albert Finney, Kevin Anderson
Above: Kevin Anderson

80

THE PRINCIPAL

(TRI-STAR) Producer, Thomas H. Brodek; Director, Christopher Cain; Screenplay, Frank Deese; Photography, Arthur Albert; Editor, Jack Hofstra; Costumes, Marianna Astrom-DeFina; Music Supervisor, Jellybean; Music, Jay Gruska; Casting, Penny Perry; Production Manager, James T. Davis; Assistant Directors, Charles D. Myers, Tom Snyder; Art Director, Mark Billerman; Set Decorator, Rick Brown; Additional Photography, Philip Holahan; Production Supervisor, Trevor Jolly; Assistant Editor, Frank Kniest; Sound, Andy Wiskes; Special Effects, David Pier, Douglas Cattaneo, Allen S. Gross, Jr.; Stunts, Everett Creach; Songs, Jay Gruska, Bruce Roberts, Andy Goldmark, Jon Lind, Paul Gordon, and various other artists; Dolby Stereo; Technicolor; Rated R; 109 minutes; September release

CAST

Rick Latimer	James Belushi
Jake Phillips	Louis Gossett, Jr.
Hilary Orozo	Rae Dawn Chong
Victor Duncan	Michael Wright
"White Zac"	J. J. Cohen
Raymi Rojas	Esai Morales
"Baby" Emile	Troy Winbush
Arturo Diego	Jacob Vargas
Robert Darcy	Thomas Ryan
Jojo	Reggie Johnson
Treena Lester	Kelly Minter
Mrs. Jenkins	Ruth Beckford
Kevin	Julian Brooks
Secretary	Joan Valerrama
Mr. Harkley	Rick Hamilton
Security Guard	Martin Pistone
Buddies	Richard Duppell, Peter Fitzsimmons
Terhune	Joe Flood
Mrs. Ripton	Ann Armous
Kimberly	Sharon Thomas
Will	Daniel Royal
Mrs. Coswell	Delores Mitchell
P.E. Teacher	Zoltan Gray
Frank Valdis	John Allen Vick
Rolf	Sean Allen Barnes
Lance Woodbury	Yuri Lane
Stevie B.	Steve W. Birger
Gus	Gus Dimas
George Pierce	Leo Downey
Principal O'Connor	Tom Winston
Jan Buchanan	Kathryn Knotts
Charles Lester	Josh Wood
Mr. Petersen	Frank Deese
Will	J. J. Johnson
Eric	Doug White

and Tony Haney, Marshall Jones, Mark Anger, Wat Takeshita, Elliott S. Valderrama, Joel Valentin, Jessica Wilson, Kaprice Wilson, Bridgette Rodriguez, Tom Bryant, Danny Kovacs, Charmaine Anderson, James Edward Griffin, David Williams, Melanie G. Muters, Linda Throwbridge, Danny Williams, Bill Yarbrough, Terry Coleman, Melissa Lee Hollowman, Luis Zuno, Nemo Wade, Wural Wills

Right: James Belushi, Kelly Minter
Above: Troy Winbush, Belushi, J. J. Cohen
Top: James Belushi, Louis Gossett, Jr.
© *Tri-Star Pictures*

CHUCK BERRY HAIL! HAIL! ROCK 'N' ROLL

(UNIVERSAL) Producers, Stephanie Bennett, Chuck Berry; Director, Taylor Hackford; Music Producer, Keith Richards; Associate Producers, Albert Spevak, Jane Rose; Photography, Oliver Stapleton; Editor, Lisa Day; Concert Production Designer, Kim Colefax; Production Manager, Thomas D. Adelman; Assistant Directors, Beau Marks, K. C. Colwell; Creative Consultants, Robbie Robertson, Scott Richardson; Concert Lighting, Bill Klages; Sound, Michael Frondelli; Set Decorator, Rosemary Brandenburg; Costumes, Dewey Perrigo; Assistant Designer, Tom Randol; Associate Producer, George Nierenberg; Documentary/Concert; Dolby Stereo; DuArt Color; Rated PG; 120 minutes; October release

CAST

Eric Clapton, Robert Cray, Etta James, Julian Lennon, Keith Richards, Linda Ronstadt, Ingrid Berry, Johnnie Johnson, Steve Jordan, Bobby Keys, Chuck Leavell, Joey Spampinato, Chuck Clay, Frank Dunbar

Chuck Berry, Julian Lennon, Ingrid Berry
© *Universal City Studios*

BABY BOOM

(MGM/UA) Producer, Nancy Meyers; Director, Charles Shyer; Screenplay, Nancy Meyers, Charles Shyer; Photography, William A. Fraker; Designer, Jeffrey Howard; Editor, Lynzee Klingman; Associate Producer, Bruce A. Block; Costumes, Susan Becker; Casting, Pam Dixon; Music, Bill Conti; Production Manager, Michele Ader; Assistant Directors, John Kretchmer, Carole Keligian, Barbara Gelman; Art Director, Beala Neel; Set Decorator, Lisa Fischer; Assistant Editors, Larry Falick, Dorothy McGowan; Sound, Bill Nelson; Orchestrations, Jack Eskew; Special Effects, John Frazier; Baby Coordinator, Jimmy "Bubbles" Wagner; Casting Associate, Carol Lefko; Song, *"Everchanging Times"* by Burt Bacharach, Carole Bayer Sager, Bill Conti; Vocals, Siedah Garrett; Song Producers, Burt Bacharach, Carole Bayer Sager, David Foster; Color; Rated PG; 103 minutes; October release

CAST

J. C. Wiatt	Diane Keaton
Steven Buchner	Harold Ramis
Fritz Curtis	Sam Wanamaker
Ken Arrenberg	James Spader
Hughes Larrabee	Pat Hingle
Vern Boone	Britt Leach
Elizabeth Wiatt	Kristina and Michelle Kennedy
Dr. Jeff Cooper	Sam Shepard
Narrator	Linda Ellerbee
Robin	Kim Sebastian
Charlotte	Mary Gross
Secretary	Patricia Estrin
Mrs. Atwood	Elizabeth Bennett
Maitre D'	Peter Elbling
Cloak Room Attendant	Shera Danese
Ann Bowen	Beverly Todd
Stockboy	Angel David
Delivery Boy	Nicholas Cascone
Merle White	William Frankfather
Wilma White	Annie O'Donnell
Everett Sloane	George O. Petrie
Eve	Victoria Jackson
Food Chain Secretary	Marianne Doherty
Dwayne	John C. Cooke
Helga	Carol Gillies
Ben	Benjamin Diskin
"Center" Instructor	Paxton Whitehead
Receptionist	Constance Forslund
Sam Potts	Hansford Rowe
Roofer	Billy Beck
Realtor	Margaret Hussey
Katie Potts	Mary O'Sullivan
Stacy	Lisa Fuller
Store Owner	Kate O'Connell
PostMaster	Mary Peters
Nurse/Mayor	Elizabeth Philbin
Little Girl in Vermont	Annie Meyers-Shyer

and Patti Johns, Annie Golden, Jennifer Balgobin, Eugenie Ross-Leming, Dori Brenner, Jane Elliot, John J. Philbin, Richard Humphreys, Katherine Borowitz, Robin Bartlett, Christopher Noth, Barry Heins

Top Right: Diane Keaton, and below with Harold Ramis © *United Artists*

Diane Keaton, Kristina/Michelle Kennedy

Diane Keaton, Sam Shepard

ANNA

(VESTRON) Producers, Zanne Devin, Yurek Bogayevicz; Director, Yurek Bogayevicz; Executive Producers, Julianne Gilliam, Deirdre Gainor; Screenplay, Agnieszka Holland; Story, Yurek Bogayevicz, Agnieszka Holland; Music, Greg Hawkes; Production Manager/Associate Producer, Brenda Goodman; Costumes, Hali Breindel; Designer, Lester Cohen; Editor, Julie Sloane; Lighting, Larry Banks; Photography, Bobby Bukowski; Casting, Caroline Thomas; Assistant Directors, Lisa Zimble, Ellen Davis, Amy Herzig; Art Director, Daniel Talpers; Assistant Art Director, Pam Woodbridge; Set Decorator, John Tatlock; Stills Sequence, Bobby Bukowski, Abigayle Tarchs; Sound, William Sarokin; Hair Design, Theodore Mayes of Glemby; Assistant Costume Designers, Lori Stone, Beatrix Aruna Pasztor; Production Coordinator, Donna Amato; Assistant Production Coordinator, Chris Quinn; Casting, Caroline Thomas; Assistant Editor, Elizabeth Rich; A Magnus Films Production; TVC Color; Rated PG-13; 100 minutes; October release

CAST

Anna	Sally Kirkland
Daniel	Robert Fields
Krystyna	Pauline Porizkova
Director #1	Gibby Brand
Director #2	John Robert Tillotson
Woman Author	Julianne Gilliam
Stage Manager	Joe Aufiery
Assistant #1	Lance Davis
Assistant #2	Deirdre O'Connell

"Seven Women of Different Ages":

Woman #1/Gloria	Ruth Maleczech
Woman #2/Woman with bird	Holly Villaire
Woman #3/Woman in white veil	Shirl Bernheim
Woman #4/Woman in bonnet	Rene Coleman
Woman #5/Woman in black	Gabriella Farrar
Woman #6/Woman in turban	Jordana Levine
Woman #7/Woman in gold	Rosalia Traina
Actress D	Maggie Wagner
Agent	Charles Randall
Agent's Secretary	Mimi Wedell
Baskin	Larry Pine
Producer	Lola Pashalinski
Professor	Stefan Schnabel
Tonda	Steven Gilborn
George	Rand Stone
Daniel's Mother	Geena Goodwin
Daniel's Father	David Ellis
Jonathan	Brian Kohn
Interviewer	Caroline Aaron
Czech Demonstrators	Vasek Simek, Paul Leski, Larry Attile
Noodle	Sofia Coppola

Right: Sally Kirkland (C)
Top: Robert Fields, Sally Kirkland
© Vestron Pictures

Robert Fields, Paulina Porizkova, Sally Kirkland

Sally Kirkland, Paulina Porizkova

DANCERS

(CANNON) Producers, Menahem Golan, Yoram Globus; Director, Herbert Ross; Screenplay, Sarah Kernochan; Executive Producers, Nora Kaye, Jack Brodsky; Associate Producers, Charles France, John Thompson; Costumes, Adriana Spadaro, Anna Anni, Enrico Serafini, Tirelli Costumes; Photography, Ennio Guarneri; Designer, Gianni Quaranta; Editor, William Reynolds; Music, Pino Donaggio, Adolphe Adam; Conductor, Michael Tilson-Thomas; In association with Hera/Baryshnikov Productions; Ballet Sequences Staged by Mikhail Baryshnikov (after Jean Coralli, Jules Perrot, and Marius Petipa); Libretto, Theophile Gautier; Production Supervisor. Alessandro Von Normann; Production Manager, Franco Balati; Assistant Directors, Gianni Arduini Plaisant, David Turchi; Casting, Francesco Cenieri; Art Director, Luigi Marchione; Set Decorator, Elio Altamura; Sound, Clive Winter; Associate Editor, Michael Polakow; Assistant Editors, David Dresher, Walter Diotallevi, Paul Murphy; Music Supervisor, Jack Fishman; Music Coordinator, Stephanie Lee; Production Supervisors, Michael Alden, Alain Jakubowixz; Production Coordinator, Omneya "Nini" Mazen; Dolby Stereo; Color; Rated PG; 99 minutes; October release.

CAST

Tony	Mikhail Baryshnikov
Francesca	Alessandra Ferri
Nadine	Leslie Browne
Patrick	Thomas Rall
Muriel	Lynn Seymour
Wade	Victor Barbee
Lisa	Julie Kent
Contessa	Mariangela Melato
Paolo	Leandro Amato
Guido	Gianmarco Tognazzi
Duke of Courland	Desmond Kelly
Bathilde	Chrisa Keramidas
Interviewer	Amy Werba
Jack	Jack Brodsky
Impresario	Robert Argand
Moyna	Amanda McKerrow
Zulma	Bonnie Moore

and Deanne, Melissa Allen, Shawn Black, Ethan Brown, Gabrielle Brown, Wes Chapman, Jeremy Collins, Christine Dunham, Christina Fagundes, Elizabeth Ferrell, Alina Hernandez, Careen Hobart, Lucette Katerndahl, Ellen Krafft, Valerie Madonia, Kathleen Moore, Lisa Rinehart, Amy Rose, Hilary Ryan, Scott Schlexer, Loren Schmalle, Anna Spelman, Christine Spizzo, Dana Stackpole, John Summers, Thomas Titone, Roger Van Fleteren, Mary Wilson, Craig Wright, Ross Yearsley, Jennet Zerbe.

Left: Mikhail Baryshnikov, Julie Kent and above with Leandro Amato Top: Alessandra Ferri, Mikhail Baryshnikov © *Cannon Films*

DEADLY ILLUSION

(CINETEL FILMS) Producer, Irwin Meyer; Executive Producers, Michael Shapiro, Rodney Sheldon; Directors, William Tannen, Larry Cohen; Photography, Daniel Pearl; Editors, Steve Mirkovich, Ronald Spang; Music, Patrick Gleeson; Sound, David Lewis Yewdall; Art Directors, Marina Zurkow, Ruth Lounsbury; Assistant Director, Michael Tadross; Associate Producers, Steve Mirkovich, Michael Tadross, Bill Elliott; Casting, Louis DiGiamo; A Pound Ridge Films production; Ultra-Stereo; DeLuxe Color; Rated R; 87 minutes; October release

CAST

Hamberger	Billy Dee Williams
Rina	Vanity
Jane/Sharon	Morgan Fairchild
Alex Burton	John Beck
Detective Lefferts	Joe Cortese
Fake Burton	Dennis Hallahan
Gloria Reid	Jenny Cornuelle
Costillion	Michael Wilding, Jr.
Nancy Costillion	Allison Woodward
Man with gun	Joe Spinell
Medical Examiner	Michael Emil

(No photos available)

Leslie Brown, Victor Barbee

BARFLY

(CANNON) Producers, Barbet Schroeder, Fred Roos, Tom Luddy; Director, Barbet Schroeder; Screenplay, Charles Bukowski; Executive Producers, Menahem Golan, Yoram Globus; Associate Producer, Jack Baran; Photography, Robby Muller; Editor, Eva Gardos; Designer, Bob Ziembicki; Costumes, Milena Canonero; Production Manager, Christopher Pearce; Assistant Directors, Jack Baran, Nilo Otero; Production Executive, Rony Yacov; Creative Consultant, Stanton Kaye; Editing Consultant, Denise De Casablanca; Visual Consultant, Milena Canonero; Casting, Robert MacDonald, Pat Orseth, Nancy Lara; Sound, Petur Hliddal; Set Decorator, Lisa Dean; Stunts, Webster Whinery; Production Supervisor, Michelle Solotar; Production Coordinators, Cindy Hochman, Lesli J. Lehr; Assistant Editors, Wendy Plump, Wende Phifer Mate; Music Supervisor, Paula Erickson; Music Coordinator, Stephanie Lee; Songs by various artists; Presented with Francis Ford Coppola; TVC Color; Rated R; 99 minutes; October release

CAST

Henry	Mickey Rourke
Wanda Wilcox	Faye Dunaway
Tully	Alice Krige
Detective	Jack Nance
Jim	J. C. Quinn
Eddie	Frank Stallone
Janice	Sandy Martin
Lilly	Roberta Bassin
Grandma Moses	Gloria Leroy
Ben	Joe Unger
Rick	Harry Cohn
Joe	Pruitt Taylor Vince
Old Man in bar	Joe Rice
Hooker in bar	Julie "Sunny" Pearson
Man in alley	Donald L. Norden
Carl	Wil Albert
Mike	Hal Shafer
Roger	Zeek Manners
Helen	Pearl Shear
Jack, the Window Washer	Rik Colitti
"Elbow Inn" Bartender	Michael Collins
Liquor Store Clerk	Ron Joseph
Black Kids	Damon Hines, Lahmard J. Tate
Cops	Carlos Cervantes, Peter Conti
Alcoholic Man	Vance Colvig
Lady Manager	Stacey Pickren
Harry	Leonard Termo
Lenny	Gary Cox
Bum	Fritz Feld
Louie	Albert Henderson
Louie's Woman	Sandy Rose
Young Girl Hooker	Madalyn Carol
Loverbird Man	George Marshall Ruge
Loverbird Woman	Debbie Lynn Ross

Left: Mickey Rourke, Faye Dunaway, Alice Krige
Above: Faye Dunaway, Mickey Rourke, Barbet Schroeder
Top: Faye Dunaway, Mickey Rourke © *Cannon Films*

Frank Stallone, Mickey Rourke

Faye Dunaway, Mickey Rourke

85

HOUSE OF GAMES

(ORION) Producer, Michael Hausman; Director/Screenplay, David Mamet; Story, Jonathan Katz, David Mamet; Photography, Juan Ruiz Anchia; Designer, Michael Merritt; Costumes, Nan Cibula; Music, Alaric Jans; Editor, Trudy Ship; Production Manager, Lee R. Mayes; Assistant Directors, Ned Dowd, Michael Hausman; Casting, Cyrene Hausman; Production Coordinators, Deborah Pritchett, Cathy Sarkowsky; Sound, John Pritchett; Set Decorator, Derek Hill; Special Effects, Robert Willard/Special Effects Unlimited; Assistant Editor, Barbara Tulliver; *"This True Love Stopped For You (But Not For Me),"* Rokko Jans; Vocals, June Shellene; A Filmhaus Production; DeLuxe Color; Panavision; Rated R; 102 minutes; October release

CAST

Margaret Ford	Lindsay Crouse
Mike	Joe Mantegna
Joey	Mike Nussbaum
Dr. Littauer	Lilia Skala
The Businessman	J. T. Walsh
Girl with book	Willo Hausman
Prison Ward Patient	Karen Kohlhaas
Billy Hahn	Steve Goldstein
Bartender/House of Games	Jack Wallace
George/Vegas Man	Ricky Jay
Poker Players	G. Roy Levin, Bob Lumbra, Andy Potok, Allen Soule
Bartender/Charlie's Tavern	Ben Blakeman
Western Union Clerk	Scott Zigler
Sgt. Moran	W. H. Macy
Hotel Desk Clerk	John Pritchett
Mr. Dean	Meshach Taylor
Hotel Doorman	Sugarbear Willis
Garage Attendant	Josh Conescu
Late Student	Julie Mendenhall
Student	Rachel Cline
Patient/Ford's Office	Patricia Wolff
Man in restaurant	Paul Walsh
Restaurant Hostess	Roberta Maguire
Woman with lighter	Jacqueline De La Chaume

Left: Lindsay Crouse, Lilia Skala Above: Lindsay Crouse, Ricky Jay Top: Joe Mantegna, Lindsay Crouse
© *Orion Pictures/Lorey Sebastian*

Lindsay Crouse

Joe Mantegna, Lindsay Crouse

Karen Allen, Joanne Woodward, John Malkovich
Above: John Malkovich, Karen Allen
Top: Joanne Woodward, John Malkovich

THE GLASS MENAGERIE

(CINEPLEX ODEON) Producer, Burtt Harris; Director, Paul Newman; Playwright, Tennessee Williams; Music, Henry Mancini; Editor, David Ray; Designer/Costumes, Tony Walton; Photography, Michael Ballhaus; Production Manager, Joseph Caracciolo; Assistant Directors, Burtt Harris, Joe Caracciolo; Associate Producer, Joe Caracciolo; Sound, Nat Boxer; Art Director, John Kasarda; Set Decorator, Susan Bode; Associate Costume Designer, Merrily Murray-Walsh; This production was first staged at The Williamstown Theatre Festival and The Long Wharf Theatre by Nikos Psacharopoulos; Music Archivist, Leo Chears; Menagerie by Milon Townsend; DuArt Color; Rated PG; 135 minutes; October release

CAST

Amanda	Joanne Woodward
Tom	John Malkovich
Laura	Karen Allen
Gentleman Caller	James Naughton

Top Right: James Naughton, Karen Allen
Below: Karen Allen, Joanne Woodward
© Cineplex Odeon Films

Joanne Woodward

LIKE FATHER LIKE SON

(TRI-STAR) Producers, Brian Grazer, David Valdes; Director, Rod Daniel; Screenplay, Lorne Cameron, Steven L. Bloom; Story, Lorne Cameron; Photography, Jack N. Green; Designer, Dennis Gassner; Editor, Lois Freeman-Fox; Costumes, Robert Turturice; Music, Miles Goodman; Casting, Judith Weiner; Production Manager, Penelope L. Foster; Assistant Directors, Dan Kolsrud, Tena Psyche Yatroussis; Set Decorator, John T. Walker; Associate Editor, Mallory Gottlieb; Additional Editor, Marilyn Madderom; Assistant Editor, Richard Leeman; Music Coordinators, Ken Kushnick, David Passick; Sound, C. Darin Knight; Special Effects, John Frazier; Stunts, Michael Tillman; Casting Associate, Linda Phillips-Palo; Lighting Designer for Concert, Marc Brickman; Songs by various artists: Dolby Stereo; Technicolor; Rated PG-13; 97 minutes; October release

CAST

Dr. Jack Hammond	Dudley Moore
Chris Hammond	Kirk Cameron
Ginnie Armbruster	Margaret Colin
Dr. Amy Larkin	Catherine Hicks
Dr. Armbruster	Patrick O'Neal
Trigger	Sean Astin
Lori Beaumont	Cami Cooper
Rick Anderson	Micah Grant
Uncle Earl	Bill Morrison
Medicine Man	Skeeter Vaughan
Navajo Helper	Larry Sellers
Navajo Girl	Tami David
Phyllis	Maxine Stuart
Dr. Roger Hartwood	David Wohl
Dr. Mike O'Donald	Michael Horton
Dr. Spellner	Randolph Dreyfuss
Mr. Racine	Art Frankel
Norma	Carol Swarbrick
Sidney	Kedric Wolfe
Hal Gilden	Robert Balderson
Old Man Morrison	Dakin Matthews
Coach Ellis	Les Lannom
Mrs. Davis	Lorna Hill
Janice Stenfield	Alexandra Kenworthy
Rick's Friend	Todd Selby
Trigger's Dad	Armin Shimerman
Trigger's Mom	Kitty Swink

and Christine Healy, Mary Jane Courier, Chera Holland, Debbie Zipp, Teresa Bowman, Brian Peck, John Stinson, Bill Stevenson, Lloyd Nelson, John Tokatlian, Mark McCannon, Jan Duncan, Lisa Robins, Richard Gilberts, James Lashly, Corki Grazer, Nancy Lenehan, Edwin Brecht, Johnathan Brecht; Steve Plunkett, Randy Rand, Steve Lynch, Keni E. Richards, Steven Isham, James Deeth

Right: Kirk Cameron, Sean Astin
Above: Kirk Cameron, Cami Cooper
Top: Margaret Collin, Dudley Moore
© Tri-Star Pictures

Kirk Cameron, Dudley Moore

Dudley Moore

GABY—A TRUE STORY

(TRI-STAR) Producer/Executive Producer, Pinchas Perry; Director/Co-Producer/Developed by Luis Mandoki; As told to him by Gabriela Brimmer; Screenplay, Martin Salinas, Michael James Love; Associate Producers, Jacobo Feldman, Marcos Salame, Rafael Jauregui, Marc A. Solomon; Executive Consultant, John Huddy; Photography, Lajos Koltai; Music, Maurice Jarre; Editor, Garth Craven; Art Director, Alejandro Luna; Sound, Robert Grieve, Ike Magal, Jose Antonio Garcia; Casting, Johanna Ray; Assistant Directors, Alfonso Cuaron, Emmanuel Lubeski; Set Designer, Olivia Bond; Production Associate, Luciana S. De Cabarga; Production Managers, Luz Maria Rojas, Hugo Green; Production Coordinator, Rosalia Salazar; Development Associate, Abraham Cherem; Development Consultant, Francisco Drohojowski; Consultant to Director, Eduardo Linder; Additional Casting, Margarita Mandoki, Kimba Hills; Assistant Director of Photography, Gyula Kovacs; Production Supervisor, Marc A. Solomon; Associate Editor, Steven Weisberg; Assistant Editors, Samuel Craven, Lisa Davis; Music Supervisor, Morris I. Diamond; Music Coordinator, Ezra Kliger; Costumes, Tolita Figueroa, Lucile Donay; Stunts, Margot Shaw; Songs by various artists; Technicolor; Rated R; 110 minutes; October release

CAST

Sari	Liv Ullmann
Florencia	Norma Aleandro
Michel	Robert Loggia
Gaby	Rachel Levin
Fernando	Lawrence Monoson
Luis	Robert Beltran
Fernando's Mother	Beatriz Sheridan
David	Tony Goldwyn
Carlos	Danny De La Paz
Gaby—3 years old	Paulina Gomez
Minister of Education	Enrique Lucero
Hector Bulle Goyri	Eduardo Lopez Rojas
Nurse at Brimmer house	Ana Ofelia Murguia
University Professor	Hugh Harleston
Teacher—rehabilitation Center	Carolyn Valero
Bureaucrat	Eduardo Noriega
Neighbor Maid	Alejandra Flores
Hospital Nurse	Zaide Silva
Terry	Nailea Norvind
Lupe	Cecilia Tijerina
High School Teacher	Carlos Romano
Betty	Susana Alexander
Otto	George Belanger
Roberto	Miguel Andrade
Therapy Doctor	Dr. Juan Mandoki
Professor at Exam	Enrique Kahan
Professor's Assistant	Ramon Barragan
Secretary Newspaper Publisher	Anais De Melo
Hospital Admitting Orderly	Arturo Fernandez
Rabbi at funeral	Manuel Kaminer
Guys Drinking Beer	Jesus Romero Chiapa, Fernando Moreno

Right: Norma Aleandro, Rachel Levin Above: Lawrence Monoson Top: Liv Ullmann, Rachel Levin
© *Tri-Star Pictures*

Liv Ullmann, Robert Loggia

Rachel Levin, Norma Aleandro

SLAMDANCE

(ISLAND PICTURES) Producers, Rupert Harvey, Barry Opper; Director, Wayne Wang; Screenplay, Don Opper; Executive Producer, Cary Brokaw; Designer, Eugenia Zanetti; Music, Mitchell Froom; Casting, Lora Kennedy, Carol Rosenthal; Editor, Lee Percy; Photography, Amir Mokri; Production Manager, Daryl Kass; Art Director, Philip Dean Foreman; Assistant Directors, John R. Woodward, Chip Vucelich; Editor, Sandy Nervig; Drood's Artwork, Robert Kopecky; Costumes, Malissa Daniel; Sound, Drew Kunin, David Lewis Yewdall; Set Decorator, Michael C. Marcus; Special Effects, Jerry Williams, Joe Knott, John Milinac; Choreographer, David Titchnell; Stunts, Mike Cassidy; Songs by various artists; Additional Music, John Lurie; US/British; Color; Rated R; 100 minutes; October release

CAST

C. C. Drood	Tom Hulce
Helen Drood	Mary Elizabeth Mastrantonio
Jim	Adam Ant
Bean	Judith Barsi
Mrs. Bell	Rosalind Chao
Girl at nursery	Sasha Delgado
Boy at nursery	Joshua Caceras
Buddy	Don Opper
Gilbert	John Doe
Detective	Marty Levy
Junkie	Jon C. Slade
Mean Drunk	Dennis Hayden
Smiley	Harry Dean Stanton
Frank	Robert Beltran
Yolanda	Virginia Madsen
Mrs. Raines	Herta Ware
Bartender	Marc Anthony Thompson
Librarian	Lin Shaye
Morgue Clerk	Michael Ennis
Ms. Schell	Lisa Niemi
Cops	Julian Deyer, Jerris L. Poindexter, Christopher Keene
Bobbie Nye	Millie Perkins
Pat Minninger	Laura Campbell
George	Philip Granger
Opera Singer	John Fleck
Minister	Buckley Norris
Radio DJ	Frazer Smith

**Left: Virginia Madsen, Tom Hulce
Above: Tom Hulce, Don Opper
Top: Tom Hulce
© *Island Pictures***

Adam Ant

John Doe

NO MAN'S LAND

(ORION) Producers, Joseph Stern, Dick Wolf; Director, Peter Werner; Screenplay, Dick Wolf; Executive Producers, Ron Howard, Tony Ganz; Music, Basil Poledouris; Photography, Hiro Narita; Designer, Paul Peters; Editor, Steve Cohen; Costumes, Jodie Tillen; Casting, Judith Holstra, Marcia Ross; Associate Producers, Jack Behr, Sandy Kroopf; Production Manager, Duncan Henderson; Assistant Directors, Josh McLaglen, Matt Early Beesley, Philip J. Gallegos; Production Coordinator, Susan Vanderbeek, Sound, Charlie Wilborne; Set Decorator, Ethel Robins Richards; Assistant Art Director, Eva Anna Bohn; Special Effects, Dennis Petersen, Scott Forbes; Stunts, Corey Eubanks; Editor, Daniel Hanley; Assistant Editors, Joseph McJimsey, Mark Magione, Michael Amundsen; *Leave My Heart Alone* by James House, Todd Sharp, Jack Conrad, and songs by various other artists; Dolby Stereo; DeLuxe Color; Rated R; 106 minutes; October release

CAST

Benjy Taylor	D. B. Sweeney
Ted Varrick	Charlie Sheen
Ann Varrick	Lara Harris
Lieutenant Vincent Bracey	Randy Quaid
Malcolm	Bill Duke
Frank Martin	R. D. Call
Lieutenant Curtis Loos	Arlen Dean Snyder
Captain Haun	M. Emmet Walsh
Danny	Al Shannon
Ridley	Bernard Pock
Leon	Ken Endosa
Brandon	James F. Kelly
Suzanne	Lori Butler
Deborah	Clare Wren
Michel	Philip Benichou
Party Girl	Linda Carol
Magot	Danitza Kingsley
Benjy's Mom	Peggy McCay
Peggy	Linda Shayne
Jim	Robert Pierce
Uncle Ray	Claude Earl Jones
Aunt Rhea	Jan Burrell
Aunt Fran	Channing Chase
Mary Jean	Jessica Puscas
Colleen	Molly Carter
Apartment Manager	Florence Schauffler
Jaws	Guy Boyd
Heath	Henry Sanders
Cal	Gary Riley
Tory Bracey	Jenny Gago
Bailey	Scott Lincoln
Shopping Center Guards	James W. Smith, Jack Yates
Julio	Tom Santo
Supplier	Anthony Palmer
Valets	Jeff L. O'Haco, Mario Roberts
Horton	Michael Riley
Duncan	Denis Hartigan
Club Band	The Untouchables

Left: D. B. Sweeney, J. W. Smith
Above: D. B. Sweeney, Lara Harris, Charlie Sheen
Top: Charlie Sheen, D. B. Sweeney
© Orion Pictures/Sidney Baldwin

Charlie Sheen, Randy Quaid

Lara Harris

STACKING

(SPECTRAFILM) Producer/Director, Martin Rosen; Screenplay, Victoria Jenkins; Executive Producer, Lindsay Law; Co-Producers, Peter Burrell, Patrick Markey; Editor, Patrick Dodd; Photography, Richard Bowen; Additional Photography, Paul Elliot; Music, Patrick Gleeson; Designer, Linda Bass; Casting, Amanda Mackey; Production Manager, Patrick Markey; Assistant Directors, Dick Feury, Eric Heffron, Lisa Samford; Production Coordinator, Kerry Peterson; Sound, Hans Roland; Art Director, Sharon Seymour; Set Decorator, Sandy Reynolds Wasco; Special Effects, Loren Cerkoney; Stunts, Loren Janes, Larry Holt; Orchestrations, Dwight Okamura; "Dream Chaser," Brent Maher, Jeff Bullock; Vocals, Lisa Silver; A Nepenthe Production Presented by Nelson Entertainment and American Playhouse Theatrical Productions; Color; Rated PG; 97 minutes; October release

CAST

Kathleen Morgan	Christine Lahti
Buster McGuire	Frederic Forrest
Anna Mae Morgan	Megan Follows
Gary Connaloe	Jason Gedrick
Dan Morgan	Ray Baker
Photographer	Peter Coyote
Clate Connaloe	James Gammon
Connie Van Buskirk	Kaiulani Lee
Mrs. Connaloe	Jacqueline Brookes
Mrs. McGuire	Irene Dailey
Auctioneer	Pat Goggins
Duane Connaloe	Darrin Schreder
Stella Martindale	Pat Ponich
Bartender	Jess Schwidde
Nurse	Amy Krempasky
Len Diltz	Eric Hendricks
Harry Van Buskirk	Mark Jenkins

Christine Lahti, Megan Follows

Fredric Forrest, Megan Follows
© *International Spectrafilm*

SOMEONE TO WATCH OVER ME

(COLUMBIA) Executive Producer/Director, Ridley Scott; Producers, Thierry de Ganay, Harold Schneider; Director, Ridley Scott; Screenplay, Howard Franklin; Photography, Steven Poster; Designer, Jim Bissell; Editor, Claire Simpson; Costumes, Colleen Atwood; Casting, Joy Todd; Music, Michael Kamen; Associate Producer, Mimi Polk; Production Manager, Max Stein; Assistant Directors, Joseph P. Reidy, Robert Yannetti; Set Decorators, Linda DeScenna, Steve Jordan; Sound, Gene Cantamessa, Jim Shields, Gerry Humphreys; Assistant Editors, Robert Frazen, William Webb, Sarah Thomas; Associate Editor, Brian Peachey; Art Directors, Chris Burian-Mohr, Jay Moore; Set Desingers, Jim Teegarden, Ann Harris; Production Coordinator, Jane Prosnit; Stunts, Glenn Wilder, Ronnie Rondell; Songs, "Someone to Watch Over Me" by George and Ira Gershwin, and songs by various other artists; Dolby Stereo; Deluxe Color; Rated R; 106 minutes; October release

CAST

Mike Keegan	Tom Berenger
Claire Gregory	Mimi Rogers
Ellie Keegan	Lorraine Bracco
Lt. Garber	Jerry Orbach
Neil Steinhart	John Rubinstein
Joey Venza	Andreas Katsulas
T. J.	Tony DiBenedetto
Koontz	James Moriarty
Win Hickings	Mark Moses
Scotty	Daniel Hugh Kelly
Tommy	Harley Gross
Helen Greening	Joanne Baron
Waiter	Anthony Bishop
Cop #1	David Berman
Bimbo	Sharon Brecke
Doorman	Peter Carew
Rookie Cop	Christopher Cass
Sparks	Jim Paul Eilers
Pretty Young Thing	Susi Gilder
Mary the Maid	Mary Gillis
Brooklyn	Billy Kane
Met Benefactress	Helen Lambros
Bartender	Jack McGeed
Antonia	Meg Mundy
Tie Salesman	Jeff Neilsen
Killer	Harlan Cary Poe
Marge	Marilyn Rockafellow
Vietnamese Girl	Helen Tran
Giddings	Harvey Vernon
Plainclothesman #1	Mark Voland

Tom Berenger, Harley Cross, Lorraine Bracco

Left Center: Tom Berenger, Jerry Orbach, John Rubinstein, Mimi Rogers
© *Columbia Pictures*

SUSPECT

(TRI-STAR) Producer, Daniel A. Sherkow; Director, Peter Yates; Screenplay Eric Roth; Executive Producer, John Veitch; Photography, Billy Williams; Designer, Stuart Wurtzel; Editor, Ray Lovejoy; Costumes, Rita Ryack; Music, Michael Kamen; Associate Producer/ Production Manager, Jennifer Ogden; Casting, Howard Feuer; Assistant Directors, Pat Kehoe, Carol Louise Green, Matt Bearson, Brian Whitley; Art Director, Steve Sardanis; Set Decorator, Arthur Jeph Parker; Production Coordinator, Sarah Carson; Associate Editor, Emily Paine; Assistant Editors, Simon Harris, John Downer, Mayin Lo; Sound, Tod A. Maitland; Special Effects, Jim Fredburg, Joe Ramsey; Stunts, Jeff Smolek; Color; Rated R; 121 minutes; October release

CAST

Kathleen Riley	Cher
Eddie Sanger	Dennis Quaid
Carl Wayne Anderson	Liam Neeson
Judge Matthew Helms	John Mahoney
Charlie Stella	Joe Mantegna
Paul Gray	Philip Bosco
Grace Comisky	E. Katherine Kerr
Morty Rosenthal	Fred Melamed
Marilyn	Lisbeth Bartlett
Michael	Paul D'Amato
Walter	Bernie McInerney
Justice Lowell	Thomas Barbour
Elizabeth Quinn	Katie O'Hare
Justice Lowell's Secretary	Rosemary Knower
Forensic Pathologist	Aaron Schwartz
Detective	Lloyd White
April	Myra Taylor
Judge Franklin	Bill Cobbs
Judge Louis Weiss	Sam Gray
Everett Bennett	Richard Gant
Doris/Video Typist	Sandi Ross
Helms' Court Clerk	Paul de la Rosa
Helms' Court Steno	Siona Dixon
Helms' Court Marshals	Gene Mack, Jim Walton
Marvin Johnson	Stefan Graham
Club Congressman	Robert Walsh
Congressman	Edwin M. Adams
Dr. Alan Alpert	Billy Williams
Judge Ansel Stewart	Ralph Cosham
Mr. Davis	Jack Jessop
Anthony Hall	Edward Everard Williams

and Michael Beach, Prudence Barry, Carl Jackson, Tony Craig, Sandra Bowie, Fred Strother, Jaye Tyrone Stewart, Paul Hjelmervik, Wendy E. Taylor, R. C. Coleman, Djanet Sears, Diane Marie L. Tomajczyk, Richard Bertone, Laura J. Dalton, Greg McKinney, Michael Emmett, Darryl Palmer, David Lyle.

Left: Cher, Joe Mantegna Above: Liam Neeson, Cher Top: Dennis Quaid, Cher
© *Tri-Star Pictures*

Cher, John Mahoney

Cher, Dennis Quaid

NEAR DARK

(DE LAURENTIIS) Producer, Steven-Charles Jaffe; Director, Kathryn Bigelow; Screenplay, Eric Red, Kathryn Bigelow; Co-Producer, Eric Red; Executive Producers, Edward S. Feldman, Charles R. Meeker; Music, Tangerine Dream; Photography, Adam Greenberg; Designer, Stephen Altman; Editor, Howard Smith; Costumes, Joseph Porro; Casting, Karen Rea; Associate Producer, Diane Nabatoff; Associate Producer/Production Manager, Mark Allan; Special Effects Makeup, Gordon Smith; Assistant Directors, Guy Louthan, John J. C. Scherer, Chuck Williams; Art Director, Dian Perryman; Stunts, Everett Creach; Sound, Donald Summer; Songs by various artists; F/M Entertainment; Ultra Stereo; Technicolor; Rated R; 95 minutes; October release

CAST

Caleb	Adrian Pasdar
Mae	Jenny Wright
Jesse	Lance Henriksen
Severen	Bill Paxton
Diamondback	Jenette Goldstein
Loy	Tim Thomerson
Homer	Joshua Miller
Sarah	Marcie Leeds
Deputy Sheriff	Kenny Call
Ticket Seller	Ed Corbett
Plainclothes Officer	Troy Evans
Sheriff Eakers	Bill Cross
Cajun Truck Driver	Roger Aaron Brown
Bartender	Thomas Wagner
Patron in bar	Robert Winley
Teenage Cowboy	James LeGros
Waitress	Jan King
Biker in bar	Danny Kopel
Motel Manager	Billy Beck
Police Officer	S. A. Griffin

and Bob Terhune, William T. Lane, Gary Littlejohn, Paul Michael Lane, Eddie Mulder, Don Pugsley, Neith Hunter, Theresa Randle, Tony Pierce, Gordon Haight, Leo Geter, Gary Wayne Cunningham

Lance Henriksen, Joshua Miller, Jenette Goldstein, Bill Paxton © *DEG*

WEEDS

(DE LAURENTIIS) Producer, Bill Badalato; Director, John Hancock; Screenplay, Dorothy Tristan, John Hancock; Executive Producers, Mel Pearl, Billy Cross; Music, Angelo Badalamenti; Songs, Melissa Etheridge, Orville Stoeber; Photography, Jan Weincke; Designer, Joseph T. Garrity; Supervising Editor, Dennis O'Connor; Editors, David Handman, Jon Poll, Chris Lebenzon; Costumes, Mary Kay Stolz; Casting, Cathy Henderson, Barbara Hanley; Associate Producers, Fred Baron, Patti Carr, Ken Kitch; Assistant Directors, Paul Deason, Randall Badger; Art Director, Pat Tagliaferro; Set Decorator, Jerie Kelter; Choreography, Jerry Evans; Production Associates, Jeffrey Harlacker, Susan Willett; Theatrical Lighting, Chuck Cattotti; Assistant Set Decorator, Richard Villalobos; Special Effects, Mike Menzel, Marvin Gardner, Rick Barefoot; Sound, James Thorton; Set Design, Francine Mercadante; Additional Casting, Slater-Willett; Additional Editing, Robert Lederman; Assistant Editors, Rod Dean, Christian A. Wagner, Ken Morrisey, Leslie Jones, Kris Bergen, Kris Garfield, Tom Scurry, John Spence, Tommy Dorsett; Stunts, Joe Dunne; Production Supervisor, Jim Honore; Additional Songs by various artists; Vocals, The Cast; Soundtrack on Varese Sarabande; Dolby Stereo; Technicolor; Rated R; 115 minutes; October release

CAST

Lee Umstetter	Nick Nolte
Claude	Lane Smith
Burt	William Forsythe
Navarro	John Toles-Bey
Carmine	Joe Mantegna
Bagdad	Ernie Hudson
Dave	Mark Rolston
Lazarus	J. J. Johnston
Lillian	Rita Taggart
Lead Guitar	Orville Stoeber
Thurman	Essex Smith
Percussion	Cyro Baptista
Keyboard	Sam L. Waymon
Mom Umstetter	Anne Ramsey
Pop Umstetter	Ray Reinhardt
Bagdad's Girlfriend	Amanda Gronich
Associate Wardens	Felton Perry, Nicholas Wyman
Godot Players	Barton Heyman, Walter Charles
Rabble Rousers	William Lucas, Reggie Montgomery
Grad Student	Amy C. Bass
Derrick Mann	Richard Olsen
Fisher Cobb	Drew Elliot
Charlie Rich	Himself
House Manager	Howard Spiegel
Waiter	Louis Criscuolo
Caterer	Denny Burt
Busboy	Raymond Rivera
Doorman	Billy Badalato
Dean	John Bonitz
Pound Attendant	Billy Cross
Saleswoman	Rhesa Stone
Motel Manager	James Deuter
Kirsten	Kirsten Baker

and Arnold Johnson, Gerald Orange, Leonard Johnson, Paul Herman, Frank Gio, Gift Harris, Paul Weeden, Maximo Cerda, Richard Portnow, Michael Luciano, Daniel Kent, John Ring, Robert Miano, Sam Stoneburner

Rita Taggert, Nick Nolte

Left Center: Nick Nolte
© *DeLaurentiis Entertainment Group*

THE WHALES OF AUGUST

(**ALIVE FILMS**) Producers, Carolyn Pfeiffer, Mike Kaplan; Director, Lindsay Anderson; Screenplay, David Berry, Based on his play of same title; Executive Producer, Shep Gordon; Photography, Mike Fash; Designer, Jocelyn Herbert; Music, Alan Price; Production Executive, Victoria Lee Pearman; Editor, Nicolas Gaster; Arranger/Conductor, Derek Wadsworth; Associate Producer, Stuart Besser; Production Manager, Dixie J. Capp; Production Coordinator, Janice Reynolds; Assistant Directors, Broderick Miller, Matthew Clark; Art Directors, K. C. Fox, Bob Fox; Costumes, Rudy Dillon; Miss Davis' Costumes, Julie Weiss; Set Decorator, Sosie Hublitz; Assistant Art Director, Evan Klein; Sound, Donald Summer; Assistant Editor, Laurie McDowell; Presented with Circle Associates, Ltd; In association with Nelson Entertainment; CIF Color; Not rated; 90 minutes; October release

CAST

Libby Strong	Bette Davis
Sarah Webber	Lillian Gish
Mr. Maranov	Vincent Price
Tisha Doughty	Ann Southern
Joshua Brackett	Harry Carey, Jr.
Mr. Beckwith	Frank Grimes
Old Randall	Frank Pitkin
Young Randall	Mike Bush
Young Libby	Margaret Ladd
Young Tisha	Tisha Sterling
Young Sarah	Mary Steenburgen

**Below: Harry Carey, Jr., Ann Sothern
Top Right: Lillian Gish, Bette Davis
Below: Vincent Price**
© *Alive Films*

Vincent Price, Lillian Gish

Lillian Gish, Bette Davis

ZOMBIE HIGH

(CINEMA GROUP) Producers, Marc Toberoff, Aziz Ghazal; Executive Producer, Cassian Elwes; Director, Ron Link; Editors, Shawn Hardin, James Whitney; Designer, Matthew Kozinets; Production Managers, Seth Front, Richard Scruggs; Assistant Directors, David Householdter, K. C. Hodenfield, Kip Konweiser; Music, Daniel May; Songs, Kent Richards, Tymm Rocco; Photography, Jay Roach, Harris Done, Rusty Gorman; Sound, Jon Oh, Michael Sabo, Bill Navarro; Special Effects Makeup, Chris Biggs, Mark Messenger, Bill Mertz, Bernard David; Art Director, Hisham Abed; Set Decorator, Arabella Serrell-Watts; Assistant Editor, Sharon Anton; Production Coordinator, Linda Buckel; Stunts, Harry Terzian; Special Effects, Scott Haas; Music Performances, K. Richards, T. Rocco, B. Gabriele, N. Roche; Additional Songs by various artists; Color; Rated R; 91 minutes; October release

CAST

Andrea	Virginia Madsen
Philo	Richard Cox
Dean Eisner	Kay Kuter
Barry	James Wilder
Suzi	Sherilyn Fenn
Emerson	Paul Feig
Felner	T. Scott Coffey
Ignatius	Paul Williams
Bell	Henry Sutton
Phillip	Christopher Peters
Mary Beth	Clare Carey
Biff	Christopher Crews
Senator Felner	John Sack
Mom	Susan Barnes
Nurse	Abigail Hanness
Doctor	Arvid Holmberg
Chief Hillis	Walter Addison

and Dan Garrity, John Cook, Tom Sheppard, Phil Weinstock, Kent Snyder, Diana Lands, Brett Gathrid, Alan Milligan, Diana Darby, Gary Maynard, Phil Tracy, Sam Ginsberg, Brass Adams, Gilbert Purvis, "Tease" (Kipper, Derek O, Thommy O, Jay), Hugh Kelly, Lisa Smith, Janet Cagliano, Dennis Nolette, Buzz Hays, Bob Ducsay, Kirk Bodyfelt, Leslie Ann Bushka, Lisa Cach, Mark Decew, Carey Gerwig, Michael Gretza, John Hirovat, Adam Litman, Kyle Markgraf, Sean Nevelt, Will Plyer, Eric Stachowski, Dawn Thompson, Melissa Toy, Rick White, Stephanie Willis, John Stewart, Paul Short, Solly Marks, Nicole Praveck, Bob Ivy, Ben Darricks.

Top Right: Virginia Madsen
© Cinema Group Pictures

Keith Coogan, Jon Cryer

HIDING OUT (aka ADULT EDUCATION)

(DE LAURENTIIS ENTERTAINMENT GROUP) Producer, Jeff Rothberg; Executive Producer, Martin Tudor; Director, Bob Giraldi; Screenplay, Joe Menosky, Jeff Rothberg; Photography, Daniel Pearl; Editor, Edward Warschilka; Music, Anne Dudley; Designer, Dan Leigh; Art Director, Carol Wood; Set Decoration, Leslie Rollins; Costumes, Susan Gammie; Sound, Kim Ornitz; Assistant Director, Robert Girolami; Second Unit Director, Carol Wood; Casting, Bonnie Ginnegan, Steve Jacobs; An Evenmore Entertainment/Locomotion Pictures Production; Technicolor; Dolby Stereo; Rated PG-13; 98 minutes; November release

CAST

Andrew Morenski	Jon Cryer
Patrick Morenski	Keith Coogan
Ryan Campbell	Annabeth Gish
Aunt Lacy	Gretchen Cryer
Killer	Oliver Cotton
Clinton	Claude Brooks
Ezzard	Lou Walker
Kevin O'Roarke	Tim Quill
Grandma Jennie	Anne Pitoniak
Mrs. Billings	Nancy Fish

© DeLaurentiis Entertainment Group

SURRENDER

(WARNER BROS.) Producers, Aaron Spelling, Alan Greisman; Director/Screenplay, Jerry Belson; Executive Producers, Menahem Golan, Yoram Globus; Photography, Juan Ruiz Anchia; Editor, Wendy Greene Bricmont; Designer, Lilly Kilvert; Costumes, Betsy Heimann; Music, Michel Colombier; Associate Producers, Jim Van Wyck, Wendy Greene Bricmont; Production Manager, Ted Swanson; Assistant Directors, Princess McLean, Chuck Rowley; Production Executive, Rony Yacov; Casting, Bonnie Pietila; Stunts, Peter T. Stader; Sound, Steve Nelson; Art Director, Jon Hutman; Set Designer, Richard Mays; Paintings, Dale Gottlieb; Set Decorator, Cricket Rowland; Assistant Decorator, Jacqueline Sartino; Production Executive, Nancy Stone; Production Coordinator, Claire Baker; Casting Assistant, Julie Pyken; Special Effects, Charles Spurgeon; Music Supervisor, Paula Erickson; Music Coordinator, Lorrie Behrhorst; Songs by various artists; Ultra-Stereo; TVC Color; Rated PG; 95 minutes; October release

CAST

Daisy	Sally Field
Sean	Michael Caine
Marty	Steve Guttenberg
Jay	Peter Boyle
Ace	Jackie Cooper
Ronnie	Julie Kavner
Joyce	Louise Lasser
Hedy	Iman
Hooker	Michael Andrews
Mr. Chobanian	Jerry Lazarus
Tony	Tony Borgia
Thugs	Frank Dicopoulos, Charles Noland, Dominic Messina
Judge	Paddie Edwards
Palimony Judge	Bill McIntyre
Dream Lawyers	Bruce French, Steven Rotblatt, Mark Pilon, Stan Roth, Lee Ryan, Ted Lehmann, Christian Clemenson
Daisy's Lawyer	Channing Chase
Hedy's Lawyer	Joan McMurtrey
Joyce's Lawyer	F. J. O'Neil
Sam	Donald Grant
Stewardess	Karen Huie

and David Hess, Timothy Jecko, Ann Walker, Selwyn Emerson Miller, Duke Moosekian, Robert Nadder, Bunny Kacher, Dan Navratil, Frank Lugo, Eduardo Ricard, Yacub Salih, Julie Silliman, Jim Van Wyck

Right: Michael Caine, Sally Field
Top: Sally Field, Michael Caine
© *Cannon Films*

Steve Guttenberg, Sally Field, Michael Caine

Corbin Bernsen, Shelley Long
© *Touchstone Pictures*

Corbin Bernsen, Sela Ward

HELLO AGAIN

(TOUCHSTONE) Producer/Director, Frank Perry; Screenplay, Susan Isaacs; Photography, Jan Weincke; Executive Producer, Salah M. Hassanein; Editors, Peter C. Frank, Trudy Ship; Co-Producers, G. Mac Brown, Martin Mickelson, Susan Isaacs, Thomas Folino; Music, William Goldstein; Casting, Donna Isaacson, John Lyons; Designer, Edward Pisoni; Costumes, Ruth Morley; Production Manager, G. Mac Brown; Assistant Directors, Joel B. Segal, Michael Ingber; Art Director, William Barclay; Set Decorator, Robert J. Franco; Sound Gary Alper; Additional Costumes, Sandra Culotta; Production Coordinators, Blair Bellis Mohr, Lynn Goldman; Associate Editor, Farrel Levy; Assistant Editors, Barbara Tulliver, Guy Barresi, David Siegel; Special Visual Effects, Balsmeyer & Everett, Inc.; In association with Silver Screen Partners III; Buena Vista Pictures Distribution; Dolby Stereo; Color; Rated PG; 96 minutes; November release

CAST

Lucy Chadman	Shelley Long
Zelda	Judith Ivey
Kevin Scanlon	Gabriel Byrne
Jason Chadman	Corbin Bernsen
Kim Lacey	Sela Ward
Junior Lacey	Austin Pendleton
Regina Holt	Carrie Nye
Phineas Devereux	Robert Lewis
Felicity	Madeleine Potter
Danny Chadman	Thor Fields
Bruce Holt	John Cunningham
Butler	I. M. Hobson
Maid	Mary Fogarty
Tough Guy	Tony Sirico
Burns	Elkan Abramowitz
Miss Tammy	Shirley Rich
Miss Lee	Kaiulani Lee
Bearded Man	John Rothman
T.V. Moderator	John Tillinger
E.R. Nurse	Debra D. Stewart

and Kate McGregor-Stewart, Lynne Thigpen, Royce Rich, Chip Zien, Anna Marie Wieder, Robert Lempert, Susan Isaacs, Marcell Rosenblatt, Catherine Tambini, Everett Quinton, Patricia Gage, Mary Armstrong, Colin R. Fox, Rose Indri, Elyzabeth Chrystea, Suzanne Barnes, Karen Shallo, Paul Royce, Illeana Douglas, Ester Gordon, John J. Healey, Jo Jones, Anna Marie Wieder

Judith Ivey, Shelley Long

Shelley Long, Gabriel Byrne

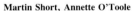
Martin Short, Annette O'Toole

CROSS MY HEART

(**UNIVERSAL**) Producer, Lawrence Kasdan; Director, Armyan Bernstein; Screenplay, Armyan Bernstein, Gail Parent; Co-Producers, Charles Okun, Michael Grillo; Executive Producers, Aaron Spelling, Alan Greisman; Photography, Thomas DelRuth; Designer, Lawrence G. Paull; Editor, Mia Goldman; Music, Bruce Broughton; Costumes, Marilyn Vance-Straker; Casting, Wally Nicita; Production Manager, Charles Okun; Assistant Directors, Michael Grillo, Stephen Dunn; Sound, David McMillan; Set Decorator, Bruce Gibeson; Set Designer, Nick Navarro; Special Effects, George Zamora; Production Coordinator, Diane Baxter; Casting Associate, Joanne Zaluski; Songs by various artists; Dolby Stereo; DeLuxe Color; Rated R; 90 minutes; November release

CAST

David	Martin Short
Kathy	Annette O'Toole
Bruce	Paul Reiser
Nancy	Joanna Kerns
Jessica	Jessica Puscas
Parking Attendant	Lee Arenberg
Susan	Corinne Bohrer
Waiter	Jason Stuart
Woman in restaurant	Shelley Taylor Morgan
Stud	Michael D. Simms
Maitre d'	Eric Poppick
Woman outside restaurant	Lori Hall
Cashier	Mary Gillis
Waitress	Patty Regan
Girl in car	Marti Muller
Convenience Store Clerk	David Nail

Top: Martin Short, Annette O'Toole
Right: Martin Short
© *Universal City Studios*

Annette O'Toole, Martin Short

LESS THAN ZERO

(20th CENTURY FOX) Producers, Jon Avnet, Jordan Kerner; Director, Marek Kanievska; Screenplay, Harley Peyton; Based on novel by Bret Easton Ellis; Photography, Edward Lachman; Designer, Barbara Ling; Editors, Peter E. Berger, Michael Tronick; Costumes, Richard Hornung; Casting, David Rubin; Music Supervisor, Rick Rubin; Music, Thomas Newman; Production Manager, Kurt Neumann; Assistant Directors, Deborah Love, Robin Holding; Art Director, Stephen Rice; Set Decorator, Nancy Nye; Assistant Art Director, Cosmas Demetriou; Sound, Glenn Berkovitz; Special Effects, Dan Lester; Assistant Editor, George C. Villasenor; Production Coordinator, Lata Ryan; Casting Assistant, Lisa Beach; Produced in association with Marvin Worth and with Amercent Films and American Entertainment Partners L.P.: Song, *"You And Me" ("Less Than Zero")* by Glen Danzig, Rick Rubin; Songs by various artists; Soundtrack on Def Jam Recordings/Columbia Records; Dolby Stereo; DeLuxe Color; Rated R; 98 minutes; November release

CAST

Clay	Andrew McCarthy
Blair	Jami Gertz
Julian	Robert Downey, Jr.
Rip	James Spader
Bradford Easton	Tony Bill
Benjamin Wells	Nicholas Pryor
Elaine Easton	Donna Mitchell
Hop	Michael Bowen
Markie	Sarah Buxton
Patti	Lisanne Falk
Robert Wells	Michael Greene
Alana	Neith Hunter
Kim	Afton Smith
Trent	Brian Wimmer
Lile	Kelly Wolf
Kid #3	David Colby
Musician #3	Cole Dammett
Musician #1	Flea
Teenager #2	Brittain Frye
Musician #4	Jack Irons
D. J.	Afrika Islam
Bouncer	Kris Jorgenson
Margery Easton	Jeannette Kerner
Photographer	Lee Kissinger
Liz	Moya Kordick
Cindy	Jayne Modean
Alice	Jude Mussetter
Little Girl	Jessica Puscas
Jenny	Jandi Swanson
Seth Wells	Eric Walker
Teenager #1	Scott Warner
Naked Man	John Yurasek

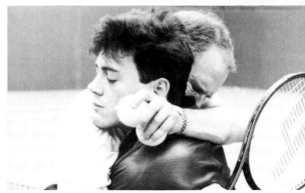

Right: Robert Downey, Jr., Nicholas Pryor
Above: Andrew McCarthy, Jami Gertz
Top: Robert Downey, Jr, James Spader
© 20th Century Fox/John Clifford

Jami Gertz, Robert Downey, Jr., Andrew McCarthy

Robert Downey, Jr., Andrew McCarthy

HOUSEKEEPING

(COLUMBIA) Producer, Robert F. Colesberry; Director/Screenplay, Bill Forsyth; Based on novel *"Housekeeping"* by Marilynne Robinson; Photography, Michael Coulter; Designer, Adrienne Atkinson; Editor, Michael Ellis; Costumes, Mary-Jane Reyner; Music, Michael Gibbs; Casting, Lynne Carrow, Margery Simkin; Production Manager, Robert Frederick; Assistant Directors, Lee Kniffelberg, David Webb, Richard Cowan; Art Director, John Willett; Set Decorator, Jim Erickson; Production Coordinator, Elaine Fleming; Sound, Ralph Parker; Special Effects, John Thomas; Assistant Costume Designer, Maureen Hiscox; Costume Supervisor, Linda Lee Langdon; Assistant Set Decorator, Della Mae Johnston; Art Director (Alberta), John Stuart Blackie; Stunts, Betty Thomas; Assistant Editors, Tony Trompetto, Richard Martin, Debra Rurak; Soundtrack on Varese Sarabande Records; Dolby Stereo; Color; Rated PG; 117 minutes; November release

CAST

Sylvie	Christine Lahti
Ruth	Sara Walker
Lucille	Andrea Burchill
Aunt Lily	Anne Pitoniak
Aunt Nona	Barbara Reese
Helen	Margot Pinvidic
Sheriff	Bill Smillie
Principal	Wayne Robson
Mrs. Jardine	Betty Phillips
Mrs. Patterson	Karen Austin
Mrs. Walker	Delores Drake
Grandmother	Georgie Collins
Young Ruth	Tonya Tanner
Young Lucille	Leah Penny
Deputy Sheriff	Brian Linds
Boys on cliff	Clayton W. Okell, Clay Barton
Sandy	Erik Richardson
Charlie	Bob Hughes
Bernice	Sheila Paterson
Ice Cream Lady	Judi Pustil
Gas Station Attendant	Ron Koukal
Grandmother's Friends	Bob Elsdon, Hans "Fritz" Farenholtz
Etta	Enid Saunders
Hoboes	Mike Daley, Gunter Voight
Fisherman	Michael Davidoff
Woman on train	Isobel Louie
Mr. Wallace	Anthony Holland
Mrs. Dickson	Elizabeth Strong
Georgette	Juli Bailey
Marie	Tiffany Ward
Miss Royce	Jeannette Grittani
Grandpa as a young boy	Adrian Naqvi

Right: Andrea Burchill, Christine Lahti, Sara Walker
Above: Andrea Burchill, Sara Walker
Top: Christine Lahti
© *Columbia Pictures*

Andrea Burchill, Christine Lahti, Sara Walker

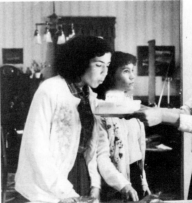

Sara Walker, Andrea Burchill, Christine Lahti

NUTS

(WARNER BROS.) Producer, Barbra Streisand; Director, Martin Ritt; Screenplay, Tom Topor, Darryl Ponicsan, Alvin Sargent; Based on play of same title by Tom Topor; Executive Producers, Teri Schwartz, Cis Corman; Photography, Andrzej Bartkowiak; Designer, Joel Schiller; Editor, Sidney Levin; Costumes, Joe Tomkins; Casting, Marion Dougherty; Music, Barbra Streisand; Production Manager, George Goodman; Assistant Directors, Aldric La'Auli Porter, Martina Ritt, Concetta Rinaldo; Arranger/Conductor, Jeremy Lubbock; Art Director, Eric Orbom; Set Decorator, Anne McCulley; Additional Editors, Rick Sparr, Jeff Werner; Assistant Editors, Mike Klein, Robert Frazen, Robert Hedland; Sound, Thomas Causey; Stunts, Roydon Clark; Special Effects, Larry Fuentes; Production Associate, Philip E. Thomas; Assistant Casting, Gail Levin; Set Designer, Greg Papalia; *"Here We Are At Last"* Music, Barbra Streisand, Lyrics, Richard Baskin; A Barwood Film Presentation; Dolby Stereo; Technicolor; Rated R; 116 minutes; November release

CAST

Claudia Draper	Barbra Streisand
Aaron Levinsky	Richard Dreyfuss
Rose Kirk	Maureen Stapleton
Arthur Kirk	Karl Malden
Dr. Herbert A Morrison	Eli Wallach
Francis MacMillan	Robert Webber
Judge Stanley Murdoch	James Whitmore
Allen Green	Leslie Nielsen
Clarence Middleton	William Prince
1st Judge	Dakin Matthews
Harry Harrison	Paul Benjamin
Saul Kreiglitz	Warren Manzi
Dr. Johnson	Elizabeth Hoffman
Dr. Arantes	Castulo Guerra
16 year-old Claudia	Stacy Bergman
11 year-old Claudia	Hayley Taylor-Block
Court Reporter	Matt Riivald
Holding Cell Guard	John Wesley
Arraignment Court Clerk	Ron Cummins
Defendent Davis	Noel Walcott, III
Defendent Gonzales	Tony Rolon
Card-Playing Patient	Suzanne Kent

and Sarina Grant, Tyra Ferrell, Nicole Burdette, Valentina Quinn, Carlos Cervantes, Gerry Okuneff, Conni Marie Brazelton, Roydon Clark, Dana Dru Evenson, Bruce Barbour, Pamela Seamon, Tina Lifford, Stephannie Howard, Rocco Karega, Armando Diaz, Alphonse V. Walter, Joseph Romeo, Ernest-Frank Taylor, Edward Blackoff, Darryl Ponicsan, Billy Kane, Lavelle Roby, Shirley Jo Finney, Sharon Barr, Annie LaRussa, Babbie Green, Barbara Ann Grimes, Cecilia Garcia, Leontine Guilliard

Left: Richard Dreyfuss, James Whitmore, Barbra Streisand
Above: Maureen Stapleton, Karl Malden
Top: Richard Dreyfuss, Barbra Streisand
© *Warner Bros.*

Eli Wallach, Robert Webber

Barbra Streisand

MADE IN HEAVEN

(LORIMAR) Producers, Raynold Gideon, Bruce A. Evans, David Blocker; Director, Alan Rudolph; Screenplay, Bruce A. Evans, Raynold Gideon; Photography, Jan Kiesser; Editor, Tom Walls; Designer, Paul Peters; Art Director, Steven Legler; Costumes, April Ferry; *"We've Never Danced"* Music & Lyrics, Neil Young; Music, Mark Isham; Casting, Pam Dixon; Associate Producer, Stuart Besser; Production Manager, Jack Grossberg; Assistant Directors, David McGiffert, Pamela Eilerson, Cara Giallanza; Special Visual Effects, Max W. Anderson; Sound, Ron Judkins, Robert Jackson; Associate Editor, John Rosenberg; Assistant Editor, Scott Brock; Set Decorators, Rosemary Brandenburg, Lynn Wolverton; Assistant Art Director, Kellie Davis; Set Designers, David Boatwright, Gershon Ginsburg; Casting Associate, Benjamin Rubin; Production Coordinators, Joan Wolpert, Peggy Moore; Stunts, Greg Walker; Special Effects, Doug DeGrazzio; Songs by various artists; Soundtrack on Elektra/Asylum; Dolby Stereo; Technicolor; Rated PG; 102 minutes; November release

CAST

Mike Shea/Elmo Barnett	Timothy Hutton
Annie Packert/Ally Chandler	Kelly McGillis
Aunt Lisa	Maureen Stapleton
Annette Shea	Ann Wedgeworth
Steve Shea	James Gammon
Brenda Carlucci	Mare Winningham
Ben Chandler	Don Murray
Tom Donnelly	Timothy Daly
Donald Sumner	David Rasche
Wiley Foxx	Amanda Plummer
Guy Blanchard/Brian Dutton	Willard Pugh
Lyman McCray	Vyto Ruginis
Truck Driver	Neil Young
Stanky	Tom Petty
Shark	Ric Ocasek
Mrs. Packert	Marj Dusay
Mr. Packert	Ray Gideon
Billy Packert	Zack Finch
Orrin	Rob Knepper
Mr. Bjornstead	James Tolkan
Sam Morrell	Gailard Sartain
Angel	John Considine
Woody-Talent Coordinator	Elliott Rabinowitz
Mario the Toymaker	Tom Robbins
Miss Barnett	Debra Dusay
Mrs. Burwell	Patricia Earnest
Reginald/TV Interviewer	Leon Martell
TV Interviewers	Dave Michaels, Billi Jo Rucker
Young Elmo	Paul Sloan
Uncle Gus	Larry Sloan
Young Ally	Lauren Hill
Grandmother Chandler	Ann Owens
C. C. Stank	Tom Walls
Andy	Elliot Street
Murray	Michael Klastorin
Ally's Assistant	Meeghan Ochs
Henry	Henry Sanders
Emmett	Debra Winger
Lucille	Ellen Barkin

and David Bethany, Pete Munro, Johnny Popwell, Alveda King Beale, Stuart Manne, Randy Cash, Christen Childers, Jim L. Gassman, Jack Hager, Jennifer Deer Johnson, Dirk Blocker, Irv Gorman, Rick West, Jon Kohler, Danielle Aubuchon, Amy Van Nostrand, Kelly Wellman, Ed Yousefian, Denise Stephens, Doug DeGrazzio, Gladys Lavitan, Kerry Lyn McKissick, Sonya Maddox, John Rosenberg, David Paradis, Paul A. Simmons, The Cabelleros, Robert Ivey Ballet, Daniel J. Vaganek, George Pappas, Kerrie Cullen, Carrie Paddock, Matthew Paddock

Top Left: Timothy Hutton, Maureen Stapleton
Below: Amanda Plummer; Ann Wedgeworth, James Gammon
© Lorimar Motion Pictures

Kelly McGillis, John Considine, Timothy Hutton
Above: Timothy Hutton, Kelly McGillis

THE RUNNING MAN

(TRI-STAR) Producers, Tim Zinnemann, George Linder; Director, Paul Michael Glaser; Screenplay, Steven E. deSouza; Based on novel *"The Running Man"* by Richard Bachman; Executive Producers, Keith Barish, Rob Cohen; Photography, Thomas Del Ruth; Designer, Jack T. Collis; Editors, Mark Roy Warner, Edward A. Warschilka, John Wright; Music, Harold Faltermeyer; Costumes, Robert Blackman; Casting, Jackie Burch; Production Manager, Gary D. Daigler; Assistant Directors, Richard Peter Schroer, Barry Thomas; Stunts, Bennie Dobbins; Additional Photography, Reynaldo Villalobos; Choreography, Paula Abdul; Theatrical Lighting Designer, Mark Brickman; Assistant Art Directors, Gene Nollmann, Joseph E. Hubbard; Set Decorator, Jim Duffy; Set Designers, Nancy Patton, Nick Navarro, Richard G. Berger; Sound, Richard Bryce Goodman; Special Make-up Effects, The Burman Studio; Special Effects, Larry Cavanaugh, Bruce Steinheimer; Production Coordinator, Dana Miller Schornstein; Special Animated Effects, Chris Casady; *"Running Away With You"* Music & Lyrics, Harold Faltermeyer, John Parr; "The Death March"/ "Paula's Theme" by Jackie Jackson, Glen Barbee; Taft Entertainment Pictures/Keith Barish Productions; Dolby Stereo; Technicolor; Rated R; 101 minutes; November release

CAST

Ben Richards	Arnold Schwarzenegger
Amber Mendez	Maria Conchita Alonso
Laughlin	Yaphet Kotto
Fireball	Jim Brown
Captain Freedom	Jesse Ventura
Dynamo	Erland Van Lidth
Weiss	Marvin J. McIntyre
Buzzsaw	Gus Rethwisch
Subzero	Professor Toru Tanaka
Mic	Mick Fleetwood
Stevie	Dweezil Zappa
Damon Killian	Richard Dawson
Brenda	Karen Leigh Hopkins
Sven	Sven Thorsen
Lenny	Eddie Bunker
Mad Tech	Bryan Kestner
Valdez	Anthony Penya
Tony	Kurt Fuller
Agent	Kenneth Lerner
Amy	Dey Young
Don Pardo	Roger Bumpass
Mrs. McArdle	Dona Hardy
Edith Wiggins	Lynne Stewart
Leon	Bill Margolin
Narrator	Joe Leahy
Lieutenant Saunders	George P. Wilbur
Chico	Tom Rosales, Jr.
Suzie Checkpoint	Sondra Holt

and Anthony Brubaker, Joel Kramer, Billy Lucas, Daniel Celario, Mario Celario, Sidney Chankin, Kim Pawlik, Roger Kern, Barbara Lux, Franco Columbu, Lin Shaye, Boyd R. Kestner, Wayne Grace, Charlie Phillips, Greg Lewis, John William James, Jon Cutler, Kerry Brennan, Paula Brown, Megan Gallivan, Suzie Hardy, Debby Harris, Melissa Hurley, Marlene Lange, Morgan Lawley, Cindy Millican, Andrea Moen, Mary Ann Oedy, Karen Owens, Sharon Owens, Pamela Rossi, Mia Togo

**Right: Gus Rethwisch, Arnold Schwarzenegger
Above: Yaphet Kotto, Schwarzenegger Top:
Richard Dawson, Schwarzenegger
© Taft Entertainment Pictures**

Arnold Schwarzenegger, Richard Dawson

Maria Conchita Alonso

PLANES, TRAINS AND AUTOMOBILES

(PARAMOUNT) Producer/Director/Screenplay, John Hughes; Photography, Donald Peterman; Designer, John W. Corso; Editor, Paul Hirsch; Associate Producer, Bill Brown; Music, Ira Newborn; Costumes, April Ferry; Casting, Janet Hirshenson, Jane Jenkins; Executive Producers, Michael Chinich, Neil Machlis; Music Supervisor, Tarquin Gotch; Production Manager, Neil A. Machlis; Assistant Directors, Mark Radcliffe, Arthur Anderson, Jeanne Caliendo; Music Coordinator, Ron Payne; Set Decorators, Jane Bogart, Linda Spheeris; Art Director, Harold Michelson; Additional Editors, Peck Prior, Andrew London, Adam Bernardi; Assistant Editors, Jim Prior, David Dresher; Set Designer, Louis Mann; Sound, James Alexander; Orchestrator, Don Nemitz; Special Effects, Stan Parks, Bill Aldridge, Roger Lifsey; Stunts, Bennie Dobbins; Soundtrack on Hughes Music/MCA Records; Dolby Stereo; Technicolor; Rated R; 93 minutes; November release

CAST

Neal Page	Steve Martin
Del Griffith	John Candy
Susan Page	Laila Robbins
State Trooper	Michael McKean
Taxi Racer	Kevin Bacon
Owen	Dylan Baker
Joey	Carol Bruce
Marti	Olivia Burnette
Peg	Diana Douglas
Motel Clerk	Martin Ferrero
Doobie	Larry Hankin
Walt	Richard Herd
Waitress	Susan Kellerman
Little Neal	Matthew Lawrence
Car Rental Agent	Edie McClurg
Martin	George O. Petrie
Motel Thief	Gary Riley
Gus	Charles Tyner
Marie	Susan Isaacs
Owen's Wife	Lulie Newcomb
Cab Dispatcher	John Randolph Jones
New York Lawyer	Nicholas Wyman
Cab Driver-New York	Gaetano Lisi
Stewardess	Diana Castle
Man on plane	Bill Erwin
New York Ticket Agent	Ruth De Soza
Stripper	Debra Lamb
Wichita Airport Rep	Ben Stein
Receptionist	Kim Genell
Brand Manager	Grant Forsberg
Cafe Patron	David Raiport
Bus Lover	Andrew J. Hentz
Bus Loverette	Karen Meisinger
Pilot	Gary Palmer

and Diane Nieman, Sylvia Vitrungs, Joann Taylor, Julie A. Herbert, Jennifer Allswang, Wendy Lee Avon, Amy Meyers, Bob Jaurequi, Jeff Jenson, Rick LeFevour, John Moio, Victoria Vanderkloot, Corey Eubanks, Mike Tillman, Kent Hays, Bill Lane

Right: John Candy, Steve Martin (also Top)
© *Paramount/Joyce Rudolph/Theo Westenberger*

John Randolph Jones, Steve Martin, John Candy

Steve Martin (L), John Candy (R)

THREE MEN AND A BABY

(TOUCHSTONE) Producers, Ted Field, Robert W. Cort; Director, Leonard Nimoy; Screenplay, James Orr, Jim Cruickshank; Based on *"Trois Hommes Et Un Couffin"* written by Colien Serreau; Executive Producer, Jean Francois Lepetit; Co-Producer, Edward Teets; Photography, Adam Greenberg; Designer, Peter Larkin; Editor, Michael A. Stevenson; Music, Marvin Hamlisch; Casting, Dianne Crittenden; Production Manager, David Shepherd; Assistant Directors, Robert Cowan, Rocco Gismondi, Rose Tedesco; Art Director, Dan Yarhi; Assistant Art Director, Dennis Davenport; Set Decorator, Hilton Rosemarin; Assistant Set Decorator, Dan Conley; Orchestrations, Jack Hayes; Production Coordinators, Patt McCurdy, Susan Kavesh; Consultant, Coline Serreau; Comic Character Designer, David A. Pacheco; Sound, Todd Maitland, Owen Langevin; Costumes, Larry Wells; Special Effects, Michael Kavanagh; Additional Casting, Jan Stefoff, Stuart Akins; Assistant Editors, Dennis E. Lew, Cherie MacNeill, Robin Russell, Toni Telo, Barbara Gandolfo; Distributed by Buena Vista; Dolby Stereo; DeLuxe Color; Rated PG; 102 minutes; November release

CAST

Peter	Tom Selleck
Michael	Steve Guttenberg
Jack	Ted Danson
Sylvia	Nancy Travis
Rebecca	Margaret Colin
Patty	Alexandra Amini
Woman at gift shop	Francine Beers
Mary	Lisa Blair/Michelle Blair
Detective Melkowitz	Philip Bosco
Dramatic Actress	Barbara Budd
Handsome Man at party	Michael Burgess
Angelyne	Claire Cellucci
Man at party #1	Eugene Clark
Jan Clopatz	Derek deLint
Tawnya	Michele Duquet
Telephone Installer	David Ferry
Grocery Store Clerk	David Foley
Vince	Paul Guilfoyle
Mrs. Hathaway	Cynthia Harris
Satch	Earl Hindman
Jack's Mother	Celeste Holm
Cab Driver	Mario Joyner
Detective #1	Gary Klar
One of Jack's girls	Christine Kossak
Detective #2	Joe Lynn
Security Guard	Edward D. Murphy
Gate Attendant	Jacqueline Murphy
Gift Shop Clerk	Colin Quinn
Mounted Policeman	Thomas Quinn
Edna	Jackie Richardson
Paul Milner	John Gould Rubin
Cherise	Camilla Scott
Swimming Instructor	Daniele Scott
Vanessa	Sharolyn Sparrow
Sally	Louise Vallance
Adam	Jonathan Whitaker

Left: Celeste Holm, Ted Danson
Top: Tom Selleck, Steve Guttenberg
© *Touchstone Pictures*

Steve Guttenberg, Tom Selleck, Ted Danson

Steve Guttenberg, Tom Selleck

Sheila E., Prince, Cat

SIGN O' THE TIMES

(CINEPLEX ODEON) Producers, Robert Cavallo, Joseph Ruffalo, Steven Fargnoli; Director/Songs/Song Producer, Prince; Co-Producer, Simon Fields; Photography, Peter Sinclair; Additional Photography, Jerry Watson; Production/Lighting Design, Leroy Bennett; Editor, Steve Purcell; Music Supervision, Billy Youdelman, Susan Rogers; Production Manager, Victoria Niles; Associate Producer, Tim Clawson; Assistant Directors, Randy Carter, Fred Eisenlohr, Selannie Tyc, Betsy Bangs; Additional Editors, Dan Blevin, Jeff U'ren, Bob Jenkins, Dave Blum, Kevin Duckett, Don Wilson, David Pincus, Fred Raimondi, Charley Randazzo; Associate Editor, Judy Reidel; Assistant Editor, D. D. Stenehjem; Art Director for Bignettes, Michael Hanan; Assistant Art Director, Joel Lang; Set, Chanhasen Dinner Theatre; Wardrobe, Elizabeth Dorr; Sound, Robert "Cubby" Colby, Gary Sanguinet, Harald Danker, William Head, Robin Fox; "U Got the Look" Directed by David Hogan; Additional Songwriters, Carole Raphaelle Davis, Charlie Parker, Eric Leeds, Dr. Fink; Color; Rated PG-13; 85 minutes; November release

CAST

Prince, Sheila E., Sheena Easton, Dr. Fink, Miko Weaver, Levi Seacer, Jr., Wally Safford, Gregory Allen Brooks, Boni Boyer, Eric Leeds, Atlanta Bliss, Cat

Prince

STEEL DAWN

(VESTRON) Producers, Lance Hool, Conrad Hool; Director, Lance Hool; Executive Producers, William J. Quigley, Larry Sugar; Associate Producer, Edgar Bold; Screenplay, Doug Lefler; Photography, George Tirl; Music, Brian May; Designer, Alex Tavoularis; Editor, Mark Conte; Costumes, Poppy Cannon; Casting, Fern Champion, Pamela Basker; Assistant Directors, Terry Buchinsky, Gavin Sweeney, Christa Schamberger; Production Manager, Stanley Roup; Sound, David Stone; Special Effects, Joe Quinlivan, Chris Pieterse; Art Director, Hans Van Den Zanden; Assistant Art Director, Mike Owens; Stunts, John Barrett; Assistant Editors, Margaret A. Smith, Grant Gatzke; Presented by Silver Lion Films; CFI Color; Rated R; 102 minutes; November release

CAST

Nomad	Patrick Swayze
Kasha	Lisa Niemi
Sho	Christopher Neame
Tark	Brion James
Cord	John Fujioka
Jux	Brett Hool
Damnil	Anthony Zerbe
Lann	Marcel Van Heerden
Makker	Arnold Vosloo
Tooey	James Whyle
Off	Russell Savadier
Cali	Joe Ribeiro
Priest	Alex Heyns
Bluto	Brad Morris
Henchman	Tullio Moneta
Merchant	David Sherwood

Right: Patrick Swayze, Christopher Neame
Top: Patrick Swayze, Lisa Niemi
© Vestron Pictures/Umberto Abaggi

Eddie Murphy

EDDIE MURPHY "RAW"

(PARAMOUNT) Producers, Robert D. Wachs, Keenen Ivory Wayans; Director, Robert Townsend; Screenplay, Eddie Murphy; Sketch Written by Eddie Murphy, Keenen Ivory Wayans; Executive Producers, Eddie Murphy, Richard Tienken, Ernest Dickerson; Photography, Ernest Dickerson; Designer, Wynn P. Thomas; Editor, Lisa Day; Co-Producer, Jefrey Chernov; Casting, Pat Golden; Production Manager, Jeffrey Chernov; Assistant Directors, Dwight Williams, Micheal Caye; Set Decorator, James T. Fredericks; Assistant Editor, Eric Strand; Assistant Photographers, Algernon Ramirez, Angelo DiGiacomo, Craig Haagensen, Marc D. Hirschfeld, Chris Lanzenberg, Joe Ritter, Deborah J. Sarjeant, John Cambria, Elizabeth Dubelman, Paul Gaffney, Stan Keitt; Sound, Frank Graziadei; Mr. Murphy's Wardrobe, Darlene Jackson; Production Coordinator, Dru Whitacre; Concert Sound, Bill Fertig; Concert Lighting, Jeff Bolderwick; "Raw" by Eddie Murphy, David Allen Jones, Rod Antoon, and Songs by various other artists; Dolby Stereo; Technicolor; Rated R; 91 minutes; December release

CAST

Singing Child	Tatyana Ali
Eddie's Aunt	Billie Allen
Card Player #1	Edye Byrde (Butts)
Uncle Lester	Clebert Ford
Card Player #2	Geri Gibson
Aunt Rose	Bidie M. Hale
Card Player #3	Tiger Haynes
Uncle Gus	Leonard Jackson
Eddie's Uncle	Samuel L. Jackson
Eddie's Cousin	Jody Jones
Eddie's Aunt	Davenia McFadden
Eddie's Mother	Gwen McGee
Card Player #4	Lex Monson
Poetry Reader	Warren Morris
Eddie Murphy	Eddie Murphy
Little Eddie	Deon Richmond
Eddie's Father	Basil Wallace
Child Running in house	Damien Wayans
Eddie's Uncle	Ellis Williams
Eddie's Aunt	Carol Woods
Thanksgiving Guests	James Brown III, Michelle Davison, J. D. Hall, Barbara Iley, John Lafayette

© Paramount Pictures/Bruce Talamon

THROW MOMMA FROM THE TRAIN

(ORION) Producer, Larry Brezner; Director, Danny DeVito; Screenplay, Stu Silver; Executive Producer, Arne L. Schmidt; Photography, Barry Sonnenfeld; Designer, Ida Random; Editor, Michael Jablow; Costumes, Marilyn Vance-Straker; Music, David Newman; Co-Producer, Kristine Johnson; Casting, Dennison/Selzer; Production Manager, Charles J. Newirth; Assistant Directors, Joe Napolitano, Michele A. Panelli, Michael A. Amundson; Associate Producer, J. Marina Muhlfriedel; Production Coordinator, Allegra Clegg; Production Associate, Linda Kwasha; Set Decorator, Anne D. McCulley; Art Director, William Elliott; Sound, Jeff Wexler, Don Coufal, Jim Stuebe; Set Designers, R. Gilbert Clayton, Joseph G. Pacelli, Jr.; Special Makeup Effects, Tom Burman, Bari Dreiband-Burman; Special Effects, John Frazier, Rocky A. Gehr; Stunts, Vince Deadrick, Sr.; Casting Assistant, Parick Rush; Additional Casting, Todd Thaler; Additional Editor, Duwayne Dunham; Assistant Editors, Lynne Southerland, Jay Ignaszewski, Carrie Ellison, Kelly Mahan; Songs, Branford Marsalis, James Kaholokula, Sipho Mabuse; Dolby Stereo; DeLuxe Color; Rated PG-13; 88 minutes; December release

CAST

Owen	Danny DeVito
Larry	Billy Crystal
Beth	Kim Greist
Momma	Anne Ramsey
Margaret	Kate Mulgrew
Lester	Branford Marsalis
Joel	Rob Reiner
Detective DeBenedetto	Bruce Kirby
Sargeant	Joey DePinto
Mrs. Hazeltine	Annie Ross
Pinsky	Raye Birk
Oprah Winfrey	Herself
Ms. Gladstone	Olivia Brown
Mr. Perlman	Philip Perlman
Ramon	Stu Silver
Millington	J. Alan Thomas
Bucky	Randall Miller
Rosey	Andre "Rosey" Brown
Mr. Lopez	Tony Ciccone
Steward	William Ray Watson
Announcer	Larry McCormick
Old Man	Peter Brocco
Reporter	Hettie Lynne Hurtes
Laughing Woman	Karen J. Westerfield
Cab Driver	Stanley L. Gonsales
Priest	Fred Gephart
Radio DJ	Don Burns

and Billy Childs, Ralph Penland, Tony Dumas, Ne Kaholokula

Right: Anne Ramsey, Danny DeVito
Above: Kate Mulgrew, Danny DeVito
Top: Billy Crystal, Danny DeVito
© Orion Pictures/Laurel Moore

Danny DeVito, Billy Crystal

Danny DeVito, Anne Ramsey

THE DEAD

(VESTRON) Producers, Wieland Schulz-Keil, Chris Sievernich; Director, John Huston; Screenplay, Tony Huston; Based on short story *"The Dead"* from the collection *Dubliners* by James Joyce; Photography, Fred Murphy; Editor, Roberto Silvi; Music, Alex North; Production Manager/Assistant Director, Tom Shaw; Executive Producer, William J. Quigley; Costumes, Dorothy Jeakins; Designer, Stephen Grimes; In collaboration with Dennis Washington; 2nd Assistant Director, John "Joe" Brooks; Casting Nuala Moiselle; Set Decorator, Josie MacAvin; Sound, Bill Randall, David Stafford, Bill Randall, Jr.; Hair, Anthony Cortino; Makeup, Fern Buchner; Orchestrations, Richard Bronskill; Assistant Editor/Production Supervisor, Keith M. Sheridan; Special Effects, Candy Flanagin; Production Coordinator, Anne M. Shaw; Choreographer, Paul Gleason; Song, *"The Lass of Aughrim"* performed by Frank Patterson; In association with Vestron Pictures (USA), Zenith and Channel 4 (London), Delta Film (Berlin); Made by Liffey Films, Inc; Dolby Stereo; FotoKem Color; Rated PG; 83 minutes; December release

CAST

Aunt Kate	Helena Carroll
Aunt Julia	Cathleen Delany
Lily	Rachael Dowling
Miss Furlong	Katherine O'Toole
Miss Higgins	Bairbre Dowling
Miss O'Calaghan	Maria Hayden
Mr. Kerrigan	Cormac O'Herlihy
Mr. Bergin	Colm Meaney
Mary Jane	Ingrid Craigie
Mr. Brown	Dan O'Herlihy
Gretta	Anjelica Huston
Gabriel	Donal McCann
Bartell D'Arcy	Frank Patterson
Mrs. Malins	Marie Kean
Freddy Malins	Donal Donnelly
Mr. Grace	Sean McClory
Molly Ivors	Maria McDermottroe
Miss Daly	Lyda Anderson
Young Lady	Dara Clarke
Young Gentlemen	Paul Grant, Paul Carroll, Patrick Gallagher
Cabman	Brendan Dillon
Nightporter	Redmond M. Gleeson

Right: Sean McClory, Ingrid Craigie
Above: Marie Kean, Donal Donnelly
Top: Donal McCann, Angelica Huston
© *Vestron Pictures/Francois Duhamel*

Dan O'Herlihy, Helena Carroll, Cathleen Delany

Cathleen Delany, Helena Carroll, Angelica Huston

BATTERIES NOT INCLUDED

(UNIVERSAL) Producer, Ronald L. Schwary; Director, Matthew Robbins; Screenplay, Brad Bird, Matthew Robbins, Brent Maddock, S. S. Wilson; Story, Mick Garris; Executive Producers, Steven Spielberg, Kathleen Kennedy, Frank Marshall; Associate Producer, Gerald R. Molen; Photography, John McPherson; Designer, Ted Haworth; Casting, Penny Perry; Music, James Horner; Editor, Cynthia Scheider; Production Manager, Gerald R. Molen; Assistant Directors, Jerry Grandey, Bruce Cohen; Visual Effects, Bruce Nicholson; Art Director, Angelo Graham; Production Coordinator, Lata Ryan; Set Decorator, George R. Nelson; Assistant Art Director, Jim Murakami; Sound, Gene Cantamessa, Steve Cantamessa; Special Effects, Ken Pepiot, Al Winiger, Dan Lester; Stunts, Thomas Rosales, Jr.; Production Associate, Brian Steward; Casting Assistant, Mae Williams; Orchestrations, Greig McRitchie, Billy May; Visual Effects produced at Industrial Light & Magic; Soundtrack on MCA; Dolby Stereo; DeLuxe Color; Rated PG; 106 minutes; December release

CAST

Frank	Hume Cronyn
Faye	Jessica Tandy
Harry	Frank McRae
Marisa	Elizabeth Pena
Carlos	Michael Carmine
Mason	Dennis Boutsikaris
Sid	Tom Aldredge
Muriel	Jane Hoffman
Gus	John DiSanti
Kovacs	John Pankow
DeWitt	MacIntyre Dixon
Lacey	Michael Greene
Mrs. Thompson	Doris Belack
Pamela	Wendy Schaal
Goons	Jose Santana, James LeGross
Louie	Ronald Schwary
Receptionist	Susan Shoffner
Policemen	Shelly Kurtz, Joseph Hamer, H. Clay Dear
Reporters	Howard Renensland, Judy Grafe
Nurse	Alice Beardsley
Fireman	Dick Martinsen
Hector	Charles Raymond
Band Members	Charles Raymond, Riki Colon, Jon Imparato
Chauffer	John Arceri

Top: Jessica Tandy, Frank McRae, Elizabeth Pena, Hume Cronyn, Dennis Boutsikiris Right: Tandy, Cronyn
© *Universal City Studios*

Dennis Boutsikiris, Hume Cronyn, Elizabeth Pena
Above: Jessica Tandy, Elizabeth Pena

111

BROADCAST NEWS

(20th CENTURY FOX) Producer/Director/Screenplay, James L. Brooks; Executive Producer, Polly Platt; Co-Producer, Penney Finkelman Cox; Photography, Michael Ballhaus; Designer, Charles Rosen; Editor, Richard Marks; Music, Bill Conti; Casting, Ellen Chenoweth; Associate Producers, Kristi Zea, Susan Zirinsky; Costumes, Molly Maginnis; Additional Casting, Paula Herald; Production Executive for Gracie Films, Richard Sakai; Production Manager, David V. Lester; Assistant Directors, Yudi Bennett, David Sardi, Barbara Bruno; Special Advisor, David Davis; Set Decorator, Jane Bogart; Sound, Thomas Causey; Production Associates, Diane Brooks, Paul Germain; Executive Assistant, Barbara Duncan; Set Designer, Harold Fuhrman; Additional Editors, David Rawlins, M. Pam Blumenthal, Barbara Marks; Assistant Editors, Karen I. Stern, David Mortiz, Margaret Goodspeed, Mike Mulconnery; Production Coordinator, Cyndy Streit; Stunts, Jery Hewitt; In association with Amercent Films and American Entertainment Partners L.P.: Orchestrations, Jack Eskew; *"Newsroom Theme"* by Michel Camilo; Songs, Francis Cabrel, Jim Weatherly; Dolby Stereo; DeLuxe Color; Rated R; 131 minutes; December release

CAST

Tom Grunick	William Hurt
Aaron Altman	Albert Brooks
Jane Craig	Holly Hunter
Ernie Merriman	Robert Prosky
Jennifer Mack	Lois Chiles
Blair Litton	Joan Cusack
Paul Moore	Peter Hackes
Bobby	Christian Clemenson
Martin Klein	Robert Katims
George Weln	Ed Wheeler
Gerald Grunick	Stephen Mendillo
Young Tom	Kimber Shoop
Young Aaron	Dwayne Markee
Young Jane	Gennie James
Jane's Dad	Leo Burmester
Elli Merriman	Amy Brooks
Anne Merriman	Jane Welch
Clifford Altman	Jonathan Benya
Mercenary	Frank Doubleday
Lila	Sally Knight
General McGuire	Richard Thomsen
Commander	Nathan Benchley
Date-Rape Woman	Marita Geraghty
Weekend News Producer	Nicholas D. Blanchet
Makeup Woman	Maura Moynihan
Floor Manager	Chuck Lippman
Paul's Secretary	Nannette Rickert
Edward Towne	Tim White
Tom's Soundwoman	Peggy Pridemore
Emily	Emily Crowley
Newsroom Worker	Gerald Ender
Donny	David Long
Chyron Operator	Josh Billings
Control Room Director	Richard Pehle
Weekend News Director	James V. Franco
News Theme Writers	Glen Roven, Marc Shaiman
Lecture Host	Alex Mathews
Ellen	Susan Marie Feldman
Tom's Female Colleague	Jean Bourne Carinci
Cab Driver	M. Fekade-Salassie
Uniformed Cop	Jerry Gough
Defense Dept. Spokesman	Robert Rasch
NATO Spokesman	Robert Walsh
Angry Messenger	John Cusack
Bill Rorich	Jack Nicholson

and Manny Alvarez, Luis Valderrama, Francisco Garcia, Glenn Faigen, Robert Grevemberg, Jr., Jimmy Mel Green, Raoul N. Rizik, Mike Skehan, Franklyn L. Bullard, Steve Smith, Martha L. Smith, Cynthia B. Hayes, Dean Nitz, Phil Ugel, Lance Wain, John Badila, Heather Ehlers, Arlene M. Dillon, Sam Samuels, Rochelle Deering, Albert Murphy, Sr., Eleanore C. Kopecky, Jeffrey Alan Thomas

Top Left: Holly Hunter, William Hurt, Albert Brooks
Below: William Hurt
© 20th Century Fox/Kerry Hayes

Albert Brooks, Holly Hunter
Above: Albert Brooks, William Hurt

Albert Brooks, Holly Hunter, William Hurt Top Left: Albert Brooks,
William Hurt Below: Holly Hunter Top Right: Lois Chiles,
Holly Hunter Below: Joan Cusack, Albert Brooks, Peter Hackes

GOOD MORNING, VIETNAM

(TOUCHSTONE) Producers, Mark Johnson, Larry Brezner; Director, Barry Levinson; Screenplay, Mitch Markowitz; Photography, Peter Sova; Designer, Roy Walker; Editor, Stu Linder; Music, Alex North; Co-Producers, Ben Moses, Harry Benn; Casting, Louis DiGiaimo; Assistant Directors, M. Mathis Johnson, Bill Westley, Gerry Toomey, Sompol Sungkawes; Production Executive, Santa Pestonji; Art Director, Steve Spence; Set Decorator, Tessa Davies; Costumes, Keith Denny; Sound, Clive Winter; Music Consultant, Allan Mason; Orchestrations, Henry Brant; Thailand Casting, Marie Row, Rassami Paoluengtong; Casting Assistant, William Dowd; Production Coordinators, Joyce Turner, Kanokporn Sae Tang; Stunts, Clive Curtis; Special Effects, Fred Cramer; Soundtrack on A&M Records; Dolby Stereo; Buena Vista Distribution, Inc.; DeLuxe Color; Rated R; 120 minutes; December release

CAST

Adrian Cronauer	Robin Williams
Edward Garlick	Forest Whitaker
Tuan	Tung Thanh Tran
Trinh	Chintara Sukapatana
Lt. Steven Hauk	Bruno Kirby
Marty Lee Dreiwitz	Robert Wuhl
Sgt. Major Dickerson	J. T. Walsh
Gen. Taylor	Noble Willingham
Pvt. Abersold	Richard Edson
Phil McPherson	Juney Smith
Dan "The Man" Levitan	Richard Portnow
Eddie Kirk	Floyd Vivino
Jimmy Wah	Cu Ba Nguyen
Censors	Dan R. Stanton, Don E. Stanton
MPs	Danny Aiello, III, J. J.
Sergeants at Jimmy Wah's	James McIntire, Peter MacKenzie
Chaplain Noel	Ralph Tabakin

and No Tran, Hoa Nguyen, Uikey Kuay, Suvit Abakaz, Panas Wiwatpanachat, Lerdcharn Namkiri, Hanh Hi Nguyen, Tuan Lai, Boonchai Jakraworawut, Joe B. Veokeki, Wichien Chaopramong, Kien Chufak, Prasert Tangpantarat, Tim O'Hare, John Goyer, Louis Hood, Christopher Mangan, Kenneth Pitochelli, Jonathan MacLeod, Gregg T. Knight, Sangad Sangkao, Vanlap Sangkao

Right: Robin Williams, Tung Thanh Tran
Above: Chintara Sukapatana, Robin Williams
Top: Bruno Kirby, Floyd Vivino, Richard Portnow,
Robert Wuhl, Forest Whitaker, Robin Williams (center)
© *Touchstone Pictures*

Robin Williams, Forrest Whitaker

Robin Williams

114

OVERBOARD

(MGM) Producers, Alexandra Rose, Anthea Sylbert; Director, Garry Marshall; Screenplay, Leslie Dixon; Executive Producer, Roddy McDowall; Photography, John A. Alonzo; Art Directors, James Shanahan, Jim Dultz; Editors, Dov Hoenig, Sonny Baskin; Associate Producer, Nick Abdo; Costumes, Wane Finkelman; Visual Consultant, Lawrence Miller; Music, Alan Silvestri; Casting, Wallis Nicita Associates, JoAnne Zaluski; Production Managers, Michelle Ader, James Herbert; Assistant Directors, Katy Emde, Matt Earl Beesley; Sound, Bruce Bisenz; Assistant Editors, Mark Sadusky, Angel Pine, Bobby Bell, Joe Mosca; Special Effects, Alan E. Lorimer, Lambert A. Powell, Ralph A. Winiger, Richard C. Ratliff; Set Decorator, Tom Bugenhagen; Set Designers, Judy Cammer, Ron Yates, William James Teegarden; Stunts, Hal Burton; Production Coordinator, Anita Terrian; Orchestrations, James Campbell; Songs by various artists; *"I Love You Madly"* Music & Lyrics, Harvey Miller; Dolby Stereo; Technicolor; Rated PG; 112 minutes; December release

CAST

Joanna/Annie	Goldie Hawn
Dean Proffitt	Kurt Russell
Grant Stayton III	Edward Herrmann
Edith Mintz	Katherine Helmond
Billy Pratt	Michael Hagerty
Andrew	Roddy McDowall
Charlie	Jared Rushton
Joey	Jeffrey Wiseman
Travis	Brian Price
Greg	Jamie Wild
Captain Karl	Frank Campanella
Dr. Norman Korman	Harvey Alan Miller
Wilbur Budd	Frank Buxton
Rose Budd	Carol Williard
Adele Burbridge	Doris Hess
Thud Gittman	Ed Cree
Gertie	Mona Lyden
Tess	Lucinda Crosby
Sheriff Earl	Bing Russell

and Richard Stahl, Ray Combs, Marvin Braverman, Tim Wright, Tom Wright, John McDowell, Steven Walker, Israel Juarbe, Paul Fonteyn, Antonio Martinez Garcia, Robert Goldman, Keith Syphers, Robert Meadows, Lisa Hunter, Erin Grant, Lisa Beth Ross, Liz Stewart, Laura Fabian, Julie Paris, Paul Tinder, Scott Marshall, Bill Applebaum, Don Thompson, Charley Marie Morgan, Gary Pike, Geof Brewer

**Right: Kurt Russell, Goldie Hawn
Top: Jamie Wild, Goldie Hawn, Jared Rushton,
Jeffrey Wiseman, Kurt Russell, Brian Price**
© *M-G-M/Aaron Rapoport*

Goldie Hawn

Roddy McDowall, Goldie Hawn, Edward Herrmann

Sam Waterston, Dianne Wiest
Above: Dianne Wiest, Mia Farrow

Jack Warden, Elaine Stritch
Above: Mia Farrow, Denholm Elliott

SEPTEMBER

(ORION) Producer, Robert Greenhut; Director/Screenplay, Woody Allen; Executive Producers, Jack Rollins, Charles H. Joffe; Photography, Carlo Di Palma; Designer, Santo Loquasto; Editor, Susan E. Morse; Costumes, Jeffrey Kurland; Casting, Juliet Taylor; Production Manager, Joseph Hartwick; Assistant Directors, Thomas Reilly, Ken Ornstein; Associate Producer, Gail Sicilia; Production Coordinator, Helen Robin; Art Director, Speed Hopkins; Assistant Art Directors, Tom Warren, Matthew Bliss; Set Decorator, George DeTitta, Jr.; Sound, James Sabat, Louis Sabat, Frank Graziadei; Assistant Costume Designers, Judianna Makovsky, Jessica Fasman; Assistant Editors, Jon Neuburger, Janice Keuhnelian; Casting Associate, Ellen Lewis; De-Luxe Color; Rated PG; 82 minutes; December release

CAST

Howard	Denholm Elliott
Stephanie	Dianne Wiest
Lane	Mia Farrow
Diane	Elaine Stritch
Peter	Sam Waterston
Lloyd	Jack Warden
Mr. Rains	Ira Wheeler
Mrs. Raines	Jane Cecil
Mrs. Mason	Rosemary Murphy

Top Left: Mia Farrow, Sam Waterston
Below: Mia Farrow, Dianne Wiest
© *Orion Pictures/Brian Hamill*

IRONWEED

(TRI—STAR) Producers, Keith Barish, Marcia Nasatir; Director, Hector Babenco; Screenplay, William Kennedy based on his novel; Executive Producers, Joseph H. Kanter, Denis Blouin, Rob Cohen; Co-Producers, Gene Kirkwood, C. O. Erickson; Photography, Lauro Escorel; Designer, Jeannine C. Oppewall; Editor, Anne Goursaud; Costumes, Joseph G. Aulisi; Music, John Morris; Casting, Bonnie Timmermann; Production Managers, C. O. Erickson, Myron Adams; Assistant Directors, Albert Shapiro, Robert Roda, Sarah M. Brim; Art Director, Robert Guerra; Set Decorators, Leslie Pope, Elaine O'Donnell; Assistant to Production Designer, Berta Segall; Assistant Art Directors, Teresa M. Carriker, Beth Kuhn, Enno Poersch, Clare Scarpulla; Orchestrator, Jack Hayes; Sound, Danny Michael; Special Effects, Steve Kirshoff, William Dale Harrison; Stunts, Alan Gibbs; Production Coordinators, Danis Regal-O'Connell, Katherine A, Kennedy; Special Production Consultant, Robert Dawson; Songs by various artists; In association with Home Box Office; Taft Entertainment/ Keith Barish Productions; Dolby Stereo; Technicolor; Rated R; 144 minutes; December release

CAST

Francis Phelan	Jack Nicholson
Helen	Meryl Streep
Annie Phelan	Carroll Baker
Billy	Michael O'Keefe
Peg	Diane Venora
Oscar Reo	Fred Gwynne
Katrina	Margaret Whitton
Rudy	Tom Waits
Pee Wee	Jake Dengel
Harold Allen	Nathan Lane
Reverend Chester	James Gammon
Rowdy Dick	Will Zahrn
Nora	Laura Esterman
Jack	Joe Grifasi
Rosskam	Hy Anzell
Librarian	Bethel Leslie
Donovan	Richard Hamilton
Clara	Black-Eyed Susan

and Louise Phillips, Marjorie Slocum, Lena Spencer, Lola Pashalinski, Paul A. DiCocco, Jr., Priscilla Smith, James Dukas, Jared Swartout, Ted Levine, Martin Patterson, Terry O'Reilly, Michael O'Gorman, Frank Whaley, Jordan Valdina, Louis St. Louis, John Wright, Robin Wood-Chappelle, Nicole Weden, Peter Pryor, Duane Scholz, Matt McGrath, Lois Barden Stilley, Cori Irwin, Pamela Payton-Wright, Boris McGiver, Phyllis Gottung, James Yoham, Ean Egas, Nebraska Brace, Jeff Morris, William Duell, George Rafferty, Robert Manion, Pat Devane

Top Right: Meryl Streep, Jack Nicholson
Below: Jack Nicholson, Tom Waits
© *Taft Entertainment Pictures*

Meryl Streep

Carroll Baker, Michael O'Keefe, Diane Venora,
Jack Nicholson

MOONSTRUCK

(MGM) Producers, Patrick Palmer, Norman Jewison; Director, Norman Jewison; Screenplay, John Patrick Shanley; Photography, David Watkin; Designer, Philip Rosenberg; Editor, Lou Lombardo; Costumes, Theoni V. Aldredge; Music, Dick Hyman; Associate Producer, Bonnie Palef-Woolf; Casting, Howard Feuer; Production Associate, Christopher Cook; Art Directors, Barbra Matis, Dan Davis; Sound, Dennis L. Maitland; Production Managers, Roger Paradiso, Bonnie Palef-Woolf; Assistant Directors, Lewis Gould, Gregory Palmer, Stephen Wertimer, David McAree, Andrew Shea; Set Decorator, Philip Smith; Production Coordinator, Jackie Martin; Casting Assistant, Sam Broomall; Special Effects, David Lemmem; Assistant Editors, Lee Michael Searles, Rosmary Conte; Soundtrack on Capital Records; Dolby Stereo; Technicolor; Rated PG; 102 minutes; December release

CAST

Loretta Castorini	Cher
Ronny Cammareri	Nicolas Cage
Cosmo Castorini	Vincent Gardenia
Rose Castorini	Olympia Dukakis
Mr. Johnny Cammareri	Danny Aiello
Rita Cappomaggi	Julie Bovasso
Perry	John Mahoney
Raymond Cappomaggi	Louis Guss
Old Man	Feodor Chaliapin
Mona	Anita Gillette
Chrissy	Nada Despotovich
Shy Waiter	Joe Grifasi
Old Crone	Gina DeAngeles
Barbara	Robin Bartlett
Lotte	Helen Hanft
Irv	David S. Howard
Bobo	Robert Weil
Bonnie	Amy Aquino
Conti	Tony Azito
Florist	Frankie Gio
Nancy	Ann McDonough
Lowell	John Christopher Jones
Patricia	Lisa Howard
Sheila	Cynthia Dale
Priest	Anthony Messuri
Mimi	Martha Collins
Rodolfo	John Fanning
Vesta	Antonia Minella
Eddie	Nicholas Pasco
Bob	Al Therrien
Mook	Lou Pitoscia
Rocco	Gilberto Godoy
Jimmy	Louis DiBianco
Pietro	Michael Barbaro
Franco	Antonio Pariselli
Ruby	Mimi Lizio
Al	Tim Koetting
Harvey	Gerald Flannery

and Betti Orsatti, Corrado Gianna, Tommy Hollis, Matt Meyers, Michael Dunster, Stella Bruno, Mimi Cecchini, Robert Payson, Catherine Scorsese, Jack Tsirakis

Top Left: Julie Bovasso, Olympia Dukakis, Louis Guss, Vincent Gardenia, Danny Aiello, (seated) Nicolas Cage, Cher, Feodor Chaliapin Below: Cher, Danny Aiello
© M-G-M/Greg Gorman

1988 Academy Awards for Best Actress (Cher), Supporting Actress (Olympia Dukakis), and Original Screenplay

Anita Gillette, Vincent Gardenia

Cher, Nicolas Cage Top: Olympia Dukakis, Danny Aiello

WALKER

(UNIVERSAL) Executive Producer, Edward R. Pressman; Director, Alex Cox; Screenplay, Rudy Wurlitzer; Producers, Lorenzo O'Brien, Angel Flores Marini; Associate Producer, Debbie Biaz; Music, Joe Strummer; Sound, Richard Beggs; Editors, Carlos Puente, Alex Cox; Photography, David Bridges; Additional Photography, Dennis Crossan, Frank Pineda, Steve Fierberg, Tom Richmond, Rafael Ruiz; Designer, Bruno Rubeo; Costumes, Pam Tait; Casting, Victoria Thomas, Miguel Sandoval; Production Supervisor, Michael Flynn; Line Producer, Carlos Alvarez; Production Manager, Chris Brigham; Assistant Directors, Mary Ellen Woods, Miguel Lima, Fernando Altschul, James O'Brien; Sound, Peter Glossop, David Batchelor; Art Directors, Cecilia Montiel, Jorge Sainz; Set Decorator, Bryce Perrin; Special Effects, Marcelino Pacheco Guzman; Stunts, Rick Barker; Orchestrations, Dick Bright; Soundtrack on Virgin Records America; In association with Incine; Released in association with Northern Distribution Partners; Color; Rated R; 95 minutes; December release

CAST

William Walker	Ed Harris
Ephraim Squier	Richard Masur
Major Siegfried Henningson	Rene Auberjonois
Timothy Crocker	Keith Szarabajka
Captain Hornsby	Sy Richardson
Byron Cole	Xander Berkeley
Stebbins	John Diehl
Cornelius Vanderbilt	Peter Boyle
Ellen Martin	Marlee Matlin
Raousset	Alfonso Arau
Munoz	Pedro Armendariz
Mayorga	Roberto Lopez Espinoza
Norvell Walker	Gerrit Graham
James Walker	William O'Leary
Yrena	Blanca Guerra
Don Domingo	Alan Bolt
Parker French	Miguel Sandoval
Doctor Jones	Rene Assa
Achilles Kewen	Bennet Guillory
Prange	Norbert Weisser
Anderson	Bruce Wright
Turley	Richard Edson
Bruno Van Namzer	Charley Braun
Mrs. Bingham	Linda Callahan
Judge	Milton Selzer
Lemuel	Richard Zobel
Alta Kewen	Ren Woods
Wiley Marshall	Frederick Neumann
Father Rossiter	David Hayman
Doubleday	Edward Tudor Pole
Faucet	Joe Strummer
Darlene	Sharon Barr
Annie Mae	Kathy Burke
District Attorney	Fox Harris
Corral	Enrique Beraza
Benito	Luis Contreras
Major Angus	Ed Pansullo
Sanders	Jack Slater
Davenport	Spider Stacey
Padre Vigil	Del Zamora
Rudler	Biff Yeager
Fry	William Utay
Assistant Deputy	George Belanger
Huey	Zander Schloss
Dewey	William Rothlein
Lul	David Chung
Castellon	Paulino Rodriquez
Washburn	Dick Rude
Morgan	Rudy Wurlitzer
Garrison	Bob Tzudiker
Mendez	Nestor Mendez Garcia
Breckenridge	Rick Barker
Huston	J. D. Silvester

and Robert Dickman, Joe Celeste, Martin Aylett, Ramon Alvarez, Raymund Kettless, Tom Collins, Louis Mathews, Dexter Taylor, Michele Winstanley

Top Right: Marlee Matlin, Ed Harris
Below: Ed Harris (center)
© *Universal City Studios*

Charley Braun, J. D. Sylvester, Ed Harris, Rene Auberjonois Above: Ed Harris (center)

SHY PEOPLE

(CANNON) Producers, Menahem Golan, Yoram Globus; Director/ Story, Andrei Konchalovsky; Screenplay, Gerard Brach, Andrei Konchalovsky, Marjorie David; Editor, Alain Jakubowicz; Photography, Chris Menges; Designer, Stephen Marsh; Music, Tangerine Dream; Casting, Robert MacDonald; Production Manager, Michael Fottrell; Assistant Directors, Michael Schroeder, Frank Capra, III; Production Executive, Rony Yacov; Art Director, Leslie McDonald; Set Decorator, Leslie Morales; Assistant Set Decorator, Alice Baker; Sound, Mark Ulano; Costumes, Katherine Dover; Production Supervisor, Marc S. Fischer; Production Coordinator, Lark Bernini; Special Effects, Calvin V. Acord, Timothy J. Moran, Samuel Marquez, Brian Loft; Visual Effects, Sean MacLeod Phillips; Stunts, Michael Adams, Cherie Tash, Steve Kelso; Assistant Editors, Axel Anton Hubert, Marcelo Sansevieri, Pietro Scalia, Michael Murphy, Galit Lidsky, Alexander Renskoff, Anthony Sherin; Music Supervisor, Paula Erickson; Music Coordinator, Stephanie Lee; *"Shy People"*, *"Goin' to Town"* Music, Tangerine Dream, Lyrics, Ron Boustead/*"Hummin' the Blues"* by Michael Bishop/*"Goodbye"* by Shelley Speck, and songs by other artists; Vocals, Michael Bishop, John Bigham, Janey Clewer, Shelley Speck, Ruth Etting; Color; Dolby Stereo; Rated R; 118 minutes; December release

CAST

Diana	Jill Clayburgh
Ruth	Barbara Hershey
Grace	Martha Plimpton
Mike	Merritt Butrick
Tommy	John Philbin
Mark	Don Swayze
Paul	Pruitt Taylor Vince
Candy	Mare Winningham
Louie	Michael Audley
Larry	Brad Leland
Jake	Tony Epper
Henry	Paul Landry
Dick	Warren Battiste
Chuck	Edward Bunker
Welder	Vladimir Bibic
Chief	Dominic Barto
Sheriff	Dave Petitjean
Policemen	William Anderson, David Avne, Ronn Wright
Stewardesses	Cheryl Starbuck, Claire Acerno
Black Man	J. Larry McGill
Vietnamese Pimp	Ernest Tan
Cab Driver	Jack McGee
Pal #1	Jack Radosta
Margo	Phyllis Guerrini
Man	Greg Guirard

Top Right: Jill Clayburgh, Barbara Hershey
Below: John Philbin, Pruitt Taylor Vince
© *Cannon Films*

Barbara Hershey

Don Swayze, Barbara Hershey

WALL STREET

(20th CENTURY FOX) Producer, Edward R. Pressman; Director, Oliver Stone; Screenplay, Stanley Weiser, Oliver Stone; Co-Producer, A. Kitman Ho; Photography, Robert Richardson; Designer, Stephen Hendrickson; Editor, Claire Simpson; Costumes, Ellen Mirojnick; Music, Stewart Copeland; Casting, Risa Bramon, Billy Hopkins; Production Manager, Judith Stevens; Assistant Directors, Steve Lim, Amy Sayres, Vebe Borge; Associate Producer, Michael Flynn; Associate Editor, David S. Brenner; Technical Advisor, Ken Lipper; Art Directors, John Jay Moore, Hilda Stark; Production Supervisor, Budd Carr; Set Decorators, Leslie Bloom, Susan Bode; Sound, Chris Newman; Assistant Costume Designer, Judy Wong; Production Coordinator, Jackie Martin; Additional Casting, Todd Thaler, Judy Fixler; Stunts, Harry Madsen, Jim Lovelett; Produced in association with American Entertainment Partners L.P.; Dolby Stereo; DeLuxe Color; Rated R; 124 minutes; December release

CAST

Bud Fox	Charlie Sheen
Carolyn	Tamara Tunie
Dan	Franklin Cover
Chuckie	Chuck Pfeiffer
Marvin	John C. McGinley
Lou Mannheim	Hal Holbrook
Lynch	James Karen
Natalie	Leslie Lyles
Gordon Gekko	Michael Douglas
Charlie	Frank Adonis
Dominick	John Capodice
Carl Fox	Martin Sheen
Alex	Francois Giroday
Ollie	Josh Mostel
Susan	Ann Talman
Gina	Lisa Zebro
Sir Larry Wildman	Terence Stamp
Maitre'd "Le Cirque"	George Vlachos
Woman at "Le Cirque"	Liliane Montevecchi
Kate Gekko	Sean Young
Candice Rogers	Cecelia Peck
Stone Livingston	Paul Guilfoyle
Muffie Livingston	Annie McEnroe
Darien Taylor	Daryl Hannah
Sam Ruspoli	Jack Pruett
Houseboy	Ronald Yamamota
Roger Barnes	James Spader
Panos	Yanni Sfinias
Harold Salt	Saul Rubinek
Rudy Gekko	Sean Stone
Nicole	Astrid De Richmonte
Janet	Adelle Lutz
Realtor	Sylvia Miles
Cromwell	Richard Dysart
Duncan Wilmore	William G. Knight
Toni Carpenter	Jean DeBaer
Mrs. Fox	Millie Perkins

and Suzen Murakoshi, Dani Klein, Rocco Anacarola, Monique Van Vooren, Andrea Thompson, George Blumenthal, Ronald Von Klaussen, Michael O'Donoghue, Pirie McDonald, Thomas Anderson, Grant Shaud, Carol Schneider, Christopher Burge, Richard Feigen, James Rosenquist, John Galateo, Marlene Bielinska, Bruce Diker, Jeff Beck, Diego Del Vayo, Pat Skipper, John Deyle, Michael A. Raymond, Eugene Dumaresq, Lefty Lewis, Michael Rutigliano, Heather Evans, Ken Lipper, Lauren Tom, Don Kehr, Elise Richmond, David Logan, Paul Kawecki, Dickson Shaw, Patrick Weathers, Jill Dalton, Allan Salkin, Oliver Stone, Michael C. Mahon, Jeff Rector, Pamela Riley, Jon Wool

**Top Left: Michael Douglas, Charlie Sheen
Below: Charlie Sheen, Daryl Hannah
© 20th Century Fox/Andy Schwartz**

*Michael Douglas received an Academy Award
for Best Actor of 1987*

Terence Stamp, Sean Young, Michael Douglas
Above: Charlie Sheen, Martin Sheen

Charlie Sheen, Michael Douglas Top Left: Charlie Sheen, Hal Holbrook
Below: Charlie Sheen, James Spader Top Right: Charlie Sheen,
John McGinley Below: Charlie Sheen, James Karen

Masato Ibu, Christian Bale Above; Joe
Pantoliano, Christian Bale, John Malkovich

EMPIRE OF THE SUN

(**WARNER BROS.**) Producers, Steven Spielberg, Kathleen Kennedy, Frank Marshall; Director, Steven Spielberg; Screenplay, Tom Stoppard; Based on novel by J. G. Ballard; Executive Producer, Robert Shapiro; Photography, Allen Daviau; Designer, Norman Reynolds; Editor, Michael Kahn; Music, John Williams; Associate Producer, Chris Kenny; Costumes, Bob Ringwood; Casting, Maggie Cartier; 2nd Unit Director, Frank Marshall; Assistant Directors, David Tomblin, Roy Button, Patrick Kinney, Ken Shane; Production Manager, Ted Morley; Casting-USA, Mike Fenton, Jane Feinberg, Judy Taylor; Production Coordinators, Margaret Adams, Jennie Raglan; Sound, Colin Charles, Tony Dawe; Art Directors, Charles Bishop, Frederick Hole; Set Decorators, Harry Cordwell, Michael D. Ford; Assistant Art Directors, Gavin Bocquet, Clifford Robinson; Special Effects, Kit West, David Watkins, Yves De Bono, Trevor Neighbour; Stunts, Vic Armstrong; Associate Editors, Colin Wilson, Martin Cohen, Craig Bassett; Assistant Editors, Danny Farrell, Nicholas Moore; Orchestrator, Herbert Spencer; Additional Optical Effects, Industrial Light & Magic/Dennis Muren, Michael Pangrazio, John Ellis; "Suo Gan" performance, The Ambrosian Junior Choir, Soloist, James Rainbird/Arranger-Conductor, John McCarthy; Songs by various artists; Soundtrack on Warner Bros. Records; from Amblin Entertainment; Dolby Stereo; Technicolor; Rated PG; 153 minutes; December release

CAST

Jim	Christian Bale
Basie	John Malkovich
Mrs. Victor	Miranda Richardson
Dr. Rawlins	Nigel Havers
Frank Demerest	Joe Pantoliano
Maxton	Leslie Phillips
Sgt. Nagata	Masato Ibu
Jim's Mother	Emily Richard
Jim's Father	Rupert Frazer
Mr. Victor	Peter Gale
Kamikaze Boy Pilot	Takatoro Kataoka
Dainty	Ben Stiller
Tiptree	David Neidorf
Cohen	Ralph Seymour
Mr. Lockwood	Robert Stephens
Yang	Zhai Nai She
Sgt. Uchida	Guts Ishimatsu
Amy Matthews	Emma Piper
Mr. Radik	James Walker
Singing Prisoner	Jack Dearlove
Mrs. Gilmour	Anna Turner
Mrs. Phillips	Ann Castle
Mrs. Lockwood	Yvonne Gilan
Mr. Partridge	Ralph Michael
Mrs. Hug	Sybil Maas
Mr. Chen	Burt Kwouk
Colonel Marshall	Tom Danaher
Chinese Youth	Kong-Guo-Jun
Japanese Truck Driver	Takao Yamada
Japanese Sergeant/Airfield	Hiro Arai
Lieutenant Price	Paul McGann
Frenchman	Marc De Jonge
Amah	Susan Leong
Paul	Nicholas Dastor
Paul's Sister	Edith Platten
Chinese Cook at detention centre	Shirley Chantrell
Mr. Pym	John Moore
Mrs. Pym	Ann Queensberry
Mrs. Partridge	Sylvia Marriott
Mrs. Hug's Father	Frank Duncan
Mr. Chen's Aide	Ronald Eng

and Eric Flynn, James Greene, Simon Harrison, Barrie Houghton, Paula Hamilton, Thea Ranft, Tony Boncza, Nigel Leach, Sheridan Forbes, Peter Copley, Barbara Bolton, Francesca Longrigg, Samantha Warden, Kieron Jecchinis, Michael Crossman, Gary Parker, Ray Charleson, Za Chuan Ce, Shi Rui Qing, Lu Ye, Guo Xue Liang, Ge Yan Zhao, Adam King, Shane Fry, Roy Merchant, Dickey Beer, Wendy Leech, Wayne David Michaels, Nick Gillard, Keith Harvey, Michael Durrant

Top Left: Christian Bale, Emily Richard, Rupert Frazer
Below: John Malkovich, Christian Bale
© *Warner Bros.*

WANTED DEAD OR ALIVE (New World) Producer, Robert C. Peters; Director, Gary Sherman; Screenplay, Michael Patrick Goodman, Brian Taggert, Gary Sherman; Photography, Alex Nepomniaschy; Editor, Ross Albert; Music, Joseph Renzetti; Color; Rated R; 104 minutes; January release. CAST: Rutger Hauer (Nick Randall), Gene Simmons (Malak Al Rahim), Robert Guillaume (Philmore Walker), Mel Harris (Terry), William Russ (Danny Quintz), Susan McDonald (Louise Quintz), Jerry Hardin (John Lipton), Hugh Gillin (Patrick Danahy), Robert Harper (Dave Henderson)

SWEET COUNTRY (Cinema Group) Producer/Director/Screenplay, Michael Cacoyannis; Based on the Novel by Caroline Richards; Photography, Andreas Bellis; Editor, Michael Cacoyannis, Dinos Katsourides; Music, Stavros Xarhakos; Color; Rated R; 150 minutes; January release. CAST: Jane Alexander (Anna), John Cullum (Ben), Carole Laure (Eva), Franco Nero (Paul), Joanna Pettet (Monica), Randy Quaid (Juan), Irene Papas (Mrs. Araya), Jean-Pierre Aumont (Mr. Araya), Pierre Vaneck (Father Venegas)

SOMETHING SPECIAL Producer, M. David Chilewich; Director, Paul Schneider; Screenplay, Carla Reuben, Walter Carbone; Color; Rated PG-13; 90 minutes; January release. CAST: Pamela Segall (Milly/Willy), Patty Duke (Mrs. Niceman), John Glover (Mr. Niceman), Eric Gurry (Alfie). No other credits provided.

P.K. AND THE KID (Castle Hill Prods.) Producer, Joe Roth; Director, Lou Lombardo; Screenplay, Neal Barbera; Photography, Ed Koons; Editor, Tony Lombardo; Music, James Horner; Sound, John Mason; Designer, Chet Allen; Art Director, Bill Cornford; Set Decorator, Dian Perryman; Assistant Director, Scott Maitland; Production Manager, James Margellos; Stunts, Walter Scott; from Sunn Classic Pictures; CFI Color; Rated PG-13; 89 minutes; January release. CAST: Paul Le Mat (Kid Kane), Molly Ringwald (P.K. Bayette), Alex Rocco (Lester), Charles Hallahan (Bazooka), John De Santi (Benny), Fionnula Flanagan (Flo), Bert Remsen (Al), Leigh Hamilton (Louise), Esther Rolle (Mim), John Madden, John Matuszak

BEYOND THERAPY (New World) Producer, Steven M. Haft; Director, Robert Altman; Screenplay, Christopher Durang, Robert Altman; Based on the play by Christopher Durang; Executive Producer, Roger Berlind; Photography, Pierre Mignot; Supervising Editor, Pierre Mignot; Designer, Steve Dunn; Music, Stephen Altman, Gabriel Yared; Associate Producer, Scott Bushnell; Production Executives, Paul Almond, Matthew Seig; Production Manager, Daniel Wuhrmann; Assistant Directors, Yann Gilbert, Patrick Cartoux; Costumes, John Hay; Art Director, Annie Senechal; Assistant Art Director, Arnaud De Moleron; Costumes, Claudia Perino; Sound, Philippe Lioret, Daniel Belanger; Production Coordinator, Agnes Bermejo; Casting Assistant, Guylene Pean; Editor, Jennifer Auge; Assistant Editors, Pascal Marzin, Serge Rinaldi; Song, *"Someone to Watch Over Me,"* George and Ira Gershwin; Vocals, Yves Montand, Linda Ronstadt, Lena Horne; Color; Rated R; 93 minutes; January release. CAST: Julie Hagerty (Prudence), Jeff Goldblum (Bruce), Glenda Jackson (Charlotte), Tom Conti (Stuart), Christopher Guest (Bob), Genevieve Page (Zizi), Chris Campion (Andrew), Sandrine Dumas (Cindy), Bertrand Bonvoisin (Le Gerant), Nicole Evans (Cashier), Louis-Marie Taillefer (Le Chef), Matthew Lesniak (Mr. Bean), Laure Killing (Charlie), Gilbert Blin, Vincent Longuemare (Waiters), Francoise Armel, Sylvie Lenoir, Annie Monnier, Jeanne Cellard, Helene Constantine, Yvette Prayer, Joan Tyrrell (Zizi's Friends)

Scott Strader, Mariska Hargitay in "Jocks"
© *Crown International*

JOCKS (Crown International) Producer, Ahmet Yasa; Director, Steve Carver; Screenplay, Mike Lanahan, David Oas; Photography, Adam Greenberg; Editor, Richard Halsey; Production Manager, John Broderick; Assistant Directors, Michael Schroeder, Debra Duval; Production Coordinator, Tandi Slater; Assistant Art Director, Gregory R. Wolf; Set Decorator, Gregory Melton; Sound, Mark F. Ulano; Special Effects, Gary F. Bentley; Music Coordinator, David Backstrom; Songs, David McHugh, Phillip Kennard, Linda "Peaches" Green, various other artists; DeLuxe Color; Panavision; Rated R; 90 minutes; January release. CAST: Scott Strader (The Kid), Perry Lang (Jeff), Mariska Hargitay (Nicole), Richard Roundtree (Chip), R. G. Armstrong (Beetlebom), Katherine Kelly Lang (Julie), Christopher Lee (President White), Stoney Jackson (Andy), Adam Mills (Tex), Donald Gibb (Ripper), Tom Shadyac (Chris), Christopher Murphy (Tony)

HOUR OF THE ASSASSIN (Concorde) Executive Producer, Roger Corman; Producer/Director, Luis Llosa; Co-Producer, Mary Ann Fisher; Screenplay/Production Supervisor, Matt Leipzig; Associate Producers Margarita Morales, Rolando Ore; Editor, William Flicker; Photography, Cusi Barri; Music, Fred Myrow; Production Supervisor, Deborah Brock; Sound, Edgar Lostanau; Associate Producer/Special Effects, Fernando Vasquez de Velasco; Assistant Special Effects, Carlos Casella; Stunts, Patrick Statham, Miguel Tudela, Jose Luy; Casting, Daniel Camino, Juan Manuel Ochoa; Additional Editing, Bruce Stubblefield, Ricardo Fleiss; Assistant Editors, Larry Renick, Maria Ruiz; Orchestrations/Additional Music, Richard Emmett; Special Music Contributions, Danilo Losano, Adam Rudolth; Sound, David Lewis Yewdall, Dave West; Color; Rated R; 92 minutes; January release. CAST: Erik Estrada (Fiero), Robert Vaughn (Merrick), Laura Burton (Lavalle), Alfred Calderon (Ortiz), Roland Sacha (Folco), Francisco Giraldo (Villaverde), Javier Solis (Marcelo), Oswaldo Fernandez (Casals), Ramon Garcia Ribeyso (Andujar), Alberto Montalva (Costa), German Gonzales (Santiago), Reynaldo Arenas (Paladoro), Estela Paredes (Paladoro's Wife), Gustavo Maclenan (Doc), Ramon Garcia (Navarro), David Killerby (Oakland), Paul Dillon, Francisco Torres Rosa, Andres Dasso, Daniel Camino, Walter Frank, Alfredo Alvarez Calderon

Jeff Goldblum, Julie Hagerty
in "Beyond Therapy" © *New World*

Erik Estrada in "Hour of the Assassin"

**Lorin Dreyfuss, David Landsberg
in "Dutch Treat"** © *Cannon Films*

DUTCH TREAT (Cannon) Producers, Menahem Golan, Yoran Globus; Director, Boaz Davidson; Screenplay, Lorin Dreyfuss, David Landsberg; Editor, Bruria Davidson; Designer, Randy Ser; Music Producer, Larry Lee; Music, Steve Bates; Production Manager, Ephraim Schaffer; Assistant Directors, Donald J. Newman, Gail Joyce Fortmuller, Ernest Santell; Production Executive, Rony Yacov; Casting, Bonnie Pietila; Art Director, Phil Dagort; Sound, Itzhak Magall; Set Decorator, Robert E. Johnson; Special Effects, Eric Rylander, Marty Bresin, Wynn Rylander, Michael Scorr; Production Supervisor, Michael R. Sloan; Additional Editing, Nathan Zehavi;; Assistant Editors, Marva Fucci, Ilana Ben-Gigi, Michael Murphy, Natalie Matthews; *The Dolly Dots* Costumes, Jacqueline Saint-Anne; Assistant Costume Designer, Angee Becket; Production Coordinator, Carol Kravetz; Choreographer, Eddie Baytos; Songs by Michael Bishop and various other atists; Ultrastereo; TVC Color; Rated R; 94 minutes; January release. CAST: David Landsberg (Jerry), Lorin Dreyfuss (Norm), Ria Briesfief (Ria), Angela Groothuizen (Angela), Patty Zomer (Patty), Ester Oosterbeek (Ester), Sjeel Kramers (Sjeel), Ronnie Schell (Lou Winters), Carol Potter (Betsy Winters), Lee Shepherd (Duke Clark), Hank Garrett (Vito), Jack Bernardi (Jewish Man), Terry Camilleri (Klaveman), Richard Beauchamp (Rivero), Linda Lutz (Crazy Lucy), Robie Sella (Elmo), Rosey Brown (Tyrone), Barry Dennen (Nash), Steven Lee (Herbie), Greta Blackburn (Cathy Williams), Joseph Brutzman (Man at club), Shane McCamey (Peter), Burt Van Dyke (Louis), Bill Capizzi (Franco Montoya), Fredd Wayne (Judge), Herb Muller, Gail Neely, Cal Wilson, Michael Bell, Billy Johnson, Ras-11 Beasley, Laura Bassett, Joe Mascaro, Phil Rubenstein, Ernie Fragua, Herman Roeper, Jack Karaco, Gary Hudson, Sam Nickens, George Solomon, Leonard Denato, Tim Haldeman, Ephraim Schaffe, Marilyn Morgan Holt, Robert Nadder, Wayne Hunt Anderson, Chris Oswald, Fil Formicola, Harry W. Keller, Joe Lala, R. J. Ganzert, Jane Singer, Darryl Henriques, Bobby Giordano, James Gilliam, John McCarthy, Albert Lord, Barry Pearl, Mark A. Richardson, Mark Edner, Brent Stevens, Dave Setzer, Terry Quinn, Michael Hansen, John Nyman, Kurt La Bean, Larry Hester, Greg Sutton, Tony Gilkysn, Ken Sira, Scott Hatch, Eddie Baytos, Rolf Leenderts, Bet Bunschoten, Inge Ipenburg, Monique Spijker, Francis Peach, Greg Gault, Mischa Hausserman

**Lorin Dreyfuss, David Landsberg
in "Dutch Treat"** © *Cannon Films*

WARRIOR QUEEN (Seymour Borde & Associates) Producer, Harry Alan Towers; Director, Chuck Vincent; Screenplay, Rick Marx; Based on a story by Peter Welbeck (Towers); Photography, Lorenzo Battaglia; Editors, Chuck Vincent, Joel Bender, Jim Sanders, Tony Delcampo; Music, Ian Shaw, Kai Joffe; Designer/Costumes, Lucio Parise; Sound, Larry Revene; Assistant Director, Per Sjostedt; Associate Producers, Aristide Massaccesi, Donatella Donati; A Lightning Pictures Production; Color; Rated R; 69 minutes; January release. CAST: Sybil Danning (Bernice), Donald Pleasence (Clodius), Richard Hill (Marcus), Josephine Jacqueline Jones (Chloe), Taly Chanel (Vespa), Stasia Micula (Philomena/Augusta), Suzanna Smith (Veneria), David Cain Haughton (Victor), Mario Cruciani (Roberto), Marco Tullio Cau (Goliath)

VALET GIRLS (Empire Pictures) Producer, Dennis Murphy; Director, Rafal Zielinski; Screenplay, Clark Carlton; Photography, Nicholas von Sternberg; Editor, Akiko B. Metz; Music, Robert Parr; Sound, Ed White; Art Director, Dins Danielsen; Production Manager, Bill Berry; Assistant Director, Scott White; Costumes, Kathie Clark; Stunts, Dan Bradley; Special Effects Makeup, John Buechler; A Lexyn Production; Color; R; 82 minutes; January release. CAST: Meri D. Marshall (Lucy), April Stewart (Rosalind), Mary Kohnert (Carnation), Christopher Weeks (Dirk Zebra), Patricia Scott Michel (Tina Zebra), Jon Sharp (Lindsay), Michael Karm (Alvin Sunday), Steve Lyon (Ike), Randy Gallion (Ramon), Stuart Fratkin, John Terlesky, Jeane Byron, Charles Cooper, Kenny Sacha, Richard Erdman, Rick Lieberman, Bridget Sienna, Matt Landers, Ron Jeremy

THE KINDRED (F/M Entertainment) Producer, Jeffrey Obrow; Executive Producer Joel Freeman; Co-producer, Stacey Giachino; Directors, Jeffrey Obrow, Stephen Carpenter; Screenplay, Stephen Carpenter, Jeffrey Obrow, John Penney, Earl Ghaffari, Joseph Stefano; Photography, Stephen Carpenter; Editors, John Penny, Earl Ghaffari; Music, David Newman; Designer, Chris Hopkins; Art Director, Becky Block; Set Decorator, Susan Emshwiller; Costumes, Lynne A. Holmes; Special Creature, Michael John McCraken; Assistant Director, David Householter; Associate Producer, Diane Nabatoff; Casting, Janet Hirshenson, Jane Jenkins, Denise Chamian; Technicolor; Rated R; 91 minutes; January release. CAST: David Allen Brooks (John Hollins), Rod Steiger (Dr. Phillip Lloyd), Amanda Pays (Melissa Leftridge), Talia Balsam (Sharon Raymond), Kim Hunter (Amanda Hollins), Timothy Gobbs (Hart Phillips), Peter Frechette (Brad Baxter), Julia Montgomery (Cindy Russell), Bunki Z (Nell Valentine)

RETURN TO HORROR HIGH (New World) Executive Producer, Greg H. Sims; Producer, Mark Lisson; Director, Bill Froehlich; Screenplay, Bill Froehlich Mark Lisson, Dana Escalante, Greg H. Sim; Photography, Roy Wagner; Editor, Nancy Forner; Music, Stacy Widelitz; Designer, Greta Grigorian; Costumes, Marcy Grace Froehlich; Associate Producers, Jason Hoffs, Joan Baribeault; Casting, Linda Francis; Assistant Director, Rachel Talalay; In association with Balcor Film Investors; Color; Rated R; 95 minutes; January release. CAST: Lori Lehin (Callie), Brendan Hughes (Steven Blake), Alex Rocco (Barry Sleerik), Scott Jacoby (Josh Forbes), Andy Romano (Principal Kastleman), Richard Brestoff (Arthur Lyman), Al Fann (Amos), Pepper Martin (Chief Deyner), Maureen McCormick (Officer Tyler), Vince Edwards (Richard Birnbaum)

HUNTER'S BLOOD (Concorde) Executive Producer, Judith F. Schuman; Producer, Myrl A. Schreibman; Director, Robert C. Hughes; Screenplay, Emmet Alston; Based on novel by Jere Cunningham; Photography, Tom DeNove; Editor, Barry Zetlin; Costumes, Jacqueline Johnson; Art Director, Douglas Forsmith; Music, John D'Andrea; Songs, Dan Hamilton; Vocals, Dan Hamilton, Joe Frank, Weber Reynolds; Associate Producer, George Springmeyer; Casting, Al Onorato, Jerold Franks; Production Manager, Andrew LaMarca; Stunts, Rawn Hutchinson; Production Associate, Kathy Kusner; Assistant Directors, Richard Kanter, Tom Seldon, John Keefer; Set Decorator, Catherine Wilshire; Sound, Larry Hooberry; Mechanical Effects, Scott Haas; Special Make-Up Effects, Douglas J. White, John R. Fifer, Allan A. Apone, Steve Frakes; Co-Assistant Producer, Alexander Beck; Assistant Editor, Lisa Davis; Color; Rated R; 102 minutes; January release. CAST: Samuel Bottoms (David Rand), Kim Delaney (Melanie), Clu Gulager (Mason Rand), Ken Swofford (Al Coleman), Joey Travolta (Marty Adler), Mayf Nutter (Ralph Coleman), Lee de Broux (Red Beard), Bruce Glover (One Eye), Billy Drago (Snake), Mickey Jones (Wash Pot), Charles Cyphers (Woody), Bryan Rasmussen (Purty Boy), Joe Verroca (Ants), David DeShay (Tull), Michael Muscat (Bubba), Connie Danese (Tracy), Gene Glazer (Harris), Ray Young (Brinkley), Burr Middleton, Billy Million, Allen Lerner, Ron LaPere, Billy Bob Thornton, Beverly E. Schwartz, Nan J. Seitz, Jerry Ratay, Dennis Dorantes, Daniel McFeeley

DEATH BEFORE DISHONOR (New World) Producer, Lawrence Kubik; Director, Terry J. Leonard; Story/Screenplay, John Gatliff, Lawrence Kubik; Photography, Don Burgess; Editor, Steve Mirkovich; Music, Brian May; Color; Rated R; 96 minutes; February release. CAST: Fred Dryer (Burns), Joey Gian (Ramirez), Sasha Mitchell (Ruggieri), Peter Parros (James), Brian Keith (Halloran), Paul Winfield (Ambassador), Joanna Pacula (Elli), Kasey Walker (Maude), Rockne Tarkington (Jihad), Dan Chodos (Amin), Muhamad Bakri (Gavril)

MORGAN STEWART'S COMING HOME aka "Homefront" (New Century/Vista) Producer, Stephen Friedman Director, Alan Smithee; Screenplay, Ken Hixon, David Titcher; Photography, Richard Brooks; Editor, Bob Letterman; Music, Peter Bernstein; Designer, Charles Bennett; Set Decorator, Victor Kempster; Sound, Danny Michael; Assistant Director, Lewis Gould; Associate Producer, Patrick McCormick; Costumes, Molly Maginnis; A Kings Road Production; DeLuxe Color; Rated PG-13; 96 minutes; February release. CAST: Jon Cryer (Morgan Stewart), Lynn Redgrave (Nancy Stewart), Nicholas Pryor (Tom Stewart), Viveka Davis (Emily), Paul Gleason (Jay Sprinsteen), Andrew Duncan (General Fenton), Savely Kramorov (Ivan), John David Cullum (Garrett), no other credits supplied.

MY DARK LADY (Film Gallery) Executive Producer/Director, King Keller; Producers, Carole Terranova, Stratton Rawson; Screenplay, Fred A. Keller, Gene Brook, Frederick King Keller; From origiinal story by Fred A. Keller; Photography, Thom Marini; Editor, Darren Kloomok; Music, Ken Kaufman; Designer, Stratton Rawson; Set Decorator, Gary Matwijkow; Costumes, Elizabeth Haas Keller; Sound, Dan Sack; Assistant Director, Rick Seeberg; Color; Not rated; 104 minutes; February release. CAST: Fred A. Keller (Sam Booth), Lorna Hill (Lorna Dahomey), Raymond Holder (Malcolm Dahomey), John Buscaglia (Jonathan Park), Evan Perry (Samuel T. MacMillan), Barbara Cady (Sarah Teasdale), Stuart Roth (Horace Babinski), Tess Spangler (Minnie O'Hara), Steven Cooper (Terry Terranova)

CRY WILDERNESS (Visto International) Producers, Philip Yordan, Jay Schlossberg-Cohen; Executive Producer, William F. Messeli; Co-producer, Gene S. Ruggiero; Associate Producer, James E. Davis; Director, Jay Schlossberg-Cohen; Screenplay, Philip Yordan; Photography, Joseph D. Urbanczyk; Music, Fritz Heede; Music Supervisor, Ralph Ives; Sound, Bruce Bell; Color; Rated PG; 95 minutes; February release. CAST: Eric Foster (Paul Cooper), Maurice Grandmaison (Will Cooper), Griffin Casey (Morgan), John Tallman (Jim), Faith Clift (Dr. Helen Foster) no other credits supplied

NICE GIRLS DON'T EXPLODE (New World) Producers, Doug Curtis, John Wells; Director, Chuck Martinez; Screenplay, Paul Harris; Photography, Steven Katz; Editor, Wende Phifer Mate; Music, Brian Banks, Anthony Marinelli; Designer, Sarina Rothstein; Costumes, Belinda Wells; Production Executive, Bob Stein; Associate Producers, Jim Moores, Belinda Wells, Paul Harris; Makeup, Margaret Sunshine; Color; Rated PG; 92 minutes; February release. CAST: Barbara Harris (Mom), Michelle Meyrink (April), William O'Leary (Andy), Wallace Shawn (Ellen), James Nardini (Ken), Margot Gray (Little April), Jonas Baugham (Little Andy), William Kuhlke (Dr. Stewart)

WINNERS TAKE ALL (Apollo Pictures, Inc.) Producers, Tom Tatum, Christopher W. Knight; Director, Fritz Kiersch; Executive Producer, David R. Axelrod; Screenplay, Ed Turner; Music, Doug Timm; Color; Rated PG-13; 105 minutes; February release. CAST: Don Michael Paul, Kathleen York, Robert Krantz, Deborah Richter (No other credits submitted)

R. E. M. in "Athens, GA."
© *ASA Communications*

ATHENS, GA (ASA Communications, Inc.) Producer, Bill Cody; Director/Screenplay, Tony Gayton; Executive Producers, Spotlight Productions, Inc.; Photography, Jim Herbert; Editor, Adam Wolfe; Assistant Producers, Clark Hunter, Lisa Mae Wells; Assistant Camera, Lance Wyatt; Sound, Jim Hawkins; Assistant Editor, Amy Tomkins; Sound, B & B Sound; Editorial Advisor, Thom Noble; A Subterranean Productions & Spotlight, Inc. Production; Songs by various artists; Soundtrack on IRS Records; Documentary; Not rated; 82 minutes; February release. CAST: The B-52's, Bar-B-Q Killers, Dreams So Real, Flat Duo Jets, Kilkenny Cats, Limbo District, Love Tractor, Pylon, R.E.M., The Squalls, Time Toy, Jeremy Ayers, William Orten Carlton, Rev. Howard Finster, Jim Herbert, Rev. John D. Ruth, John Seawright, Chris Slay, Herbert Abrahams, David Giles, Paul Lombard, Bucky Redwine, Walter Rittenberry, Errol Stewart, Mike Webb, J. J., Orf

SWEET REVENGE (Concorde) Producers, Brad Krevoy, Steven Stabler; Director, Mark Sobel; Screenplay, Steven M. Krauzer, Tim McCoy; Additional Dialogue, Jim Beaver; Story, Michael Jones, Randy Kornfeld; Executive Producers, Roger Corman, Brad Krevoy; Associate Producers, Victor Ordonez, Vivian Recio; Production Executive, Bob Waters; Casting, Cecily Adams, Stacey Noel; Music, Ernest V. Troost; Orchestrations/Music Production Supervisor, Barb Luby; Music Sound Design, Gilbert Kaufman; Additional Casting, Dadalee May, Chuck Bismark, Ernie Davie; Story Consultant, Matt Leipzig; Production Coordinators, Ann Narus, Germaine Simiens; Production Manager, Bugsy Dabao; Assistant Directors, Dennis Marasigan, Noli Tomacruz; Photography, Shane D. Kelly; Designer, Vic Dabao; Sound, George Mahlberg; Stunts, Ray Lykins, Mandy Bustamante, Kay Kimler, Kathy Lykins; Effects, Chagar, Mariano Garcia, Joe Cadores, Benjamin Luciano; A Motion Picture Corp. of America Film; Songs, Ron Artis; Vocals, Victoria Artis; Editor, Michael S. Murphy; Associate Editor, Patrick Rand; Production Coordinator, Eric Brooks; Assistant Editors, Tim Bismark, Chantel Feghali; Color; Rated R; 78 minutes; February release. CAST: Nancy Allen (Jillian Gray), Ted Shackelford (Boone), Martin Landau (Cicero), Sal Landi (Gil), Michelle Little (Lee), Gina Gershon (K. C.), Lotis Key (Sonya), Stacey Adams (Tina), Leo Martinez (Buddah), Angelo Castro, Jr. (Ricardo), Ramone D'Salva (Dok), Paul Holme (Auction M.C.), Ruth Arras (Jaimie Gray), Betty Mae Peccio (Mai), Crispin Medina (Tak), Richard Kind (Tho), Ronnie Lazaro (Jimmy Lee), Jeffrey Hammet (Frank), Ernie David (Fat Man), Tony Gonzalvez (Count), Cecile Krevoy (Countess), Billy Gyenes (First Mate), John Kater (Derelict)

Martin Landau in "Sweet Revenge"
© *Concorde*

Nancy Allen, Ted Shackelford in "Sweet Revenge"
© *Concorde*

Sho Kosugi in "Rage of Honor"
© *Trans World Entertainment*

IRA, YOU'LL GET INTO TROUBLE (New Line Cinema) Producer/Director/Photography, Stephen A. Sbarge; Editor, Mark Rappaport; Documentary, 1970; Black & White; Not rated; 85 minutes; February release

FILMING OTHELLO (FILM FORUM) Producers, Klaus Hellwig, Juergen Hellwig; Director, Orson Welles; Photography, Gary Graver; Music, Francesco Lavagnino, Alberto Barbaris; Editor, Marty Roth; Documentary; West Germany, 1978; In English; Not rated; 90 minutes; February release. CAST: Orson Welles, Michael MacLiammoir, Hilton Edwards, others not listed

MANNEQUIN (20th Century Fox) Producer, Art Levinson; Director, Michael Gottlieb; Screenplay, Edward Rugoff, Michael Gottlieb; Executive Producers, Edward Rugoff, Joseph Farrell; Photography, Tim Suhrstedt; Designer, Josan Russo; Editor, Richard Halsey; Music Producer, Joel Sill; Music, Sylvester LeVay; Casting, Marci Liroff; Production Manager, John J. Smith; Assistant Directors, Michael Haley, James Skotchdopole, Carla Corwin; Choreography, Vincent Paterson; Animation Sequence, Sally Cruikshank; Associate Producer, Catherine Paura; Additional Editor, Frank Jimenez; Production Supervisor, Norman Wallerstein; Art Director, Richard Amend; Set Decorator, Elise "Cricket" Rowland; Assistant Set Decorators, Abbee Goldstein, Kara Lindstrom; Costumes, Lisa Jensen; Special Effects, Phil Cory, Hans Metz, Ray Svedin; Sound, Jan Brodin; Mannequins by Tanya Wolf-Ragir; Assistant Editor, Cheryl Bloch; Animation, Ted and Gerry Wollery, Playhouse Pictures; Songs, *"Nothing's Gonna Stop Us Now"* by Albert Hammond, Diane Warren/*"In My Wildest Dreams"* by Bob Crewe, Jerry Corbetta, Charlotte Caffey/*"Do You Dream About Me"* by Diane Warren; Music Performances, Starship, Belinda Carlisle, Alisha, The Temptations; Presented by Gladden Entertainment; DuArt Color; Rated PG; 90 minutes; February release. CAST: Andrew McCarthy (Jonathan Switcher), Kim Cattrall (Emmy), Estelle Getty (Claire Timkin), James Spader (Richards), G. W. Bailey (Felix), Carole Davis (Roxie), Stephen Vinovich (B. J. West), Christopher Maher (Armand), Meshach Taylor (Hollywood), Phyllis Newman (Emmy's Mother), Phil Rubenstein, Jeffery Lampert, Kenneth Lloyd, Jake Jundeff, Harvey Levine, Thomas J. McCarthy, R. L. Ryan, Glenn Davish, Steve Lippe, Lee Golden, Vernon R. DeVinney, Olivia Frances Williams, Charles N. Lord, Ben Hammer, Jane Moore, Jane Carol Simms, Judi Goldhand, Lara Harris, Dan Lounsberry, Kitty Minehart, Katherine Conklin, Andrew Hill Newman, Bill Greene

Andrew McCarthy, Kim Cattrall in "Mannequin"
© *20th Century Fox/Gale Adler*

RAGE OF HONOR (Trans World Entertainment) Exeuctive Producers, Moshe Diamant, Moshe Barkat, Sunil R. Shah; Producer, Don Van Atta; Director, Gordon Hessler; Screenplay, Robert Short, Wallace Bennet; Story, Robert Short; Photography, Julio Bragado; Editor, Robert Gordon; Music, Stelvio Cipriani; Designer, Adrain Gorton; Art Direction, Kirk Demusiak, Abel Fagellio; Special Effects, Paul Staples; Martial Arts Choreography/Special Weapons Designer, Kosugi; Production Supervisor, Barry Parnell; Casting, Barbara Hanley, Kathy Henderson; A Rage Production; Dolby Stereo; Technicolor; Rated R; 91 minutes; February release. CAST: Sho Kosugi (Shiro Tanaka), Lewis Van Bergen, Robin Evans, Gerry Gibson, Chip Lucia, Richard Wiley, Carlos Estrada, Alan Amiel

CRYSTAL HEART (New World) Producer, Carlos Vasallo; Director, Gil Bettman; Screenplay, Linda Shayne; From a story by Alberto Vazquez-Figueroa; Photography, Alexander (Alejandro) Ulloa; Editor, Nicholas Wentworth; Music, Joel Goldsmith; Designer, Jose Maria Alarcon; Sound, Manuel Rincon; Costumes, Etta Leff; Choreography, Marcea D. Lane; Assistant Director, Alvaro Forque; Casting, Vikkie Vicars; Dolby Stereo; Technicolor; Rated R; 103 minutes; February release. CAST: Lee Curreri (Christopher Newley), Tawny Kitaen (Alley Daniels), Lloyd Bochner (Frank Newley), May Heatherly (Diana Newley), Simon Andreu (Jean-Claude), Marina Saura (Justine), LeGena Lookabill (Jasper).

THE BIKINI SHOP (Int. Film Marketing) Producers, Gary Mehlman, J. Kenneth Rotcop; Co-producer, Leo Leichter; Executive Producers, Charles C. Thieriot, Andrew Bullians, Jean Bullians, Sandy Climan; Director/Screenplay, David Wechter; Photography, Tom Richmond; Editor, Jean-Marc Vasseur; Music Supervisor, Don Perry; Art Director, Dian Perryman; Set Decorator, Kayla Koeber; Costumes, Rita Riggs; Sound, Dana Gray; Associate Producer, Ron Bechtel; Assistant Director, Cliford C. Coleman; A Westcom production; In association with Romax Prods.; Dolby Stereo; CFI Color; Rated R; 99 minutes; February release. CAST: Michael David Wright (Alan), Bruce Greenwood (Todd), Barbra Horan (Ronnie), Debra Blee (Jane), Jay Robinson (Ben), Galyn Gorg (Cindy), Ami Julius (Kathy), Frank Nelson (Richard J. Remington), no other credits supplied

ALIEN PREDATOR (Trans World Entertainment) Executive Producers, Helen Sarlui, Eduard Sarlui; Producers, Deran Sarafian, Carlos Aured; Director/Screenplay, Deran Sarafian; Based on Screenplay *"Massacre at R.V. Park"* By Noah Blogh; Photography, Tote Trenas; Editors, Dennis Hill, Peter Teschner; Music, Chase/Rucker Prods.; Sound, Anthony Bloch; Co-producer, Michael Sourapas; Production Manager, Joe Ochoa; Special Effects, John Balandin; Casting, Lee Payne; A Continental Motion Pictures production; Color; Rated R; 90 minutes; February release. CAST: Dennis Christopher (Damon), Martin Hewitt (Michael), Lynn-Holly Johnson (Samantha), Luis Prendes (Prof. Tracer), J. O. Bosso (Capt. Wells), no other credits supplied

WORKING GIRLS (Miramax Films) Producer, Lizzie Borden, Andi Gladstone; Director/Story, Lizzie Borden; Screenplay, Lizzie Borden, Sandra Kay; Photography, Judy Irola; Music, David van Tieghem; Color; Not rated; 90 minutes; February release. CAST: Louise Smith (Molly), Ellen McElduff (Lucy), Amanda Goodwin (Dawn), Marusia Zach (Gina), Janne Peters (April), Helen Nicholas (Mary), No other credits provided.

EAT AND RUN (New World) Producer, Jack Briggs; Director, Christopher Hart; Screenplay, Stan Hart, Christopher Hart; Photography, Dyanna Taylor; Editor, Pamela S. Arnold; Music, Scott Harper; Color; Rated R; 85 minutes; February release. CAST: Ron Silver (Mickey McSorely), Sharon Schlarth (Judge Cheryl Cohen), R. L. Ryan (Murray Creature), John F. Fleming (Captain), Derek Murcott (Sorely McSorely), Robert Silver (Pusher), Mimi Cecchini (Grandmother)

CYCLONE (CineTel) Producer, Paul Hertzberg; Director, Fred Olen Ray; Screenplay, Paul Garson, T. L. Lankford; Story, Fred Olen Ray; Photography, Paul Elliot; Music, David A. Jackson, James Saad; Art Director, Maxine Shepard; Costumes, Dorothy Amos; Special Effects, Kevin McCarthy, Tracy Design Inc; Color; Rated R; 83 minutes; February release; CAST: Heather Thomas (Teri Marshall), Jeffrey Combs (Rick Davenport), Ashley Ferrare (Carla Hastings), Dar Robinson (Rolf), Martine Beswicke (Waters), Robert Quarry (Knowles), Martin Landau (Bosarian), Huntz Hall (Long John), Troy Donahue (Bob Jenkins), Michael Reagan (McCardy), Tim Conway, Jr. (Barrell), Dawn Wildsmith (Henna), Bruce Fairbairn (Lt. Cutter), Sam Hiona (Buyer), John Stewart, Paul Short, Bob Bragg (Scruffies), Lauren Hertzberg, Jordan Hertzberg (Children with groceries), Billy Joe Brown, David Jackson, Tony Brewster, Gary Bettmann, Grant Waldman (Policemen), Paul Stuart, Neil Lundell (Paramedics), Jesse Long (Photographer), Jack Davidson (Lava Club Manager), Michael Sonye, Tom Cush, Joe Ramirez, Kingsley Candler (Haunted Garage), Russ Tamblyn

WALK LIKE A MAN (MGM/UA) Producer, Leonard Kroll; Executive Producer/Screenplay, Robert Klane; Director, Melvin Frank; Photography, Victor J. Klemper; Editors, Bill Butler, Steve Butler; Music, Lee Holdridge; Designer, Bill Malley; Set Design, Richard J. Lawrence; Sound, Gary Bourgeois, Chris Carpenter, Dean Okrand; Assistant Director, Roger Joseph Pugliese; Casting, Jane Jenkins, Janet Hirshenson, Denise Chamian; from MGM Pictures; Metrocolor; Rated PG; 86 minutes; March release. CAST: Howie Mandel (Bobo Shand), Christopher Lloyd (Reggie Henry), Cloris Leachman (Margaret Shand), Colleen Camp (Rhonda Shand), Amy Steel (Penny), no other credits supplied

HARD TICKET TO HAWAII (Malibu Bay Films) Producer, Arlene Sidaris; Director/Screenplay, Andy Sidaris; Photography, Howard Wexler; Editor, Michael Haight; Music, Gary Stockdale; Assistant Director, M. M. Freedman; Designers Sal Grasso, Peter Munneke; Costumes, Fionn; Martial Arts Choreography, Harold Diamond; Skateboard Stunts, Russell Howell; Associate Producer, Tina Scott; United Color; Rated R; 96 minutes; March release. CAST: Ronn Moss (Rowdy Abilene), Dona Speir (Donna), Hope Marie Carlton (Taryn), Harold Diamond (Jade), Rodrigo Obregon (Seth Romero), Cynthia Brimhall (Edy), Patty Duffek (Pattycakes), Wolf Larson (Jimmy-John Jackson), Lory Green (Rosie), Rustam Branaman (Kimo), David DeShay (Ashley), Michael Andrews (Michelle.Michael), Andy Sidaris (Whitey), Kwan Hi Lim, Joseph Hieu, Peter Bromilow, Glen Chin, Russell Howell, Richard LePore, Joey Meran, Shawne Zarubica

OMEGA SYNDROME (New World) Executive Producer, George Zecevic; Producer, Luigi C. Cingolani; Director, Joseph Manduke; Screenplay, John Sharkey; Photography, Harvey Genkins; Editor, Stephen A. Isaacs; Music, Nicholas Carras, Jack Cookerly; Sound, Kim Ornitz; Art Director, Nancy Arnold; Assistant Director, James M. Freitag; Production Manager, John Curran; Stunts, Spiro Razatos; Production Supervisor, Bud S. Isaacs; Associate Producer, Paul Di Salvo; Casting, Barbara Remsen & Associates, Ann Remsen; In association with Prey Presentations and Smart Egg Pictures; United Color; Rated R; 85 minutes; March, release. CAST: Ken Wahl (Jack Corbett), George DiCenzo (Phil), Nicole Eggert (Jessie), Doug McClure (Det. Milnor), Xander Berkeley, Ron Kuhlman, Bill Morey, Robert Gray, Colm Meaney, Bob Tzudiker, Al White, Pati Tippo, Robert Kim, George Fisher, Christopher Doyle

HEAT (New Century/Vista Film Company) Producers, Keith Rotman, George Pappas; Director, R. M. Richards; Screenplay, William Goldman; Based on the novel by William Goldman; Photography, James Contner; Editor, Jeffrey Wolf; Music, Michael Gibbs; Color; Rated R; 101 minutes; March release. CAST: Burt Reynolds (Nick Escalante), Karen Young (Holly), Peter MacNicol (Cyrus Kinnick), Howard Hesseman (Pinchus Zion), Neill Barry (Danny DeMarco), Diana Scarwid (Cassie), Joe Mascola (Baby), Alfie Wise (Felix)

"Hell Squad"
© *Cannon Films*

HELL SQUAD (Cannon International) Producer/Director/Screenplay, Kenneth Hartford; Executive Producers, Menahem Golan, Yoram Globus; Photography, John McCoy; Editor, Robert Ernst; Music, Charles P. Barnett; Production Coordinator, Ben Brothers; Production Manager, Maryann Zvoleff; Assistant Director, Steve Wallace; Production Staging, Ewing Brown; Choreography, Andrea Hartford; Sound, Robert Bourne, Dave Fisher, Jasper Watt; Costumes, Connie Porter, Claire Clair; Showgirl Costumes, Suzy Vegas; Special Effects, Harry Woolman; Song, Kenneth Hartford; A Cinevid presentation of an Eastern Hemisphere Production; Color; Rated PG; 87 minutes; March release. CAST: Bainbridge Scott, Glen Hartford, Tina Ledderman, Maureen Kelly, Penny Prior, Kim Baucum, Delynn Gardner, Lisa Nottingham, Kathy Jinnett, Loren Chamberlain, Marvin Miller, William Bryant, Walter Cox, Lee Coy, Sally Swift, Jace Damon, Robert Searles, Robert Herts, Frank Romano, Steve Wallace, Maryann Zvoleff, Gary Sebunia, Dennis MacArthur, Larry Lyons, Philip Rhee, Tony, Dawn Smith, Sheyla Havard, Joyce Rush, Mary Asta, Marcia Reibel, Hisham Wer, John Diaz, William Meyers, Hugo Limon, Mark Brandon, Toni Alessandrini, Karey Sinclair, Anaheed, Narayana, Hubert Wells, Julian Sylvester

DOLLS (Empire Pictures) Producer, Brian Yuzna; Executive Producer, Charles Band; Director, Stuart Gordon; Screenplay, Ed Naha; Photography, Mac Ahlberg; Doll Effects, John and Vivian Brunnee, Giancarlo Del Brocco, David Allen; Color; Rated R; 77 minutes; March release. CAST: Ian Patrick Williams (David Bower), Carolyn Purdy-Gordon (Rosemary Bower), Carrie Lorraine (Judy Bower), Guy Rolfe (Gabriel Hartwicke), Hilary Marson (Hilary Hartwicke), Bunty Bailey (Isabel Prange), Cassie Stuart (Enid Tilley), Stephen Lee (Ralph Morris), no other credits provided

THE HERO'S JOURNEY: THE WORLD OF JOSEPH CAMPBELL (Direct Cinema) Executive Producer, Stuart L. Brown; Producer, William Free; Co-Producer, Janelle Balnicke; Directors, Janelle Balnicke, David Kennard; Screenplay, William Free, Phil Cousineau, Janelle Balnicke; Editor, Yasha Aginsky; Narrator, Peter Donat; Associate Executive Producer, Robert Cockrell; Associate Producer, Phil Cousineau; Consulting Producer, David Kennard; New York Sequences Producer, Michael G. Lemle; Music, Rand Weatherwax, Mickey Hart; Photography, Erik Daarstad, H. J. Brown, Stephen Lighthill, Joseph Montgomery; Sound, Courtney Goodin, Will Harvey; Assistant Editor, Laura Stuchinsky; Documentary; Not rated; 58 minutes; March release

Peter MacNicol, Burt Reynolds in "Heat"
© *New Century/Vista*

Joseph Campbell in "A Hero's Journey"
© *Direct Cinema*

David Birney in "Prettykill"
© *Spectrafilm*

EVIL DEAD 2: DEAD BY DAWN (Rosebud Releasing Corp.)
Producer, Robert G. Tapert; Director, Sam Raimi; Screenplay, Sam
Raimi, Scott Spiegel; Music, Joseph LoDuca; Special Make-up, Mark
Shostrom; Photography, Peter Deming; Night Photography, Eugene
Shlugleit; Editor, Kaye Davis; Production Manager, Joseph C. Still-
man; Assistant Directors, Joseph Winogradoff, K. Siobhan Phelan; Art
Directors, Philip Duffin, Randy Bennett; Set Decorator, Elizabeth
Moore; Sound, Tom Morrison; Special Effects, Vern Hyde, Dale
Johnson, Dave Thiry; Production Coordinator, Elaine Dysinger; An-
imated Dance Sequence, Doug Beswick; Choreography, Susan Labatt,
Andrea Brown, Tam G. Warner; Technicolor; Not Rated; 85 minutes;
March release. CAST: Bruce Campbell (Ash), Sarah Berry (Annie),
Dan Hicks (Jake), Kassie Wesley (Bobby Joe), Theodore Raimi (Pos-
sessed Henrietta), Denise Bixler (Linda), Richard Domeier (Ed), John
Peaks (Prof. Knowby), Lou Hancock (Henrietta), William Preston
Robertson (Voice)

PRETTY SMART (New World) Producers, Ken Solomon, Jeff Be-
gun; Co-producer, Melanie J. Alschuler; Director, Dimitri Logothetis;
Screenplay, Dan Hoskins; Story, Jeff Begun, Melanie J. Alschuler;
Photography, Dimitri Papacostantis; Editor, Daniel Gross; Music, Jay
Levy, Eddie Arkin; Designer Beau Peterson; Costumes, Gaelle Allen;
Casting, F. Daniel Somrack, Kostanti Tzoumas; Presented by Balcor
Film Investors in association with Chroma III and First American Film
Capital; Color; Rated R; 84 minutes; March release. CAST: Tricia
Leigh Fisher (Daphne Ziegler), Lisa Lorient (Jennifer Ziegler), Dennis
Cole (Richard Crawley), Patricia Arquette (Zero), Paris Vaughan
(Torch), Kimberly B. Delfin (Yuko), Brad Zutaut (Alexis), Kim Wal-
trip (Sara)

THE SUPERNATURALS (Republic Entertainment International)
Executive Producers/Screenplay, Michael S. Murphey, Joel Soisson;
Director, Armand Mastroianni; Executive Producers, Mel Pearl, Don
Levin; Photography, Peter Collister; Music, Robert O. Ragland; Pro-
duction Manager, Angela Heald; Art Director, Jo-ann Chorney; Special
Effects, Gregory Landerer; Associate Producers, Victoria Plummer,
William Fay; Color; Rated R; 80 minutes; March release. CAST:
Maxwell Caulfield (Pvt. Ray Ellis), Nichelle Nichols (Sgt. Leona
Hawkins), Talia Balsam (Ptc. Angela Lejune), Bradford Bancroft (Ptc.
Tom Weir), Levar Burton (Ptc. Michael Osgood), Bobby Di Cicco
(Ptc. Tim Cort), Margaret Shendal (Melanie), Patrick "Grampy" David
(Old Man), James Kirkwood (Captain), no other credits supplied

PRETTYKILL (Spectrafilm) Executive Producer, Sandy Howard;
Producers, John R. Bowey, Martin Walters; Director, George Kac-
zender; Screenplay, Sandra K. Bailey; Photography, Joao Fernandes;
Associate Producers, David Witz, Michael Masciarelli; Music, Robert
Ragland; Editor, Tom Merchant; Casting, Paul Bengston, David Cohn,
Anne Tait, Diane Polley, David Tochterman; Production Executive,
Gary Johnson; Production Associates, Risa Gertner, Chris Koseluk;
Production Manager, Daniel Nyberg; Assistant Directors, Richard
Flower, Rocco Gismondo, Yaseen Lachporia; Art Directors, Andris
Hausmanis, Jimmy Williams; Set Decorator, Jeff Cutler; Production
Coordinators, Justine Estee, Kristin Smith, Sandra Sereda; Sound,
Daniel Latour, Margaret Duke; Costumes, Trish Bakker; Stunts, Shane
Cardwell, Dan Bradley; Assistant Editors, Margaret Carlton, David
Finkelstein, Marion Siwek, Carol Hogan; Color; Rated R; 95 minutes;
March release. CAST: David Birney (Sgt. Larry Turner), Season
Hubley (Heather Todd), Susannah York (Toni), Yaphet Kotto (Harris),
Suzanne Snyder (Francie), Germaine Houde (Jacque Mercier), Lenore
Zann (Carrie), Vito Rezza (Bartender), Marsha Moreau (Stephie),
Sarah Polley (Karla), Peter Colvey (Assistant), Tim Burd (Cab Driver),
Anna Louise Richardson (Courtney), O. L. Duke (Eddie K.), Heather
Smith (Eve), Erik King (Sullivan), Richard Fitzpatrick (Policeman),
Ron White (Rickert), Gary Majchrizak (Lightnin' Boy), Louis Turenne
(Ambassador), J. Winston Carroll (Smiley), Catherine Gallant (Det.
Green), Philip Akin (Joey), Al Bernado (Vendor), Belinda Metz (Es-
cort), Garrick Hagon (Chambers), Paul Haddad (Lover), Allan Royal
(Conley Reid)

LILY TOMLIN (Broomfield Churchill Productions) Producers/
Directors, Joan Churchill, Nicholas Broomfield; Photography, Joan
Churchill; Sound/Editor, Nicholas Broomfield; In association with
Channel Four Television, Public Television Stations and the Corpora-
tion for Public Broadcasting; Documentary; Color; Not rated; 90
minutes; March release. WITH: Lily Tomlin, Jane Wagner, and others.
No other credits provided

THE HANOI HILTON (Cannon Group) Producers, Menahem
Golan, Yoram Globus; Director/Screenplay, Lionel Chetwynd; Editor,
Penelope Shaw; Music, Jimmy Webb; Designer, R. Clifford Searcy;
Photography, Mark Irwin; Production Manager, Joel Glickman; Assis-
tant Directors, Bob Bender, Mike Katleman, Robert Engelman; Pro-
duction Executives, Rony Yacov, Nancy Rae Stone; Co-Executive
Producer, Stephen Dart; Casting, Perry Bullington; Art Director, Carol
Bosselman; Assistant Art Director, Everett Wilson; Costumes, Richard
LaMotte; Set Decorator, Ian Cramer; Sound, Gary Cunningham;
Stunts, Kenny Endoso; Special Effects Make-up, Dee Mansano;
Special Effects, Lloyd Hamlett, Dale Brady, Robert Burman; Produc-
tion Coordinator, Janis Benjamin Collister; Production Supervisor,
Michael Alden; Assistant Editors, Cathy Welch, Matthew Geeves-
Booth; *"What Makes You So Special?"* Music/Lyrics, Jimmy Webb;
Dolby Stereo/Ultrastereo; TVC Color; Rated R; 123 minutes; March
release. CAST: Michael Moriarty (Williamson), John Edwin Shaw
(Mason), Ken Wright (Kennedy), Paul LeMat (Hubman), David Soul
(Oldham), Stephen Davies (Miles), Lawrence Pressman (Cathcart),
Doug Savant (Ashby), David Anthony Smith (Gregory), Jeffrey Jones
(Fischer), John Vargas (Oliviera), Rick Fitts (Turner), Scotty Sachs
(Soles), John Diehl (Murphy), Jesse Dabson (Rasmussen), Bruce Fair-
bairn (Shavick), James Acheson (Cummins), Tony Markes (Rookie),
Bill Cakmis (Considine), Nicolas Freccia (Morrison), Robert Ligouri,
Brian Demonbreun, Tony Gray, Peter Gray, Mark Brennan, Le Tuan,
Elizabeth Reiko Kubota, Peter Pan, Leslie Hung, Aki Aleong, Baoan
Coleman, Augustine Lam, Joseph Hieu, April Tran, Glen Lee, Kevin
Lee, Bill Lee, Michael Russo, Marii Mak, Cloria Carlin, Mark Kem-
ble, Gary Guidinger, D. Paul Thomas, Ron Barker, Janet Travers, Col.
Leo Thorsness, USAF (Ret.), Col. Kenneth Hughey, USAF (Ret.),
Capt. Rod Knutson, USN

Lily Tomlin

John Diehl, Rick Fitts, Michael Moriarty,
Doug Savant in "Hanoi Hilton" © *Cannon*

GHOST FEVER (Miramax) Producers, Edward Coe, Ron Rich; Director, Alan Smithee; Screenplay, Oscar Brodney, Ron Rich, Richard Egan; Photography, Zavier Cruz Ruvalcaba; Music, James Hart; Editor, James Ruxin; Production Designer, Dora Corona; Costumes, Susan Chevalier, Leslie Levin; Special Effects, Miguel Vasquez; Color; Rated PG; 86 minutes; March release. CAST: Sherman Hemsley (Buford/Jethro), Luis Avalos (Benny), Jennifer Rhodes (Mme. St. Espirt), Deborah Benson (Linda), Diana Brookes (Lisa), Pepper Martin (Beauregard Lee/Sheriff Clay), Myron Healey (Andrew Lee), Joe Frazier (Terrible Tucker), Kenneth Johnston (Terrible Tucker's Manager), Roger Cudney (TV Announcer), Patrick Welch (Ring Announcer), Steve Stone (Reporter), Ramon Beramen (Referee), George Palmiero (Terrible Tucker's Trainer).

MUNCHIES (Concorde) Producer, Roger Corman; Director, Bettina Hirsch; Screenplay, Lance Smith; Co-Producer, Ginny Nugent; *Munchies* Created by Robert Short; Production Manager, Jamie Beardsley; Production Coordinator, Kelly Jones; Assistant Directors, Whitney Hunter, Diane Friedman, David Reskin; Casting Associate, Rosemary Weldon; Sound, Jose Araujo; Costumes, Katie Sparks; Art Director, John Ballowe; Assistant Art Director, Quinn Monahan; Set Decorator, Naomi Shohan; Special Visual Effects, Roger George, Lisa Romanoff; Stunts, John Stewart; Assistant Editors, Terry Hubbard, Leslie Jones, Martha Rubin; Sond Design, Dave Yewdall; Orchestrations/Music Supervisor, Barb Luby; *"Get Even"* by Bruce Goldstein, Joel Raney, Steve Gideon/Performed by Bruce Goldstein, Joel Raney; Color; Rated PG; 83 minutes; March release. CAST: Harvey Korman (Cecil/Simon), Charles Stratton (Paul), Nadine Van Der Velde (Cindy), Alix Elias (Melvis), Charlie Phillips (Eddie), Hardy Rawls (Big Ed), Jon Stafford (Dude), Robert Picardo (Bob Marvelle), Wendy Schaal (Marge Marvelle), Scott Sherk (Buddy Holly), Lori Birdsong (Terry), Traci Huber-Sheridan (Amy), Paul Bartel (Dr. Crowder), Ellen Albertini Dow (Little Old Lady), Jerado De Cordovier (Old Indian), Roberto A. Jomeniz (Ramon), Chip Heller, Michael Lee Gogin, Larry Nicholas, Kevin Thompson, Justin Dreyfuss, Jan Kuljis, Paul Short, Steven Bernstein, Frank Welker, Fred Newman

BURGLAR (Warner Bros) Producers, Kevin McCormick, Michael Hirsh; Director, Hugh Wilson; Screenplay, Joseph Loeb III, Matthew Weisman, Hugh Wilson; Based on books by Lawrence Block; Executive Producer, Tom Jacobson; Photography, William A. Franker; Designer, Todd Hallowell; Editor, Frederic Steinkamp, William Steinkamp; Casting, Marsha Kleinman; Costumes, Susan Becker; Associate Producer, Michael Green; Co-Producers, Joseph Loeb III, Matthew Weisman; Music, Sylvester Levay; Songs, Sylvester Levay, Kathy Wakefield, and various other artists; Song Producer, Bernard Edwards; Production Manager, Penelope Foster; Assistant Directors, Michael Green, Chris Griffin, Maggie Parker, David L. D'Ovidio; Art Director, Michael Corenblith; Set Director, Daniel Loren May; Stunts, David Ellis; Set Designer, Dan Maltese; Sound, Darin Knight; Special Effects, Stan Parks; Dolby Stereo; Technicolor; Rated R; 102 minutes; March release. CAST: Whoopi Goldberg (Bernice Rhodenbarr), Bob Goldthwait (Carl Hefler), G. W. Bailey (Ray Kirschman), Lesley Ann Warren (Dr. Cynthia Sheldrake), James Handy (Carson Verrill), Anne DeSalvo (Det. Todras), John Goodman (Det. Nyswander), Elizabeth Ruscio (Frankie), Vyto Ruginis (Graybow), Larry Mintz (Knobby), Raye Birk, Eric Poppick, Scott Lincoln, Thom Bray, Nathan Davis, Brenda Hayes, Lia Sargent, Brett Marx, Steve Shellen, Fredi Oster, Rick Hamilton, Barbara Simpson, Dennis Richmond, Robert Ernst, Bill Jelliffe, Michael Pniewski, Jay Hirsh, Gary Hershberger, John H. Fields, Jo Anna March, David J. Partington, Jack O'Leary, John LeFan, Margaret Lenzey, Ethan Phillips, Ron Molina, James Terry, Amy Michelson, The Distance, Michael Nesmith, Spike Sorrentino, Hugh Wilson, Jack Andreozzi, John-Frederick Jones, Al Pugliese, Justin DeRosa, Vincent Pantone, Brian Ann Zoccola, Elaine Corral

Jimmy Woodard, Robert Townsend
in "Hollywood Shuffle" © *Samuel Goldwyn Co.*

HOLLYWOOD SHUFFLE (Goldwyn) Director/Producer, Robert Townsend; Executive Producer, Carl Craig; Screenplay, Robert Townsend, Keenen Ivory Wayans; Photography, Peter Deming; Music, Patrice Rushen, Udi Harpaz; Editor, W. O. Garrett; Art Director, Melba Katzman Farquhar; Casting, Brown & Livingston; Sound, William Shaffer; Costumes, Andre Allen; Special Photography, Paul Slaughter; Lighting, Michael LaViolette; Special Effects, Howard A. Anderson Co.; Choreographer, Donald Douglass; Stunts, Steve W. James; Color; Rated R; 82 minutes; March release. CAST: Robert Townsend (Bobby Taylor), Anne-Marie Johnson (Lydia), Starletta Dupois (Mother), Helen Martin (Grandmother), Craigus R. Johnson (Stevie). Domenick Irrera (Manvacum), Paul Mooney (NAACP President), Lisa Mende (Producer), Robert Shafer (Director), John Witherspoon (Mr. Jones), Ludie Washington (Tiny), Keenen Ivory Wayans (Donald), Steven Fertig (Agent), Brad Sanders (TV Actor), Roy Fegan (Jesse Wilson)

DOWN TWISTED aka "The Treasure of San Lucas" (Cannon) Producers, Menahem Golan, Yoram Globus; Director/Story, Albert Pyun; Screenplay, Gene O'Neill, Noreen Tobin; Associate Producers, Karen Koch, Tom Karnoski; Editor, Dennis O'Connor; Photography, Walt Lloyd; Designer, Chester Kaczenski; Music, Berlin Game; Production Manager, Christopher Pearce; Assistant Directors, Ramiro G. Jaloma, Tony Perez; Production Executive, Rony Yacov; Costumes, Renee Johnston; Casting, Perry Bullington; Art Directors, Richard Hummel, Douglas H. Leonard; Sound, Drew Kunin; Set Designer, Edward L. Rubin; Set Decorator, A. Rosalind Crew; Production Coordinator, Beth Marks Nelson; Special Effects, Bet Dalton, Larry Roberts, Frank L. Pope; Stunts, Alan Gibbs; Music Supervisor, Paula Erickson; Music Coordinator, John Stuckmeyer; Songs, Berlin Game and various other artists; TVC Color; Rated R; 88 minutes; March release. CAST: Carey Lowell (Maxine), Charles Rocket (Reno), Trudi Dochtermann (Michelle), Thom Mathews (Damalas), Norbert Weisser (Deltoid), Linda Kerridge (Soames), Nicholas Guest (Brady), Gaylyn Gorg (Blake), Courteney Cox (Tarah), Bambi Jordan (Suzie), Ken Wright (Mr. Wicks), Alec Markham (Captain), Eduardo Cassab (Sargento), Christabel Wigley (Theona), Tim Holland (Mickey), Paula Nichols (Shayne), Shayne Farris (Electra), Eric Bartsch, Tony Kienitz (Customers), Ana De Sade (Cafe Owner), Alejandro Tamayo (Funeral Director); Lucy Reyna (Anna), Magda Pablos (Tour Guide), Spike Silver (Farnsworth)

Raye Birk, Whoopi Goldberg, Scott Lincoln
in "Burglar" © *Warner Bros.*

Carey Lowell, Charles Rocket in "The Treasure
of San Lucas" © *Cannon*

131

Robert Ginty in "Programmed to Kill"
© *Trans World Entertainment*

SLAUGHTER HIGH (Vestron) Producers, Steve Minasian, Dick Randall; Director/Screenplay, George Dugdale, Mark Ezra, Peter Litten; Photography, Alain Pudney; Music, Harry Manfredini; Editor, Jim Connock; Production Designer, Geoff Sharpe; Costumes, Lee Scott; Special Effects, Coast to Coast Productions, Peter Litten; Color; Rated R; 88 minutes; April release. CAST: Caroline Munro (Carol), Simon Scuddamore (Marty), Carmine Iannaccone (Skip), Donna Yaeger (Stella), Gary Hartman (Joe), Billy Martin (Frank), Michael Saffran (Ted), John Segal (Carl), Kelly Baker (Nancy), Sally Cross (Susan), Josephine Scandi (Shirley), Marc Smith (Coach), Dick Randall (Manny), Jon Clark (Digby)

THE MESSENGER (Snizzlefritz) Producers, Fred Williamson, Pier Luigi Ciriaci; Director/Story, Fred Williamson; Screenplay, Brian Johnson, Conchita Lee, Anthony Wisdom; Photography, Giancarlo Ferrando, Craig Greene; Editor, Meuller; Music, William Stuckey; Casting, Jaki Baskow; A Realta Cinematografica-Po'Boy production; US/Italian; Fujicolor; Rated R; 92 minutes; April release. CAST: Fred Williamson (Jake Sebastian Turner), Sandy Cummings (Sabrina), Val Avery (Clark), Michael Dante (Emerson), Chris Connelly (FBI Agent Parker), Cameron Mitchell (Capt. Carter), Peter Turner (Harris), Joe Spinell (Rico), no other credits provided.

THE NIGHT STALKER (Almi) Producer, Don Edmonds; Director, Max Kleven; Executive Producers, Stephen Chrystie, Michael Landes, Albert Schwartz; Co-Producers, Buck Flower, Jef Richard; Screenplay, John Goff, Don Edmonds; Music, David Kitay, Kos Kosinski, Samuel Winans; Associate Producer, Jack Lorenz; Photography, Don Burgess; Designer, Allan Terry; Editor, Stanford C. Allen; Production Manager, Stanford Hampton; Assistant Directors, Thomas A. Irvine, Matt Hinkley; Special Effects, Paul Staples; Assistant Editor, Ray DeVally Jr.; Sound, Craig Felburg; Color; Rated R; 93 minutes; April release. CAST: Charles Napier (J. J. Striker), Michelle Reese (Rene Talbot), Katherine Kelly Lang (Denise), Robert Viharo (Charlie Garrett), Joey Gian (Buddy Brown), Robert Zdar (Chuck Summers), Leila Carlin (Terry Hollander), Gary Crosby (Gallagher), Diane Sommerfield (Lannie Roberts), John F. Goff (Capt. Markham), James Louis Watkins (Julius Parker), Richard Cansino (Antonio Vargas), Joan Chen (Mai Wong), Marcia Karr (M. J. Salters), Karen Bryson (Josanne), Tally Chanel (Brenda), Ola Ray (Sable Fox), Rebecca Lynn (Laurel Baxter), Travis McKenna (Hugh Punker), Roy Jenson (Cook), Clifford Pellow (Clerk), John Lorenz (Det. Haller), Mary Mercier (Lynette Stanfield), Muni Zano (Guru)

PROGRAMMED TO KILL (Trans World Entertainment) Producers, Don Stern, Allan Holtzman; Director, Allan Holtzman; Additional Scenes Directed by/Screenplay, Robert Short; Photography, Nitcho Lion Nissim, Ernest Holtzman; Editor, Michael Kelly; Music, Jerry Immel, Craig Huxley; Sets, Michael Parker, Pola Schreiber; Sound, Pat Moriarty, Eli Yarkoni; Makeup, Maria Haro; Special Effects, Vern Hyde, John Carter; Costumes, Vicki Graff, Lennie Barin; A Retaliator Production; Color; Rated R; 92 minutes; April release. CAST: Robert Ginty (Eric), Sandahl Bergman (Samira), James Booth (Broxk), Alex Courtney (Blake), Paul W. Walker (Jason), Louise Caire Clark (Sharon), Peter Bromilow (Donovan), George Fisher (Mike), Jim Turner (Chris), Arnon Tzador (Hassim)

THE PRINCESS ACADEMY (Empire Pictures) Executive Producer, Fred Weintraub; Producer, Sandra Weintraub; Director, Bruce Block; Screenplay, Sandra Weintraub; From an idea by Fred Weintraub; Photography, Kent Wakeford; Editor, Martin Cohen; Music, Roger Bellon; Sound, M. Curtis Price, Gregory H. Watkins, Leonard Peterson; Eva Gabor's Wardrobe, Nolan Miller; Casting, Myrna Meth, Paul Defreitas; A Cloverleaf-Jadran-Sofracima production; US/Yugoslav/French; Color; Rated R; 90 minutes; April release. CAST: Eva Gabor (Countess), Lar Park Lincoln (Cindy), Lu Leonard (Fraulein Stickenschmidt), Richard Paul (Drago), Carole Davis (Sonia), Bedar Howar (Sarah), Barbara Rovsek (Izzie), Yolande Palfrey (Pamela), Britt Helfer (Lulu)

THREE FOR THE ROAD (New Century/Vista) Producers, Herb Jaffe, Mort Engelberg; Director, B. W. L. Norton; Screenplay, Richard Martini, Tim Metcalfe, Miguel Tejada-Flores; Story, Richard Martini; Photography, Steve Posey; Editor, Christopher Grenbury; Music, Barry Goldberg; Designer, Linda Allen; Art Direction, William Buck; Set Decorator, Linda Allen; Sound, Glenn Berkovitz; Costumes, Hillary Wright; Associate Producers, Christopher Greenbury, Jay Cassidy; Assistant Director, Dennis Maguire, Casting, Nina Axelrod; A Vista Organization production; DeLuxe Color; Rated PG; 88 minutes; April release. CAST: Charlie Sheen (Paul), Kerri Green (Robin), Alan Ruck (T. S.), Sally Kellerman (Blanche), Blair Tefkin (Missy), Raymond J. Berry (Sen. Kitteridge), Alexa Hamilton (Virginia), no other credits supplied

BLOOD HOOK (Troma) Producer, David Herbert; Director, James Mallon; Executive Producers, Lloyd Kaufman, Michael Herz; Screenplay, Larry Edgerton, John Galligan; Story, Gail Anderson, David Herbert, James Mallon, Douglas Rand; Production Manager, Gail Anderson; Editor/Photography, Marsha Kahm; Music, Thomas A. Naunas; Assistant Directors, Joanne Garrett, Lee Stanford; Costumes, Patsy Herbert; Special Make-Up Design, Dale Kuipers; Sound, Tom Naunas; Lighting, Rob Reed; Assistant Editor, Ali Selim; Songs by various artists; A Golden Chargers Production/Spider Lake Films Limited Partnership; Color; Rated R; 95 minutes; April release. CAST: Mark Jacobs (Peter Van Clease), Don Cosgrove (Roger Swain), Patrick Danz (Rodney), Paul Drake (Wayne Duerst), Dale Dunham (Denny Dobyns), Donald Franke (Grandfather), Ryan Franke (Young Peter), John Galligan (Emcee), Sara Hauser (Kiersten), Paul Heckman (Sheriff), Ron Kaiser (Emcee), Bonnie Lee (Sheila), Bill Lowrie (Evelyn), Sandra Meuwissen (Bev D.), Greg Nienas (Irving), Dana Rember (Dickie), Lisa Todd (Ann), Julie Vortanz (Ruth-Ann), Christopher Whiting (Finner), Don Winters (LeRoy)

SAMUEL BECKETT: SILENCE TO SILENCE (Film Forum) Director, Sean O Mordha for Radio Telefis Eireann; Screenplay, Richard Ellmann, Declan Kiberd; Documentary Ireland, 1984; Not rated; 80 minutes; April release. CAST: David Warrilow, Billie Whitelaw, Jack McGowran, Patrick Magee

**Michelle Reese, Robert Zdar
in "The Night Stalker"** © *Almi*

Don Winters in "Blood Hook"
© *Troma Team*

SILENT NIGHT, DEADLY NIGHT PART II (Ascot Entertainment Group/Silent Night Releasing) Producer, Lawrence Appelbaum; Director, Lee Harry; Screenplay, Lee Harry, Joseph H. Earle; Story, Lee Harry, Joseph H. Earle, Dennis Paterson, Lawrence Appelbaum and a character created by Michael Hickey, Paul Caimi; Photography, Harvey Genkins; Music, Michael Armstrong; United Color; Rated R; 88 minutes; April release. CAST: Eric Freeman, James L. Newman, Elizabeth Clayton, Jean Miller, Lilyan Chauvin

SUMMER CAMP NIGHTMARE aka "The Butterfly Revolution" (Concorde) Producers, Robert T. Crow, Emilia Lesniak-Crow; Director, Bert L. Dragin; Screenplay, Bert L. Dragin, Penelope Spheeris; Based on novel *The Butterfly Revolution* by William Butler; Co-Producer, Andy Howard; Photography, Don Burgess; Music, Ted Neeley, Gary Chase; Editor, Michael Spence; Casting, Bengston & Cohn; Production Manager, Andy Howard; Assistant Directors, Tom Irvine, Mike Topoozian, Kenneth Brewer; Designer, Richard McGuire; Art Director, Barry Franenberg; Set Decorator, Jennifer Pray; Assistant Set Decorator, Teresa St. Clair; Sound, Stephan Von Hase; Assistant Editor, Mark Rosenbaum; Production Coordinator, Cynthia A. Gifford; United Color Lab Color; Rated PG-13; 88 minutes; April release. CAST: Chuck Connors (Mr. Warren), Charles Stratton (Franklin Reilly), Harold 'P' Pruett (Chris Wayne), Adam Carl (Donald Poultry), Tom Fridley (John Mason), Melissa Brennan (Heather), Stuart Rogers (Stanley Runk), Shawn McLemore (Hammond Pumpernil), Samantha Newark (Debbie), Nancy Calabrese (Trixie), Michael Cramer (Jerome Blackridge), Rick Fitts (Ed Heinz), Doug Toby (Manuel Rivaz), Shirley Mitchell (Mrs. Knute), Chris Hubbell (Jack Caldwell), Scott Curtis (Peter), Jennifer McGrath (Laurie), John Louie (Paul Indian), Brad Kestin (GoGo), Tina Blum (Nurse Newman), Tom Rayhall (Det. Stone), Wade Crow (Wade), Rick Dorio, Bradley Lieberman, David Hern, Lynda Nichols, Nicole Normand, Desiree Simpers, Mandy McEnnan, Danielle Rioux, John Maninger, Christopher Gosch, Sally Piper, Tony Willard, Christianna Billman, John Branagan, Andrew Epper, Patrick J. Statham, Bobby Porter, Michael Gronenman

CLUB LIFE (Troma) Producer/Director/Screenplay, Norman Thaddeus Vane; Story, Bleu McKenzie, Norman Thaddeus Vane; Music, Jack Conrad, FM Songs (America), Inc.; Choreography, Dennon Rawles; Executive Producers, Charles Aperia, Guy Collins; Editor, David Kern; Line Producer, Patrick Wright; Photography, Joel King; Executive Music Producers, Frank Musker, Evros Stakis; Casting, Stanzi Stokes; Associate Producers, Sandy Horowitz, Herb Linsey, Mark Madero; Music Supervisor, Philip Moores; Music Coordinator, David Minns; Production Executive, Jean Ovrum; Production Managers, Herb Linsey, Larry Gitlin; Assistant Directors, Patrick Wright, Kelly Schroeder, Kurt Benjamin, Tony DiSalvo; Assistant Choreographer, Michael Rooney; Costumes, Elisabeth Scott; Sound, Jim Murphy; Production Coordinator, Mark Madero; Set Decorators, Sherry Dreizen, Michelle Hormel; Art Directors, Cynthia Sowder, Phillip Duffin; Set Designer, Katherine Vallin; Special Effects, SPFX, Inc., Court Wizard; Stunts, Michael Walters, Speed Sterns; Songs by Frank Musker and various other artists; CFI Color; Rated R; 92 minutes; April release. CAST: Tom Parsekian (Cal), Michael Parks (Tank), Jamie Barrett (Sissy), Tony Curtis (Hector), Dee Wallace (Tilly), Ron Kuhlman (Doctor), Pat Ast (Butch), Bruce Reed (Punk), Sal Landi (Sonny), Robert Miano (Ferd), Ron Gilbert (Mace), Bleu McKenzie, Michael Aaron, Herb Abrams, Dominick Allen, Gene Scott Casey, Ross Fenton, Kate Finlayson, Whip Hubley, Jay Arlen Jones, Elizabeth Lamers, Barbara Powers, Yvonne Smith, Valerie Shaldene, John Vidor, Charles Prior, Yana Nirvana, Lisa LeCover, Kimberlee Carlson, Michael Rooney, Nell Alano, Richard Sullivant

Alec Baldwin, Hanna Schygulla
in "Forever, Lulu" © *Tri-Star Pictures*

FOREVER, LULU (Tri-Star) Producer/Director/Screenplay, Amos Kollek; Executive Producer, Michael Steinhardt; Photography, Lisa Rinzler; Editor, Jay Freund; Designer, Stephen McCabe; Casting, Marcia Shulman; Assistant to Producer/Director, Julia Robinson; Editing Consultant, Ralph Rosenblum; Production Manager, Sarah Green; Costumes, Canda Clements; Assistant Production Manager, Trudy Elins; Sound, Felipe Borrero; Assistant Directors, Gary Marcus, Howard Mason; Assistant Designer, Jocelyne Beaudoin; Set Decorator, Victor Zolfo; Special Effects, Willie Caban; Ms. Schygulla's Costumes, Barbara Weiss, Lesleigh; Color; Rated R; 86 minutes; April release. CAST: Hanna Schygulla (Elaine), Deborah Harry (Lulu), Alec Baldwin (Buck), Annie Golden (Diana), Paul Gleason (Robert), Dr. Ruth Westheimer (Herself), Raymond Serra (Alphonse), George Kyle (Pepe), Harold Guskin (Archie), Bill Corsair (Blackmailer), Jonathan Freeman (Don), Amos Kollek (Larry), Charles Ludlam (Harvey), Cathy Gati (Lisa), Beatrice Pons (Fortune Teller), Sally Jane Heit (Martha), Helen Lloyd Breed (Landlady), Justine Johnston (Judith Cabot), Susan Blommaert (Jackie Coles), Kenny Marino (Det. Calhoun), Joanne Carlo (Donna), Wayne Knight (Stevie), Jennifer Leigh Warren (Hooker), Yvette Edelhart (Dolores), Antonia Rey (Clara), Charles Prior, Andrew Craig, Everett Quinton, Christine Jensen, Anthony Powers, Dennis Green, Pattis Astor, Judith Cohen, Ernest Abuba, Sydney D. Sheriff, Jr., Michael Steinhardt, Felix Mintz, Lazar Mintz, Adriane Lenox, R. L. Ryan, Mike Hodge, Clifford Arashi, Ron Ryan, Sassy Gearhardt, Bill Masters, James Langrall, Joe Lissi, Bernie Friedman, Martina Ferenczy, Samantha Louca, Julia Robinson, Judith Zimmer, Erik Koniger

SORORITY HOUSE MASSACRE (Concorde) Producer/Production Manager, Ron Diamond; Director/Screenplay, Carol Frank; Assistant Directors, David B. Householter, Bruce Carter; Sound, Don Sanders, Walt Martin, Charles Kelly; Set Decorator, Gene Sardena; Assistant Editor, Eve Gage; Additional Editing, Mike Miller; Sound Designer, Dave Lewis Yewdall; Color; Rated R; 73 minutes; April release. CAST: Angela Maegan O'Neil (Laura/Beth), Wendy Martel (Linda), Pamela Ross (Sara), Nicole Rio (Tracy), John C. Russell (Killer/Bobby), Marcus Vaughter (Andy), Vinnie Bilancio (John), Joe Nassi (Craig), Gillian Frank (Dr. Lindsey), Joseph Mansier (Technician), Mary Anne (Mrs. Lawrence) Axel Roberts (Larry), Fitzhough Houston (Dep. Gilbert), Marsha Carter (Nurse), Maureen Hawkes (Professor), Alan Eugster (Orderly), Phyllis Frank (Teacher), Thomas Muston (Steve), Susan Bollman (Cindy), Ray Spinka, Bobby Ivy, Hammer, Todd Darling

Dee Wallace in "Club Life"
© *Troma Team*

Angela O'Neill, Wendy Martel in "Sorority
House Massacre" © *Concorde*

Kathleen Quinlan in "Wild Thing"
© *Atlantic Entertaining Group*

Betty Buckley, Rob Knepper in "Wild Thing"
© *Atlantic Entertaining Group*

WILD THING (Atlantic) Executive Producer, Thomas Coleman, Michael Rosenblatt; Director, Max Reid; Screenplay, John Sayles; Story, Larry Stamper, John Sayles; Producers, David Calloway, Nicolas Clermont; Editors, Battle Davis, Steven Rosenblum; Casting, Paul Ventura; Music Supervisor, Steve Tyrell; Stunts, Peter Cox; Costumes, Paul-Andre Guerin; Production Manager, Lyse Lafontaine; Assistant Directors, Pedro Gandol, Bruno Bazin, Lorne Goloff; Production Coordinator, Jean Gerin; Sound, Henri Blondeau; Production Coordinators, Kelly A. Schumann; Special Effects, Jacques Godbout; Color; Rated PG-13; 92 minutes; April release. CAST: Rob Knepper (Wild Thing), Kathleen Quinlan (Jane), Robert Davi (Chopper), Maury Chaykin (Trask), Betty Buckley (Leah), Guillaume Lemay-Thivierge (Wild Thing-aged 10), Robert Bednarski (Free/Wild Thing aged 3), Clark Johnson (Winston), Sean Hewitt (Father Quinn), Teddy Abner (Rasheed), Cree Summer Francks (Lisa), Shawn Levy (Paul), Rod Torchia (Hud), Christine Jones (Laurie), Robert Austern (Wiz), Tom Rack (Braindrain), Alexander Chapman (Shakes), Robert Ozores (El Borracho), Lorena Gale (Scooter), Sonny Forbes (Doowop), and Johnny O'Neil, Alastair Chartey, Richard Raybourne, Freddie James, George Popovich, Ken Roberts, Ron Lea, Jose Miguel Luis, Claire Rodger, Lynne Adams, Elizabeth Turbide, Diana Sookedeo, Mitsumi Takahashi, Doug Price, Michael Hunter, Susan Seymour, Wally Martin, Audie Grant, Jodie Resther, Carol Ann Francis, Douglas Leopold, Patricia Hanganu, Neil Kroetsch, Harry Stanjofski, Tyrone Benskin, Neil Affleck, Arthur Corber, Griffith Brewer, Anthony Sherwood, Joe Cazalet, Arthur Holden, Donald Lamoreux, Sandra Blackie, Ray Roth, Real Andrews, Bonnie Beck, Jeffrey Chong, Richard Campbell, Leon Darnell Ramsoondar

HEAVEN (Island Pictures) Producer, Joe Kelly; Director, Diane Keaton; Executive Producers, Tom Kuhn, Charles Mitchell, Arlyne Rothberg; Editor, Paul Barnes; Photography, Frederick Elmes, Joe Kelly; Art Director, Barbara Ling; Music, Howard Shore; Sound, Skip Livesay; Associate Editor, Bruce Shaw; Production Executives/RCA, Arnold J. Holland, Phillip L. Rosen; Archival Footage Consultants, William K. Everson, Richard Prelinger; Assistant Editor, Mame Kennedy; Synclavier Effects, Paul Friedman; Associate Producers, Tom Stovall, Susan Emerling; Sound, Peter F. Chaikin, John E. Kaufer, Tom Moore; Production Coordinator, Kate Kevorkian; Title Song, Nick Laird-Clowes, Gilbert Gabriel; Songs by various artists; Produced by Perpetual Productions, Inc. for RVP Productions; Documentary; Rated PG-13; 80 minutes; April release. CAST: Michael Agbabian,

James Allport, Swami Prem Amitabh, Lazaro Aruizu, Steven Augustine, Tracy Bauer, Nancy Block, Robert Boettger, Pinkietessa Braithwaite, Dorothy Brunett, Christine Calame, Josie Campo, Abram Christ, Jacob Christ, Moses Christ, Candice Clark, Inell Clark, Michael Darwin, Ruben Ben David, Kim Dozier, Isaac Fields, Johnny "Paul" Fiore, Marvin Ford, Ida Foreman-Flick, Peter Fraser, Lisa Friedman, Lawrence Goldblum, Brent Gordon, Richard Gordon, Heather Granger, Dorrie Hall, Jack and Dorothy Hall, Mary Hall, Evangelists Robert and Joyce Hanan, Dr. R. Michael Hands, Ted "Pops" Hawkins, Jr., Leslie Heath, Myra Henderson, Millie Hobbs, Barry Holt, Mark Hornbacher, Andrea Christensen Hunter, Dr. Robert L. Hymers, Jr., Ma Deva Jessica, Grace Johansen, Lucas Johnson-Yahraus, Bernard Kaye, Tim Kelly, Jean Kepley, Jack Kimbrough, Don King, Stan Levy, Robert Liddil, Julie and Bryan Ling, Dino Lomedico, Pastor William H. Luke, Randall McAlister, James McClellan, Leoma McKinney, Susan McNabb, Tracy Moe, Marjorie Moritz, James Morrill, Curt Morton, Olive Mott, Kenneth Ostin, Tony Ford Rapisarda, Cpt. and Mrs. Fred Rasmussen, Matthew and Jean Rattner, Alfred Robles, Emily Romero, Brother Ron, Tracy Ryan, Charla Sampsel, Victoria Sellers, Pastor L. D. Shaw, Madlen Stappung, Rev. John Steer, Emery Tang, The Tripp Family, Soorya Townley, Kathy and Nicole Tracy, Rosie Vasquez, Florence Wander, Nadine Watt, Ruby and Ruben Wein, Lorene Williams, Mary Woods, Corey Young

CREEPSHOW 2 (New World) Producer, David Ball; Director, Michael Gornick; Screenplay, George A. Romero; Based on stories by Stephen King; Photography, Dick Hart, Tom Hurwitz; Editor, Peter Weatherly; Music, Les Reed; Color; Not rated; 92 minutes; May release. CAST: George Kennedy (Ray Spruce), Dorothy Lamour (Martha Spruce), Lois Chiles (Annie Lansing), Page Hannah (Rachel), Tom Wright (Hitchhiker), Tom Savini (The Creep). No other credits provided

THEY STILL CALL ME BRUCE (Shapiro Entertainment) Producers/Directors/Screenplay, Johnny Yune, James Orr; Photography, R. Michael Delahoussaye; Editor, Roy Watts; Music, Morton Stevens; Executive Producer, Ji Hee Choi; Associate Producers, Stephen Sharff, Bert Weil; Color; Rated PG; 91 minutes; May release. CAST: Johnny Yune, Robert Guillaume, Pat Paulsen, David Mendenhall, Joey Travolta, Bethany Wright, Don Gibb and others (no other credits submitted)

George Kennedy, Dorothy Lamour in "Creepshow 2"
© *New World Pictures*

Johnny Yune in "They Still Call Me Bruce"
© *JiHee Productions*

Zarah Leander, Paul Seller in "My Life . . ."
© *Christian Blackwood Productions*

"I Married a Vampire"
© *Troma Team*

RETURN TO SALEM'S LOT (Warner Bros.) Producer, Paul Kurta; Director/Story, Larry Cohen; Screenplay, Larry Cohen, James Dixon; Based on characters created by Stephen King; A Larco Production; Color; Rated R; 95 minutes; May release. CAST: Michael Moriarty (Joe Weber), Samuel Fuller (Dr. Van Meer), Ricky Addison Reed (Jeremy Weber), Andrew Duggan (Judge Axel), June Havoc (Aunt Clara), Evelyn Keyes (Mrs. Axel), Ronee Blakley (Sally). No other credits provided

HAPPY HOUR (The Movie Store) Executive Producer, J. Stephen Peace; Produers, J. Stephen Peace, John De Bello; Director, John De Bello; Screenplay John De Bello, Constantine Dillon, J. Stephen Peace; Photography Kevin Morrisey; Editor, John De Bello; Music, Rick Patterson, Neal Fox; Song, Devo; Sound, Joe Thompson, Jr.; Designer, Dillon; Stunts, Monty Jordan; Production Supervisor, Robert Matzenauer; Casting, Samuel Warren & Associates; A Four Square Production; Ultra-Stereo; CFI Color; Rated R; 86 minutes; May release. CAST: Richard Gilliland (Blake Teegarden), Jamie Farr (Fred), Tawny Kitaen (Misty Roberts), Ty Henderson (Bill), Rich Little (Mr. X), Eddie Deezen (Hancock), Kathi Diamant (Cathy Teegarden), Debbie Gates (Meredith Casey), James Newell, Beverly Todd, Debi Fares, Eric Christmas, no other credits provided

SIZZLE BEACH, U.S.A. (Troma Team) Producer, Eric Louzil; Director, Richard Brander; Photography, John Sprung; Screenplay, Craig Kusaba; Assistant Director, Charles Domokos; Sound, David Gaines; Casting, Leslie Braude; Assistant Editors, David Gaines, Fred Gerhart, Pamela Kleibrink; Costumes, Mary Gerhart; Production Supervisor, Howard Heard; Presented by Lloyd Kaufman, Michael Herz; Color; Rated R; 93 minutes; May release. CAST: Terry Congie (Janice Johnston), Leslie Brander (Dit McCoy), Roselyn Royce (Cheryl Percy), Robert Acey (Steve), Kevin Costner (John Logan), Larry DeGraw (Brent Richardson), James Pascucci (Von Titale), Justin Michael Scott (Gary), Peter Risch (Pete Fargo), Lulu Nicholson (Acting Instructor), Ronald Kieptke, Joe Marmo, Sylvia Wright, Blaine Nicholson, Toni Serritell, Ted Naimy, Jr., Victoria Taft (Candi), Richard Brander (Cowboy), Jennifer Stewart, Claudia Lowe, Bert Kelly, Lee Grover, Tiffany Renee Naimy, Maureen Ochon, Gregory Falk, Dot Kuhne, Bonnie Class, Barbara Wiltzer, Roy Freeman, Wendy Thompson, Kenneth Landon, Jams Fidelis, Laura L. Stewart, Ken Cummings, Bill Gross, Patty Dobashi, John Kayden, Martin Braude, Julius Metoyer, Kathryn Morris, Jeff Roberts, Elizabeth Carroll, Steve Moos, Chris Pascucci, Elaine Chan, Corinne Cook, Howard Heard, Lindarea Goldstein, Beverly Urman, Sheldon Urman

I MARRIED A VAMPIRE (Troma) Producer/Director/Screenplay/Editor, Jay Raskin; Producer/Art Director/Assistant Editor, Vicky Prodromidou; Photography, Oren Rudavsky; Lighting, Lon Caracappa; Sound, Phil Caracappa, Chris O'Donnell; Assistant Director, Maria Mann-Scherzer; Lighting, W. A. Simpson, Emmet Kane, David Phillips, Ken Roerden, Daniel Sterne; Assistant Art Director/Sound, Saudra Stephen; Music, Steve Monahan; Color; Rated R; 90 minutes; May release. CAST: Rachel Golden (Viola), Brendan Hickey (Robespierre), Ted Zalewski (Gluttonshire), Deborah Carroll (Olivia), Temple Aaron (Portia), David Dunton (Morris), Kathryn Karnes (Doris), Marcus Chase (M.B.C. Lecturer), Steve Monahan (M.B.C. Salesman), Ken Skeer (Lawyer), Rit Friedman (Landlord), Ellen Boscov (Ex-M.B.C. Member), James Beauregard (Man in club), Jo-Anne Raskin (Bagwoman), Bruce Barker (Nightguard), Jeff Vidianos (Bouncer)

MY LIFE FOR ZARAH LEANDER Producer/Director/Screenplay/Photography/Editor, Christian Blackwood; Sound, Fritz Berg, Isolde Kaiser, Michael Eiler; Documentary; Germany; German with subtitles; Color; Not rated; 90 minutes; May release. WITH: Zarah Leander, Paul Seiler, Margot Hielscher, Douglas Sirk, Michael Jary, Bruno Blaz, Harold Prince

AMERICAN NINJA 2 (Cannon) Producers, Menahem Golan, Yoram Globus; Director, Sam Firstenberg; Screenplay, Gary Conway, James Booth; Story, Gary Conway; Based on characters created by Avi Kleinberger, Gideon Amir; Executive Producer, Avi Lerner; Editor, Michael J. Duthie; Music, George S. Clinton; Production Manager, Peter Warnaby; Assistant Directors, Richard Green, Jonathan Finnegan, Sheldon Kaplan; Martin Jacobsen; Production Executive, Rony Yacov; Casting, Perry Bullington; Art Director, Robert Jenkinson; Sound, Phillip Key; Stunts, BJ Davis; Martial Arts Choreography, Michael Stone; Costumes, Audrey M. Bansmer; Production Coordinator, Gillian Pearson; Special Effects, Paul Staples, Laszlo Stumpf, Hennie Muller, Rod Dyson; Assistant Editor, Paul Elman; Color; Rated R; 89 minutes; May release. CAST: Michael Dudikoff (Joe), Steve James (Jackson), Larry Poindexter (Charlie), Gary Conway (Lion), Jeff Weston (Wild Bill), Michelle Botes (Alicia Sanborn), Michael Stone (Tojo Ken), Len Sparowhawk (Pat McCarthy), Jonathan Pienaar (Taylor), Bill Curry (Sgt. Singh), Dennis Folbigge (Sir Cloudsly Smith), Elmo Fillis (Toto), Ralph Draper (Prof. Sanborn), John Pasternak (Vesuvius), Gary Ford (Ambassador Scruggs), Melvin Jones (Chuck), Adrian Waldon (Karl), Jamie Bartlett (Sinclair), Gavin Van Der Berg (Bert Ballard), Anne Curtis (Lady Smith), Nava Halmi (Girlfriend)

Kevin Costner in "Sizzle Beach"
© *Troma Team*

Michael Dudikoff, Steve James in
"American Ninja 2" © *Cannon*

135

John Cusack, Wendy Gazelle
in "Hot Pursuit" © *RKO Pictures*

Sela Ward, Martin Kove
in "Steele Justice" © *Atlantic*

HOT PURSUIT (Paramount) Producers, Pierre David, Theodore R. Parvin; Director, Steven Lisberger; Screenplay, Steven Lisberger, Steven Carabatsos; Story, Steven Lisberger; Photography, Frank Tidy; Production Designer, William J. Creber; Costumes, Taryn "Teri" De Chellis; Art Directors, Fernando Ramirez, Chris Dorrington; Music, Rareview; Editor, Mitchell Sinoway; Executive Producers, Tom Mankiewicz, Jerry Offsay; Assistant Director, Max Kleven; An RKO Pictures production; Metrocolor; Rated PG-13; 93 minutes; May release. CAST: John Cusack (Dan Bartlett), Wendy Gazelle (Lori Cronenberg), Robert Loggia (Mac MacLaren), Jerry Stiller (Victor Honeywell), Monte Markham (Bill Cronenberg), Shelley Fabares (Buffy Cronenberg), Dah-Ve Chodan (Ginger Cronenberg), Ben Stiller (Chris Honeywell), Terrence Cooper (Capt. Andrew), Andaluz Russell (Carmelina), Ursaline Bryant (Roxanne), Keith David (Alphonso), Paul Bates (Cleon), Ted White, Andrew Cochrane.

MALONE (Orion) Producer, Leo L. Fuchs; Director, Harley Cokliss; Screenplay, Christopher Frank; From the novel *"Shotgun"* by William Wingate; Photography, Gerald Hirschfeld; Designer, Graeme Murray; Editor, Todd Ramsay; Casting, Joseph D'Agosta, Carole Kenneally; Music, David Newman; Associate Producers, Gerard Croce, Mary Eilts; Additional Photography, Graeme Cowley; Stunts, Bud Davis; Production Manager, Gerard Croce; Assistant Directors, Brad Turner, Karen Robyn, Rachael Leiterman, Jack Hardy; Production Coordinators, Gayle Goldin, Heather Boyd; Sound, Richard Van Dyke; Set Decorator, Barry Brolly; Costumes, Norman Salling; Special Effects, Dennis Dion, Dean Lockwood; Assistant Editors, Carolle Alain, Lisa Morlas; Orchestration, Shirley Walker; DeLuxe Color; Rated R; 93 minutes; May release. CAST: Burt Reynolds (Malone), Cliff Robertson (Delaney), Kenneth McMillan (Hawkins), Cynthia Gibb (Jo Barlow), Scott Wilson (Paul Barlow), Lauren Hutton (Jamie), Philip Anglim (Harvey), Tracey Walter (Calvin Bollard), Dennis Burkley (Dan Bollard), Alex Diakun (Madrid), Brooks Gardner (Patterson), Mike Kirton (Frank), Duncan Fraser (Malone's Target), Janne Mortil (Helen), Campbell Lane (Tom Riggs), Tom McBeath (Stringbean), Don Mackay (Dr. Florian), Tom Herton (Eli), Blu Mankuma (Rev. Danby), Walter Marsh (Congressman), Graydon Gould (Lawyer), Bill Buck (Banker), Don Davis (Buddy), Frank C. Turner (Andy), Mavor Moore (Hausmann), Stephen E. Miller (Clinton), Donna White (Nurse), Dwight McFee (Harry), Christianne Hirt (Girl in Wagon).

STEEL JUSTICE (Atlantic) Executive Producers, Thomas Coleman, Michael Rosenblatt; Producer, John Strong; Director/Screenplay, Robert Boris; Associate Producer, John O'Connor; Production Manager/Assistant Director, Thomas A. Irvine; Music, Misha Segal; Photography, John M. Stephens; Editors, John O'Connor, Steve Rosenblum; Casting, Paul Ventura; Assistant Directors, R. P. Sekon, Michael Drobashevsky, James Steele; Sound, Clifford Gynn; Designer, Richard N. McGuire; Associate Art Director, Gary R. Bailard; Set Decorator, John Nelson Tichler; Costumes, Leslie Wilshire; Production Coordinator, Julie P. Freund; Special Effects, SPFX, Inc., James Wayne Beauchamp; Color; Rated R; 95 minutes; May release. CAST: Martin Kove (John Steele), Sela Ward (Tracy), Ronny Cox (Bennett), Bernie Casey (Reese), Joseph Campanella (Harry), Soon-Teck Oh (Gen. Bon Soong Kwan), Jan Gan Boyd (Cami), David Froman (Kelso) Sarah Douglas (Kay), Kimiko Hiroshige (Grandmother), Sheila Gale (Anchorwoman), Robert Kim (Lee Van Minh), Peter Kwong (Pham)

UNDER COVER (Cannon) Producers, Menahem Golan, Yoram Globus; Director, John Stockwell; Screenplay, John Stockwell, Scott Fields; Associate Producers, Susan Hoffman, Scott Fields; Photography, Alexander Gruszynski; Editor, Sharyn L. Ross; Designer, Beck Block; Music, Todd Rundgren; Casting, Pat Orseth; Production Executive, Ronny Yacov; Production Manager, Neil Rapp; Assistant Directors, Allan Nichols, James Lansbury; Special Effects, Paul Staples; Sound, Glenn Berkovitz; Set Decorator, Tom Talbert; Assistant Set Decorator, Phoebe Schmidt; Costumes, Ernest Misko; Production Coordinator, Susan Watt Kydd; Assistant Editors, Gina Mittelman, Denise Cochran; Stunts, Greg Walker; Music Supervisor, Paula Erickson; Music Coordinator, Lorrie Behrhorst; *"Shef's Theme"* by Wayne Coster; Songs by various artists; Soundtrack on Enigma Records; Color Ultrastereo; Rated R; 94 minutes; May release. CAST: David Neidorf (Shef Hauser), Jennifer Jason Leigh (Tanille Laroux), Barry Corbin (Sgt. Irwin Lee), David Harris (Lucas Morris), Kathleen Wilhoite (Corinne Armor), Carmen Argenziano (Lt. Leonard), Brad Leland (Terry Vaughn), John Philbin (Officer Vic Peterson), David Denney (Hassie Pearl), Brent Hadaway (Peyton Lewis), Mark Holton (Denny), Lauri Riley (Secretary), Diana Bellamy (Lynette Dettons), Ed Bernard (Chief Haller), Rommy Vistart (Harley), Kirstie Tice (Mary Anne), Piper Cochrane (Penny), Jorli McLain (Marla), Charles Viracola (Stevie Barkin), Wendy Wilkins (Lindy Parker), James Curley (Commander), Beth Grant (Miss Randolph), Franny Parrish, Eve Smith, Lou Hancock, Pamela London, Eugene Townsend Ellis

Cliff Robertson, Burt Reynolds
in "Malone" © *Orion/Douglas Curran*

Kathleen Wilhoite, David Neidorf
in "Under Cover" © *Cannon*

SALVATION! (aka "Have You Said Your Prayers Today") (Circle Releasing) Producers, Beth B, Michael H. Shamberg; Director/Sound/Music Supervisor, Beth B; Screenplay, Beth B, Tom Robinson; Executive Producer, Ned Richardson; Photography, Francis Kenny; Editor, Elizabeth Kling; Designer, Lester Cohen; Co-Executive Producers, Michel Duval, Irving Ong; Associate Producer, Arthur Baker; Line Producers, John Sylbert, Matthew Titone, Elizabeth White; Production Manager, Phil Betz; Production Coordinator, Wendy Kaplan; Casting, Isabelle Kramer, Susie Shopmaker; Assistant Directors, Sandy Tate, Matthew Handle, David Backus, Bob Hurrie, Jon Sylbert; Associate Editor, Geraldine Peronie; Assistant Editor, Tamar Bahari; Art Director, Jessica Lanier; Wardrobe, Pamela Goldman, Tanya Seeman; Special Effects, David Dumont; Stunts, Jeffrey Lee Gibson; Songs, New Order and various other artists; Music Producer, Michael H. Shamberg; Color; Rated R; 80 minutes; May release. CAST: Stephen McHattie (Rev. Edward Randall), Dominique Davalos (Lenore Finley), Exene Cervenka (Rhonda Stample), Viggo Mortensen (Jerome Stample), Rockets Redglare (Oliver), Billy Bastiani (Stanley)

Dominique Davalos, Stephen McHattie
in "Salvation" © Circle Films

THE CHIPMUNK ADVENTURE (Goldwyn) Producer, Ross Bagdasarian; Director, Janice Karman; Music, Randy Edelman; Chipmunk & Chipettes Design, Sandra; Character Design, Louis Zingarelli; Backgrounds, Ron Dias; Designer, Carol Holman Grosvenor; Associate Producer, Gwendolyn Sue Shakespeare; Directing Animators, Skip Jones, Don Spencer, Andrew Gaskill, Mitch Rochon, Becky Bristow; Production Executive, Hope London; Production Supervisor, Rocky Solotoff; Orchestrations, Ralph Ferraro; Music Editor, Doug Lackey; Songs by various artists; Animated; Color; Rated G; 90 minutes; May release. VOICE CAST: Ross Bagdasarian, Janice Karman, Dody Goodman, Susan Tyrell, Anthony DeLongis, Frank Welker, Nancy Cartwright, Philip Clark, Ken Sansom, George Poulos, Charles Adler, Pat Pinney

ADVENTURE OF THE ACTION HUNTERS (Troma) Producer, Mary Holland; Director/Editor, Lee Bonner; Screenplay, Lee Bonner, Leif Elsmo; Photography, David Insley; Music/Songs, John Palumbo; Assistant Director, Leif Elsmo; Casting, Jane Brinker, Martha Royall; Production Executive, Gilbert Armiger; Production Manager, Terri Trupp; Sound, Richard Angellella; Production Coordinator, Peter Mullett; Art Director, Vincent Peranio; Special Effects, Fred Buccholtz, Howard Donahue, Controlled Demolition Inc.; Stunts, Archie Murphy, The Flying Alaimo; Assistant Editors, Randy Aitken, Lorraine Claggett, Leif Elsmo; Sound, Bill Bruechner; Color; Rated PG; 90 minutes; May release. CAST: Ronald Hunter (Walter), Sean Murphy (Betsy), Joseph Cimino, Art Donovan (Gangsters), Steve Beauchamp (Skipper), Peter Walker (Oliver), Bert Michaels, Stu Kerr, Leif Elsmo, David Deboy, Hans Kramm, Morris Engle, Tilda Wolpert, Carole Copeland, Harry Davenport, Ed Weber, Wayne Gruen, Daniel Solloway, Gorham Scott, Tom Small, Prentiss Rowe, Scott Elliott, Michael Desanto, Robert Witte, Elaine Dunstan, Vincent Peranio, Ted Talbert, Marcello Rolando, George Stover, Bobo Lewis, Laura Summer, Linda Abitbal, Didier Kilatte, Judy Thornton, Kathleen Wooley, C. Douglas Penniman, Vinnie Bratten Penniman, Harry Davenport, Nancy Davenport, Delores Deluxe, Linda Heyman, Nancy Irving, Bob Miser, Ed Weber, Ethel Weber, David Bosley, Bruce Bonner, Janet Bonner, David Burrows, Deborah Burrows, Chris Cimino, Beatrice Deane, Gordon Gilbert, Eileen Halpren, David Insley, Mary Katherine Kasyer, Kathi Bell, M. Margaret Green, Claire T. Hartman, Chris Neufer, John R. Sullivan, Alison Bonner, Linda Bonner, Patricia Bonner, Meredith Copeland, Bernie Cropfelder, Donald Cropfelder, Mike Divine, Laurie Hart, Chris Held, Richie Hunt, Audrey Kennedy, Terry Kernan, John Kulacki, Elissa Mocko, Ramsay Muhley, Greg Naughton, Beth Rose, John Sybert

I WAS A TEENAGE T.V. TERRORIST (Troma) Producer, Susan Kaufman; Director, Stanford Singer; Screenplay, Kevin McDonough, Stanford Singer; Photography, Lisa Rinzler; Art Director, Ann Williams; Editor, Richard King; Music, Cengiz Yaltkaya; Associate Producer, Evan Edelist; Production Manager/Assistant Director, Stan Bickman; Assistant Director, Robert Sherman; Production Coordinator, Jolie Gorchov; Casting, Suzanne Rees; Assistant Art Director, Susan Shopmaker; Set Decorator, Susan Goulder; Sound, Judith Karp; Assistant Editor, Lindsey Hicks; Costumes, Jeanne Button Eaton, Muriel Stockdale; Color; Rated R; 90 minutes; May release. CAST: Adam Nathan (Paul Pierce), Julie Hanlon (Donna Rose), John MacKay (John Reid), Walt Willey (Bill Johnson), Saul Alpiner (Frank Romance), Mikhail Druhan (Miss Murphy), Michael Griffith (Marcel Pederewsky), Guillermo Gonzalez (Rico), Warren Shapiro (Mitchel), Natalie O'Connell, Marilyn Kray, Tony Kruk, Howard Korder, Edmund Loughlin, Joel Von Ornsteiner, George Ratchford, Russ Pennington, Dawn Brzezinski, Cheryl Josephson, Suzanne Rees, Jami Simon, Mindy Morgenstern, Amy McLellan, Kate Green, James Sheenan, Tracy Jabara, Mike Atkin, Stanford Singer, Kevin McDonough

THE BARBARIANS (Cannon) Producer, John Thompson; Director, Ruggero Deodato; Screenplay, James R. Silke; Music, Pino Donaggio; Conductor, Natale Massaro; Photography, Lorenzo Battaglia; Editor, Eugene Alabiso; Designer, Giuseppe Mangano; Production Supervisor, Claudio Grassetti; Production Manager, Luciano Balducci; Assistant Director, Roberto Palmerini; Stunts, Benito Stefanelli; Choreographer, Pino Pennese; Sound, Massimo Loffredi; Assistant Designer, Atos Mastrogirolami; Costumes, Francesca Panicali, Michela Gisotti; Assistant Costume Designer, Stefania Del Guerra; Assistant Editors, Nadia Boggian, Silvana Di Legge; Dolby Stereo Marchio; Telecolor; Rated R; 88 minutes; May release. CAST: David Paul (Kutchek), Peter Paul (Gore), Richard Lynch (Kadar), Eva La Rue (Ismene), Virginia Bryant (Canary), Sheeba Alahani (China), Michael Berryman (Dirtmaster), Nanni Bernini (Sligot), Angelo Ragusa (Dead Bone), Lucio Rosato (One Ear), Franco Pistoni (Ibar), Raffaella Baracchi (Allura), Benito Stefanelli (Greyshaft), Pasquale Bellazecca (Child Kutchek), Luigi Bellazecca (Child Gore), Tiziana Di Gennaro (Kara), Giovanni Cinafriglia (Ghedo), Renzo Pevarello (Bones), L. Caroli (Nose), Paolo Risi (Pin the Dwarf), Wilma Marzilli (Fat Lady)

"Adventure of the Action Hunter"
© *Troma Team*

Theodore, Dave, Alvin, Simon
in "The Chipmunk Adventure" © *Samuel Goldwyn Co.*

Jim Varney in "Ernest Goes to Camp"
© *Buena Vista Pictures*

MY LITTLE GIRL (Hemdale) Producer/Director, Connie Kaiserman; Screenplay, Connie Kaiserman, Nan Mason; Photography, Pierre L'Homme; Music, Richard Robbins; Editor, Katherine Wenning; Production Designer, Dan Leigh; Costumes, Susan Gammie; Black Swan Productions/Merchant-Ivory; Color; Rated R; 119 minutes; May release. CAST: Mary Stuart Masterson (Franny Bettinger), James Earl Jones (Ike Bailey), Geraldine Page (Grandmother Molly), Pamela Payton-Wright (Mrs. Bettinger), Peter Michael Goetz (Mr. Bettinger), Traci Lin (Alice), Erika Alexander (Joan), Anne Meara (Mrs. Chopper), Peter Gallagher (Kai), Naeemah Wilmore (Camille), Jordan Charney, Page Hannah, Jennifer Lopez, George Newberth, Bill O'Connell

HANGMEN (Shapiro Entertainment) Producers, J. Christian Ingvordsen, Steven W. Kaman, Richard R. Washburn; Director, J. Christian Ingvordsen; Photography, Steven W. Kaman; Screenplay, J. Christian Ingvordsen, Steven Kaman; Music, Michael Montes; Associate Producers, Marc L. Bailin, Peggy Jacobson; Executive Producers, C. Steven Duncker, Robert Anderson; Color; Not rated; 90 minutes; May release. CAST: Richard R. Washburn, Jake Lamotta, Dog Thomas, Kosmo Vinyl, Keith Bogart. No other credits provided

IT'S ALIVE III: ISLAND OF THE ALIVE (Warner Bros.) Producer, Paul Strader; Executive Producer/Director/Screenplay, Larry Cohen; Creature Design, Rick Baker; *"It's Alive" Theme,* Bernard Herrmann; A Larco Production; Editor, David Kern; Photography, Daniel Pearl; Music, Laurie Johnson; Color; Rated R; 91 minutes; May release. CAST: Michael Moriarty (Stephen Jarvis), Karen Black (Ellen Jarvis), Laurene Landon (Sally), Gerrit Graham (Ralston), James Dixon (Lt. Perkins), Neal Isreal (Dr. Brewster), Macdonald Carey (Judge Milton Watson), Art Lund (Dr. Swenson), Ann Dane (Dr. Morrell), Patch Mackenzie (Robbins), Rick Garcia (Tony), William Watson (Cabot), Bobby Ramsen (TV Host)

UNFINISHED BUSINESS . . . (American Film Institute) Producers, Dale Ann Stieber, Chrisann, Suzanne Kent; Director/Screenplay, Viveca Lindfors; Photography, Sean McLin; Music, Patricia Lee Stotter; Don Rebic, Matt Sullivan; Editor, Dale Ann Stieber, Sharyn C. Blumenthal; Costumes, Marty Rodenbush; Production Designer, Johanna Leovey; Color; Not rated; 65 minutes; May release. CAST: Viveca Lindfors (Helena), Peter Donat (Ferenzy), Gina Hecht (Vickie), James Morrison (Jonathan), Anna Devere Smith (Anna), Haley Taylor-Block (Kristina), Herriett Guiar (Cynthia), James Ward (Chauffeur), Chuck Cochran (Manager)

Susanna Hoffs, Michael Ontkean
in "The Allnighter" © *Universal City Studios*

MONSTER IN THE CLOSET (Troma Team) Producers, David Levy, Peter L. Bergquist; Director/Screenplay, Bob Dahlin; Executive Producers, Lloyd Kaufman, Michael Herz; Story, Bob Dahlin, Peter L. Bergquist; Photography, Ronald W. McLeish; Music, Barrie Guard; Editors, Raja Gosnell, Stephanie Palewski; Designer, Lynda Cohen; Associate Producers, Michel Billot, Terrence Corey, Robert Rock; Casting, Sally Ann Stiner, Cindy Pierson, Patrice Messina; Production Manager, Mitch Factor; Assistant Directors, Peter L. Bergquist, Bob Simon; Production Coordinators, Sly Lovegren, Cynthia Colegrove; Sound, Don Parker; Sound, Bill Dager, George Marshall Jr.; Voices, Ken Kessler, William Kirksey, Kathleen McGrath, Paul McIsaac; Art Director, Lynda Cohen; Assistant Art Directors, Randy Alexander, Laurence Bennett, Gary Frimann; Set Decorator, Patricia Hall; Monster Design, William Stout; Monster Effects, Bill Sturgeon, Mark Wilson; Special Effects, Martin Becker, Frank Diaz, John Hartigan, Ken Sher; Stunts, Doc Duhame; Color; Rated PG; 93 minutes; May release. CAST: Donald Grant (Richard Clark), Denise DuBarry (Diane Bennett), Henry Gibson (Dr. Pennyworth), Howard Duff (Father Finnegan), Donald Moffat (Gen. Turnball), Claude Aikins (Sheriff Ketchum), Paul Walker (Professor), Frank Ashmore (Scoop Johnson), John Carradine (Old Joe), Paul Dooley (Roy Crane), Stella Stevens (Margo Crane), Jesse White (Ben Bernstein), Kevin Peter Hall (Monster), Stacy Ferguson, Ritchie Montgomery, Arthur Berggren, Darly Ann Lindley, Gordon Metcalfe, David Anthony, Annie Glynn, Arlee Reed, James Arone, Andrew Cofrin, Benny Baker, Doc Duhame, Jonna Lee, Arthur Taxier, Archie Lang, Claire Nono, John Walsh, Wycliffe Young, Paul Latchaw, David McCharen, Patricia Richarde, Carole Kean, Jack Tate, Sheldon Feldner, Terrence Beasor, Katherine Lyons, Jack Shearer, Richie Egan, Jonathan Aluzas, Brad Kester, Evan Arnold, Corky Pigeon, Stephanie White, Tony Carlin

ERNEST GOES TO CAMP (Touchstone) Producer, Stacy Williams; Director, John R. Cherry III; Screenplay, John R. Cherry III, Coke Sams; Executive Producers, Elmo Williams, Martin Erlichman; Photography, Harry Mathias, Jim May; Art Director, Kathy Emily Cherry; Editor, Marshall Harvey; Music, Shane Keister; Casting, Hank McCann; Creative Consultant, Coke Sams; Production Manager, Tara Sad; Assistant Directors, Patrice Leung, Sandra Mayo, Jeff Shirk; Production Coordinator, Loolee DeLeon; Set Decorator, Kathy Emily Cherry; Sound, Rich Schirmer; Costumes, Ann Payne; Special Effects, Jaime Bird, Mike Weesner, Bruce Kuroyama; Music Supervisor, Robert Randles; Presented in association with Silver Screen Partners III; Buena Vista Pictures Distribution; DeLuxe Color; Dolby Stereo; Rated PG; 90 minutes; May release. CAST: Jim Varney (Ernest P. Worrell), Victoria Racimo (Nurse St. Cloud), John Vernon (Sherman Krader), Iron Eyes Cody (Old Indian Chief), Lyle Alzado (Bronk Stinson), Gailard Sartain (Jake), Daniel Butler (Eddy), Patrick Day (Bobby Wayne), Scott Menville (Crutchfield), Jacob Vargas (Bubba Vargas), Danny Capri (Danny), Hakeem Abdul-Samad (Moustafa Hakeem-Jones), Todd Loyd (Chip Ozgood), Andy Woodworth (Pennington), Richard Speight, Jr. (Borrks), Buck Ford (Attny. Elliott Blatz), Larry Black (Mr. Tipton), Eddy Schumacher (Stennis), Hugh Sinclair (Sparks), Johnson West (Puckett), Jean Wilson, Mac Bennett, John Brown, Robert G. Benson, III, Adam Ruff, Michael Chappelear, Lance Bridgesmith, Paulo DeLeon, Harvey Godwin, Jr., Jeff Standing Bear, Ivan Green, Christian Haas, Brenda Haynes, Keith Teller, Doc Duhame

THE ALLNIGHTER (Universal) Producer/Director, Tamar Simon Hoffs; Screenplay, M. L. Kessler, Tamar Simon Hoffs; Co-Producer/Production Manager, Nancy Israel; Executive Producer, James L. Stewart; Photography, Joseph Urbanczyk; Designer, Cynthia Sowder; Editor, Dan M. Rich; Music, Charles Bernstein; Casting, Carrie Frazier, Shani Ginsberg; Associate Producer, Margot Kessler; Assistant Directors, H. Gordon Boos, Matt Bearson, Cynthia Riddle, Robin Randal Oliver; Production Supervisor, Aron Warner; Costumes, Isis Mussenden; Special Photography, George Billinger III; Additional Editors, Jonas Thaler, Bette Cohen; Assistant Art Director, Jose Montano; Set Decorator, Debra Combs; Choreographer, Sarah Elgart; Production Coordinator, Benjamin Allanoff; Sound, David Brownlow; An Aurora Production; CFI Color; Rated PG-13; 108 minutes; May release. CAST: Susanna Hoffs (Molly), Dedee Pfeiffer (Val), Joan Cusack (Gina), John Terlesky (C. J.), James Anthony Shanta (Killer), Michael Ontkean (Mickey Leroi), Pam Grier (Sgt. MacLeish), Phil Brock (Brad), Kaaren Lee (Connie Alvarez), Janelle Brady (Mary Lou), Meshach Taylor (Det. Philip), Will Seltzer (Det. Ted), Denise Dummont (Julie), Mary Petrie (Anna), Kelly Lynn Pushkin (Nancy), Todd Field, Bradford Bancroft, Danyi Deats, Sarah Elgart, Gordon Boos, Joshua Richmond, Molly Cleator, Robert Goldman, Max Perlich, Dr. Walter Bracklemanns, Ruth Zakarian, Christina Lane, Christopher Doyle, Reese Patterson, Davey Miller, Richard Zanderwhyk, Louis and Clark, Larry Chapman, Michael Gurley, Louis Gutierrez, David Salinas, Steve Ferguson

CAMPUS MAN (Paramount) Producers, Peggy Fowler, Jon Landau; Executive Producers, Barbara D. Boyle, Marc E. Platt; Associate Producer, Todd Headlee; Director, Ron Casden; Screenplay, Matt Dorff, Alex Horvat, Geoffrey Baere; Screen Story, Matt Dorff, Alex Horvat; Photography, Francis Kenny; Designer, David Gropman; Editor, Steven Polivka; Music, James Newton Howard; Music Supervisor, Richard Rudolph; Production Manager, Jon Landau; Assistant Directors, John Jopson, Christopher Griffin, Richard Feld, Lisa Horowitz; Art Director, Karen Schulz; Set Decorator, J. Allen Highfill; Sound, Bruce Litecky; Costumes, Elisabetta Rogiani; Production Coordinator, Ingrid Johanson; Stunts, Greg Barnett; Assistant Editor, Tony Kadell; Music Consultant, Beck Mancuso; Songs by various artists; Vocals by Michael Sembello and various other artists; An RKO Picture; Metrocolor/Technicolor; Rated PG; 94 minutes; May release. CAST: John Dye (Todd Barrett), Steve Lyon (Brett Wilson), Kim Delaney (Dayna Thomas), Kathleen Wilhoite (Molly Gibson), Miles O'Keeffe (Cactus Jack), Morgan Fairchild (Katherine Van Buren), John Welsh (Prof. Jarman), Josef Rainer (Charles McCormick), Dick Alexander (Mr. Bowersox), Steve Archer (Coach Waters), Eden Brandy (Party Girl), Marty Miller (Party Animal), Gayn Erickson, Zibby Miles, Isabelle Bailey, Paul Mancuso, Jason Scott, Bob G. Anthony, Deborah Dee, Lorin Young, Cheli Ayn Chew, Mark Curtis, Bill Stull, Tracy Tanen, Ivan Schwarz, James Sanich, Danny Sullivan, Stuart Grant, Janet Osgood, Tiny Wells, Henry Tank, Linda Williams, Val Ross, Holly Davis, Julie Lamm, Larry Swanson, Michael Byun, Michael Spiller, Ellen Ruffalo, Charley Gilleran, Kristen Danielson, David Draves, John Meier, Susan C. Smith, Scott P. Anthony, Duwan Erickson, Randy Mastey, Ron Piemonte, Bill Travis, Jim Sullivan, Steve Voelker, Christopher Ambrose, James A. Quistorff, D. Sidney Potter, Robert Donahue, Ricky Austin Hill, David T. Moran, John Jaqua, Brad Huestis, Guy R. Vick, Mark P. Bastin

ISHTAR (Columbia) Producer, Warren Beatty; Director/Screenplay, Elaine May; Photography, Vittorio Storaro; Designer, Paul Sylbert; Costumes, Anthony Powell; Sound/Music Coordinator, John Strauss; Associate Producers David L. MacLeod, Nigel Wooll; Editors, Stephen A. Rotter, William Reynolds, Richard Cirincione; Production Representative, John Thomas Lenox; Production Manager, G. Mac Brown; Assistant Directors, Don French, Louis Desposito; Songs, Paul Williams, Elaine May; Sound, Ivan Sharrock; NY Casting, Howard Feuer; Art Directors, Bill Groom, Vicki Paul; Set Decorators, Steve Jordan, Alan Hicks; Stunts, Victor Magnotta; Associate Editor, William S. Scharf; Assistant Editors, Richard Freidlander, William Joseph Kruzykowski, Joseph Gutowski, Dorian Harris; Special Effects, George Gibbs, Garth Inns, Terence Cox, Brian Lince; Additional Songs, Dustin Hoffman and various other artists; Moroccan Music, Bahjawa; Soundtrack on Capitol Records; From Columbia-Delphi V Productions; Technicolor; Technovision; Rated PG-13; 107 minutes; May release. CAST: Warren Beatty (Lyle Rogers), Dustin Hoffman (Chuck Clarke), Isabelle Adjani (Shirra Assel), Charles Grodin (Jim Harrison), Jack Weston (Marty Freed), Tess Harper (Willa), Carol Kane (Carol), David Margulies (Mr. Clark), Aharon Ipale (Emir Yousef), Rose Arrick (Mrs. Clarke), Fuad Hageb (Abdul), Julie Garfield (Dorothy), Christine Rose (Siri Darma), Bob Girolami (Bartender), Abe Kroll (Mr. Thomopoulos), Hannah Kroll (Mrs. Thomopoulos), Herb Gardner (Rabbi Pierce), Bill Moor (U.S. Consulate), Edgar Smith (Prof. Barnes), J. C. Cutler (Omar), Bill Bailey (Gen. Westlake), Ian Gray (Manager Chez Casablanca), Maati Zaari, Bouhaddane Larbi, Fred Melamed, Ron Berglass, Matt Frewer, Alex Hyde White, Stefan Fryff, Alexei Jawdocimov, Mark Ryan, Stuart Abramson, John Freudenheim, Bruce Gordon, Paul Standig, Joseph Gmerek, John Trumpbour, Marie Jean-Charles, Patrice Jean-Charles, Danielle Jean-Charles, Aziz Ben Driss, Kamarr, Eddy Nedari, Adam Hussein, George Masri, Warren Clarke, Arthur Brauss, Sumar Khan, Jon Paul Morgan, Nadim Sawalha, Haluk Belginer, George Marshall Ruge, Konrad Sheehan, Denise Amirante, Peter Bucossi

BODY SLAM (De Laurentiis Entertainment Group) Producers, Shel Lytton, Mike Curb; Director, Hal Needham; Screenplay, Shel Lytton, Steve Burkow; Story, Shel Lytton; Photography, Mike Shea; Editor, Randy Thornton; Music, Michael Lloyd, John D'Andrea; Art Director, Pamela Warner; Assistant Director, Tom Connolly; Co-Producer, Graham Henderson; Rock & Wrestling Consultant, David Wolff; a Hemdale presentation of a Musifilm production; CFI Color; Ultra-Stereo; Rated PG; 89 minutes; May release. CAST: Dirk Benedict (Harry Smilac), Tanya Roberts (Candace Van Der Vegen), Rowdy Roddy Piper (Rick Roberts), Capt. Lou Albano (Capt. Lou Milano), Barry Gordon (Sheldon), Charles Nelson Reilly (Vic Carson), Billy Barty (Tim McClusky), John Astin (Scotty), Dani Janssen (Mrs. Van Der Vegen), Sam "Tama" Fatu (Tonga Tom), Dennis Fimple (Elmo), Kick, Ric Flair, Bruno Sammartino, Afa & Sika, Freddie Blassie, Sheik Adnan Al Kaissy

Steve Lyon, John Dye, Morgan Fairchild
in "Campus Man" © *RKO Pictures*

ENEMY TERRITORY (Empire Pictures) Producers, Cynthia DePaula, Tim Kincaid; Executive Producer, Charles Band; Director, Peter Manoogian; Screenplay, Stuart M. Kaminsky, Bobby Liddell; Story, Stuart M. Kaminsky; Photography, Ernest Dickerson; Editor, Peter Teschner; Music, Sam Winans, Richard Koz Kosinaki; Sound, Mik Cribben; Visual Consultant, Ruth Lounsbury; Designer, Medusa Studios, Marina Zurkow; Art Director, Joanne Besinger; Assistant Director, Michael Speero; Production Manager, Joe Derrig; Special Makeup Effects, John Bisson; Stunts, Dave Copeland; Pyrotechnic Special Effects, Matt Vogel; Casting, Judy Henderson, Alycia Amuller, Anthony Barnao; Associate Producer, Hope Perello; A Millennial Production; Precision Color; Rated R; 90 minutes; May release. CAST: Gary Frank (Barry), Ray Parker, Jr. (Jackson), Jan-Michael Vincent (Parker), Frances Foster (Elva Briggs), Tony Todd (Count), Stacey Dash (Toni Briggs), Dean Richmond (Chet), Tiger Haynes (Barton), Charles Randall (Mr. Beckhorne)

NECROPOLIS (Empire Pictures) Producers, Cynthia DePaula, Tim Kincaid; Director/Screenplay, Bruce Hickey; Photography, Arthur D. Marks; Editors, Barry Zetlin, Tom Mesherski; Music, Don Great, Tom Milano; Sound, Russell Fager; Art Directors, Ruth Lounsbury, Marina Zurkow; Set Design, David Morong; Assistant Director, Rebecca Rothbaum; Production Manager, Michael Spero; Special Makeup Effects, Ed French; Special Effects, Matt Vogel; Choreography, Taunie Vrenon; A Tycin Entertainment Production; Precision Color; Rated R; 76 minutes; May release. CAST: LeeAnne Baker (Eva), Jacquie Fitz (Dawn), Michael Conte (Billy), William K. Reed (Rev. Henry James), George Anthony, Jeff Julian, Nadine Hart, Anthony Gioia, Gy Mirano, Jennifer Stall, Paul Ruben, Adrianne Lee

PSYCHOS IN LOVE (ICN Bleecker) Executive Producer, Gary Bechard; Producer/Director/Editor/Photography, Gorman Bechard; Screenplay/Music, Carmine Capobianco Gorman Bechard; Sound/Associate Producer, Shaun Cashman; Production Manager/Assistant Director/Associate Producer, H. Shep Pamplin; Costumes, Debi Thibeault; Special Effects, H. Shep Pamplin, Matt Brooks, Jan Radder, Jan Pdis, Nina Port, Carmine Capobianco; Special Effects Props, Jennifer Aspinall, Tom Molinelli; Makeup/Hair, Frank Stewart; A Wizard Video Presentation of a Generic Films Production; Precision Color; Not rated; 87 minutes; May release. CAST: Carmine Capobianco (Joe), Debi Thibeault (Kate), Frank Stewart (Herman), Cecilia Wile (Nikki), Donna Davidge (Heather), Shawn Light, LeeAnn Baker, Tressa Zannino, Kate McCamy

Dustin Hoffman, Warren Beatty in "Ishtar" (Columbia)

139

Eric Douglas (C), Paul LaGreca (R)
in "Student Confidential" © *Troma Inc.*

THE HEARST METROTONE NEWSREEL SHOW (Film Forum) Original films produced by the Hearst Corporation 1929–1940; Compilation selected by Michael Friend for the UCLA Film and Television Archive; Distributed by the UCLA Film and Television Archive, Robert Rosen, Director; Made from original 35mm nitrate materials; Black and white; Not rated; 100 minutes; May release.

SLAMMER GIRLS (Lightning) Producer/Director, Chuck Vincent; Screenplay, Craig Horrall, Chuck Vincent, Rick Marx, Larue Watts; Photography, Larry Revene; Music, Ian Shaw, Kai Joffe; Editor, Marc Ubell; Costumes, Eddie Heath; Color; Rated R; 80 minutes; June release. CAST: Devon Jenkin (Melody), Jeff Eagle (Harry Wiener), Jane Hamilton (Miss Crabapples), Ron Sullivan (Gov. Caldwell), Tally Brittany, Darcy Nychols, Stasia Micula, Sharon Cain, Beth Broderick, Sharon Kelly, Kim Kafkaloff, Philip Campanaro, Michael Hentzman, Louis Bonanno, Janice Doskey, Jane Kreisel, Captain Haggerty

ANDY WARHOL Producer, Michael Blackwood; Director, Lana Jokel; Photography, Mark Woodcock, Roger Murphy, Lana Jokel; Documentary; Not rated; 53 minutes; June release. WITH: Andy Warhol, Holly Woodlawn, Ingrid Superstar, Viva, Sylvia Miles, Joe Dallesandro, Barbara Rose, and others

LUGGAGE OF THE GODS (General Pictures) Producer, Jeff Folmsbee; Director/Screenplay, David Kendall; Photography, Steven Ross; Editor, Jack Haigis; Music, Cengiz Yaltkaya; Art Director, Joshua Harrison; Color; Not rated; 80 minutes; June release. CAST: Mark Stolzenberg, Gabriel Barre, Gwen Ellison, No other credits provided.

PARTY CAMP (Lightning Pictures) Producer, Mark Borde; Director, Gary Graver; Screenplay, Paul L. Brown; Photography, Gary Graver; Music, Dennis Dreith; Editors. Michael B. Hoggan, Joyce L. Hoggan; United Color; Rated R; 96 minutes; June release. CAST: Andrew Ross (Jerry Riviera), Kerry Brennan (Heather), Billy Jacoby (D.A.), Jewel Shepard (Dyanne), Peter Jason (Sarge), Kirk Cribb (Tad), Dean R. Miller (Cody), Corky Pigeon (Winslow), Stacy Baptist (Kelly), Paula Irvine (Devil), Betsy Chasse (Lisa), Jon Pine (Ned-Man), April Wayne (Nurse Brenda), Cherie Franklin (Mrs. Beadle), Troy Shire (Les), Erika Smith (Paul), Kevin Telles (Ferris), Rashad Barzaghi (Camper), Marsha McClelland (Miss Hollywood)

John Moulder Brown, Amy Irving
in "Rumpelstiltskin" © *Cannon*

STUDENT CONFIDENTIAL (Troma) Producer/Director/Screenplay/Music/Editor, Richard Horian; Executive Producer, James Horian; Photography, James Dickson; Production Executive, H. Kaye Dyle; Designer, David Wasco; Art Director, Robert Joyce; Lighting, Al Goldenhar; Sound, Gerald B. Wolfe; Second Editor, Danny Retz; Casting Assistant, Ninon Messina; Production Coordinator, Harry Haskell; Assistant Directors, Steven Pomeroy, Amanda Gill, Art Payne; Assistant Editor, William T. Gentry; Costumes, Cassandra Voison; Set Decorators, Sharon Seymour, Steve Baumann, Evan Ensign, Len Levine, Keith Vidger; DeLuxe Color; Rated R; 100 minutes; June release. CAST: Eric Douglas (Johnny Warshetsky), Marlon Jackson (Joseph Williams), Susan Scott (Susan Bishop), Elizabeth Singer (Elaien Duvat), Ronee Blakely (Jenny Selden), Richard Horian (Michael Drake), Paula Sorenson (Carla), John Mildord (Mr. Warshetsky), Kip King (Milton Goldman), Sarina Grant (Mrs. Williams), Billy Jean Thomas (Maggie Murkill), Joel Mills (Rob), Corwyn Anthony (Greg), Katherine Kriss, Mindy Levy, Ed Karvoski, Paul LaGreca, Shawn Lieber, Andre Rosey Brown, Daniel Morong, John Willamette, Nadia Cota, Jace Julee, Tara Wade, Robert Varney, Joan McGough

CAPTIVE HEARTS (MGM/UA) Producer, John A. Kuri; Executive Producer, Milton Goldstein; Director, Paul Almond; Screenplay, Pat Morita, John A. Kuri; From a work by Sargon Tamimi; Photography, Thomas Vamos; Editor, Yurij Luhovy; Music, Osamu Kitajima; Costumes, Nicoletta Massone; Designers, Steve Sardanis, Francois DeLucy; Set Decorators, Claudine Charbonneau, Anne Galea; Sound, Patrick Rousseau; Metrocolor; Rated PG; 97 minutes; June release. CAST: Noriyuki "Pat" Morita (Fukushima), Chris Makepeace (Robert), Mari Sato (Miyoko), Michael Sarrazin (Sgt. McManus), Seth Sakai (Takayama), Denis Akiyama (Masato)

COMMANDO SQUAD (Trans World Entertainment) Producer, Alan Amiel; Executive Producer, Yoram Pelman; Co-producer/Director, Fred Olen Ray; Screenplay, Michael D. Sonye; Photography, Gary Graver; Editor, Kathie Weaver; Sound, David Waelder; Art Director, Corey Kaplan; Special Effects, Kevin McCarthy, Sandy McCarthy; Assistant Directors, Gary M. Bettmann; Associate Producer, Herb Linsey; Foto-Kem Color; Rated R; 89 minutes; June release. CAST: Brian Thompson (Clint), Kathy Shower (Cat), William Smith (Morgan), Sid Haig (Iggy), Robert Quarry (Milo), Ross Hagen (Long John), Marie Windsor (Casey), Mel Welles (Quintano), Benita Martinez (Anita), Dawn Wildsmith, Russ Tamblyn, Tane McClure, Michael D. Sonye

NIGHTMARE AT SHADOW WOODS (Film Concept Group) Executive Produer, J. W. Stanley; Producer, Marianne Kanter; Director, John W. Grissmer; Screenplay, Richard Lamden; Photography, Richard E. Brooks; Editor, Michael R. Miller; Music, Richard Einhorn; Designer, Jim Rule; Special Effects, Ed French; Casting, Amanda Mackey; CFI Color; Rated R; 84 minutes; June release. CAST: Louise Lasser (Maddy), Mark Soper (Todd/Terry), Marianne Kanter (Dr. Berman), Julie Gordon (Karen), Jayne Bentzen (Julie), William Fuller (Brad)

RUMPLESTILTSKIN (Cannon) Producers, Menahem Golan, Yoram Globus; Director/Screenplay, David Irving; Associate Producer, Patricia Ruben; Executive Producer, Itzik Kol; Photography, David Gurfinkel; Designer, Marek Dobrowolski; Editor, Tova Neeman; Music, Max Robert; Art Director, Charlie Leon; Production Manager, Asher Gat; Assistant Directors, Mike Katzin, Haim Rinsky, Yael Golan; Production Coordinator, Charlotte Rosa; Music Supervisor, Stephen Lawrence; Sound, Eli Yarkoni; Set Decorator, Albert Segal; Special Effects, Carlo de Marchis, Juan Ferrer, Yoram Zargary, Jackie Boaz; Makeup Design, Marie-Helen Yatchenkoff; Casting, Hadassa Degani, Wendy Murray; Assistant Editors, Tali Halter, Elinora Hardy; Choreographer, Dari Shai; Musical Directors, Yohushua Ben Yohushua, Jack Fishman; Orchestrations, Frank Barber; Music Performance, Kevin Stanton, Spencer Lee; Songs, Max Robert, Jules Irving, David Irving; Vocals, Amy Irving, Stuart Zagni, Clive Revill, Billy Barty; Soundtrack on Kid Stuff Audio & Video/IJE Inc.; Dolby Stereo; Color; Rated G; 84 minutes; June release. CAST: Amy Irving (Katie), Billy Barty (Rumpelstiltskin), Clive Revill (King Mezzer), Priscilla Pointer (Queen Grizelda), Robert Symonds (Victor), John Moulder-Brown (Prince), Yehuda Efroni (Count Flax), Johnny Phillips (Ralph), Jack Messinger (Alf), Michael Schneider (Peasant), Yael Uziely (Emily), Julian Chagrin (Blacksmith), Danny Segev (Clerk), Susan Berlin (Clerk's Wife), Austin Irving, Yael Neeman, Jonathan Gurfinkel (Clerk's Children), Igor Borisov (Cook), Jerry Hyman (Advisor), Joseph Lee (Farmer), Yankale Ben Sira (Guard), Ely Shi (Executioner), Samini Koresh (Midget Driver)

Silvio Oliviero, Helen Papas
in "Graveyard Shift" © *Cinema Ventures*

Victoria Barrett, Shakti
in "Three Kinds of Heat" © *Cannon*

THE PUPPETOON MOVIE (Expanded Entertainment) Producer/Voice Director/Screenplay, Arnold Leibovit; Animation, Peter Kleinow; Animation Director, Gene Warren, Jr.; Music, Buddy Baker; Associate Producer, Fantasy II; *New Animation Sequences:* Photography, Gene Warren, Jr,; Editor, Arnold Leibovit; Script Consultant, Peter Kleinow; Gumby Advisor, Art Clokey; Additional Photography, John Huneck; Assistant Camera, Michael Griffen; Art Directors, Gene Warren, Jr., Michael Minor; Supervisor Set/Minature Construction, Gary Campsie; Gumby Maker, Kurt Hanson; Arnie the Dinosaur/Artistic Finishing, Charlie Chiodo, Steve Chiodo; Title Design/George Pal Book Refinishing, Walt Disney Graphic Services/Ed Garbert; Animation Camera, Nick Vasu; Sound, John 'Doc' Wilkinson, Lajon Productions; Additional Puppet Figures, David Allen Productions, Coast Special Effects, The Chiodo Brothers; Time Machine, Bob Burns; Songs by various artists; Soundtrack on Talking Rings Record Company; featuring Animation Produced by George Pal at the Pal Studio in Eindhoven, Netherlands/Puppetoons Produced by George Pal for Paramount (1930's-40's); Color and Black & White; Not rated; 80 minutes; June release

GRAVEYARD SHIFT (Shapiro Entertainment) Producer, Michael Bockner; Director/Screenplay, Gerard Ciccoritti; Photography, Robert Bergman; Music, Nicholas Pike; Editors, Robert Bergman, Norman Smith; Executive Producers, Arnold H. Bruck, Stephen R. Flaks; Associate Producers, Peter Boboras, Richard Borciver; Supervising Producer, Lester Berman; Presented in association with Cinema Ventures, Inc.; A Lightshow Communications production; Color; Rated R; 89 minutes; June release. CAST: Silvio Oliviero, Helen Papas, Cliff Stoker. No other credits provided

THREE KINDS OF HEAT (Cannon) Producer, Michael Kagan; Director/Screenplay, Leslie Stevens; Associate Producer, Michael Hartman; Editor, Bob Dearberg; Designer, Duncan Cameron; Photography, Terry Cole; Music, Michael Bishop with Scott Page; Production Managers, Clive Challis, William E. Roe; Assistant Directors, Steve Bernstein, Paul Lowin, Martin Lee; Production Coordinator, Christine Fenton; Sound, Stan Phillips; Art Director, Alan Hunter Craig; Assistant Art Director, Tom Brown; Set Decorator, Robyn Hamilton-Doney; Special Effects, John Gant, Chris Gant, Ian Biggs; Stunts, Peter Diamond; Assistant Editors, Martin Crane, Mark Thomson, Carolann Sanchez; Music Supervisor, Paula Erickson; Music Coordinator, Stephanie Lee; Arranger, Michael Bishop; "*Spin*"/"*3 Kinds of Heat*" by Michael Bishop; "*Blast*" by Steve Bates; Song Performances, Wane Lindsay, Michael Bishop, Susie Sexton, Suzie Benson; Dolby/Ultra-Stereo; Rated R; 87 minutes; June release. CAST: Robert Ginty (Elliot Cromwell), Victoria Barrett (Terry O'Shea), Shakti (Major Shan), Sylvester McCoy (Harry Pimm), Barry Foster (Norris), Paul Gee (Eddie Wing), Malcolm Connell (Jingmao), Trevor Martin (Haggard) Mary Tamm (Pilou), Jeannie Brown (Angelica), Keith Edwards (Kaufman), Jack Hedley (Kirkland), Bridget Khan (Adrianna), Eddie Yeoh (Messenger Boy), D'Artagnan (Woodrow), Lekiddo (Lamont), Steven McFarlen (Delivery Boy), Sydney Coll (Parking Attendant), Jerry Harte (Haig), Patrick Durkin (Trainer), Michael Mellinger (Reggio), Les Clack (Duclos), Reginald Marsh (Sir Hugh), Oscar James (Uncle Joe), Robert Grange (Peterson), Paul Ridley (Collins), Edwin Craig (Scibillia), Arnold Lee (Cho), Vincent Wong (Fan), Natasha Williams (Fran), Samantha Fox (Charleen), Linda May Harris (Coco)

TOO MUCH (Cannon) Producers, Menahem Golan, Yoram Globus; Director/Screenplay, Eric Rochat; Narration written by Joan Laine; Line Producer, Yosuke Mizuno; Associate Producer, Dov Maoz; Music, George S. Clinton; Editor, Alaine Jakubowicz; Photography, Daisaku Kimura; Production Manager, Kenichi Horii; Assistant Directors, Toshiaki Arai, Shinichiro Nakada, Takaaki Hayashi; Production Executive, Rony Yacov; Stunts, Chihiro Mitsuishi, Yoshifumi Nonaka, Tsuyoshi Matsumoto; Art Director, Tsuneo Kantake; Assistant Art Director, Takeshi Shimizu; Set Decorators, Satoshi Sakuma, Hirokazu Minagawa; Sound, Shyotaro Yoshida; Costumes, Kyoto Isho; Production Coordinator, Riuko Tominaga; Special Effects, Osamu Kune; Robot, Masaharu Ogawa, Toshio Komiya, Yasushi Ishizu, Studio Nue; Production Supervisor, Michael R. Sloan; Assistant Editors, Marcelo Sansevieri, Galit Lidsky, Marianne Skweres, Alexander Renskoff; Music Supervisor, Paula Erickson; Additional Orchestrations, Joey Rand; Songs, Coby Recht, Ole Georgg; Vocals, Coby Recht, Hilya Recht, The Knowles, Beverly Nero; Dolby Stereo/Ultra-Stereo; TVC Color; Rated PG; 89 minutes; June release. CAST: Masao Fukazawa (Too Much), Bridgette Andersen (Susie), Morikiyo Bowhay (Mata), Hiroyuki Watanabe (Tetsuro), David N. Spencer (Tom), Rachel Huggett (Jane), Karen Hammer (Currie), Char Fontana (Dr. Finkel), Uganda (Bernie), Shigeru Khoyama (Police Chief), Noboru Mitani (Doorman), Ryota Mizushima (Mechanic), Hachiro Misumi, Hiroshi Murayama, Tsuyoshi Matsumoto, Hidekazu Nagae, Naoto Yokouchi, Minoru Inaba, Masayoshi Takigawa, Masuji Fujiwara, Nenji Kobayashi, Yoshifumi Nonaka, Yoichi Kikukawa, Satoru Fukasaku, Hirobumi Nakase, Kazunori Arai, Isao Kishimoto

Brian Thompson, Kathy Shower
in "Commando Squad" © *Trans World*

Morikiyo Bowhay, TM, Bridgette Andersen
in "Too Much" © *Cannon*

Dennis Hopper, Grace Jones
in "Straight to Hell" © *Island Pictures*

PRIVATE INVESTIGATIONS (MGM) Producers, Steven Golin, Sigurjon Sighvatsson; Director, Nigel Dick; Screenplay, John Dahl, David Warfield; Story, Nigel Dick; Photography, David Bridges, Bryan Duggan; Music, Murray Munro; Editor, Scott Chestnut; Production Designer, Piers Plowden; Art Director, Nick Rafter; Costumes, Charmin Espinoza; Executive Producers, Michael Kuhn, David Hockman; Sound, Bob Dreebin; Associate Producer, David Warfield; Songs by various artists; Color; Dolby Stereo; Rated R; 91 minutes; June release. CAST: Clayton Rohner (Joey Bradley), Ray Sharkey (Ryan), Paul LeMat (Detective Wexler), Talia Balsam (Jenny Fox), Phil Morris (Eddie Gordon), Martin Balsam (Cliff Dowling), Anthony Zerbe (Charles Bradley), Robert Ito (Kim), Vernon Wells (Detective North), Anthony Geary (Larry), Justin Lord (Howard White), Robert Cummings, Jr. (Hollister), Desiree Boschetti (Denise), Andy Romano (Mr. Watson), Sydney Walsh (Janet), Jon St. Elwood (Gil), Rex Ryon (Lou), Richard Herkert (Kim's Driver), Frank Gargani (Wire Tapper), Big Yank (Clay), Nigel Dick (Photographer), Dennis Phung (Cafe Owner), Sharonlee McLean (Cafe Waitress), Michelle Seipp (Woman in restaurant), Stan Yale (Bum), Hugh Slate (Himself), Robert Torti, Jean Glaude (Burglars), Del Zamora, Luis Manuel ("Car Thieves")

MILLION DOLLAR MYSTERY (De Laurentiis Entertainment Groups) Producer, Stephen F. Kesten; Director, Richard Fleischer; Screenplay, Tim Metcalfe, Miguel Tejada-Flores, Rudy DeLuca; Photography, Jack Cardiff; Editor, John W. Wheeler; Stunts, George Fisher; Associate Producer, Kuki Lopez Rodero; Music Design, Ryrell-Mann; Score, Al Gorgoni; Designer, Jack G. Taylor, Jr.; Casting, Marilyn Black; Costumes, Clifford Capone; Production Manager, Brooke Kennedy; Assistant Directors, Juan Carlos Lopez Rodero, Ian Foster Woolf, Margaret Krueger; Production Coordinator, Judi Rosner; Sound, Kirk Francis; Special Effects, John Stirber, Stephen Humphrey; Assistant Editor, Timothy Board; Art Director, Dawn Snyder; Set Decorators, Stephen Potter, Richard Boris, Ron Green, Bob Trow, Bruce Ayres; Songs. Barry Mann, John Lewis Parker, Stephanie Tyrell, Ashley Hall, and various other artists; Ultra-Stereo; Technicolor; Rated PG; 95 minutes; June release. CAST: Eddie Deezen (Rollie), Wendy Sherman (Lollie), Rick Overton (Stuart Briggs), Mona Lyden (Barbara Briggs), Douglas Emerson (Howie Briggs), Royce D. Applegate (Tugger), Pam Matteson (Dotty), Daniel McDonald (Crush), Penny Baker (Charity), Tawny Fere (Faith), LaGena Hart (Hope), Tom Bosley (Sidney Preston), Mack Dryden (Fred), Jamie Alcroft (Bob), Rich Hall (Slaughter), Gail Neely (Officer Gretchen), Kevin Pollak (Officer Quinn), H. B. Haggerty (Awful Abdul), Bob

Schott (Bad Obris), Peter Pitofsky (Toxic Werewolf), Greg Travis, Tommy Sledge, Christopher Cary, Rudy DeLuca, Mark Regan, John Gilgreen, Katie LaBourdette, Pat McGroarty, Clark Coleman, Paul Strader, Rosemary Johnston, David Trim, Susann Benn, John Hammil, Gary Kelson, Sal Lopez, Augustine Lam, Jack Carpenter, Andy Epper, George Fisher, Dar Robinson

STRAIGHT TO HELL (Island Pictures) Producer, Eric Fellner; Director, Alex Cox; Screenplay, Dick Rude, Alex Cox; Photography, Tom Richmond; Editor, Dave Martin; Designer, Andrew McAlpine; Production Manager, Paul Raphael; Costumes, Pam Tait; Sound, Ian Voight; Art Director, Caroline Hanania; Assistant Directors, Joe Ochoa, Bill Rudgard, Paul Wood; Assistant Editors, Justin Krish, Angelica Landry; Special Effects, Juan Ramon Molina; An Initial Pictures Production of a Commies From Mars Film; Color; Rated R; 86 minutes; June release. CAST: Sy Richardson (Norwood), Joe Strummer (Simms), Dick Rude (Willy), Courtney Love (Velma), Zander Schloss (Karl), Del Zamora (Poncho), Luis Contreras (Sal), Jim Jarmusch (Mr. Dade), Miguel Sandoval (George), Jennifer Balgobin (Fabienne), Biff Yeager (Frank), Sue Kiel (Leticia), Michele Winstanley (Louise), Edward Tudor-Pole (Rusty), Xander Berkeley (Preacher), Fox Harris (Kim Blousson), Dennis Hopper (I. G. Farben), Grace Jones (Sonya), Graham Fletcher Cook (Whitey/Jeeves), Spider Stacy (Angel Eyes), Shane MacGowan (Bruno). Jem Finer (Granpa), Terry Woods (Tom), Cait O'Riordan (Slim), Kathy Burke (Sabrina), James Fearnley (Jimmy), Sara Sugarman (Chuch), Juan Torres (Churbo), Anne-Marie Ruddock (Molly), Sharon Bailey (Porter), Andrew Rankin (Lance), Frank Murray (Biff), Philip Chevron (Ed), Elvis Costello (Hives), Jose Pomedio Monedero (Gomez), Ed Pansullo (Mac MacMahon)

NUMBER ONE (Film Forum) Director/Screenplay, Dyan Cannon; A project of the American Film Institute's Directing Workshop for Women; 1976; Not rated; 48 minutes; June release. CAST: Allen Garfield (Principal) and others

SURF NAZIS MUST DIE (Troma) Executive Producer/Director, Peter George; Producer/Production Manager, Robert Tinnell; Screenplay, Jon Ayre; Editor, Craig Colton; Associate Producer/Surf Coordinator, Antonyia Verna; Photography, Rolf Kesterman; Art Director/Costumes, Byrnadette diSanto; Music, Jon McCallum; Assistant Directors, John Bick, Nancy Mott; Production Coordinator, Andrew Sands; Sound, Robert Janiger, Jan Ove Hogman; Stunts, Frank diSanto; Casting, Sahara Productions/Mahmud Abudaber, Donna Besse, Nancy Mott; Assistant Editors, Dan McCann, Corina Zuniga; Narration, Jon Ayre, Young Tom Productions; Song, Andrew Spindler; Color; Ultra-Stereo; Rated R; 80 minutes; July release. CAST: Gail Neely (Mama Washington), Robert Harden (LeRoy Washington), Barry Brenner (Adolf), Dawn Wildsmith (Eva), Michael Sonye (Mengele), Joel Hile (Hook), Gene Mitchell (Brutus), Tom Shell (Smeg), Bobbie Briese (Mom), Ty Thomas/Tom Demenkoff (Aerial), John Willamette (Mex), Rand Hogen (Teeth), Daniel Kong/Dennis Phung (Wang), Steve Ried (Yin), Terry Lee (Yang), Brian Krutoff (Curl), Ted Prior (Blow), Andrew Bick (Dry), Dawne Ellison (Nurse Withers), Berta Dahl (Matron), Willa Reynolds (Anne), Eva Goodrich (Maggie), Esther Lloyd (Esther), Thomas Searle (Wheels), Karan Hanson, Cristina Garcia, Dominique/Byrnadette diSanto, Sherry Dreizen, Ross Allman/Jon McCallum, Maurice E. Brooks III, Daniel R. Flynn, Cosme T. Mata, Douglas D. Meyer, Don Lee Weiler, Jason Collier, Antonyia Verna, Scott Baker, Brian Curry, Jason Dreizen, Gary Frye, Miles Guarneri, Ian Meno, Jodi Shapiro, Josh Mott, Justin Dalton, Jeremy Mullen, Jessica Mullen, Mike Yoder, Eric DeYoung, Kenneth Scherr, Laura Gregory, Dianne Copeland, John Bick, Peter George, Mel Sparks, Garry Levinson, Carrie Joseph/June March, Jan Ove Hogman, Robert Tinnell, Anders Olausson, Andrew Sands, David Bergeson, Chris Andrae, Brandi Bigler, Richard Hill, Mark Foo, Christopher Gardner, Tony Higa

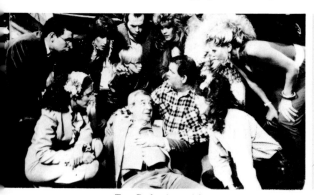

Tom Bosley (center) in
"Million Dollar Mystery" © *DEG*

"Surf Nazis Must Die"
© *Troma Inc.*

THE SQUEEZE (Tri-Star) Producers, Rubert Hitzig, Michael Tannen; Director, Roger Young; Screenplay, Daniel Taplitz; Executive Producers, Harry Colomby, David Shamroy Hamburger; Photography, Arthur Albert; Designer, Simon Waters; Editor, Harry Keramidas; Costumes, Jane Greenwood; Music, Miles Goodman; Associate Producers, James Chory, Gayle Scott; Casting, Lynn Kressel; Production Manager, Terence A. Donnelly; Assistant Directors, James Chory, Johanna Jenson, Nina Kostroff; Art Director, Christopher Nowak; Music Supervisor, Michael Tannen; Set Decorators, Ted Glass, Elaine O'Donnell; Assistant Set Decorator, Stephen Davis; Additional Editing, David Holden; Assistant Editors, Alexandra Leviloff, Janet Fiona Mason, Lewis Schoenbrun; Sound, Danny Michael, Franklin D. Stettner; Special Effects, Gary Elmendorf, John Gray, Steve Kirshoff; Assistant Costume Designers, David Charles, Judianna Makovsky; Stunts, Victor Magnotta; Production Coordinators, Victoria W. Hsu, Liz Galloway; Songs by various artists; from Tri-Star-ML Delphi Premier Productions; Dolby Stereo; DuArt Color; Rated PG-13; 102 minutes; July release. CAST: Michael Keaton (Harry Berg), Rae Dawn Chong (Rachel Dobs), Joe Pantoliano (Norman), Ronald Guttman (Rigaud), John Davidson (Honest Tom T. Murray), George Gerdes (Joe), Leslie Bevis (Gem Vigo), Liane Langland (Hilda), Pat MacNamara (Arnold Drisco), Meat Loaf (Titus), Richard Portnow (Ruben), Paul Herman (Freddy), Ric Abernathy (Bouncer), Danny Aiello III (Ralph Vigo), Bobby Bass, Jophrey Brown, Lou Criscoulo, Ray Gabrield, Richard E. Huhn, John Dennis Johnston, Jeffrey Josephson, Diana Lewis, Frank Lugo, Andrew Magarian, Mick Muldoon, Jack Murray, Gerald J. Quimby, John S. Rushton, Peg Shirley

I WAS A TEENAGE ZOMBIE (Horizon Releasing) Producers, Richard Hirsh, John Elias Michalakias; Director, John Elias Michalakias; Screenplay, James Martin, George Seminara, Steve McCoy; Photography, Peter Lewnes; Music, Jonathan Roberts, Craig Seeman; Editor, John Elias Michalakias; Art Directors, Tom Stampa, Dora Katsoulogiannakis; Costumes, Dora Katsoulogiannakis; Special Effects, Carl Sorenson, Mike Lacky; a Periclean production; Color; Not rated; 92 minutes; July release. CAST: Michael Rubin (Dan Wake), George Seminara (Gordy), Steve McCoy (Mussolini), Peter Bush (Rosencrantz), Cassie Madden (Cindy Faithful), Cindy Keiter (Miss Lugae), Gwyn Drischell (Margo), Allen L. Rickman (Lieberman), Lynnea Benson (Hilda), Ray Stough (Lenny), Robert C. Sabin (Chuckie), Kevin Nagle (The Byrd), Ted Polites (Moon), Steve Reidy (Policeman), Caren Pane (Poetry Teacher), Sal Lumetta, Tom Caldoro (Gangsters), Ken Baggett, Jim Martin, Brian Doyle, Denise Texeira, Joan Bostwick, Gail Lucas, Frank Devlin

MASTERBLASTER (Artist Entertainment Group) Executive Producer, William Grefe; Producer/Story, Randy Grinter; Director, Glenn R. Wilder; Screenplay, Randy Grinter, Glenn R. Wilder, Jeff Moldovan; Photography, Frank Pershing Flynn; Editor, Angelo Ross; Music, Alain Salvati; Sound, Henry Lopez; Stunts, Scott Wilder; Assistant Directors, Don Moody, Marty Swartz; Production Manager, Jon Williams; Associate Producers, Chuck Greenfield, Angela Greenfield, Jeanna Plafsky, Richard Pitt; From Radiance Films Intl.; A First American Entertainment Production; Color; Rated R; 84 minutes; July release. CAST: Jeff Moldovan (Jeremy Hawk), Donna Rosae (Samantha), Joe Hess (DeAngelo), Peter Lundblad (Lewis), Robert Goodman (Mike), Richard St. George, George Gill, Earleen Carey, Jim Reynolds, Julian Byrd, Ron Urgs, Tracy Hutchinson, Bill Whorman, Ray Forchion, Lou Ann Carroll, Kari Whitman

SUMMER SCHOOL (Paramount) Producers, George Shapiro, Howard West; Director, Carl Reiner; Screenplay, Jeff Franklin; Story, Stuart Birnbaum, David Dashev, Jeff Franklin; Executive Producer, Marc Trabulus; Photography, David M. Walsh; Designer, David L. Snyder; Editor, Bud Molin; Music, Danny Elfman; Associate Producer, Jeff Franklin; Casting, Penny Perry; Production Manager, Jack

Rae Dawn Chong, Michael Keaton in "The Squeeze" © *Tri-Star*

Roe; Assistant Directors, Marty Ewing, James Dillon, Nilo Otero; Art Director, Joe Wood; Set Decorator, Linda DeScenna; Set Designer, John Warnke; Sound, Joe Kenworthy; Orchestrations, Steve Bartek; Costumes, Ray Summers, Production Coordinator, Janet Lee Siegel; Casting Assistant, Donna Anderson; Choreography, Tony Fields; Special Effects, Richard Helmer; Assistant Editor, Stephen Myers; Songs, Danny Elfman, Steve Bartek and various other artists; Technicolor; Rated PG-13; July release. CAST: Mark Harmon (Freddy Shoop), Kirstie Alley (Robin Bishop), Robin Thomas (Phil Gills), Patrick Labyorteaux (Kevin), Courtney Thorne Smith (Pam), Dean Cameron (Chainsaw), Gary Riley (Dave), Kelly Minter (Denise), Ken Olandt (Larry), Shawnee Smith (Rhonda), Richard Steven Horvitz (Alan Eakian), Fabiana Udenio (Anna-Marie), Frank McCarthy (Principal Kelban), Tom Troupe (Judge), Lucy Lee Flippin (Substitute Teacher), Amy Stock (Kim), Bo (Wondermut), Beau Starr (Chainsaw's Dad), Laura Waterbury (Chainsaw's Mom), Robin Kaufman (Chainsaw's Sister), Dottie Archibald (Dave's Mom), Patricia Conklin (Larry's Mom), Vivian Bonnell (Denise's Mom), Judy Heinz (Rhonda's Mom), Michael MacRae (Kevin's Dad), Carl Reiner (Mr. Dearadorian), Lillian Adams (Grandma Eakian), Duane Davis (Jerome), David Wakefield (Scuzzy Kid), Conroy Gedeon (Mr. Winnick), Bill Capizzi, Andrea Howard, Deedee Rescher, Christopher Kriesa, Carlos Lacamara, Jeff Silverman, Thomas Ryan, Judy Nagy, Darwyn Swalve, Prince Hughes, Courtney Gebhart, Terry Logan, Nels Van Patten, Leigh French, Jack Blessing, Gigi Vorgan, Lynne Marie Stewart, John Stark, Susan Elliott, Lora Staley, Laurie Faso, Brian Stevens, Gary Imhoff

A MAN IN LOVE (Cinecom) Director, Diane Kurys; Executive Producer, Michael Seydoux, Camera One; Co-Producer, Alexandre Films; Associate Producers, Marjorie Israel, Armand Barbault; Line Producer, Roberto Guissani, Dolly Cinematografica; Music, Georges Delerue; Assistant Directors, Paolo Barzman, Pericles Prokopiades; Art Director, Dean Tavoularis; Photography, Bernard Zitzermann; Editor, Joele Van Effenterre; Screenplay, Diane Kurys; Adaptation, Diane Kurys, Olivier Schatzky; Costumes, Brigitte Nierhaus; Sound, Bernard Bats, Gerard Lamps; Production Manager, Bertrand Van Effenterre; Color; Rated R; 108 minutes; July release. CAST: Peter Coyote (Steve), Greta Scacchi (Jane), Peter Riegert (Michael), John Berry (Harry), Vincent Lindon (Bruno), Jean Pigozzi (Pizani), Elia Katz (Sam), Constantin Alexandrov (De Vitta), Michele Melega (Paolo), Jean-Claude De Goros (Dr. Sandro), Claudia Cardinale (Julia), Jamie Lee Curtis (Susan)

Mark Harmon, Kirstie Alley in "Summer School" © *Paramount/Fred Sabine*

Peter Coyote, Peter Riegert in "A Man in Love" © *Cinecom*

"Berserker"
© *American Video Group*

WHITE WATER SUMMER (Columbia) formerly *Rites of Summer;* Producer, Mark Tarlov; Director, Jeff Bleckner; Screenplay, Mayna Starr, Ernest Kinoy; Photography: John Alcott; Music, Michael Boddicker; Editor, David Ray; Art Director, Jeffrey L. Goldstein; Costumes, Thomas Dawson; Executive Producer, Wolfgang Glattes; Sound, Kirk Francis; Associate Producers, Christopher Dalton, Dennis Palumbo, Bob Roe, Larry Rapaport; Assistant Director, Bob Roe; Songs by various artists; a Columbia-Delphi V production from Polar Entertainment; Technicolor; Rated PG; 90 minutes; July release. CAST: Kevin Bacon (Vic), Sean Astin (Alan Block), Jonathan Ward (Mitch), K. C. Martel (George) Matt Adler (Chris), Caroline McWilliams (Virginia Block), Charles Siebert (Jerry Block), Joseph Passarelli (Storekeeper)

BERSERKER (Shapiro Entertainment) Producer, Jules Rivera; Director/Screenplay, Jef Richard; Executive Producers, Robert A. Foti, Robert M. Seibert; Music, Chuck Francour, Gary Griffin; Production Manager, Joan Weidman; Photography, Henning Shellrup; Editor, Marcus Manton; Color; Not rated; 85 minutes; July release. CAST: Joseph Alan Johnson, Valerie Sheldon, Greg Dawson. No other credits provided

BLOOD DINER (Lightning Pictures) Producer, Jimmy Maslon; Director/Co-Producer, Jackie Kong; Creative Consultant, Mr. Osco; Executive Producers, Lawrence Kasanoff, Ellen Steloff; Screenplay, Michael Sonye; Music, Don Preston; Photography, Jurg Walther; Production Manager, Jay Koiwai; Designer, Ron Peterson; Art Director, Keith Barrett; Assistant Art Director, Brenda Plantt; Costumes, Shiz Herrera; Assistant Costume Designer, Diane Winesburg; Assistant Directors, Bill Laxson, Paul LeClair, Val Norwood; Special Effects, Bruce Zahlava; Editor, Thomas Meshelski; Music Coordinator, Art Fein; Stunts, Joe Fury; Color; Rated R; 90 minutes; July release. CAST: Rick Burks (Michael Tutman), Carl Crew (George Tutman), Roger Dauer (Mark Shepard), LaNette La France (Sheba Jackson), Lisa Guggenheim (Connie Stanton), Max Morris (Chief Miller), Roxanne Cybelle (Little Michael), Sir Rodenheaver (Little George), Dino Lee (King of White Trash), The Luv Johnsons (White Trash Review), Drew Godderis (Anwar), Bob Loya (Stan Saldin), Alan Corona (Paul Stanton), Deseree Rose (Mrs. Stanton), Laurie Guzda (Joanne), Tanya Papanicolas (Sheetar/Bitsy), Karen Hazelwood (Babs), Effie Bilbrey (Peggy), Michael Barton (Vitamin), Cynthia Baker (Cindy), John Randall (Buzz), Jane Cantillion (Mrs. Namtut), John Barton Shields (Little Jimmy Hitler)

O.C. AND STIGGS (MGM) Producers, Robert Altman, Peter Newman; Director, Robert Altman; Screenplay, Donald Cantrell, Ted Mann; Based on story by Tod Carroll, Ted Mann from a story in *National Lampoon* magazine; Photography, Pierre Mignot; Music, King Sunny Ade and his African Beats; Editor, Elizabeth Kling; Production Designer, Scott Bushnell; Art Director, David Gropman; Set Decorator, John Hay; Executive Producer, Lewis Allen; Sound, John Pritchett; Assistant Directors, Stephen P. Dunn, Paula Mazur; Associate Producer, Scott Bushnell; Metrocolor; Rated R; 109 minutes; July release. CAST: Daniel H. Jenkins (Oliver Cromwell "O.C." Ogilvie), Neill Barry (Mark Stiggs), Paul Dooley (Randall Schwab), Jane Curtin (Elinore Schwab), Jon Cryer (Randall Schwab, Jr.), Ray Walston (Gramps), Louis Nye (Garth Sloan), Tina Louise (Florence Beaugereaux), Martin Mull (Pat Coletti), Dennis Hopper (Sponson), Melvin Van Peebles (Wino Bob), Donald May (Jack Stiggs), Carla Borelli (Stella Stiggs), Cynthia Nixon (Michelle), Laura Urstein (Lenore Schwab), Victor Ho (Frankie Tang), Stephanie Elfrink (Missie Stiggs), James Gilsenan (Barney Beaugereaux), Greg Mangler (Jefferson Washington), Alan Autry (Goon), Dan Ziskie (Rusty Calloway), Tiffany Helm (Charlotte), Dana Andersen (Robin), Bob Vecker (Himself), Margery Bond (Mrs. Bunny), Jeannine Ann Cole (Nancy Pearson), Nina Van Pallandt (Claire Dejavve), Thomas Hal Phillips (Hal Phillip Walker), Danny Darst (Schwab Commercial Singer), Caroline Aaron (Janine), Tom Flagg (Policeman), Maurice Orozco (Bandito), Louis Enriques (Promoter), Frank Sprague (Actor in play), Robert Fortier (Wino Jim), Allan Berne, Bob Reilly, Robert Carter, Richard Thompson, Roy Gunsberg, Wayne Wallace, Robert Ledford, D. C. Warren, Lobo, Florence White (Winos), Fred Newman (Bongo Voice), King Sunny Ade and his African Beats

JAWS THE REVENGE (Universal) Producer/Director, Joseph Sargent; Screenplay, Michael de Guzman; Based on character created by Peter Benchley; Photography, John McPherson; Designer, John Lloyd; Editor, Michael Brown; Associate Producer, Frank Baur; *Theme from "JAWS",* John Williams; Music, Michael Small; Casting, Nancy Nayor; Production Manager, Frank Baur; Assistant Directors, Wes McAfee, Stephen Southard, Lynda Gilman, Karen Miller Ehrlich; Costumes, Marla Denise Schlom, Hugo Pena; Art Director, Don Woodruff; Set Decorators, Hal Gausman, John Dwyer; Set Designer, Steve Schwartz; Production Coordinators, Nanette Siegert, Jo Ann Mathue; Sound, Willie Burton; Special Effects, Henry Millar, Doug Hubbard, Michael J. Millar; Orchestrations, Jack Hayes, Christopher Dedrick; Director, Jordan Klein; Underwater Stunt Sequences, Gavin McKinney; Songs, Arnie Roman, Stephen Broughton Lunt, Rupert Holmes; Dolby Stereo; Rated PG-13; 110 minutes; July release. CAST: Lorraine Gary (Ellen Brody), Lance Guest (Michael), Mario Van Peebles (Jake), Karen Young (Carla), Michael Caine (Hoagie), Judith Barsi (Thea), Lynn Whitfield (Louisa), Mitchell Anderson (Sean), Jay Mello (Young Sean), Cedric Scott (Clarence), Charles Bowleg (William), Melvin Van Peebles (Mr. Witherspoon), Mary Smith (Tiffany), Edna Billotto (Polly), Fritzi Jane Courtney (Mrs. Taft), Cyprian R. Dube, Lee Fierro, John Griffin, Diane Hetfield, Daniel J. Manning, William E. Marks, James Martin, David Wilson, Romeo Farrington, Anthony Delaney, Heather Thompson, Levant Carey, Darlene Davis, Thomas Friedkin, Chuck Wentworth, James W. Gavin, Karl Wickman

STORY OF A JUNKIE (Troma) Producers, Lech Kowalski, Ann S. Barish; Director, Lech Kowalski; Executive Producer, Gareth E. Newell; Associate Producer, Karen O'Toole; Editor, Val Kiklowsky; Photography, Raffi Ferrucci; Music, Chuck Kentis; Assistant Director, Georgia Kacandes; Sound, Benoit Deswarte, John McCormick; Special Effects, Lester Larrain; Assistant Editors, Chip Cronkite, Tom Crawford, Benoit Deswarte; Color; Rated R; 95 minutes; July release. CAST: John Spacely (no other cast members provided)

Carl Crew, Rick Burks in "Blood Diner"
© *Lightning Pictures*

Karen Young, Lance Guest, Lorraine Gary, Judith Barsi (child) in "Jaws the Revenge"
© *Universal City Studios*

LUST FOR FREEDOM (Troma) Producer/Director, Eric Louzil; Co-Producer, Laurel A. Koernig; Executive Producers, Lloyd Kaufman, Michael Herz; Associate Producers, William J. Kulzer, Riley Carsey; Music, John Massari; Editors, Steve Mann, Thomas R. Rondinella, David Khachatorian; Photography, Ron Chapman; Screenplay, Craig Kusaba, Duke Howard, Eric Louzil; Production Manager/Assistant Director, Rob Rosen; Sound, Steve Mann, Ann Krupa; Assistant Editors, Brianne Siddall, Diane Graham, Christopher Kentis; Art Director, Riley Carsey; Special Effects/Stunts, William J. Kulzer, Jan Washburn, Jim Cooper; Stunts, William J. Kulzer; Songs, Brian Scavo, Carlton Dinnall, Steve Grimmett, Nick Bowcott; Color; Rated R; 91 minutes; July release. CAST: Melanie Coll (Gillian Kaites), William J. Kulzer (Sheriff Coale), Judi Trevor (Ms. Pusker), Howard Knight (Warden Maxwell), Elizabeth Carlisle (Vicky), Dee Booher (Big Eddie), Shea Porter (Scruggs), Rob Rosen (Pete Andrews), John Tallman (Jud), Donna Lederer (Donna), Rick Crews (J. T.), Elizabeth Carroll (Sharon), Lor Stickel (Warren), Joan Tinei (Evelyn), Raymond Oceans (Petey), Dana Palmer (Susan), Richard Vega (Bill), Amy Lyndon (Mary), Lisa Stagno (Lynn), Michelle Bauer (Jackie), Denise Webb (Sally), Adrian Scott (Karen), George J. Engelson (Doc), Karl Anthony Smith (Cody), Jan Washburn, Marc Christopher, John Martin, Pamela Gilbert, Sam Crespi, Terri Beck, Rosemary Marston, Wendy Forman, Nick Kranovich, Nealie Gerard, Richard Newkirk, James Barron, Richard Escobedo, Budha Khan, Dennis Benda, Charles McFarlin, John Arnet, Martha Garcia, Precious, Beverly Urman, Brian Scavo, Riley Carsey, Jim Cooper, Chuck Koernig, Lynne Troupe, Ron Chapman, Jesse Chavez, Greg Trevor, Maxine Spencer, Brianne Siddall, Lori Hemmingway, Barbara Kane, Caprena Nowicki, Sylvia Smith, Rebecca Smith, Shay Howard, Jessica Pompei, Dianna Plumlee, Lorilei Harris, Danny Upton, Maria Stockel, Lindsay Stockel, Bryan Louzil, Eric R. Louzil, Steve Kulzer, Veronica Kulzer, Jessica Pompei, Ty Arnold, Diane Demartelaere, Renee Hudson, Patty Stahl, Tony Davidson

REVENGE OF THE NERDS II: NERDS IN PARADISE (20th Century Fox) Producers, Ted Field, Robert Cort, Peter Bart; Director/Executive Producer, Joe Roth; Screenplay, Dan Guntzelman, Steve Marshall; Based on characters created by Tim Metcalfe, Miguel Tejada-Flores, Steve Zacharias, Jeff Buhai; Photography, Charles Correll; Designer, Jeffrey Kurland; Casting, Pam Dixon; Music, Mark Mothersbaugh, Gerald V. Casale; Music Performance, Devo; Editor, Richard Chew; Associate Producers, Richard Chew, Paul Schiff; Production Manager, Art Seidel; Assistant Directors, Jim Chory, Ellen Schwartz; Additional Editor, Curtis Schulkey; Set Decorator, Don Ivey; Assistant Editors, Albert Coleman, Eric Whitfield, Gaston M. Santiso, Kristen McCray; Sound, Jack Dalton; Special Effects, Wayne Beauchamp, Bruce Hanover, Kevin Harris, March Banich, David Robinson; Stunts, Glenn Wilder; Choreography, Larry B. Scott; Additional Casting, The Casting Directors/Dee Miller, Carol Lefko; An Interscope Communications Production; In Association with Amercent Films and American Entertainment Partners L.P.; Songs by various artists; Dolby Stereo; DeLuxe Color; Rated PG-13; 94 minutes; July release. CAST: Robert Carradine (Lewis), Curtis Armstrong (Booger), Larry B. Scott (Lamar), Timothy Busfield (Poindexter), Courtney Thorne-Smith (Sunny), Andrew Cassese (Wormser), Donald Gibb (Ogre), Bradley Whitford (Roger), Ed Lauter (Buzz), Barry Sobel (Stewart), Tom Hodges (Tiny), Jack Gilpin (Mr. Comstock), Anthony Edwards (Gilbert), James Hong (Snotty), Priscilla Lopez (Aldonza), James Cromwell (Mr. Skolnick), Jason Julien (Winston), Marilyn Caskey (Mrs. Comstock), Richard Joseph Paul (Gundy), Rhonda Waymire (Indian Maiden), Donna Rosae (Lori), Susan Vanech (Michelle), Robert Goodman (Jerry), James O'Doherty (Stan), Michael Fitzgerald (Pot Roast), Huey Laborde, Raymond Forchion, Teresa Blake, Carmen Thomas, Anthony Tracy, Miles Greadington, Victor Morris, Eddie Knott, Jr., Tom Boykin, Bonnie Lockwood, Robert Lockwood, Don Samuels, Ruben Rabasa

"Lust for Freedom"
© *Troma Inc.*

HOUSE II: THE SECOND STORY (New World) Producer, Sean S. Cunningham; Director/Screenplay, Ethan Wiley; Photography, Mac Ahlberg; Editor, Marty Nicholson; Color; Rated PG-13; 88 minutes; August release. CAST: Arye Gross (Jesse), Jonathan Stark (Charlie), Royal Dano (Gramps), Bill Maher (John), John Ratzenberger (Bill), Lar Park Lincoln (Kate), Amy Yasbeck (Lana), No other credits provided.

OUTTAKES (Marketechnics) Producers, Jack M. Sell, Adrianne Richmond; Director, Jack M. Sell; Screenplay, Jack M. Sell, Adrianne Richmond, Jim Fay; Photography, Ron Bell, Jack M. Sell; Music, Jack M. Sell, Rich Daniels, Chris Lay; Editor, Jack M. Sell; Sell Pictures; Color; Not Rated; 71 minutes; August release. CAST: Forrest Tucker, Bobbi Wexler, Joleen Lutz, Curt Colbert, Marilyn Abrams, Warren Davis, Coleen Downey, Jim Fay, Jack M. Sell

NORTH SHORE (Universal) Executive Producer, Randal Kleiser; Producer, William Finnegan; Director, William Phelps; Screenplay, Tim McCanlies, William Phelps; Story, William Phelps, Randal Kleiser; Music, Richard Stone; Associate Producers, Tim McCanlies, Gregory Hinton; Production Manager, Douglas E. Green; Assistant Directors, Bruce Shurley, James Dillon; Production Executives, Margaret E. Fannin, David Roessell; Production Coordinator, Scott Hancock; Music Supervisor, Rick Brown; Set Decorator, Wally White; Sound, Tim Himes; Costumes, Kathe James; Stunts, Tom Lupo; Additional Editors, Barbara Pokras, Charles Tetoni; Special Effects, Paul Tremaine; Songs, Paul Delph, Rebecca Parnell, Rick Parnell, various other artists; Dolby Stereo; Color; Rated PG; 92 minutes; August release. CAST: Matt Adler (Rick), Gregory Harrison (Chandler), Nia Peeples (Kiani), John Philbin (Turtle), Gerry Lopez (Vince), Laird Hamilton (Lance Burkhart), Robbie Page (Alex Rogers), Mark Occhilupo (Occy), John Parragon (Professor), Rocky Kauanoe (Rocky), Lokelani Lau (Anela), Cristina Raines, Tiffany Pestana, Corky Carroll, Joe Teipel, Lord "Tally Ho" Blears, Jim "Poor Man" Trenton, Tavita Tu, David Ige, Kelly Hager, Lionel Tarape, Steven Yoshikawa, Timothy Kamaka, Randy Kauhane, Kawika Stant, Shawn Donahue, Danny Allen, Amy Heutmaker, Alan Cole, Charlene Silva, Susan Kagehiro, Freya Singer, John Michael Hydo, Norman Compton, Shaun Tomson, Hans Hedemann, Derek Ho, Mark Foo, Ken Bradshaw, Mike Latronic, Michael Ho, James Jones, Max Madeiros, Scott Daley, Aaron Napoleon, Christian Fletcher, Davey Miller, Mickey Nielsen

Anthony Edwards, Robert Carradine in "Revenge of the Nerds II" © *20th Century Fox/Zade Rosenthal*

Matt Adler, Nia Peeples in "North Shore"
© *Universal City Studios*

Belinda Bauer, Donald Sutherland in
"The Rosary Murders" © *New Line*

LIONHEART (Orion) Producers, Stanley O'Toole, Talia Shire; Director, Franklin J. Schaffner; Screenplay, Menno Meyjes, Richard Outten; Story, Menno Meyjes; Executive Producers, Francis Coppola, Jack Schwartzman; Photography, Alec Mills; Editor, David Bretherton, Richard Haines; Music, Jerry Goldsmith; Production Designer, Gil Parrondo; Costumes, Nana Cecchi; Production Supervisor, Scott Wodehouse; Assistant Director, Gary Daigler; Color; Rated PG; 104 minutes; August release. CAST: Eric Stoltz (Robert Nerra), Gabriel Byrne (The Black Prince), Deborah Barrymore (Mathilda), Nicholas Clay (Charles de Montfort), Bruce Purchase (Simon Nerra), Neil Dickson (King Richard), Chris Pitt (Odo)

THE ROSARY MURDERS (New Line Cinema) Producer, Robert G. Laurel; Director, Fred Walton; Screenplay, Elmore Leonard, Fred Walton; Based on the novel by William X. Kienzle; Executive Producers, Robert G. Laurel, Michael R. Mihalich; Photography, David Golia; Visual Consultant, Stewart Campbell; Costumes, Judy Dolan; Music, Bobby Laurel, Don Sebesky; Arrangment/Conductor, Don Sebesky; Associate Producer/Production Manager, Chris Coles; Casting, Pennie du Pont; Assistant Directors, Steve McRoberts, Scott Kohlrust; Sound, Jim Webb; Set Decorator, Diane Campbell; Special Effects, Rick Josephsen; Stunts, Gary Combs; Production Coordinator, Marlana Geha; Assistant Art Director, Peter Gurski; Assistant Set Decorator, Michelle Poulik; Songs, Bobby Laurel, Dennis Leahy/Antonio Lottia; Dolby Stereo; Metrocolor; Rated R; 101 minutes; August release. CAST: Donald Sutherland (Father Koesler), Charles Durning (Father Nabors), Josef Sommer (Lt. Koznicki), Belinda Bauer (Pat Lennon), James Murtaugh (Javison), John Danelle (Det. Harris), Addison Powell (Father Killeen), Kathleen Tolan (Sister Ann Vania), Tom Mardirosian (Det. Fallon), Anita Barone (Irene Jimenez), and Howard Andress, Roger Angelini, Constance Barry, Doris Biscoe, Sandy Broad, Keith Brooks, Bethany Carpenter, Joseph Conrad, Divina Cook, Richard Cottrell, Leila Danette, Harry Davis, Bruce Economou, Rex Everhart, Lillian Ferguson, Stefan Gierasch, Georgine Hall, Harald Hansen, Cordis Heard, Robert Heller, Ann Hilary, Dorothy Hutton, Jihmi Kennedy, Don Lessnau, Maria Lopez, Mark Margolis, Robert C. Maxwell, Anna Minot, Joel Nash, Ed Oldani, Lupe Ontiveras, Burt Pearson, Sam Pollack, David Regal, Jordan Rodriguez, Ed Ruffalo, Ed Seamon, John Seitz, Steven Sosa, Peter Van Norden, Josephine Vassalo, Jo Mullin White, Dennis Wrosch

THE GARBAGE PAIL KIDS MOVIE (Atlantic) Producer/Director, Rod Amateau; Screenplay, Melinda Palmer/Rod Amateau; Co-Producers, Michael Lloyd, Melinda Palmer; Executive Producers, Thomas Coleman, Michael Rosenblatt; Supervising Producer, John Serong; Garbage Pail Kids Animatronics, John Buechler, Mechanical Make-up Imageries, Inc; Editor, Leon Carrere; Music, Michael Lloyd; Photography, Harvey Genkins; Designer, Robert I. Jillson; Costumes, Judie Champion; Production Manager, Gilles A. de Turenne; Assistant Directors, Thomas A. Irvine, Dan Steinbrocker; Sound, Clifford "Kip" Gynn; Design Consultant, Gary L. Hudson; Set Decorator, Hub Braden; Production Coordinator, Jill Vandermeer; Assistant Production Coordinator, Felice Genkins; Assistant Editor, Michael Sale; Special Mechanical Effects, Los Angeles Effects; Special Effects, Ted Koerner, Ted Coplen; Stunts, Todd Amateau; Color; Rated PG; 100 minutes; August release. CAST: Anthony Newley (Captain Manzini), MacKenzie Astin (Dodger), Katie Barberi (Tangerine), Ron MacLachlan (Juice), J. P. Amateau (Wally), Marjory Graue (Blythe), Debbie Lee Carrington (Valerie Vomit), Kevin Thompson (Ali Gator), Phil Fondacaro (Greaser Greg), Robert Bell (Foul Play), Larry Green (Nat Nerd), Arturo Gil (Windy Winston), Sue Rossitto (Messy Tessie), John Cade (Bartender), and Lynn Cartwright, Chester Grimes, Patty Lloyd, Leo V. Gordon, Gavin Moloney, Lindy Huddleson, Kristine McKeon, Debbie Lytton, John Herman Shaner, Joan L. Burton, Kevin Thompson, Debbie Lee Carrington, Arturo Gil, Jim Cummings, Chloe Amateau, Teri Benaron, Gray Johnson

WHERE THE HEART ROAMS (New Yorker Films) Producer/Director/Editor, George Paul Csicsery; Photography, John Knoop; Music, Mark Adler; Documentary; Not rated; 83 minutes; August release

STEWARDESS SCHOOL (Columbia) Producer, Phil Feldman; Director/Screenplay, Ken Blancato; Photography, Fred J. Koenekamp; Designer, Daniel A. Lomino; Editors, Lou Lombardo, Kenneth C. Paonessa; Co-Producers, Michael Kane, Jerry A. Baerwitz; Associate Producers, Don McFarlane, Elizabeth A. Bardsley; Music, Robert Folk; Production Manager, Jerry A. Baerwitz; Assistant Directors, Bill Scott, Dennis Capps, David D'Ovidio; Casting, Melissa Skoff; Production Coordinator, Beverly Setlowe; Set Decorator, Robert L. Zilliox; Set Designer, Sue Lomino; Sound, Dick Raguse; Costumes, Wayne Finkleman; Stunts, Bill Couch, Jimmy Lynn Davis; Special Effects, John Stirber, Danny Gill, Stephen Humphrey, Peter Geyer; Assistant Editor, Joseph Delia; "Stew School" Music, Robert Folk, Lyrics, Ken Blancato, and songs by various other artists; From Columbia-Delphi V Productions; DeLuxe Color; Rated R; 84 minutes; August release. CAST: Brett Cullen (Philo Henderson), Mary Cadorette (Kelly Johnson), Donald Most (George Bunkle), Sandahl Bergman (Wanda Polanski), Wendie Jo Sperber (Jolean Winters), Judy Landers (Sugar Dubois), Dennis Burkley ("Snake" Pellino), Julia Montgomery (Pimmie Polk), Corinne Bohrer (Cindy Adams), Rob Paulsen (Larry Falkwell), William Bogert (Roger Weidermeyer), Sherman Hemsley (Mr. Buttersworth), Vicki Frederick (Miss Grummet), Alan Rosenberg (Mad Bomber), Rod McCary (Capt. Biff), Vito Scotti (Carl Stromboli), Yuliis Ruval (Beautiful Blonde), Earl Boen (Mr. Adams), Toni Sawyer (Mrs. Adams), Joe Dorsey (Captain), Casey Sander (Dudley), John Allen (Bubba Brock), Brooke Bundy (Mrs. Polk), Gloria LeRoy (Grandma Polk), Leslie Huntley (Allison), Pilar DelRey (Sarah Stromboli), Mark Neely, Barbara Whinnery, Paul Eiding, Ruth Manning, Paul Barselou, Richard Lineback, Ron Ross, Lenore Woodward, Anita Dangler, Timothy Hoskins, Bert Hinchman, Rowena Balos, John O'Leary, Paddi Edwards, Larry Grenna, Felix Nelson, William O'Connell, Richard Erdman, Tom Ashworth, Justin Lord, William Erwin, Conrad Dunn, Billy Varga, Joan Lemmo, Robert Towers, Dian Gallup, Denise Gallup, Fran Ryan, Marie Denn, Theodore Wilson, Kathleen O'Haco, Linda Lutz, Andrew J. Kuehn, Carole Kean, Lela Rochon, Lenora Logan, Hartley Silver, Phyllis Cowan, Suzanne Dunn, Priscilla Linn, Paul Bradley, Cathleen MacIntosh, Viola Kates Stimpson, David Sterago, Alexandra Rodzianko

THE CURSE (Trans World) Producer, Ovidio G. Assonitis; Director, David Keith; Screenplay, David Chaskin; Photography, Robert D. Forges; Editor, Claude Kutry; Music, John Debney; Designer, Frank Vanorio; Color; Rated R; 100 minutes; September release. CAST: Wil Wheaton (Zachary), Claude Akins (Nathan Hayes), Kathleen Jordan Gregory (Frances), Steve Davis (Mike), Amy Wheaton (Alice), Malcolm Danare (Cyrus), Cooper Huckabee (Dr. Alan Forbes), John Schneider (Carl Willis)

MISS . . . OR MYTH? (Cinema Guild) Producers, Geoffrey Dunn, Mark Schwartz, Claire Rubach; Directors, Geoffrey Dunn, Mark Schwartz; Photography/Editor, Mark Schwartz; Documentary; Not rated; 60 minutes; September release

Wil Wheaton, Kathleen Jordan Gregory,
Claude Akins in "The Curse" © *Trans World*

REAL MEN (MGM/UA) Producer, Martin Bregman; Executive Producer, Louis A. Stroller; Director/Screenplay, Dennis Feldman; Photography, John A. Alonzo; Art Directors, William J. Cassidy, James Allen; Set Director, Tom Pedigo; Set Designer, Dan Maltese; Costumes, Jodie Tillen; Sound, Keith Wester; Assistant Director, Allan Wertheim; Casting, Lynn Stalmaster David Rubin; Color; Rated PG-13; 96 minutes; September release. CAST: James Belushi (Nick Pirandello), John Ritter (Bob Wilson), Barbara Barrie (Mom), Bill Morey (Cunard), Iva Andersen (Dolly), Gail Berle (Sherry), Mark Herrier (Bradhwaw), Matthew Brooks (Bob, Jr.)

THE RETURN OF RUBEN BLADES Producer/Director, Robert Mugge; A Mug-Shot Production in association with Channel Four (U.K.); Documentary; Color; Not rated; 82 minutes; September release. WITH: Ruben Blades, Seis del Solar, Linda Ronstadt

GOSPEL ACCORDING TO AL GREEN Producer/Director/ Screenplay, Robert Mugge; Documentary; 94 minutes; September release. WITH: Al Green, Willie Mitchell, Ken Tucker, No other credits provided.

SURVIVAL GAME (Trans World Entertainment) Executive Producer, Moshe Diamant; Producer, Gideon Amir; Director/Story, Herb Freed; Screenplay, Herb Freed, Susannah de Nimes, P. W. Swann; Photography, Avraham Karpick; Editors, Charles Simmons, Karen Gebura; Music, Tom Simonec, Michael Linn; Sound, Jacob Goldstein; Designer, Diana Morris; Assistant Director, Paul Samuelson; Fight Coordinator, Aaron Norris; Production Manager/Associate Producer, Mel A. Bishop; Production Consultant, Steven E. de Souza; Casting, Caro Jones; Dolby Stereo; Rated R; 97 minutes; September release. CAST: Mike Norris (Mike), Deborah Goodrich (C. J. Forrest), Seymour Cassel (Dave Forrest), Ed Bernard (Sugar Bear), Jon Sharp (Charles), Rick Grassi (Ice), Arlene Golonka (Mom), Michael Halton (Harlan), no other credits provided

YOU TALKIN' TO ME? (United Artists) Producer, Michael Polaire; Director/Screenplay, Charles Winkler; Photography, Paul Ryan; Editor, David Handman; Music, Joel McNeely; Color; Rated R; 97 minutes; September release. CAST: Jim Youngs (Bronson Green), James Noble (Peter Archer), Mykel T. Williamson (Thatcher Marks), Faith Ford (Dana Archer), Bess Motta (Judith Margolis), Rex Ryon (Kevin), Brian Thompson (James), Alan King (Alan King), No other credits provided.

CHINA GIRL (Vestron) Producer, Michael Nozik; Director, Abel Ferrara; Screenplay, Nicholas St. John; Executive Producers, Mitchell Cannold, Steve Reuther; Photography, Bojan Bazelli; Editor, Anthony Redman; Designer, Dan Leigh; Music, Joe Delia; Associate Producer/ Production Manager, Mary Kane; Costumes, Richard Hornung; Casting, Marcia Shulman; Production Executive, Alan Grabelsky; Color; Rated R; 89 minutes; September release. CAST: James Russo (Alberto "Alby" Monte), Richard Panebianco (Tony Monte), Sari Chang (Tyan-Hwa), David Caruso (Johnny Mercury), Russell Wong (Yung-Gan), Joey Chin (Tsu-Shin), Judith Malina (Maria), James Hong (Gung-Tu), Robert Miano (Perito), Paul Hipp (Nino), Doreen Chan (Gau-Shing), Randy Sabusawa (Ma-Fan/Cyclops), Keenan Leung (Ying-Tz), Lum Chang Pan (Da-Shan), Sammy Lee (Mohawk), Johnny Shia (Jimmy Bing), Stephen Chen (Tang), Raymond Moy (Tommy Chyan), Josephina Gallego-Diaz (Rosetta), Caprice Benedetti (Theresa), Anthony Dante (Costare) Robert Lasardo (Forza), Chi Moy (Yang), David Kelsey Reilly, Joseph Pentangelo (Cops), Anthony Esposito (Don Carlucci), Diane Cheng (Nyu-Ren), Frank Young (Waiter), John Ciarcia (Cha Cha), Jon Orofino (Nicky), Ida Bernadini (Rosa), Nancy Moo (Nightclub Owner), Jadin Wong (Mrs. Lei), Carole Cortland (Italian Woman), Denise Leong (Mei), Edna Holt (Singer)

Leon Isaac Kennedy (R) in "Penitentiary III"
© *Cannon*

PENITENTIARY III (Cannon) Producers, Jamaa Fanaka, Leon Isaac Kennedy; Director/Screenplay/Based on characters created by Jamaa Fanaka; Photography, Marty Ollstein; Editor, Ed Harker; Costumes, Maria Burrell Fanaka; Designer Marshall Toomey; Assistant Directors, Brent Sellstrom, Pat Kirck, Tony Major, Chip Vecelich; Art Director, Craig Freitag; Assistant Art Director, Wayne Pigford; Sound, Oliver Moss; Set Designer, Robert L. Gordon, Jr.; Set Decorator, Beverly Esteredge; Jim Bailey's Costumes, Jerry Skeels; Special Effects Makeup, Mike Spatola; Production Coordinator, Susan Kydd; Special Effects, Reel Effects, Frank Russo; Production Supervisor, Michael Alden; Production Coordinator, Omneya "Nini" Mazen; Additional Editors, Woodward Smith, Ray Icely, Earl Ghaffari; Assistant Editors, Marcelo Sansevieri, Hope Moskowitz, Doran Shauly; Stunts, John Sherrod, George Perry; Martial Arts, Hugh Van Patton, Glen Eaton; Music Supervisor, Paula Erickson; Music Producer, Robby Weaver; Music Performance, The Gap Band; Soundtrack by McHenry/ Lombard on RCA Records; TVC Color; Rated R; 89 minutes; September release. CAST: Leon Isaac Kennedy (Too Sweet), Anthony Geary (Serenghetti), Jim Bailey (Cleopatra), Steve Antin (Roscoe), Ric Mancini (Warden), Marie Burrell Fanaka (Chelsea Remington), The Haiti Kid (Midnight Thud Jessup), Rick Zumwalt (Joshua), Magic Schwarz (Hugo), Big Bull Bates (Simp), Big Yank (Rock), Bert Williams (Tim Shoah), Mark Kemble (Rufus), Jack Rader (Fred), Madison Campudoni (El Cid), Mike Payne (Jess), Drew Bundini Brown (Sugg), Ty Randolph (Sugar), J. J. Johnson, Earl Garnes (Announcers), Jim Phillips (Gentleman), Faith Minton, Macella Ross, Ray Hollitt (Female Boxers), Danny Trejo (See Veer), Mary O'Conner, Cardella DeMilo (Female Guards), "Dr. De" Ron Demps (Referee)

RACHEL RIVER (American Playhouse Theatrical Films) Producer, Timothy Marx; Executive Producer, Lindsay Law; Director, Sandy Smolan; Screenplay Judith Guest; Based on the stories of Carol Bly; Photography, Paul Elliott; Editor, Susan Crutcher; Music, Arvo Part; Designer, David Wasco; Associate Producer, Nan Simons; Costumes, Linda Fisher; A Marx/Smolan production; Color; Not rated; 90 minutes; September release. CAST: Željko Ivanek (Momo), Pamela Reed (Mary), Craig T. Nelson (Marlyn), James Olson (Jack), Alan North (Beske), Viveca Lindfors (Harriet), Jo Henderson (Estona), Jon De Vries (Baker), Ailene Cole, Courtney Kjos, Ottie Osterberg, Wellington Nelson, Richard Jenkins, Michael Gallagher, Richard Riehle, Ron Duffy, Don Cosgrove, Stephen Yoakum, Cliff Rakerd, Patricia Mary Van Oss

Sari Chang, Richard Panebianco
in "China Girl" © *Vestron/Mitch Epstein*

Rick Grassi, Seymour Cassel, Deborah Goodrich
in "Survival Game" © *Trans World*

Jon Cryer in "Dudes"
© International Video Entertainment

STREET TRASH (Lightning Pictures) Producer/Screenplay, Roy Frunkes; Director, Jim Munro; Photography, David Sperling; Editor, Dennis Werner; Music, Rick Ulfik; Designer, Rob Marcucci; Art Directors, Denis Labelle, Tom Molinelli; Special Makeup Effects, Jennifer Aspinall, Mike Lackey; Associate Producer, Frank Farel; Assistant Director, Robert J. Hurrie; Costumes, David Tripet; Costumes, Michele Leifer; Special Sound Effects, Pawel Wdowczak; Assistant Editor, Brian Evans; A Chaos Production; Color; Not rated; 91 minutes; September release. CAST: Bill Chepil (Bill the Cop), Mike Lackey (Fred), Vic Noto (Bronson), Mark Sferrazza (Kevin), Jane Arakawa (Wendy), Nicole Potter (Winette), R. L. Ryan (Frank Schnizer), Clarenze Jarmon (Burt), Bernard Perlman (Wizzy), Miriam Zucker (Wench), M D'Jango Krunch (Ed), James Loinz (Doorman), Morty Storm (Black Suit), Bruce Torbet (Paulie), Sam Blasco (Jimmy), Roman Zack (Forensics Expert), Gary Auerbach (Hit Man), Tony Darrow (Nick Duran), Roy Frumkes, Jeanne Laporta, Colin Derouin, Julian Davis, Victoria Lacas, Eddie Bay, Frank Farel, Robynne White, Kevin Simmons, Glenn Andreiev, Allan Lozito, Bill Bondanza, Stephen Patterson, Fred Schomaker, Peter Iasillo, Karl Schroeder, Stephen Santiago, Carmel Pugh, Robert Depietro, Frank Dassaro, Joseph Vero, Raymond Ristau, Raul Velez, Thomas Fuzia, Donald Ascher, Gary Rozanski, Bobby Faust, John Hukushi, Sylvia Wong, Judy Chin, Kevin Chin, William Elijah Tyre, David Paul Rubenstein, Nathaniel Young, Paul Sansone, Michael Maurer, James D. Clements, Terrence Devlin, Eliezer Diaz, Robert Audin, Lawrence Sufrin, Alan Brustein, Gail Feinsod, Buddy Mantia, Jet, Jennifer Muro, Melanie Borsack, Robyn Borsack

HE'S MY GIRL (Scotti Brothers Pictures) Producers, Lawrence Taylor Mortorff, Angela Schapiro; Director, Gabrielle Beaumont; Screenplay, Taylor Ames, Charles F. Bohl; Photography, Peter Lyons Collister; Editor, Roy Watts; Production Manager, Fred Wardell; Color; Rated PG-13; 104 minutes; September release. CAST: T. K. Carter (Reggie/Regina), David Hallyday (Bryan), Misha McK (Tasha), Jennifer Tilly (Lisa), Warwick Sims (Simon Sledge), David Clennon (Mason Morgan), Monica Parker (Sally), No other credits provided.

LADY BEWARE (Scotti Brothers Entertainment Industries), Producers, Lawrence Taylor Mortorff, Tony Scotti; Director, Karen Arthur; Screenplay, Susan Miller, Charles Zev Cohen; Photography, Tom Neuwirth; Editor, Roy Watts; Music, Craig Safan; Color; Rated R; 108 minutes; September release. CAST: Diane Lane (Katya Yarno), Michael Woods (Jack Price), Cotter Smith (Mac Odell), No other credits provided.

James Woods, Victoria Tennant in "Best Seller"
© Orion/Lorey Sebastian

TOUGH GUYS DON'T DANCE (Cannon) Producers, Menahem Golan, Yoram Globus; Director/Screenplay, Norman Mailer; Executive Producers, Francis Coppola, Tom Luddy; Designer, Armin Ganz; Costumes, Michael Kaplan; Visual Consultant, John Bailey; Sound, Leslie Shatz, Drew Kunin; Editor, Debra McDermott; Music, Angelo Badalamenti; Production Executive, Rony Yacov; Casting, Robert MacDonald, Bonnie Pietilia, Bonnie Timmerman, Fred Roos; Stunts, Don Pike, Rob Bloch, Siane Peterson; Additional Photography, Danny Dukovny; Set Decorator, Gretchen Rau; Assistant Costume Designer, Monique Montgomery; Special Effects, Jerry D. Williams, Lou Carlucci; Production Supervisor, Marc Fischer; Production Coordinator, Caroline Baron; Assistant Editors, Kate MacDonald, Aaron D. Weisblatt, James H. Nau; Music Supervisor, Paula Erickson; Music Coordinator, Stephanie Lee; Musical Director, Angelo Badalamenti; Orchestrations, Angelo Badalamenti, Joe Turrin, Andy Barret; *"You'll come Back (You Always Do)"* Music Angelo Badalamenti/Lyrics, Norman Mailer, Angelo Badalamenti/Vocal, Mel Tillis; *"Real Man"* Music, Angelo Badalamenti/Lyrics, Danielle Badalamenti/Vocal, Pam Tillis; Ultra-Stereo; TVC Color; Rated R; 108 minutes; September release. CAST: Ryan O'Neal (Tim Madden), Isabella Rossellini (Madeleine) Debra Sandlund (Patty Lareine), Wings Hauser (Regency), John Bedford Lloyd (Wardley Meeks, III), Lawrence Tierney (Dougy Madden), Penn Jillette (Big Stoop), Frances Fisher (Jessica Pond), R. Patrick Sullivan (Lonnie Pangborn), John Snyder (Spide), Stephan Morrow (Stoodie), Clarence Williams III (Bolo), Kathryn Sanders (Beth), Ira Lewis (Mervyn Finney), Ed Setrakian (Lawyer), Faith Cahn (Rhonda), Edward Bonetti (Old Cellmate), Joel Meyerowitz (2nd Cellmate), Greg Hodal (Bartender), Katrina Marshall (Topless Girl), Sally Moffett, Carol Stevens (Wiches' Vocies)

CASTAWAY (Cannon) Producer, Rick McCallum; Director, Nicolas Roeg; Screenplay, Allan Scott; Based on the book by Lucy Irvine; Editor, Tony Lawson; Photography, Harvey Harrison; Music, Stanley Myers; Designer, Andrew Sanders; Executive Producers, Peter Shaw, Richard Johnson; Production Supervisor, Selwyn Roberts; Assistant Directors, Michael Zimbrich, Waldo Roeg, Lee Cleary; Production Coordinator, Clare St. John; Casting, Mary Selway, Liz Mullinar; Sound, Paul Le Mare; Art Directors, Stuart Rose, George Galitzine; Assistant Editors, Margaret Thompson, Michael Danks; Additional Music, Hans Zimmer, Bary Guy; Orchestrations, Christopher Palmer; Costumes, Nick Ede; Special Effects, Alan Whibley, Dave Eltham, Richard Roberts, Nick Middleton; Songs, Kate Bush, Brian Eno, Richard Messer, David Mills; Pub Piano Music, Lionel Robinson; Dolby Stereo; Color; Rated R; 118 minutes; September release. CAST: Oliver Reed (Gerald Kingsland), Amanda Donohoe (Lucy Irvine), Tony Rickards (Jason), Todd Rippon (Rod), Georgina Hale (Sister Saint Margaret), Frances Barber (Sister Saint Winnifred), John Sessions (Man in pub), Virginia Hey (Janice), Richard Johnson (Davenport), Sorrel Johnson (Lara), Len Peihopa (Ronald), Paul Reynolds (Mike Kingsland), Sean Hamilton (Geoffrey Kingsland), Sarah Harper (Swimming Teacher), Stephen Jenn (Shop Manager), Joseph Blatchley (Registrar), Simon Dormandy (Jackson), Ruth Hudson (Receptionist), Gordon Honeycombe (TV Newsreader)

THE PICK-UP ARTIST (20th Century Fox) Producer, David L. MacLeod; Director/Screenplay, James Toback; Photography, Gordon Willis; Designer, Paul Sylbert; Editor, David Bretherton, Angelo Corrao; Costumes, Colleen Atwood; Casting, Howard Feuer; Music, Georges DeLerue; Production Manager, G. Mac Brown; Assistant Director, Tom Reilly, Ken Ornstein; Art director, Bill Groom; Set Decorator, John Alan Hicks; Sound, Les Lazarowitz, Vito Ilardi; Production Associate, Maggie Kusik; Assistant Editors, Deborah Wallach, Diane Schwab, Richard Haines, Marva Fucci; *"The Pick-Up Artist"* by Stevie Wonder/Vocals, Keith John, and songs by various other artists; In association with Amercent Films and American Entertainment Partners L.P.; Dolby Stereo; DeLuxe Color; Rated PG-13; 90 minutes; September release. CAST: Molly Ringwald (Randy Jensen), Robert Downey (Jack Jericho), Dennis Hopper (Flash), Danny Aiello (Phil), Mildred Dunnock (Nellie), Harvey Keitel (Alonzo), Brian Hamill (Mike), Tamara Bruno (Karen), Vanessa Williams (Rae), Angie Kempf (Student), Polly Draper (Pat), Frederick Koehler (Richie), Robert Towne (Stan), Victoria Jackson (Lulu), Lorraine Bracco (Carla), Bob Gunton (Portacarrero), Clemenze Caserta (Clem), John Butera (Gene), Phoebe Ungerer (Gene's Girl), Victor Argo (Harris), Fred Melamed (George), Patrick Johnson (Bruce), Kenny Kieran (OTB Cashier), Anne Marie Bobby (Mona), Don Peoples (Harry), Sidney Armus (Sidney), Bea Soong (Museum Employee), Christina Sclafani (Angie), Alexis Cruz (Charlie), Brad Frankel, Eric Jason, Mary Griffin, Marc Joseph, Beverly Kaik, Meghan Lahey, Bianca Levin, Anna Lee (Joan), Michelle Eabry (Michelle), Isabel Garcia-Lorca (Information Lady), Raisen Cain, James Jackson, Randall Jackson, Melvin Shepherd, Bob Maroff, Rene Santoni, Geoffrey Nauffts, Edward Rowan, Christine Baranski, Jilly Rizzo

THE OFFSPRING aka "From a Whisper to a Scream" (Conquest Entertainment) Producers, Darin Scott, William Burr; Executive Producer, David Shaheen; Director, Jeff Burr; Screenplay, C. Courtney Joiner, Jeff Burr, Darin Scott; Photography, Craig Greene; Editor, W. O. Garrett; Music, Jim Manzie, Pat Regan; Sound, Jerry Wolfe; Assistant Director, Mark Hannah; Special Makeup Effects, Rob Burman; United Color; Rated R; 96 minutes; September release. CAST: Vincent Price (Julian White), Clu Gulager (Stanley Burnside), Terry Kiser (Jess Hardwick), Harry Caesar (Felder Evans), Rosalind Cash (Sideshow Owner), Cameron Mitchell (Sergeant), Susan Tyrrell (Bess Chandler), Ron Brooke (Stephen), Didi Lanier (Amaryllis), Martine Beswick (Katherine White), Angelo Rossitte (Carny Barker), Lawrence Tierney (Official)

LADY BEWARE (Scotti Bros.) Producers, Tony Scotti, Lawrence Taylor Mortorff; Executive Producers, Ben Scotti, Fred Scotti; Director, Karen Arthur; Screenplay, Susan Miller, Charles Zev Cohen; Photography, Tom Neuwirth; Editor, Roy Watts; Music, Craig Safan; Set Decorator, Tom Wells; Costumes, Patricia Fields; Sound, Larry Loewinger; Associate Producer/Assistant Director, Paula Marcus; Casting, Diane Dimeo, Joy Todd Inc,. Sharon & Clayton Hill; In association with Intl. Video Entertainment; Dolby Stereo; Color; Rated R; 108 minutes; September release. CAST: Diane Lane (Katya Yarno), Michael Woods (Jack Price), Cotter Smith (Mac Odell), Peter Nevargic (Lionel), Edward Penn (Thayer), Tyra Ferrell (Nan)

THOU SHALT NOT KILL . . . EXCEPT (Filmworld) Executive Producers, Shirley Becker, Arnold Becker; Producer, Scott Spiegel; Director, Josh Becker; Screenplay, Josh Becker, Scott Spiegel; Story, Josh Becker, Sheldon Lettich, Bruce Campbell; Music, Joseph Lo Duca; An Action Pictures production; Color; Not rated; 94 minutes; September release. CAST: Brian Schulz (Stryker), John Manfredi (Miller), Robert Rickman (Jackson), Tim Quill (Tyler), Sam Raimi (Cult Leader), Cheryl Hanson (Sally), Perry Mallette (Otis), Sayle Jackunas (Eddie Munster), Rick Hudson, Connie Craig, Terry Brumfield, Ted Raimi, Al Johnson, Kirk Haas, Glen Barr, Gary O'Conner, Dave Gerney, Scott Mitchell

CREEPOZOIDS (Urban Classics) Producers, David DeCoteau, John Schouweiler; Director, David DeCoteau; Screenplay, Burford Hauser, David DeCoteau; Photography, Thomas Callawa; Editor, Miriam L. Preissel; Music, Guy Moon; Music Supervisor, Jonathan Scott Bogner; Sound, Marty Kasparia; Designer, Royce Mathew; Production Manager, Ellen Cabot; Assistant Director, Nigel Parker; Special Makeup/Creature Effects, Next Generation Effects/Thom Floutz, Peter Carsillo; Special Mechanical Effects, John Criswell; Stunts, John Stewart; Production Supervisor, Juliet Avola; Casting, Stan Shaffer; A Titan Production; Foto-Kem Color; Rated R; 71 minutes; September release. CAST: Linnea Quigley (Bianca), Ken Abraham (Butch), Michael Aranda (Jesse), Richard Hawkins (Jake), Kim McKamy (Kate), Joi Wilson (Scientist)

NIGHTSTICK (Production Distribution Co.) Producer, Martin Walters; Director Joseph L. Scanlan; Screenplay, James J. Docherty; Photography, Robert Fresco; Editors, Richard Wells, Daniel Radford; Music, Robert O. Ragland; Art Director, Reuben Freed; Set Decorator, Tony Duggan-Smith; Costumes, Eva Gord; Special Effects, Carere Special Effects; Associate Producer, Risa Gertner; Assistant Director, Ken Girotti; Casting, Paul Bengston, David Cohn, Ann Tait; A Sandy Howard presentation; Color; Rated R; 92 minutes; September release. CAST: Bruce Fairbairn (Jack Calhoun), Kerrie Keane (Robin Malone), Robert Vaughn (Ray Melton), John Vernon (Adam Beardsley), Leslie Nielsen (Evans), Walker Boone (Roger Bantam), Tony De Santis (Jerry Bantam), David Mucci (Pat Bantam)

SLAVE GIRLS FROM BEYOND INFINITY (Urban Classics) Producer/Director/Screenplay, Ken Dixon; Co-producers, John Eng, Mark Wolf; Photography, Ken Wiatrak, Thomas Callaway; Editors, Bruce Stubblefield, James A. Stewart; Music, Carl Dante; Music Supervisor, Jonathan Scott Bogner; Sound, Rick Fine, Paul Bacca; Art Director, Escott Norton; Assistant Directors/Production Managers, Don Daniels, Devorah Hardberger; Special Effects, Mark Wolf; Special Visual Effects, John Eng; Androids & Phantazoid Warrior by John Buechler; Zombie & Mutant by Joe Reader; Special Effects Makeup, David Cohen; Stunts, Mike Cooper, Greg Cooper; Production Coordinator, Juliet Avola; A Titan Production; Foto-Kem Color; Rated R; 72 minutes; September release. CAST: Elizabeth Cayton (Daria), Cindy Beal (Tisa), Brinke Stevens (Shel), Don Scribner (Zed), Carl Horner (Rik), Kirk Graves (Vak), Randolph Roehbling (Krel)

THE WOMEN'S CLUB (Lightning Pictures) Producer, Fred Weintraub; Director/Screenplay, Sandra Weintraub; Photography, Kent Wakeford; Editor, Martin Cohen; Music, David Wheatley, Paul F. Antonelli; Art Director, Tim Duffey; Sound, Bob Abbott; Co-producer, Martin Hornstein; In association with Scorsese Prods.; United Color; R; 89 minutes; September release. CAST: Michael Pare (Patrick), Maud Adams (Angie), Eddie Velez (Carlos), no other credits provided

Ryan O'Neal, Lawrence Tierney in "Tough Guys Don't Dance" © *Cannon*

DUDES (New Century/Vista Film) Producer, Herb Jaffe; Executive Producer, Morth Engelberg; Line Producer, Gordon Wolf; Director, Penelope Spheeris; Screenplay, J. Randal Johnson; Photography, Robert Richardson; Editor, Andy Horvitch; Sound, Walter Martin; Designer, Robert Ziembjcki; Assistant Director, Guy Louthan; Casting, Nina Axelrod; A Vista Organization production; Color; Ultra-Stero; Rated R; 90 minutes; September release. CAST: Jon Cryer (Grant), Daniel Roebuck (Biscuit), Flea (Milo), Lee Ving (Missoula), Catherine Mary Stewart (Jessie), Billy Ray Sharkey, Glenn Withrow, Michael Melvin, Axxel G. Reese, Marc Rude, Calvin Bartlett, Pete Willcox, Vance Colvig, Pamela Gidley

BEST SELLER (Orion) Producer, Carter DeHaven; Director, John Flynn; Screenplay, Larry Cohen; Executive Producers, John Daly, Derek Gibson; Photography, Fred Murphy; Designer, Gene Rudolf; Editor, David Rosenbloom; Music, Jay Ferguson; Casting, Michael McLean, Diane Dimeo & Assoc.; Production Manager, Jack Roe; Assistant Directors, David Anderson, Leonid Zisman, Karen Miller Ehrlich; Production Executive, Graham Henderson; Music Supervisor, Budd Carr; Art Director, Robert Howland; Set Decorator, Chris Butler; Production Coordinator, Janet Lee Smith; Assistant Editors, Deborah Zimmerman, Jody Levine; Sound, Lee Alexander; Music Coordinator, Joanne Weiss; Stunts, Steve Lambert, Roydon Clark, Glenn Randall, Chuck Hicks; Special Effects, Ken Speed, Robert Olmstead; "*Perfect Ending*," Lamont Dozier; Vocals, Ben E. King; Songs, Jean Paul Martini, Claude Debussy; Soundtrack on Manhattan Records; Presented by Hemdale Film Corporation; Color; Rated R; 110 minutes; September release. CAST: James Woods (Cleve), Brian Dennehy (Dennis Meechum), Victoria Tennant (Roberta Gillian), Allison Balson (Holly Meechum), Paul Shenar (David Madlock), George Coe (Graham), Ann Pitoniak (Mrs. Foster), Mary Carver (Cleve's Mother), Sully Boyar (Monks), Kathleen Lloyd (Annie), Harold Tyner (Cleve's Father), E. Brian Dean (Taxi Driver), Jeffrey Josephson (Pearlman), Edward Blackoff (Thorn), Branscombe Richmond, J. P. Bumstead, William Bronder, Jenny Gago, Michael Crabtree, Clare Fields, Claudia Stenke, David Byrd, Loyda Ramos, Obaka Adedunyo, Ted Markland, Phil Hoover, David Blackwood, David Ursin, Jay Ingram, Daniel Trent, Gary Kirk, Dean Abston, David Cass, Bill Mitchell, John Howard Swain, Dennis Acree, Mark Venturini, Larry Holt, Jeff Ramsey, James Winburn, Peter Stader, Samuel V. Baldoni, Hank Woessner, Brian Gaffikin, Michael White, Martin West, Wally Burr, Arlin Miller, Sands Hall,

Robert Downey, Jr., Molly Ringwald in "Pick-up Artist" © *20th Century Fox/Brian Hamill*

Darius McCrary, Ricky Busker
in "Big Shots" © *Lorimar Pictures*

THE CURE IN ORANGE (ASA Communications/Movie Visions) Producer, Gordon Lewis; Executive Producer, Chris Parry; Director, Tim Pope; Photography, Chris Ashbrook; Editor, Peter Goddard; Stage Lighting, Angus MacPhail; Film Lighting, Zenith Lighting; Sound, David Allen, Steve Riddell, Mark Phillips; Production Managers, Berney Jeffrey, Mick Kluczynski, Serge Touboul; A Fiction Film Production; Documentary; Color; Dolby Stereo; Not rated; 96 minutes; October release. WITH: The Cure—Robert Smith, Simon Gallup, Porl Thompson, Boris Williams, Laurence Tolhurst

BORN AGAIN: LIFE IN A FUNDAMENTALIST BAPTIST CHURCH Producers/Directors, James Ault, Michael Camerini; Associate Director, Adrienne Miesmer; Photography, Michael Camerini; Editor, Sarah Stein; Music, Paul Moravec; Sound, Carol Ramsey; Narrator, Norman Rose; Assistant Editor, Adrienne Miesmer; A presentation of the South Carolina Educational Television Network, Columbia, S.C.; Produced with funding from New England Foundation for The Humanities, the Corporation for Public Broadcasting, and the Massachusetts Foundation for The Humanities and Public Policy; Documentary; Color; Not rated; 87 minutes; October release

PRINCE OF DARKNESS (Universal) Producer, Larry Franco; Director, John Carpenter; Screenplay, Martin Quatermass (John Carpenter); Photography, Gary B. Kibbe; Editor, Steve Mirkovich; Music, John Carpenter, in association with Alan Howarth; Designer, Daniel Lomino; Executive Producers, Shep Gordon, Andre Blay; Photography, Gary B. Kibbe; Editor, Steve Mirkovich; Designer, Daniel Lomino; Set Design, Rick Gentz; Costumes, Deahdra Scarano; Sound, Terry Porter, Mel Metcalfe, David J. Hudson; Stunts, Jeff Imada; Assistant Director, Larry Franco; Casting, Linda Francis; An Alive Films presentation; DeLuxe Color; Ultra-Stereo; Panavision; Rated R; 101 minutes; October release. CAST: Donald Pleasence (Priest), Jameson Parker (Brian), Victor Wong (Birack), Lisa Blount (Catherine), Dennis Dun (Walter), Susan Blanchard (Kelly), Anne Howard (Susan), Ann Yen (Lisa), Ken Wright (Lomax), Dirk Blocker (Mullins), Jessie Lawrence Ferguson (Calder), Peter Jason (Dr. Leahy), Alice Cooper (Street Schizo) No other credits provided

FIRE FROM THE MOUNTAIN Producer, Adam Friedson, Deborah Shaffer; Director, Deborah Shaffer; Photography, Frank Pineda; Editor, Virginia Reticker; Music, Charlie Haden; Documentary; Not rated; 60 minutes; October release

Victor Wong, Donald Pleasence
in "Prince of Darkness"
© *Universal City Studios*

BIG SHOTS (20th Century Fox) Producers, Joe Medjuck, Michael C. Gross; Director, Robert Mandel; Screenplay, Joe Eszterhas; Executive Producer, Ivan Reitman; Photography, Miroslav Ondricek; Designer, Bill Malley; Editors, Sheldon Kahn, William Anderson, Dennis Virkler; Music, Bruce Broughton; Casting, Lynn Stalmaster, Mali Finn; Costumes, Richard Bruno; Production Manager, John G. Wilson; Assistant Directors, Peter Giuliano, Robert J. Wilson, Linnea Wicklund; Set Decorator, Jean Alan; Set Designers, Gary Baugh, Bundy Trinz; Music Supervisor, David Kershenbaum; Orchestrations, Mark McKenzie, Chris Boardman; Special Effects, Bob Shelley, Bob Shelley, Jr.; Sound, Bill Randall; Associate Editor, Judith Blume; Assistant Editors, Karen Kory, Emmy Schallert, Jeffrey Bell, Howard Davis; Stunts, Spike Silver; Songs by various artists; Presented by Lorimar Pictures; Dolby Stereo; Panavision; DeLuxe Color; Rated PG-13; 90 minutes; October release. CAST: Ricky Busker (Obie), Darius McCrary (Scam), Robert Joy (Dickie), Robert Prosky (Keegan), Jerzy Skolimowski (Doc), Paul Winfield (Johnnie Red), Brynn Thayer (Mom), Bill Hudson (Dad), Jim Antonio (Uncle Harry), Andrea Bebel (Alley), Hutton Cobb (Bible Salesman), Joe Seneca (Ferryman), Beah Richards (Miss Hanks), Olivia Cole (Mrs. Newton), Mitch Beasley (Duane Henderson), Pauline Brailsford (Science Teacher), Cedric Young (Bartender), Timothy Scott (Smiley), Elise Langan, Sephus Booker, Wilbert Bradley, Bernard Chestleigh, Ron Dean, Tim Halligan, Jeffrey Harris, Shirley Spiegler Jacobs, Oscar Jordan, Michael Krawic, Lorraine Matthews, Maria McCrary, Sherry Narens, Jack R. Orend, Frank Rice, Antoine Roshell, Dick Sollenberger, James Spinks, Michael Stoyanov, Ken White, Dave Adams, Hank Underwood, Ellen Geer, Janet MacLachlan, David S. Dunard, Richard Caine

87 DAYS + 11 Producer/Director, Whitney Blake; Photography, Frances Reid; Editor, Joanne D'Antonio; A Go For It! production; Documentary; Color; Not rated; 99 minutes; October release

ISLANDS a film by Albert Maysles, Charlotte Zwerin and David Maysles; Producers, Susan Froemke, Joel Hinman; Photography, David Maysles, Albert Maysles; Editor, Kate Hirson; Music, Scott Cossu; Documentary; Color; Not rated; 58 minutes; October release

THE OUTING (TMS Pictures) Producer/Screenplay, Warren Chaney; Director, Tom Daley; Photography, Herbert Ratischnig; Music, Joel Rosenbaum, Bruce Miller; Color; Rated R; 89 minutes; October release. CAST: Deborah Winters (Eve Farrell), James Huston (Dr. Al Wallace), Andra St. Ivanyi (Alex Wallace), Scott Barkston (Ted Pinson), Mark Mitchell (Mike Daley), No other credits provided.

CATCH THE HEAT (Trans World Entertainment) Producer, Don Van Atta; Executive Producers, Moshe Diamant, Stirling Silliphant; Director, Joel Silberg; Screenplay, Stirling Silliphant; Photography, Nissim Nitcho, Frank Harris; Editors, Christopher Holmes, Darren Holmes; Music, Thomas Chase, Steve Rucker; Sound, Enrique Sansalvador Viale; Designer, Jorge Marchegiani; Production Manager, Jorge Velasco; Stunts, Alan Amiel; Casting, Caro Jones; A Negocios Cinematograficos production; In association with M'Amsel Tea Entertainment; Dolby Stereo; Cinecolor; Rated R; 87 minutes; October release. CAST: David Dukes (Waldo), Tiana Alexandra (Checkers Goldberg), Rod Steiger (Jason Hannibal), Brian Thompson (Danny), Jorge Martinez (Raul), John Hancock (Ike), Brian Libby (Brody), Jessica Schultz (Maria), Prof. Toru Tanaka (Dozu)

SLUMBER PARTY MASSACRE II (Concorde) Producers, Deborah Brock, Don Daniel; Director/Screenplay, Deborah Brock; Photography, Thomas L. Callaway; Editor, William Flicker; Music, Richard Cox; Sound, David Waelder; Designer John Eng; Art Director, Franc Novak; Set Decorator, Rozanne Taucher; Special Makeup Effects, James Cummins; Production Supervisor, Matt Leipzig; Assistant Director/Production Manager, Don Daniel; Production Supervisor, Steve Barnett; Casting, Kevin Alber, Bruce Boll; Foto-Kem Color; Rated R; 75 minutes; October release. CAST: Crystal Bernard (Courtney Bates), Kimberly McArthur (Amy), Juliette Cummins (Sheila), Patrick Lowe (Matt), Heidi Kozak (Sally), Atanas Ilitch (Driller Killer), Joel Hofman (T. J.), Scott Westmoreland (Jeff), Jennifer Rhodes (Mrs. Batehs), Cynthia Eilbacher (Valerie), Michael DeLano (Office Kreuger)

NIGHTFLYERS (New Century/Vista) Producer/Screenplay, Robert Jaffe; Executive Producer, Herb Jaffe; Director, T. C. Blake (Robert Collector); Based on the novel by George R. R. Martin; Photography, Shelly Johnson; Editor, Tom Siiter; Music, Doug Timm; Designer, John Muto; Art director, Mike Bingham; Set Decorator, Anne Huntley-Ahrens; Costumes, Brad R. Loman; Special Makeup/Mechanical Effects, Robert Short; Special Visual Effects, Gene Warren, Jr.; Sound, Steve Nelson; Assistant Director, Kristine Peterson; Casting, Nina Axelrod; Ultra-Stereo; DeLuxe Color; Rated R; 89 minutes; October release. CAST: Catherine Mary Stewart (Miranda), Michael Praed (Royd), John Standing (O'Branin), Lisa Blount (Audrey), Glenn Withrow (Keelor), James Avery (Darryl), Helene Udy (Lilly), Annabel Brooks (Eliza), Michael Des Barres (Jon Winderman)

Stacey Glick, Casey Siemaszko in "3 O'Clock High"
© Universal City Studios

Sam Elliott, Whoopi Goldberg in "Fatal Beauty"
© M-G-M/Len Hekel

THREE O'CLOCK HIGH (Universal) Producer, David E. Vogel; Director, Phil Joanou; Screenplay, Richard Christian Matheson, Thomas Szollosi; Executive Producers, Aaron Spelling, Alan Greisman; Lighting Consultant, Barry Sonnenfeld; Designer, William F. Matthews; Editor, Joe Ann Fogle; Co-Producers, John Davis, Neal Israel; Music, Tangerine Dream; Additional Music, Sylvester Levay; Costumes, Jane Ruhm; Casting, Nancy Nayor; Production Manager, Lynn M. Morgan; Assistant Directors, David Beanes, Martha Elcan; Set Decorator, Tom C. Bugenhagen, David D'Ovidio; Sound, Darin Knight; Special Effects, Michael A. Thompson, Wendell Winegar; Production Coordinators, Teri Fettis, Janice Pelin; Casting Assistant, Valerie McCaffrey; Stunts, Buddy van Horn: *"Something to Remember Me By"* by Jim Walker; Soundtrack on Varese Sarabande Records; Dolby Stereo; DeLuxe Color; Rated PG-13; 97 minutes; October release. CAST: Casey Siemaszko (Jerry Mitchell), Anne Ryan (Franny Perrins), Richard Tyson (Buddy Revell), Stacey Glick (Brei Mitchell), Jonathan Wise (Vincent Costello), Jeffrey Tambor (Mr. Rice), Philip Baker Hall (Det. Mulvahill), John P. Ryan (Mr. O'Rourke), Liza Morrow (Karen Clarke), Scott Tiler (Bruce Chalmer), Guy Massey (Scott Cranston), Theron Read (Mark Bojeekus), Mike Jolly (Craig Mattey), Charles Macaulay (Voytek Dolinski), Mitch Pileggi (Duke Herman), E. Katherine Kerr (Mrs. Phillips), Caitlin O'Hearney (Miss Farmer), Vivian Brown (Miss Vail), John Rothman (Mr. Medved), Sterling E. Gardner (Mr. Boal), Shirley Stoler (Eva), Alice Nunn (Nurse Palmer), Brooke Stevens, Helle K. Grimmer, Michael Alex, Michael Alvarez, John Amador, Brian Andrews, Bob Apisa, Geoffrey Bennett, Stanton Davis, Geoffrey Douglas, Paul Feig, Anthony Godfrey, Deanne Gunderson, Byron Jensen, John Kendrick, Tracey Lewis, Jeffrey Charles Michaelson, Brooke Montgomery, Adam Jay Sadowsky, Joel Sahleen, Jamie Shuman, Yeardley Smith, David Michael Taylor, Tom Taylor, Howard F. Flynn, Tom Ellito, Sandy Leavenworth, Bill McIntosh, Jerry Wills

POSITIVE I.D. (Universal) Producer/Director/Screenplay, Andy Anderson; Photography, Paul Barton; Editors, Andy Anderson, Robert J. Castaldo; Color; Rated R; 102 minutes; October release. CAST: Stephanie Rascoe (Julie Kenner), John Davies (Don Kenner), Steve Fromholz (Roy/Lt. Mercer), Laura Lane (Dana), Gail Cronauer (Melissa), Audeen Casey (Dr. Sterling), Matthew Sacks (Mr. Tony), Steven Jay Hoey (Johnny), John Williamson (Scotty), Erin White (Katie Kenner), April White (Mary Kenner), Terry Leeser (Vinnie DeStephano)

FATAL BEAUTY (MGM) Producer, Leonard Kroll; Director, Tom Holland; Screenplay, Hilary Henkin, Dean Riesner; Story, Bill Svanoe; Photography David M. Walsh; Designer, James William Newport; Editor, Don Zimmerman; Costumes, Aggie Guerard Rodgers; Music, Harold Faltermeyer; Casting, Richard Pagano, Sharon Bialy; Production Manager/Associate Producer, Art Schaefer; Assistant Directors, Michael Green, Barry Thomas, Richard Abramitis; Set Decorator, Rick Simpson; Set Designer, E. C. Chen; Sound, William Nelsn, Jules Strasser, Mychal Smith; Assistant Editors, Paul Cichocki, Rick Meyer, Carmen Baker; Production Coordinator, Ingrid C. Michaels; Special Effects, Kenneth D. Pepiot, Grant Burdette; Stunts, Walter Scott; Songs by various artists; Soundtrack on Atlantic Records; Dolby Stereo; DeLuxe Color; Rated R; 104 minutes; October release. CAST: Whoopi Goldberg (Rita Rizzoli), Sam Elliott (Mike Marshak), Ruben Blades (Carl Jimenez), Harris Yulin (Conrad Kroll), John P. Ryan (Lt. Kellerman), Jennifer Warren (Cecile Jaeger), Brad Dourif (Leo Nova), Mike Jolly (Earl Skinner), Charles Hallahan (Dep. Getz), David Harris (Raphael), James Le Gros (Zack Jaeger), Neill Barry (Denny Miflin), Mark Pellegrino (Frankenstein), Clayton Landey (Jimmy Silver), Fred Asparagus (Delgadillo), Catherine Blore (Charlene), Michael Champion (Buzz), Steve Akahoshi (Shigeta), Richard Milholland (Charlie), David Dunard (Cowboy Hat), Cheech Marin (Bartender), James Smith (Ritchie), Larry Hankin (Jerry Murphy), Michael DeLorenzo (Falco), Rick Telles (Epifanio), Carlos Cervantes (Basqual), Emilia Ayarza (Candy), Ebbe Roe Smith (Marty), Walter Robles (Clay), M. C. Gainey (Barndollar), Bernie Hern (Mike Weinstein), Prince Hughes (Big Bubba), Jim Bentley, Lucia Lexington, Jane Chung, Ellarye, Phil Chong, Joycelyne Lew, Jonathan Wong, Tom Spiroff, William Martin Brennan, Dower Phillips, Josh Pickard, Read Morgan, Cliff Murdock, Belinda Mayne, Celeste Yarnall, Sandra Bogan, Parker Whitman

THE HIDDEN (New Line Cinema) Producers, Robert Shaye, Gerald T. Olson, Michael Meltzer; Director, Jack Sholder; Screenplay, Bob Hunt; Casting, Annette Benson; Music, Michael Convertino; Editor, Michael Knue; Photography, Jacques Haitkin; Executive Producers, Stephen Diener, Lee Muhl, Dennis Harris, Jeffrey Klein; Special Effects Makeup, Kevin Yagher; Designers, C. J. Strawn, Mick Strawn; Presented with Heron Communications, Inc.; Color; Rated R; 96 minutes; October release. CAST: Michael Nouri (Tom Beck), Kyle MacLachlan (Lloyd Galagher), Ed O'Ross (Cliff Willis), Clu Gulager (Ed Flynn), Claudia Christian (Brenda Lee), Clarence Felder (John Masterson), William Boyett (Jonathan Miller), Richard Brooks (Sanchez), Catherine Cannon (Barbara Beck), Larry Ceder (Brem), John McCann (Holt), Chris Mulkey (Jack DeVries)

"Positive I.D."
© Universal City Studios

Michael Nouri, Kyle MacLachlan
in "The Hidden" © New Line Cinema

**Lisa Howard, Don Michael Paul
in "Rolling Vengeance"** © *Apollo Pictures*

NORMAN ROCKWELL'S WORLD . . . AN AMERICAN DREAM (Columbia) Producer, Concepts Unlimited; Executive Producer, Richard Barclay; Director, Robert Deubel; Concept/Screenplay, Gaby Monet; Photography, Carroll Ballard, Bob Bailin, David Watts; Editor, Burt Rashby; Music, John Kander, Song, *"Faces"* Music by John Kander, Lyrics by Fred Ebb; Vocals, Patrick Fox; Arranger/Conductor, Harold Hastings; Assistant Photographers, William Beautyman, Jr., Sal Guida, Wolfgang Zippel; Sound, Michael Scott, Vincent Deleo; Production Assistant, Miller Lide; Costumes, Maija; Documentary; 1973 Academy Award/Best Short Subject-Live Action; Not rated; thirty minutes; October release. CAST: Norman Rockwell & others

ROLLING VENGEANCE (Apollo Pictures, Inc.) Producer/Director, Steven H. Stern; Executive Producer, Jack E. Freedman; Screenplay, Michael Montgomery; Photography, Laszlo George; Editor, Ron Wisman; Art Director, H. E. Thrasher; Music, Phil Marshall; Color; Rated R; 90 minutes; October release. CAST: Don Michael Paul, Lawrence Dane, Ned Beatty, Lisa Howard (no other credits submitted)

SIGNED, LINO BROCKA Producer/Director/Screenplay/Photography, Christian Blackwood; Editor, Monika Abspacher; Sound, John Murphy; Documentary; Color; Not rated; 90 minutes; October release

HOSTAGE (Noble Entertainment) Executive Producers, James Aubrey, Michael Leighton; Producers, Thys Heyns, Paul Raleigh; Director, Hanro Mohr; Screenplay, Norman Winski, Michael Leighton; Photography, Johan van der Vyver; Editor, Simon Grimley; Sound, Shaunh Murdoch; Assistant Director, Richard Green; Art Director, Geoff Hill; Set Design, Caron Hill; Stunts, Reo Ruiters; A Blue Flower/Alpine production; Color; Rated R; 95 minutes; October release. CAST: Wings Hauser (Sam Striker), Karen Black (Laura Lawrence), Kevin McCarthy (Col. Tim Shaw), Nancy Locke (Nicole) Robert Whitehead, Billy Second, Ian Steadman, Iain Winter, Robert K. Brown, John Donovan, Michael Brunner, Pamela Perry, At Botha, Marcel van Heerden, Gerhard Hametner, Limpie Basson

THE KILLING TIME (New World) Producers, Peter Abrams, Robert L. Levy; Executive Producer, J. P. Guerin; Director, Rick King; Screenplay, Don Bohlinger, James Nathan, Bruce Franklin Singer; Photography, Paul H. Goldsmith; Editor, Lorenzo de Stefano; Music, Paul Chihara; Designer, Bernt Amadeus Capra; Set Decorator, Byrnadete Di Santo; Sound, Ron Judkins, Bob Jackson; Costumes, Jean-Pierre Dorleac; Assistant Director, Matthew Carlisle; Casting, Paul Ventura; Foto-Kem Color; Rated R; 95 minutes; October release. CAST: Beau Bridges (Sam Wayburn), Kiefer Sutherland (Brian Mars), Wayne Rogers (Jake Winslow), Joe Don Baker (Carl Cunningham), Camelia Kath (Laura Winslow), Janet Carroll (Lila Dagget), Michael Madsen (Stu)

RETRIBUTION (United Film) Executive Producers, Scott Lavin, Brian Christian Producer/Director, Guy Magar; Screenplay, Guy Magar, Lee Wasserman; Photography, Gary Thieltges; Editors, Guy Magar, Alan Shetland; Music, Alan Howarth; Sound, Peter Bentley; Designer, Robb Wilson King; Production Manager, Jeanne N. van Cott; Assistant Director, Douglas F. Dean 3d; Special Makeup Effects, Kevin Yagher; Special Effects, Court Wizard; Stunts, Bob Yerkes; Production Supervisor, Jeffrey Reiner; Associate Producer, Lee Wasserman; In association with Unicorn Motion Pictures; A Renegade Film production; Dolby Stereo; Fuji Color; Rated R; 107 minutes; October release. CAST: Dennis Lipscomb (George Miller), Leslie Wing (Jennifer Curtis), Suzanne Snyder (Angel), Jeff Pomerantz (Alan Falconer), George Murdock (Dr. Talbot), Pamela Dunlap (Sally Benson), Susan Peretz (Mrs. Stroller), Clare Peck (Carla Minelli), Chris Caputo (Dylan), Hoyt Axton (Lt. Ashley), Ralph Manza (Amos)

THE SICILIAN (20th Century Fox) Producers, Michael Cimino, Joann Carelli; Director, Michael Cimino; Screenplay, Steve Shagan; Based on the novel by Mario Puzo; Executive Producer, Sidney Beckerman; Assistant Directors, Brian Cook, Michael Stevenson; Production Executive, Malcolm R. Harding; Photography, Alex Thomson; Designer, Wolf Kroeger; Costumes, Wayne Finkelman; Editor, Francoise Bonnot; Music, David Mansfield; Casting, Deborah Brown; Choreographer, Claire Hutchins; Stunts, Vic Armstrong; Production Associate, Katherine Haber; Special Production Coordinators, Roberto Ando, Lia Pasqualino De Marineo; Associate Editor, Lizabeth Gelber; Assistant Editors, Gilberto Costa Nunes, Lesley Topping, Sue Kesler; Production Supervisor, Robert Cocco; Production Managers, Franco Coduti, Gianni Stellitano, Michael Fuller; Sound, David Crozier; Special Effects, Jeff Jarvis, Richard Hill, Scott Forbes, John McLeod; Art Director, Stefano Ortolani; Set Decorator, Joseph Mifsud Chevalier; Arrangements, David Mansfield, Don Swan; Presented by Gladden Entertainment Corp.; Technicolor; Rated R; 115 minutes; October release. CAST: Christopher Lambert (Salvatore Giuliano), Terence Stamp (Prince Borsa), Joss Ackland (Don Masino Croce), John Turturro (Aspanu Pisciotta), Richard Bauer (Prof. Hector Adonis), Barbara Sukowa (Camilla), Giulia Boschi (Giovanna Ferra), Ray McAnally (Minister Trezza), Barry Miller (Dr. Nattore), Andreas Katsulas (Passatempo), Michael Wincott (Corp. Silvestro Canio), Derrick Branche (Terranova), Richard Venture (Cardinal), Ramon Bieri (Quintana), Stanko Molnar (Silvio Ferra), Oliver Cotton (Comm. Roccofino), Joe Regalbuto (Father Doldana), Tom Signorelli (Abbot Manfredi), Aldo Ray (Don Siano), Nicholas Kepros, Justin Clark, Trevor Ray, Barone Giovanni Gagliardo Di Carpinello, Barone Guglielmo Inglese, Don Luciano Cappucino, Anita Laurenzi, Massimo Sarchielli, Emanuella Torri, Riccoardo De Torrebruna, Gaspare Canzoneri, Barone Francesco Agnello, Geoffrey Copplestone, Claudio Collova, Tony Sperandeo, Marino Matranga, Accursio Di Leo, Leonardo Treviglio, Franco Trevisi, Danilo Mattei, Carlo Pavone, Enrico Stassi, Chiara Carrafa, Francesco Plaia, Isidoro Passanante, Leonardo Plaia, Matteo Ingrao, Vito Ingoglia, Gaspare Mirrione, Carmelo Annelo, Marchesa Anna Lanza Di Mazzirino, Don Pepito Moncado Di Paterno, Donna Laura Moncada Di Paterno, Donna Olga Gagliardo Di Carpinello, Donna Matilda Gagliardo Di Carpinello, Lia Pasqualino Di Marineo, Prof. Antonio Pasqualino, Giovanna Carducci, Pietro De Spuches, Delia Bucca, Principe Filiberto Di Camporeale

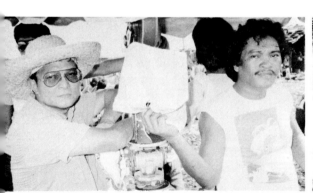

Lino Brocka (L) in "Signed: Lino Brocka"
© *Christian Blackwood*

**John Turturro, Christopher Lambert
in "The Sicilian"** © *20th Century Fox/David James*

FUNLAND (Double Helix Films, Inc.) Producers, William Vanderkloot, Michael A. Simpson; Director, Michael A. Simpson; Screenplay, Michael A. Simpson, Bonnie Turner, Terry Turner; Photography, William Vanderkloot; Editors, William Vanderkloot, Wade Watkins, Teresa Garcia; Music, James Oliverio; Color; Rated R; 87 minutes; October release. CAST: William Windom (Angus Perry), David L. Lander (Bruce Burger), Bruce Mahler (Spencer), Robert Sacchi (DiMaurio/Bogie), Clark Brandon (Doug Sutterfield), Jill Carroll (Denise Wilson), Mike McManus (T. G. Hurley), Mary McDonough (Kristin Cumming), Terry Beaver (Carl DiMaurio), Lane Davies (Chad Peller)

BIG BAD MAMA II (Concorde) Producer, Roger Corman; Director, Jim Wynorski; Screenplay, R. J. Robertson, Jim Wynorski; Based on characters created by William Norton & Frances Doel; Executive Producer, Lois Luger; Associate Producer, Matt Leipzig; Production Manager, Reid Shane; Assistant Directors, Michael Snyder, Julie Bloom; Art Director, Billie Breenbaum; Set Decorator, Archie D'Amico; Assistant Decorator, Beth Lamure; Additional Photography, Sean McLin; Sound, Chat Gunter, Gary Theard, Jeff Wilson; Costumes, Ellen Gross; Special Effects, Paul Hickerson; Casting, Rosemary Wildon; Production Supervisor, Steve Barnett; Assistant Editors, Tom Calderon, Robin Toor; Sound Design/Sound Editor, David John West; Music Performances, Steve Gornall, Carl Stewart, Chris Culverhouse, Chuck Cirino/"The Pocono Rangers"; Color; Rated R; 83 minutes; October release. CAST: Angie Dickinson (Wilma McClatchie), Robert Culp (Darly Pearson), Danielle Brisebois (Billy Jean), Julie McCullough (Polly), Jeff Yagher (Jordan Crawford), Bruce Glover (Morgan Crawford), Ebbe Roe Smith (Lucus Stroud), Charles Cyphers (Capt. Stark), H. Ray Huff (Police Chief), Ace Mask (Maitre D'), Nick La Tour (Doc Robey), Jacque Lynn Colton (Alma), Tom Finnegan (Bank President), Yvonne Peattie (Marton), Arthur Roberts (Mr. Sanders), Art Hern (Music Lover), Hardy Rawls (Police Capt.), Ed Cook (Truck Driver), John Dresden (Aaron McClatchie), Linda Shayne (Teller), Arnie Miller (Businessman), Kelli Maroney (Willie Crawford)

HOLY TERROR (Cinema Guild) Producers, Hudson River Prods. and Helsinki Films; Producer/Screenplay, Victoria Schultz; Directors, Victoria Schultz, Nancy Kanter; Photography, Peter Pearce, Jeff Wayman; Editor, Nola Schiff; Music, Sorrel; Produced by Hudson River Prods. and Helsinki Films, NY; Documentary; Color; Not rated; 60 minutes; October release

DERANGED (Platinum Pictures) Producer/Director, Chuck Vincent; Screenplay, Craig Horrall; Photography, Larry Revue; Music, Bill Heller; Editor, James Davalos; Costumes, Lorraine Altamura; Line Producer, Bill Tasgal; Associate Producer, Bill Slobodian; Sound, Peter Penguin; Art Director, Marc Ubell; Set Decorator, Mark Hammond; Special Effects, Vincent Guastini; Casting, Lem Amero; Assistant Director, Chip Lambert; Color; Rated R; 84 minutes; October release. CAST: Jane Hamilton (Joyce), Paul Siederman (Frank), Jennifer Delora (Maryann), James Gillis (Eugene), Jill Cumer (Sheila), Loretta Palma (Margaret), John Brett (Darren), Jessica Rose (Young Maryann), Gary Goldman (Nick), Harvey Siegel (Dr. Freemont), Frank Cole (Merrick), Daniel Chapman (Minister), Bob Fitzpatrick (Valet), Nancy Groff (Teacher), Max Hamilton (Baby Frankie)

OFF THE MARK (Fries Entertainment) Producer, Temple Matthews; Executive Producer, Marisa Arango; Director, Bill Berry; Screenplay, Temple Matthews, Bill Berry; Photography, Arledge Armenaki; Music, David Frank; Co-producer, Ira Trattner; Color; Rated R; 90 minutes; November release. CAST: Mark Neely, Terry Farrell, Clarence Gilyard, Jr., Norman Alden, Virginia Capers, Jon Cypher, Barry Corbin, Billy Barty. No other credits provided.

Angie Dickinson, Julie McCullough, Danielle Brisebois
in "Big Bad Mama II" © *Concorde*

FLOWERS IN THE ATTIC (New World) Producers, Sy Levin, Thomas Fries; Director/Screenplay, Jeffrey Bloom; Based on the novel by V. C. Andrews; Photography, Frank Byers, Gil Hubbs; Editor, Gregory F. Plotts; Music, Christopher Young; Designer, John Muto; Color; Rated PG-13; 95 minutes; November release. CAST: Louise Fletcher (Grandmother), Victoria Tennant (Mother), Kristy Swanson (Cathy), Jeb Stuart Adams (Chris), Ben Ganger (Cory), Lindsay Parker (Carrie), Marshall Colt (Father), Nathan Davis (Grandfather)

HEART (New World) Producer, Randy Jurgensen; Executive Producer, Michael Nicklous; Director, James Lemmo; Screenplay, James Lemmo, Randy Jurgensen; Photography, Jacek Laskus; Editor, Lorenzo Marinelli; Music, Geoff Levin, Chris Many; Designer, Vicki Paul; Art Director, Susan Raney; Costumes, Ticia Blackburn; Sound, Rolf Pardula; Associate Producer, Chris D'Antoni; Casting, Henry Alford; TVC Color; Rated R; 90 minutes; November release. CAST: Brad Davis (Eddie), Francis Fisher (Jeannie), Steve Buscemi (Nicky), Robinson Frank Adu (Buddy), Jesse Doran (Diddy), Sam Gray (Leo), Bill Costello (Fighter)

HONEYMOON (International Film Marketing) Producers, Xavier Gelin, Rene Malo; Director, Patrick Jamain; Screenplay, Patrick Jamain, Philippe Setbon, Robert Geoffrion; Story, Patrick Jamain, Philippe Setbon; Photography, Daniel Diot; Editor, Robert Rongier; Music, Robert Charlebois; Rated R; 100 minutes; November release. CAST: Nathalie Baye (Cecille), John Shea (Zack), Richard Berry (Michel), Marla Lukofsky (Sally), Peter Donat (Novak), Greg Ellwand (Bill), Cec Linder (Barnes), Alf Humphreys (Sonny), Michel Beaune (Garnier), Arthur Grossner (Forrester), Adriana Roach (Thelma), No other credits provided.

MARILYN MONROE: BEYOND THE LEGEND Producers/Screenplay, Gene Feldman, Suzette Winter; Director, Gene Feldman; Photography, Rick Robertson, Richard Francis; Editor, Les Mulkey; Associate Producer, Stephen Janson; Narrator, Richard Widmark; Documentary; Black & White; Not rated; 60 minutes; November release. WITH: Robert Mitchum, Shelley Winters, Joshua Logan, Susan Strasberg, Don Murray, Celeste Holm, Sheree North, Clark Gordon, John Springer, Laszlo Willinger

Jane Hamilton, Gary Goldman, Paul Siederman
in "Deranged" © *Platinum Pictures*

"Holy Terror"
© *Cinema Guild*

Andy Minsker (center)
in "Broken Noses"

Florence Shauffler, Brendan Hughes, Dennis Vero
in "Stranded" © *New Line Cinema*

BROKEN NOSES (Weber/Bush) Producers, Nan Bush in association with Steven Cohen, Kira Films; Director, Bruce Weber; Photography, Jeff Preiss; Sound, John Boisseau; Editor, Phyllis Famiglietti; Music Coordinator, Cherry Vanilla; Music, Julie London, Chet Baker, Robert Mitchum, Danny Small, Gerry Mulligan, Joni James, Ken Nordine; Documentary; Color; Not rated; 75 minutes; November release. WITH: Andy Minsker

BORDER RADIO (Coyote Films) Producer, Marcus De Leon; Directors/Screenplay, Allison Anders, Dean Lent, Kurt Voss; Additional Dialogue, the cast; Photography, Dean Lent; Music, Dave Alvin with Steve Berlin, Bill Bateman, John Bazz, D. J. Bonebrake, John Doe; Sound, Nietzehka Keene; Associate Producer, Robert Rosen; Black & White; Not rated; 84 minutes; November release. CAST: Chris D. (Jeff), John Doe (Dean), Luana Anders (Lu), Chris Shearer (Chris), Dave Alvin (Dave), Iris Berry (Scenester), Texacala Jones (Babysitter), Devon Anders (Devon), Chuck Shepard (Expatriot), Craig Stark, Eddie Flowers, Sebastian Copeland (Thugs), Green On Red (Themselves)

DATE WITH AN ANGEL (De Laurentiis) Producer, Martha Schumacher; Director/Screenplay, Tom McLoughlin; Photography, Alex Thomson; Editor, Marshall Harvey; Music, Randy Kerber; Designer, Craig Stearns; Art Director, Jeffrey S. Ginn; Set Designer, Randy Moore; Costumes, Donna O'Neal; Sound, Gary Bourgeois, Dean Okrand, Chris Carpenter; Visual Effects, Richard Edlund; Assistant Director, Bruce Moriarty; Casting, Fern Champion, Pamela Basker; In association with De Laurentiis Film Partners; Dolby Stereo; Technicolor; JDC Widescreen; Rated PG; 105 minutes; November release. CAST: Michael E. Knight (Jim Sanders), Phoebe Cates (Patty Winston), Emmanuelle Beart (Angel), David Dukes (Ed Winston), Phil Brock (George), Albert Macklin (Don), Pete Kowanko (Rex), Vinny Argiro (Ben Sanders), Bibi Besch (Grace Sanders)

TEEN WOLF TOO (Atlantic Releasing) Producer, Kent Bateman; Executive Producers, Thomas Coleman, Michael Rosenblatt; Director, Christopher Leitch; Screenplay, R. Timothy Kring; Story, Joseph Loeb 3d, Matthew Weisman; Photography, Jules Brenner; Editors, Steven Polivka, Kim Secrist, Harvey Rosenstock, Raja Gosnell; Music, Mark Goldenberg; Art Director, Peg McClellan; Sound, Richard Wadell; Assistant Director, Tana Manners; Casting, Pamela Rack; Color; Rated PG; 95 minutes; November release. CAST: Jason Bateman (Todd Howard), Kim Darby (Prof. Brooks), John Astin (Dean Dunn), Paul Sand (Coach Finstock), James Hampton (Uncle Howard), Mark Holton (Chubby), Estee Chandler (Nicki), Robert Neary (Gustavson), Stuart Fratkin (Stiles), Beth Ann Miller (Lisa), Rachel Sharp (Emily)

DEATH WISH 4: THE CRACKDOWN (Cannon) Producer, Pancho Kohner; Director, J. Lee Thompson; Screenplay, Gail Morgan Hickman; Based on characters created by Brian Garfield; Executive Producers, Menahem Golan, Yoram Globus; Photography, Gideon Porath; Music, Paul McCallum, Valentine McCallum, John Bisharat; Casting, Perry Bullington, Robert McDonald; Art Director, Whitney Brooke Wheeler; Production Executive, Rony Yacov; Assistant Directors, Robert J. Dougherty, Robert C. Ortwin, Jr.; Production Manager, John Zane; Production Supervisor, Marc S. Fischer; Production Coordinator, Barbara A. Hall; Sound, Craig Felburg; Set Decorator, Mark Andrew Haskins; Costume Supervisor, Michael Hoffman; Special Effects, Michael Wood; Assistant Editors, Mary E. Jochem, Christopher J. Notarthomas; Music Supervisor, Paula Erickson; Music Coordinator, Stephanie Lee; Color; Rated R; 99 minutes; November release. CAST: Charles Bronson (Paul Kersey), Kay Lenz (Karen Sheldon), John P. Ryan (Nathan White), Perry Lopez (Ed Zacharias), George Dickerson (Det. Reiner), Soon-Teck Oh (Det. Nozaki), Dana Barrow (Erica Sheldon), Jesse Dabson (Randy Viscovich), Peter Sherayko (Nick Franco), James Purcell (Vince Montono), Michael Russo (Danny Moreno), Danny Trejo (Art Sanella), Daniel Sabia (Al Arroyo), Mike Moroff (Jack Romero), Dan Ferro (Tony Romero), Tom Everett (Max Green), David Fonteno (Frank Bauggs), Michael Wise (Hood), Irwin Keyes (Chauffeur), Tim Russ (Jesse), Hector Mercado (JoJo), Derek Rydall (Kid), Mark Pellegrino (Punk)

Phoebe Cates, Michael Knight, Emmanuelle Beart
in "Date with an Angel" © *DeLaurentiis Entertainment*

Charles Bronson in "Death Wish 4:
the Crackdown" © *Cannon*

RUSSKIES (New Century Entertainment) Producers, Mark Levinson, Scott Rosenfelt; Director, Rick Rosenthal; Screenplay, Alan Jay Glueckman, Sheldon Lettich, Michael Nankin; Photography, Reed Smoot; Editor, Anthony Gibbs; Music, James Newton Howard; Designer, Linda Pearl; Color; Rated PG; 98 minutes; November release. CAST: Whip Hubley (Mischa), Lea` Phoenix (Danny), Peter Billingsley (Adam), Stefan DeSalle (Jason), Susan Walters (Diane), Patrick Kilpatrick (Raimy), Vic Polizos (Sulock), Charles Frank (Mr. Vandermeer), Susan Blanchard (Mrs. Vandermeer), Benjamin Hendrickson (Sgt. Kovac), Carole King (Mrs. Kovac).

SIESTA (Lorimar) Producer, Gary Kurfirst; Director, Mary Lambert; Screenplay, Patricia Louisianna Knop; Based on a Novel by Patrice Chaplin; Photography, Bryan Loftus; Editor, Glenn A. Morgan; Music, Marcus Miller; Designer, John Beard; Color; Rated R; 97 minutes; November release. CAST: Ellen Barkin (Claire), Gabriel Byrne (Augustine), Julian Sands (Kit), Isabella Rosselini (Marie), Martin Sheen (Del), Alexi Sayle (Cabbie), Grace Jones (Conchita), Jodie Foster (Nancy), Anastassia Stakis (Desdra), Gary Cady (Roger), No other credits provided.

CAUGHT (World Wide Pictures) Producer, Jerry Ballew; Director/Screenplay, James F. Collier; Photography, Eddie Van Der Enden; Production Designer, J. Michael Hooser; Music, Ted Neeley; Color; Rated PG-13; 113 minutes; November release. CAST: John Shepherd (Tim Devon), Amerjit Deu (Rejam Prasad), Jill Ireland (Janet Devon), Alex Tetteh-Lartey (Abraham Abimue), Frederik DeGroot (Jacques), Marnix Kappers (Erik de Bie), Kimberly Simms (Aimee Lynn), Hans Kenna (Tourist Clerk), Pim Vosmaer (Wouter), Erik J. Meijer (Sprug), Bruni Heincke (Mrs. de Bie), Rene Klijn (Tibbe), Peter Blok (Dude), Ethel Smyth, Kerry Cederberg, Deborah Smyth, Iris Misset, Martin Versluys, Annie de Jong, Bart Romer, Edward Kolderwijn, Elvira Wilson, Leontien de Rijiter, Billy Graham.

DEAR AMERICA (HBO COUTURIE) Producers, Bill Couturie, Thomas Bird; Director, Bill Couturie; Screenplay, Richard Dewhurst, Bill Couturie; Photography, stock footage from NBC Video Archives; Editor, Stephen Stept; Music, Todd Boekelheide; Sound, Robert Shoup, Mark Berger; Production Manager, EZ Petroff; Documentary; Dolby Stereo; Color; Not rated; 87 minutes; November release. WITH VOICES OF: Tom Berenger, Ellen Burstyn, J. Kenneth Campbell, Richard Chaves, Josh Cruze, Willem Dafoe, Robert De Niro, Brian Dennehy, Kevin Dillon, Matt Dillon, Robert Downey Jr., Michael J. Fox, Mark Harmon, John Heard, Fred Hirz, Harvey Keitel, Elizabeth McGovern, Judd Nelson, Sean Penn, Randy Quaid, Tim Quill, Eric Roberts, Ray Robertson, Howard Rollins Jr., John Savage, Raphael Sbarge, Martin Sheen, Tucker Smallwood, Roger Steffens, Jim Tracy, Kathleen Turner, Tico Wells, Robin Williams.

THE AMERICAN WAY, aka *Riders of the Storm* (Miramax Films) Producers, Laurie Keller, Paul Cowan; Director, Maurice Phillips; Screenplay, Scott Roberts; Photography, John Metcalfe; Editor, Tony Lawson; Music, Brian Bennett; Production Designer, Evan Hercules; Color; Rated R; 92 minutes; December release. CAST: Dennis Hopper (Captain), Michael J. Pollard (Tesla), Eugene Lipinski (Ace), James Aubrey (Claude), All Matthews (Ben), William Armstrong (Jerry), Michael Ho (Minh), Derek Hoxby (Sam), Nigel Pegram (Mrs. Westinghouse).

BLIND (Zipporah Films) Producer/Director/Sound, Frederick Wiseman; Photography, John Davey; Documentary; Not rated; 132 minutes; December release. WITH: Students, teachers and staff of the Alabama School for the Deaf and Blind.

THE TROUBLE WITH SPIES (De Laurentiis Entertainment Group) Producer/Director/Screenplay, Burt Kennedy; Executive Producer, Constantine P. Karos; Based on the book *"Apple Pie in the Sky"* by Marc Lovell; Photography, Alex Phillips; Editor, Warner E. Leighton; Music, Ken Thorne; Designer, Jose Maria Tapiador; An HBO Pictures presentation of a Brigade production; Eastmancolor; Rated PG; 91 minutes; December release. CAST: Donald Sutherland (Appleton Porter), Ned Beatty (Harry Lewis), Ruth Gordon (Mrs. Arkwright), Lucy Gutteridge (Mona Smith), Michael Hordern (Jason Lock), Robert Morley (Angus Watkins), Gregory Sierra (Capt. Sanchez), Suzanne Danielle (Maria Sola), Fima Noveck (Col. Novikov).

SULLIVAN'S PAVILION (Adirondack Alliance) Producer/Director/Screenplay, Fred G. Sullivan; Photography, Hal Landen; Music, Kenneth Higgins, James Calabrese; Editor, Fred G. Sullivan; DuArt Color; Rated PG; 83 minutes; November release. CAST: Polly Sullivan, Tate Sullivan, Kurt Sullivan, Ricky Sullivan, Fred G. Sullivan (Themselves), Jon Granik (Bear/Narrator), James R. Hogue (Conrad P. Drizzle), Jan Jalenak (The Temptress), Judith Mayes (Sister Mary Anthony), Don Samuels (The Cretin Beer Lover), Roberta Schwebel (Gillian Solomon, M.D.)

Mura Dehn (center)
in "The Spirit Moves"

THE SPIRIT MOVES: A HISTORY OF BLACK SOCIAL DANCE ON FILM *Parts 1 and 2* (Filmmakers Library) Producer/Director, Mura Dehn; Documentary; 119 minutes; December release; shown in tandem with *In a Jazz Way: A Portrait of Mura Dehn* Directors, Louise Ghertler, Pamela Katz; Documentary; Not rated; 30 minutes; December release

STRANDED (New Line Cinema) Producers, Scott Rosenfelt, Mark Levinson; Executive Producer, Robert Shaye; Director, Tex Fuller; Screenplay, Alan Castle; Photography, Jeff Jur; Editor, Stephen E. Rivkin; Music, Stacy Widelitz; Sound, Peter Bentley; Aliens created and designed by Michele Burke; Special Visual Effects, VCE Inc./Peter Kuran; Special Effects, Allen Hall; Assistant Director, Mike Topoozian; Production Manager, Marie Cantin; Set Decorator, Lisette Thomas; Stunts, John Branagan; Associate Producer, Sara Risher; Casting, Annette Benson; Additional Editor, Steven Schoenberg; Alien World Sequence: Director, Marina Sargenti; Photography, Robert Brinkmann; United Color; Rated PG-13; 80 minutes; December release. CAST: Ione Skye (Deirdre), Joe Morton (Sheriff McMahon), Maureen O'Sullivan (Grace Clark), Susan Barnes (Helen Anderson), Cameron Dye (Lt. Scott), Michael Greene (Vernon Burdett), Brendan Hughes (Prince), Gary Swanson (Sergeant), Flea (Jester), Spice Williams (Warrior)

CHRISTMAS EVIL Producers, Burt Kleiner, Pete Kameron; Director/Screenplay, Lewis Jackson; Color; Rated R; 92 minutes; December release. CAST: Brandon Maggart (Harry), Jeffrey DeMunn (Phillip), Diane Hull (Jackie), No other credits provided.

DEATHROW GAMESHOW (Crown International) Executive Producer/Sound, Sergio Bandera; Producer, Brian J. Smith; Director/Screenplay, Mark Pirro; Additional material, Alan Gries; Photography, Craig Bassuk; Supervising Editor, Tim Shoemaker; Music, Gregg Gross; Designer, Mark Simon; Assistant Director, Tom Milo; Production Manager, Devorah Hardburger; Stunts, Eric Megison; Casting, John McCafferty Kent Butler; Co-producer, Glenn Campbell; Color; Rated R; 83 minutes; December release. CAST: John McCafferty (Chuck Toedan), Robin Blythe (Gloria Sternvirgin), Beano (Luigi Pappalardo), Mark Lasky (Momma), Darwyn Carson (Trudy), Debra Lamb (Shanna Shallow), Paul Farbman (Dinko)

Joe Morton, Maureen O'Sullivan
in "Stranded" © *New Line Cinema*

155

**Valri Bromfield, Martin Mull
in "Home Is Where the Hart Is"** © *Atlantic*

COLD STEEL (Cinetel) Producer, Lisa M. Hansen; Executive Producer, Paul Hertzberg; Director, Dorothy Ann Puzo; Screenplay, Michael Sonye, Moe Quigley; Story, Michael Sonye, Ann Puzo, Lisa M. Hansen; Photography, Tom Denove; Editor, David Bartlett; Music, David A. Jackson; Art Director, Maxine Shepard; Set Decoration, Scott Ambrose; Sound, Rob Janifer; Assistant Director, Richard Kanter; Associate Producer, Peter Combs; Casting, Barbara Claman, Margie Clark; Foto Kem Color; Rated R; 90 minutes; December release. CAST: Brad Davis (Johnny Modine), Sharon Stone (Kathy), Jonathan Banks (Iceman), Jay Acovone (Cookie), Adam Ant (Mick), Eddie Egan (Lt. Hill), Sy Richardson (Rashid), Anne Haney (Anna Modine), Ron Karabatso (Fishman)

THIS IS OUR HOME, IT IS NOT FOR SALE (RIVERSIDE PRODUCTIONS) Producer/Director, Jon Schwartz; Photography, Levie Isaacks; Editor, Ronald Medico; Sound, Brenda Reiswerg; Documentary; Color; Not rated; 190 minutes; December release

THE WILD PAIR (Trans World Entertainment) Producer, Paul Mason; Director, Beau Bridges; Screenplay, Joseph Gunn, Story, Joseph Gunn; John Crowther; Photography, Peter Stein; Editor, Christopher Holmes, Scott Conrad; Music, John Debney; Designer, Stephen M. Berger; Color; Rated R; 86 minutes; December release. CAST: Beau Bridges (Jo Jennings), Bubba Smith (Benny Avalon), Lloyd Bridges (Col. Hester), Gary Lockwood (Capt. Kramer), Raymond St. Jacques (Ivory), Danny de la Paz (Tucker), Lela Rochon (Debby)

THE MAGIC SNOWMAN (Miramax) Producers, Pavlina Proevska, Jovan Markovic; Director, C. Stanner; Screenplay, Dennis Maitland, Lyle Morris; Adaptation, Jovan Markovic; Story, Dennis Maitland; Photography, Karpo Godina; Music, John Berenzy; Production Supervisor, Simon Nuchtern; A Pavlina Ltd. (N.Y.) and Film i Ton (Belgrade) production; U.S./Yugoslav; CFS Color; Not rated; 84 minutes; December release. CAST: Justin Fried (Jamie), Dragana Marjanovic (Mandy), Jack Aronson, Christian James, Kyle Morris, Roger Moore (Voice of Lumi Ukko, the Snowman)

SCARED STIFF Color; Rated R; 87 minutes; December release. CAST: Mary Page Keller (Kate Christopher), Andrew Stevens (David Young), Josh Segal (Jason). No other credits provided.

**Gloria Foster, Bill Cosby, Pat Colbert
in "Leonard Part 6"** © *Columbia*

HOME IS WHERE THE HART IS (Atlantic Entertainment Group) Executive Producers, Ralph Scobie, Richard Strafehl; Producer, John M. Eckert; Director/Screenplay, Rex Bromfield; Photography, Robert Ennis; Editor, Michael Todd; Art Director, Jill Scott; Music, Eric N. Robertston; Casting, Ingrid Fischer; Production Manager, Harold Tichenor; Assistant Directors, T. W. Peacocke, Mick Mackay, Paul Pollio; Sound, Martin Fossum; Assistant Art Director, Eric Norlin; Set Decorator, Lesley Beale; Costumes, Jane Still; Production Supervisor, Don Haig; Color; Rated PG-13; 94 minutes; December release. CAST: Valri Bromfield (Belle Haimes), Stephen E. Miller (Rex Haimes), Deanne Henry (Selma Dodge), Martin Mull (Carson Boundy), Eric Christmas (Martin Hart), Ted Stidder (Art Hart), Leslie Nielsen (Sheriff Nashville Schwartz), Joe Austin (Slim Hart), Enid Saunders (Minnie Hart), Leslie Jones (Night Nurse), Dana Still (Blind Man), Jeni LeGon (Wanda Fuch), Jackson Davis (Minister), Hagan Beggs (Gravedigger), Marc Bourrel (Chester Nimms), Joe Sala (Nun), Mark Acheson (Customer), Adrien Dorval (Dep. Worse), Jeanette Lewis (Millie), Ian Tracey (Punk Kid), Simon Webb (Justice of the Peace), Janet Wright (J.P.'s wife)

LEONARD PART 6 (Columbia) Producer/Story, Bill Cosby; Director, Paul Weiland; Screenplay, Jonathan Reynolds; Executive Producers, Alan Marshall, Steve Sohmer; Photography, Jan DeBont; Designer, Geoffrey Kirkland; Editor, Gerry Hambling; Visual Effects, Richard Edlund; Costumes, Aggie Guerard Rodgers; Choreography, Louis Falco; Casting, Victoria Thomas; Music, Elmer Bernstein; Production Manager, Nancy Giebink; Assistant Directors, Aldric Porter, Joseph Ray; Associate Producer, Ned Kopp; Art Director, Blake Russell; Set Decorator, Jim Poynter; Sound, David MacMillan; Additional Editing, Peter Boita; Assistant Editors, Carlyn Montes De Oca, Richard Fettes, Wayne Smith, Larry Moten, Leonard Green, Bob Marty, Michelle Perrone, Alexander Parker, Barry Dresner; Set Designers, Bill Beck, Paul Kraus; Stunts, Alan Oliney; Special Effects, Jeff Gillam, John McLeod, Casey Cavanaugh, Dan Nelson, Chuck Ray, Josie Cornell, Ross Lorente, Dana Fuller; A SAH Enterprises, Inc. Production; Songs, *"Without You (Love Theme)"* by Lamont Dozier, *"Positive"* by Peter Quigley, Alaster Campbell, *"Hurt"* by Jimmie Crane, Al Jacobs; Vocals, Peabo Bryson, Regina Belle; Dolby Stereo; DeLuxe Color; Rated PG; 85 minutes; December release. CAST: Bill Cosby (Leonard), Tom Courtenay (Frayn), Joe Don Baker (Snyderburn), Moses Gunn (Giorgio), Pat Colbert (Allison), Gloria Foster (Medusa), Victoria Rowell (Joan), Anna Levine (Nurse Carvalho), David Maier (Man Ray), Grace Zabriskie (Jefferson), Hal Bokar (Andy), George Maguire (Madison), John Hostetter (Adams), William Hall (Monroe), George Kirby (Dochamp), Mel A. Tomlinson, Ann Armour, Reggie Waldon, Reed Kirk Rahlmann, Keith Joe Dick, Eva Gholson, Leona Harris, Cab Covay, Darlene Barrett, Alan Liss, Sarah Wagner, Darry Porter, Derek Benton, Alex Adams, Katie McKelley, Rose Wong, Harry Wong, Babatunde, Larry Alexander, Zoltan Gray, Eugene Robinson, Ted Young, Clint Jung, Gordon Kimbrough, George Abrams, Jr., Larry Gates, David Rowe, Chitti Sookvamdee, Eric Hanes, Leo Rossi, Ren Reynolds, Gianni Giacri, Bruno Pella, Alan Oliney

PINOCCHIO AND THE EMPEROR OF THE NIGHT (New World) Producer, Lou Scheimer; Director, Hal Sutherland; Screenplay, Robby London, Barry O'Brien, Dennis O'Flaherty; Photography, Ervin L. Kaplan; Editor, Jeffrey Patrick Gehr; Music, Anthony Marinelli, Brian Banks; Songs, Will Jennings, Barry Mann, Steve Tyrell; Production Supervisor, Erika Scheimer; Art Director, John Grusd; Sound, B & B Sound Studios; Animated; Dolby Stereo; CFI Color; Rated G; 87 minutes; December release. VOICE CAST: Edward Asner, Tom Bosley, Lana Beeson, Linda Gary, Jonathan Harris, James Earl Jones, Ricky Lee Jones, Don Knotts, William Windom

THE ORDER OF THE BLACK EAGLE (International Film Marketing) Executive Producers, Betty J. Stephens, John A. Stephens; Producers, Betty J. Stephens, Robert P. Eaton; Director, Worth Keeter; Screenplay, Phil Behrens; Photography, Irl Dixon; Editor, Matthew Mallinson; Music, Dee Barton; Sound, David Henson; Art Director, Mack Pittman; Production Manager, Thom McIntyre; Associate Producer, Matthew Mallinson; Technicolor; Rated R; 93 minutes; December release. CAST: Ian Hunter (Duncan Jax), C. K. Bibby (Star), William Hicks (Baron), Anna Rapagna (Maxie Ryder), Jill Donnellan (Tiffany), Flo Hyman (Spike), Shan Tai Tuan (Sato), Stephan Krayk, Gene Scherer, Wolfgang Linkman, Typhoon the Baboon

LOVE STORIES: WOMEN, MEN & ROMANCE (Cine Research) Producers, Richard Broadman, John Grady, Judith Smith, Kersti Yllo; Director/Editor, Richard Broadman; Photography, John Bishop, John Hoover; Sound, Stephen Olech; Line Producer, Susan Steiner; Production Manager, Kate Davis; Archival Research, Judith Smith, Media Research; Narrator, Janice Gray; Documentary; Color; Not rated; 83 minutes; December release

PROMISING NEW ACTORS OF 1987

KATHY BAKER

ALEC BALDWIN

JOAN CHEN

JOHN LONE

JENNIFER GREY

ESAI MORALES

LOU DIAMOND PHILLIPS

GLENNE HEADLY

HOLLY HUNTER

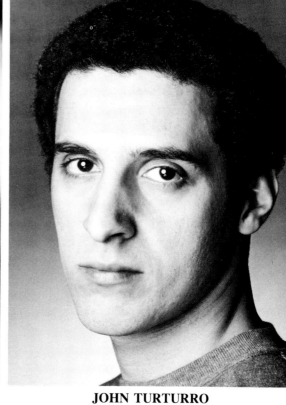

JOHN TURTURRO

COURTNEY B. VANCE

MARY STUART MASTERSON

THE LAST EMPEROR

(COLUMBIA) Producer, Jeremy Thomas; Director, Bernardo Bertolucci; Screenplay, Mark Peploe with Bernardo Bertolucci; Associate Producer, Franco Giovale, Joyce Herlihy; Music, Ryuichi Sakamoto, David Byrne, Cong Su; Photography, Vittorio Storaro; Editor, Gabriella Cristiani; Designer, Ferdinando Scarfiotti; Costumes, James Acheson; Production Supervisor, Mario Cotone; Initial Screenplay Collaboration, Enzo Ungari; Casting, Joanna Merlin; Assistant Directors, Gabriele Polverosi, Serena Canevari, Nicoletta Peyran, Franco Angeli, Giulio Levi, Ning Ying, Basil Pao; Additional Casting, Ulrike Koch (China), Patricia Pao (Hong Kong); Production Managers, Attilio Viti, Lamberto Palmieri, Pietro Sassaroli, Alberto Passone, Stefano Bolzoni; Production Coordinator, Manuela Pineskj Berger; Production Consultant, Shirley Sun; Sound, Ivan Sharrock, Bill Rowe, Colin Wood, Don Banks, David Motta; Assistant Editors, Elvio Sordoni, Martin Crane, Nadia Mazzoni, Fiorella Giovanelli, Catherine Hodgson; Special Effects, Gino De Rossi, Fabrizio Martinelli; Assistant Costume Designers, Frank Gardiner, Gilly Hebden, Thomas Casterline, Collette Koo; Military Costumes, Ugo Pericoli, Millina Deodata; Hair Designers, Giancarlo De Leonardis, Iole Cecchini; Art Directors, Gianni Giovagnoni, Gianni Silvestri, Maria Teresa Barbasso; Songs, *"Kaiser Walzer"* Johann Strauss/*"Am I Blue"* Harry Akst, Grant Drake; Made by Yanco Films Limited and Tao Films SRL in association with Recorded Picture Company Limited/Screenframe Limited/AAA Soprofilms; Presented by Hemdale Film Corporation; Dolby Stereo; Eastman Color/Technicolor; Technovision; Rated PG-13; 160; November release

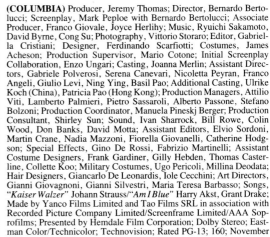

CAST

Pu Yi (Adult)	John Lone
Wan Jung	Joan Chen
Reginald Johnston (R. J.)	Peter O'Toole
The Governor	Ying Ruocheng
Chen Pao Shen	Victor Wong
Big Li	Dennis Dun
Amakasu	Ryuichi Sakamoto
Eastern Jewel	Maggie Han
Interrogator	Ric Young
Wen Hsiu	Wu Jun Mimei
Chang	Cary Hiroyuki Tagawa
Ar Mo	Jade Go
Yoshioka	Fumihiko Ikeda
Pu Yi (3 years)	Richard Vuu
Pu Yi (8 years)	Tijger Tsou
Pu Yi (15 years)	Wu Tao
Pu Chieh (Adult)	Fan Guang
Pu Chieh (7 years)	Henry Kyi
Pu Chieh (14 years)	Alvin Riley III
Tzu Hsui	Lisa Lu
General Ishikari	Hideo Takamatsu
Japanese Translator	Hajime Tachibana
Prince Chun	Basil Pao
Lord Chamberlain	Jiang Xi Ren
Captain of Imperial Guard	Chen Kai Ge
Big Foot	Zhang Liangbin
Hunchback	Huang Wenjie
Lady Aisin-Gioro	Liang Dong
Old Doctor	Dong Zhendong
Doctor	Dong Jiechen
Ocultist	Constantine Gregory
Lung Yu	Soong Huaikuei
First High Consort	Shao Ruzhen
Second High Consort	Li Yu
Third High Consort	Li Guangli
Grey Eyes	Xu Chunqing
Old Tutor	Zhang Tianmin
Sleeping Old Tutor	Luo Hongnian
Hsiao Hsiu	Yu Shihong
Wen Hsiu (12 years)	Wu Jun
Lady of the Book	Lucia Hwong
Lady of the Pen	Cui Jingping
Republican Officer	Wu Hai
Tang	Gu Junguo
Captain of Feng's Army	Xu Tongrui
Minister of Trade	Li Fusheng

Top Left: Lisa Lu, Richard Vuu (also below)
Academy Awards for Best Picture, Director, Screen Adaptation, Cinematography, Editing, Original Score, Art Direction, Costume Design, and Sound © Columbia Pictures

Peter O'Toole (center)
Above: John Lone

BEST PICTURE OF 1987

Maggie Han, Joan Chen Above: John Lone,
Joan Chen Top: Wu Tao, Joan Chen Below:
John Lone

John Lone, Joan Chen
Above and Top: John Lone

MICHAEL DOUGLAS

in "Wall Street" © *20th Century Fox/Andy Schwartz*
ACADEMY AWARD FOR BEST ACTOR OF 1987

CHER

in "Moonstruck" © *M-G-M Pictures*
ACADEMY AWARD FOR BEST ACTRESS OF 1987

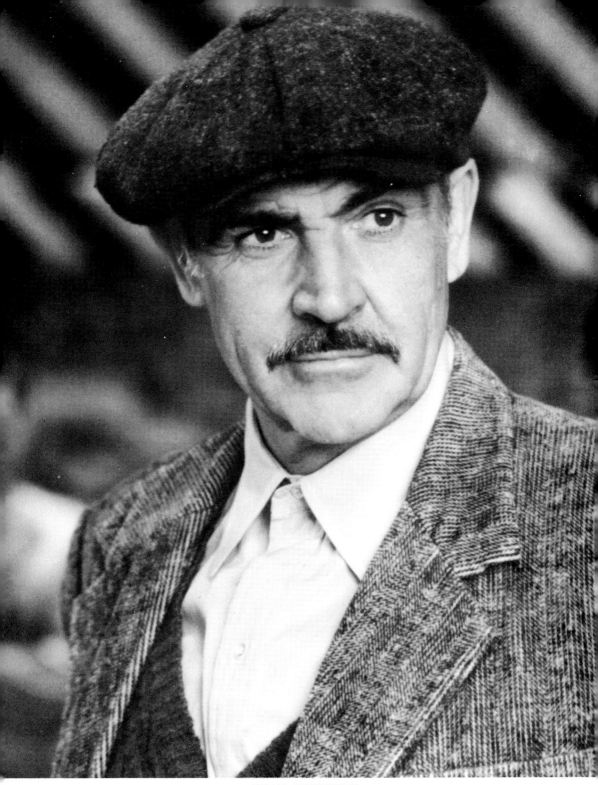

SEAN CONNERY

in "The Untouchables" © *Paramount Pictures/Zade Rosenthal*
ACADEMY AWARD FOR BEST SUPPORTING ACTOR OF 1987

OLYMPIA DUKAKIS

in "Moonstruck" © *M-G-M Pictures*
ACADEMY AWARD FOR BEST SUPPORTING ACTRESS OF 1987

BABETTE'S FEAST

(ORION CLASSICS) Executive Producer, Just Betzer; Producer, Bo Christensen; Director, Gabriel Axel; Assistant Director, Tom Hedegaard; Screenplay, Gabriel Axel from short story by Isak Dinesen; Photography, Henning Kristiansen; Designer, Sven Wichman; Music, Per Norgard; Sound, Michael Dela, John Nielson; Light, Michael Sorensen, Michael Wils Jensen; Editor, Finn Henriksen; Costumes, Annelise Hauberg, Pia Myrdal, Karl Lagerfeld; Make-up, Lydia Pujol, Bente Moller, Elisabeth Bukkehave; Special Effects, Henning Bahs; Production Manager, Lene Nielsen; A Just Betzer/Panorama Film International production in cooperation with Nordisk Film A/S and the Danish Film Institute (Claes Kastholm Hansen); Denmark; Danish and French with subtitles; Color; Rated G; 102 minutes; March release

CAST

Babette Hersant	Stephane Audran
Achille Papin	Jean-Philippe Lafont
Lorens Lowenhielm (young)	Gudmar Wivesson
Lorens Lowenhielm (old)	Jarl Kulle
Swedish Royal Opera Patron	Bibi Andersson
Philippa (young)	Hanne Stengard
Philippa (old)	Bodil Kjer
Martina (young)	Vibeke Hastrup
Martina (old)	Birgitte Federspiel
Old Nielsen	Bendt Rothe
The Widow	Lisbeth Movin
The Captain	Preben Lerdorff Rye
The Coachman	Axel Strobye
Christopher	Ebbe Rode
The General's Aunt	Ebba With
The Vicar	Pouel Kern
Erik	Erik Petersen
Karlsen	Holger Perfort
Anna	Asta Esper Andersen
Solveig	Else Petersen
The Grocer	Finn Nielsen
Martha	Therese Hojgard
The Fisherman	Lars Lohmann
Lorens' Wife	Tine Miehe-Renard
Singing Voice for Philippa	Tina Kiberg

Left: The parishioners enjoy Babette's feast
Above: Hanne Stensgard, Pouel Kern, Vibeke Hastrup
Top: Stephane Audran, Lars Lohmann
© Orion Pictures

Bodil Kjer, Birgitte Federspiel

Stephane Audran

ACADEMY AWARD FOR BEST FOREIGN-LANGUAGE FILM OF 1987

THE TEN-YEAR LUNCH: THE WIT AND LEGEND OF THE ALGONQUIN ROUND TABLE (Aviva Films) Producer/Director, Aviva Slesin; Co-Executive Producer, Stephen Samuels; A Production of Aviva Films in association with American Masters/WNET; Documentary; Winner 1988 Academy Award; Color; Not rated; 60 minutes; March release. WITH: Marc Connelly, Averell Harriman, Ruth Gordon, Helen Hayes, Margalo Gillmore, Heywood Hale Broun and others

Top: "The Algonquin Round Table"
as drawn by Al Hirschfeld
© *Margo Feiden Galleries*

Dorothy Parker

ACADEMY AWARD FOR BEST FEATURE-LENGTH DOCUMENTARY OF 1987   **167**

Katharine
Hepburn

Timothy
Hutton

Celeste
Holm

Dustin
Hoffman

Goldie
Hawn

Gregory
Peck

PREVIOUS ACADEMY AWARD WINNERS

(1) Best Picture, (2) Actor, (3) Actress, (4) Supporting Actor, (5) Supporting Actress, (6) Director, (7) Special Award, (8) Best Foreign Language Film, (9) Best Feature Documentary

1927–28: (1) "Wings," (2) Emil Jannings in "The Way of All Flesh," (3) Janet Gaynor in "Seventh Heaven," (6) Frank Borzage for "Seventh Heaven," (7) Charles Chaplin.

1928–29: (1) "Broadway Melody," (2) Warner Baxter in "Old Arizona," (3) Mary Pickford in "Coquette," (6) Frank Lloyd for "The Divine Lady."

1929–30: (1) "All Quiet on the Western Front," (2) George Arliss in "Disraeli," (3) Norma Shearer in "The Divorcee," (6) Lewis Milestone for "All Quiet on the Western Front."

1930–31: (1) "Cimarron," (2) Lionel Barrymore in "A Free Soul," (3) Marie Dressler in "Min and Bill," (6) Norman Taurog for "Skippy."

1931–32: (1) "Grand Hotel," (2) Fredric March in "Dr. Jekyll and Mr. Hyde" tied with Wallace Beery in "The Champ," (3) Helen Hayes in "The Sin of Madelon Claudet," (6) Frank Borzage for "Bad Girl."

1932–33: (1) "Cavalcade," (2) Charles Laughton in "The Private Life of Henry VIII," (3) Katharine Hepburn in "Morning Glory," (6) Frank Lloyd for "Cavalcade."

1934: (1) "It Happened One Night," (2) Clark Gable in "It Happened One Night," (3) Claudette Colbert in "It Happened One Night," (6) Frank Capra for "It Happened One Night," (7) Shirley Temple.

1935: (1) "Mutiny on the Bounty," (2) Victor McLaglen in "The Informer," (3) Bette Davis in "Dangerous," (6) John Ford for "The Informer," (7) D. W. Griffith.

1936: (1) "The Great Ziegfeld," (2) Paul Muni in "The Story of Louis Pasteur," (3) Luise Rainer in "The Great Ziegfeld," (4) Walter Brennan in "Come and Get It," (5) Gale Sondergaard in "Anthony Adverse," (6) Frank Capra for "Mr. Deeds Goes to Town."

1937: (1) "The Life of Emile Zola," (2) Spencer Tracy in "Captains Courageous," (3) Luise Rainer in "The Good Earth," (4) Joseph Schildkraut in "The Life of Emile Zola," (5) Alice Brady in "In Old Chicago," (6) Leo McCarey for "The Awful Truth," (7) Mack Sennett, Edgar Bergen.

1938: (1) "You Can't Take It with You," (2) Spencer Tracy in "Boys' Town," (3) Bette Davis in "Jezebel," (4) Walter Brennan in "Kentucky," (5) Fay Bainter in "Jezebel," (6) Frank Capra for "You Can't Take It with You," (7) Deanna Durbin, Mickey Rooney, Harry M. Warner, Walt Disney.

1939: (1) "Gone with the Wind," (2) Robert Donat in "Goodbye, Mr. Chips," (3) Vivien Leigh in "Gone with the Wind," (4) Thomas Mitchell in "Stagecoach," (5) Hattie McDaniel in "Gone with the Wind," (6) Victor Fleming for "Gone with the Wind," (7) Douglas Fairbanks, Judy Garland.

1940: (1) "Rebecca," (2) James Stewart in "The Philadelphia Story," (3) Ginger Rogers in "Kitty Foyle," (4) Walter Brennan in "The Westerner," (5) Jane Darwell in "The Grapes of Wrath," (6) John Ford for "The Grapes of Wrath," (7) Bob Hope.

1941: (1) "How Green Was My Valley," (2) Gary Cooper in "Sergeant York," (3) Joan Fontaine in "Suspicion," (4) Donald Crisp in "How Green Was My Valley," (5) Mary Astor in "The Great Lie," (6) John Ford for "How Green Was My Valley," (7) Leopold Stokowski, Walt Disney.

1942: (1) "Mrs. Miniver," (2) James Cagney in "Yankee Doodle Dandy," (3) Greer Garson in "Mrs. Miniver," (4) Van Heflin in "Johnny Eager," (5) Teresa Wright in "Mrs. Miniver," (6) William Wyler for "Mrs. Miniver," (7) Charles Boyer, Noel Coward.

1943: (1) "Casablanca," (2) Paul Lukas in "Watch on the Rhine," (3) Jennifer Jones in "The Song of Bernadette," (4) Charles Coburn in "The More the Merrier," (5) Katina Paxinou in "For Whom the Bell Tolls," (6) Michael Curtiz for "Casablanca."

1944: (1) "Going My Way," (2) Bing Crosby in "Going My Way," (3) Ingrid Bergman in "Gaslight," (4) Barry Fitzgerald in "Going My Way," (5) Ethel Barrymore in "None but the Lonely Heart," (6) Leo McCarey for "Going My Way," (7) Margaret O'Brien, Bob Hope.

1945: (1) "The Lost Weekend," (2) Ray Milland in "The Lost Weekend," (3) Joan Crawford in "Mildred Pierce," (4) James Dunn in "A Tree Grows in Brooklyn," (5) Anne Revere in "National Velvet," (6) Billy Wilder for "The Lost Weekend," (7) Walter Wanger, Peggy Ann Garner.

1946: (1) "The Best Years of Our Lives," (2) Fredric March in "The Best Years of Our Lives," (3) Olivia de Havilland in "To Each His Own," (4) Harold Russell in "The Best Years of Our Lives," (5) Anne Baxter in "The Razor's Edge," (6) William Wyler for "The Best Years of Our Lives," (7) Laurence Olivier, Harold Russell, Ernst Lubitsch, Claude Jarman, Jr.

1947: (1) "Gentleman's Agreement," (2) Ronald Colman in "A Double Life," (3) Loretta Young in "The Farmer's Daughter," (4) Edmund Gwenn in "Miracle On 34th Street," (5) Celeste Holm in "Gentleman's Agreement," (6) Elia Kazan for "Gentleman's Agreement," (7) James Baskette, (8) "Shoe Shine," (Italy).

1948: (1) "Hamlet," (2) Laurence Olivier in "Hamlet," (3) Jane Wyman in "Johnny Belinda," (4) Walter Huston in "The Treasure of the Sierra Madre," (5) Claire Trevor in "Key Largo," (6) John Huston for "The Treasure of the Sierra Madre," (7) Ivan Jandl, Sid Grauman, Adolph Zukor, Walter Wanger, (8) "Monsieur Vincent," (France).

1949: (1) "All the King's Men," (2) Broderick Crawford in "All the King's Men," (3) Olivia de Havilland in "The Heiress," (4) Dean Jagger in "Twelve O'Clock High," (5) Mercedes McCambridge in "All the King's Men," (6) Joseph L. Mankiewicz for "A Letter to Three Wives," (7) Bobby Driscoll, Fred Astaire, Cecil B. DeMille, Jean Hersholt, (8) "The Bicycle Thief," (Italy).

1950: (1) "All about Eve," (2) Jose Ferrer in "Cyrano de Bergerac," (3) Judy Holliday in "Born Yesterday," (4) George Sanders in "All about Eve," (5) Josephine Hull in "Harvey," (6) Joseph L. Mankiewicz for "All about Eve," (7) George Murphy, Louis B. Mayer, (8) "The Walls of Malapaga," (France/Italy).

1951: (1) "An American in Paris," (2) Humphrey Bogart in "The African Queen," (3) Vivien Leigh in "A Streetcar Named Desire," (4) Karl Malden in "A Streetcar Named Desire," (5) Kim Hunter in "A Streetcar Named Desire," (6) George Stevens for "A Place in the Sun," (7) Gene Kelly, (8) "Rashomon," (Japan).

1952: (1) "The Greatest Show on Earth," (2) Gary Cooper in "High Noon," (3) Shirley Booth in "Come Back, Little Sheba," (4) Anthony Quinn in "Viva Zapata," (5) Gloria Grahame in "The Bad and the Beautiful," (6) John Ford for "The Quiet Man," (7) Joseph M. Schenck, Merian C. Cooper, Harold Lloyd, Bob Hope, George Alfred Mitchell, (8) "Forbidden Games," (France).

1953: (1) "From Here to Eternity," (2) William Holden in "Stalag 17," (3) Audrey Hepburn in "Roman Holiday," (4) Frank Sinatra in "From Here to Eternity," (5) Donna Reed in "From Here to Eternity," (6) Fred Zinnemann for "From Here to Eternity," (7) Pete Smith, Joseph Breen, (8) no award.

1954: (1) "On the Waterfront," (2) Marlon Brando in "On the Waterfront," (3) Grace Kelly in "The Country Girl," (4) Edmond O'Brien in "The Barefoot Contessa," (5) Eva Marie Saint in "On the Waterfront," (6) Elia Kazan for "On the Waterfront," (7) Greta Garbo, Danny Kaye, Jon Whitely, Vincent Winter, (8) "Gate of Hell," (Japan).

1955: (1) "Marty," (2) Ernest Borgnine in "Marty," (3) Anna Magnani in "The Rose Tattoo," (4) Jack Lemmon in "Mister Roberts," (5) Jo Van Fleet in "East of Eden," (6) Delbert Mann for "Marty," (8) "Samurai," (Japan).

1956: (1) "Around the World in 80 Days," (2) Yul Brynner in "The King and I," (3) Ingrid Bergman in "Anastasia," (4) Anthony Quinn in "Lust for Life," (5) Dorothy Malone in "Written on the Wind," (6) George Stevens for "Giant," (7) Eddie Cantor, (8) "La Strada," (Italy).

1957: (1) "The Bridge on the River Kwai," (2) Alec Guinness in "The Bridge on the River Kwai," (3) Joanne Woodward in "The Three Faces of Eve," (4) Red Buttons in "Sayonara," (5) Miyoshi Umeki in "Sayonara," (6) David Lean for "The Bridge on the River Kwai," (7) Charles Brackett, B. B. Kahane, Gilbert M. (Bronco Billy) Anderson, (8) "The Nights of Cabiria," (Italy).
1958: (1) "Gigi," (2) David Niven in "Separate Tables," (3) Susan Hayward in "I Want to Live," (4) Burl Ives in "The Big Country," (5) Wendy Hiller in "Separate Tables," (6) Vincente Minnelli for "Gigi," (7) Maurice Chevalier, (8) "My Uncle," (France).
1959: (1) "Ben-Hur," (2) Charlton Heston in "Ben-Hur," (3) Simone Signoret in "Room at the Top," (4) Hugh Griffith in "Ben-Hur," (5) Shelley Winters in "The Diary of Anne Frank," (6) William Wyler for "Ben-Hur," (7) Lee de Forest, Buster Keaton, (8) "Black Orpheus," (Brazil).
1960: (1) "The Apartment," (2) Burt Lancaster in "Elmer Gantry," (3) Elizabeth Taylor in "Butterfield 8," (4) Peter Ustinov in "Spartacus," (5) Shirley Jones in "Elmer Gantry," (6) Billy Wilder for "The Apartment," (7) Gary Cooper, Stan Laurel, Hayley Mills, (8) "The Virgin Spring," (Sweden).
1961: (1) "West Side Story," (2) Maximilian Schell in "Judgment at Nuremberg," (3) Sophia Loren in "Two Women," (4) George Chakiris in "West Side Story," (5) Rita Moreno in "West Side Story," (6) Robert Wise for "West Side Story," (7) Jerome Robbins, Fred L. Metzler, (8) "Through a Glass Darkly," (Sweden).
1962: (1) "Lawrence of Arabia," (2) Gregory Peck in "To Kill a Mockingbird," (3) Anne Bancroft in "The Miracle Worker," (4) Ed Begley in "Sweet Bird of Youth," (5) Patty Duke in "The Miracle Worker," (6) David Lean for "Lawrence of Arabia," (8) "Sundays and Cybele," (France).
1963: (1) "Tom Jones," (2) Sidney Poitier in "Lilies of the Field," (3) Patricia Neal in "Hud," (4) Melvyn Douglas in "Hud," (5) Margaret Rutherford in "The V.I.P.'s," (6) Tony Richardson for "Tom Jones," (8) "8½," (Italy).
1964: (1) "My Fair Lady," (2) Rex Harrison in "My Fair Lady," (3) Julie Andrews in "Mary Poppins," (4) Peter Ustinov in "Topkapi," (5) Lila Kedrova in "Zorba the Greek," (6) George Cukor for "My Fair Lady," (7) William Tuttle, (8) "Yesterday, Today and Tomorrow," (Italy).
1965: (1) "The Sound of Music," (2) Lee Marvin in "Cat Ballou," (3) Julie Christie in "Darling," (4) Martin Balsam in "A Thousand Clowns," (5) Shelley Winters in "A Patch of Blue," (6) Robert Wise for "The Sound of Music," (7) Bob Hope, (8) "The Shop on Main Street," (Czech).
1966: (1) "A Man for All Seasons," (2) Paul Scofield in "A Man for All Seasons," (3) Elizabeth Taylor in "Who's Afraid of Virginia Woolf?," (4) Walter Matthau in "The Fortune Cookie," (5) Sandy Dennis in "Who's Afraid of Virginia Woolf?," (6) Fred Zinnemann for "A Man for All Seasons," (8) "A Man and A Woman," (France).
1967: (1) "In the Heat of the Night," (2) Rod Steiger in "In the Heat of the Night," (3) Katharine Hepburn in "Guess Who's Coming to Dinner," (4) George Kennedy in "Cool Hand Luke," (5) Estelle Parsons in "Bonnie and Clyde," (6) Mike Nichols for "The Graduate," (8) "Closely Watched Trains," (Czech).
1968: (1) "Oliver!," (2) Cliff Robertson in "Charly," (3) Katharine Hepburn in "The Lion in Winter" tied with Barbra Streisand in "Funny Girl," (4) Jack Albertson in "The Subject Was Roses," (5) Ruth Gordon in "Rosemary's Baby," (6) Carol Reed for "Oliver!," (7) Onna White for "Oliver!" choreography, John Chambers for "Planet of the Apes" make-up, (8) "War and Peace," (USSR).
1969: (1) "Midnight Cowboy," (2) John Wayne in "True Grit," (3) Maggie Smith in "The Prime of Miss Jean Brodie," (4) Gig Young in "They Shoot Horses, Don't They?," (5) Goldie Hawn in "Cactus Flower," (6) John Schlesinger for "Midnight Cowboy," (7) Cary Grant, (8) "Z," (Algeria).
1970: (1) "Patton," (2) George C. Scott in "Patton," (3) Glenda Jackson in "Women in Love," (4) John Mills in "Ryan's Daughter," (5) Helen Hayes in "Airport," (6) Franklin J. Schaffner for "Patton," (7) Lillian Gish, Orson Welles, (8) "Investigation of a Citizen above Suspicion," (Italy).
1971: (1) "The French Connection," (2) Gene Hackman in "The French Connection," (3) Jane Fonda in "Klute," (4) Ben Johnson in "The Last Picture Show," (5) Cloris Leachman in "The Last Picture Show," (6) William Friedkin for "The French Connection," (7) Charles Chaplin, (8) "The Garden of the Finzi-Continis," (Italy).
1972: (1) "The Godfather," (2) Marlon Brando in "The Godfather," (3) Liza Minnelli in "Cabaret," (4) Joel Grey in "Cabaret," (5) Eileen Heckart in "Butterflies Are Free," (6) Bob Fosse for "Cabaret," (7) Edward G. Robinson, (8) "The Discreet Charm of the Bourgeoisie," (France).
1973: (1) "The Sting," (2) Jack Lemmon in "Save the Tiger," (3) Glenda Jackson in "A Touch of Class," (4) John Houseman in "The Paper Chase," (5) Tatum O'Neal in "Paper Moon," (6) George Roy Hill for "The Sting," (8) "Day for Night," (France).

Liza Minnelli

Robert Redford

Audrey Hepburn

1974: (1) "The Godfather Part II," (2) Art Carney in "Harry and Tonto," (3) Ellen Burstyn in "Alice Doesn't Live Here Anymore," (4) Robert DeNiro in "The Godfather Part II," (5) Ingrid Bergman in "Murder on the Orient Express," (6) Francis Ford Coppola for "The Godfather Part II," (7) Howard Hawks, Jean Renoir, (8) "Amarcord," (Italy).
1975: (1) "One Flew over the Cuckoo's Nest," (2) Jack Nicholson in "One Flew over the Cuckoo's Nest," (3) Louise Fletcher in "One Flew over the Cuckoo's Nest," (4) George Burns in "The Sunshine Boys," (5) Lee Grant in "Shampoo," (6) Milos Forman for "One Flew over the Cuckoo's Nest," (7) Mary Pickford, (8) "Dersu Uzala," (U.S.S.R.), (9) "The Man Who Skied Down Everest."
1976: (1) "Rocky," (2) Peter Finch in "Network," (3) Faye Dunaway in "Network," (4) Jason Robards in "All the President's Men," (5) Beatrice Straight in "Network," (6) John G. Avildsen for "Rocky," (8) "Black and White in Color" (Ivory Coast), (9) "Harlan County U.S.A."
1977: (1) "Annie Hall," (2) Richard Dreyfuss in "The Goodbye Girl," (3) Diane Keaton in "Annie Hall," (4) Jason Robards in "Julia," (5) Vanessa Redgrave in "Julia," (6) Woody Allen for "Annie Hall," (7) Maggie Booth (film editor), (8) "Madame Rosa" (France), (9) "Who Are the DeBolts?"
1978: (1) "The Deer Hunter," (2) Jon Voight in "Coming Home," (3) Jane Fonda in "Coming Home," (4) Christopher Walken in "The Deer Hunter," (5) Maggie Smith in "California Suite," (6) Michael Cimino for "The Deer Hunter," (7) Laurence Olivier, King Vidor, (8) "Get Out Your Handkerchiefs" (France), (9) "Sacred Straight."
1979: (1) "Kramer vs. Kramer," (2) Dustin Hoffman in "Kramer vs. Kramer," (3) Sally Field in "Norma Rae," (4) Melvyn Douglas in "Being There," (5) Meryl Streep in "Kramer vs. Kramer," (6) Robert Benton for "Kramer vs. Kramer," (7) Robert S. Benjamin, Hal Elias, Alec Guinness, (8) "The Tin Drum" (Germany), (9) "Best Boy."
1980: (1) "Ordinary People," (2) Robert DeNiro in "Raging Bull," (3) Sissy Spacek in "Coal Miner's Daughter," (4) Timothy Hutton in "Ordinary People," (5) Mary Steenburgen in "Melvin and Howard," (6) Robert Redford for "Ordinary People," (7) Henry Fonda, (8) "Moscow Does Not Believe in Tears" (Russia), (9) "From Mao to Mozart: Isaac Stern in China."
1981: (1) "Chariots of Fire," (2) Henry Fonda in "On Golden Pond," (3) Katharine Hepburn in "On Golden Pond," (4) John Gielgud in "Arthur," (5) Maureen Stapleton in "Reds," (6) Warren Beatty for "Reds," (7) Fuji Photo Film Co., Barbara Stanwyck, (8) "Mephisto" (Germany/Hungary), (9) "Genocide."
1982: (1) "Gandhi," (2) Ben Kingsley in "Gandhi," (3) Meryl Streep in "Sophie's Choice," (4) Louis Gossett, Jr. in "An Officer and a Gentleman," (5) Jessica Lange in "Tootsie," (6) Richard Attenborough for "Gandhi," (7) Mickey Rooney, (8) "Volver a Empezar" (To Begin Again) (Spain), (9) "Just Another Missing Kid."
1983: (1) "Terms of Endearment," (2) Robert Duvall in "Tender Mercies," (3) Shirley MacLaine in "Terms of Endearment," (4) Jack Nicholson in "Terms of Endearment," (5) Linda Hunt in "The Year of Living Dangerously," (6) James L. Brooks for "Terms of Endearment," (7) Hal Roach, (8) "Fanny and Alexander" (Sweden), (9) "He Makes Me Feel Like Dancin'."
1984: (1) "Amadeus," (2) F. Murray Abraham in "Amadeus," (3) Sally Field in "Places in the Heart," (4) Haing S. Ngor in "The Killing Fields," (5) Peggy Ashcroft in "A Passage to India," (6) Milos Forman for "Amadeus," (7) James Stewart, (8) "Dangerous Moves" (Switzerland), (9) "The Times of Harvey Milk."
1985: (1) "Out of Africa," (2) William Hurt in "Kiss of the Spider Woman," (3) Geraldine Page in "The Trip to Bountiful," (4) Don Ameche in "Cocoon," (5) Anjelica Huston in "Prizzi's Honor," (6) Sydney Pollack for "Out of Africa," (7) Paul Newman, Alex North, (8) "The Official Story" (Argentina), (9) "Broken Rainbow."
1986: (1) "Platoon," (2) Paul Newman in "The Color of Money," (3) Marlee Matlin for "Children of a Lesser God," (4) Michael Caine for "Hannah and Her Sisters," (5) Dianne Wiest for "Hannah and Her Sisters," (6) Oliver Stone for "Platoon," (7) Ralph Bellamy, (8) "The Assault" (Netherlands), (9) "Artie Shaw: Time Is All You've Got" tied with "Down and Out in America"

MY SWEET LITTLE VILLAGE

(CIRCLE RELEASING CORP.) Director, Jiri Menzel; Screenplay, Zdenek Sverak; Photography, Jaromir Sofr; Art Director, Zbynek Hloch; Music, Jiri Sust; Czechoslovakia; Color; Rated PG; 100 minutes; January release

CAST

Otik	Janos Ban
Pavek	Marian Labuda
Skruzny	Rudolf Hrusinsky
Mrs. Pavek	Milena Dvorska
Rumlena	Ladislav Zupanic
Turek	Petr Cepek
Mrs. Turek	Libuse Safrankova
Kaspar	Jan Hartl
Odvarka	Evzen Jegorov
Kunc	Oldrich Vlach

Below: Janos Ban, Marian Labuda Right: Janos
Ban Top: Marian Labuda, Rudolf Hrusinsky, Janos Ban
© *Circle Films*

Libuse Safrankova, Jan Hartl

Janos Ban

ALPINE FIRE

(VESTRON) Executive Producer, Bernard Lang; Director/Screenplay, Fredi M. Murer; Assistant Director, Mathias Von Gunten; Photography, Pio Corradi; Additional Photography, Patrick Linenmaier, Yvonne Griss, Martin Witz; Sound, Florian Eidenbenz; Music, Mario Beretta; Editor, Helena Gerber; Assistant Editor, Manuela Stingelin; Set Design, Bernhard Sauter; Lighting, Werner Santschi, Willy Kopp; Scenery, Edith Peier, Greta Roderer; Costumes, Greta Roderer; Switzerland; In Swiss-German dialect; Color; Rated R; 117 minutes; January release

CAST

The Boy	Thomas Nock
Belli	Johanna Lier
The Mother	Dorothea Moritz
The Father	Rolf Illig
The Grandmother	Tilli Breidenbach
The Grandfather	Joerg Odermatt

Left: Thomas Nock, Johanna Lier
© *Vestron Pictures*

THE FRINGE DWELLERS

(ATLANTIC) Executive Producers, Damien Nolan, Hilary Heath; Producer, Sue Milliken; Director, Bruce Beresford; Screenplay, Bruce Beresford, Phoisin Beresford; Adapted from the novel by Nene Gare; Photography, Don McAlpine; Editor, Tim Wellburn; Music, George Dreyfus; Casting, Alison Barrett; Designer, Herbert Pinter; Production Manager, Helen Watts; Assistant Director, Mark Egerton; Costumes, Kerri Barnett; Sound, Max Bowring; Production Coordinator, Tatts Bishop; Art Director, Stewart Way; Presented by Virgin Films Limited in Association with Damien Nolan Productions & Ozfilm Limited; Color; Australia; Rated PG; 98 minutes; January release

CAST

Trilby	Kristina Nehm
Mollie	Justine Saunders
Joe	Bob Maza
Noonah	Kylie Belling
Bartie	Denis Walker
Phil	Ernie Dingo
Charlie	Malcolm Silva
Hannah	Marlene Bell
Audrena	Michelle Torres
Blanchie	Michele Miles
Eva	Kath Walker
Skippy	Bill Sandy
Rene	Maureen Watson
Tim	Robert Ugle
Bruce	Alan Dargin
Horrie	Terry Thompson
May	Annie Saward
Matron	Dianne Eden
Dr. Symons	Wilkie Collins
Nurse McCarthy	Lisa-Jane Stockwell
Nurse Creswell	Sandra Lehane
School Girl	Theresa Stafford
Stockman	Leo Wockner
Bert	Wilf Campagnoni
Headmaster	David Clendinning
Miss Simmons	Noanie Wood
Mrs. Henwood	Gabrielle Lambros

Kristina Nehm, Ernie Dingo
© *Atlantic Entertainment Group*

Alberto Isola (center)
"The City and the Dogs"

THE CITY AND THE DOGS

(CINEVISTA) Producer/Director, Francisco J. Lombardi; Screenplay, Jose Watanabe; Based on the novel by Mario Vargas Llosa; Photography, Pili Flores Guerra; Peru, 1985; Spanish with subtitles; Not rated; 133 minutes; January release

CAST

Poet	Pablo Serra
Lieut. Gamboa	Gustavo Bueno
Jaguar	Juan Manuel Ochoa
Colonel	Luis Alvarez
Slave	Eduardo Adrianzen
Teresa	Liliana Navarro
Arrospide	Miguel Iza

© *Cinevista*

OPERA DO MALANDRO

(SAMUEL GOLDWYN) Executive Producer, Alberto Graca; Director, Ruy Guerra; Screenplay, Chico Buarque, Orlando Senna, Ruy Guerra; Based on the play *"Opera Do Malandro"* by Chico Buarque; Dialogue/Music/Lyrics, Chico Buarque; Arrangements/Conductor, Chiquinho De Moraes; Set, Mauro Monteiro, Irenio Maia; Costumes, Maria Cecilia Motta; Choreography, Regina Miranda; Photography, Antonio Luis Mendes; Editor, Mair Tavares, Ide LaCreta, Kenout Peltier; Sound, Claude Villand, Bernard Le Roux; Brazil; Color; Dolby Stereo; Not rated; 109 minutes; January release

CAST

Max	Edson Celulari
Lu	Claudia Ohana
Margot	Elba Ramalho
Tigrao	Ney Latorraca
Otto Strudell	Fabio Sabag
Geni	J. C. Violla
Satiro Bilhar	Wilson Grey
Victoria Strudell	Maria Silvia
Fiorella	Claudia Gimenez
Fichinha	Andreia Dantas
Doris Pelanca	Ilva Nino
Dorinha Tubao	Zenaide
Shirley Paquete	Djenane Machado
Mimi Bibelo	Katia Bronstein
Porfirio	Luthero Luiz

and Angel Morsi, Angela De Castro, Denise Telles, Leticia B. De Mello, Lia Rodrigues, Valeria Rowena, Ataide, Arcoverde, Breno Moroni, Julio Levy, Marcus Vicinius, Mauro Cesar Cunha, Padilha, Ruben Gabira, Sergio Maia, Thiago Justino, Aluisio Gomes Flores, Carlos Jesus, Claudio Moreno, Christovam Netto, Estevam Santos, Jean Paul Rajzman, Jitman Vibranoski, Jorge Paulo, Bebel, Delta Araujo, Fernanda Caetano, Luzia Dos Santos, Maria Odete Garnier, Marina Salomon, Sophie Paznakhet, Bernard Seygnoux, Conceicao Senna, John Doo, Paulo Henrique, Mauro Gorini, Breno Bonin, Candido Damn, Charles Myara, Gilles Gwizdek, Savvas Karydakis, Alain Vial, Carlos Loffler

Anthony Hopkins, Jim Broadbent
© *Skouras Pictures*

HOUR OF THE STAR

(KINO INTERNATIONAL) Director, Suzana Amaral; Screenplay, Suzana Amaral, Alfredo Oroz; Based on the novel *"A Hora da Estrela"* by Clarice Lispector; Production Director, Eliane Bandeira; Executive Producer, Assuncao Hernandes; Photography, Edgar Moura; Art Director, Clovis Bueno; Editor, Ide N. Lacreta; Music, Marcus Vinicius; Assistant Director, Silvia Bahiense; Production Company, Raiz Producoes Cinematograficas; Brazil; Portugese with subtitles; Color; Not rated; 96 minutes; January release

CAST

Macabea	Marcelia Cartaxo
Olympico	Jose Dumont
Gloria	Tamara Taxman
Madame Carlota	Fernanda Montenegro
Seu Raimundo	Umberto Magnani
Pereira	Denoy de Olivera
Maria de Penha	Claudia Rezende
Maria	Lizete Negreiros
Maria do Carmo	Maria do Carmo Soares
Mrs. Joana	Sonia Guedes

Top Left: Jose Dumont, Marcelia Cartaxo
© *Kino International*

Edson Celulari, Claudia Ohana
© *Samuel Goldwyn Co.*

THE GOOD FATHER

(SKOURAS) Producer, Ann Scott; Director, Mike Newell; Screenplay, Christopher Hampton; Based on the novel by Peter Prince; Photography, Michael Coulter; Designer, Adrian Smith; Editor, Peter Hollywood; Music, Richard Hartley; A Film Four International Presentation of a Greenpoint Films Production; Color; Rated R; 90 minutes; February release

CAST

Bill Hooper	Anthony Hopkins
Roger Miles	Jim Broadbent
Emmy Hooper	Harriet Walter
Cheryl Miles	Fanny Viner
Mark Varda	Simon Callow
Mary Hall	Joanne Whalley
Jane Powell	Miriam Margolyes
Leonard Scruby	Michael Byrne
Bill's Friends	Jennie Stoller, Johanna Kirby
Creighton	Stephen Fry
Judge	Clifford Rose
Punk	Chris Bradshaw
Bill's Son	Harry Grubb
Roger's Son	Tom Jamieson

CLASS RELATIONS

(NEW YORKER FILMS) Director/Screenplay, Jean-Marie Straub, Daniele Huillet; Based on Franz Kafka's *"Amerika"*; Photography, Willy Lubtchansky; Assistant Camera Operators, Caroline Champetier, Christopher Pollock; Sound, Louis Hochet; Sound Assistant, Georges Vaglio; Editor, Straub-Huillet; Electrician, Jim Howe; Production, Klaus Feddermann, Manfred Blank; Produced by NEF-Diffusion (Paris), Janus Film (Frankfort), Straub-Huillet, Television de Hesse; Germany/France, 1984; German with subtitles; Black & White; Not rated; 126 minutes; February release

CAST

Karl Rossmann	Christian Heinisch
Soutier	Reinald Schnell
Line	Anna Schnell
The Captain	Klauss Traube
Cashier	Hermann Hartmann
Stewart	Jean-Francois Quinque
Uncle Jacob	Mario Adorf
Schubal	Gerard Semaan
Pollunder	Willi Voebel
Chauffeur	Willi Dewelk
Klara	Anne Bold
Green	Tilmann Heinisch
Sevant	Aloys Pompetzki
Mack	Burckhardt Stoelck
Delamarche	Harun Farocki
Robinson	Manfred Blank
Cook	Kathrin Bold
Server	Alf Bold
Therese	Libgart Schwarz
Giacomo	Nazzareno Bianconi
Hotelboy	Salvatore Sammartino
Manage	Alfred Edel
Porter	Andi Engel
Taxi Driver	Franz Hillers
Policemen	Klaus Feddermann, Henning
Brunelda	Laura Betti
Student	Georg Brintrup
Leader	Thom Andersen
Other Man	Barton Byg

(No photos available)

**Top right: Sigfrit Steiner, Julie Andrews, Alan Bates
Below: Max von Sydow, Julie Andrews**
© *Cannon*

DUET FOR ONE

(CANNON GROUP) Producers, Menahem Golan, Yoram Globus; Director, Andrei Konchalovsky; Screenplay, Tom Kempinski, Jeremy Lipp, Andrei Konchalovsky; Based on the play by Tom Kempinski; Editor, Henry Richardson; Costumes, Evangeline Harrison; Designer, John Graysmark; Photography, Alex Thomson; Associate Producer, Michael J. Kagan; Production Supervisor, Alexander De Grunwald; Assistant Directors, David Tringham, Michael Stevenson, Kate Goodwin; Production Co-ordinator, Sally Hayman; Sound, David Crozier; Production Coordinator, Stephen Barker; Music Consultant, Alan Smyth; Music Coach, Peter Daniels; Set Decorator, Peter Young; Assistant Art Directors, Reg Bream, Steve Cooper; Special Effects, John Gant, Chris Gant, Michael Dawson; Casting, Noel Davis, Jeremy Zimmerman; Conductor, Anthony Randall; Violin Solos, Nigel Kennedy; Orchestrations, Michael Linn; British; Dolby Stereo; Rank Film Laboratories Colour; Rated R; 108 minutes; February release

CAST

Stephanie Anderson	Julie Andrews
David Cornwallis	Alan Bates
Dr. Louis Feldman	Max von Sydow
Constantine Kassanis	Rupert Everett
Sonia Randvich	Margaret Courtenay
Penny Smallwood	Cathryn Harrison
Leonid Lefimov	Sigfrit Steiner
Totter	Liam Neeson
Anya	Macha Meril
Mrs. Burridge	Janette Newling
Drunk	John Delaney
Derek	Kevin Ranson
Betty	Dorthea Phillips
Gail	Marcia Linden
Charlie	David Miller
Terry	Gary Fairhall
Joan	Nicola Davies
Woman in pub	Pam Brighton
Betsy	Nicola Perring

**Sigfrit Steiner, Julie Andrews
Above: Alan Bates, Julie Andrews**

GOSPEL ACCORDING TO VIC

(SKOURAS) Producer, Michael Relph; Director/Screenplay, Charles Gormley; Executive Producer, Ann Skinner; Associate Producer, Clive Reed; Photography/Lighting, Michael Coulter; Editor, John Gow; Music, B. A. Robertson; Musical Director, Simon Webb; Designer, Rita McGurn; Art Director, Annette Gillies; Costumes, Lindy Hemming; Casting, Anne Henderson; Production Manager, Liz Kerry; Sound, Louis Kramer; Sound Editor, Nicolas Gaster; Dubbing, Peter Maxwell; Location manager, Eric Coulter; Camera, Jan Pester; An Island Film in association with Skreba for Film Four International in Association with the National Finance Corporation; Scottish; Color; Rated PG-13; 92 minutes; March release

CAST

Vic Mathews	Tom Conti
Ruth Chancellor	Helen Mirren
Jeff Jeffries	David Hayman
Father Cobb	Brian Pettifer
Nurse	Jennifer Black
Headmaster	Dave Anderson
Brusse	Tom Busby
Doctor	Sam Graham
McAllister	Kara Wilson
MacKrimmond	Robert Paterson
Gibbons	John Mitchell

KANGAROO

(CINEPLEX ODEON) Producer, Ross Dimsey; Director, Tim Burstall; Screenplay, Evan Jones; Adapted from novel by D. H. Lawrence; Photography, Dan Burstall; Designer, Tracy Watt; Editor, Edward McQueen-Mason; Costumes, Terry Ryan; Production Manager, Darryl Sheen, Production Coordinator, Jennie Crowley; Assistant Directors, Stuart Freeman, Stephen Saks, Ian Freeman; Sound, Paul Clark; Casting, Liz Mullinar Casting/Greg Apps; Assistant Editors, Irwin Hirsh, Stephen Radic; Sound, Phil Heywood; Music, Nathan Waks; Australia; Produced with the Assistance of Film Victoria; Color; Panavision; Rated R; 105 minutes; March release

CAST

Richard Somers	Colin Friels
Harriet Somers	Judy Davis
Jack Calcott	John Walton
Vicki Calcott	Julie Nihill
Kangaroo	Hugh Keays-Byrne
Jaz	Peter Hehir
Struthers	Peter Cummins
O'Neill	Tim Robertson
Publisher	Malcolm Robertson
Cornwall Detective	David Hutchins
Army Captain	Victor Kazan
Army Sergeant at medical	Bill Richardson
Collier	Alan Lee
Major	Richard Moss
Doctors	Howard Priddle, Denzil Howson
Male Nurse	Roy Baldwin
Dug	Ron Pinnell
Taxi Driver	Geoff Brooks
Drummer	Bob Butcher
Fyfe Player	Don Laughton
Digger Bill	David Bickerstaff
Digger Gary	Christopher Stevenson
Shearer's Leader	Jack Perry
Unionist Dave	Phil Sumner
Unionist Bert	Roderick Williams
Mac	Steve Payne
Digger Fred	Ian Shrives
Digger Sam	Nield Schneider
Ted	Steve Hutchinson
Manservant	John Chu
Hall Sergeant	Roy Edmunds
Cell Sergeant	Terry Trimble
Arresting Sergeant	John Mortimore
Nurse	Kerry Bannister

(No photos available)

Left: Tom Conti, Helen Mirren
Above: Brian Pettifer, Tom Conti
© *Skouras Pictures*

BROKEN MIRRORS

(FIRST RUN FEATURES) Producer, Matthijs Van Heijningen; Director/Screenplay, Marleen Gorris; Photography, Frans Bromet; Sound, George Bossaers; Editor, Hans Van Dongen; Music, Lodewijk de Boer; Art Director, Harry Ammerlaan; Dutch, 1984; Dutch with subtitles; Not rated; 110 minutes; March release

CAST

Diane	Lineke Rijxman
Dora	Henriette Tol
Bea	Edda Barends
Ellen	Coby Stunnenberg
Jean/Pierre	Eddy Brugman

and Carly Hardy, Marijke Veugelers, Arline Renfurm, Hedda Tabet, Anke Van'T Hof, Johan Leysen

A PROMISE

Producer, Yasuyo Saito, Matsuo Takahashi; Director, Yoshishige Yoshida; Screenplay, Yoshishige Yoshida, Fukiko Miyauchi; From the Novel *"Rojuko Kazoku"* by Shuichi Sae; Photography, Yoshihiro Yamazaki; Editor, Akira Suzuki; Music, Haruomi Hosono; Production Companies, Seibu Saison Group, TV Asahi, Kinema Tokyo; Japan; Japanese with English subtitles; Color; Not rated; 123 minutes; March release

CAST

Ryosaku Morimoto	Renataro Mikuni
Tatsu	Sachiko Murase
Yoshio	Choichiro
Ritsuko	Orie Sato
Takao	Tetsuta Sugimoto
Naoko	Kumiko Takeda
Saeko Nogawa	Reiko Tajima
Inspector Tagami	Tomisaburo Wakayama
Sergeant Miura	Sakatoshi Yonekura
Takeya Nakamura	Choei Takahashi
Noriko Nakamura	Mieko Yuki

(No photos available)

PADRE NUESTRO

(INTERNATIONAL FILM EXCHANGE) Producers, Eduardo Ducay, Julian Marcos; Director, Francisco Regueiro; Screenplay, Angel Fernandez Santos, Francisco Regueiro; Photography, Juan Amoros; Production Manager, Emiliano Otegui; Art Director/Designer, Enrique Alarcon; Editor, Pedro Del Rey; Sound, Bernardo Menz; Wardrobe, Gumersindo Andres; Presented by Heritage Entertainment; A production of Classic Films Productions; Spanish with subtitles; Not rated; 90 minutes; April release

CAST

Cardenal	Fernando Rey
Abel	Francisco Rabal
Cardenala	Victoria Abril
Maria	Emma Penella
Valentina	Amelia de la Torre
Jeronima	Rafaela Aparicio
Blanca	Lina Canalejas
El Papa	Jose Vivo
Lolita	Yolanda Cardama
Sagrario	Luis Barbero
Guevines	Franciso Vidal
La Muda	Diana Penalver
Monja	Maria Elena Flores

Top Right: Fernando Rey, Victoria Abril
Below: Francisco Rabal
© *International Film Exchange*

SOREKARA
"And Then"

(NEW YORKER FILMS) Producers, Mitsuru Kurosawa, Sadatoshi Fujimine; Executive Producer, Shigeru Okada; Director, Yoshimitsu Morita; Screenplay, Tomomi Tsutsui; Based on the novel by Suseki Natsume; Photography, Yonezo Maeda; Editor, Akira Suzuki; Art Director, Isutomu Imamura; Lighting, Kazuo Yabe; Sound, Fumio Hacimoto, Hisoyuki Miyamata; Music, Shigaru Umnhoyoshi; Costumes, Michiko Kitamura; A Toei Co. release and production; Japanese; Japanese with subtitles; Color; Not rated; 130 minutes; April release

CAST

Daisuke	Yusaku Matsuda
Michiyo	Miwako Fujitani
Hiraoka	Kaoru Kobayashi
Father	Chishu Ryu
Sister-in-law Mitsuko	Kusabue
Brother	Katsuo Nakamura

Miwako Fujitani, Yasaku Matsuda
Above: Yasaku Matsuda, Chisu Ryu
© *New Yorker Films*

PRICK UP YOUR EARS

(GOLDWYN) Producer, Andrew Brown; Director, Stephen Frears; Screenplay, Alan Bennett; Photography, Oliver Stapleton; Music, Stanley Myers; Editor, Mick Audsley; Production Manager, Ann Wingate; Production Coordinator, Lorraine Goodman; Assistant Directors, Michael Zimbrich, Lee Cleary, Adam Walton; Casting, Debbie McWilliams; Designer, Hugo Luczyc-Wyhowski; Art Director, Philip Elton; Sound, Tony Jackson; Costumes, Bob Ringwood; A Civilhand Zenith Film; British; Color; Rated R; 111 minutes; April release

CAST

Joe Orton	Gary Oldman
Kenneth Halliwell	Alfred Molina
Peggy Ramsey	Vanessa Redgrave
John Lahr	Wallace Shawn
Anthea Lahr	Lindsay Duncan
Elsie Orton	Julie Walters
William Orton	James Grant
Mrs. Sugden	Janet Dale
Mr. Sugden	Dave Atkins
Madame Lambert	Margaret Tyzack
Education Officer	Eric Richard
Janet	Charlotte Wodehouse
RADA Instructor	Linda Spurrier
Mr. Cunliffe	Charles McKowen
Miss Datersby	Selina Cadell
Wigmaker	John Bailey
Brickie	Liam Staic
Magistrate	Bert Parnaby
Leonie Orton	Frances Barber
George Barnett	Stephen Bill
London Evening Standard Awards Chairman	Max Stafford-Clark

Julie Walters

Wallace Shawn
Above: Vanessa Redgrave

Top: Gary Oldman, Alfred Molina
© *Samuel Goldwyn Co.*

PERSONAL SERVICES

(VESTRON) Producer, Tim Bevan; Director, Terry Jones; Screenplay, David Leland; Photography, Roger Deakins; Designer, Hugo Luczyc-Wyhowski; Art Director, Jane Coleman; Editor, George Akers; Production Manager, Jane Frazer; Production Coordinator, Sarah Cellan-Jones; Assistant Directors, Micky Finch, Fraser Copp, Tim Dennison; Casting, Debbie McWilliams; Costumes, Shuna Harwood; Sound, Garth Marshall; British; Color; Rated R; 103 minutes; May release

CAST

Christine Painter	Julie Waters
Wing Commander Morton	Alec McCowen
Shirley	Shirley Stelfox
Dolly	Danny Schiller
Rose	Victoria Hardcastle
Timms	Tim Woodward
Sydney	Dave Atkins
Mr. Popozogolou	Leon Lissek
Mr. Marsden	Benjamin Whitrow
Mr. Marples	Peter Cellier
Mr. Dunkley	Stephen Lewis
Mr. Webb	Anthony Collin
Edward	Ewan Hooper

Below: Alec McCowen, Julie Walters
Right: Julie Walters, client, Shirley Stelfox
Top: Julie Walters © *Vestron Pictures*

Andrei Mironov, Nina Ruslanova
Above: Nina Ruslanova

MY FRIEND IVAN LAPSHIN

(INTERNATIONAL FILM EXCHANGE) Director, Alexei Gherman; Screenplay, Eduard Volodarsky; Based on short stories of Yri Cherman; Photography, Valery Fedosov; Music, Arkady Ganulashvili; Designer, Yuri Pugach; A Lenfilm Production; Russia, 1986; "Golden Leopard." Locarno Film Festival/International Press Critics Award; Black & White/Color/Sepia; Not Rated; 100 minutes; May release

CAST

Lapshin	Andrei Boltnev
Adashova	Nina Ruslanova
Khanin	Andrei Mironov
Okoshkin	A. Zharkov
Patri Keyevna	Z. Adamovich
Zanadvorov	Z. Filippenko

© *International Film Exchange*

Marco Bellocchio's
DEVIL IN THE FLESH

(ORION CLASSICS) Director, Marco Bellocchio; Screenplay, Marco Bellocchio, Enrico Palandri with the collaboration of Ennio De Concini; Photography, Giuseppe Lanci; Art Director, Andrea Crisanti; Costumes, Lina Nerli Taviani; Music, Carlo Crivelli; Editor, Mirco Garrone; Production Managers, Angelo Barbagallo, Stefano Bolzoni; Executive Producer, Leo Pescarolo; Line Producers, Eric Heumann, Stephane Sorlat; An Italian/French co-production of LP Films SRL (Rome)/Istituto Luce (Rome)/Films Sextile (Paris)/FR3 Films Production (Paris); Italian with subtitles; Color; Rated X; 110 minutes; May release

CAST

Giulia Dozza	Maruschka Detmers
Andrea Raimondi	Federico Pitzalis
Mrs. Pulcini	Anita Laurenzi
Giacomo Pulcini	Riccardo De Torrebruna
Dr. Raimondi	Alberto Di Stasio
Mrs. Dozza	Anna Orso
Don Piscane, the priest	Claudio Botosso
Mrs. Raimondi	Catherine Diamant
The Terrorists	Lidia Broccolino, Stefano Abbati

Federico Pitzalis, Maruschka Detmers
© *Orion Pictures*

TAMPOPO

(NEW YORKER FILMS) Producers, Juzo Itami, Yasushi Tamaoki, Seigo Hosogoe; Director/Screenplay, Juzo Itami; Photography, Masaki Tamura; Lighting, Yukio Inoue; Sound, Fumio Hashimoto; Art Director, Takeo Kimura; Editor, Akira Suzuki; Music, Kunihiko Murai; Costumes, Emiko Kogo; Food Design, Izumi Ishimori; Graphic Design, Kenichi Samura; Casting, Kosaburo Sasaoka; Assistant Director, Kazuki Shiroyama; Presented by Itami Productions and New Century Producers; Japan, 1986; Japanese with subtitles; Color; Not rated; 117 minutes; May release

CAST

Goro	Tsutomu Yamazaki
Tampopo (Dandelion)	Nobuko Miyamoto
Man in white suit	Koji Yakusho
Gun	Ken Watanabe
Pisken	Rikiya Yasuoka
Shohei	Kinzo Sakura
Tabo	Mampei Ikeuchi
Master of Ramen Making	Yoshi Kato
Rich Old Man	Shuji Otaki
Mistress of Man in white suit	Fukumi Kuroda
Rich Old Man's Mistress	Setsuko Shinoi
Girl Catching Oysters	Yoriko Doguchi
Supermarket Manager	Mashaiko Tsugawa
Company Executives	Motoo Noguchi, Yoshihei Saga, Tsuguho Narita, Akio Tanaka, Choei Takahashi
Young Company Employee	Toshimune Kato
Waiter	Isao Hashizume
Rude Owner of Competing Ramen Shop	Akira Kubo
Owner of Efficient Ramen Shop	Saburo Satoki
Owner of Ramen Stand	Mario Abe
Owner of Chinatown Ramen Shop	Hitoshi Takagi
His Neighbor	Tadao Futami
Chinese Ramen Chef	Akio Yokoyama
Small Bum	Masato Tsujimura
Thin Bum	Ei Takami
Bum with long face	Gilliark Amagasaki
Fat Bum	Norio Matsui
Bum with red nose	Noboru Sato
Dentist	Tadakazu Kitami
Lady Owner of Soba Shop	Kyoko Oguma
Man with toothache	Toshiya Fujita
Old Lady in supermarket	Izumi Hara
Man Who Runs to dying wife	Hisashi Igawa
Dying Wife	Kazuyo Mita
Old Con Man	Nobuo Nakamura
Con Man Who Is Conned	Naritoshi Hayashi
Master of Ramen Eating	Ryutaro Otomo
Teacher of table manners	Mariko Okada

Koji Yakusho, Fukumi Kuroda
Above: Ken Watanabe, Ryutaro Otomo
© *New Yorker Films*

MY LIFE AS A DOG

(SKOURAS) Producer, Waldemar Bergendahl; Director, Lasse Hallstrom; Screenplay, Lasse Hallstrom, Reidar Jonsson, Brasse Brannstrom, Per Berglund; Based on the novel by Reider Jonsson; Photography, Jorgen Persson; Editors, Christer Furubrand, Susanne Linnman; Sound, Eddie Axberg, Goran Carmback; Music, Bjorn Isfalt; Art Director, Lasse Westfelt; A Svenske Filmindustri Picture; Swedish with subtitles; Not rated; 101 minutes; May release

CAST

Ingemar	Anton Glanzelius
Uncle Gunnar	Tomas von Bromssen
Mother	Anki Liden
Saga	Malinda Kinnaman
Aunt Ulla	Kicki Rundgren
Berit	Ing-Mari Carlsson

Below: Ing-Mari Carlsson, Anton Glanzelius
Top Right: Melinda Kinnaman, Anton Glanzelius,
Jan-Philip Hollstrom Below Center: Anton Glanzelius,
Melinda Kinnaman Bottom: Glanzelius (right)
© *Skouras Pictures*

Ganjiro Nakamura, Shoichi Ozawa
© *East-West Classics*

THE PORNOGRAPHERS

(EAST-WEST CLASSICS) Producers, Shohei Imamura, Jiro Tomoda, Issei Yamamoto; Director, Shohei Imamura; Screenplay, Shohei Imamura, Koji Numata; Story, Akiyuki Nozaka; Photography, Shinsaku Himeda; Music, Toshiro Mayuzumi; Japan; Japanese with English subtitles; Color; Not rated; 128 minutes; May release

CAST

Subuyan Ogata	Shoichi Ozawa
Haru Matsuda	Sumiko Sakamoto
Elderly Executive	Ganjiro Nakamura
Banteki	Haruo Tanaka
Keiko Matsuda	Keiko Sakawa
Koichi Matsuda	Masaomi Kondo
Detective Sanada	Akira Nishimura

THE MOST BEAUTIFUL

(RF/S8) Producer, Motohiko Ito; Director Screenplay, Akira Kurosawa; Art Director, Teruaki Abe; Music, Seichi Suzuki; Photography, Joji Ohara; Semi-Documentary; Japanese, April 13, 1944; A Toho Production; New Titles, Audie Bock; 85 minutes; June release

CAST

Wanatabe .... Yoko Yaguchi
Mizushima, the teacher .... Takako Ire
The Director .... Takashi Shimura
Sanada, his assistant .... Ichiro Sugai
Workers .... Asako Suzuki, Koyuri Tanima,
Toshiko Hattori

Right: Yoko Yaguchi © R5/S8

RENDEZ-VOUS

(SPECTRAFILM) Director, Andre Techine; Executive Producer, Armand Barbault; Producer, Alain Terzian; Screenplay, Andre Techine, Olivier Assayas; Photography, Renato Berta; Editor, Martine Giordano; Music, Philippe Sarde; Art Director, Jean-Pierre Kohut-Svelko; Sound, Jean-Louis Huguetot; Costumes, Christian Gasc; France; French with subtitles; Cinemascope; Not rated; 82 minutes; June release

CAST

Nina .... Juliette Binoche
Quentin .... Lambert Wilson
Paulot .... Wadeck Stanczak
Scrutzler .... Jean-Louis Trintignant

Juliette Binoche, Jean-Louis Trintignant
Above: Wadeck Stanczak, Juliette Binoche
© International Spectrafilm

SUMMER NIGHT WITH GREEK PROFILE, ALMOND EYES, & SCENT OF BASIL

(NEW LINE CINEMA) Director/Screenplay, Lina Wertmuller; Photography, Camillo Bazzoni; Photographer, Tonino Benetti; Art Director, Enrico Job; Dresses, Valentino; General Organizer, Gino Millozza; Cameraman, Roberto Brega; Make-up, Cesare Paciotti; Sound, Mario Bramonti; Music, Bixio C.E.M.S.A.; Produced by Gianni Minervini for A.M.A. Film, Leone Film & Medusa Distribution with the collaboration of Reteitalia S.p.a.; Color by Cinecitta; Italian with subtitles; Not rated; 94 minutes; June release

CAST

Fulvia .... Mariangela Melato
Beppe .... Michele Placido
Miki .... Roberto Herlitzka
Turi .... Massimo Wertmuller

Mariangela Melato, Michele Placido
© New Line Cinema

SCARECROW

(INTERNATIONAL FILM EXCHANGE) Director, Rolan Bykov; Screenplay, Rolan Bykov, Vladimir Zheleznikov; Photography, Anatoly Mukasei; Music, Sofya Gabaidulina; Art Director, Yevgeny Markovich; Production Company, Mosfilm Studios; A Heritage Entertainment Film; USSR 1983; Russian with subtitles; Color; 130 minutes; June release

CAST

Nikolai Nikolayevich .... Yuri Nikulin
Lena .... Christina Orbakaite
(no other credits supplied)

Top Right: Christina Orbakaite, Yuri Nikulin
© *International Film Exchange*

Jose Isbert (left)
© *Kino International*

EL COCHECITO (THE LITTLE COACH)

(KINO INTERNATIONAL) Producer, Pedro Portabella; Director, Marco Ferreri; Screenplay, Marco Ferreri, Rafael Azcona; Photography, Juan Julio Baena; Music, Miguel Asins Arbo, Marco Ferreri; Spain, 1960; Not rated; 88 minutes; June release

CAST

Don Anselmo .... Jose Isbert
Don Lucas .... Jose A. Bepe
and Pedro Porcel, Maria Luisa Ponte, Jose Luis Lopez Vazquez

WITHNAIL AND I

(CINEPLEX ODEON) Executive Producers, George Harrison, Denis O'Brien; Producer, Paul M. Heller; Director/Screenplay, Bruce Robinson; Co-Producer, David Wimbury; Photography, Peter Hannan; Camera, Bob Smith; Designer, Michael Pickwoad; Art Director, Henry Harris; Editor, Alan Strachan; Sound, Clive Winter; Casting, Mary Selway; Music, David Dundas; Production Manager, Matthew Binns; Production Coordinator, Valerie Craig; Assistant Directors, Peter Kohn, Kathy Sykes; Costumes, Andrea Galer; Special Effects, Paul Corbould; British; Color; Rated R; 104 minutes; June release

CAST

Withnail .... Richard E. Grant
. . . & I .... Paul McGann
Monty .... Richard Griffiths
Danny .... Ralph Brown
Jake .... Michael Elphick
Irishman .... Daragh O'Malley
Isaac Parkin .... Michael Wardle
Mrs. Parkin .... Una Brandon-Jones
General .... Noel Johnson
Waitress .... Irene Sutcliffe
Tea Shop Proprietor .... Llewellyn Rees
Policemen .... Robert Oates, Anthony Wise
Presuming Ed .... Eddie Tagoe

**Richard E. Grant, Paul McGann, and
above with Richard Griffiths**
© *HandMade Films*

JEAN de FLORETTE

(ORION CLASSICS) Director, Claude Berri; Screenplay, Claude Berri, Gerard Brach; from the novel by Marcel Pagnol; Original Dialogue, Marcel Pagnol; Photography, Bruno Nuytten; Music, Jean-Claude Petit; Music Performance, The Paris Orchestra; Designer, Bernard Vezat; Costumes, Sylvie Gautrelet; Executive Producer, Pierre Grunstein; Associate Producer, Alain Poire; Sound, Pierre Gamet, Bernard Chaumeil, Dominique Hennequin; Editors, Arlette Langmann, Herve De Luze, Noelle Boisson; Production Manager, Polan Thenot; Hair/Make-up, Michele Deruelle, Jean-Pierre Eychenne; Assistant Directors Xavier Castano, Pascal Baeumeler; Assistant Editors, Jeanne Kef, Corine Lazare; Casting, Marie-Christine Lafosse; Dedicated to Marcel and Jacqueline Pagnol; A Renn Productions/Films A2/RAI 2/DD Productions Production; France; French with subtitles; Color; Technovision; Dolby Stereo; Rated PG; 122 minutes; June release

CAST

Cesar Soubeyran, "Le Papet"	Yves Montand
Jean de Florette	Gerard Depardieu
Ugolin	Daniel Auteuil
Aimee	Elisabeth Depardieu
Manon	Ernestine Mazurowna
Pique-Bouffigue	Marcel Champel
Philoxene	Armand Meffre
Pamphile	Andre Dupon
Casimir	Pierre Nougaro
Martial	Marc Betton
Anglade	Jean Maurel
Ange	Roger Souza
Giuseppe	Bertino Benedetto
Baptistine	Margarita Lozano
Pascal	Pierre Jean Rippert
Eliacin	Didier Pain
The Florist	Fransined
The Doctor	Christian Tamisier
The Notary	Marcel Berbert
The Muledriver	Jo Doumerg
Amadine, Papet's Servant	Chantal Liennel

Left: Ernestine Mazurowna, Gerard Depardieu
Above: Gerard Depardieu, Ernestine Mazurowna,
Elisabeth Depardieu Top: Daniel Auteuil, Yves Montand
© *Orion Pictures*

Gerard Depardieu, Elisabeth Depardieu

Yves Montand

Victoria Wicks, Ric Young Above: David
Yip, Lucy Sheen © *Samuel Goldwyn Co.*

PING PONG

(GOLDWYN) Producers, Malcolm Craddock, Michael Guest; Director, Po Chih Leong; Screenplay, Jerry Liu; Based on an idea by Po Chih Leong; Editor, David Spiers; Designer, Colin Pigott; Photography, Nick Knowland; Music, Richard Harvey; Production Manager, Annie Rees; Production Coordinator, Faye Perkins; Assistant Directors, John O'Connor, Iain Whyte, Trevor Puckle, Sean Fleming; Casting, John & Ros Hubbard, Tina Liu; Sound, Nick Hosker; Set Decorator, Bryony Foster; Wardrobe, Sally Cairney; Make-Up, Sally Harrison; A Picture Palace Production for Film Four International; Chinese; Not rated; 95 minutes; July release

CAST

Mike Wong	David Yip
Elaine Choi	Lucy Sheen
Mr. Chen	Robert Lee
Ah Ying	Lam Fung
Siu Loong	Victor Kan
Cherry	Barbara Yu Ling
Alan Wong	Ric Young
Alan's Wife	Victoria Wicks
Uncle Choi	Stephen Kuk
A Chee	Rex Wei
Jimmy	Hi Ching
Siu Loong's Kids	Won Hun Tse, Chad Lee
Sam Wong	K. C. Leong
Peter	David Lyon
Susie	Karen Seacombe
Mortician	Nigel Fan
Probate Official	Jonathan Elsom
Winnie	Yee San Foo
Mr. Orbach	Olivier Pierre
W P C Rainbird	Susan Leong
Sarah Lee	Juliet Hammond
Sam Wong at 40	Alan Wong
Young Mike	Ryan Yap

and Eddie Yeoh, Lu Sang Wong, Clive Panto, Jonathan Docker-Drysdale, Nicholas Pritchard, Errol Shaker, Trevor Baxter, San Lee, Phillip Voon, Pat Starr, Kate Harper, Manning Redwood, Bruce Boa, Romolo Bruni, Kim Teoh

GOOD MORNING, BABYLON

(VESTRON) Producer, Giuliani De Negri; Directors/Screenplay, Vittorio Taviani, Paolo Taviani; Executive Producer, Edward Pressman; Associate Producers, Lloyd Fonvielle, Caldecott Chubb, Milena Canonero; French Co-Producer, Marin Karmitz; Photography, Giuseppe Lanci; Editor, Roberto Perpignani; Art Director, Gianni Sbarra; Costumes, Lina Nerli Taviani; General Organizer, Grazia Volpi; Choreography, Gino Landi; Music, Nicola Piovani; Production Supervisor, Tommaso Calevi; Assistant Director, Mimmola Girosi; Sound, Carlo Palmieri, Michael Billingsley; U.S. Casting, Jose Villaverde; Assistant Art Director, Lorenzo D'Ambrosio; Assistant Costumes, Cristiana Bentivoglio; Assistant Editors, Carmena Lombardi, Dan Hoffman; Assistant Choreographer, Mirella Aguiaro; Presented with Rai-Radiotelevisione Italiana; US/Italy/France; Color; Rated PG-13; 115 minutes; July release

CAST

Nicola	Vincent Spano
Andrea	Joaquim De Almeida
Edna	Greta Scacchi
Mabel	Desiree Becker
Bonanno	Omero Antonutti
D. W. Griffith	Charles Dance
Moglie Griffith	Berangere Bonvoisin
Grass	David Brandon
Thompson	Brian Freilino
La Veneziana	Margarita Lozano
Duccio	Massimo Venturiello
Operat Irlandese	Andrea Prodan

and Dorotea Ausenda, Ugo Bencini, Daniel Bosch, Renzo Cantini, Marco Cavicchioli, Fiorenza D'Alessandro, Lionello Pio De Savoia, Maurizio Fardo, Domenico Fiore, Miro Guidelli, John Francis Lane, Ubalso Lo Presti, Luciano Macherelli, Sandro Mallegni, Elio Marconato, Michele Melega, Mauro Monni, Lamberto Petrecca, Diego Ribon, Antonio Russo, Giuseppe Scarcella, Leontine Snel, Egidio Termine, Francesco Tola, Pino Toska

Charles Dance

Right Center: Joaquim De Almeida, Desiree Becker,
Greta Scacchi, Vincent Spano
© *Vestron Pictures/Umberto Montiroli*

183

WISH YOU WERE HERE

(ATLANTIC) Producer, Sarah Radclyffe; Director/Screenplay, David Leland; Photography, Ian Wilson; Editor, George Akers; Designer, Caroline Amies; Costumes, Shuna Harwood; Music, Stanley Myers; Casting, Susie Figgis; Production Manager, Caroline Hewitt; Assistant Directors, Steve Finn, Nick Laws, Pat Aldersley; Production Coordinator, Ginny Roncoroni; Additional Voices, Brendan Donnison; Stunts, Jim Dowdall; Sound, Billy McCarthy; Art Director, Nigel Phelps; Assistant Editors, Dennis McTaggart, Christopher Cook; Music Coordinator, Gerry Butler; resented with Film Four International; A Zenith Production in association with Working Title; British; Technicolor; Rated R; 92 minutes; July release

CAST

Tap Dancing Lady	Trudy Cavanagh
Lynda	Emily Lloyd
Mrs. Parfitt	Clare Clifford
Valerie	Barbara Durkin
Hubert	Geoffery Hutchings
Gillian	Charlotte Barker
Eric	Tom Bell
Margaret	Chloe Leland
Lynda (aged 11)	Charlotte Ball
Aunt Millie	Pat Heywood
Margaret (aged 7)	Abigail Leland
Lynda's Mother	Susan Skipper
Harry Figgis	Geoffrey Durham
Joan Figgis	Sheila Kelley
Cinema Manager	Neville Smith
Lady with hurt knee	Marjorie Sudell
Brian	Lee Whitlock
Dave	Jesse Birdsall
Passenger with Brolly	Frederick Hall
Mental Patient	Bob Flag
Dr. Holroyd	Heathcote Williams
Uncle Brian	William Lawford
Mrs. Hartley	Pamela Duncan
Fish And Chip Shop Van Customer	David Hatton
Policeman	Ben Daniels
Maisie Mathews	Val McLane
Vickie	Kim McDermott
Cafe Manager	Barrie Houghton
Cook	Jim Dowdall
The Baby	Danielle Phelps
Mitch the Dog	George

Right: Charlotte Ball, Emily Lloyd, Tom Bell
Above: Emily Lloyd, Jesse Birdsall
Top: Emily Lloyd
© *Atlantic Entertainment Group*

Le Cung Bac, Phuong Dung

KARMA

(FILM FORUM) Producer/Director, Ho Quang Minh; Screenplay, Ho Quang Minh; Screenplay, Ho Quang Minh, Nguy Ngu; Based on a stopry by Nguy Ngu; Photography, Tran Dinh Muu, Tran Ngoc Huynh; Music, Trinh Cong Son; Vietnam, 1985; Vietnamese with subtitles; The first Vietnamese features to play in the U.S.; Black and white; Not rated; 100 minutes; July release

CAST

Binh	Tran Quang
Nga	Phuong Dung
Tri	Le Cung Bac
Binh's Mother	Ba Nam Sa Dec
Van (Prostitute)	Thuy An

THE LIVING DAYLIGHTS

(MGM/UA) Producers, Albert R. Broccoli, Michael G. Wilson; Director, John Glen; Screenplay, Richard Maibaum, Michael G. Wilson; Associate Producers, Tom Pevsner, Barbara Broccoli; Music, John Barry; Designer, Peter Lamont; Main Title Designer, Maurice Binder; Photography, Alec Mills; Additional Photography, Arthur Wooster; Special Visual Effects, John Richardson; Costumes, Emma Porteous; Casting, Debbie McWilliams; Editors, John Grover, Peter Davies; Production Supervisor, Anthony Waye; Production Managers, Philip Kohler, Sparky Greene, Arno Ortmair, Leonhard Gmur, Denise O'Dell; Assistant Directors, Gerry Gavigan, Callum McDougall, Crispin Reece, Nick Heckstall-Smith, Terry Blyther, Urs Egger, Ahmed Hatimi, Mohamed Hassini; Sound, Derek Ball; Stunts, Paul Weston, Remy Julienne, B. J. Worth; Art Director, Terry Ackland-Snow; Set Decorator, Michael Ford; Production Coordinators, Pam Parker, Janine Lodge, Daniela Stibitz, Ihsanne Khalafaoui, Brenda Ramos, Dawn Severdia, May Capsaskis; Additional Art Directors, Michael Lamont, Ken Court, Fred Hole, Bert Davey, Thomas Riccabona, Peter Manhard; Assistant Art Directors, James Morahan, Ted Ambrose, Dennis Bosher; Assistant Set Decorators, Jille Brown, Christoph Kanter; Video Effects, Richard Hewitt; Additional Sound, Brian Marshall, Roby Guever; Orchestrations, Nicholas Raine; Special Effects, Chris Corbould, Joss Williams, Brian Smithies, Ken Morris, Willy Neuner; Songs, *The Living Daylights* by Pal Waaktaar, John Barry, Performed by a-ha/ *Where Has Every Body gone?* & *If There Was a Man* by John Barry, Chrissie Hynde, performed by The Pretenders; *The James Bond Theme* by Monty Norman; Soundtrack, Warner Bros.; Dolby Stereo; Panavision; Technicolor; British; Rated PG; 130 minutes; July release

CAST

James Bond	Timothy Dalton
Kara Milovy	Maryam d'Abo
General Georgi Koskov	Jeroen Krabbe
Brad Whitaker	Joe Don Baker
General Leonid Pushkin	John Rhys-Davies
Kamran Shah	Art Malik
Necros	Andreas Wisniewski
Saunders	Thomas Wheatley
Q	Desmond Llewelyn
M	Robert Brown
Minister of Defense	Geoffrey Keen
General Anatol Gogol	Walter Gotell
Miss Moneypenny	Caroline Bliss
Felix Leiter	John Terry
Rubavitch	Virginia Hey
Col. Feyador	John Bowe
Rosika Miklos	Julie T. Wallace
Linda	Kell Tyler
Liz	Catherine Rabett
Ava	Dulice Liecier
Chief of Security, Tangiers	Nadim Sawalha
Koskov's KGB Minder	Alan Talbot
Imposter	Carl Rigg
Chief of Snow Leopard Brotherhood	Tony Cyrus
Achmed	Atik Mohamed
Kamran's Men	Michael Moor, Sumar Khan
Jailer	Ken Sharrock
Gas-works' Supervisor	Peter Porteous
Male Secretary, Blayden	Antony Carrick
Trace Centre Toastmaster	Richard Cubison
004	Frederick Warder
002	Glyn Baker
Sergeant Stagg	Derek Hoxby
Butler, Blayden	Bill Weston
Trace Centre Toastmaster	Richard Cubison
Concierege, Vienna Hotel	Heinz Winter
Lavatory Attendant	Leslie French

and Odette Benatar, Dianna Casale, Sharon Devlin, Femi Gardiner, Patricia Keefer, Ruddy Rodriguez, Mayte Sanchez, Cela Savannah, Karen Seeberg, Waris Walsch, Karen Williams

Top Right: Timothy Dalton
Below: Maryam d'Abo
© *United Artists/MGM*

LA GRAN FIESTA

(ZAGA FILMS) Producer/Editor, Roberto Gandara; Director/Photography, Marcos Zurinaga; Screenplay, Ana Lydia Vega, Marcos Zurinaga; Music, Angel Pena; presented by MC Releasing; The first full-length film from Puerto Rico; Spanish with English subtitles; Not rated; 101 minutes; July release

CAST

Jose Manule	Daniel Lugo
Attorney Vazquez	Miguelangel Suarez
Don Manolo Gonzalez	Luis Prendes
Raquel Cordelia Gonzalez	Cordelia Gonzalez
Rita Laura Delano	Laura Delano
Master of Ceremonies	Raul Carbonell Jr.
Angel Luis	Carlos Augusto Cestero
Don Miguel de la Torre	Raul Davila
Poet	Raul Julia
Judge Cropper	E. G. Marshall
Don Antonia Jimenez	Julian Pastor

(No photos available)

THE SEA AND POISON

(FILM FORUM) Producer, Kanou Otsuka; Director/Screenplay, Kei Kumai; Based on the novel by Shusaku Endo; Photography, Masao Tochizawa; Music performance, Tokyo Symphony Orchestra; Japan, 1986; Japanese with subtitles; Not rated; 123 minutes; July release

CAST

Suguro	Eiji Okuda
Toda	Ken Watanabe
Professor Gondo	Shigeru Kamiyama
Professor Hashimoto	Takahiro Tamura

Ken Watanabe, Eiji Okuda

THE WHISTLE BLOWER

(HEMDALE) Producer, Geoffrey Reeve; Director, Simon Langton; Screenplay, Julian Bond; Executive Producer, James Reeve; Associate Producer, Peter Dolman; Photography, Fred Tammes; Camera, Neil Binney; Designer, Morley Smith; Art Director, Chris Burke; Costumes, Raymond Hughes; Editor, Bob Morgan; Assistant Editor, John Nuth; Casting, Maude Spector; British; Color; Rated PG; 100 minutes; July release

CAST

Frank Jones	Michael Caine
Lord	James Fox
Bob Jones	Nigel Havers
Cynthia Goodburn	Felicity Dean
Sir Adrian Chapple	John Gielgud
Bill Pickett	Kenneth Colley
Bruce	Gordon Jackson
Charles Greig	Barry Foster
Secretary to the Cabinet	David Langton
Rose	Dinah Stabb
Mark	James Simmons
Dodgson	Bill Wallis
Allen Goodburn	Andrew Hawkins
Tiffany	Katherine Reeve
Inspector Bourne	Trevor Cooper
Coroner's Officer	Gregory Floy

Left: Nigel Havers, Felicity Dean
Above: John Gielgud, Michael Caine
© Hemdale

LIVING ON TOKYO TIME

(SKOURAS) Producers, Lynn O'Donnell, Dennis Hayashi; Director/Editor, Steven Okazaki; Screenplay, John McCormick, Steven Okazaki, Photography, Steven Okazaki, Zand Gee; Sound, Giovanni De Simone, Sara Chin; Assistant Director, Judith Nihei; A Farallon Films Production; Color; R; 83 minutes; August release

CAST

Kyoko	Minako Ohashi
Ken	Ken Nakagawa
Mimi	Mitzie Abe
Carl	Bill Bonham
Michelle	Brenda Aoki
Lana	Kate Connell
Richie	John McCormick
Nina	Sue Matthews
Jimbo	Jim Cranna
Warren	Alex Herschlag
Lambert	Keith Choy
Sheri	Judi Nihei
Lane	Lane Nishikawa

Minako Ohashi and director Steve Okazaki
© Skouras Pictures

THE FOURTH PROTOCOL

(LORIMAR) Producer, Timothy Burrill; Director, John Mackenzie; Screenplay, Frederick Forsyth; Photography, Phil Meheux; Editor, Graham Walker; Music, Lalo Schifrin; British; Color; Rated R; 120 minutes; August release; No other credits provided

CAST

John Preston	Michael Caine
Petrofsky	Pierce Brosnan
Vassileva	Joanna Cassidy
Borisov	Ned Beatty
Brian Harcourt-Smith	Julian Glover
Sir Bernard Hemmings	Michael Gough
General Karpov	Ray McAnally
Sir Nigel Irvine	Ian Richardson
George Berenson	Anton Rodgers

Pierce Brosnan, Joanna Cassidy
© *Lorimar Motion Pictures*

THE CARE BEARS ADVENTURE IN WONDERLAND

(CINEPLEX ODEON FILMS) Producers, Michael Hirsh, Patrick Loubert, Clive A. Smith; Supervising Producer, Lenora Hume; Director, Raymond Jafelice; Story, Peter Saunder; Screenplay, Susan Snooks, John De Klein; Songs, John Sebastian; Music, Patricia Cullen; "*Rise and Shine*" Music & Lyrics, Maribeth Solomon/Vocal, Natalie Cole/Arrangement, Mickey Erbe; Creative Consultants, Jack Chojnacki, Harvey Levin; Care Bears Character Development Supervision, Ralph Shaffer, Linda Edwards, Tom Schneider; Editors, Rob Kirkpatrick, Evan Landis; Animation Director, John Laurence Collins; Story Editor, Patrick Loubert; Coordinating Producer, Heather Walker; Line Producer, Stephen Hodgins; Production Supervisor, Dale Cox; Voice Director, Rob Kirkpatrick; Casting, Arlene Berman, Deborah Patz; Additional Scenes, Heather MacGillvray; Art Directors, Wayne Gilbert, Gabe Csakany, Kim Cleary; Layout Director, Arna Selznick; Special Effects, Core Animated Effects; Production Manager, Steve Fraser; Music Producers, David Greene, Scott McCrorie; Musical Director, Eugene Martynec; Orchestrations/Conductor, Milton Barnes; Vocals, John Sebastian, Keith Hampshire, Colin Fox; Animated; Canadian; Color; Rated G; 75 minutes; August release

CAST (voices)

Grumpy Bear	Bob Dermer
Swift Heart Rabbit	Eva Almos
Brave Heart Lion/Dum	Dan Hennessey
Tenderheart Bear	Jim Henshaw
Good Luck Bear	Marla Lukofsky
Lotsa Heart Elephant	Luba Goy
White Rabbit	Keith Knight
Alice	Tracey Moore
Wizard	Colin Fox
Dim/Cheshire Cat	John Stocker
Caterpillar	Don McManus
Queen of Wonderland	Elizabeth Hanna
Flamingo	Alan Fawcett
Mad Hatter/Jabberwocky	Keith Hampshire
Princess	Alyson Court

Alice and Dinah
© *Cineplex Odeon Films*

BACKLASH

(SAMUEL GOLDWYN) Producer/Director/Screenplay, Bill Bennett; Photography, Tony Wilson; Editor, Denis Hunter; Music, Michael Atkinson, Michael Spicer; Sound, Leo Sullivan; Sound, Brett Robinson; Sound Editors, Dany Cooper, Denise Hunter; Production Manager, Sue Seeary; A Mermaid Beach Productions Pty. Ltd. Film; Australian; Color; Not Rated; 90 minutes; August release

CAST

Trevor Darling	David Argue
Nikki Iceton	Gia Carides
Kath	Lydia Miller
Lyle	Brian Syron
Mrs. Smith	Anne Smith
Mr. Smith	Don Smith
Waitress	Jennifer Cluff

Lydia Miller, David Argue
© *Samuel Goldwyn Co.*

187

ON THE LINE

(MIRAMAX FILMS) Producers, Steven Kovacs, Jose Luis Borau; Director, Jose Luis Borau; Screenplay, Jose Luis Borau, Barbara P. Solomon; Photography, Teo Escamilla; Music, Joel Goldsmith; Editors, Curtiss Clayton, Cari Coughlin; Art Director, Philip Thomas; Executive Producer, Jose Jacoste; Associate Producer, Antonio Isasi; Production Managers, Mark Tarnawsky, Paul Kimatian; Assistant Directors, Victor Albarran, Cara Giallanza, Michael Proust; Additional Photography, Steven Posey, Mikhail Suslov, Joan Gelpi, Nicholas Von Sternberg; Sound Editors, Nicholas Wentworth, Jose Salcedo; Music Editor, Patricia Summers; Sound, Walter Martin; Costumes, Sawnie Ruth Baldridge; Casting, Liz Keigley; Stunts, B. J. Davis; Assistant Production Manager, Jean-Marc Felio; Production Coordinators, Judith Schneider, Barbara Martinelli; Production-Direction Coordinator, Santiago Pozo; Set Decorators, Ellen Freund, John Stadleman; Assistant Set Decorator, David Pearce; Casting Assistant, Malsy Maniquis; *"It's Always Fickle"* by Shanklin-Jensen, and Songs by A Manzanero, Pam Savage, Miguel Munoz; Vocals, Michael McGinnis, Liz Lemers, Mariachi Vargas de Tecalitlan, Pam Savage; Spanish, 1984; In English; DeLuxe Color; Not rated; 103 minutes; September release

CAST

Bryant	David Carradine
Mitch	Scott Wilson
Engracia	Victoria Abril
Chuck	Jeff Delger
Jonathan	Paul Richardson
Chief	Jesse Vint
El Gabacho	Sam Jaffe
Pimp	David Estuardo
Stephens	Mitch Pileggi
Rooney	Christopher Saylors
Adela	Susana Zepeda
Rita	Stacey Sanchez
Texan Lawyer	Celso Martinez
Mexican Consul	Carlos Cantu
Smuggler	Roberto Arredondo
Duty Officer	Richard Rutowski
Customs Officer	Michael Bowen
Law Professor	Steven Polinsky
Academy Director	Walter Anderson
Reverend Snyder	Ronald Gottesman
Mrs. Snyder	Annette Barath

Jeff Delger, David Carradine
Top: Jeff Delger, Victoria Abril
© *Miramax Films*

Bob Hoskins, Mickey Rourke
Above: Alan Bates, Christopher Fulford
© *Samuel Goldwyn Co.*

A PRAYER FOR THE DYING

(GOLDWYN) Producer, Peter Snell; Director, Mike Hodges; Screenplay, Edmund Ward, Martin Lynch; Music, Bill Conti; Photography, Mike Garfath; Production Supervisor, Christabel Albery; Designer, Evan Hercules; Costumes, Evangeline Harrison; Assistant Director, Terry Needham; Sound, Chris Munro; British; Color; Dolby Stereo; Rated R; 104 minutes; September release

CAST

Martin Fallon	Mickey Rourke
Jack Meehan	Alan Bates
Father DaCosta	Bob Hoskins
Anna	Sammi Davis
Billy	Christopher Fulford
Liam Docherty	Liam Neeson
Siobhan Donovan	Alison Doody
Jenny	Camille Coduri
Kristou	Ian Bartholomew
Ainsley	Mark Lambert
Varley	Cliff Burnett
Rupert	Anthony Head
Donner	David Lumsden
Bonati	Lenny Termo

TOO OUTRAGEOUS!

(SPECTRAFILM) Producer, Roy Krost; Director/Screenplay, Dick Benner; Photography, Fred Guthe; Art Director, Andris Hausmanis; Costumes, Alisa Alexander; Editor, George Appleby; Music/Arrangements, Russ Little; Production Manager, Dan Nyberg; Assistant Directors, Tony Thatcher, David Till, Reid Dunlop; Sound, Daniel Latour; Assistant Art Director, Andrew Poulos; Set Decorators, Liz Calderhead, Marlene Graham; Make-Up, Inge Klaudi; Hairdresser, Madeleine Russell; Stunts, Shane Cardwell; Casting, John Drury, Risa Gertner; Assistant Editors, Jay Houpt, Kelly Makin; Production Coordinator, Justine Estee; Canadian; Colour; Rated R; 105 minutes; September release

CAST

Robin Turner	Craig Russell
Liza Connors	Hollis McLaren
Bob	David McIlwraith
Luke	Ron White
Betty Treisman	Lynne Cormack
Lee Sturges	Michael J. Reynolds
Rothchild	Timothy Jenkins
Tony Sparks	Paul Eves
Manuel	Frank Pellegrino
Homeless Lady	Norma Dell'Agnese
Man in drag (N.Y.)	Norman Duttweiler
Snotty Waiter	Kent Staines
Jack Rabbit Club Bartender	Rusty Ryan
Audience Member	Doug Millar
Betty's Receptionist	Kate Davis
Executives	Doug Paulson, George Hevenor
Phil the Waiter, Monroe Impersonator	Jimmy James
Phil Kennedy, Talk Show Host	Barry Flatman
Chuck the Bartender	Ray Paisley
French Director	Raymond Accolas
French Announcer	Francois Klanfer
Hospital Receptionist	Linda Goranson
TV Emcee	Doug Inear

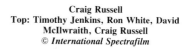

Craig Russell
Top: Timothy Jenkins, Ron White, David McIlwraith, Craig Russell
© *International Spectrafilm*

DARK EYES

(ISLAND PICTURES) Producers, Silvia D'Amico Bendico, Carlo Cucchi; Director, Nikita Mikhalkov; Screenplay, Alexander Adabachian, Nikita Mikhalkov, with the collaboration of Suso Cecchi D'Amico; Based on the short stories by Anton Chekhov; Photography, Franco de Giacomo; Editor, Enzo Meniconi; Music, Francis Lai; Production Supervisor, Vittorio Noia; Italy; Color; Not rated; 118 minutes; September release; No other credits provided

CAST

Romano	Marcello Mastroianni
Elisa	Silvana Mangano
Tina	Marthe Keller
Anna	Elena Sofonova
Elisa's Mother	Pina Cei
Pavel	Vsevolod Larionov
The Governor of Sisoiev	Innokenti Smoktunovski
The Lawyer	Roberto Herlitzka

Elena Sofonova, Marcello Mastroianni
Above: Silvana Mangano, Marcello Mastroianni
© *Island Pictures*

HEY BABU RIBA

(ORION CLASSICS) Executive Producers, George Zecevic, Petar Jankovic; Producers, Dragoljub Popovich, Nikola Popovic; Director, Jovan Acin; Screenplay, Jovan Acin from the memories of Petar Jankovic, George Zecevic and Jovan Acin; Photography, Tomislav Pinter; Editor, Shezana Ivanovic; Art Director, Sava Acin; Music, Zoran Simjanovic; Sound, Marko Rodic; Costumes, Shezana Kojic, Divna Jovanovic; Paintings/Drawings, Kolja Milunovic, Momo Kapor; An Avala Films/Smart Egg Pictures/Esplandor/Inex Film Production; Yugoslavia 1986; Color; Rated R; 109 minutes; September release

CAST

Miriana Zivkovic ("Ester")	Gala Videnovic
Glen	Relja Basic
Young Glen	Nebojsa Bakocevic
Sacha	Marko Todorovic
Young Sacha	Dragan Bjelogrlic
Kicha	Milos Zutic
Young Kicha	Srdjan Todorovic
Pop	Djordge Nenadovic
Young Pop	Goran Radakovic
Rile Ristic ("Joe")	Dragomir Borjanic-Gidra
Young Rile Ristic (Young "Joe")	Milan Strljic
Glen's Father	Ljubisa Samardjic
Kicha's Mother	Ruzica Sokic
Esther's Mother	Spela Rozin
Rada	Danica Maksimovic
Sacha's Grandmother	Tatjana Lukjanova
Dr. Popovic, Pop's Father	Rade Markovic
Major Zivkovic, Esther's Father	Petar Banicevic
Chief Policeman	Dusan Janicijevic
Artist	Predrag Ejdus
Joe's Boss	Josif Tatic
Esther's Daughter (at the funeral)	Tatjana Mirasevic
High School Teacher	Svetlana Novak
Boarder in Kicha's house	Sladjana Radenkovic
First Policeman	Bozidar Pavicevic-Longa
Joe's Friends	Boris Komenic, Branko Vidakovic
Speaker at art exhibition	Milutin Micovic
Speaker at crew competition	Drago Cumic
Waiter on Baueau-Mouche	Izet Curi
Esther's Attacker (at the dance)	Momir Radevic

Gerard Depardieu, Bernard Blier
© *Interama*

I'VE HEARD THE MERMAIDS SINGING

(MIRAMAX FILMS) Producers, Patricia Rozema, Alexandra Raffe; Director/Screenplay/Editor, Patricia Rozema; Executive Producer, Don Haig; Production, VOS Productions, Inc.; Photography, Douglas Koch; Production, John Pace; Assistant Directors, Arlene Hazzan, Thomas Quinn, Louise Shekter; Art Director, Valanne Ridgeway; Assistant Art Director, Jake Fry; Art Consultant, Carla Garnet; Costumes, Martine Mathews, Alexzandra Z.; Assistant Editor, Ron Sanders; Sound, James Musselman, Steven Munro; Music, Mark Korven; Music Coordinator, John Switzer; Mermaid Voices, Rebecca Jenkins; Production Manager, Alexandra Raffe; Songs by various artists; Stunts, Dwayne Maclean; Casting, Maria Armstrong, Ross Clydesdale; Produced with Ontario Arts Council, Canada Council, National Film Board (PAFFPS), Ontario Film Development Corporation, Telefilm Canada; Color; Not rated; 81 minutes; September release

CAST

Polly Vandersma	Sheila McCarthy
Gabrielle St-Peres	Paule Baillargeon
Mary Joseph	Ann-Marie McDonald
Warren	John Evans
Japanese Waitress	Brenda Kamino
Critic	Richard Monette

Top Left: Sheila McCarthy
© *Miramax Films*

Gala Videnovic, Milan Strljic
Above: Nebojsa Bakocevic, Srdjan Todorovic,
Goran Radakovic, Gala Videnovic, Dragan
Bjelogrlic © *Orion Pictures*

BUFFET FROID

(INTERAMA) Producer, Sara Films-Antenne 2; Executive Producer, Alain Sarde; Director/Screenplay, Bertrand Blier; Photography, Jean Penzer; Editor, Claudine Merlin; Set Design, Theo Meurisse; French; Color; Not rated; 98 minutes; September release

CAST

Alphonse Tram	Gerard Depardieu
Inspector	Bernard Blier
Assassin	Jean Carmet
Widow	Genevieve Page
Witness	Jean Rougerie
Doctor	Bernard Crommbey
Man in subway	Michel Serrault

FAMILY BUSINESS

(EUROPEAN CLASSICS) Producer, Michele Ray-Gavras; Director/Screenplay, Costa-Gavras; From the book by Francis Ryck; Photography, Robert Alazraki; Editor, Marie-Sophie Dubus; Music, George Delerue; Art Director, Eric Simon; France; Color; Not rated; 98 minutes; September release; No other credits provided

CAST

The Father	Johnny Hallyday
The Mother	Fanny Ardant
Faucon	Guy Marchand
Francois 1	Laurent Romor
Francois 2	Remi Martin
Martine 1	Juliette Rennes
Martine 2	Caroline Pochon

Top Left: Fanny Ardant, Johnny Hallyday
© *European Classics*

THE FUNERAL

(NEW YORKER FILMS) Producers, Yasushi Tamaoki, Yutaka Okada; Associate Producer, Seigo Hosogoshi; Director/Screenplay, Juzo Itami; Photography, Yonezo Maeda; Lighting, Shosaku Kato; Sound, Minoru Nobuoka; Art Director, Hiroshi Tokuda; Music, Joji Yuasa; Editor, Akira Suzuki; Photography for Monochrome Sequence, Shinpei Asai; Casting, Kosaburo Sasaoka; Assistant Director, Hideyuki Hirayama; Production Manager, Yoshinori Fujita; Japan, 1984; Color/Monochrome; Not rated; 124 minutes; September release

CAST

Wabisuke Inoue	Tsutomu Yamazaki
Chizuko Amamiya	Nobuko Miyamoto
Kikue Amamiya	Kin Sugai
Shokichi Amamiya	Shuji Otaki
Satomi	Ichiro Zaitsu
Ebihara	Nekohachi
Shinkichi Amamiya	Koen Okumura
Ayako	Chikako Yuri
Shigeru	Isao Bito
Akira	Ittoku Kishibe
Aoki	Takashi Tsumura
Mrs. Kimura	Michiyo Yokoyama
Mrs. Hanamura	Hikaru Nishikawa
Kiyo	Midori Ebina
Shokichi's Wife	Hiroko Futaba
Instructress	Hiroko Seki
Old Mrs. Iwakiri	Mitsuko Yoshikawa
The Little Man	Kamatari Fujiwara
The Other Old Man	Haruko Tanaka
Chairman of the Golden Agers' Club	Ryosuke Kagawa
Kurosaki	Asao Sano
Okumura	Koji Sekiyama
Sakakibara	Ippei Soda
Ebihara's Assistant	Yoshihiro Kato, Saburo Satoki
Fuku	Akio Kaneda
The Man Who Climbs the Tree	Go Riju
The Hospital Cashier	Mariko Nakamura
TV Studio Guard	Hideo Fukuhara
Dr. Kimura	Masahiko Tsugawa
Inose	Kaoru Kobayashi
Yoshiko Saito	Haruna Takase
The Priest	Chishu Ryu

Tsutomu Yamazaki, Nobuko Miyamato
Above: Nobuko Miyamato, ?, Kim Sugai
© *New Yorker Films*

COMING UP ROSES

(SKOURAS) Producer, Linda James; Director, Stephen Bayly; Screenplay, Ruth Carter; Music, Michael Storey; Photography, Dick Pope; Editor, Scott Thomas; Designer, Hildegard Bechtler; Costumes, Maria Price; Sound, Simon Fraser; A Red Rooster Films Production for S4C; Welsh with subtitles; Color; Rated PG; 90 minutes; September release

CAST

Trevor	Dafydd Hywel
Mona	Iola Gregory
Gwen	Olive Michael
June	Mari Emlyn
Eli Davies	W. J. Phillips
Dino	Glan Davies
Sian	Gillian Elisa Thomas
Dave	Ifan Huw Dafydd
Pete	Rowan Griffiths
Mr. Valentine	Bill Paterson
Councillor	Clyde Pollitt

Iola Gregory, Dafydd Hywel
© *Skouras Pictures*

James Wilby, Rupert Graves
Top right: Denholm Elliot, James Wilby
Below: James Wilby, Hugh Grant
© Cinecom

MAURICE

(CINECOM) Producer, Ismail Merchant; Director, James Ivory; Screenplay, Kit Hesketh-Harvey, James Ivory; Photography, Pierre Lhomme; Music, Richard Robbins; Editor, Katherine Wenning; Designer, Brian Ackland-Snow; Costumes, Jenny Beavan, John Bright; Casting, Celestia Fox; Associate Producer, Paul Bradley; Production Supervisor, Raymond Day; Production Coordinator, Joyce Turner; Assistant Directors, Michael Zimbrich, Lee Cleary; Art Director, Peter James; Sound, Mike Shoring; Soundtrack on RCA Red Seal; England; Color; Rated R; 140 minutes; September release

CAST

Maurice	James Wilby
Clive	Hugh Grant
Alec	Rupert Graves
Dr. Barry	Denholm Elliott
Mr. Ducie	Simon Callow
Mrs. Hall	Billie Whitelaw
Lasker-Jones	Ben Kingsley
Mrs. Durham	Judy Parfitt
Anne Durham	Phoebe Nicholls
Risley	Mark Tandy
Ada Hall	Helena Mitchell
Kitty Hall	Kitty Aldridge
Simcox	Patrick Godfrey
Archie	Michael Jenn
Dean Cornwalis	Barry Foster
Mr. Borenius	Peter Eyre
Pippa Durham	Catherine Rabett
Young Maurice	Orlando Wells

Rupert Graves, James Wilby
Above: Hugh Grant, Phoebe Nicholls

DOGS IN SPACE

(SKOURAS) Producer, Glenys Rowe; Director/Screenplay, Richard Lowenstein: Executive Producers, Robert Le Tet, Dennis Wright; Production Executive, John Kearney; Photography, Andrew De Groot; Editor, Jill Bilcock; Musical Director, Ollie Olsen; Strange Noises, John Murphy; Sound, Dean Gawen, Stephen Vaughan, Roger Savage, Bruce Emery; Production Manager, Lynda House; Art Director, Jody Borland; Wardrobe, Lynne-Maree Milburn, Karen Ansell; Special Effects, Visual Effect P/L, Peter Stubbs, Jeff Little; Stunts, Glenn Boswell; Music Consultant, Bruce Milne; *"Shivers"* Video Directors, Paul Goldman, Evan English; *"3RRR I.D."* by Martin Armiger/Vocal, Jane Clinton; Songs, Sam Sejavka, Mike Lewis, Ollie Olsen, Brian Eno, Marcus Bergner, Marie Hoy, Roland S. Howard, Thrush and the C . . . s, The Primitive Calculators, The Birthday Party, Gang of Four, Chuck Rio; Vocals, Iggy Pop, Whirlywirld, the Marching Girls, Boys Next Door; Produced with assistance from Film Victoria; An Entertainment Media/Burrowes Film Group Presentation; Digital Stereo/Dolby Stereo; Color; Not Rated; 108 minutes; October release

CAST

Sam	Michael Hutchence
Anna	Saskia Post
Tim	Nique Needles
The Girl	Deanna Bond
Luchio	Tony Helou
Chainsaw Man	Chris Haywood
Anthony	Peter Walsh
Clare	Laura Swanson
Grant	Adam Briscomb
Leanne	Sharon Jessop
Nick	Edward Clayton-Jones
Mark	Martii Coles
Charles	Chuck Meo
Jenny	Caroline Lee
Barbara	Fiona Latham
Erica	Stephanie Johnson
Barry	Gary Foley
Lisa	Glenys Osborne
Anna's Girlfriends	Allanah Hill, Robyn McLellan
Skinhead	Troy Davies
Leanne's Brothers	John Murphy, Troy Davies, Owen Robertson
Stacey	Helen Phillips
Chainsaw Woman	Kelly Hoare
Chainsaw Baby	Robyn Lowenstein
The Dealer	Robert Ratti
Sam's Mother	Barbara Jungwirth
Hardcore Hippie	Beamish Elliot
Policemen	Noel Pennington, Ted Fahrner
Grant's Girls	Michelle Bennett, Lian Lunson
Crazy George	George Maleckas
Pierre	Hugo Race
Terry Towelling Man	Joe Camilleri
Sales People	Liz Meyers, Tim Mclaughlan
Mount Waverley Mum	Lillian Wilson
Champion Girls	Emma De Clario, Sybil Gibb
TV Interviewer	Helen Gianevsky
Anna's Mum	Jean Osborne
Countdown Announcer	Gavin Wood
3RRR D.J.	Bohdan

and Martha Butler, Kate Doherty, Harriet Freeman, Kelly Gallagher, Angela Howard, Tim Millikan, Marie Hou, John Murphy, Sarah Newsome, Ollie Olsen, Miriam Smith, Miles Standish, Noah Taylor, *Dogs in Space:* Edward Clayton-Jones, Michael Hutchence, Chuck Meo, Nique Needles, Glenys Osborne, *Whirlywirld:* Arnie Hanna, David Hoy, John Murphy, Ollie Olsen, *Too Fat to Fit Through the Door:* Marcus Bergner, Marie Hoy, John Murphy, James Rogers, Ollie Olsen, *Primitive Calculators:* Terry Dooley, Denise Grant, Stuart Grant, David Light, *Thrush and the C . . . S:* Marie Hoy, Denise Grant, Danila Stirpe, Jules Taylor, *Marie Hoy and Friends:* Marie Hoy, Loki, Tim Millikan, John Murphy, Ollie Olsen.

Right Center: Michael Hutchence
Above: Tony Helou, Nique Needles
Top: Michael Hutchence, Saskia Post
© *Skouras Pictures*

DIARY FOR MY LOVED ONES

Director, Marta Meszaros; Screenplay, Marta Meszaros, Eva Pataki; Photography, Miklos Jancso Jr.; Editor, Eva Karmento; Music, Zsolt Dome; Set Designer, Eva Martin; A Mafilm-Budapest Studio production; Hungary; Hungarian with English subtitles; Not rated; 135 minutes; September release.

CAST

Juli	Zsuzsa Czinkoczi
Magda	Anna Polony
Janos	Jan Norwicki
Grandpa	Pal Zolnay
Grandma	Mari Szemes
Erzsi	Erzsebet Kutvolgyi
Anna Pavlovna	Irina Kuberskala
Natasha	Adel Kovacs

(No photos available)

MAN ON FIRE

(TRI-STAR) Producer, Arnon Milchan; Director, Elie Chouraqui; Screenplay, Elie Chouraqui, Sergio Donati; Based on novel *"Man on Fire"* by A. J. Quinnell; Associate Producer, Robert Benmussa; Production Executives, Claudio Mancini, Steven Hirsch; Photography, Gerry Fisher; Music, John Scott; Editor, Noelle Boisson; Sound, Claude Villand, Bernard Leroux, Guillaume Sciama; Costumes, Alberte Barsacq; Art Director, Giantito Burchiellaro; Assistant Directors, Inigo Lezzi, Serge Pescetelli, Jacques Eberhard; Casting, Barbara Claman, Daniele Luchetti; Assistant Art Directors, Mauro Borrelli, Maria Sabina Segatori, Luigi Ubani; Set Decorator, Bruno Amalfitano; Assistant Editors, Michelle Hollander, Roberto Garzelli, Anne Manigand, Agnes Schwab, Fabrizzio Palmisano, Catherine Blocus, Corrine Rozenberg; Special Effects, Remy Julienne, Giovanni Corridori, Renato Agostini; Stunts, Sergio Mioni, Ricardo Mioni; Production Supervisor, Walter Massi; Production Manager, Tullio Lullo; Production Coordinator, Shneor Ratzkovsky; Songs, George and Ira Gershwin, Chuck Berry, Vito Pallavicini, Paolo Conte; Italy/France; Dolby Stereo; Color; Rated R; 93 minutes; October release

CAST

Creasy	Scott Glenn
Sam	Jade Malle
David	Joe Pesci
Jane	Brooke Adams
Michael	Jonathan Pryce
Ettore	Paul Shenar
Conti	Danny Aiello
Julia	Laura Morante
Satta	Giancarlo Prati
Bellu	Inigo Lezzi
Sandri	Alessandro Haber
Rabbia	Franco Trevisi
Violente	Lou Castel
Bruno	Lorenzo Piani
Snake	Giuseppe Caderna
Elio	Giovani Mauriello
Elio's Wife	Frederica Tatulli
Conti's Wife	Anita Zagaria
Maria	Enrica Rosso
Nurse	Anna Guerrieri
Foot Race Pro	Angela Finocchiaro
Marco	Giovanni Visentin
School Guard	James Bradell
Claudio	Enrico Papa

and Luigi Mezza Notte, Piero Vida, Antoine Reb, Alexandre Lopez, Alessandro Spadorcia, Henri-Charles Alexandre, Lucas Orlandini, Martine Malle, Marie Sellers, Antonio Petrocelli, Fabio Bussotti, Manfredi Aliquo, Leonardo Petrillo

Right: Scott Glenn, Paul Shenar
Above: Jade Malle Top: Jade
Malle, Scott Glenn
© *Tri-Star Pictures*

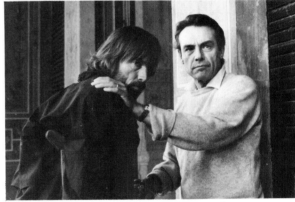

UNDER SATAN'S SUN

Producer, Daniel Toscan du Plantier; Director, Maurice Pialat; Screenplay Sylvie Danton, Maurice Pialat; From the novel by Georges Bernanos; Photography, Willy Kurant; Editor, Yann Dedet; Art Director, Katia Vischikof; Production Companies, Erato Films, Films A2, Flach Films, Action Films, Sofica Investimage, Sofica Creations with the participation of the National Center of Cinematography; France; French with English subtitles; Color; Not rated; 97 minutes; October release

CAST

Donissan	Gerard Depardieu
Mouchette	Sandrine Bonnaire
Menou-Segrais	Maurice Pialat
Cadignan	Alain Artur
Gallet	Yann Dedet
Mouchette's Mother	Brigitte Legendre
Malorthy	Jean-Claude Bourlat
Horse-trader	Jean-Christophe Bouvet
Quarryman	Philippe Pallut
Msgr. Gerbier	Marcel Anselin
Marthe	Yvette Lavogez
Havret	Pierre D'Hoffelize

(No photos available)

Brooke Adams

HOPE AND GLORY

(COLUMBIA) Producer/Director/Screenplay, John Boorman; Co-Producer, Michael Dryhurst; Executive Producers, Jake Eberts, Edgar F. Gross; Photography, Philippe Rousselot; Designer, Anthony Pratt; Costumes, Shirley Russell; Editor, Ian Crafford; Sound Editor, Ron Davis; Music/Arranger/Conductor, Peter Martin; Casting, Mary Selway; Special Effects Design, Phil Stokes; Assistant Director, Andy Armstrong; Sound, Peter Handford, John Hayward; Art Director, Don Dossett; Assistant Art Director, Keiron Phipps; Set Decorator, Joan Wollard; Additional Photography, John Harris; Assistant Directors, Melvin Lind, Julian Wall; Special Effects, Rodney Fuller, Michael Collins; Production Coordinator, Sheila Collins; Choreography, Anthony Van Laast; Assistant Editor, Pat Brennan; Presented in association with Nelson Entertainment; Soundtrack on Varese/Sarabande Records; England; Eastmancolor by Technicolor; Rated PG-13; 113 minutes; October release

CAST

Bill	Sebastian Rice Edwards
Sue	Geraldine Muir
Grace	Sarah Miles
Olive	David Hayman
Dawn	Sammi Davis
Mac	Derrick O'Connor
Molly	Susan Woolridge
Bruce	Jean-Marc Barr
Grandfather George	Ian Bannen
Grandma	Annie Leon
Faith	Jill Baker
Hope	Amelda Brown
Charity	Katrine Boorman
Clive's Pal	Colin Higgins
WVS Woman	Shelagh Fraser
Headmaster	Gerald James
Teacher	Barbara Pierson
Roger	Nicky Taylor
Roger's Gang	Jodie Andrews, Nicholas Askew, Jamie Bowman, Colin Dale, David Parkin, Carlton Taylor
Pauline	Sarah Langton
Jennifer	Imogen Cawrse
Mrs. Evans	Susan Brown
Luftwaffe Pilot	Charley Boorman
Policeman	Peter Hughes
Honeymoon Couple	Ann Thornton, Andrew Bicknell
Pianist	Christine Crowshaw
Canadian Sergeant	William Armstrong
Fireman	Arthur Cox

Right: Sammi Davis, Jean-Marc Barr
Above: Sebastian Rice Edwards, David Hayman
Top: Sarah Miles, Sebastian Rice Edwards, Annie Leon, Ian Bannen, Sammi Davis, Geraldine Muir
© *Columbia Pictures*

Sarah Miles, Geraldine Muir

Derrick O'Connor, Sarah Miles

SAMMY AND ROSIE GET LAID

(CINECOM) Producers, Tim Bevan, Sarah Radclyffe; Director, Stephen Frears; Screenplay, Hanif Kureishi; Lighting/Photography, Oliver Stapleton; Sound, Albert Bailey; Designer, Hugo Luczyc Wyhowski; Editor, Mick Audsley; Costumes, Barbara Kidd; Assistant Director, Guy Travers; Production Manager, Jane Frazer; Casting, Debbie McWilliams; Stunts, Gareth Milne; British; Color; Rated R; 100 minutes; October release

CAST

Rafi	Shashi Kapoor
Rosie	Frances Barber
Alice	Claire Bloom
Sammy	Ayub Khan Din
Danny	Roland Gift
Anna	Wendy Gazelle
Vivia	Suzette Llewellyn
Rani	Meera Syal
Ghost	Badi Uzzaman

Top Left: Shashi Kapoor, Claire Bloom
Left: Frances Barber, Roland Gift, Shashi Kapoor
Below: Frances Barber, Ayub Khan Din
© Cinecom

THE THEME

(INTERNATIONAL FILM EXCHANGE) Director, Gleb Panfilov; Screenplay, Gleb Panfilov, Alexander Chernivsky; Photography, Leonid Kalashnikov; Music, Vadim Bibergan; Art Director, Marksen Gaukman-Sverdlov; Production Company, Mosfilm Studios; USSR 1979; Golden Bear, 1987 Berlin Film Festival/Intl. Press Critics Award; Color; 100 minutes; Not rated; 100 minutes; October release

CAST

Sasha Nikolaeva	Inna Churikova
Kim Esenin	Mikhail Ulyanov
The Gravedigger	Stanislav Lyubshin
Igor	Evgeny Vesnik
Jr. Lt. Sinitsyn	Sergei Nikonenko
Svetelana	Natalia Selezyova
Maria Alexandrova	Yevgenia Nechayeva

Inna Churikova Above: Mikhail Ulyanov
© International Film Exchange

MANON OF THE SPRING

(ORION CLASSICS) Director, Claude Berri; Screenplay, Claude Berri, Gerard Brach; From the Novel *L'Eau des Collines* by Marcel Pagnol; Original Dialogue, Marcel Pagnol; *Sequel to Claude Berri's "Jean de Florette"*; Photography, Bruno Nuytten; Music, Jean-Claude Petit; *"Jean's Theme"* inspired by Giuseppe Verdi's *"La Forza del Destino"*; Music Performance, The Paris Orchestra; Designer, Bernard Vezat; Costumes, Sylvie Gautrelet; Executive Producer, Pierre Grunstein; Associate Producer, Alain Poire; Sound, Pierre Gamet; Editors, Genevieve Louveau, Herve De Luze; Hair/Make-up, Michele Deruelle, Jean-Pierre Eychenne; Production Manager, Roland Tehnot; Assistant Director, Xavier Castana; Assistant Editor, Mireille Leroy; Casting, Marie-Christine Lafosse; Renn Productions/Films A2/RAI 2/DD Productions; France; French with subtitles; Color; Technovision; Dolby Stereo; Rated PG; 113 minutes; November release

CAST

Cesar Soubeyran, "Le Papet"	Yves Montand
Ugolin	Daniel Auteuil
Manon	Emmanuelle Beart
Bernard Olivier, the Schoolteacher	Hippolyte Girardot
Aimee	Elisabeth Depardieu
Victor	Gabriel Bacquier
Baptistine	Margarita Lozano
Belloiseau	Lucien Damiani
The Water Specialist	Tiki Olgado
Philoxene	Armand Meffre
Pamphile	Andre Dupon
Casimir	Pierre Nougaro
Martial	Marc Betton
Ange	Roger Souza
Anglade	Jean Maurel
Pascal	Pierre Jean Rippert
Eliacin	Didier Pain
The Florist	Fransined
The Priest	Jean Bouchaud
Delphine	Yvonne Gamy
Amandine, Papet's Servant	Chantal Liennel

Top: Yves Montand Right: Emmanuelle Beart
Below: Daniel Auteuil, Yves Montand
© *Orion Pictures*

(Center) Emmanuelle Beart, Bernard Olivier

197

LA VIE EST BELLE

(LAMY FILMS) Producers, Benoit Lamy, Vera Belmont; Directors, Benoit Lamy, Ngangura Mweze; Screenplay, Ngangura Mweze, Maryse Leon, Benoit Lamy; Photography, Michel Baudour; Editor, Martine Giordano; Music, Papa Wemba, Tshala Muana, Zaiko Langa Langa and Klody; A Belgium, Zaire and France co-production; French with English subtitles; Not rated; 85 minutes; November release

CAST

Kourou .... Papa Wemba
Kabibi .... Bibi Krubwa
Mamou .... Landu Nzunzimbu
Nvouandou .... Kanku Kasongo
Nzazi .... Lokinda Mengi Feza
Mongali .... Kalimazi (Riva) Lombume
Mama Dingari .... Mazaza Mukoko
Cherie Bondowe .... Mujinga Mbuji Inabanza
Nganga, the Lawyer .... Bwanando Ngimbi
Emoro, the Dwarf .... Tumba (Emoro) Ayila
Grandpa Kalle .... Pepe Kalle
Nvouandou's Chauffeur .... Alamba Engongo

Top Left: Landu Nzunzimbu, Kanku Kasongo

CRIME AND PUNISHMENT (CRIME ET CHATIMENT)

(CINEMA GUILD) Producer, Michael Kagansky for General Productions; Director, Pierre Chenal; Screenplay, Pierre Chenal, Christian Stengel, Wladimir Strijevsky; Based on novel by Fyodor Dostoyevsky; Additional Dialogue, Marcel Ayme; Photography, Joseph-Louis Mundviller; Camera, Rene Colas; Designer, Aime Bazin; Editors, Andre Galitzine, Pierre Chenal; Music, Arthur Honegger; Assistant Director, Louis Daquin; Production Manager, Christian Stengel; Unit Manager, Ben Barkay; Studio, Gaumont-Franco-Films-Aubert (Paris); Sound, Guy Moreau; U.S. release in association with Ruth Zorn, Cinema Central New York, with the assistance of Unifrance Films and the Centre National de la Cinematographie; Paris Premiere, July 1935; French with subtitles; Black & white; Not rated; 110 minutes; November release

CAST

Raskolnikov .... Pierre Blanchar
Porfiry .... Harry Baur
Sonia .... Madeleine Ozeray
Louzhin .... Aime Clariond
Raskolnikov's Mother .... Marcelle Geniat
Razhoumikhin .... Alexandre Rignault
Dunia .... Lucienne Lemarchand
Aliona Ivanovna .... Magdeleine Berubet
Lizaveta .... Catherine Hessling
Nicolas .... Georges Douking
Marmeladov .... Marcel Delaitre
Zamiatov .... Daniel Gilbert
Lieutenant Poudre .... Paul Asselin
One-Eyed Man .... Eugene Chevalier
Commissioner's Assistant .... Geo Ferny
Polia .... Paulette Elambert
Pestriakov .... Charles Lemontier
Koch .... Leon Larive
Nastassia .... Claire Gerard
and Paul Bonifas, Maurice Devienne, Jean Gehret, Ernest Ferny, Eugene Stube, Etienne Decroux

Pierre Blanchar, Harry Baur Above: Blanchar, Madeleine Ozeray © Cinema Guild

A BOY FROM CALABRIA

(INTERNATIONAL FILM EXCHANGE) Producer, Fulvio Lucisano; Director, Luigi Comencini; Screenplay, Luigi Comencini, Ugo Pirro; Story, Demetrio Casile; Photography, Franco Di Giacomo; Editor, Nino Baragli; Music, Vivaldi; An Italian-French Co-production; Italian International Film-U.P. Schermo Video-Rome; Carthago Film S.R.L.-Canal Plus Productions General Image-Paris in collaboration with RAI Channel 1; Italian with English subtitles; Not rated; 106 minutes; November release

CAST

Felice .... Gian Maria Volonte
Nicola .... Diego Abatantuono
Mariuccia .... Therese Liotard
Mimi .... Santo Polimeno
Crisolinda .... Giada Faggioli
and Jacques Peyrac, Enzo Ruoti, Jean Masrevery

Santo Polimeno, Therese Liotard
© International Film Exchange

CRY FREEDOM

(UNIVERSAL) Producer/Director, Richard Attenborough; Screenplay, John Briley; Based on the books *"Biko"* and *"Asking For Trouble"* by Donald Woods; Executive Producer, Terence Clegg; Photography, Norman Spencer; Co-Producers, Norman Spencer, John Briley; Editor, Lesley Walker; Designer, Stuart Craig; Music, George Fenton, Jonas Gwangwa; Sound, Simon Kaye, Jonathan Bates, Gerry Humphreys; Costumes, John Mollo; Consultants, Donald Woods, Wendy Woods, Hamilton Zolile Keke, Majakathata Mokoena; Special Advisor, Dalindlela Tambo; Arranger/Conductor, George Fenton; Assistant Directors, David Tomblin, Steve Chigorimbo, Roy Button, Patrick Kinney, Steve Fillis, Sue Sheldon, Clive Stafford, David Bennett; Art Directors, Norman Dorme, George Richardson, John King; Assistant Art Director, Gavin Bocquet; Set Decorator, Michael Seirton; Stunts, Peter Brace; Vocals, Thuli Dumakude, Nicola Emmanuel, Jonas Gwangwa; Additional Orchestrations, Peter Whitehouse; Casting, Susie Figgis, Andrew Whaley; Production Managers, Allan James, Gerry Levy; Production Coordinator, Judy Thornton; Special Effects, David Harris, Martin Grant, Paul Knowles, Alan Poole, Gift Nyaniandi; Color; Panavision; Dolby Stereo; British; Rated PG; 157 minutes; November release

CAST

Dr. Ramphele	Josette Simon
Tenhy	Wabei Siyolwe
Mapetla	John Matshikiza
Ntsiki Biko	Juanita Waterman
Donald Woods	Kevin Kline
Ken	Kevin McNally
Alec	Albert Ndinda
Steve Biko	Denzel Washington
Wendy Woods	Penelope Wilton
Jane Woods	Kate Hardie
Dillon Woods	Graeme Taylor
Duncan Woods	Adam Stuart Walker
Gavin Woods	Hamish Stuart Walker
Mary Woods	Spring Stuart Walker
Evalina	Sophie Mgcina
Peter Jones	Jim Findley
Captain De Wet	Timothy West
Dilima	Tichatonga Mazhindu
Father Kani	Zakes Mokae
Kruger	John Thaw
Lemick	Miles Anderson
Lemick's Assistant	Neil McPherson
Soga	Hepburn Graham
Samora Biko	Munyaradzi Kanaventi
Nkosinathi Biko	George Lovell
Policeman Nel	Andrew McCulloch
Nel's Partner	Graham Fletcher Cook
Biko's Brother	Fishoo Tembo
'Helen Suzman'	Peggy Marsh
Don Card	Julian Glover
Bruce	John Hargreaves
Major Boshoff	Philip Bretherton
Beukes	Paul Herzberg
Judge Boshoff	Michael Turner
State Prosecutor	Ian Richardson
Jason	Mawa Makondo
Magistrate Prins	Kalie Hanekom
Sergeant Louw	Paul Jerricho
Tami	Tommy Buson
Moses	Joseph Marcell
Wendy's Mother	Gwen Watford
Wendy's Stepfather	John Paul
Mcelrea	Garrick Hagon
Richie	Nick Tate
Acting High Commisioner	Alec McCowen

and Evelyn Sithole, Xoliswa Sithole, James Coine, Andrew Whaley, Shelley Borkum, Patricia Gumede, Angela Gavaza, Nocebo Mlambo, Walter Matemavi, Clement Muchachi, Ruth Chinamando, Basil Chidyamathamba, Marcy Mushore, Alton Kumalo, Lawrence Simbarashe, Carl Chase, Morgan Sheppard, Claude Maredza, Carlton Chance, Glen Murphy, Russell Keith Grant, Karen Drury, Niven Boyd, Tony Vogel, Christopher Hurst, Gerald Sim, Peter Cartwright, Gary Whelan, Dudley Dickin, David Trevena, Badi Uzzaman, Robert Phillips, Gwyneth Strong, Robert MacNamara, Hans Sittig, Kimpton Mativenga, David Henry, Star Ncube, David Guwaza, Hilary Minster, James Aubrey, Peter Cary, Dominic Kanaventi, Sam Mathambo, Walter Muparutsa, Judy Cornwell, Louis Mahoney, Michael Graham Cox, John Hartley, Simon Shumba, Marilyn Poole, William Marlowe

Top Right: Denzel Washington, Kevin Kline
Below: Kevin Kline, Penelope Wilton; Denzel
Washington
© *Universal City Studios*

Kevin Kline, Denzel Washington

199

POUVOIR INTIME
(BLIND TRUST)

(CINEMA GROUP) Producer, Claude Bonin; Director, Yves Simoneau; Associate Producers, Francine Forest, Jacques Bonin; Screenplay, Yves Simoneau, Pierre Curzi; Photography, Guy Dufaux; Editor, Andre Corriveau; Sound, Michel Charron; Music, Richard Gregoire; In association with Roger Frappier; Canadian; Color; Rated PG-13; 88 minutes; November release

CAST

Roxanne	Marie Tifo
Gildor	Pierre Curzi
Theo	Jacques Godin
Martial	Robert Gravel
Meurseault	Jean-Louis Milette
H. B.	Yvan Ponton
Robin	Eric Brisebois
Janvier	Jacques Lussier

Right: Eric Brisebois
Top: Marie Tifo, Pierre Curzi
© *Cinema Group Pictures*

THE MAN FROM NOWHERE
(L'HOMME DE NULLE PART)

(CINEMA GUILD) Producers, Christian Stengel, Michel Kagansky for General Productions, Alessandro Ghenzi, Antonio Baroni for Ala-Colosseum Films; Director, Pierre Chenal; Screenplay, Armand Salacrou, Pierre Chenal, Christian Stengel; Based on novel by Luigi Pirandello; Additional Dialogue, Roger Vitrac; Photography, Joseph-Louis Mundwiller, Andre Bac, Francesco Izzarelli; Set Decoration, Guido Fiorini, A. Arduini; Music, Jacques Ibert; Costumes, Gino Sensani; Sound, Bittmann; U.S. release in association with Ruth Zorn, Cinema Central New York; Paris Premiere, March 1937; French with subtitles; Black & white; Not rated; 98 minutes; November release

CAST

Mathias Pascal/Adrien Meis	Pierre Blanchar
Louis Paleari	Isa Miranda
Papiano	Robert Le Vigan
The Widow Pescatore	Catherine Fonteney
Paleari	Sinoel
Romilda	Ginette Leclerc
Malagna	Pierre Alcover
Mlle. Caporale	Margo Lion
The Mayor	Marcel Vallee
Titus	Pierre Palau
Pomino	Jean Hebey
Scholastique	Maximilienne
Railwayman	Rene Genin
Mme. Pascal	Charlotte Barbier-Krauss
Cousin Meis	Charles Granaval
Cousine Meis	Yvonne Yma
The Idiot	Georges Douking
Newspaper Editor	Gaston Dupray
Beraldez	Marcel Lupovic
The Doctor	Henri Giquel
Hotel Keeper	Leonce Corne
Pepita	Paquita Claude
The Grave Digger	Robert Moor
The Librarian	Charles Leger
The Tradesman	Leduc
The Hairdresser	Enrico Glori
The Priest	Dax Berthy
Desk Clerk	Louis Daquin

Pierre Blanchar (left) and above center
© *Cinema Guild*

THE LONELY PASSION
OF JUDITH HEARNE

(ISLAND PICTURES) Producers, Peter Nelson, Richard Johnson; Director, Jack Clayton; Screenplay, Peter Nelson; Executive Producers, George Harrison, Denis O'Brien; Photography, Peter Hannan; Designer, Michael Pickwood; Editor, Terry Rawlings; Music, Georges Delerue; Costumes, Elizabeth Waller; Production Associate, Elton John; Production Supervisor, David Barron; Camera, Bob Smith; Sound, Alistair Crocker; Assistant Director, Gary White, Nick Laws, Adam Walton; Casting, Irene Lamb; Production Coordinator, Gillian Bates; Sound, Bruno Heller; Assistant Editors, Tim Grover, Rony Tromp; Set Decorator, Josie MacAvin; Art Director, Henry Harris; Presented by Hemdale Films; A United British Artists/Peter Nelson Production; British; Color; Rated R; 110 minutes; December release

CAST

Judith Hearne	Maggie Smith
James Madden	Bob Hoskins
Aunt D'Arcy	Wendy Hiller
Mrs. Rice	Marie Kean
Bernard	Ian McNeice
Father Quigley	Alan Devlin
Mary	Rudi Davies
Moira O'Neill	Prunella Scales
Edie Marinan	Aine Ni Mhuiri
Miss Friel	Sheila Reid
Mr. Lenahan	Niall Buggy
Sister Ignatius	Kate Binchy
Sister Mary Paul	Martina Stanley
Mrs. Mullen	Veronica Quilligan
The Major	Frank Egerton
Doctor Bowe	Leonard McGuire
Owen O'Neill	Kevin Flood
Una O'Neill	Catherine Cusack
Kevin O'Neill	Peter Gilmore
Shaun O'Neill	James Holland
Youth at liquor store	Aiden Murphy
Young Judith	Emma Jane Lavin
Priest	Dick Sullivan
Young Priest	Alan Radcliffe
Taxi Drivers	Seamus Newham, Paul Boyle
Old Women	Isolde Cazelet, Marjorie Hogan
Waiter	Gerard O'Hagan
Girl Gigglers	Anna Murphy, Gemma Murphy
Drunk in pub	Paddy Joyce
Tin Whistle Player	Richard Taylor
Cellist at Aunt D'Arcy's	Sue Hampson
Violinist at Aunt D'Arcy's	Mike Rennie

Right and Top: Maggie Smith, Bob Hoskins
© *Island Pictures*

Wendy Hiller

Marie Kean

HIGH TIDE

(TRI-STAR) Producer, Sandra Levy; Director, Gillian Armstrong; Screenplay, Laura Jones; Executive Producers, Antony I. Ginnane, Joseph Skrzynski; Photography, Russell Boyd; Editor, Nicholas Beauman; Music, Mark Moffiatt, Ricky Fataar; Production Designer, Sally Campbell; Sound, Ben Osmo; Production Manager, Julie Forster; Assistant Director, Mark Turnbull; Casting, Liz Mullinar; Associate Producer, Greg Rickertson; Australian; Color; Rated PG-13; 104 minutes; December release

CAST

Lilli	Judy Davis
Bet	Jan Adele
Ally	Claudia Karvan
Mick	Colin Friels
Col	John Clayton
Lester	Frankie J. Holden
Tracey	Monica Trapaga
Mechanic	Mark Hembrow
Mary	Toni Scanlon
Jason	Marc Gray
Michelle	Emily Stocker

Right: Jan Adele, Claudia Karvan
Top: Judy Davis
© Tri-Star Pictures

Katevan Abuladze, Edisher Giorgobiani
© Cannon Films

REPENTANCE

(CANNON) Producer, Gruziafilm Studio; Director, Tengiz Abuladze; Screenplay, Nana Djanedlidze, Tengiz Abuladze, Rezo Kveselava; Photography Mikhail Agranovich; Designer, Georgy Mikeladze; Music Arranger, Nana Djanelidze; Russian; 1984; Georgian with subtitles; Rated PG; 145 minutes; December release

CAST

Varlam Aravidze/Avel Aravidze	Avtandil Makharadze
Katevan Baratelli	Zeinab Botsvadze
Sandro Baratelli	Edisher Giorgobiani
Nino Baratelli	Katevan Abuladze
Guliko Aravidze	Iya Ninidze
Tornike	Merab Ninidze
with Kakhi Kavsade	

AU REVOIR, LES ENFANTS
(Goodbye, Children)

(ORION CLASSICS) Producer/Director/Screenplay, Louis Malle; Photography, Renator Berta; Editor, Emmanuelle Castro; Art Director, Willy Holt; Sound, Jean-Claude Larreux, Claude Villand; Costumes, Corinne Jorry; Production Manager, Gérald Molto; Assistant Director, Yann Gilbert; Music, Franz Schubert, Camille Saint-Saens; Casting, Jeanne Biras, Iris Carrière, Sylvie Meyer; Associate Producer, Christian Ferry; Nouvelles Editions de Films S.A./M.K.2. Productions/ Stella Film GmbH/N.E.F.; French-West German; Eastmancolor; Rated PG; 104 minutes; December release

CAST

Julien Quentin	Gaspard Manesse
Jean Bonnet	Raphaël Fejtö
Mme. Quentin	Francine Racette
Francois Quentin	Stanislas Carré De Malberg
Father Jean	Philippe Morier-Genoud
Father Michel	Francois Berléand
Joseph	Francois Négret
Muller	Peter Fitz
Boulanger	Pascal Rivet
Ciron	Benoit Henriet
Sagard	Richard Leboeuf
Babinot	Xavier Legrand
Negus	Arnaud Henriet
Laviron	Jean-Sébastien Chauvin
Moreau	Luc Étienne
Tinchaut	Daniel Edinger
Guibourg	Marcel Bellot
Florent	Ami Flammer
Mlle. Davenne	Irène Jacob
Father Hippolyte	Jean-Paul Dubarry
Infirmary Nurse	Jacqueline Staup
Mme. Perrin	Jacqueline Paris

and Rene Bouloc, Alain Clement, Michael Rottstock, Detlef Gericke, Michael Becker, Thomas Friedl, Christian Sohn, Michel Ginot, Philippe Despaux

Top Right: Gaspard Manesse, Francine Racette, Stanislas Carre de Malberg, Raphael Fejto
Below: Raphael Fejto, Damien Salot, Arnaud Henriet, Philippe Morier-Genoud
© Orion Pictures

Francine Racette, Gaspard Manesse

Raphael Fejto, Gaspard Manesse
(also above)

Gabriel Byrne, Denholm Elliott
in "Defense of the Realm" © *Hemdale*

AMULET OF OGUM (New Yorker Films) Producer, Regina Films; Director/Screenplay, Nelson Pereira dos Santos; Photography, Helio Silva; Editors, Severino Dada, Paulo Pessoa; Music, Jards Macale; Brazil, 1975; Portuguese with English subtitles; Not rated; 117 minutes; February release. CAST: Ney Snat'Anna (Gabriel), Jofre Soares (Severiano), Annecy Rocha (Eneida), Emmanuel Cavalcanti (Dr. Barauna), Jards Macale (Blind Singer), Maria Ribeiro (Gabriel's Mother), Jose Marinho (Francisco Santos)

PACKAGE TOUR (New Yorker Films) Director, Gyula Gazdag; Photography, Elemer Ragalyi; A Mafilm (Budapest) production; Documentary; Hungary, 1984; Hungarian with subtitles; 75 minutes; Not rated; January release

COMIC MAGAZINE (Cinecom) Director, Yojiro Takita; Screenplay, Yuya Uchida, Isao Takagi; Photography, Yoichi Shiga; Editor, Masatsugi Kanazawa; Music, Katsuo Ono; A Zune Keisatsu Production with Kitty Films and New Century Producers; Japan; Japanese with English subtitles; Not rated; 120 minutes; January release. CAST: Yuya Uchida, Yumi Asou, Hiromi Go, Beat Takeshi, Yoshio Harada, Taiji Tonoyama, Masahiro Kuwana, Rikiya Yasuoka, Tsurutaro Kataoka, Daisuke Shima, Kazuyoshi Miura, Pussycat Club

MES PETITES AMOUREUSES (New Yorker Films) Producer, Pierre Cottrell; Director/Screenplay, Jean Eustache; Photography, Nestor Almendros; Editors, Francoise Belleville, Alberto Yaccelini, Vincent Cottrell; Music, Theodore Botrel; France, 1974; French with English subtitles; Not rated; 110 minutes; January release. CAST: Ingrid Caven (Mother), Martin Loeb (Daniel), Jacqueline Dufranne (Girl), Maurice Pialat (Client), Dionys Mascolo (Jose), Pierre Edelman (Boss)

IRON WARRIOR aka "Echoes of Wizardry" (Trans World Entertainment) Producer, Sam Sill (Ovidio G. Assonitis); Director, Al Bradley (Alfonso Brescia); Screenplay, Steven Lutto, Alfonso Brescia; Photography, Waly Gentleman; Editor, Tom Kezner; Music, Charles Scott; Special Effects, Mario Cassar; Costumes, Dana Kwitney; Casting, Joanna Lester; Italian; Fujicolor/Technicolor; Rated PG-13; 82 minutes; January release. CAST: Miles O'Keeffe (Ator), Savina Gersak (Janna), Iris Peynado (Deeva), Elisabeth Kaza (Phodra), Tim Lane (King), no other credits supplied

LA REPUBLICA PERDIDA II (THE LOST REPUBLIC: PART II) (Cinema Guild) Producers, Noran Productions, Enrique Vanoli; Director/Screenplay, Miguel Perez; Textbook, Maria Elena Walsh; Music, Luis Maria Serra; Argentina, 1985; Spanish with subtitles; Documentary; Color and B & W; Not rated; 140 minutes; January release

CEU ABERTO (OPEN SKY) (Cinema Guild) Producers, Raiz Producoes Cinematograficas Ltda.; Director/Screenplay, Joao Batista de Andrade; Photography, Francisco Botelho; Editor, Walter Rogerico; Brazil, 1985; Documentary; Portuguese with subtitles; Color; Not rated; 80 minutes; January release

AMARGO MAR (BITTER SEA) (Cinema Guild) Producers, Productora Cinematografica UKAMAU; Director/Shooting Script, Antonio Eguino; Screenplay, Oscar Soria; Photography, Antohio Eguino; Armando Urioste; Editor, Just Vega; Production Manager, Paolo Agazzi; Music, Alberto Villalpando; Bolivia, 1985; Spanish with subtitles; Color; Not rated; 100 minutes; January release. CAST: Eddy Bravo (Gen. Hilarion Daza), Orlando Sacha (Dr. Guillermo Reyes Argandona), Edgar Vargas (Gen. Narcizo Campero), German Calderon (Manual Davalos), Enriqueta Ulloa (Alcira, "la Vidita")

UNA NOVIA PARA DAVID (A GIRLFRIEND FOR DAVID) (Cinema Guild) Producer, Sergio San Padro; Director, Orlando Rojas; Screenplay, Senel Paz, Orlando Rojas; Editor, Nelson Rodriguez; Photography, Livio Delgado; Sound, Carlos Fernandez, Raul Garcia; Music, Pablo Milanes, interpreted by Elena Burke; Produced by the Instituto Cubano del Arte y Industria Cinematograficos (ICAIC); Cuba, 1985; Spanish with subtitles; Color; Not rated; 103 minutes; January release. CAST: Maria Isabel Diaz Lago (Ofelia/"la gordita"), Jorge Luis Alvarez (David), Francisco Gattorno (Miguel), Edith Massola (Olga), Thais Valdes (Marisela), Rolando Tarajano (Tunas)

PLACE OF WEEPING (New World) Producer, Anant Singh; Director/Screenplay, Darrell Roodt; Photography, Paul Witte; Editor, David Heitner; Art Director, Dave Barkham; Sound, Craig Walmsley, Chris Pieterse; South African; Color; Rated PG; 90 minutes; January release. CAST: James Whyte (Philip Seago), Gcina Mhlophe (Grace), Charles Comyn (Tokkie), Norman Coombes (Father Eagen), Michelle du Toit, Ramolao Makhene, Patrick Shai

DEFENSE OF THE REALM (Hemdale Releasing Corp.) Producers, Robin Douet, Lynda Myles; Director, David Crury; Screenplay, Martin Stellman; Photography, Roger Deakins; Editor, Michael Bradsell; Music, Richard Hartley; Designer, Roger Murray-Leach; Art Director, Daian Charnley; Costumes, Louise Frogley; Sound, Tony Jackson, Howard Lanning; Executive Producer, David Puttnam; A Rank Film Distributors presentation of an Enigma film, in association with the National Film Finance Corp; British; Color; Not rated; 96 minutes; January release. CAST: Gabriel Byrne (Nick Mullen), Greta Scacchi (Nina Beckman), Denholm Elliott (Vernon Bayliss), Ian Bannen (Dennis Markham), Fulton Mackay (Victor Kingsbrook), Bill Paterson (Jack MacLeod), David Calder (Harry Champion), Frederick Treves (Arnold Reece), Robbie Coltrane (Leo McAskey)

Jorge Luis Alvarez, Francisco Gattorno
in "Una Novia para David" © *Cinema Guild*

Maria Isabel Diaz Lago, Edith Massola
in "Una Novia para David" © *Cinema Guild*

THE GOOD WIFE (Atlantic) Producer, Jan Sharp; Director, Ken Cameron; Screenplay, Peter Kenna; Photography, James Bartle; Associate Producer/Production Manager, Helen Watts; Production Executive, Michael Nolin; Production Consultant, Greg Ricketson; Designer, Sally Campbell; Music, Cameron Allen; Costumes, Jennie Tate; Editor, John Scott; Production Coordinator, Elizabeth Symes; Assistant Directors, Phil Rich, Craig Bolles, Grant Lee; Sound, Ben Osmo; Casting, Liz Mullinar; Stunts, Chris Anderson; Assistant Editors, Pamela Barnetta, Liz Goldfinch, Gai Steele; Australia; Color; Rated R; 97 minutes; February release. CAST: Rachel Ward (Marge Hills), Bryan Brown (Sonny Hills), Steven Vidler (Sugar Hills), Sam Neill (Neville Gifford), Jennifer Claire (Daisy), Bruce Barry (Archie), Peter Cummins (Ned Hopper), Carole Skinner (Mrs. Gibson), Clarissa Kay-Mason (Mrs. Jackson), Barry Hill (Mr. Fielding), Susan Lyons (Mrs. Fielding), Helen Jones (Rosie Gibbs), Lisa Hensley (Sylvia), May Howlett (Mrs. Carmichael), Maureen Green (Sal Day), Garry Cook (Gerry Day), Harold Kissin (Davis), Oliver Hall (Mick Jones), Sue Ingleton (Rita), Robert Barrett (Heckler), Maurice Hughes (Sgt. Larkin), Margarita Haynes (Greta), Bill Bader, Dick May, Trevor Thomas, Philip Wilton, Craig Fuller, Peter Ford

FACES OF WOMEN (New Yorker Films) Producer/Director/Screenplay, Desire Ecare; Photography, Francois Migeat, Dominique Gentil; Editors, Giselle Miski, Mme. Dje-dje, Nicholas Barrachin; Sound, Jean-Pierre Kaba, N'Guessan Konacou; A Films de la Lagune (Abidjan) Production with the assistance of the French Ministry of Foreign Affairs; Ivory Coast, 1985; Color; In indigenous languages and French with English subtitles; Not rated; 105 minutes; February release. CAST: Eugenie Cisse Roland (the fish-seller), Sidiki Bakaba (Kouassi), Albertine N'Guessan (N'Guessan), Kouadio Brou (Brou), Mahile Veronique (Affoue), Carmen Levry, Anny Brigitte, Alexis Leatche, Desire Bamba, Fatou Sall, and the Adioukrou people of Lopou Village

UNSANE (Bedford Entertainment/Film Gallery) Producer, Claudio Argento; Director, Dario Argento; Screenplay, Dario Argento, George Kemp; Story, Dario Argento; Photography, Luciano Tovoli; Editor, Franco Fraticelli; Music, Claudio Simonetti, Fabio Pignatelli, Massimo Morante; Art Direction, Giuseppe Bassan; Set Decoration, Maurizio Garrone; Production Manager, Giuseppe Mangogna; Assistant Directors, Lamberto Bava, Michele Soavi; Special Effects, Giovanni Corridori; Executive Producer, Salvatore Argento; A Sigma Production; Italian; Eastmancolor; Technovision; R; 100 minutes; February release. CAST: Anthony Franciosa (Peter Neal), John Saxon (Bulmer), Daria Nicolodi (Anne), Giuliano Gemma (Inspector), Mirella D'Angelo, Veronica Lario, John Steiner, Lara Wendel, Christian Borromeo, Ania Pieroni, Eva Robins, Mirella Banti, Isabella Amadeo, Carola Stagnaro

ONE WOMAN OR TWO (Orion Classics) Producer, Rene Cleitman; Director, Daniel Vigne; Screenplay, Daniel Vigne, Elisabeth Rappeneau; Photography, Carlo Varini; Art Director, Jean-Pierre Kohut-Svelko; Sound, Guillaume Sciama; Editor, Marie-Josephe Yoyotte; Music, Kevin Mulligan, Evert Verhees, Toots Thielemans; Assistant Directors, Renald Calcagni, Michel Debats, Hiromi Rollin; Choreography, Lydie Callier; Costumes, Catherine Leterrier; Sets, Regis Des Plas, Michelle Abbe-Vannier, Marc Denize, Jean-Louis Laher, Florence Lhebrard, Michel Grimaud, Vincente Mateu-Ferrer; Casting, Francoise Menidrey, Gerard Moulevrier; Production Manager, Michel Choquet; Executive Producer, Philippe Dussart; *"Tracks of Love,"* Talkback; An Hachette Premiere/Philippe Dussart S.A.R.L./FR3 Films/D.D. Productions Production; Color; In English and French with subtitles; Rated PG-13; 91 minutes; February release. CAST: Gerard Depardieu (Julien Chayssac), Sigourney Weaver (Jessica Fitzgerald), Dr. Ruth Westheimer (Mrs. Heffner), Michel Aumont (Pierre Carrier), Zabou (Constance), Jean-Pierre Bisson (Gino), Yann Babilee (Alex), Maurice Barrier (Mayor), Robert Blumenfeld (Patrick), Michael Goldman (Maxwell), Adrian Howard (Patrick's Assistant), Jean-Quentin Chatelain (Homere), Axel Bogousslavsky (Antoine), Andre Julien (Old Man), Jean-Paul Muel (Marc), Jean-Francois Perrier (Concierge), Andre Haber (Bellman), Philippe Dehesdien, Mathe Souberbie, Philippe Desboeub (Academicians), Dion Anderson (Doorman), Janet Aldrich (Secretary), Seth Allen (Assistant), Kyle Scott Jackson (Chauffeur)

MAN FACING SOUTHEAST (Filmdallas Pictures) Producer, Lujan Pflaum; Director/Screenplay, Eliseo Subiela; Photography, Ricardo de Angelis; Editor, Luis Cesar d'Angiolillo; Music, Pedro Aznar; Argentina; Spanish with subtitles; Color; Rated R; 105 minutes; March release. CAST: Lorenzo Quinteros (Dr. Julio Denis), Hugo Soto (Rantes), Ines Vernengo (Beatriz the Saint), Rubens W. Correa (Dr. Prieto), David Edery (Hospital Director), Tomas Voth (Mental Patient)

Rachel Ward, Bryan Brown, Steven Vidler
in "The Good Wife" © *Atlantic*

IN THE JAWS OF LIFE Producer, Alexsander Stojanovic; Director, Rajko Grlic; Screenplay, Rajko Grlic, Dubravke Ugresic; Photography, Tomislav Pinter; Editor, Zivka Toplak; Music, Brane Zivkovic; Yugoslavia, 1984; Serbo-Croatian with English subtitles; Not rated; 96 minutes; March release. CAST: Gorica Popovic, Bogdan Diklic, Vitomira Loncar

WILD MOUNTAINS Director, Yan Xueshu; Screenplay, Yan Xueshu, Zhu Zi; From the novella *"Jiwowade Renjia"* (*"The People of Jiwowa"*) by Jia Ping'ao; Photography, Mi Jiaqing; Music, Xu Youfu; Production Company, Xi'an Film Studio; Chinese; Chinese with English subtitles; Color; Not rated; March release. CAST: Yue Hong (Guilan), Xin Ming (Huihui), Du Yuan (Hehe), Xu Shouli (Qiurong), Tan Xihe (Ershui), Qiu Yuzhen (Ershen)

THE NIGHT OF THE PENCILS Producer, Fernando Ayala; Director, Hector Olivera; Screenplay, Hector Olivera, Daniel Kon; Based on the historical essay by Maria Seoane and Hector Ruiz Nunez; Photography, Leonardo Rodriguez Solis; Editor, Miguel Mario Lopez; Music, Jose Luis Castineira de Dios; Production Company, Aries Cinematografica Argentina S.A.; Spanish with English subtitles; Not rated; 101 minutes; March release. CAST: Alejo Garcia Pintos (Pablo), Vita Escardo (Claudia), Pablo Novarro (Horacio), Leonardo Sbaraglia (Daniel), Jose Ma. Monje Berbel (Panchito), Pablo Machado (Claudio), Adriana Salonia (Maria Claudia), Hector Bidonde (Dr. Falcone), Tina Serrano (Nelva de Falcone), Lorenzo Quinteros (Raul)

TASIO Producer, Elias Querejeta; Director/Screenplay, Montxo Armendariz; Photography, Jose Luis Alcaine; Editor, Pablo G. DelAmo; Music, Angel Illarramendi; Spain; Spanish with English subtitles; Color; Not rated; 96 minutes; March release. CAST: Patxi Bisquert (Tasio, adult), Isidro Jose Solano (Tasio, adolescent), Garikoitz Mendigutxia (Tasio, child), Amaia Lasa (Paulina), Nacho Martinez (Brother), Jose Maria Asin (Friend), Paco Sagarzazu (Guard), Enrique Giocoechea (Father), Elena Uriz (Mother)

A WOMAN ALONE Director, Agnieszka Holland; Screenplay, Agnieszka Holland, Maciej Karpinski; Photography, Jacek Petrycki; Editor, roman Kolski; Music, Jan Kanty Pawluskiewicz; Poland; Polish with English subtitles; Not rated; 110 minutes; March release. CAST: Maria Chwalibog, Boguslaw Linda, Pawel Witczak, Krzysztof Zaleski, Bohdana Majda

Sigourney Weaver, Gerard Depardieu
in "One Woman or Two" © *Orion Pictures*

Donald Ewer, Rita Tushingham
in "The Housekeeper" © *Castle Hill*

Michael Elphick, Kim, Lars von Trier
in "The Element of Crime" © *Reel Movies*

THE HOUSEKEEPER (Castle Hill) Producer, Harve Sherman; Director, Ousama Rawi; Screenplay, Elaine Waisglass; Based on the novel "*A Judgement in Stone*" by Ruth Rendell; Photography, David Herrington; Editor, Stan Cole; Music, Paul Zaza; Executive Producers, David Pady, Ousama Rawi, Harve Sherman; Line Producer, Jim Cole; A Rawfilm Inc./Schulz Productions Presentation; Canadian; Rated R; 96 minutes; March release. CAST: Rita Tushingham (Eunice Parchman), Ross Petty (George Coverdale), Shelley Peterson (Jackie Coverdale), Jonathan Crombie (Bobby Coverdale), Jessica Steen (Melinda Coverdale), Jackie Burroughs (Joan Smith), Tom Kneebone (Norman Smith), Peter MacNeill (William), Donald Ewer (Mr. Parchman), Joyce Gordon (Aunt), Aisha Tushingham (Young Eunice)

PASSE TON BAC D'ABORD (New Yorker Films) Director/Screenplay, Maurice Pialat; France, 1979; French with subtitles; Not rated; 85 minutes; March release. CAST: Sabine Haudepin (Elisabeth), Philippe Marlaud (Philippe), Bernard Tronczyk (Bernard), Agnes Makowiak (Agnes). No other credits provided.

DARK HAIR Producer/Director, Midori Kurisaki; Photography, Hideo Fujii, Fujio Morita; Documentary; Not rated; 60 minutes; March release

BLACK AND WHITE Producer, Les Films du Volcan, Ministere de la Culture; Director/Screenplay, Claire Devers; Photography, Daniel Desbois, Christopher Doyle, Alain Lasfargues, Jean Paul Da Costa; Editors, Fabienne Alvarez, Yves Sarda; Music sung by Chorale Rhapsodes Black & White; Not rated; 80 minutes; March release. CAST: Francis Frappat (Antoine), Jacques Martial (Dominique), Josephine Fresson (Josy), Marc Berman (M. Roland), Benoit Regent (Night Watchman), Claire Rigollier (Edith), Catherine Belkodja (Housekeeper), Arnaud Carbonnier (Masseur)

THE REALM OF FORTUNE (Azteca Films) Director, Arturo Ripstein; Screenplay, Paz Alicia Garciadiego; Based on a Story by Juan Rulfo; Photography, Angel Goded; Editor, Carlos Savage; Music, Lucia Alvarez; Production Company, Imcine/Conacine; Mexico; Spanish with English subtitles; Color; Not rated; 132 minutes; March release. CAST: Ernesto Gomez Cruz (Dionisio Pinzon), Blanca Guerra (Bernarda Cutino/La Caponera), Alejandro Parodi (Lorenzo Benavides), Zaide Silvia Gutierrez (La Pinzona), Margarita Sanz (Cara de Canario), Ernesto Yanez (Patilludo)

THE ELEMENT OF CRIME (Reel Movies Inl./Metro Cinema) Executive Producer, Per Holst; Director, Lars von Trier; Screenplay, Lars von Trier, Niels Vorsel; Photography, Tom Elling; Editor/Sound, Thomas Gislason; Music, Bo Holten; Production, Per Holst Filmproduktion in co-operation with the Danish Film Institute; Danish; Original English Version; Not rated; 104 minutes; March release. CAST: Michael Elphick (Fisher), Esmond Knight (Osbourne), Jerold Wells (Kramer), Me Me Lei (Kim), Preben Lerdorff Rye (Grandfather), Astrid Henning-Jensen (Housekeeper), Ghota Andersen (Judge)

THE DARK SIDE OF THE MOON Director/Screenplay, Erik Clausen; Photography, Morten Bruus, Jens Schlosser; Editors, Ghita Beckendorff, Jack Thuesen; Music, Robert Broberg; Production Company, Film-Cooperativet Danmark/Metronome Productions A/S for the Danish Film Institute; Danish; Not rated; 93 minutes; March release. CAST: Peter Thiel (John), Catherine Poul Jupont (Maria Bianca), Christina Bengtsson (John's daughter), Kim Jansson (Husband), Yavuzer Cetinkaya (The Turc), Berthe Qvistgaard, Erik Truxa, Anne Nojgaard, Marianne Mortensen, Stig Hoffmeyer, Ramezan Arslan, Meliha Saglanmak, Roy Richards, Dogan Arslan, Elmas Yildiz

LAW OF DESIRE (LA LEY DEL DESEO) (Cinevista) Executive Producer, Miguel A. Perez Campos; Director/Screenplay, Pedro Almodovar; Associate Producer, Agustin Almodovar; Photography, Angel Luis Fernandez; Editor, Jose Salcedo; Costumes, Jose Maria Cossio; Decoration, Javier Fernandez; Production Chief, Ester Garcia; Spain, 1987; Not rated; 100 minutes; March release. CAST: Eusebio Poncela (Pablo Quintero), Carmen Maura (Tina Quintero), Antonio Banderas (Antonio Benitez), Miguel Molina (Juan Bermudez), Manuela Velasco (Ada-Child), Bibi Anderssen (Ada-Mother), Fernando Guillen (Inspector), Nacho Martinez (Dr. Martino), Helga Line (Antonio's Mother), Fernando G. Cuervo (Policeman), German Cobos (Priest), Maruchi Leon (Juan's Sister), Marta Fernandez Muro (Gropie), Alfonso Vallejo (Sgt.), Tinin Almodovar (Lawyer), Lupe Barrado (Nurse), Roxy Von Donna, Jose Manuel Bello, Angie Gray, Jose Ramon Fernandez, Jose R. Pardo, Juan A. Granja, Pepe Patatin, Hector Saurit

REICHSAUTOBAHN (Film Forum) Producer/Director/Screenplay, Harmut Bitomsky; A Big Sky Film Production; Photography, Carlos Bustamante; Presented in association with Goethe House, New York; Documentary; West Germany, 1985; German with subtitles; Not rated; 90 minutes; March release

Astrid Henning-Jenson, Michael Elphick
in "The Element of Crime" © *Reel Movies*

"Reichsautobahn"

Yasujiro Ozu in "I Lived, But . . ."

"The Only Son"

A WOMAN FROM THE PROVINCES Director, Andrzej Baranski; Screenplay, Andrzej Baranski, Waldemar Sieminski; From a Novel by Waldemar Sieminski; Photography, Ryszard Lenczewski; Editor, Marek Denys; Music, Henryk Kuzniak; Production Company, Oko Film Unit; Polish; Polish with English subtitles Color; Not rated; 104 minutes; March release. CAST: Ewa Dalkowska (Andzia), Ryszarda Hanin (Mother), Bozena Dykiel (Jadzka), Magdalena Michalak (Celinka), Halina Wyrodek (Acquaintance), Kazimierz Wichniarz (Solski), Aleksander Fogiel (Father), Maciej Goraj (Szczepan), Jan Jankowksi (Henius), Hanna Giza (Siejwa)

ALADDIN (Cannon) Producer, Ugo Tucci; Director, Bruno Corbucci; Screenplay, Mario Amendola, Marcello Fondato, Bruno Corbucci; Photography, Silvano Ippoliti; Editor, Daniele Alabiso; Music, Fabio Frizzi; Costumes, Mario Russo; Italian; Technicolor; Rated PG; 97 minutes; April release. CAST: Bud Spencer (Genie), Luca Venantini (Al Haddin), Janet Agren (Mrs. Haddin), Fred Buck (Sgt. O'Connor), Tony Adams (Monty Siracusa), Carlo Carbucci (Red), Cristiano Ciancio (Harry), Giancarlo Bastianoni (Randy), Sergio Smacchi (Mark), Riccardo Rainieri (Larry), Umberto Raho, Julian Voloshin, Daimy Spencer

CAPTIVE (Virgin-CineTel) Producer, Don Boyd; Director/Screenplay, Paul Mayersberg; Music, Edge, Michael Berkeley; Color; Rated R; 103 minutes; April release. CAST: Irina Brook (Rowena), Oliver Reed (Gregory), Hiro Arai (Hiro), Xavier Deluc (D), Corinne Dacla (Bryony)

CHILE:HASTA CUANDO? (Filmakers Library) Producer/Director, David Bradbury; Photography, David Knaus, Peter Schnall; Australian 1986; Documentary; 57 minutes; April release

MALABRIGO (Cinema Guild) Producers, Andres Malatesta, Emilio Salomon; Director, Alberto Durant; Screenplay, Jorge Guerra, Alberto Durant; Photography, Mario Garcia Joya; Sound, Guillermo Palacios; Editor, Justo Vega; Set Design, Jose Watanabe, Eduardo Cayo; Peru, 1986; Produced by Perfo Studio; Co-Produced by ICAIC (Cuba), ZDF, Kleine Fernshspiel (Germany) and Channel Four (England); Spanish with subtitles; Color; Not rated; 84 minutes; April release. CAST: Charo Verastegui (Sonia), Luis Alvarez (Otoniel), Ricardo Blume (Montero Sheaffer), Felix Alvarez (Paco), Annia (Linares (Rebeca), Ramon Garcia (Domingo Perez), Jose Maria Salcedo (Ortega), Ricardo Valasquez (Belisario), Bertha Malabrigo (Sra. Huapaya), Jose Luis Bocanegra

GOTHIC (Vestron) Executive Producers, Al Clark, Robert Devereux; Producer, Penny Corke; Director, Ken Russell; Screenplay, Stephen Volk; Photography, Mike Southon; Music, Thomas Dolby; Editor, Michael Bradsell; Designer, Christopher Hobbs; Costumes, Victoria Russell; Assistant Director, Iain Patrick; Art Director, Michael Buchanan; Production Manager, Laura Julian; Sound, Bruce White; Casting, Mary Selway; British; Color; Rated R; 90 minutes; April release. CAST: Gabriel Byrne (Byron), Julian Sands (Shelley), Natasha Richardson (Mary), Myriam Cyr (Claire), Timothy Spall (Dr. Polidori), Andreas Wisniewski (Fletcher), Alex Mango (Murray), Dexter Fletcher (Rushton), Pascal King (Justice), Tom Hickey (Tour Guide), Linda Coggin (Mechanical Doll), Kristine Landon-Smith (Mechanical Woman)

THE ONLY SON (Films Inc.) Director, Yasujiro Ozu; Japan, 1936; Japanese with subtitles; Not rated; 87 minutes; April release

I LIVED, BUT . . . (Shochiku Company Ltd.) Director/Screenplay, Kazuo Inoue; Japan, 1983; Japanese with subtitles; Not rated; 118 minutes; April release

BUSTED UP (Shapiro Entertainment) Producers, Damian Lee, David Mitchell; Director, Conrad E. Palmisano; Screenplay, Damian Lee; Editor, Gary Zubek; Photography, Ludvik Bogner; Associate Producer, Curt Petersen; Executive Producer, Lawrence Nesis; Music, Charles Barnett; Presented by Rose & Ruby; Canadian; Color; Rated R; 90 minutes; April release. CAST: Irene Cara, Paul Coufos, Stan Shaw, Tony Rosato, Frank Pellegrino, Gordon Judges and others (no other credits supplied)

RAWHEAD REX (Empire Pictures) Producers, Kevin Attew, Don Hawkins; Director, George Pavlou; Screenplay, Clive Barker; Photography, John Metcalfe; Editor, Andy Horvitch; Art Director, Lee Huntingford; Executive Producers, Al Burgess, Paul Gwynn; Creature Effects, Peter Litten; Sound, Pat Hayes; Assistant Director, Martin O'Malley; Casting, Michael McLean, Diane Dimeo and Associates, An Alpine Pictures-Paradise Pictures-Green Man production; British; Rank Color; Rated R; 89 minutes; April release. CAST: David Dukes (Howard Hallenbeck) Kelly Piper (Elaine Hallenbeck), Ronan Wilmot (Declan O'Brien), Niall Toibin (Rev. Coot), Heinrich Von Schellendoft (Rawhead Rex), Niall O'Brian (Det. Insp. Gissing), no other credits supplied

"Chile: Hasta Cuando?"

Irene Cara, Paul Coufos
in "Busted Up" © *Shapiro*

207

Rebecca DeMornay, John Savage
in "Beauty and the Beast" © *Cannon*

Micheline Presle, Claude Pieplu
in "Good Weather . . ."

BEAUTY AND THE BEAST (Cannon) Producers, Menahem Golan, Yoram Globus; Director, Eugene Marner; Screenplay, Carole Lucia Satrina; Based on the classic fairy tale by Madame De Villeneuve; Executive Producer, Itzik Kol; Associate Producer, Patricia Ruben; Music, Lori McKelvey; Costumes, Buki Shiff; Designer, Merek Dobrowolski; Editor, Tova Ascher; Photography, Avi Karpick; Assistant Director, Tamir Paul; Production Manager, Dov Keren; Assistant Production Manager, Ron Isak; Assistant Directors, Shaul Gorodesky, Liora Rodan, Rozelle Vogelman; Music Supervisors, Stephen Lawrence/Yehoshua Ben Yehoshua; Choreographer, Christine Oren; Sound, Danny Natovich; Assistant Editors, Hagit Anin, Tivi Zichroni; Art Director, Yoram Shayer; Special Effects, Terry Glass, John Hargreaves, Ran Charash, Yoram Zargari, Nane Rosenstein; Casting, Daliah Hovers, Chava Nachum, Wendy Murray; Character Desin/Make-up, Mony Monsano; Make-up Special Effects, Jon Price, Deborah Eastwood; Set Decorator, Moshe Magnesi; Production Coordinator, Hadas Ruchin; Songs/Orchestrations, Lori McKelvey; Vocals, Rebecca De Mornay, John Savage, Ruth Harlap, Carmela Marner, Jack Messinger, Nick Curtis, George Little; Color; Dolby Stereo; Rated G; 93 minutes; April release. CAST: John Savage (Beast/Prince), Rebecca De Mornay (Beauty), Yossi Graber (Father), Michael Schneider (Kuppel), Carmela Marner (Bettina), Ruth Harlap (Isabella), Joseph Bee (Oliver), Jack Messinger (Frederick) Tzipi Mor, Fira Kanter, Yacov Ben Sira (Maids), Rafi Goldvasser, Eduardo Hobshar, Nitzan Zytzer, Eran Lavy (Acrobats/Jugglers), Deborah Sherph (Innkeeper), Amiram Atias (Statue)

L'ANNEE DES MEDUSES aka *The Year of the Jellyfish* (European Classics) Producer, Alain Terzian; Director/Screenplay, Christopher Frank; Based on the novel by Christopher Frank; Photography, Renato Berta; Editor, Nathalie Lafaurie; Music, Alain Wisniak; Art Director, Jean-Jacques Cazior; A T Films-FR3-Parafrance co-production; Not rated; 110 minutes; April release. CAST: Valerie Kaprisky (Chris), Bernard Giraudeau (Romain), Caroline Cellier (Claude), Jacques Perrin (Vic), Beatrice Agenin (Marianne), Betty Assenza (Dorothee) Charlotte Kadi (Miriam), Pierre Vaneck (Pierre), Philippe Lemaire (Lamotte), Antoine Nikola (Peter)

LA VIE EST A NOUS Director, Jean Renoir; Screenplay, Jean Renoir, Paul Vaillant-Couturier, Jean-Paul Le Chanois, Andre Zwoboda, and others; Photography, Louis Page, Jean Isnard, Jean-Serge Bourgoin, A. Douarinou, Claude Renoir; Editor, Marguerite Renoir; Music, *"The International," "La Cucaracha", "Aupres de Ma Blonde";* Documentary; France, 1936; Not rated; 66 minutes; May release

Rebecca DeMornay, John Savage
in "Beauty and the Beast" © *Cannon*

GOOD WEATHER, BUT STORMY LATE THIS AFTERNOON (Coralie Films International) Director, Gerard Frot-Coutaz; Screenplay, Gerard Frot-Coutaz, Jacques Davila; France; French with subtitles; Not rated; 85 minutes; May release. CAST: Micheline Presle (Jacqueline), Claude Pieplu (Jacques), Xavier Deluc (Bernard), Tonie Marshall (Brigitte)

THE GATE (New Century Entertainment/Vista Organization) Producer, John Kemeny; Director, Tibor Takacs; Screenplay, Michael Nankin; Photography, Thomas Vamos; Editor, Rit Wallis; Music, Michael Hoenig, J. Peter Robinson; Designer, William Beeton; Sound, Doug Ganton; Special Effects, Randall William Cook; Makeup, Craig Rearson; Co-producer, Andras Hamori; Assistant Directors, Michael Zenon, Bill Bannerman, Kathleen Meade; Casting, Mary Gail Artz, Clare Walker; An Alliance Entertainment Production; Canadian; Color; Dolby Stereo; Rated PG-13; 92 minutes; May release. CAST: Stephen Dorff (Glen), Christa Denton (Al), Louis Tripp (Terry), Kelly Rowan (Lori Lee), Jennifer Irwin (Linda Lee), Deborah Grover (Mom), Scot Denton (Dad)

MEMED, MY HAWK (Filmworld) Producer, Fuad Kavur; Director/Screenplay, Peter Ustinov; Based on the novel by Yashar Kemal; Photography, Freddie Francis; Editor, Peter Honess; Music, Manos Hadjidakis; Color; Rated PG-13; 104 minutes; May release. CAST: Peter Ustinov (ABDI Aga), Herbert Lom (Ali Safa), Simon Dutton (Memed), Denis Quilley (Rejeb), Michael Elphick (Jabbar), Leonie Mellinger (Hatche), Vladeck Sheybal (Lame Ali), Michael Gough (Kerimoglu), Walter Gotell (Sgt. Asim)

THE SECOND VICTORY (Filmworld Distributors Inc.) Producer/Director, Gerald Thomas; Screenplay, Morris West; Photography, Alan Hume; Editor, Leslie Healey; Music, Stanley Myers; Designer, Harry Pottle; Color; Not rated; 95 minutes; May release. CAST: Anthony Andrews (Major Hanion), Max Von Sydow (Dr. Huber), Helmut Griem (Karl Fischer), Mario Adorf (Dr. Sepp Kunzil), Brigit Doll (Anna Kunzli), Wolfgang Reichmann (Max Holzinger), Renee Soutendijk (Traudi Holzinger), Gunther Maria Halmer (Rudi Winkler), Jimmy Schell (Liesl Holzinger) No other credits provided.

ROSA LUXEMBURG (New Yorker Films) Producer, Eberhard Junkersdorf; Director/Screenplay, Margarethe von Trotta; Editor, Dagmar Hirtz; Music, Nicholas Economou; Art Directors, Bernd Lepel, Karel Vacek; Germany; German and Polish with English subtitles; Not rated; 122 minutes; May release. CAST: Barbara Sukowa (Rosa Luxemburg), Daniel Olbrychski (Leo Jogiches), Otto Sander (Karl Liebknecht), Adelheid Arndt (Luise Kautsky), Doris Schade (Clara Zetkin), Hannes Jaenicke (Kostia Zetkin), Jan-Paul Biczycki (August Bebel), Karin Baal (Mathilde Jacob), Winfried Glatzeder (Paul Levi)

THEATRE IN RUINS (CHRONOS-FILM) Producer, Bengt von zur Muehlen; Director, Irmgard von zur Muehlen; Screenplay, Dieter Hildebrandt; Narrator, Erich Schwarz; Documentary; Germany; German with English subtitles; Not rated; 56 minutes; June release. WITH: Friederich Luft, Hans Borgelt, Boleslaw Barlog, Ita Maximowna, Hildegard Knef, Klaus Schwarzkopf

Patrick Macnee, Antony Sher in "Shadey"
© *Skouras Pictures*

**Robert Koltai, Magda Vasaryova
in "Quiet Happiness"**

SHADEY (Skouras) Producer, Otto Plaschkes; Director, Philip Saville; Screenplay, Snoo Wilson; Music, Colin Towns; Photography, Roger Deakins; Designer, Norman Garwood; Editor, Chris Kelly; Costumes, Tudor George; Production Manager, Paul Sparrow; Assistant Director, Guy Travers; Sound, Sandy Macrae; Production Consultant, Nina Zuckerman; from Film Four International; Color; British; Rated PG-13; 90 minutes; June release. CAST: Antony Sher (Oliver Shadey), Billie Whitelaw (Dr. Cloud), Patrick Macnee (Sir Cyril Landau), Leslie Ash (Carol Landau), Bernard Hepton (Capt. Amies), Larry Lamb (Dick Darnley), Katherine Helmond (Lady Constance Landau), Jon Cartwright (Shulman), Jessie Birdsall (Carl), Oliver Pierre (Manson), Stephen Persaud (Winston), Basil Henson (Bishop), Madhav Sharma, Susan Engel (Orators), Jane Myerson (Penelope), Simon Prebble (Hotel Manager), Zabu (Maid), Rita Keegan (Minder), Zohra Segal (Indian Lady), Bill Bingham (TV Interviewer), Jonathan Perkins/Silver Spurs (Pop Group)

A VIRUS KNOWS NO MORALS (EIN VIRUS KENNT KEINE MORAL) Producer/Director/Screenplay, Rosa von Praunheim; Photography, Elfi Mikesch; Editors, Rosa von Praunheim, Michael Schaefer; Music, Maran Gosov and The Bermudas; Sound, Michael Schaefer, Reinhard Sterger; Executive Producer, Renee Gundelach; West Germany 1985; German with subtitles; Color; Not rated; 82 minutes; June release. CAST: Rosa von Praunheim (Rudiger), Dieter Dicken (Christian), Maria Hasenaecher (Dr. Blut), Christian Kesten (Student), Eva Kurz (Carola), Regina Rudnick (Therapist), Thilo von Trotha (Mother), the 3 Tornados, Craig Russel, Ellen Reichard, The Bermudas

QUIET HAPPINESS (Film Forum) Director, Dusan Hanak; Screenplay, Dusan Hanak, Ondrej Sulaj; Photography, Viktor Svoboda; Distributor, International Film Exchange; Czech with subtitles; Not rated; 89 minutes; June release. CAST: Magda Vasaryova (Sonia), Robert Koltai (Emil), Jiri Bartoska (Dr. Macko), Jana Brejchova (Dr. Galova)

BURKE AND WILLS (Hemdale) Producers, Graeme Clifford, John Sexton; Director, Graeme Clifford; Screenplay, Michael Thomas; Photography, Russell Boyd; Editor, Tim Wellburn; Music, Peter Schulthorpe; Designer, Ross Major; Australia; Rated PG-13; 140 minutes; June release. CAST: Jack Thompson (Robert O'Hara Burke), Nigel Travers (William John Wills), Greta Scacchi (Julie Matthews), Matthew Farger (John King), Ralph Cotterill (Charley Gray), Drew Forsythe (William Brahe), Chris Haywood (Tom McDonagh), Monroe Reimers (Dost Mahomet)

MIX-UP Producers, Dominique Rouchand, Jacques Merlino; Director, Francoise Romand; Photography, Emile Navarro; Editor, Maguy Alziari; Music, Nicolas Frize; In association with Antenne 2 and with the participation of the Ministry of Culture; Documentary-fiction; France; Not rated; 60 minutes; July release. No other credits provided.

SINGING ON THE TREADMILL (Hungarofilm) Producer, Mafilm-Hunnia Studio; Director, Gyula Gazdag; Screenplay, Gyula Gazdag, Miklos Gyorffy; Photography, Elemer Ragalyi; Music Arranger, Ferenc Gyulai Gaal; Hungary, 1974; Hungarian with English subtitles; Not rated; 76 minutes; July release. CAST: Ewald Schorm (Mr. Dezso), Istvan Iglodi (Mr. Rezso), Lili Monori (Anna), Robert Koltai (Peter), Judit Pogany (Boszi), Sandor Halmagyi (Odon), Mari Kiss (Kati), Zoltan Papp (Joska), Eszter Csakanyi (Tini), Laszlo Helyey (Rudi), Hedi Temessy (Elvira), Lajos Oze (Patko), Hanna Honthy (Ageless Goddess of the Operetta)

THE WOLF AT THE DOOR (International Film Marketing) Director, Henning Carlsen; Screenplay, Christopher Hampton; Based on a script by Henning Carlsen, Jean-Claude Carriere; Photography, Mikael Salomon; Editor, Janus Billeskov Jansen; Music, Ole Schmidt; Sound, Rene Levert; Designers, Andre Guerin, Karl-Otto Hedal; Costumes, Charlotte Clason; Assistant Directors, Gert Fredholm, Else Heidary, Terje Dragseth; Production Managers, Bo Christensen Didier Gyuard; Production Associates, Jean-Pierre Cottet, Alain Moreau, Leon Zuratas, Henning Dam Kargaard; A Dagmar Film Prod., Henning Dam Kargaard (Denmark), Cameras Continentales, Famous French Films, TF-1 Film Prod. (France) production in association with the Danish Film Institute and the French Cultural Affairs Ministry; From Karne Film (Copenhagen); French-Danish; Eastmancolor; No rated; 140 minutes; July release. CAST: Donald Sutherland (Paul Gaugin), Valerie Glandut (Annah), Max von Sydow (August Strindberg), Sofie Grabol (Judith), Merete Voldstedlund (Mette), Jorgen Reenberg (Edward Brandes), Yves Barsack (Degas), Thomas Antoni (Jourdan), Bill Dunn, Fanny Bastien, Morten Grunwald, Hans Henrik Lehrfeldt, Jean-Claude Flamant, Solbjorg Hojfeldt, Jesper Bruun Rasmussen, Anthony Michael, Chili Turell

RITA, SUE AND BOB TOO! (Orion Classics) Producer, Sandy Lieberson; Director, Alan Clarke; Screenplay, Andrea Dunbar; Executive Producer, Oscar Lewenstein; Co-Producer, Patsy Pollock; Production Supervisor, Garth Thomas; Production Coordinator, Laura Grumitt; Casting, Beverly Keogh; Assistant Directors, Mike Gowans, John Older, Cordelia Hardy; Music, Michael Kamen; Art Director, Len Huntingford; Sound, Mike McDuffie; Costumes, Catherine Cooke; Assistant Costume Designer, Katharine Naylor; Editor, Steve Singleton; Assistant Editor, Tony Morris; British; Color; Rated R; 95 minutes; July release. CAST: George Costigan (Bob), Siobhan Finneran (Rita), Michelle Holmes (Sue), Lesley Sharp (Michelle), Kulvinder Ghir (Aslam), Willie Ross (Sue's Father), Patti Nicholls (Sue's Mother), Paul Oldham (Lee), Bryan Heeley (Michael), Joyce Pembroke (Rita's Mother), Jane Atkinson (Helen), Mark Crompton (Stuart Goodwin, Andrew Krauz, Simon Waring, Max Jackman, David Britton (Rita's Brother's), Bernard Wringley (Terry Middleton), Marie Jelliman (Teacher), Joanna Steele (Sulvia) Alison Goodman (Hilda), Joanne Barrow (Judy), Paula Jayne (Schoolgirl), Ken Hainsworth (Billy), Miss Nancy (Mavis), Niall Costigan (Simon), Raeesa Mehmodd, (Aslam's Sister), Usma Islam, Naeela Jabeen Sabir, Shabar Hussain (Aslam's Niece's), Danny O'Dea (Paddy), Laura Devon, Charles Meek, Claude Powell, Nelson Fletcher, Mel Fredericks, Blake Roberts, Paul Hedges, Alexander Cruise

**Michelle Holmes, George Costigan, Siobhan Finneran
in "Rita, Sue and Bob Too"** © *Orion Pictures*

Stephen Brennan, Eamon Morrissey
in "Eat the Peach" © *Skouras Pictures*

Clare Powney, Franco Nero
in "The Girl" © *Shapiro Entertainment*

EAT THE PEACH (Skouras) Producer, John Kelleher; Director, Peter Ormrod; Executive Producer, David Collins; Screenplay, Peter Ormrod, John Kelleher; Designer, David Wilson; Editor, J. Patrick Duffner; Photography, Arthur Wooster; Music, Donal Lunny; Presented by Jonathan Demme; from Film Four International, Strongbow Marketing in association with Bord Scannan na hEireann/The Irish Film Board; A Strongbow Production; Ireland; Color; Not rated; 95 minutes; July release. CAST: Stephen Brennan (Vinnie), Eamon Morrissey (Arthur), Catherine Byrne (Nora), Niall Toibin (Boots), Joe Lynch (Boss Murtagh), Tony Doyle (Sean Murtagh), Takashi Kawahara (Bunzo), Victoria Armstrong (Vicky), Barbara Adair (Mrs. Fleck), Bernadette O'Neill (Nuala), Paul Raynor (O'Hagen), Martin Dempsey (Quiz Master), Maeliosa Stafford (Priest), Jill Doyle (Aileen), Don Foley (Journalist), Brian J. Hogg (Danny), Pat Kenny (TV Reporter), Barry Kelly (Cameraman), Edmund Lynch (Soundman)

SLEEPWALK (First Run Features) Director, Sara Driver; Screenplay, Sara Driver, Lorenzo Mans; Story, Sara Driver, Kathleen Brennon; Photography, Frank Prinzi, Jim Jarmusch; Editor, Li Shin Yu; Music, Phil Kiline; Production Company, Ottoskop Filmproduktion GmBh, Munich, West Germany, and Driver Films Inc., New York; Production Team, Dave Bromberg, Dan Shulman, J. C. Hardin, Jane Weinstock; West Germany; Not rated; 78 minutes; July release. CAST: Suzanne Fletcher (Nicole), Ann Magnuson (Isabelle), Dexter Lee (Jimmy), Steven Chen (Dr. Gou), Ako (Ecco Ecco)

LA GRAN FIESTA (MC Releasing) Executive Producer/Editor, Roberto Gandara; Producer Roberto Gandara, Marcos Zurinaga; Director/Photography, Marcos Zurinaga; Screenplay, Ana Lydia Vega, Marcos Zurinaga; Music, Angel (Cucco) Pena; Set Design, Maria Teresa Pecanins; Costumes, Gloria Saez, Federico Castillo A Zaga Films Production; Puerto Rican; Spanish with subtitles; Color; Not rated; 101 minutes; July release. CAST: Daniel Lugo, Miguelangelo Suarez, Luis Prendes, Cordelia Gonzalez, Laura Delano, Raul Julia, E. G. Marshall, Julian Paster, no other credits submitted

CRAZY MOON (Miramax Films) Producers/Screenplay, Tom Berry, Stefan Wodoslawsky; Director, Allan Eastman; Photography, Savas Kalogeras; Editor, Franco Battista; Music, Lou Forestieri; Art Director, Guy Lalande; Canadian; Color; Rated PG-13; 90 minutes; July release. CAST: Kiefer Sutherland (Brooks), Vanessa Vaughan (Anne), Peter Spence (Cleveland), Ken Pogue (Alec), Eve Napier (Mimi), Sean McCann (Anne's father), Bronwen Mantel (Anne's mother)

THE GIRL (Shapiro Entertainment) Producer/Director, Arne Mattsson; Screenplay, Ernest Hotch; Photography, Tomislav Pinter; Editor, Derek Trigg; Designer, Anders Barreus; Costumes, Mago; Music, Alfi Kabiljo; Production Manager, Bjorn Ulfung; Make-up, Eva Helene Wiktorson, Jan Kindahl; Continuity, Stina Klemming; Props, Pontus Lindblad; Sound, Lasse Lundberg, Asa Lindgren; Lux Film Productions; Color; Sweden; in English; Not rated; 194 minutes; August release. CAST: Franco Nero (John Berg), Bernice Stegers (Eva Berg), Clare Powney (Pat-The Girl), Frank Brennan (Lindberg), Mark Robinson (Hans), Clifford Rose (The General), Rosy Jauckens (General's Wife), Derek Benfield (Janitor), Mark Dowling (Zilenski), Leonore Zann (Viveca), Christopher Lee (Peter Storm), Tim Earle (Journalist), Sam Cook (Antonio), Heinz Hopf (David), Ragnar Ulfung (Grandenz)

COLEGAS (PALS) (David Whitten Promotions) Producer, J. A. Perez Giner; Director, Eloy de la Iglesia; Screenplay, Gonzalo Goicoechea, Eloy de la Iglesia; An Opalo Films Production; Spanish; Eastman Color; Not rated; 117 minutes; August release. CAST: Antonio Gonzalez (Antonio), Rosario Gonzalez (Rosario), Jose Luis Manzano (Jose), Enrique San Francisco (Rogelio), Queta Claver (Mother)

SERA POSIBLE EL SUR: A TRIP THROUGH ARGENTINA WITH MERCEDES SOSA (Cinema Guild) Producers, Gerd Unger, Chris Sievernich; Director, Stefan Paul; Photography, Hans Schalk, Hans Warth, Jorge Casal; Sound, Roland Engele, Hans Warth, Pepe Grammatico; Editor/Postproduction Supervisor, Hildegard Schroeder; Production Assistant/Translator, Karin Hartschuh; Graphics, Michael Wagner; West Germany; 1985; An Arsenal Film Production; Documentary; Spanish with subtitles; Color; Stereo; Not rated; 76 minutes; August release. CAST: Mercedes Sosa

VAMPRIES IN HAVANA (Cinema Guild) Director/Screenplay, Juan Padron; Principal Animators, Jose Reyes, Mario Garcia Montes, Noel Lima; Colorist, Gisela Gonzalez; Photography, Adalberto Hernandez; Editor, Rosa M. Carreras; Music, Rembert Egues; Trumpeter, Arturo Sandoval; A Coproduction of the Instituto del Arte y Industria/Cinematograficos (ICAIC), and TVE, S.A. (Espana), Spanish Television; Cuba, 1985; Spanish with subtitles; Color; Not rated 30 minutes; August release

THE URGE TO KILL (EL ANSIA DE MATAR) (Peliculas Mexicanas) Executive Producers, Gilberto Trujillo, Raul Trujillo; Producer/Director/Screenplay, Gilberto de Anda; Photography, Antonio de Anda; Editor, Sergio Soto; Music, Diego Herrera; A Cinemagrafica de Sol production; Mexican; Color; Not rated; 82 minutes; August release. CAST: Mario Almada (Roberto Robles), Gilberto Trujillo (Quillo), Jorge Luke (Guerrilla Capt.), Diana Golden (Lorena), Tere Velazquez (Magda), Gabriela Ruffo (Maria), Raul Trujillo (Deaf Guerrilla), Valentin Trujillo (Major), Jorge Munoz, Alfonso Davila, Xorge Noble, Agustin Bernal, Luis Guevara, Alberto Arvizu, Jose Chavez, Carlos East, Ricardo de Loera, Jaime Reyes, Arturo Martinez Jr., Gilberto de Anda

WINDRIDER (MGM/UA) Producer, Paul Barron; Director, Vincent Monton; Screenplay, Everett De Roche, Bonnie Harris; Photography, Joe Pickering; Editor, John Scott; Music, Kevin Peak; Sound Mark Lewis; Art Director, Steve Jodrell; Production Manager, Terri Vincent; Associate Producer, Bonnie Harris; Casting, Michael Lynch; A Hoyts release of a Barron Films Production; Australia; Eastmancolor; Not rated; 92 minutes; July release. CAST: Tom Burlinson (P. C. Simpson), Nicole Kidman (Jade), Charles Tingwell (Simpson Sr.), Jill Perryman (Miss Dodge), Simon Chilvers, Kim Bullad, Matt Parkinson, Penny Brown

Pepito in "Vampires in Havana"
© *Cinema Guild*

John Savage in "Hotel Colonial"
© Orion Pictures

Mark Pilisi, Matthew Hunter, Kim Willoughby,
Rebecca Saunders in "Tearaway" © Spectrafilm

RIO QUARENTA GRAUS (RIO 40°C/-RIO 100°F) (New Yorker Films) Producer/Director/Screenplay, Nelson Pereira dos Santos; Photography, Helio Silva; Editor, Rafael Justo Valverde; Set Designers, Julio Romito, Adrian Samailoff; Music, Radames Gnatalli; Songs, Zeaketi, Tau Silva, Moacir Soares Pereira; Assistant Director, Jece Valadao; Brazilian, 1955; Black & White; Not rated; 90 minutes; August release. CAST: Glauce Rocha (Maid), Roberto Batalin (Marine), Ana Beatriz (Girl on the beach), Jece Valadao (Miro the Hoodlum), Al Ghiu (Daniel the Soccer Player), Sady Cabral (Bookmaker), Haroldo de Oliveira (The Kid)

HOTEL COLONIAL (Orion) Producers, Mauro Berardi, William M. Siegel; Executive Producer, Ira R. Barmak; Director, Cinzia Th Torrini; Screenplay, Enzo Monteleone, with the participation of Cinzia Th Torrini, Ira R. Barmak; Consultant, Robert Katz; Photography, Giuseppe Rotunno; Editor, Nino Baragli; Music, Pino Donaggio; Art Director, Cianitito Burchilliaro; A Yarno Cinematografica/Legei Theatrical co-production; US/Italian; Technicolor; R; 104 minutes; September release. CAST: John Savage (Marco Venieri), Robert Duvall (Carrasco), Rachel Ward (Irene), Massimo Troisi (Werner), Anna Galiena

HELLRAISER (New World) Executive Producers, Christopher Webster, Mark Armstrong, David Saunders; Producer, Christopher Figg; Director/Screenplay, Clive Barker, Based on his novel "The Hellbound Heart"; Photography, David Worley; Music, Christopher Young; Sound, John Midgely; Assistant Director, Selwyn Roberts; Art Director, Jocelyn James; Stunts, Jim Dowdall; Released in association with Cinemarque Entertainment; A Film Futuras Production; British; Dolby Stereo; Technicolor; R; 90 minutes; September release. CAST: Andrew Robinson (Larry Cotton), Clare Higgins (Julia Cotton), Ashley Laurence (Kirsty), Sean Chapman (Frank Cotton), Oliver Smith (Frank the Monster), Robert Hines (Steve), Antony Allen, Leon Davis, Michael Cassidy, Frank Baker, Kenneth Nelson, Gay Barnes, Niall Buggy

JANE AND THE LOST CITY (New World) Producer/Music, Harry Robertson; Director, Terry Marcel; Screenplay, Mervyn Haisman; Based on the comic strip by Norman Pett; Photography, Paul Beeson; Editor, Alan Jones; Designer, Mick Pickwood; Sound, Alan Gerhardt; Assistant Director, Graham Hickson; In association with Glen Films Prods.; British; Rank Color; Not rated; 93 minutes; September release. CAST: Sam Jones (Jungle Jack Buck), Maud Adams (Lola Pagola), Kirsten Hughes (Jane), Jasper Carrott (Heinrich), Robin Bailey (Colonel), Ian Roberts (Carl), Elsa O'Toole (Leopard Queen), Graham Stark, John Rapley. No other credits submitted

A WINTER TAN Producer, Louise Clark; Director, Louise Clark, Jackie Burroughs, John Frizzell, John Walker, Aerlyn Weissman; Screenplay, Jackie Burroughs; Based on the Book "Give Sorrow Words" by Maryse Holder; Photography, John Walker; Editors, Alan Lee, Susan Martin; Music, Ahmend Hassan, John Lang; Sound, Aerlyn Weissman; Associate Producer, Dulce Kuri; Color; Not rated; 91 minutes; September release. CAST: Jackie Burroughs (Maryse Holder), Erando Gonzalez (Miguel Novaro), Javier Torres (Lucio Salvador), Anita Olanick (Pam), Diane D'Aquila (Edith), Fernando Perez de Leon, Dulce Kuri, Ruben Dario Hernandez, Abraham Hernandez Castillo, Maricarmen Dominguez, Reyna Lobato Mariche, John Frizzell, John Walker, Jorge Galcedo, Luis Lobato, Servando Gaja, Alberta Chalulas, Librado Jiminez

FLAMES IN THE ASHES (Film Forum) Producer, Monia Avrahami; Directors, Haim Guri, Jacquot Erlich for the Ghetto Fighter's House; Advisors, Prof. Yehuda Bauer, Mulka Bernchock; Music, Yossi Mar-Haim; Israel 1985; Yiddish, Hebrew & other languages with subtitles; Documentary; Not rated; 90 minutes; September release

TEARAWAY (SpectraFilm) Producer, Larry Parr; Director, Bruce Morrison; Associate Producer, Finola Dwyer; Editor, Michael Hacking; Photography, Kevin Hayward; Musical Director, Dave McArtney; Screenplay, Bill Baer; Sound, George Lyle; Production Manager, Chloe Smith; Assistant Directors, Chris Short, Victoria Hardy, Richard Lawrence, Kara Dodson; Designer, Mike Becroft; Costumes, Sue Gandy; Costumes Assistant, Nicole Williams; Assistant Editor, Wayne Cook; New Zealand; Rated R; 90 minutes; September release. CAST: Matthew Hunter (Ska), Mark Pilisi (Andrew), Ricky Bribiesca (Sniper), Kim Willoughby (Stacey), Rebecca Saunders (Fran), Peter Bland (Ryder), Pevise Vaifale (Flak), George Henare (Buyer), Michael Morrisey (Manager), Rob Jayne (Driver), Greer Robson (Ska's Sister)

JACKIE CHAN'S POLICE STORY (Golden Harvest) Producer, Edward Tang; Director, Jackie Chan; Screenplay, Edward Tang; Editor, Peter Cheung; Music, Kevin Bassinson; Art Director, Wan Fat; Not rated; 89 minutes; September release. CAST: Jackie Chan (Kevin Chan), Bridget Lin (Selina Fong), Maggie Cheung (May), Cho Yuen (Tom Koo), Bill Tung (Inspector Wong), Kenneth Tong (Frankie), Lam Kok Hung (Superintendent)

FINAL TAKE: THE GOLDEN AGE OF MOVIES (Shochiku) Producers, Yoshitaro Nomura, Shigemi Sugisaki, Nobutoshi Masmuoto, Kiyoshi Shimazu; Director, Yoji Yamada; Screenplay, Hisashi Inoue, Taichi Yamada, Yoshitaka Asama, Yoji Yamada; Photography, Tetsuo Takaba; Music, Naozumi Yamamoto; Art Director, Mitsuo Dekawa; Japanese; Color; Not rated; 118 minutes; September release. CAST: Narimi Arimori (Koharu Tanaka), Kiyoshi Atsumi (Kihachi), Kiichi Nakai (Kenjiro Shimada), Chieko Baisho (Yuki), Koshiro Matsumoto (Kida), Keiko Matsuzaka (Sumie Kawahima), Kei Suma (Ogura), Ittoku Kishibe (Ogata), Chishu Ryu (Tomo)

LA BRUTE (The Brute) (Prods. du Daunou/Marifilms) Executive Producer, Denise Petitdidier; Director/Screenplay, Claude Guillemot; From the novel by Guy des Cars; Photography, Denys Clerval; Editor, Agnes Guillemot; Music, Jean-Marie Senia; Song, Magali Llorca; Sound, Gita Gerveira; Art Director, Frederic Astich-Barre; Sign Language Advisor, Didier Flory; A Prods. du Daunon/Artistique Caumartin/Capricorne Prod./Gilmi co-production; French; Fujicolor; Not rated; 103 minutes; September release. CAST: Xavier Deluc (Jacques Vauthier), Assumpta Serna (Solange Vauthier), Jean Carmet (Deliot), Rosette (Danielle Geny), Paul Crauchet (Yves Rodallec), Magali Llorca (Phylis), Alexandre Sousa (John Bell)

"Flames in the Ashes"

John Vernon, Susan Anspach, Steve Railsback
in "Blue Monkey" © *Spectrafilm*

Veronica Lynn, Jorge Trinchet in "Lejania"
© *Cinema Guild*

BLUE MONKEY (SpectraFilm) Producer, Martin Walters; Executive Producer, Tom Fox; Director, William Fruet; Screenplay, George Goldsmith; Photography Brenton Spencer; Associate Producer, Rise Gertner; Editor, Michael Fruet; Art Director, Reuben Freed; Music, Patrick Coleman, Paul Novotny; Production Manager, John Ryan; Costumes, Gina Kiellerman; Special Effects, Jill Compton, L. Michael Roberts, Zoom EFX; Creature Effects, Sirius Effects; Stunts, Shane Cardwell; Assistant Directors, Neil Huhta, Sarah Cutts, Stephen Janisch; Assistant Art Director, Barney Bayliss; Set Decorator, Brendon Smith; Production Associate, Christine Akrey; Production Coordinator, Melody Comrie; Sound, Peter Jermyn, Urmas Rosin, Christopher Leech; Casting, Paul Bengston, David Cohn, Anne Tait, Anne Ostrenko; Casting Associate, Phyllis Newman; Assistant Editors, Peter Smits, Barry Farrell; Color; Rated R; 98 minutes; September release. CAST: Steve Railsback (Det. Jim Bishop), Gwynyth Walsh (Dr. Rachel Carson), Susan Anspach (Dr. Judith Glass), John Vernon (Roger Levering), Joe Flaherty (George Baker), Robin Duke (Sandra Baker), Don Lake (Elliot Jacobs), Sandy Webster (Fred Adams), Helen Hughes (Marwella), Joy Coghill (Dede Wilkins), Bill Lake (Paramedic), Peter Van Wart (Oscar Willets), Don Ritchie (Orderly), Stuart Stone (Joey), Marsha Moreau (Marcy), Nathan Adamson (Tyrone), Sarah Polley (Ellen), Cynthia Belliveau (Alice Bradley), Phillip Akin (Anthony Rivers), Laura Dickson, Jane Dingle (Desk Nurses), Dan Lett (Ted Andrews), Michael J. Reynolds (Albert Hooper), Michael Caruana (Technician), Gina Wilkinson (Michelle Williams), David Clement (Surgeon), Ursula Balzer (O.R. Nurse), Les Rubie (Rollo Jordan), Reg Dreger (Policeman), Karen Scanlan (I.S.O. Nurse), Ralph Small (Guard), Harry Booker (Bill Clemmins), Jo Anne Bates (Lobby Nurse), Walker Boone (Johnson), Robert Wilton (Orderly), Allan Rosenthal (Dr. Steinberg), Ken Quinn (Patient), Ivan E. Roth (The Creature)

DEADLINE (Skouras) Producer, Elisabeth Wolters-Alfs; Director, Nathaniel Gutman; Photography, Amnon Salomon, Thomas Mauch; Music, Jacques Zwart, Hans Jansen; Editor, Peter Przygodda; Story/Screenplay, Hanan Peled; Story Editor, Dieter Meichsner; Art Director, Yoram Darzily; Line Producer, Michael Scharfstein; A Virgin Vision Presentation; A Creative Film/Caro Film/Norddeutcher Rundfunk Production; West German; Color; Rated R; 99 minutes; September release. CAST: Christopher Walken (Don Stevens), Marita Marschall (Linda Larson), Hywel Bennett (Mike Jessop), Arnon Zadok (Hamdi Abu-Yussuf), Amos Lavie (Yessin Abu-Riadd), Ette Ankri (Samira),

Martin Umbach (Bernard), Moshe Ivgi (Abdul), Sason Gabay (Bassam), Shahar Cohen (Habib), Shlomo Bar-Aba (Micha), Gaby Shoshan (Salim), Igal Noar (Antoine), Jerry Weinstock (Snyder), Reuven Dayan (Karim), Nader Masraawi (Daoud), David Menachem (Phalangist), Shlomo Tarshish (Yoram), Moni Mushonov (Danny)

LEJANIA (PARTING OF THE WAYS) (Cinema Guild) Producer, Humberto Hernandez; Director/Screenplay, Jesus Diaz; Photography, Mario Garcia Joya; Editor, Justo Vega; Sound, Jeronimo Labrada; Song, *"20 Years"* by Maria Teresa Vera; Vocals, Omara Portuondo; Sets/Costumes, Jose M. Villa; Produced by the Instituto Cubano del Arte y Industria Cinematograficos (ICAIC); Cuba, 1985; Spanish with subtitles; Color; Not rated; 90 minutes; September release. CAST: Veronica Lynn (Susana), Jorge Trinchet (Reinaldo), Isabel Santos (Ana), Beatriz Valdes (Aleida), Monica Guffanti (Alejandra), Paloma Abraham (Dora), Rogelio Blain (Jacinto), Mauricio Renteria (Andresito)

THE LAST STRAW (Cinema International Canada) Producers/Screenplay, David Wilson, Giles Walker; Director, Giles Walker; Photography, Andrew Kitzanuk; Editor, David Wilson; Sound, Yves Gendron; Music, Robert Lauzon, Fernand Martel; Production Manager, Maurice Pion; Costumes, Janet Campbell; Associate Producer, Denise Beaudoin; Assistant Director, Francois Cinras; A National Film Board of Canada production; Canadian; Color; Not rated; 98 minutes; September release. CAST: Salverio "Sam" Grana (Alex), Fernanda Tavares (Laura), Maurice Podbrey (Dr. Cameron), Beverly Murray (Nurse Thompson), Stefan Wodoslawsky (Blue), Christine Pak (Hyang-Sook), Wally Martin (Manager)

A BROTHER WITH PERFECT TIMING Director, Chris Austin; Documentary; Not rated; 90 minutes; September release. WITH: Abdullah Ibrahim, Ekaya, No other credits provided.

TAKING CARE (Norstar Entertainment) Producer, Pasia Schonberg; Executive Producer/Director, Clarke Mackey; Screenplay, Rebecca Schechter; Photography, Keith Hlady; Editor, Terese Hannigan; Designer, Carol Holland; Sound, Brian Avery; Music, Jane Fair; a Telltales Ltd. production; Canadian; Color; Not rated; 90 minutes; September release. CAST: Kate Lynch (Angie), Janet Amos (Marie), Saul Rubinek (Carl), Allan Royal (Dr. Barton), Sean McCann (Ed), Bernard Behrens (Dr. O'Donnell)

Christopher Walken, Ette Ankri
in "Deadline" © *Skouras Pictures*

Abdullah Ibrahim in "A Brother
with Perfect Timing"

CONCRETE ANGELS (Shapiro-Academy Entertainment) Producers, Anthony Kramreither, Carlo Liconti; Director, Carlo Liconti; Screenplay, Jim Purdy; Photography, Karol Ike; Editor, John Harding; Art Director, Tom Doherty; Songs by various artists; a Brightstar-Leader Media film; Canadian; Color; Rated R; 97 minutes; September release. CAST: Joseph Dimambro (Bello Vecchio), Luke McKeehan (Sean), Omie Craden (Ira), Dean Bosacki (Jessie), Derrick Jones (Bullet), Rosemary Varnese (Carla), Simon Craig (Mick), Dion Farentino (Gigi), Joe Speciale (Bozo), Andrea Swartz (Sean's Sister), T. J. Criscione, Eric Herbert (Boys), Tony Nardi (Sal), Monica de Santis (Norma), Tom Maccarone (Mr. Vecchio), Anna Migliarisi (Mrs. Vecchio), Clare Barclay (Miss Hutchins), Michael Lebovic (Mr. Levinson), Cayle Chernin (Mrs. Levinson), Terry Steele (CHUK D. J.), Stephen Rusnak (Ralphie)

THE MOZART BROTHERS (First Run Features) Producer, Benjt Forslund; Director, Suzanne Osten; Screenplay/Story, Etienne Glaser, Suzanne Osten, Niklas Radstrom; Photography, Hans Welin, Solveig Warner; Editor, Lasse Hagstrom; Music, Wolfgang Amadeus Mozart, Bjorn Jason Lindh; Sweden; Swedish with subtitles; Color; Not rated; 111 minutes; September release. CAST: Etienne Glaser (Walter), Philip Zanden (Felmming/Mozart's ghost), Henry Bronett (Fritz), Loa Falkman (Eskil/Don Giovanni), Agneta Ekmanner (Marian/Donna Elvira), Lena T. Hansson (Ia/Donna Anna), Helge Skoog (Olaf/Don Ottavio), Krister St. Hill (Stone Guest), Rune Zetterstrom (Lennart/Leporello), Grith Fjeldmose (Therese/Zerlina), Malin Ek (Switchboard Operator)

BORN OF FIRE (Vidmark Entertainment) Producer/Director, Jamil Dehlavi; Screenplay, Rafico Abdulla; Photography, Bruce McGowan; Editor, Robert Hargreaves; Music, Colin Towns, Kudsi Erguner; British; Color; Rated R; 84 minutes; September release. CAST: Peter Firth (Paul Bergson), Suzan Crowley (Anoukin), Oh-Tee (Master Musician), no other credits provided

NOWHERE TO HIDE (New Century/Vista Film Company) Executive Producer, John Kemeny; Producer, Andras Hamori; Director, Mario Azzopardi; Screenplay Alex Rebar, George Goldsmith; Story, Alex Rebar; Photography, Vic Sarin; Editor, Rit Wallis; Music, Brad Fiedel; Production Executive, Susan Cavan; Costumes, Renee April; Stunts, Buddy Joe Hooker; Associate Producer, Stephane Reichel; Sound, Joe Grimaldi, Don White, Michael Liotta; Casting, Amanda Mackey, Maria Armstrong, Ross Clydesdale; An Alliance Entertainment production; Canadian; Film House Color; Rated R; 90 minutes; September release. CAST: Amy Madigan (Barbara Cutter), Daniel Hugh Kelly (Rob Cutter), Robin MacEachern (Johnny Cutter), Michael Ironside (Ben), John Colicos (Gen. Howard), Chuck Shamata (Mike Watson), Clark Johnson (Mark Halstead)

HELLO MARY LOU: PROM NIGHT II aka "The Haunting of Hamilton High (Samuel Goldwyn) Producer, Peter Simpson; Executive Producers, Peter Simpson, Peter Haley; Director, Bruce Pittman; Screenplay, Ron Oliver; Photography, John Herzog; Editor, Nick Rotundo; Designer, Sandy Kybartas; Music, Paul Zaza; Special Effects, Jim Doyle; Associate Producer, Ilana Frank; Co-producer, Ray Sager; A Simcom production; Canadian; Color; Rated R; 96 minutes; October release. CAST: Lisa Schrage (Mary Lou Maloney), Wendy Lyon (Vicki Carpenter), Michael Ironside (Principal Bill Sr.), Justin Louis (Bill Jr.), Richard Monette (Father), no other credits submitted

JOHN AND THE MISSUS (Cinema Group) Producers, Peter O'Brian, John Hunter; Direction/Screenplay, Gordon Pinsent; Based on his novel; Executive Producer, Peter O'Brian; Co-Executive Producer, S. Howard Rosen; Associate Producer/Production Manager, Gabriella Martinelli; Editor, Bruce Nyznik; Music, Michael Conway Baker; Art Director, Earl Preston; Photography, Frank Tidy; Costumes, Olga Dimitrov; Casting, Deidre Bowen; Sound, Rob Young, Bruce Nyznik; Assistant Director, William Spahic; Make-up/Hair, Suzanne Benoit; Assistant Editor, Anna Pafomow; Assistant Art Director, Fred Geringer; Assistant Costume Designer, Petra Kravjansky; Special Effects, Martin Malivoire; Assistant Photographer, Christopher Raucamp; Development Executive for Independent Pictures, Debra Henderson; Production Executive for CBC, David Pears; An Independent Pictures Production; In association with The Canadian Broadcasting Corporation; With the participation of Telefilm Canada and the Ontario Film Development Corporation; Canada; Color; PG; 100 minutes; October release. CAST: Gordon Pinsent (John Munn), Jackie Burroughs (Missus), Randy Follet (Matt), Jessica Steen (Faith), Roland Hewgill (Fred Budgell), Timothy Webber (Denny Boland), Neil Munro (Tom Noble), Michael Wade (Sid Peddigrew), Jerry Doyle (Alf Sheppard), Jane Dingle (Mavis Sheppard), Frank Holden (Nish Morris), Barry Greene (Wallace Cahill), Ricky Raymond (Robert Cahill), Austin Davis (Len Peacock), Judy Furlong (Stella Peacock), Brian Downey (Burgess), Kevin Noble (Ted Pratt), Lulu Keating (Winn), George Earle (Mr. Godden), Greg Thomey (Jimmy Ludlow), Doug Seymour (Old Man), Rick Hollett (Sax Player), Paul Steffler (Pianist), Mack Furlong (Drummer)

Jackie Burroughs, Gordon Pinsent
in "John and the Missus" © *Cinema Group*

HOWLING III (Square Pictures) Producers, Charles Waterstreet, Philippe Mora; Executive Producers, Edward Simons, Steve Lane, Robert Pringle; Director/Screenplay, Philippe Mora; Based on the book *"Howling III"* by Gary Brander; Photography, Louis Irving; Editor, Lee Smith; Music, Allan Zavod; Special Effects, Bob McCarron; Designer/Costumes, Ross Major; Co-producer, Gilda Baracchi; Sound, Bob Clayton; Assistant Director, Stuart Wood; Production Manager, Rosslyn Abernethy; Casting, Forcast; A Bacannia Entertainment presentation; Australian; Color; Rated PG-13; October release. CAST: Barry Otto (Prof. Harry Beckmeyer), Imogen Annesley (Jerboa), Dasha Blahova (Olga Gorki), Max Fairchild (Thylo), Ralph Cotterill (Prof. Sharp), Leigh Biolos (Donny Martin), Frank Thring (Jack Citron), Michael Pate (President), Barry Humphries (Dame Edna Everage), Carole Skinner (Yara), Brian Adams (Gen. Miller), Bill Collins (Doctor), Christopher Pate (Security Agent)

BAD BLOOD Director/Screenplay, Leos Carax; Photography, Jean-Yves Escoffier; Editors, Nelly Quettier, Helene Muller; A Films Plain Chang-Soprofilms-FR3 Films Production; France; French with English subtitles; Not rated; 105 minutes; October release. CAST: Denis Lavant (Alex), Juliette Binoche (Anna), Michel Piccoli (Marc), Hans Meyer (Hans), Julie Delpy (Lise), Carroll Brooks (American Woman), Hugo Pratt (Boris), Serge Reggiani (Charlie)

LE SOURD DANS LA VILLE *(Deaf to the City)* Executive Producer, Louise Carre; Director, Mireille Dansereau; Screenplay, Mireille Dansereau, Michele Mailhot, Jean-Joseph Tremblay; Story, Therese Berube; Based on a novel by Marie-Claire Blaise; Photography, Michel Caron; Editor, Louise Cote; Music, Ginette Bellavance; Sound, Dominique Chartrand, Serge Beauchemin, Philippe Schultety; Art Director, Gaudeline Sauriol; Sets, Pierre Gelinas; Costumes, Denis Sperdouklis; A Maison des Quatres Arts production, with Telefilm Canada, Societe du Cinema du Quebec, SuperEcran, Radio Quebec; Canadian; Color; Not rated; 97 minutes; October release. CAST: Beatrice Picard (Florence), Guillaume Lemay-Thivierge (Mike), Angele Coutu (Gloria), Pierre Theriaut (Tim), Han Masson (Judith), Claude Renart (Charlie), Sophie Leger (Lucia)

A DEATH IN THE FAMILY Directors, Peter Wells, Stewart Main; Screenplay, Peter Wells; Color; 60 minutes; October release. CAST: John Watson (Andrew Boyd), Jon Brazier (Simon), Nancy Flyger (Mother), Derek Hardwick (Father), Paul Gittens (Brother), No other credits provided.

John Watson (the patient) in
"A Death in the Family"

ALFRED LALIBERTE, SCULPTEUR A Les Films Francois Brault/ Les Prod. Dix-Huit production; Producer, Claude Sylvestre; Director/ Screenplay, Jean-Pierre Lefebvre; Photography, Francois Brault; Editor, Barbara Easto; Music, Dominique Tremblay; Sound, Joseph Champagne, Daniel Masse, Philippe Hochard; Documentary/Drama; Color; Not rated; 80 minutes; October release. WITH: Paul Hebert, Odette Legendre, Albert Millaire, Marcel Sabourin, Nicole Filion, Francine Ruel

EAT THE RICH (New Line) Producer, Tim Van Rellim; Director, Peter Richardson; Screenplay, Peter Richardson, Pete Richens; Photography, Witold Stok; Editor, Chris Ridsale; Art Director, Caroline Amies; Color; British; Rated R; 92 minutes; October release. CAST: Ronald Allen (Commander Fortune), Robbie Coltrane (Jeremy), Sandra Dorne (Sandra), Jimmy Fagg (Jimmy), Lemmy (Spider), Lanah Pellay (Alex), Nosher Powell (Nosher), Fiona Richmond (Fiona), Ron Tarr (Ron), Paul McCartney, Linda McCartney, Miranda Richardson

LONG LIVE THE LADY! (International Film Exchange) Director/ Screenplay, Ermanno Olmi; Photography, Maurizio Zaccaro; Music, Georg Philip Teleman; A co-production of RAI Channel 1/ Cinemaundici with the collaboration of Istituto Luce; Presented by RAI Radio-televisione Italiana; Italian; Color; Not rated; 102 minutes; October release. CAST: Marco Esposito (Libenzio), Simona Brandalise (Corinna), Stefania Busarello (Anna), Simone Dalla Rosa (Mayo), Lorenzo Paolini (Ciccio), Tarcisio Tosi (Pigi), Marisa Abbate (The Lady), Luigi Cancellara (Man with the mustache), Alberto Francescato (Libenzio's Father), Giovanna Vidotto (Grandmother), Luca Dorizzi (Priest), Michele Authier, Graziella Menichelli (Clowns), No other credits provided

HELL WITHOUT LIMITS (Azteca Films) Director/Screenplay, Arturo Ripstein; Based on the novel by Jose Donoso; Photography, Miguel Garzon; Editor, Francisco Chiu; Music, Jaoquin Gutierrez Heras; Mexico, 1978; Spanish with English subtitles; Not rated; 110 minutes; October release. CAST: Roberto Cobo (La Manuela), Ana Martin (Japonesita), Gonzalo Vega (Pancho), Lucha Villa (La Japonesa), Carmen Salinas (Lucy)

PROJECT A (PART II) (Golden Harvest/Golden Ways) Executive Producer, Raymond Chow; Producer, Leonard Ho, Director, Jackie Chan; Co-ordinator, Willie Chan; Hong Kong; Cantonese with English subtitles; Color; Not rated; 98 minutes; October release. CAST: Jackie Chan, Maggie Cheung, Rosamund Kwan, Carina Lau, No other credits provided.

THE RIGHT HAND MAN (Filmdallas Pictures) Producers, Steven Grives, Tom Oliver, Basil Appleby; Director, Di Drew; Screenplay, Helen Hodgman; Story developed by Steven Grives; Photography, Peter James; Editor, Don Saunders; Music, Allan Zavod; Designer, Neil Angwin; Australian; Color; Rated R; 101 minutes; October release. CAST: Rupert Everett (Harry Ironminster), Hugo Weaving (Ned Devine), Arthur Dignam (Dr. Redbridge), Jennifer Claire (Lady Ironminster), Catherine McClements (Sarah Redbridge), Ralph Cotterill (Sam), Adam Cockburn (Violet Head), Tim Eliott (Lord Ironminster)

THE ROMANCE OF BOOK AND SWORD Director/Screenplay, Ann Hui; Adapted from the novel by Jin Yung; Editor, Chow Mukleung; Hong Kong; Color; 180 minutes; October release. CAST: Zhang Duo Fu, Da Shi Chang, Ai Nuo, Liu Jia, No other credits provided.

VERA (Grange/Kino) Producer/Director/Screenplay, Sergio Toledo; Photography, Rodolfo Sanchez, Tercio G. da Mota; Music, Arrigo Barnabe; Designer, Rene Silber; Brazilian; Portuguese with English subtitles; Not rated; 92 minutes; October release. CAST: Ana Beatriz Nogueira (Vera), Raul Cortez (Prof. Paulo Trauberg), Aida Leiner (Clara), Carlos Kroeber (Orphanage Director), Cida Almeida (Palzao), Adriana Abujamra (Telma), Imara Reis (Helena Trauberg), Norma Blum (Izolda), Abram Faarc, Liana Duval (Librarians)

YEELEN Producer/Director/Screenplay, Souleymane Cisse; Photography, Jean-Noel Ferragut, Jean-Michel Humeau; Editors, Dounamba Coulibaly, Andree Davanture, Marie-Catherine Miqueau, Jenny Frenck, Seipati N'Xumalo; Music, Michel Portal, with the participation of Salif Keita; Mali; Bambara with English subtitles; Not rated; 105 minutes; October release. CAST: Issiaka Kane (Son), Aoua Sangare (Peul Woman), Niamanto Sanogó (Father), Balla Moussa Keita (Peul King), Soumba Traore (Mother), Ismaila Sarr (Uncle), Youssouf Tenin Cisse (Boy), Koke Sangare (Komo Chief)

JEAN RENOIR, THE BOSS Directors, Jacques Rivette, Andre S. Labarthe; American version by Cherryl Carlissimo, Suzanne Fenn, Jackie Raynal; Presented by Zanzibar Productions; Documentary; French, 1967; French with subtitles; Not rated; 60 minutes; November release. WITH: Jean Renoir, Marcel Dalio, Jacques Rivette and others. No other credits provided

**Nosher Powell, Fiona Richmond
in "Eat the Rich"** © *New Line Cinema*

HYPOTHESIS OF A STOLEN PAINTING (Coralie Films International) Director/Screenplay, Raoul Ruiz; From an idea of Pierre Klossowski; Photography, Sacha Vierny; Editor, Patrice Royer; Music, Jorge Arriagada; France, 1978; French with English subtitles; Not rated; 70 minutes; November release. CAST: Jean Rougeul (Collector), Gabriel Gascon (Visitor's Voice), No other credits provided

STRIKE COMMANDO (Variety Film) Producer, Franco Gaudenzi; Director/Editor, Vincent Dawn (Bruno Mattei); Screenplay, Clyde Anderson; Story, Clyde Anderson, Vincent Dawn (Bruno Mattei); Photography, Richard Gras; Music, Lou Ceccarelli; Art Director, Bart Scavya; Dialog Director, Gene Luotto; A Flora Film production; Italian; Telecolor; Not rated; 102 minutes; November release. CAST: Reb Brown (Michael Ransom), Christopher Connelly (Col. Radek), Loes Kamma (Olga), Alan Collins (LeDuc), Alex Vitale (Jakoda), Edison Navarro (Lao), Karen Lopez (Cho-Li), Juliet D. Lee (Diem)

THE BURGLAR (IFEX) Producer, "Lenfilm" Studio; Director, Valeriy Ogorodnikov; Screenplay, Valeriy Priyomykhov; Photography, Valeriy Mironov; Art Director, Victor Ivanov; Music, Victor Kissin; Color; Not rated; 85 minutes; November release. CAST: Oleg Yelykomov, Konstantin Kinchev, and others

LOYALTIES (Cinema Group) Co-Producer/Director, Anne Wheeler; Producers, William Johnston, Ronald Lillie; Screenplay, Sharon Riis; Story, Sharon Riis, Anne Wheeler; Photography, Vic Sarin; Art Director, Richard Hudolin; Line Producer, Rob Iveson; Production Manager, Grace Gilroy; Assistant Director, Brad Turner; Casting, Gail Carr, Bette Chadwick; Costumes, Wendy Partridge; Sound, Garrell Clark; Special Effects, Dave Gauthier; Editor, Judy Krupanszky; Dialogue Coach, Jeremy Hart; Canadian; Color; Rated R; 98 minutes; November release. CAST: Kenneth Welsh (David Sutton), Tantoo Cardinal (Rosanne Ladouceur), Susan Wooldridge (Lily Sutton), Vera Martin (Beatrice), Diane Debassige (Leona), Tom Jackson (Eddy), Jeffrey Smith (Nicholas), Meredith Rimmer (Naomi), Alexander & Jonathan Tribiger (Jeremy), Christopher Barrington-Leigh (Robert), Yolanda Cardinal (Lisa), Dale Willier (Jesse), Wesley Semenovich (Wayne), Janet Wright (Audrey Sawchuck), Don MacKay (Mike Sawchuck), Paul Whitney (Joe Pilsudski), Tom Heaton (Pilot Henry), Sam Mottrich, Eric Kramer, Wendell Smith, Joan Hinz, Jill Dyck, Colin Vint, Veena Sood, Doris Chilcot, Terri Daniels, Susan MacNeill, Ben Cardinal, Bryan Fustukian, Larry Yachimec, Larry Musser, Eddy Washington, Joyce Vold, Eiko Waida, Emilie Chervigny, Alexandra Leigh, Joan Cole, Alison Bossy, Douglas Law, Patrick Bull, Mary Skare

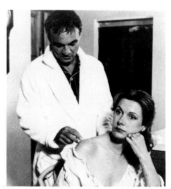

**Kenneth Welsh, Susan Wooldridge
in "Loyalties"** © *Cinema Group*

MY ENGLISH GRANDFATHER (IFEX) Producer, "Gruziafilm" Studio; Director, Nana Djordjadze; Screenplay, Irakly Kvirikadze; Photography, Levan Paatashvili; Color; Not rated; 90 minutes; November release. CAST: Zhanri Lolashvili, Ninel Chankveladze, Guram Pirtskhalava, and others.

LOVE IS A DOG FROM HELL (Cineplex Odeon) Executive Producer, Erwin Provoost; Director, Dominique Deruddere; Screenplay, Marc Didden, Dominique Deruddere; Photography, Willy Stassen; Sound, Peter Flamman; Designers, Hubert Pouille, Eric Van Belleghem; Editors, Ludo Troch, Guido Henderickx; Music, Raymond Van Het Groenewoud; a Multimedia production in cooperation with the Ministries for Culture of the Flemish Community and the French Community; Belgium/France; Not rated; 83 minutes; November release. CAST: Josse De Pauw (Harry Voss), Geert Hunaerts (Harry Voss age 12), Michael Pas (Stan), Gene Bervoets (Jeff), Amid Chakir (Bill), Florence Beliard (Princess), Karen Vanparys (Mother), Carmela Locantorc (Gina), Anne Van Essche (Liza Velani), Doriane Moretus (Marina)

THE WANNSEE CONFERENCE (Rearguard) Producer, Manfred Korytowski; Executive Producer, Siegfried B. Gloker; Director, Heinz Schirk; Screenplay, Paul Mommertz; Photography, Horst Schier; Editor, Ursula Mollinger; Art Directors, Robert Hofer-Ach, Barbara Siebner; Costumes, Diemut Remy; Sound, Sigbert Stark; Historical Advisor, Shlomo Aronson; An Infafilm GimbH Munich-Manfred Korytowski/Austrian Television-ORF/Bavarian Broadcasting Corp. co-production; West German; Color; Not rated; 87 minutes; November release. CAST: Robert Artzorn (Hofman), Friedrich Beckhaus (Mulle), Gerd Bockmann (Eichmann), Jochen Busse (Leibbrandt), Hans W. Bussinger (Luther), Harald Dietl (Meyer), Peter Fitz (Stuckart), Reinhard Glemnitz (Buhler), Dieter Groest (Neumann), Martin Luttge (Lange), Anita Mally (Secretary), Dietrich Matausch (Heydrich), Gerd Rigauer (Schongarth), Franz Rudnick (Kritzinger), Gunter Sporrle (Klopfer), Rainer Steffen (Friesler).

LE JOURNAL D'UN FOU *(The Diary of a Madman)* (Lydie Media) Director/Screenplay, Roger Coggio; Based on the story by Nicolai Gogol; Script Collaborator, Bernard G. Landry; Photography, Claude Lecomte; Editor, Helene Plemmianikoff; Music, Jean Musy; Designer, Guy-Claude Francois; Sound, Guy Rophe; Costumes, Francoise Tournafond; Co-produced by Films A2; Eastmancolor; France; Not rated; 90 minutes; November release. CAST: Roger Coggio (Auxence Popritchin), Fanny Cottencon (Sophie), Jean-Pierre Darras (Father), Charles Charras

SLATE, WYN & ME (Hemdale) Producer, Tom Burstall; Director/Screenplay, Don McLennan; Based on the novel *Slate and Wyn and Blanche McBride* by Georgia Savage; Photography, David Connell; Music, Peter Sullivan; Editor, Peter Friedrich; Costumes, Jeanie Cameron; Australian; Eastmancolor; Panavision; Not rated; 90 minutes; November release. CAST: Sigrid Thornton (Blanche McBride), Simon Burke (Wyn Jackson), Martin Sacks (Slate Jackson), Tommy Lewis (Morgan), Lesley Baker (Molly), Harold Baigent (Sammy), Michelle Torres (Daphne), Murray Fahey (Martin), Taya Straton (Pippa), Julia MacDougall (Del Downer), Peter Cummins (Old Man Downer), Reg Gorman (Sgt. Wilkinson), Warren Owens (Tommy), Eric MacPhan, Simon Westaway (Policemen), Kurt von Schneider (Truck Driver)

LAS MOVIDAS DEL MOFLES *(Mofles Escapades)* (Peliculas Mexicanas) Producers, Juan Abusaid Rios, Pedro Martin Gurrido; Director, Javier Duran; Screenplay, Francisco (Pancho) Sanchez, Marco Eduardo Contreras; Photography, Antonio Ruiz; Editor, Sergio Soto; Music, Gustavo Pimentel; A Tijuana Films production; Mexican; Color; Not rated; 89 minutes; December release. CAST: Rafael Inclan (Mofles), Manuel "Flaco" Ibanez (Abrelatas), Joaquin Garcia "Borolas" (Chopo), Charly Valentino (Don Gaston), Merle Uribe (Rebeca del Mar), Myrra Saaveda, Marla Cardenal, Alejandro Ciangherotti, Victor Junco, Raul "Chato" Padilla, Yirah Aparicio, Leo Villanuev, Oscar Fentanes, Sonia Pina, Polo Ortin, Estrella Fuentes, Alfredo "Pelon" Solares, Arturo Cobo, Gina Leal, Generaciion 2000, Los Infieles

THE ROSE KING (Filmverlag Futura) Producers, Werner Schroeter, Juliane Lorenz with FuturaFilm, Munich; Director, Werner Schroeter; Screenplay, Werner Schroeter, Magdalena Montezuma; Photography, Elfie Mikesch; Editor, Juliane Lorenz; German; German, Italian, Portuguese, Arabic, and English with English subtitles; Color; Not rated; 103 minutes; December release. CAST: Magdalena Montezuma (Anna), Mostefa Djadjam (Albert), Antonio Orlando (Fernando)

TRAGICO TERREMOTO EN MEXICO *(Tragic Earthquake in Mexico)* (Peliculas Mexicanas) Executive Producer, Miguel Kahen; Producer, Ignacio Garcia Gardelle; Director, Francisco Guerrero; Screenplay, Reyes Bercini; Based on an argument by Garcia Gardelle; Photography, Agustin Lara Alvarado; Editor, Jorge Pina; Music, Jep Epstein; A Producciones Metropolitan production, Documentary; Mexico; Color; Not rated; 96 minutes; December release

Michael Pas, Geert Hunaerts, Carmela Locantorc in "Love Is a Dog from Hell" © *Cineplex Odeon*

THE VIRGIN QUEEN OF ST. FRANCIS HIGH (Crown International) Executive Producer, Lawrence G. Ryckman; Director/Screenplay/Editor, Francesco Lucente; Photography, Kevin Alexander; Editorial Consultant, Rick Doe; Music, Danny Lowe, Brad Steckel, Brian Island; Sound, James F. Baillies, Per Asplund; Associate Producer, Alex Tadich; Assistant Director, Anisa Lalani; Casting, Olimpia Lucente, Angela Bitonti; A Pioneer Pictures production, in association with American Artists (Canada) Corp.; Canadian; Color; Rated PG; 94 minutes; December release. CAST: Joseph R. Straface (Mike), Stacy Christensen (Diane), J. T. Wotton (Charles), Anna-Lisa Iapaolo (Judy), Lee Barringer (Randy), Bev Wotton (Mother)

THE STRANGER (Columbia) Producer, Hugo Lamonica; Director, Adolfo Aristarian; Screenplay, Dan Gurskis; Photography, Horacio Maira; Designer, Abel Facello; Costumes, Felix Sanchez Plaza; Editor, Eduardo Lopez; Sound, Jose Luis Diaz; Music, Craig Safran; Executive Producer, Michael F. Nolin; Associate Producer, Peter Marai; Production Manager, Jorge Gundin; Assistant Directors, Alberto Lecchi, Antonio Barrio, Fernando Bassi; Production Manager, Noemi Nemirovsky; Production Coordinator, Luis Sartor; Special Effects, Eduardo Cundom; Assistant Editors, Brossy Reina, Fernando Guariniello, Ricardo Harrington; Set Decorator, Adriana Sforza; Stunts, Erik Cord; *"Mirrors and Lights"* Music, Craig Safan, Lyrics, Mark Mueller; Vocals, Debbie Davis; Dolby Stereo DeLuxe Color; Rated R; 88 minutes; December release. CAST: Bonnie Bedelia (Alice Kildee), Peter Riegert (Harris Kite), Barry Primus (Drake), David Spielberg (Hobby), Marcos Woinski (Macaw), Cecilia Roth (Anita Wren), Julio De Grazia (Jay), Ricardo Darin (Clark Whistler), Jacques Arndt (Rhea), Milton James (Brandt), Julio Kaufman (Dr. Hobby), Marina Magali (Actress), Tito Mendoza (Hobo), Adrian Ghio, Arturo Maly, Lala Sunblad, Nicolas Deane, Ernesto Larrese, Sacha Favelevic, Melvin Daniel, Patricia Zangaro, Heidi Froseth

LORD OF THE DANCE/DESTROYER OF ILLUSION (First Run Features) Producer, Franz-Christoph Giercke; Director, Richard Kohn; Photography, Jorg Jeshel; Sound, Barbara Becker; Editor, Noun Serra; Narrator, Peter Hudson; Story/Translations from the Tibetan, Richard Kohn; Construction, Gilles Baillot; Assistant Photographer, Alexandro Fernandez; Assistant Editor, Marie-Agnes Blum; Assistants to Mr. Kohn, Barbara Comstock, Rinchen Tsering Lama; Advisors to the Producer, Bonnie Freedman, Antony Roberts, Marie de Poncheville; Production Associates, Lisa van Gruisen, Sabine Lehmann, Charles Lambe; Sound Mixing, Elvire Lerner; Calligraphy, Yonten Gyatso; Documentary; Not rated; 113 minutes; December release

Trulshig Rinpoche (c) in "Lord of the Dance" © *First Run Pictures*

Alan Alda	Jane Alexander	Christopher Atkins	Nancy Allen	Frankie Avalon	Ann-Margret

BIOGRAPHICAL DATA

(Name, real name, place and date of birth, school attended)

AAMES, WILLIE (William Upton): 1961.

ABBOTT, DIAHNNE: NYC, 1945.

ABBOTT, JOHN: London, June 5, 1905.

ABRAHAM, F. MURRAY: Pittsburgh, PA, Oct. 24, 1939. UTx.

ADAMS, BROOKE: NYC, 1949. Dalton.

ADAMS, DON: NYC, Apr. 13, 1926.

ADAMS, EDIE (Elizabeth Edith Enke): Kingston, PA, Apr. 16, 1929. Juilliard, Columbia.

ADAMS, JULIE (Betty May): Waterloo, Iowa, Oct. 17, 1928. Little Rock Jr. College.

ADAMS, MAUD (Maud Wikstrom): Lulea, Sweden, Feb. 12, 1945.

ADDY, WESLEY: Omaha, NB, Aug. 4, 1913. UCLA.

ADJANI, ISABELLE: Germany, June 27, 1955.

ADRIAN, IRIS (Iris Adrian Hostetter): Los Angeles, May 29, 1913.

AGAR, JOHN: Chicago, Jan. 31, 1921.

AGUTTER, JENNY: Taunton, Eng, Dec. 20, 1952.

AIELLO, DANNY: June 20, 1935, NYC.

AIMEE, ANOUK (Dreyfus): Paris, Apr. 27, 1934. Bauer-Therond.

AKERS, KAREN: NYC, Oct. 13, 1945, Hunter Col.

AKINS, CLAUDE: Nelson, GA, May 25, 1936. Northwestern U.

ALBERGHETTI, ANNA MARIA: Pesaro, Italy, May 15, 1936.

ALBERT, EDDIE (Eddie Albert Heimberger): Rock Island, IL, Apr. 22, 1908. U. of Minn.

ALBERT, EDWARD: Los Angeles, Feb. 20, 1951. UCLA.

ALBRIGHT, LOLA: Akron, OH, July 20, 1925.

ALDA, ALAN: NYC, Jan. 28, 1936. Fordham.

ALDERSON, BROOKE: Dallas, Tx.

ALEJANDRO, MIGUEL: NYC, Feb. 21, 1958.

ALEXANDER, ERIKA: 1970, Philadelphia, Pa.

ALEXANDER, JANE (Quigley): Boston, MA, Oct. 28, 1939. Sarah Lawrence.

ALLEN, BYRON: 1962 Los Angeles, Ca.

ALLEN, DEBBIE: (Deborah) Jan. 16, 1950, Houston, Tx.; HowardU.

ALLEN, JOAN: Rochelle, IL, Aug. 20, 1956, EastIllU.

ALLEN, KAREN: Carrollton, IL. Oct. 5, 1951. UMd.

ALLEN, NANCY: NYC June 24, 1950.

ALLEN, REX: Wilcox, AZ, Dec. 31, 1922.

ALLEN, STEVE: New York City, Dec. 26, 1921.

ALLEN, WOODY (Allen Stewart Konigsberg): Brooklyn, Dec. 1, 1935.

ALLYSON, JUNE (Ella Geisman): Westchester, NY, Oct. 7, 1917.

ALONSO, MARIA CONCHITA: Cuba 1957.

ALT, CAROL: Dec. 1, 1960, Queens, NY. HofstraU.

ALVARADO, TRINI: NYC, 1967.

AMECHE, DON (Dominic Amichi): Kenosha, WI, May 31, 1908.

AMES, ED: Boston July 9, 1929.

AMES, LEON (Leon Wycoff): Portland, IN, Jan. 20, 1903.

AMIS, SUZY: Oklahoma City, Ok., Jan. 5, 1958. Actors Studio.

AMOS, JOHN: Newark, NJ, Dec. 27, 1940. Colo. U.

ANDERSON, JUDITH: Adelaide, Australia, Feb. 10, 1898.

ANDERSON, LONI: St. Paul, Mn., Aug. 5, 1946.

ANDERSON, LYNN: Grand Forkes, ND; Sept. 26, 1947. UCLA.

ANDERSON, MELODY: Canada 1955, Carlton U.

ANDERSON, MICHAEL, JR.: London, Eng., 1943.

ANDERSON, RICHARD DEAN: Minneapolis, Mn, 1951.

ANDERSSON, BIBI: Stockholm, Nov. 11, 1935. Royal Dramatic Sch.

ANDES, KEITH: Ocean City, NJ, July 12, 1920. Temple U., Oxford.

ANDRESS, URSULA: Switz., Mar. 19, 1936.

ANDREWS, ANTHONY: London, 1948.

ANDREWS, DANA: Collins, MS, Jan. 1, 1909. Sam Houston Col.

ANDREWS, HARRY: Tonbridge, Kent, Eng., Nov. 10, 1911.

ANDREWS, JULIE (Julia Elizabeth Wells): Surrey, Eng., Oct. 1, 1935.

ANNABELLA (Suzanne Georgette Charpentier): Paris, France, July 14, 1912/1909.

ANN-MARGRET (Olsson): Valsjobyn, Sweden, Apr. 28, 1941. Northwestern U.

ANSARA, MICHAEL: Lowell, MA, Apr. 15, 1922. Pasadena Playhouse.

ANTHONY, TONY: Clarksburg, WV, Oct. 16, 1937. Carnegie Tech.

ANTON, SUSAN: Yucaipa, CA. Oct. 12, 1950. Bernardino Col.

ANTONELLI, LAURA: Pola, Italy.

ARANHA, RAY: Miami, Fl, May 1, 1939. FlaA&M, AADA.

ARCHER, ANNE: Los Angeles, Aug. 25, 1947.

ARCHER, JOHN (Ralph Bowman): Osceola, NB, May 8, 1915. USC.

ARDEN, EVE (Eunice Quedens): Mill Valley, CA, Apr. 30, 1912.

ARKIN, ALAN: NYC, Mar. 26, 1934. LACC.

ARNAZ, DESI, JR.: Los Angeles, Jan. 19, 1953.

ARNAZ, LUCIE: Hollywood, July 17, 1951.

ARNESS, JAMES (Aurness): Minneapolis, MN, May 26, 1923. Beloit College.

ARTHUR, BEATRICE (Frankel): NYC, May 13, 1924. New School.

ARTHUR, JEAN: NYC, Oct. 17, 1905.

ASHCROFT, PEGGY: London, Eng., Dec. 22, 1907.

ASHLEY, ELIZABETH (Elizabeth Ann Cole): Ocala, FL, Aug. 30, 1939.

ASSANTE, ARMAND: NYC, Oct. 4, 1949. AADA.

ASTIN, JOHN: Baltimore, MD, Mar. 30, 1930. U. Minn.

ASTIN, MacKENZIE: 1973, Los Angeles.

ASTIN, SEAN: 1971, Los Angeles.

ASTIN, PATTY DUKE: (see Patty Duke)

ATHERTON, WILLIAM: Orange, CT, July 30, 1947. Carnegie Tech.

ATKINS, CHRISTOPHER: Rye, NY, Feb. 21, 1961.

ATTENBOROUGH, RICHARD: Cambridge, Eng., Aug. 29, 1923. RADA.

AUBERJONOIS, RENE: NYC, June 1, 1940. Carnegie Tech.

AUDRAN, STEPHANE: Versailles, Fr., 1933.

AUGER, CLAUDINE: Paris, Apr. 26, 1942. Dramatic Cons.

AULIN, EWA: Stockholm, Sweden, Feb. 14, 1950.

AUMONT, JEAN PIERRE: Paris, Jan. 5, 1909. French Nat'l School of Drama.

AUTRY, GENE: Tioga, TX, Sept. 29, 1907.

AVALON, FRANKIE (Francis Thomas Avallone): Philadelphia, Sept. 18, 1940.

Kevin
Bacon

Carroll
Baker

Gene
Barry

Bonnie
Bedelia

Richard
Benjamin

Candice
Bergen

AYKROYD, DAN: Ottawa, Can., July 1, 1952.

AYRES, LEW: Minneapolis, MN, Dec. 28, 1908.

AZNAVOUR, CHARLES (Varenagh Aznourian): Paris, May 22, 1924.

BACALL, LAUREN (Betty Perske): NYC, Sept. 16, 1924. AADA.

BACH, BARBARA: Aug. 27, 1946.

BACKER, BRIAN: NYC, Dec. 5, 1956. Neighborhood Playhouse.

BACKUS, JIM: Cleveland, Ohio, Feb. 25, 1913. AADA.

BACON, KEVIN: Philadelphia, PA., July 8, 1958.

BAILEY, PEARL: Newport News, VA, March 29, 1918.

BAIN, BARBARA: Chicago, Sept. 13, 1934. U. ILL.

BAIO, SCOTT: Brooklyn, NY, Sept. 22, 1961.

BAKER, BLANCHE: NYC, Dec. 20, 1956.

BAKER, CARROLL: Johnstown, PA, May 28, 1931. St. Petersburg Jr. College.

BAKER, DIANE: Hollywood, CA, Feb. 25, 1938. USC.

BAKER, KATHY WHITTON: Midland, TX., June 8, 1950. UCBerkley.

BALABAN, ROBERT (Bob); Chicago, Aug. 16, 1945. Colgate.

BALDWIN, ADAM: Chicago, IL. 1962.

BALDWIN, ALEC: Massapequa, NY, Apr. 3, 1958. NYU.

BALE, CHRISTIAN: 1974, Bournemouth, Eng.

BALIN, INA: Brooklyn, Nov. 12, 1937. NYU.

BALL, LUCILLE: Celaron, NY, Aug. 6, 1910. Chatauqua Musical Inst.

BALSAM, MARTIN: NYC, Nov. 4, 1919. Actors Studio.

BANCROFT, ANNE (Anna Maria Italiano): Bronx, NY, Sept. 17, 1931. AADA.

BANES, LISA: Chagrin Falls, Oh, July 9, 1955, Juilliard.

BANNEN, IAN: Airdrie, Scot., June 29, 1928.

BARANSKI, CHRISTINE: Buffalo, NY, May 2, 1952, Juilliard.

BARBEAU, ADRIENNE: Sacramento, CA. June 11, 1945. Foothill Col.

BARDOT, BRIGITTE: Paris, Sept. 28, 1934.

BARKIN, ELLEN: Bronx, NY, 1959. Hunter Col.

BARNES, BINNIE (Gitelle Enoyce Barnes): London, Mar. 25, 1906

BARNES, C. B. (Christopher): 1973, Portland, Me.

BARRAULT, JEAN-LOUIS: Vesinet, France, Sept. 8, 1910.

BARRAULT, MARIE-CHRISTINE: Paris, 1946.

BARRETT, MAJEL (Hudec): Columbus, OH, Feb. 23. Western Reserve U.

BARRON, KEITH: Mexborough, Eng., Aug. 8, 1936. Sheffield Playhouse.

BARRY, GENE (Eugene Klass): NYC, June 14, 1921.

BARRY, NEILL: NYC, Nov. 29, 1965.

BARRYMORE, DEBORAH: London, London Acad.

BARRYMORE, DREW: Los Angeles, Feb. 22, 1975.

BARRYMORE, JOHN BLYTH: Beverly Hills, CA, June 4, 1932. St. John's Military Academy.

BARTHOLOMEW, FREDDIE: London, Mar. 28, 1924.

BARYSHNIKOV, MIKHAIL: Riga, Latvia, Jan. 27, 1948.

BASINGER, KIM: Athens, GA., Dec. 8, 1953. Neighborhood Playhouse.

BATEMAN, JASON: 1968 Los Angeles

BATEMAN, JUSTINE: Rye, NY, Feb. 19, 1966.

BATES, ALAN: Allestree, Derbyshire, Eng., Feb. 17, 1934. RADA.

BATES, JEANNE: San Francisco, CA., May 21. RADA.

BAUER, STEVEN: (Steven Rocky Echevarria): Havana, Cuba, Dec. 2, 1956. UMiami.

BAXTER, KEITH: South Wales, Apr. 29, 1933. RADA.

BEAL, JOHN (J. Alexander Bliedung): Joplin, MO, Aug. 13, 1909. PA. U.

BEART, EMMANUELLE: 1965, Gassin, France.

BEATTY, NED: Louisville, KY. July 6, 1937.

BEATTY, ROBERT: Hamilton, Ont., Can., Oct. 19, 1909. U. of Toronto.

BEATTY, WARREN: Richmond, VA, March 30, 1937.

BECK, MICHAEL: Horseshoe Lake, AR, 1948.

BEDELIA, BONNIE: NYC, Mar. 25, 1952. Hunter Col.

BEDI, KABIR: India, 1945.

BEERY, NOAH, JR.: NYC, Aug. 10, 1916. Harvard Military Academy.

BEGLEY, ED, JR.: NYC, Sept. 16, 1949.

BELAFONTE, HARRY: NYC, Mar. 1, 1927.

BELASCO, LEON: Odessa, Russia, Oct. 11, 1902.

BEL GEDDES, BARBARA: NYC, Oct. 31, 1922.

BELL, TOM: Liverpool, Eng., 1932.

BELLAMY, RALPH: Chicago, June 17, 1904.

BELLER, KATHLEEN: NYC, 1957.

BELLWOOD, PAMELA (King): Scarsdale, NY June 26.

BELMONDO, JEAN PAUL: Paris, Apr. 9, 1933.

BELUSHI, JAMES: Chicago, May 15, 1954.

BENEDICT, DIRK (Niewoehner): White Sulphur Springs, MT. March 1, 1945. Whitman Col.

BENJAMIN, RICHARD: NYC, May 22, 1938. Northwestern U.

BENNENT, DAVID: Lausanne, Sept. 9, 1966.

BENNETT, BRUCE (Herman Brix): Tacoma, WA, May 19, 1909. U. Wash.

BENNETT, JILL: Penang, Malay, Dec. 24, 1931.

BENNETT, JOAN: Palisades, NJ, Feb. 27, 1910. St. Margaret's School.

BENSON, ROBBY: Dallas, TX, Jan 21, 1957.

BERENGER, TOM: Chicago, May 31, 1950, UMo.

BERENSON, MARISSA: NYC, Feb. 15, 1947.

BERGEN, CANDICE: Los Angeles, May 9, 1946. U. PA.

BERGEN, POLLY: Knoxville, TN, July 14, 1930. Compton Jr. College.

BERGER, HELMUT: Salzburg, Aus., 1942.

BERGER, SENTA: Vienna, May 13, 1941. Vienna Sch. of Acting.

BERGER, WILLIAM: Austria, Jan. 20, 1928. Columbia.

BERGERAC, JACQUES: Biarritz, France, May 26, 1927. Paris U.

BERLE, MILTON (Berlinger): NYC, July 12, 1908.

BERLIN, JEANNIE: Los Angeles, Nov. 1, 1949.

BERLINGER, WARREN: Brooklyn, Aug. 31, 1937. Columbia.

BERNHARD, SANDRA: June 6, 1955, Flint, Mi.

BERNSEN, CORBIN: Los Angeles, Sept. 7, 1954, UCLA.

BERRI, CLAUDE (Langmann): Paris, July 1, 1934.

BERRIDGE, ELIZABETH: Westchester, NY, May 2, 1962. Strasberg Inst.

BERTO, JULIET: Grenoble, France, Jan. 1947.

BEST, JAMES: Corydon, IN, July 26, 1926.

BETTGER, LYLE: Philadelphia, Feb. 13, 1915. AADA.

BEYMER, RICHARD: Avoca, IA, Feb. 21, 1939.

BIEHN, MICHAEL: Ala. 1957.

BIKEL, THEODORE: Vienna, May 2, 1924. RADA.

BIRNEY, DAVID: Washington, DC, Apr. 23, 1939. Dartmouth, UCLA.

BIRNEY, REED: Alexandria, VA., Sept. 11, 1954. Boston U.

BISHOP, JOEY (Joseph Abraham Gottlieb): Bronx, NY, Feb. 3, 1918.

BISHOP, JULIE (formerly Jacqueline Wells): Denver, CO, Aug. 30, 1917. Westlake School.

BISSET, JACQUELINE: Waybridge, Eng., Sept. 13, 1944.

BIXBY, BILL: San Francisco, Jan. 22, 1934. U. CAL.

BLACK, KAREN (Ziegler): Park Ridge, IL, July 1, 1942. Northwestern.

BLADES, RUBEN: Panama 1948, Harvard.

BLAINE, VIVIAN (Vivian Stapleton): Newark, NJ, Nov. 21, 1923.

BLAIR, BETSY (Betsy Boger): NYC, Dec. 11, 1923.

BLAIR, JANET (Martha Jane Lafferty): Blair, PA, Apr. 23, 1921.

BLAIR, LINDA: Westport, CT, Jan. 22, 1959.

BLAKE, AMANDA (Beverly Louise Neill): Buffalo, NY, Feb. 20, 1921.

BLAKE, ROBERT (Michael Gubitosi): Nutley, NJ, Sept. 18, 1933.

BLAKELY, SUSAN: Frankfurt, Germany 1950. U. TEX.

BLAKLEY, RONEE: Stanley, ID, 1946. Stanford U.

BLOOM, CLAIRE: London, Feb. 15, 1931. Badminton School.

BLYTH, ANN: Mt. Kisco, NY, Aug. 16, 1928. New Wayburn Dramatic School.

BOCHNER, HART: Toronto, 1956. U. San Diego.

BOGARDE, DIRK: London, Mar. 28, 1918. Glasgow & Univ. College.

BOHRINGER, RICHARD: 1942 Paris

BOLKAN, FLORINDA (Florinda Soares Bulcao): Ceara, Brazil, Feb. 15, 1941.

BOND, DEREK: Glasgow, Scot., Jan. 26, 1920. Askes School.

BONET, LISA: Nov. 16, 1967, San Francisco

BONO, SONNY (Salvatore): Detroit, MI, Feb. 16, 1935.

BOONE, PAT: Jacksonville, FL, June 1, 1934. Columbia U.

BOOTH, SHIRLEY (Thelma Ford): NYC, Aug. 30, 1907.

BORGNINE, ERNEST (Borgnino): Hamden, CT, Jan. 24, 1918. Randall School.

BOSCO, PHILIP: Jersey City, NJ, Sept. 26, 1930, CatholicU.

BOSTWICK, BARRY: San Mateo, CA., Feb. 24, 1945. NYU.

BOTTOMS, JOSEPH: Santa Barbara, CA, Aug. 30, 1954.

BOTTOMS, TIMOTHY: Santa Barbara, CA, Aug. 30, 1951.

BOULTING, INGRID: Transvaal, So. Africa, 1947.

BOVEE, LESLIE: Bend, OR, 1952.

BOWIE, DAVID: (David Robert Jones) Brixton, South London, Eng. Jan. 8, 1947.

BOWKER, JUDI: Shawford, Eng., Apr. 6, 1954.

BOXLEITNER, BRUCE: Elgin, IL., May 12, 1950.

BOYLE, PETER: Philadelphia, PA, Oct. 18, 1933. LaSalle Col.

BRACKEN, EDDIE: NYC, Feb. 7, 1920. Professional Children's School.

BRADLEY, BRIAN: Philadelphia, UFla.

BRAEDEN, ERIC: (Hans Gudegast): Braeden, Germany.

BRAGA, SONIA: Maringa, Brazil, 1951.

BRAND, NEVILLE: Kewanee, IL, Aug. 13, 1920.

BRANDO, JOCELYN: San Francisco, Nov. 18, 1919. Lake Forest College, AADA.

BRANDO, MARLON: Omaha, NB, Apr. 3, 1924. New School.

BRANDON, CLARK: NYC 1959.

BRANDON, HENRY: Berlin, Ger., June 18, 1912. Stanford.

BRANDON, MICHAEL (Feldman): Brooklyn, NY.

BRANTLEY, BETSY: Rutherfordton, NC, 1955. London Central Sch. of Drama.

BRAZZI, ROSSANO: Bologna, Italy, Sept. 18, 1916. U. Florence.

BRENNAN, EILEEN: Los Angeles, CA., Sept. 3, 1935. AADA.

BRIALY, JEAN-CLAUDE: Aumale, Algeria, 1933. Strasbourg Cons.

BRIAN, DAVID: NYC, Aug. 5, 1914. CCNY.

BRIDGES, BEAU: Los Angeles, Dec. 9, 1941. UCLA.

BRIDGES, JEFF: Los Angeles, Dec. 4, 1949.

BRIDGES, LLOYD: San Leandro, CA, Jan. 15, 1913.

BRINKLEY, CHRISTIE: Malibu, CA., Feb. 2, 1954.

BRISEBOIS, DANIELLE: Brooklyn, June 28, 1969.

BRITT, MAY (Maybritt Wilkins): Sweden, Mar. 22, 1936.

BRITTANY, MORGAN: (Suzanne Caputo): Los Angeles, 1950.

BRITTON, TONY: Birmingham, Eng., June 9, 1924.

BRODERICK, MATTHEW: NYC, Mar. 21, 1963.

BRODIE, STEVE (Johnny Stevens): Eldorado, KS, Nov. 25, 1919.

BROLIN, JAMES: Los Angeles, July 18, 1940. UCLA.

BROMFIELD, JOHN (Farron Bromfield): South Bend, IN, June 11, 1922. St. Mary's College.

BRONSON, CHARLES (Buchinsky): Ehrenfield, PA, Nov. 3, 1920.

BROOKES, JACQUELINE: Montclair, NJ, July 24, 1930, RADA.

BROOKS, ALBERT (Einstein): Los Angeles, July 22, 1947.

BROOKS, MEL (Melvyn Kaminski): Brooklyn, June 28, 1926.

BROSNAN, PIERCE: County Meath, Ireland, May 16, 1952.

BROWN, BLAIR: Washington, DC, 1948; Pine Manor.

BROWN, BRYAN: Panania, Aust., 1947.

BROWN, GARY (Christian Brando): Hollywood, Ca., 1958.

BROWN, GEORG STANFORD: Havana, Cuba, June 24, 1943. AMDA.

BROWN, JAMES: Desdemona, TX, Mar. 22, 1920. Baylor U.

BROWN, JIM: St. Simons Island, NY, Feb. 17, 1935. Syracuse U.

BROWNE, CORAL: Melbourne, Aust., July 23, 1913.

BROWNE, LESLIE: NYC, 1958.

BUCHHOLZ, HORST: Berlin, Ger., Dec. 4, 1933. Ludwig Dramatic School.

BUCKLEY, BETTY: Big Spring, Tx., July 3, 1947. TxCU.

BUETEL, JACK: Dallas, TX, Sept. 5, 1917.

BUJOLD, GENEVIEVE: Montreal, Can., July 1, 1942.

BURGHOFF, GARY: May 24, 1943 Bristol, Ct.

BURGI, RICHARD: July 30, 1958, Montclair, NJ

BURKE, DELTA: Orlando, FL, July 30, 1956, LAMDA.

BURKE, PAUL: New Orleans, July 21, 1926. Pasadena Playhouse.

BURNETT, CAROL: San Antonio, TX, Apr. 26, 1933. UCLA.

BURNS, CATHERINE: NYC, Sept. 25, 1945. AADA.

BURNS, GEORGE (Nathan Birnbaum): NYC, Jan. 20, 1896.

BURR, RAYMOND: New Westminster, B.C., Can., May 21, 1917. Stanford, U. CAL., Columbia.

BURSTYN, ELLEN (Edna Rae Gillooly): Detroit, MI, Dec. 7, 1932.

BURTON, LeVAR: Los Angeles, CA. Feb. 16, 1958. UCLA.

BUSEY, GARY: Goose Creek, Tx, June 29, 1944.

BUSKER, RICKY: 1974 Rockford, Il.

BUTTONS, RED (Aaron Chwatt): NYC, Feb. 5, 1919.

BUZZI, RUTH: Wequetequock, RI, July 24, 1936. Pasadena Playhouse.

BYGRAVES, MAX: London, Oct. 16, 1922. St. Joseph's School.

BYRNES, EDD: NYC, July 30, 1933. Haaren High.

CAAN, JAMES: Bronx, NY, Mar. 26, 1939.

CAESAR, SID: Yonkers, NY, Sept. 8, 1922.

CAGE, NICOLAS: Long Beach, CA. 1964.

CAINE, MICHAEL (Maurice Michelwhite): London, Mar. 14, 1933.

CAINE, SHAKIRA (Baksh): Guyana, Feb. 23, 1947. Indian Trust Col.

CALHOUN, RORY (Francis Timothy Durgin): Los Angeles, Aug. 8, 1922.

CALLAN, MICHAEL (Martin Calinieff): Philadelphia, Nov. 22, 1935.

CALVERT, PHYLLIS: London, Feb. 18, 1917. Margaret Morris School.

CALVET, CORRINE (Corrine Dibos): Paris, Apr. 30, 1925. U. Paris.

| Kim Cattrall | Miles Chapin | Stockard Channing | Richard Chaves | Jamie Lee Curtis | Christopher Collet |

CAMERON, KIRK: Panorama City, CA, 1970.

CAMP, COLLEEN: San Francisco, 1953.

CAMPBELL, BILL: Chicago 1960.

CAMPBELL, GLEN: Delight, AR, Apr. 22, 1935.

CAMPBELL, TISHA: 1969 Newark, NJ

CANALE, GIANNA MARIA: Reggio Calabria, Italy, Sept. 12.

CANDY, JOHN: Oct. 11, 1950, Toronto, CAN.

CANNON, DYAN (Samille Diane Friesen): Tacoma, WA, Jan. 4, 1937.

CANTU, DOLORES: 1957, San Antonio, TX.

CAPERS, VIRGINIA: Sumter, SC, 1925. Juilliard.

CAPSHAW, KATE: Ft. Worth, TX. 1953. UMo.

CAPUCINE (Germaine Lefebvre): Toulon, France, Jan. 6, 1933.

CARA, IRENE: NYC, Mar. 18, 1958.

CARDINALE, CLAUDIA: Tunis, N. Africa, Apr. 15, 1939. College Paul Cambon.

CAREY, HARRY, JR.: Saugus, CA, May 16, 1921. Black Fox Military Academy.

CAREY, MACDONALD: Sioux City, IA, Mar. 15, 1913. U. of Wisc., U. Iowa.

CAREY, PHILIP: Hackensack, NJ, July 15, 1925. U. Miami.

CARMEN, JULIE: Mt. Vernon, NY, Apr. 4, 1954.

CARMICHAEL, IAN: Hull, Eng., June 18, 1920. Scarborough Coi.

CARNE, JUDY (Joyce Botterill): Northampton, Eng., 1939. Bush-Davis Theatre School.

CARNEY, ART: Mt. Vernon, NY, Nov. 4, 1918.

CARON, LESLIE: Paris, July 1, 1931. Nat'l Conservatory, Paris.

CARPENTER, CARLETON: Bennington, VT, July 10, 1926. Northwestern.

CARR, VIKKI (Florence Cardona): July 19, 1942. San Fernando Col.

CARRADINE, DAVID: Hollywood, Dec. 8, 1936. San Francisco State.

CARRADINE, JOHN: NYC, Feb. 5, 1906.

CARRADINE, KEITH: San Mateo, CA, Aug. 8, 1950. Colo. State U.

CARRADINE, ROBERT: San Mateo, CA, Mar. 24, 1954.

CARREL, DANY: Tourane, Indochina, Sept. 20, 1936. Marseilles Cons.

CARRIERE, MATHIEU: West Germany 1950.

CARROLL, DIAHANN (Johnson): NYC, July 17, 1935. NYU.

CARROLL, PAT: Shreveport, LA, May 5, 1927. Catholic U.

CARSON, JOHN DAVID: 1951, Calif. Valley Col.

CARSON, JOHNNY: Corning, IA, Oct. 23, 1925. U. of Neb.

CARSTEN, PETER (Ransenthaler): Weissenberg, Bavaria, Apr. 30, 1929. Munich Akademie.

CARTER, NELL: Birmingham, AL., Sept. 13, 1948.

CASH, ROSALIND: Atlantic City, NJ, Dec. 31, 1938. CCNY.

CASON, BARBARA: Memphis, TN, Nov. 15, 1933. U. Iowa.

CASS, PEGGY (Mary Margaret): Boston, May 21, 1925.

CASSAVETES, JOHN: NYC, Dec. 9, 1929. Colgate College, AADA.

CASSAVETES, NICK: NYC 1959, Syracuse U, AADA.

CASSEL, JEAN-PIERRE: Paris, Oct. 27, 1932.

CASSIDY, DAVID: NYC, Apr. 12, 1950.

CASSIDY, JOANNA: Camden, NJ, 1944. Syracuse U.

CASSIDY, PATRICK: Los Angeles, CA, Jan. 4, 1961.

CASSIDY, SHAUN: Los Angeles, CA., Sept. 27, 1958.

CASTELLANO, RICHARD: Bronx, NY, Sept. 3, 1934.

CATTRALL, KIM: England, Aug. 21, 1956, AADA.

CAULFIELD, JOAN: Orange, NJ, June 1, 1922. Columbia U.

CAULFIELD, MAXWELL: Glasgow, Scot., Nov. 23, 1959.

CAVANI, LILIANA: Bologna, Italy, Jan. 12, 1937. U. Bologna.

CHAKIRIS, GEORGE: Norwood, OH, Sept. 16, 1933.

CHAMBERLAIN, RICHARD: Beverly Hills, CA, March 31, 1935. Pomona.

CHAMPION, MARGE: Los Angeles, Sept. 2, 1923.

CHANNING, CAROL: Seattle, Wa., Jan. 31, 1921. Bennington.

CHANNING, STOCKARD (Susan Stockard): NYC, Feb. 13, 1944. Radcliffe.

CHAPIN, MILES: NYC, Dec. 6, 1954. HB Studio.

CHAPLIN, GERALDINE: Santa Monica, CA, July 31, 1944. Royal Ballet.

CHAPLIN, SYDNEY: Los Angeles, Mar. 31, 1926. Lawrenceville.

CHARISSE, CYD (Tula Ellice Finklea): Amarillo, TX, Mar. 3, 1922. Hollywood Professional School.

CHASE, CHEVY (Cornelius Crane Chase): NYC, Oct. 8, 1943.

CHAVES, RICHARD: Jacksonville, FL, Oct. 9, 1951, Occidental Col.

CHEN, JOAN: 1961 Shanghai, Cal-State.

CHER (Cherilyn Sarkirian) May 20, 1946, El Centro, CA.

CHIARI, WALTER: Verona, Italy, 1930.

CHONG, RAE DAWN: Vancouver, Can., 1962.

CHRISTIAN, LINDA (Blanca Rosa Welter): Tampico, Mex., Nov. 13, 1923.

CHRISTIE, JULIE: Chukua, Assam, India, Apr. 14, 1941.

CHRISTOPHER, DENNIS (Carelli): Philadelphia, PA, Dec. 2, 1955. Temple U.

CHRISTOPHER, JORDAN: Youngstown, OH, Oct. 23, 1940. Kent State.

CILENTO, DIANE: Queensland, Australia, Oct. 5, 1933. AADA.

CLAPTON, ERIC: London, Mar. 30, 1945.

CLARK, DANE: NYC, Feb. 18, 1915. Cornell, Johns Hopkins U.

CLARK, DICK: Mt. Vernon, NY, Nov. 30, 1929. Syracuse U.

CLARK, MAE: Philadelphia, Aug. 16, 1910.

CLARK, PETULA: Epsom, England, Nov. 15, 1932.

CLARK, SUSAN: Sarnid, Ont., Can., Mar. 8, 1940. RADA.

CLAY, ANDREW: Brooklyn, 1958, Kingsborough Col.

CLAYBURGH, JILL: NYC, Apr. 30, 1944. Sarah Lawrence.

CLERY, CORRINNE: Italy, 1950.

CLOONEY, ROSEMARY: Maysville, KY, May 23, 1928.

CLOSE, GLENN: Greenwich, CT., Mar. 19, 1947. William & Mary Col.

COBURN, JAMES: Laurel, NB, Aug. 31, 1928. LACC.

COCA, IMOGENE: Philadelphia, Nov. 18, 1908.

CODY, KATHLEEN: Bronx, NY, Oct. 30, 1953.

COLBERT, CLAUDETTE (Lily Chauchoin): Paris, Sept. 15, 1903. Art Students League.

COLE, GEORGE: London, Apr. 22, 1925.

COLEMAN, GARY: Zion, IL., Feb. 8, 1968.

COLEMAN, JACK: 1958. Easton, PA., Duke U.

COLLETT, CHRISTOPHER: NYC, Mar. 13, 1968. Strasberg Inst.

COLLINS, JOAN: London, May 21, 1933. Francis Holland School.

COLLINS, KATE: 1959.

COLLINS, STEPHEN: Des Moines, IA, Oct. 1, 1947. Amherst.

COLON, MIRIAM: Ponce, PR., 1945. UPR.

COMER, ANJANETTE: Dawson, TX, Aug. 7, 1942. Baylor, Tex. U.

CONANT, OLIVER: NYC, Nov. 15, 1955. Dalton.

CONAWAY, JEFF: NYC, Oct. 5, 1950. NYC.

CONDE, RITA (Elizabeth Eleanor): Cuba.

CONNERY, SEAN: Edinburgh, Scot., Aug. 25, 1930.

CONNERY, JASON: London 1962.

CONNORS, CHUCK (Kevin Joseph Connors): Brooklyn, Apr. 10, 1921. Seton Hall College.

CONNORS, MIKE (Krekor Ohanian): Fresno, CA, Aug. 15, 1925. UCLA.

CONRAD, WILLIAM: Louisville, KY, Sept. 27, 1920.

CONROY, KEVIN: 1956 Westport, Ct. Juilliard

CONVERSE, FRANK: St. Louis, MO, May 22, 1938. Carnegie Tech.

CONVY, BERT: St. Louis, MO, July 23, 1935. UCLA.

CONWAY, KEVIN: NYC, May 29, 1942.

CONWAY, TIM (Thomas Daniel): Willoughby, OH, Dec. 15, 1933. Bowling Green State.

COOK, ELISHA, JR.: San Francisco, Dec. 26, 1907. St. Albans.

COOPER, BEN: Hartford, CT, Sept. 30, 1932. Columbia U.

COOPER, CHRISTOPHER: July 9, 1951, Kansas City, Mo. UMo.

COOPER, JACKIE: Los Angeles, Sept. 15, 1921.

COPELAND, JOAN: NYC, June 1, 1922. Brooklyn Col. RADA.

CORBETT, GRETCHEN: Portland, OR, Aug. 13, 1947. Carnegie Tech.

CORBY, ELLEN (Hansen): Racine, WI, June 13, 1913.

CORCORAN, DONNA: Quincy, MA, Sept. 29, 1942.

CORD, ALEX (Viespi): Floral Park, NY, Aug. 3, 1931. NYU, Actors Studio.

CORDAY, MARA (Marilyn Watts): Santa Monica, CA, Jan. 3, 1932.

COREY, JEFF: NYC, Aug. 10, 1914. Fagin School.

CORLAN, ANTHONY: Cork City, Ire., May 9, 1947. Birmingham School of Dramatic Arts.

CORLEY, AL: Missouri, 1956. Actors Studio.

CORNTHWAITE, ROBERT: St. Helens, OR. Apr. 28, 1917. USC.

CORRI, ADRIENNE: Glasgow, Scot., Nov. 13, 1933. RADA.

CORTESA, VALENTINA: Milan, Italy, Jan. 1, 1925.

COSBY, BILL: Philadelphia, July 12, 1937. Temple U.

COSTER, NICOLAS: London, Dec. 3, 1934. Neighborhood Playhouse.

COSTNER, KEVIN: 1954, Compton, Ca., CalStaU.

COTTEN, JOSEPH: Petersburg, VA, May 13, 1905.

COURTENAY, TOM: Hull, Eng., Feb. 25, 1937. RADA.

COURTLAND, JEROME: Knoxville, TN, Dec. 27, 1926.

COYOTE, PETER (Cohon): 1942.

COX, COURTNEY: 1964, Birmingham, Al.

CRAIG, MICHAEL: India, Jan. 27, 1929.

CRAIN, JEANNE: Barstow, CA, May 25, 1925.

CREMER, BRUNO: Paris, 1929.

CRENNA, RICHARD: Los Angeles, Nov. 30, 1926. USC.

CRISTAL, LINDA (Victoria Moya): Buenos Aires, Feb. 25, 1934.

CRONYN, HUME (Blake): July 18, 1911 Ontario, Can.

CROSBY, HARRY: Los Angeles, CA, Aug. 8, 1958.

CROSBY, KATHRYN GRANT: (see Kathryn Grant)

CROSBY, MARY FRANCES: Calif., Sept. 14, 1959.

CROSS, BEN: London, 1948. RADA.

CROSS, MURPHY (Mary Jane): Laurelton, MD, June 22, 1950.

CROUSE, LINDSAY ANN: NYC, May 12, 1948. Radcliffe.

CROWLEY, PAT: Olyphant, PA, Sept. 17, 1932.

CRUISE, TOM (T. C. Mapother IV): July 3, 1962, Syracuse, NY.

CRYER, JON: NYC, Apr. 16, 1965, RADA.

CRYSTAL, BILLY: Long Beach, NY, Mar. 14, 1947. Marshall U.

CULLUM, JOHN: Knoxville, TN, Mar. 2, 1930. U. Tenn.

CULLUM, JOHN DAVID: Mar. 1, 1966, NYC

CULP, ROBERT: Oakland, CA., Aug. 16, 1930. U. Wash.

CUMMINGS, CONSTANCE: Seattle, WA, May 15, 1910.

CUMMINGS, QUINN: Hollywood, Aug. 13, 1967.

CUMMINGS, ROBERT: Joplin, MO, June 9, 1910. Carnegie Tech.

CUMMINS, PEGGY: Prestatyn, N. Wales, Dec. 18, 1926. Alexandra School.

CURTIN, JANE: Cambridge, MA, Sept. 6, 1947.

CURTIS, JAMIE LEE: Los Angeles, CA., Nov. 21, 1958.

CURTIS, KEENE: Salt Lake City, UT, Feb. 15, 1925. U. Utah.

CURTIS, TONY (Bernard Schwartz): NYC, June 3, 1924.

CUSACK, CYRIL: Durban, S. Africa, Nov. 26, 1910. Univ. Col.

CUSHING, PETER: Kenley, Surrey, Eng., May 26, 1913.

DAFOE, WILLEM: Appleton, Wi. 1955.

DAHL, ARLENE: Minneapolis, Aug. 11, 1928. U. Minn.

DALLESANDRO, JOE: Pensacola, FL, Dec. 31, 1948.

DALTON, TIMOTHY: Wales, Mar. 21, 1946, RADA.

DALTREY, ROGER: London, Mar. 1, 1945.

DALY, TYNE: Feb. 21, 1947, Madison, Wi. AMDA.

DAMONE, VIC (Vito Farinola): Brooklyn, June 12, 1928.

DANCE, CHARLES: Plymouth, Eng., 1946.

D'ANGELO, BEVERLY: Columbus, OH., Nov. 15, 1953.

DANGERFIELD, RODNEY (Jacob Cohen): Babylon, NY, Nov. 22, 1921.

DANIELS, JEFF: Georgia, 1955. EastMichState.

DANIELS, WILLIAM: Bklyn, Mar. 31, 1927. Northwestern.

DANNER, BLYTHE: Philadelphia, PA. Feb. 3, 1944. Bard Col.

DANO, ROYAL: NYC, Nov. 16, 1922. NYU.

DANSON, TED: Flagstaff, AZ, Dec. 29, 1947. Stanford, Carnegie Tech.

DANTE, MICHAEL (Ralph Vitti): Stamford, CT, 1935. U. Miami.

DANTON, RAY: NYC, Sept. 19, 1931. Carnegie Tech.

DANZA, TONY: Brooklyn, NY., Apr. 21, 1951. UDubuque.

DARBY, KIM: (Deborah Zerby): North Hollywood, CA, July 8, 1948.

DARCEL, DENISE (Denise Billecard): Paris, Sept. 8, 1925. U. Dijon.

DARREN, JAMES: Philadelphia, June 8, 1936. Stella Adler School.

DARRIEUX, DANIELLE: Bordeaux, France, May 1, 1917. Lycee LaTour.

DAVIDSON, JOHN: Pittsburgh, Dec. 13, 1941. Denison U.

DAVIS, BETTE: Lowell, MA, Apr. 5, 1908. John Murray Anderson Dramatic School.

DAVIS, BRAD: Fla., Nov. 6, 1949. AADA.

DAVIS, CLIFRON: Oct. 4, 1945, Chicago, OakwoodCol.

DAVIS, MAC: Lubbock, TX, Jan. 21, 1942.

DAVIS, NANCY (Anne Frances Robbins): NYC July 6, 1921, Smith Col.

DAVIS, OSSIE: Cogdell, GA, Dec. 18, 1917. Howard U.

DAVIS, SAMMY, JR.: NYC, Dec. 8, 1925.

DAVIS, SKEETER (Mary Frances Penick): Dry Ridge, KY. Dec. 30, 1931.

DAY, DORIS (Doris Kappelhoff): Cincinnati, Apr. 3, 1924.

DAY, LARAINE (Johnson): Roosevelt, UT, Oct. 13, 1917.

DAY-LEWIS, DANIEL: 1958, London, Bristol Old Vic.

DAYAN, ASSEF: Israel, 1945. U. Jerusalem.

DEAKINS, LUCY: NYC 1971.

DEAN, JIMMY: Plainview, TX, Aug. 10, 1928.

DeCAMP, ROSEMARY: Nov. 14, 1913, Prescott, Az.

DeCARLO, YVONNE (Peggy Yvonne Middleton): Vancouver, B.C., Can., Sept. 1, 1922. Vancouver School of Drama.

DEE, FRANCES: Los Angeles, Nov. 26, 1907. Chicago U.

DEE, JOEY (Joseph Di Nicola): Passaic, NJ, June 11, 1940. Patterson State College.

DEE, RUBY: Cleveland, OH, Oct. 27, 1924. Hunter Col.

DEE, SANDRA (Alexandra Zuck): Bayonne, NJ, Apr. 23, 1942.

DeFORE, DON: Cedar Rapids, IA, Aug. 25, 1917. U. Iowa.

DeHAVEN, GLORIA: Los Angeles, July 23, 1923.

DeHAVILLAND, OLIVIA: Tokyo, Japan, July 1, 1916. Notre Dame Convent School.

DELAIR, SUZY: Paris, Dec. 31, 1916.

DELON, ALAIN: Sceaux, Fr., Nov. 8, 1935.

DELORME, DANIELE: Paris, Oct. 9, 1927. Sorbonne.

DeLUISE, DOM: Brooklyn, Aug. 1, 1933. Tufts Col.

DeLUISE, PETER: 1967, Hollywood, Ca.

DEMPSEY, PATRICK: 1966, Maine

**Blythe
Danner**

**Tony
Danza**

**Colleen
Dewhurst**

**David
Dukes**

**Patricia
Elliott**

**Sam
Elliott**

DEMONGEOT, MYLENE: Nice, France, Sept. 29, 1938.

DeMORNAY, REBECCA: Los Angeles, Ca., 1962. Strasberg Inst.

DeMUNN, JEFFREY: Buffalo, NY, Apr. 25, 1947. Union Col.

DENEUVE, CATHERINE: Paris, Oct. 22, 1943.

DeNIRO, ROBERT: NYC, Aug. 17, 1943, Stella Adler.

DENISON, MICHAEL: Doncaster, York, Eng., Nov. 1, 1915. Oxford.

DENNEHY, BRIAN: 1938, Bridgeport, Ct., Columbia.

DENNER, CHARLES: Tarnow, Poland, May 29, 1926.

DENNIS, SANDY: Hastings, NB, Apr. 27, 1937. Actors Studio.

DEPARDIEU, GERARD: Chateauroux, Fr., Dec. 27, 1948.

DEREK, BO (Mary Cathleen Collins): Long Beach, CA, Nov. 20, 1956.

DEREK, JOHN: Hollywood, Aug. 12, 1926.

DERN, BRUCE: Chicago, June 4, 1936. U PA.

DERN, LAURA: California, 1966.

DeSALVO, ANNE: Philadelphia, PA., Apr. 3.

DEVINE, COLLEEN: San Gabriel, CA, June 22, 1960.

DeVITO, DANNY: Nov. 17, 1944. Asbury Park, NJ.

DEWHURST, COLLEEN: Montreal June 3, 1926. Lawrence U.

DEXTER, ANTHONY (Walter Reinhold Fleischmann): Talmadge, NB, Jan. 19, 1919. U. Iowa.

DEY, SUSAN: Pekin, Il, Dec. 10, 1953.

DeYOUNG, CLIFF: Los Angeles, CA, Feb. 12, 1945. Cal State.

DHIEGH, KHIGH: New Jersey, 1910.

DIAMOND, NEIL: NYC, Jan. 24, 1941. NYU.

DICKINSON, ANGIE: Kulm, ND, Sept. 30, 1932. Glendale College.

DIETRICH, MARLENE (Maria Magdalene von Losch): Berlin, Ger., Dec. 27, 1901. Berlin Music Academy.

DILLER, PHYLLIS (Driver): Lima, OH, July 17, 1917. Bluffton College.

DILLMAN, BRADFORD: San Francisco, Apr. 14, 1930. Yale.

DILLON, KEVIN: Mamaroneck, NY, 1965.

DILLON, MATT: Larchmont, NY., Feb. 18, 1964. AADA.

DILLON, MELINDA: Hope, AR, Oct. 13, 1939. Goodman Theatre School.

DOBSON, TAMARA: Baltimore, MD, 1947. MD. Inst. of Art.

DOMERGUE, FAITH: New Orleans, June 16, 1925.

DONAHUE, TROY (Merle Johnson): NYC, Jan. 27, 1937. Columbia U.

DONAT, PETER: Nova Scotia, Jan. 20, 1928. Yale.

DONNELL, JEFF (Jean Donnell): South Windham, ME, July 10, 1921. Yale Drama School.

D'ONOFRIO, VINCENT: 1960, Brooklyn.

DOOHAN, JAMES: Vancouver, BC, Mar. 3, Neighborhood Playhouse.

DOOLEY, PAUL: Parkersburg, WV, Feb. 22, 1928. U. WV.

DOUGLAS, DONNA (Dorothy Bourgeois): Baton Rouge, LA, 1935.

DOUGLAS, KIRK (Issur Danielovitch): Amsterdam, NY, Dec. 9, 1916. St. Lawrence U.

DOUGLAS, MICHAEL: New Brunswick, NJ, Sept. 25, 1944. U. Cal.

DOUGLASS, ROBYN: Sendai, Japan; June 21, 1953. UCDavis.

DOURIF, BRAD: Huntington, WV, Mar. 18, 1950. Marshall U.

DOWN, LESLEY-ANN: London, Mar. 17, 1954.

DOWNEY, ROBERT, JR.: 1965 NYC

DRAKE, BETSY: Paris, Sept. 11, 1923.

DRAKE, CHARLES (Charles Rupert): NYC, Oct. 2, 1914. Nichols College.

DREW, ELLEN (formerly Terry Ray): Kansas City, MO, Nov. 23, 1915.

DREYFUSS, RICHARD: Brooklyn, NY, Oct. 19, 1947.

DRILLINGER, BRIAN: Brooklyn, NY, June 27, 1960, SUNY/Purchase.

DRU, JOANNE (Joanne LaCock): Logan, WV, Jan. 31, 1923. John Robert Powers School.

DUBBINS, DON: Brooklyn, NY, June 28.

DUFF, HOWARD: Bremerton, WA, Nov. 24, 1917.

DUFFY, PATRICK: Townsend, Mt, Mar. 17, 1949. U. Wash.

DUKE, PATTY (Anna Marie): NYC, Dec. 14, 1946.

DUKES, DAVID: San Francisco, June 6, 1945.

DULLEA, KEIR: Cleveland, NJ, May 30, 1936. SF State Col.

DUNAWAY, FAYE: Bascom, FL, Jan. 14, 1941. Fla. U.

DUNCAN, SANDY: Henderson, TX, Feb. 20, 1946. Len Morris Col.

DUNNE, GRIFFIN: NYC June 8, 1955, Neighborhood Playhouse.

DUNNE, IRENE: Louisville, KY, Dec. 20, 1898. Chicago College of Music.

DUNNOCK, MILDRED: Baltimore, Jan. 25, 1900. Johns Hopkins and Columbia U.

DUPEREY, ANNY: Paris, 1947.

DURBIN, DEANNA (Edna): Winnipeg, Can., Dec. 4, 1921.

DURNING, CHARLES: Highland Falls, NY, Feb. 28, 1933. NYU.

DUSSOLLIER, ANDRE: Annecy, France, Feb. 17, 1946.

DUVALL, ROBERT: San Diego, CA, Jan 5, 1930. Principia Col.

DUVALL, SHELLEY: Houston, TX, July 7, 1949.

EASTON, ROBERT: Milwaukee, WI, Nov. 23, 1930. U. Texas.

EASTWOOD, CLINT: San Francisco, May 31, 1930. LACC.

EATON, SHIRLEY: London, 1937. Aida Foster School.

EBSEN, BUDDY (Christian, Jr.): Belleville, IL, Apr. 2, 1910. U. Fla.

ECKEMYR, AGNETA: Karlsborg, Swed., July 2. Actors Studio.

EDEN, BARBARA (Moorhead): Tucson, AZ, Aug. 23, 1934.

EDWARDS, ANTHONY: 1963, Santa Barbara, Ca. RADA

EDWARDS, VINCE: NYC, July 9, 1928. AADA.

EGGAR, SAMANTHA: London, Mar. 5, 1939.

EICHHORN, LISA: Reading, PA, Feb. 4, 1952. Queens Ont. U. RADA.

EILBER, JANET: Detroit, MI, July 27, 1951. Juilliard.

EKBERG, ANITA: Malmo, Sweden, Sept. 29, 1931.

EKLAND, BRITT: Stockholm, Swed. Oct. 6, 1942.

ELIZONDO, HECTOR: NYC, Dec. 22, 1936.

ELLIOTT, CHRIS: 1960, NYC

ELLIOTT, DENHOLM: London, May 31, 1922. Malvern College.

ELLIOTT, PATRICIA: Gunnison, Co, July 21, 1942, UCol.

ELLIOTT, SAM: Sacramento, CA, Aug. 9, 1944. U. Ore.

ELY, RON (Ronald Pierce): Hereford, TX, June 21, 1938.

ENGLISH, ALEX: 1954, USCar.

ERDMAN, RICHARD: Enid, OK, June 1, 1925.

ERICSON, JOHN: Dusseldorf, Ger., Sept. 25, 1926. AADA.

ESMOND, CARL: Vienna, June 14, 1906. U. Vienna.

ESTEVEZ, EMILIO: NYC 1962.

ESPOSITO, GIANCARLO: Copenhagen, Den., Apr. 26, 1958.

ESTRADA, ERIK: NYC, Mar. 16, 1949.

EVANS, DALE (Francis Smith): Uvalde, TX, Oct. 31, 1912.

EVANS, GENE: Holbrook, AZ, July 11, 1922.

EVANS, LINDA (Evanstad): Hartford, CT., Nov. 18, 1942.

EVANS, MAURICE: Dorchester, Eng., June 3, 1901.

EVERETT, CHAD (Ray Cramton): South Bend, IN, June 11, 1936.

EVERETT, RUPERT: Norfolk, Eng., 1959.

EVIGAN, GREG: 1954, South Amboy, NJ

EWELL, TOM (Yewell Tompkins): Owensboro, KY, Apr. 29, 1909. U. Wisc.

FABARES, SHELLEY: Los Angeles, Jan. 19, 1944.

FABIAN (Fabian Forte): Philadelphia, Feb. 6, 1943.

FABRAY, NANETTE (Ruby Nanette Fabares): San Diego, Oct. 27, 1920.

FAIRBANKS, DOUGLAS JR.: NYC, Dec. 9, 1907. Collegiate School.

FAIRCHILD, MORGAN: (Patsy McClenny) Dallas, TX., Feb. 3, 1950. UCLA.

FALK, PETER: NYC, Sept. 16, 1927. New School.

FARENTINO, JAMES: Brooklyn, Feb. 24, 1938. AADA.

FARINA, SANDY (Sandra Feldman): Newark, NJ, 1955.

FARR, FELICIA: Westchester, NY, Oct. 4, 1932. Penn State Col.

FARRELL, CHARLES: Onset Bay, MA, Aug. 9, 1901. Boston U.

FARROW, MIA: Los Angeles, Feb. 9, 1945.

FAULKNER, GRAHAM: London, Sept. 26, 1947. Webber-Douglas.

FAWCETT, FARRAH: Corpus Christie, TX. Feb. 2, 1947. TexU.

FAYE, ALICE (Ann Leppert): NYC, May 5, 1912.

FEINSTEIN, ALAN: NYC, Sept. 8, 1941.

FELDON, BARBARA (Hall): Pittsburgh, Mar. 12, 1941. Carnegie Tech.

FELDSHUH, TOVAH: NYC, Dec. 27, 1953, Sarah Lawrence Col.

FELLOWS, EDITH: Boston, May 20, 1923.

FERRELL, CONCHATA: Charleston, WV, Mar. 28, 1943. Marshall U.

FERRER, JOSE: Santurce, P.R., Jan. 8, 1909. Princeton U.

FERRER, MEL: Elberon, NJ, Aug. 25, 1917. Princeton U.

FERRIS, BARBARA: London, 1943.

FERZETTI, GABRIELE: Italy, 1927. Rome Acad. of Drama.

FIEDLER, JOHN: Plateville, Wi, Feb. 3, 1925.

FIELD, SALLY: Pasadena, CA, Nov. 6, 1946.

FIGUEROA, RUBEN: NYC 1958.

FINNEY, ALBERT: Salford, Lancashire, Eng., May 9, 1936. RADA.

FIORENTINO, LINDA: Philadelphia, Pa.

FIRESTONE, ROCHELLE: Kansas City, MO., June 14, 1949. NYU.

FIRTH, PETER: Bradford, Eng., Oct. 27, 1953.

FISHER, CARRIE: Los Angeles, CA, Oct. 21, 1956. London Central School of Drama.

FISHER, EDDIE: Philadelphia, Aug. 10, 1928.

FITZGERALD, BRIAN: Philadelphia, Pa, 1960, West Chester U.

FITZGERALD, GERALDINE: Dublin, Ire., Nov. 24, 1914. Dublin Art School.

FLANNERY, SUSAN: Jersey City, NJ, July 31, 1943.

FLEMING, RHONDA (Marilyn Louis): Los Angeles, Aug. 10, 1922.

FLEMYNG, ROBERT: Liverpool, Eng., Jan. 3, 1912. Haileybury Col.

FLETCHER, LOUISE: Birmingham, AL, July 1934.

FOCH, NINA: Leyden, Holland, Apr. 20, 1924.

FOLDI, ERZSEBET: Queens, NY, 1967.

FOLLOWS, MEGAN: 1967, Toronto, Ca.

FONDA, JANE: NYC, Dec. 21, 1937. Vassar.

FONDA, PETER: NYC, Feb. 23, 1939. U. Omaha.

FONTAINE, JOAN: Tokyo, Japan, Oct. 22, 1917.

FOOTE, HALLIE: NYC 1953. UNH.

FORD, GLENN (Gwyllyn Samuel Newton Ford): Quebec, Can., May 1, 1916.

FORD, HARRISON: Chicago, IL, July 13, 1942. Ripon Col.

FOREST, MARK (Lou Degni): Brooklyn, Jan. 1933.

FORREST, STEVE: Huntsville, TX, Sept. 29, 1924. UCLA.

FORSLUND, CONNIE: San Diego, CA, June 19, 1950, NYU.

FORSTER, ROBERT (Foster, Jr.): Rochester, NY, July 13, 1941. Rochester U.

FORSYTHE, JOHN (Freund): Penn's Grove, NJ, Jan. 29, 1918.

FOSTER, JODIE (Ariane Munker): Bronx, NY, Nov. 19, 1962. Yale.

FOX, EDWARD: London, 1937, RADA.

FOX, JAMES: London, May 19, 1939.

FOX, MICHAEL J.: Vancouver, BC, June 9, 1961.

FOXWORTH, ROBERT: Houston, TX, Nov. 1, 1941. Carnegie Tech.

FOXX, REDD: St. Louis, MO, Dec. 9, 1922.

FRAKES, JOHNATHAN: 1952, Bethlehem, Pa. Harvard

FRANCIOSA, ANTHONY (Papaleo): NYC, Oct. 25, 1928.

FRANCIS, ANNE: Ossining, NY, Sept. 16, 1932.

FRANCIS, ARLENE (Arlene Kazanjian): Boston, Oct. 20, 1908. Finch School.

FRANCIS, CONNIE (Constance Franconero): Newark, NJ, Dec. 12, 1938.

FRANCISCUS, JAMES: Clayton, MO, Jan. 31, 1934. Yale.

FRANCKS, DON: Vancouver, Can., Feb. 28, 1932.

FRANK, JEFFREY: Jackson Heights, NY, 1965.

FRANKLIN, PAMELA: Tokyo, Feb. 4, 1950.

FRANZ, ARTHUR: Perth Amboy, NJ, Feb. 29, 1920. Blue Ridge College.

FRAZIER, SHEILA: NYC, Nov. 13, 1948.

FREEMAN, AL, JR.: San Antonio, TX, 1934. CCLA.

FREEMAN, MONA: Baltimore, MD, June 9, 1926.

FREEMAN, MORGAN: Memphis, Tn, June 1, 1937, LACC.

FREWER, MATT: Washington, DC, 1957, Old Vic.

FREY, LEONARD: Brooklyn, Sept. 4, 1938. Neighborhood Playhouse.

FULLER, PENNY: Durham, NC, 1940. Northwestern U.

FURNEAUX, YVONNE: Lille, France, 1928. Oxford U.

FYODOROVA, VICTORIA: Russia 1946.

GABLE, JOHN CLARK: Mar. 20, 1961, Los Angeles. Santa Monica Col.

GABOR, EVA: Budapest, Hungary, Feb. 11, 1920.

GABOR, ZSA ZSA (Sari Gabor): Budapest, Hungary, Feb. 6, 1918.

GAINES, BOYD: Atlanta, GA., May 11, 1953. Juilliard.

GALLAGHER, PETER: Armonk, NY, Aug. 19, 1955. Tufts U.

GALLIGAN, ZACH: NYC, 1963. ColumbiaU.

GAM, RITA: Pittsburgh, PA, Apr. 2, 1928.

GARBER, VICTOR: Montreal, Can., Mar. 16, 1949.

GARBO, GRETA (Greta Gustafson): Stockholm, Sweden, Sept. 18, 1905.

GARCIA, ANDY: 1948, Havana, Cuba. FlaInt1U.

GARDENIA, VINCENT: Naples, Italy, Jan. 7, 1922.

GARDNER, AVA: Smithfield, NC, Dec. 24, 1922. Atlantic Christian College.

GARFIELD, ALLEN: Newark, NJ, Nov. 22, 1939. Actors Studio.

GARLAND, BEVERLY: Santa Cruz, CA, Oct. 17, 1930. Glendale Col.

GARNER, JAMES (James Baumgarner): Norman, OK, Apr. 7, 1928. Okla. U.

GARR, TERI: Lakewood, OH, 1952.

GARRETT, BETTY: St. Joseph, MO, May 23, 1919. Annie Wright Seminary.

GARRISON, SEAN: NYC, Oct. 19, 1937.

GARSON, GREER: Ireland, Sept. 29, 1906.

GASSMAN, VITTORIO: Genoa, Italy, Sept. 1, 1922. Rome Academy of Dramatic Art.

GAVIN, JOHN: Los Angeles, Apr. 8, 1935. Stanford U.

GAYLORD, MITCH: Van Nuys, CA, 1961, UCLA.

GAYNOR, MITZI (Francesca Marlene Von Gerber): Chicago, Sept. 4, 1930.

GAZZARA, BEN: NYC, Aug. 28, 1930. Actors Studio.

GEARY, ANTHONY: Coalsville, Utah, May 29, 1947.

GEDRICK, JASON: 1965, Chicago, Drake U.

GEESON, JUDY: Arundel, Eng., Sept. 10, 1948. Corona.

GEOFFREYS, STEPHEN: Cincinnati, Oh., Nov. 22, 1964. NYU.

GEORGE, BOY (George O'Dowd): London 1962.

GEORGE, SUSAN: West London, Eng. July 26, 1950.

GERARD, GIL: Little Rock, AR, Jan. 23, 1940.

GERE, RICHARD: Philadelphia, PA, Aug. 29, 1949. U. Mass.

GERROLL, DANIEL: London, Oct. 16, 1951. Central.

GETTY, ESTELLE: NYC, July 25, 1923, New School.

Morgan Fairchild   Alan Feinstein   Rochelle Firestone   Peter Gallagher   Joanna Gleason   Andy Garcia

GHOLSON, JULIE: Birmingham, AL, June 4, 1958.

GHOSTLEY, ALICE: Eve, MO, Aug. 14, 1926. Okla U.

GIAN, JOE: North Miami Beach, Fl. 1962.

GIANNINI, CHERYL: Monessen, PA., June 15.

GIANNINI, GIANCARLO: Spezia, Italy, Aug. 1, 1942. Rome Acad. of Drama.

GIBB, CYNTHIA: 1965

GIBSON, MEL: Oneonta, NY., Jan. 3, 1951. NIDA.

GIELGUD, JOHN: London, Apr. 14, 1904. RADA.

GILBERT, MELISSA: May 8, 1964, Los Angeles, CA.

GILES, NANCY: NYC, July 17, 1960, Oberlin Col.

GILFORD, JACK: NYC, July 25, 1907.

GILLIS, ANNE (Alma O'Connor): Little Rock, AR, Feb. 12, 1927.

GINTY, ROBERT: NYC, Nov. 14, 1948, Yale.

GIRARDOT, ANNIE: Paris, Oct. 25, 1931.

GIROLAMI, STEFANIA: Rome, Italy, 1963.

GISH, LILLIAN: Springfield, OH, Oct. 14, 1896.

GLASER, PAUL MICHAEL: Boston, MA, Mar. 25, 1943. Boston U.

GLASS, RON: Evansville, IN, July 10, 1945.

GLEASON, JOANNA: Winnipeg, Can, June 2, 1950, UCLA.

GLENN, SCOTT: Pittsburgh, PA, Jan. 26, 1942; William and Mary Col.

GLOVER, CRISPIN: 1964 NYC

GLOVER, DANNY: San Francisco, Ca., July 22, 1947, SFStateCol.

GLOVER, JOHN: Kingston, NY, Aug. 7, 1944.

GLYNN,CARLIN: Cleveland, Oh, Feb. 19, 1940, Actors Studio.

GODDARD, PAULETTE (Levy): Great Neck, NY, June 3, 1911.

GODUNOV, ALEKSANDR: Sakhalin, USSR, Nov. 28, 1949.

GOLDBERG, WHOOPI (Caryn Johnson): NYC, Nov. 13, 1949.

GOLDBLUM, JEFF: Pittsburgh, PA, Oct. 22, 1952. Neighborhood Playhouse.

GOLDEN, ANNIE: NYC, 1952.

GOLDSTEIN, JENETTE: Beverley Hills, CA, 1960.

GONZALEZ, CORDELIA: Aug. 11, 1958, San Juan, PR. UPR.

GONZALES-GONZALEZ, PEDRO: Aguilares, TX, Dec. 21, 1926.

GOODMAN, DODY: Columbus, OH, Oct. 28, 1915.

GORDON, GALE (Aldrich): NYC, Feb. 2, 1906.

GORDON, KEITH: NYC, Feb. 3, 1961.

GORING, MARIUS: Newport Isle of Wight, 1912. Cambridge, Old Vic.

GORMAN, CLIFF: Jamaica, NY, Oct. 13, 1936. NYU.

GORSHIN, FRANK: Apr. 5, 1933.

GORTNER, MARJOE: Long Beach, CA, 1944.

GOSSETT, LOUIS: Brooklyn, May 27, 1936. NYU.

GOULD, ELLIOTT (Goldstein): Brooklyn, Aug. 29, 1938. Columbia U.

GOULD, HAROLD: Schenectady, NY, Dec. 10, 1923. Cornell.

GOULET, ROBERT: Lawrence, MA, Nov. 26, 1933. Edmonton.

GRAF, DAVID: Lancaster, OH, Apr. 16, 1950. OhStateU.

GRAF, TODD: NYC, Oct. 22, 1959, SUNY/Purchase.

GRANGER, FARLEY: San Jose, CA, July 1, 1925.

GRANGER, STEWART (James Stewart): London, May 6, 1913. Webber-Douglas School of Acting.

GRANT, DAVID MARSHALL: Westport, CT, 1955. Yale.

GRANT, KATHRYN (Olive Grandstaff): Houston, TX, Nov. 25, 1933. UCLA.

GRANT, LEE: NYC, Oct. 31, 1930. Juilliard.

GRANVILLE, BONITA: NYC, Feb. 2, 1923.

GRAVES, PETER (Aurness): Minneapolis, Mar. 18, 1926. U. Minn.

GRAY, CHARLES: Bournemouth, Eng., 1928.

GRAY, COLEEN (Doris Jensen): Staplehurst, NB, Oct. 23, 1922. Hamline U.

GRAY, LINDA: Santa Monica, CA; Sept. 12, 1940.

GRAYSON, KATHRYN (Zelma Hedrick): Winston-Salem, NC, Feb. 9, 1922.

GREEN, KERRI: Fort Lee, NJ, 1967. Vassar.

GREENE, ELLEN: NYC, Feb. 22, 1950. Ryder Col.

GREER, JANE: Washington, DC, Sept. 9, 1924.

GREER, MICHAEL: Galesburg, IL, Apr. 20, 1943.

GREGORY, MARK: Rome, Italy. 1965.

GREY, JENNIFER: NYC 1960.

GREY, JOEL (Katz): Cleveland, OH, Apr. 11, 1932.

GREY, VIRGINIA: Los Angeles, Mar. 22, 1917.

GRIEM, HELMUT: Hamburg, Ger. U. Hamburg.

GRIFFITH, ANDY: Mt. Airy, NC, June 1, 1926. UNC.

GRIFFITH, MELANIE: NYC, Aug. 9, 1957 Pierce Col.

GRIMES, GARY: San Francisco, June 2, 1955.

GRIMES, TAMMY: Lynn, MA, Jan. 30, 1934. Stephens Col.

GRIZZARD, GEORGE: Roanoke Rapids, NC, Apr. 1, 1928. UNC.

GRODIN, CHARLES: Pittsburgh, PA, Apr. 21, 1935.

GROH, DAVID: NYC, May 21, 1939. Brown U., LAMDA.

GUARDINO, HARRY: Brooklyn, Dec. 23, 1925. Haaren High.

GUILLAUME, ROBERT: Nov. 30, 1937, St. Louis, Mo. (Robert Williams).

GUINNESS, ALEX: London, Apr. 2, 1914. Pembroke Lodge School.

GUNN, MOSES: St. Louis, MO, Oct. 2, 1929. Tenn. State U.

GUTTENBERG, STEVEN: Brooklyn, NY, Aug. 24, 1958. UCLA.

GWILLIM, DAVID: Plymouth, Eng., Dec. 15, 1948. RADA.

HACKETT, BUDDY (Leonard Hacker): Brooklyn, Aug. 31, 1924.

HACKMAN, GENE: San Bernardino, CA, Jan. 30, 1931.

HADDON, DALE: Montreal, CAN., May 26, 1949. Neighborhood Playhouse.

HAGERTY, JULIE: Cincinnati, OH, June 15, 1955. Juilliard.

HAGMAN, LARRY: (Hageman): Weatherford, TX., Sept. 21, 1931. Bard.

HAIM, COREY: Toronto, Can, 1972.

HALE, BARBARA: DeKalb, IL, Apr. 18, 1922. Chicago Academy of Fine Arts.

HALEY, JACKIE EARLE: Northridge, CA, 1963.

HALL, ALBERT: Boothton, AL, Nov. 10, 1937. Columbia.

HALL, ANTHONY MICHAEL: NYC, 1968.

HALL, KEVIN PETER: Pittsburgh, Pa, 1955. GeoWashU.

HAMILL, MARK: Oakland, CA, Sept. 25, 1952. LACC.

HAMILTON, CARRIE: Dec. 5, 1963, NYC.

HAMILTON, GEORGE: Memphis, TN, Aug. 12, 1939. Hackley.

HAMLIN, HARRY: Pasadena, CA, Oct. 30, 1951. Yale.

HAMPSHIRE, SUSAN: London, May 12, 1941.

HANKS, TOM: Oakland, CA., 1956. CalStateU.

HANNAH, DARYL: Chicago, IL., 1960, UCLA.

HANNAH, PAGE: Chicago, IL., 1964.

HARDIN, TY (Orison Whipple Hungerford II): NYC, June 1, 1930.

HAREWOOD, DORIAN: Dayton, OH, Aug. 6. U. Cinn.

HARMON, MARK: Los Angeles, CA, Sept. 2, 1951; UCLA.

HARPER, TESS: Mammoth Spring, Ark., 1952. SWMoState.

HARPER, VALERIE: Suffern, NY, Aug. 22, 1940.

HARRELSON, WOODY: Lebanon, OH, 1962.

HARRINGTON, PAT: NYC, Aug. 13, 1929. Fordham U.

HARRIS, BARBARA (Sandra Markowitz): Evanston, IL, July 25, 1935.

HARRIS, ED: Tenafly, NJ, Nov. 28, 1950. Columbia.

HARRIS, JULIE: Grosse Point, MI, Dec. 2, 1925. Yale Drama School.

HARRIS, MEL (Mary Ellen): 1957 North Brunswick, NJ, Columbia.

HARRIS, RICHARD: Limerick, Ire., Oct. 1, 1930. London Acad.

HARRIS, ROSEMARY: Ashby, Eng., Sept. 19, 1930. RADA.

HARRISON, GREG: Catalina Island, CA, May 31, 1950; Actors Studio.

HARRISON, NOEL: London, Jan. 29, 1936.

HARRISON, REX: Huyton, Cheshire, Eng., Mar. 5, 1908.

HARROLD, KATHRYN: Tazewell, VA. 1950. Mills Col.

HART, ROXANNE: Trenton, NJ, 1952, Princeton.

HARTLEY, MARIETTE: NYC, June 21, 1941.

HARTMAN, DAVID: Pawtucket, RI, May 19, 1935. Duke U.

HASSETT, MARILYN: Los Angeles, CA, 1949.

HAUER, RUTGER: Amsterdam, Hol. Jan. 23, 1944.

HAVER, JUNE: Rock Island, IL, June 10, 1926.

HAVOC, JUNE (Hovick): Nov. 8, 1916, Seattle, Wa.

HAWN, GOLDIE: Washington, DC, Nov. 21, 1945.

HAYDEN, LINDA: Stanmore, Eng. Aida Foster School.

HAYES, HELEN: (Helen Brown): Washington, DC, Oct. 10, 1900. Sacred Heart Convent.

HAYS, ROBERT: Bethesda, MD., July 24, 1947, SD State Col.

HEADLY, GLENNE: New London, Ct, Mar. 13, 1955. AmCol.

HEALD, ANTHONY: New Rochelle, NY, Aug. 25, 1944, MiStateU.

HEARD, JOHN: Washington, DC, Mar. 7, 1946. Clark U.

HEATHERTON, JOEY: NYC, Sept. 14, 1944.

HECKART, EILEEN: Columbus, OH, Mar. 29, 1919. Ohio State U.

HEDISON, DAVID: Providence, RI, May 20, 1929. Brown U.

HEGYES, ROBERT: NJ, May 7, 1951.

HEMINGWAY, MARIEL: Nov. 22, 1961.

HEMMINGS, DAVID: Guilford, Eng. Nov. 18, 1938.

HENDERSON, FLORENCE: Feb. 14, 1934.

HENDERSON, MARCIA: Andover, MA, July 22, 1932. AADA.

HENDRY, GLORIA: Jacksonville, FL. 1949.

HENNER, MARILU: Chicago, IL. Apr. 4, 1952.

HENREID, PAUL: Trieste, Jan. 10, 1908.

HENRY, BUCK (Zuckerman): NYC, 1931. Dartmouth.

HENRY, JUSTIN: Rye, NY, 1971.

HEPBURN, AUDREY: Brussels, Belgium, May 4, 1929.

HEPBURN, KATHARINE: Hartford, CT, Nov. 8, 1907. Bryn Mawr.

HERMAN, PEE-WEE (Paul Reubenfeld): 1952.

HERRMANN, EDWARD: Washington, DC, July 21, 1943. Bucknell, LAMDA.

HERSHEY, BARBARA: (Herzstein): Hollywood, CA, Feb. 5, 1948.

HESTON, CHARLTON: Evanston, IL, Oct. 4, 1922. Northwestern U.

HEWITT, MARTIN: Claremont, CA, 1960; AADA.

HEYWOOD, ANNE (Violet Pretty): Birmingham, Eng., Dec. 11, 1932.

HICKEY, WILLIAM: Brooklyn, NY, 1928.

HICKMAN, DARRYL: Hollywood, CA, July 28, 1933. Loyola U.

HICKMAN, DWAYNE: Los Angeles, May 18, 1934. Loyola U.

HIGGINS, MICHAEL: Brooklyn, NY, Jan. 20, 1926, AmThWing.

HILL, ARTHUR: Saskatchewan, CAN., Aug. 1, 1922. U. Brit. Col.

HILL, STEVEN: Seattle, WA, Feb. 24, 1922. U. Wash.

HILL, TERENCE (Mario Girotti): Venice, Italy, Mar. 29, 1941. U. Rome.

HILLER, WENDY: Bramhall, Cheshire, Eng., Aug. 15, 1912. Winceby House School.

HILLIARD, HARRIET: (See Harriet Hilliard Nelson)

HINGLE, PAT: Denver, CO, July 19, 1923. Tex. U.

HIRSCH, JUDD: NYC, Mar. 15, 1935. AADA.

HOBEL, MARA: NYC, June 18, 1971.

HODGE, PATRICIA: Lincolnshire, Eng., 1946. LAMDA.

HOFFMAN, DUSTIN: Los Angeles, Aug. 8, 1937. Pasadena Playhouse.

HOGAN, PAUL: Australia, 1939.

HOLBROOK, HAL (Harold): Cleveland, OH, Feb. 17, 1925. Denison.

HOLLIMAN, EARL: Tennesas Swamp, Delhi, LA, Sept. 11, 1928. UCLA.

HOLM, CELESTE: NYC, Apr. 29, 1919.

HOMEIER, SKIP (George Vincent Homeier): Chicago, Oct. 5, 1930. UCLA.

HOOKS, ROBERT: Washington, DC, Apr. 18, 1937. Temple.

HOPE, BOB (Leslie Townes Hope): London, May 26, 1903.

HOPPER, DENNIS: Dodge City, KS, May 17, 1936.

HORNADAY, JEFFREY: San Jose, Ca., 1956.

HORNE, LENA: Brooklyn, June 30, 1917.

HORSLEY, LEE: May 15, 1955.

HORTON, ROBERT: Los Angeles, July 29, 1924. UCLA.

HOSKINS, BOB: Bury St. Edmunds, Eng., Oct. 26, 1942.

HOUGHTON, KATHARINE: Hartford, CT, Mar. 10, 1945. Sarah Lawrence.

HOUSEMAN, JOHN: Bucharest, Sept. 22, 1902.

HOUSER, JERRY: Los Angeles, July 14, 1952. Valley Jr. Col.

HOUSTON, DONALD: Tonypandy, Wales, 1924.

HOVEY, TIM: Los Angeles, June 19, 1945.

HOWARD, ARLISS: 1955, Independence, Mo. Columbia Col.

HOWARD, KEN: El Centro, CA, Mar. 28, 1944. Yale.

HOWARD, RON: Duncan, OK, Mar. 1, 1954. USC.

HOWARD, RONALD: Norwood, Eng., Apr. 7, 1918. Jesus College.

HOWELL, C. THOMAS: 1967.

HOWELLS, URSULA: London, Sept. 17, 1922.

HOWES, SALLY ANN: London, July 20, 1930.

HOWLAND, BETH: May 28, 1941, Boston, Ma.

HUBLEY, WHIP (Grant): 1957.

HUDDLESSON, DAVID: Vinton, VA, Sept. 17, 1930.

HUDDLESTON, MICHAEL: Roanoke, VA., AADA.

HUGHES, BARNARD: Bedford Hills, NY, July 16, 1915. Manhattan Col.

HUGHES, KATHLEEN (Betty von Gerkan): Hollywood, CA, Nov. 14, 1928. UCLA.

HULCE, TOM: Plymouth, MI, Dec. 6, 1953. N.C.Sch. of Arts.

HUNNICUT, GAYLE: Ft. Worth, TX, Feb. 6, 1943. UCLA.

HUNT, LINDA: Morristown, NJ, Apr. 2, 1945. Goodman Theatre.

HUNT, MARSHA: Chicago, Oct. 17, 1917.

HUNTER, HOLLY: Atlanta, Ga, Mar. 20, 1958, Carnegie-Mellon.

HUNTER, KIM (Janet Cole): Detroit, Nov. 12, 1922.

HUNTER, TAB (Arthur Gelien): NYC, July 11, 1931.

HUPPERT, ISABELLE: Paris, Fr., Mar. 16, 1955.

HURT, JOHN: Jan. 22, 1940. Lincolnshire, Eng.

HURT, MARY BETH (Supinger): Sept. 26, 1948, Marshalltown, Ia. NYU

HURT, WILLIAM: Washington, D.C., Mar. 20, 1950. Tufts, Juilliard.

HUSSEY, RUTH: Providence, RI, Oct. 30, 1917. U. Mich.

HUTTON, BETTY (Betty Thornberg): Battle Creek, MI, Feb. 26, 1921.

HUTTON, LAUREN (Mary): Charleston, SC, Nov. 17, 1943. Newcomb Col.

HUTTON, ROBERT (Winne): Kingston, NY, June 11, 1920. Blair Academy.

HUTTON, TIMOTHY: Malibu, CA, Aug. 16, 1960.

HYDE-WHITE, WILFRID: Gloucestershire, Eng., May 13, 1903. RADA.

HYER, MARTHA: Fort Worth, TX, Aug. 10, 1924. Northwestern U.

IGLESIAS, JULIO: Madrid, Spain, Sept. 23, 1943.

INGELS, MARTY: Brooklyn, NY, Mar. 9, 1936.

IRELAND, JOHN: Vancouver, B.C., CAN., Jan. 30, 1914.

IRONS, JEREMY: Cowes, Eng. Sept. 19, 1948. Old Vic.

IVANEK, ZELJKO: Lujubljana, Yugo., Aug. 15, 1957. Yale, LAMDA.

IVES, BURL: Hunt Township, IL, June 14, 1909. Charleston ILL. Teachers College.

IVEY, JUDITH: El Paso, Tx, Sept. 4, 1951.

JACKSON, ANNE: Alleghany, PA, Sept. 3, 1926. Neighborhood Playhouse.

**Julie
Harris**

**Gregory
Harrison**

**Katharine
Houghton**

**Page
Johnson**

**Lila
Kedrova**

**Aron
Kincaid**

JACKSON, GLENDA: Hoylake, Cheshire, Eng., May 9, 1936. RADA.

JACKSON, KATE: Birmingham, AL. Oct. 29, 1948. AADA.

JACKSON, MICHAEL: Gary, Ind., Aug. 29, 1958.

JACOBI, DEREK: Leytonstone, London, Eng. Oct. 22, 1938. Cambridge.

JACOBI, LOU: Toronto, CAN., Dec. 28, 1913.

JACOBS, LAWRENCE-HILTON: Virgin Islands, 1954.

JACOBY, SCOTT: Chicago, Nov. 19, 1956.

JAECKEL, RICHARD: Long Beach, NY, Oct. 10, 1926.

JAGGER, DEAN: Lima, OH, Nov. 7, 1903. Wabash College.

JAGGER, MICK: Dartford, Kent, Eng. July 26, 1943.

JAMES, CLIFTON: NYC, May 29, 1921. Ore. U.

JAMES, JOHN (Anderson): Apr. 18, 1956, New Canaan, Ct., AADA.

JARMAN, CLAUDE, JR.: Nashville, TN, Sept. 27, 1934.

JASON, RICK: NYC, May 21, 1926. AADA.

JEAN, GLORIA (Gloria Jean Schoonover): Buffalo, NY, Apr. 14, 1927.

JEFFREYS, ANNE (Carmichael): Goldsboro, NC, Jan. 26, 1923. Anderson College.

JEFFRIES, LIONEL: London, 1927, RADA.

JERGENS, ADELE: Brooklyn, Nov. 26, 1922.

JETT, ROGER (Baker): Cumberland, MD., Oct. 2, 1946. AADA.

JILLIAN, ANN (Nauseda): Massachusetts, Jan. 29, 1951.

JOHN, ELTON: (Reginald Dwight) Middlesex, Eng., Mar. 25, 1947. RAM.

JOHNS, GLYNIS: Durban, S. Africa, Oct. 5, 1923.

JOHNSON, BEN: Pawhuska, Ok, June 13, 1918.

JOHNSON, DON: Galena, Mo., Dec. 15, 1950. UKan.

JOHNSON, PAGE: Welch, WV, Aug. 25, 1930. Ithaca.

JOHNSON, RAFER: Hillsboro, TX, Aug. 18, 1935. UCLA.

JOHNSON, RICHARD: Essex, Eng., 1927. RADA.

JOHNSON, ROBIN: Brooklyn, NY: May 29, 1964.

JOHNSON, VAN: Newport, RI, Aug. 28, 1916.

JONES, CHRISTOPHER: Jackson, TN, Aug. 18, 1941. Actors Studio.

JONES, DEAN: Morgan County, AL, Jan. 25, 1936. Actors Studio.

JONES, JACK: Bel-Air, CA, Jan. 14, 1938.

JONES, JAMES EARL: Arkabutla, MS, Jan. 17, 1931. U. Mich.

JONES, JENNIFER (Phyllis Isley): Tulsa, OK, Mar. 2, 1919. AADA.

JONES, SAM J.: Chicago, IL, 1954.

JONES, SHIRLEY: Smithton, PA, March 31, 1934.

JONES, TOM (Thomas Jones Woodward): Pontypridd, Wales, June 7, 1940.

JONES, TOMMY LEE: San Saba, TX, Sept. 15, 1946. Harvard.

JORDAN, RICHARD: NYC, July 19, 1938. Harvard.

JOURDAN, LOUIS: Marseilles, France, June 18, 1920.

JOY, ROBERT: Montreal, Can, Aug. 17, 1951, Oxford.

JULIA, RAUL: San Juan, PR, Mar. 9, 1940. U PR.

JURADO, KATY (Maria Christina Jurado Garcia): Guadalajara, Mex., Jan. 16, 1927.

KAHN, MADELINE: Boston, MA, Sept. 29, 1942. Hofstra U.

KANE, CAROL: Cleveland, OH, June 18, 1952.

KAPLAN, JONATHAN: Paris, Nov. 25, 1947. NYU.

KAPLAN, MARVIN: Brooklyn, Jan. 24, 1924.

KAPOOR, SHASHI: Bombay 1940.

KAPRISKY, VALERIE: Paris, 1963.

KATT, WILLIAM: Los Angeles, CA, Feb. 16, 1955.

KAUFMANN, CHRISTINE: Lansdorf, Graz, Austria, Jan. 11, 1945.

KAVNER, JULIE: Burbank, CA, Sept. 7, 1951, UCLA.

KAYE, STUBBY: NYC, Nov. 11, 1918.

KAZAN, LAINIE (Levine): May 15, 1942, Brooklyn

KEACH, STACY: Savannah, GA, June 2, 1941. U. Cal., Yale.

KEATON, MICHAEL: Coraopolis, Pa., 1951. KentStateU.

KEATON, DIANE (Hall): Los Angeles, CA, Jan. 5, 1946. Neighborhood Playhouse.

KEATS, STEVEN: Bronx, NY, 1945.

KEDROVA, LILA: Leningrad, 1918.

KEEL, HOWARD (Harold Leek): Gillespie, IL, Apr. 13, 1919.

KEELER, RUBY (Ethel): Halifax, N.S., Aug. 25, 1909.

KEITH, BRIAN: Bayonne, NJ, Nov. 15, 1921.

KEITH, DAVID: Knoxville, Tn., May 8, 1954. UTN.

KELLER, MARTHE: Basel, Switz., 1945. Munich Stanislavsky Sch.

KELLERMAN, SALLY: Long Beach, CA, June 2, 1938. Actors Studio West.

KELLEY, DeFOREST: Atlanta, GA, Jan. 20, 1920.

KELLY, GENE: Pittsburgh, Aug. 23, 1912. U. Pittsburgh.

KELLY, JACK: Astoria, NY, Sept. 16, 1927. UCLA.

KELLY, NANCY: Lowell, MA, Mar. 25, 1921. Bentley School.

KEMP, JEREMY: (Wacker) Chesterfield, Eng., Feb. 3, 1935, Central Sch.

KENNEDY, ARTHUR: Worcester, MA, Feb. 17, 1914. Carnegie Tech.

KENNEDY, GEORGE: NYC, Feb. 18, 1925.

KENNEDY, LEON ISAAC: Cleveland, OH., 1949.

KERR, DEBORAH: Helensburg, Scot., Sept. 30, 1921. Smale Ballet School.

KERR, JOHN: NYC, Nov. 15, 1931. Harvard, Columbia.

KEYES, EVELYN: Nov. 20, 1917, Port Arthur, Tx.

KHAMBATTA, PERSIS: Bombay, Oct. 2, 1950.

KIDDER, MARGOT: Yellow Knife, CAN., Oct. 17, 1948. UBC.

KIER, UDO: Germany, Oct. 14, 1944.

KILEY, RICHARD: Chicago, Mar. 31, 1922. Loyola.

KILMER, VAL: 1960, Juilliard.

KINCAID, ARON (Norman Neale Williams III): Los Angeles, June 15, 1943. UCLA.

KING, ALAN (Irwin Kniberg): Brooklyn, Dec. 26, 1927.

KING, PERRY: Alliance, OH, Apr. 30, 1948. Yale.

KINGSLEY, BEN (Krishna Bhanji): Snaiton, Yorkshire, Eng., Dec. 31, 1943.

KINSKI, CLAUS: (Claus Gunther Nakszynski) Sopot, Poland, 1926.

KINSKI, NASTASSJA: Germany, Jan. 24, 1960.

KIRKLAND, SALLY: 1943, NYC Actors Studio

KITT, EARTHA: North, SC, Jan. 26, 1928.

KLEMPERER, WERNER: Cologne, Mar. 22, 1920.

KLINE, KEVIN: St. Louis, Mo, Oct. 24, 1947, Juilliard.

KLUGMAN, JACK: Philadelphia, PA, Apr. 27, 1925. Carnegie Tech.

KNIGHT, MICHAEL: 1959, Princeton, NJ

KNIGHT, SHIRLEY: Goessel, KS, July 5, 1937. Wichita U.

KNOWLES, PATRIC (Reginald Lawrence Knowles): Horsforth, Eng., Nov. 11, 1911.

KNOX, ALEXANDER: Strathroy, Ont., CAN., Jan. 16, 1907.

KNOX, ELYSE: Hartford, CT, Dec. 14, 1917. Traphagen School.

KOENIG, WALTER: Chicago, IL, Sept. 14. UCLA.

KOHNER, SUSAN: Los Angeles, Nov. 11, 1936. U. Calif.

KORMAN, HARVEY: Chicago, IL, Feb. 15, 1927. Goodman.

KORVIN, CHARLES (Geza Korvin Karpathi): Czechoslovakia, Nov. 21. Sorbonne.

KOSLECK, MARTIN: Barkotzen, Ger., Mar. 24, 1907. Max Reinhardt School.

KOTTO, YAPHET: NYC, Nov. 15, 1937.

KRABBE, JEROEN: Holland 1944.

KREUGER, KURT: St. Moritz, Switz., July 23, 1917. U. London.

KRISTEL, SYLVIA: Amsterdam, Hol., Sept. 28, 1952.

KRISTOFFERSON, KRIS: Brownsville, TX, June 22, 1936. Pomona Col.

KRUGER, HARDY: Berlin Ger., April 12, 1928.

KULP, NANCY: Harrisburg, PA, Aug. 28, 1921.

KUNTSMANN, DORIS: Hamburg, 1944.

KWAN, NANCY: Hong Kong, May 19, 1939. Royal Ballet.

LaBELLE, PATTI: Philadelphia, Pa., May 24, 1944.

LACY, JERRY: Sioux City, IA, Mar. 27, 1936. LACC.

LADD, CHERYL: (Stoppelmoor): Huron, SD, July 12, 1951.

LADD, DIANE: (Ladnier): Meridian, MS, Nov. 29, 1932. Tulane U.

LaGRECA, PAUL: Bronx, NY, June 23, 1962. AADA.

LAHTI, CHRISTINE: Detroit, MI, Apr. 4, 1950; U. Mich.

LAMARR, HEDY (Hedwig Kiesler): Vienna, Sept. 11, 1913.

LAMAS, LORENZO: Los Angeles, Jan. 28, 1958.

LAMB, GIL: Minneapolis, June 14, 1906. U. Minn.

LAMBERT, CHRISTOPHER: NYC, 1958.

LAMOUR, DOROTHY (Mary Dorothy Slaton): New Orleans, LA.; Dec. 10, 1914. Spence School.

LANCASTER, BURT: NYC, Nov. 2, 1913. NYU.

LANDAU, MARTIN: Brooklyn, NY, June 20, 1931. Actors Studio.

LANDON, MICHAEL (Eugene Orowitz): Collingswood, NJ, Oct. 31, 1936. USC.

LANDRUM, TERI: Enid, OK., 1960.

LANE, ABBE: Brooklyn, Dec. 14, 1935.

LANE, DIANE: NYC, Jan. 1963.

LANGAN, GLENN: Denver, CO, July 8, 1917.

LANGE, HOPE: Redding Ridge, CT, Nov. 28, 1933. Reed Col.

LANGE, JESSICA: Cloquet, Mn, Apr. 20, 1949. U. Minn.

LANSBURY, ANGELA: London, Oct. 16, 1925. London Academy of Music.

LANGELLA, FRANK: Bayonne, NJ, Jan. 1, 1940, SyracuseU.

LANSING, ROBERT (Brown): San Diego, CA, June 5, 1929.

LaPLANTE, LAURA: Nov. 1, 1904, St. Louis, Mo.

LARROQUETTE, JOHN: Nov. 25, 1947, New Orleans, LA.

LASSER, LOUISE: Apr. 11, 1939, NYC. Brandeis U.

LAUPER, CYNTHIA: Astoria, Queens, NYC. June 20, 1953.

LAURE, CAROLE: Montreal, Can., 1951.

LAURIE, PIPER (Rosetta Jacobs): Detroit, MI, Jan. 22, 1932.

LAW, JOHN PHILLIP: Hollywood, Sept. 7, 1937. Neighborhood Playhouse, U. Hawaii.

LAWRENCE, BARBARA: Carnegie, OK, Feb. 24, 1930. UCLA.

LAWRENCE, CAROL (Laraia): Melrose Park, IL, Sept. 5, 1935.

LAWRENCE, VICKI: Inglewood, CA, Mar. 26, 1949.

LAWSON, LEIGH: Atherston, Eng., July 21, 1945. RADA.

LEACHMAN, CLORIS: Des Moines, IA, Apr. 30, 1930. Northwestern U.

LEAUD, JEAN-PIERRE: Paris, 1944.

LEDERER, FRANCIS: Karlin, Prague, Czech., Nov. 6, 1906.

LEE, BRANDON: Feb. 1, 1965. EmersonCol.

LEE, CHRISTOPHER: London, May 27, 1922. Wellington College.

LEE, PEGGY: (Norma Delores Egstrom): Jamestown, ND, May 26, 1920.

LEE, MARK: Australia, 1958.

LEE, MICHELE (Dusiak): Los Angeles, June 24, 1942. LACC.

LEIBMAN, RON: NYC, Oct. 11, 1937. Ohio Wesleyan.

LEIGH, JANET (Jeanette Helen Morrison): Merced, CA, July 6, 1926. College of Pacific.

LEMMON, JACK: Boston, Feb. 8, 1925. Harvard.

LENO, JAY: Apr. 28, 1950, New Rochelle, NY. Emerson Col.

LENZ, RICK: Springfield, IL, Nov. 21, 1939. U. Mich.

LEONARD, SHELDON (Bershad): NYC, Feb. 22, 1907, Syracuse U.

LEROY, PHILIPPE: Paris, Oct. 15, 1930. U. Paris.

LESLIE, BETHEL: NYC, Aug. 3, 1929. Brearley School.

LESLIE, JOAN (Joan Brodell): Detroit, Jan. 26, 1925. St. Benedict's.

LESTER, MARK: Oxford, Eng., July 11, 1958.

LEVELS, CALVIN: Cleveland, OH., Sept. 30, 1954. CCC.

LEVIN, RACHEL: 1954, NYC. Goddard Col.

LEWIS, CHARLOTTE: London, 1968.

LEWIS, DANIEL DAY: London, 1958, Bristol Old Vic.

LEWIS, EMMANUEL: Brooklyn, NY, March 9, 1971.

LEWIS, JERRY: Newark, NJ, Mar. 16, 1926.

LIGON, TOM: New Orleans, LA, Sept. 10, 1945.

LILLIE, BEATRICE: Toronto, Can., May 29, 1898.

LINCOLN, ABBEY (Anna Marie Woolridge): Chicago, Aug. 6, 1930.

LINDFORS, VIVECA: Uppsala, Sweden, Dec. 29, 1920. Stockholm Royal Dramatic School.

LINN-BAKER, MARK: St. Louis, Mo, 1954, Yale.

LIOTTA, RAY: 1955, Newark, NJ. UMiami.

LISI, VIRNA: Rome, Nov. 8, 1937.

LITHGOW, JOHN: Rochester, NY, Oct. 19, 1945. Harvard.

LITTLE, CLEAVON: Chickasha, OK, June 1, 1939. San Diego State.

LLOYD, EMILY: 1970, London.

LOCKE, SONDRA: Shelbyville, TN, May, 28, 1947.

LOCKHART, JUNE: NYC, June 25, 1925. Westlake School.

LOCKWOOD, GARY: Van Nuys, CA, Feb. 21, 1937.

LOCKWOOD, MARGARET: Karachi, Pakistan, Sept. 15, 1916. RADA.

LOGGIA, ROBERT: Staten Island, NY., Jan. 3, 1930. UMo.

LOLLOBRIGIDA, GINA: Subiaco, Italy, July 4, 1927. Rome Academy of Fine Arts.

LOM, HERBERT: Prague, Czechoslovakia, Jan 9, 1917. Prague U.

LOMEZ, CELINE: Montreal, Can., 1953.

LONDON, JULIE (Julie Peck): Santa Rosa, CA, Sept. 26, 1926.

LONE, JOHN: 1952, Hong Kong. AADA

LONG, SHELLEY: Ft. Wayne, IN, Aug. 23, 1949. Northwestern U.

LONOW, MARK: Brooklyn, NY.

LOPEZ, PERRY: NYC, July 22, 1931. NYU.

LORD, JACK (John Joseph Ryan): NYC, Dec. 30, 1928. NYU.

LOREN, SOPHIA (Sofia Scicolone): Rome, Italy, Sept. 20, 1934.

LOUISE, TINA (Blacker): NYC, Feb. 11, 1934, Miami U.

LOWE, CHAD: NYC, Jan, 15, 1968.

LOWE, ROB: Ohio, 1964.

LOWITSCH, KLAUS: Berlin, Apr. 8, 1936. Vienna Academy.

LOY, MYRNA (Myrna Williams): Helena, MT, Aug. 2, 1905. Westlake School.

LUCAS, LISA: Arizona, 1961.

LULU: Glasglow, Scot., 1948.

LUNA, BARBARA: NYC, Mar. 2, 1939.

LUND, JOHN: Rochester, NY, Feb. 6, 1913.

LUNDGREN, DOLPH: Stockholm, Sw., 1959. Royal Inst.

LUPINO, IDA: London, Feb. 4, 1916. RADA.

LuPONE, PATTI: Northport, NY, Apr. 21, 1949, Juilliard.

LYDON, JAMES: Harrington Park, NJ, May 30, 1923.

LYNLEY, CAROL (Jones): NYC, Feb. 13, 1942.

LYNN, JEFFREY: Auburn, MA, 1909. Bates College.

LYON, SUE: Davenport, IA, July 10, 1946.

LYONS, ROBERT F.: Albany, NY. AADA

MacARTHUR, JAMES: Los Angeles, Dec. 8, 1937. Harvard.

MACCHIO, RALPH: Huntington, NY., 1961.

MacGINNIS, NIALL: Dublin, Ire., Mar. 29, 1913. Dublin U.

MacGRAW, ALI: NYC, Apr. 1, 1938. Wellesley.

MacLAINE, SHIRLEY (Beatty): Richmond, VA, Apr. 24, 1934.

MacLEOD, GAVIN: Mt. Kisco, NY, Feb. 28, 1931.

MacMAHON, ALINE: McKeesport, PA, May 3, 1899. Barnard College.

MacMURRAY, FRED: Kankakee, IL, Aug. 30, 1908. Carroll Col.

MACNAUGHTON, ROBERT: NYC, Dec. 19, 1966.

MACNEE, PATRICK: London, Feb. 1922.

MacNICOL, PETER: Dallas, TX, Apr. 10, UMN.

MADISON, GUY (Robert Moseley): Bakersfield, CA, Jan. 19, 1922. Bakersfield Jr. College.

MADONNA (Madonna Louise Veronica Cicone): Aug. 16, 1958, Bay City, MI. UMi.

Paul
LaGreca

Angela
Lansbury

Calvin
Levels

Carol
Lynley

Peter
MacNicol

Lonette
McKee

MAHARIS, GEORGE: Astoria, NY, Sept. 1, 1928. Actors Studio.

MAHONEY, JOCK (Jacques O'Mahoney): Chicago, Feb. 7, 1919. U. of Iowa.

MAHONEY, JOHN: Manchester, Eng., June 20, 1940, WUIll.

MAILER, KATE: 1962, NYC

MAJORS, LEE: Wyandotte, MI, Apr. 23, 1940. E. Ky. State Col.

MAKEPEACE, CHRIS: Toronto, Can., 1964.

MALDEN, KARL. (Mladen Sekulovich): Gary, IN, Mar. 22, 1914.

MALET, PIERRE: St. Tropez, Fr., 1955.

MALKOVICH, JOHN: Christopher, IL, Dec. 9, 1953, IllStateU.

MALLE, JADE: 1974, France.

MALONE, DOROTHY: Chicago, Jan. 30, 1925. S. Methodist U.

MANN, KURT: Roslyn, NY, July 18, 1947.

MANOFF, DINAH: NYC, Jan. 25, 1958. CalArts.

MANTEGNA, JOE: Chicago, IL, Nov. 13, 1947, Goodman Theatre.

MANZ, LINDA: NYC, 1961.

MARAIS, JEAN: Cherbourg, France, Dec. 11, 1913. St. Germain.

MARGOLIN, JANET: NYC, July 25, 1943. Walden School.

MARIN, JACQUES: Paris, Sept. 9, 1919. Conservatoire National.

MARINARO, ED: NYC, 1951. Cornell.

MARSHALL, BRENDA (Ardis Anderson Gaines): Isle of Negros, P.I., Sept. 29, 1915. Texas State College.

MARSHALL, E. G.: Owatonna, MN, June 18, 1910. U. Minn.

MARSHALL, KEN: NYC, 1953. Juilliard.

MARSHALL, PENNY: Bronx, NY, Oct. 15, 1942. U. N. Mex.

MARSHALL, WILLIAM: Gary, IN, Aug. 19, 1924. NYU.

MARTIN, DEAN (Dino Crocetti): Steubenville, OH, June 17, 1917.

MARTIN, GEORGE N.: NYC, Aug. 15, 1929.

MARTIN, MARY: Weatherford, TX, Dec. 1, 1914. Ward-Belmont School.

MARTIN, STEVE: Waco, TX, 1945. UCLA.

MARTIN, TONY (Alfred Norris): Oakland, CA, Dec. 25, 1913. St. Mary's College.

MASON, MARSHA: St. Louis, MO, Apr. 3, 1942. Webster Col.

MASON, PAMELA (Pamela Kellino): Westgate, Eng., Mar. 10, 1918.

MASSEN, OSA: Copenhagen, Den., Jan. 13, 1916.

MASSEY, DANIEL: London, Oct. 10, 1933. Eton and King's Col.

MASTERS, BEN: Corvallis, Or, May 6, 1947, UOr.

MASTERSON, MARY STUART: NYC, 1967, NYU.

MASTERSON, PETER: Angleton, TX, June 1, 1934. Rice U.

MASTRANTONIO, MARY ELIZABETH: Chicago, Il., Nov. 17, 1958. UIll.

MASTROIANNI, MARCELLO: Fontana Liri, Italy, Sept. 28, 1924.

MATHESON, TIM: Glendale, CA, Dec. 31, 1947. CalState.

MATHIS, JOHNNY: San Francisco, Ca., Sept. 30, 1935. SanFranStateCol.

MATLIN, MARLEE: Morton Grove, IL., Aug. 24, 1965.

MATTHAU, WALTER (Matuschanskayasky): NYC, Oct. 1, 1920.

MATTHEWS, BRIAN: Philadelphia, PA, Jan. 24, 1953. St. Olaf.

MATURE, VICTOR: Louisville, KY, Jan. 29, 1915.

MAY, ELAINE (Berlin): Philadelphia, Apr. 21, 1932.

MAYEHOFF, EDDIE: Baltimore, July 7. Yale.

MAYO, VIRGINIA (Virginia Clara Jones): St. Louis, MO, Nov. 30, 1920.

McCALLUM, DAVID: Scotland, Sept. 19, 1933. Chapman Col.

McCAMBRIDGE, MERCEDES: Jolliet, IL, Mar. 17, 1918. Mundelein College.

McCARTHY, ANDREW: NYC, 1963, NYU.

McCARTHY, KEVIN: Seattle, WA, Feb. 15, 1914. Minn. U.

McCLANAHAN, RUE: Healdton, OK, Feb. 21, 1935.

McCLORY, SEAN: Dublin, Ire., Mar. 8, 1924. U. Galway.

McCLURE, DOUG: Glendale, CA, May 11, 1935. UCLA.

McCOWEN, ALEC: Tunbridge Wells, Eng., May 26, 1925. RADA.

McCRARY, DARIUS: 1976, Walnut, Ca.

McCREA, JOEL: Los Angeles, Nov. 5, 1905. Pomona College.

McDERMOTT, DYLAN: 1962, NYC. Neighborhood Playhouse

McDOWALL, RODDY: London, Sept. 17, 1928. St. Joseph's.

McDOWELL, MALCOLM (Taylor): Leeds, Eng., June 15, 1943. LAMDA.

McENERY, PETER: Walsall, Eng., Feb. 21, 1940.

McFARLAND, SPANKY: Dallas, TX, Oct. 2, 1926.

McGAVIN, DARREN: Spokane, WA, May 7, 1922. College of Pacific.

McGILLIS, KELLY: Newport Beach, CA, July 9, 1957. Juilliard.

McGOVERN, ELIZABETH: Evanston, IL, July 18, 1961. Juilliard.

McGREGOR, JEFF: 1957, Chicago. UMn.

McGUIRE, BIFF: New Haven, CT, Oct. 25, 1926. Mass. State Col.

McGUIRE, DOROTHY: Omaha, NE, June 14, 1918.

McHATTIE, STEPHEN: Antigonish, NS, Feb. 3. AcadiaU, AADA.

McKAY, GARDNER: NYC, June 10, 1932. Cornell.

McKEE, LONETTE: Detroit, MI, 1954.

McKELLEN, IAN: Burnley, Eng., May 25, 1939.

McKENNA, VIRGINIA: London, June 7, 1931.

McKEON, DOUG: New Jersey, 1966.

McKUEN, ROD: Oakland, CA, Apr. 29, 1933.

McLERIE, ALLYN ANN: Grand Mere, Can., Dec. 1, 1926.

McNAIR, BARBARA: Chicago, Mar. 4, 1939. UCLA.

McNALLY, STEPHEN (Horace McNally): NYC, July 29, 1913. Fordham U.

McNICHOL, KRISTY: Los Angeles, CA, Sept. 11, 1962.

McQUEEN, ARMELIA: North Carolina, Jan. 6, 1952. Bklyn Consv.

McQUEEN, BUTTERFLY: Tampa, FL, Jan. 8, 1911. UCLA.

McQUEEN, CHAD: Los Angeles, CA, 1961. Actors Studio.

MEADOWS, AUDREY: Wuchang, China, 1924. St. Margaret's.

MEADOWS, JAYNE (formerly, Jayne Cotter): Wuchang, China, Sept. 27, 1920. St. Margaret's.

MEARA, ANNE: Brooklyn, NY, Sept. 20, 1929.

MEDWIN, MICHAEL: London, 1925. Instut Fischer.

MEISNER, GUNTER: Bremen, Ger., Apr. 18, 1926. Municipal Drama School.

MEKKA, EDDIE: Worcester, MA, 1932. Boston Cons.

MELATO, MARIANGELA: Milan, Italy, 1941. Milan Theatre Acad.

MELL, MARISA: Vienna, Austria, Feb. 25, 1939.

MERCADO, HECTOR JAIME: NYC, 1949. HB Studio.

MERCOURI, MELINA: Athens, Greece, Oct. 18, 1915.

MEREDITH, BURGESS: Cleveland, OH, Nov. 16, 1908. Amherst.
MEREDITH, LEE (Judi Lee Sauls): Oct., 1947. AADA.
MERRILL, DINA (Nedinia Hutton): NYC, Dec. 9, 1925. AADA.
MERRILL, GARY: Hartford, CT, Aug. 2, 1915. Bowdoin, Trinity.
METZLER, JIM: Oneonda, NY. Dartmouth Col.
MICHELL, KEITH: Adelaide, Aus., Dec. 1, 1926.
MIDLER, BETTE: Honolulu, HI., Dec. 1, 1945.
MIFUNE, TOSHIRO: Tsingtao, China, Apr. 1, 1920.
MILANO, ALYSSA: Brooklyn, NY, 1975.
MILES, JOANNA: Nice, France, Mar. 6, 1940.
MILES, SARAH: Ingatestone, Eng., Dec. 31, 1941. RADA.
MILES, SYLVIA: NYC, Sept. 9, 1932. Actors Studio.
MILES, VERA (Ralston): Boise City, OK, Aug. 23, 1929. UCLA.
MILFORD, PENELOPE: Winnetka, IL.
MILLER, ANN (Lucille Ann Collier): Chireno, TX, Apr. 12, 1919. Lawler Professional School.
MILLER, BARRY: Los Angeles, Ca., Feb. 6, 1958
MILLER, JASON: Long Island City, NY, Apr. 22, 1939. Catholic U.
MILLER, LINDA: NYC, Sept. 16, 1942. Catholic U.
MILLER, REBECCA: 1962, Roxbury, Ct. Yale.
MILLS, HAYLEY: London, Apr. 18, 1946. Elmhurst School.
MILLS, JOHN: Suffolk, Eng., Feb. 22, 1908.
MILNER, MARTIN: Detroit, MI, Dec. 28, 1931.
MIMIEUX, YVETTE: Los Angeles, Jan. 8, 1941. Hollywood High.
MINNELLI, LIZA: Los Angeles, Mar. 12, 1946.
MIOU-MIOU: Paris, Feb. 22, 1950.
MITCHELL, CAMERON (Mizell): Dallastown, PA, Nov. 4, 1918. N.Y. Theatre School.
MITCHELL, JAMES: Sacramento, CA, Feb. 29, 1920. LACC.
MITCHUM, JAMES: Los Angeles, CA, May 8, 1941.
MITCHUM, ROBERT: Bridgeport, CT, Aug. 6, 1917.
MODINE, MATTHEW: 1960, Utah
MOLINA, ALFRED: 1954, London. Guildhall
MONTALBAN, RICARDO: Mexico City, Nov. 25, 1920.
MONTAND, YVES (Yves Montand Livi): Mansummano, Tuscany, Oct. 13, 1921.
MONTGOMERY, BELINDA: Winnipeg, Can., July 23, 1950.
MONTGOMERY, ELIZABETH: Los Angeles, Apr. 15, 1933. AADA.
MONTGOMERY, GEORGE (George Letz): Brady, MT, Aug. 29, 1916. U. Mont.
MOOR, BILL: Toledo, OH, July 13, 1931. Northwestern.
MOORE, CONSTANCE: Sioux City, IA, Jan. 18, 1919.
MOORE, DEMI (Guines): Roswell, NMx, Nov. 11, 1962.
MOORE, DICK: Los Angeles, Sept. 12, 1925.
MOORE, DUDLEY: Apr. 19, 1935, Dagenham, Essex, Eng.
MOORE, FRANK: Bay-de-Verde, Newfoundland, 1946.

MOORE, KIERON: County Cork, Ire., 1925. St. Mary's College.
MOORE, MARY TYLER: Brooklyn, Dec. 29, 1936.
MOORE, ROGER: London, Oct. 14, 1927. RADA.
MOORE, TERRY (Helen Koford): Los Angeles, Jan. 7, 1929.
MORALES, ESAI: Brooklyn, 1963.
MOREAU, JEANNE: Paris, Jan. 23, 1928.
MORENO, RITA (Rosita Alverio): Humacao, P.R., Dec. 11, 1931.
MORGAN, DENNIS (Stanley Morner): Prentice, WI, Dec. 10, 1910. Carroll College.
MORGAN, HARRY (HENRY) (Harry Bratsburg): Detroit, Apr. 10, 1915. U. Chicago.
MORGAN, MICHELE (Simone Roussel): Paris, Feb. 29, 1920. Paris Dramatic School.
MORIARTY, CATHY: Bronx, NY, 1961.
MORIARTY, MICHAEL: Detroit, MI, Apr. 5, 1941. Dartmouth.
MORISON, PATRICIA: NYC, 1915.
MORITA, NORIYUKI "PAT": June 28, 1933, Isleton, Ca.
MORLEY, ROBERT: Wiltshire, Eng., May 26, 1908. RADA.
MORRIS, ANITA: Durham, NC, 1932.
MORRIS, GREG: Cleveland, OH, Sept. 27, 1934. Ohio State.
MORRIS, HOWARD: NYC, Sept. 4, 1919. NYU.
MORSE, DAVID: Hamilton, MA, 1953.
MORSE, ROBERT: Newton, MA, May 18, 1931.
MORTON, JOE: NYC, Oct. 18, 1947, HofstraU.
MOSS, ARNOLD: NYC, Jan. 28, 1910. CCNY.
MOUCHET, CATHERINE: Paris, 1959, Ntl. Consv.
MOYA, EDDY: El Paso, TX, Apr. 11, 1963. LACC.
MULL, MARTIN: N. Ridgefield, Oh., Aug. 18, 1941. RISch. of Design.
MULLIGAN, RICHARD: NYC, Nov. 13, 1932.
MURPHY, EDDIE: Brooklyn, NY, Apr. 3, 1961.
MURPHY, GEORGE: New Haven, CT, July 4, 1902. Yale.
MURPHY, MICHAEL: Los Angeles, CA, May 5, 1938, UAz.
MURRAY, BILL: Evanston, IL, Sept. 21, 1950. Regis Col.
MURRAY, DON: Hollywood, July 31, 1929. AADA.
MURRAY, KEN (Don Court): NYC, July 14, 1903.
MUSANTE, TONY: Bridgeport, CT, June 30, 1936. Oberlin Col.
NABORS, JIM: Sylacauga, GA, June 12, 1932.
NADER, GEORGE: Pasadena, CA, Oct. 19, 1921. Occidental College.
NADER, MICHAEL: Los Angeles, CA, 1945.
NAMATH, JOE: Beaver Falls, Pa, May 31, 1943. UAla.
NAPIER, ALAN: Birmingham, Eng., Jan. 7, 1903. Birmingham University.
NATWICK, MILDRED: Baltimore, June 19, 1908. Bryn Mawr.
NAUGHTON, DAVID: 1955
NAUGHTON, JAMES: Middletown, CT, Dec. 6, 1945. Yale.

NAVIN, JOHN P., JR.: Philadelphia, PA, 1968.
NEAL, PATRICIA: Packard, KY, Jan. 20, 1926. Northwestern U.
NEFF, HILDEGARDE (Hildegard Knef): Ulm, Ger., Dec. 28, 1925. Berlin Art Academy.
NELL, NATHALIE: Paris, Oct. 1950.
NELLIGAN, KATE: London, Ont., Can., Mar. 16, 1951. U Toronto.
NELSON, BARRY (Robert Nielsen): Oakland, CA, Apr. 16, 1920.
NELSON, DAVID: NYC, Oct. 24, 1936. USC.
NELSON, GENE (Gene Berg): Seattle, WA, Mar. 24, 1920.
NELSON, HARRIET HILLIARD (Peggy Lou Snyder): Des Moines, IA, July 18, 1914.
NELSON, JUDD: Maine, 1959, Haverford Col.
NELSON, LORI (Dixie Kay Nelson): Santa Fe, NM, Aug. 15, 1933.
NELSON, WILLIE: Texas, Apr. 30, 1933.
NETTLETON, LOIS: Oak Park, IL. Actors Studio.
NEWHART, BOB: Chicago, IL, Sept. 5, 1929. Loyola U.
NEWLEY, ANTHONY: Hackney, London, Sept. 21, 1931.
NEWMAN, BARRY: Boston, MA, Mar. 26, 1938. Brandeis U.
NEWMAN, PAUL: Cleveland, OH, Jan. 26, 1925. Yale.
NEWMAR, JULIE (Newmeyer): Los Angeles, Aug. 16, 1935.
NEWTON-JOHN, OLIVIA: Cambridge, Eng., Sept. 26, 1948.
NGUYEN, DUSTIN: 1962, Saigon.
NICHOLAS, PAUL: London, 1945.
NICHOLS, MIKE (Michael Igor Peschkowsky): Berlin, Nov. 6, 1931. U. Chicago.
NICHOLSON, JACK: Neptune, NJ, Apr. 22, 1937.
NICKERSON, DENISE: NYC, 1959.
NICOL, ALEX: Ossining, NY, Jan. 20, 1919. Actors Studio.
NIELSEN, BRIGITTE: 1963, Denmark.
NIELSEN, LESLIE: Regina, Saskatchewan, Can., Feb. 11, 1926. Neighborhood Playhouse.
NIMOY, LEONARD: Boston, MA, Mar. 26, 1931. Boston Col., Antioch Col.
NIXON, CYNTHIA: NYC, Apr. 9, 1966. Columbia U.
NOBLE, JAMES: Dallas, TX, Mar. 5, 1922, SMU.
NOLAN, KATHLEEN: St. Louis, MO, Sept. 27, 1933. Neighborhood Playhouse.
NOLTE, NICK: Omaha, NE, Feb. 8, 1940. Pasadena City Col.
NORRIS, CHRISTOPHER: NYC, Oct. 7, 1943. Lincoln Square Acad.
NORRIS, CHUCK (Carlos Ray): Ryan, OK, 1939.
NORTH, HEATHER: Pasadena, CA, Dec. 13, 1950. Actors Workshop.
NORTH, SHEREE (Dawn Bethel): Los Angeles, Jan. 17, 1933. Hollywood High.
NORTON, KEN: Aug. 9, 1945.
NOURI, MICHAEL: Washington, DC, Dec. 9, 1945.
NOVAK, KIM (Marilyn Novak): Chicago, Feb. 18, 1933. LACC.
NUREYEV, RUDOLF: Russia, Mar. 17, 1938.
NUTE, DON: Connellsville, PA, Mar. 13, Denver U.

Dina
Merrill

Barry
Miller

Cynthia
Nixon

Don
Nute

Maureen
O'Sullivan

Anthony
Perkins

NUYEN, FRANCE (Vannga): Marseilles, France, July 31, 1939. Beaux Arts School.

O'BRIAN, HUGH (Hugh J. Krampe): Rochester, NY, Apr. 19, 1928. Cincinnati U.

O'BRIEN, CLAY: Ray, AZ, May 6, 1961.

O'BRIEN, MARGARET (Angela Maxine O'Brien): Los Angeles, Jan. 15, 1937.

O'CONNOR, CARROLL: Bronx, NY, Aug. 2, 1925. Dublin National Univ.

O'CONNOR, DONALD: Chicago, Aug. 28, 1925.

O'CONNOR, GLYNNIS: NYC, Nov. 19, 1956. NYSU.

O'CONNOR, KEVIN: Honolulu, HI, May 7, 1938, U. Hi.

O'DAY, DAWN: aka Anne Shirley (see).

O'HANLON, GEORGE: Brooklyn, NY, Nov. 23, 1917.

O'HARA, MAUREEN (Maureen FitzSimons): Dublin, Ire., Aug. 17, 1920. Abbey School.

O'HERLIHY, DAN: Wexford, Ire., May 1, 1919. National U.

O'KEEFE, MICHAEL: Paulland, NJ, Apr. 24, 1955, NYU, AADA.

OLDMAN, GARY: 1959, New Gross, South London, Eng.

OLIVIER, LAURENCE: Dorking, Eng., May 22, 1907. Oxford.

OLMOS, EDWARD JAMES: Feb. 24, 1947, Los Angeles, CA. CSLA.

O'LOUGHLIN, GERALD S.: NYC, Dec. 23, 1921. U. Rochester.

OLSON, NANCY: Milwaukee, WI, July 14, 1928. UCLA.

O'NEAL, GRIFFIN: Los Angeles, 1965.

O'NEAL, PATRICK: Ocala, FL, Sept. 26, 1927. U. Fla.

O'NEAL, RON: Utica, NY, Sept. 1, 1937. Ohio State.

O'NEAL, RYAN: Los Angeles, Apr. 20, 1941.

O'NEAL, TATUM: Los Angeles, Nov. 5, 1963.

O'NEIL, TRICIA: Shreveport, LA, Mar. 11, 1945. Baylor U.

O'NEILL, JENNIFER: Rio de Janeiro, Feb. 20, 1949. Neighborhood Playhouse.

O'SULLIVAN, MAUREEN: Byle, Ire., May 17, 1911. Sacred Heart Convent.

O'TOOLE, ANNETTE (Toole): Houston, TX, Apr. 1, 1952. UCLA.

O'TOOLE, PETER: Connemara, Ire., Aug. 2, 1932. RADA.

PACINO, AL: NYC, Apr. 25, 1940.

PAGE, TONY (Anthony Vitiello): Bronx, NY, 1940.

PAGET, DEBRA (Debralee Griffin): Denver, Aug. 19, 1933.

PAIGE, JANIS (Donna Mae Jaden): Tacoma, WA, Sept. 16, 1922.

PALANCE, JACK (Walter Palanuik): Lattimer, PA, Feb. 18, 1920. UNC.

PALMER, BETSY: East Chicago, IN, Nov. 1, 1929. DePaul U.

PALMER, GREGG (Palmer Lee): San Francisco, Jan. 25, 1927. U. Utah.

PAMPANINI, SILVANA: Rome, Sept. 25, 1925.

PANEBIANCO, RICHARD: 1971 NYC

PANTALIANO, JOEY: Hoboken, NJ. 1952.

PAPAS, IRENE: Chiliomodion, Greece, Mar. 9, 1929.

PARE, MICHAEL: Brooklyn, NY, 1959.

PARKER, ELEANOR: Cedarville, OH, June 26, 1922. Pasadena Playhouse.

PARKER, FESS: Fort Worth, TX, Aug. 16, 1927. USC.

PARKER, JAMESON: Baltimore, MD, Nov. 18, 1947. Beloit Col.

PARKER, JEAN (Mae Green): Deer Lodge, MT, Aug. 11, 1912.

PARKER, RAY, JR.: 1957, Detroit

PARKER, SUZY (Cecelia Parker): San Antonio, TX, Oct. 28, 1933.

PARKER, WILLARD (Worster Van Eps): NYC, Feb. 5, 1912.

PARKINS, BARBARA: Vancouver, Can., May 22, 1943.

PARSONS, ESTELLE: Lynn, MA, Nov. 20, 1927. Boston U.

PARTON, DOLLY: Sevierville, TN, Jan. 19, 1946.

PATINKIN, MANDY: Chicago, IL, Nov. 30, 1952. Juilliard.

PATRIC, JASON: 1966, NYC

PATRICK, DENNIS: Philadelphia, Mar. 14, 1918.

PATTERSON, LEE: Vancouver, Can., Mar. 31, 1929. Ontario Col.

PATTON, WILL: Charleston, SC, June 14, 1954.

PAVAN, MARISA (Marisa Pierangeli): Cagliari, Sardinia, June 19, 1932. Torquado Tasso College.

PAYNE, JOHN: Roanoke, Va., March 23, 1912.

PEACH, MARY: Durban, S. Africa, 1934.

PEARL, MINNIE (Sarah Cannon): Centerville, TN, Oct. 25, 1912.

PEARSON, BEATRICE: Denison, TX, July 27, 1920.

PECK, GREGORY: La Jolla, CA, Apr. 5, 1916. U. Calif.

PELIKAN, LISA: Paris, July 12. Juilliard.

PENHALL, BRUCE: Balboa, CA, 1958.

PENN, SEAN: Burbank, Ca., Aug. 17, 1960.

PENNY, JOE: London, 1957.

PEPPARD, GEORGE: Detroit, Oct. 1, 1928. Carnegie Tech.

PEREZ, JOSE: NYC 1940.

PERKINS, ANTHONY: NYC, Apr. 14, 1932. Rollins College.

PERKINS, ELIZABETH: Queens, NY, Nov. 18, 1960. Goodman School.

PERLMAN, RON: Apr. 13, 1950 in NYC. UMn.

PERREAU, GIGI (Ghislaine): Los Angeles, Feb. 6, 1941.

PERRINE, VALERIE: Galveston, TX, Sept. 3, 1944. U. Ariz.

PESCOW, DONNA: Brooklyn, NY, 1954.

PETERS, BERNADETTE (Lazzara): Jamaica, NY, Feb. 28, 1948.

PETERS, BROCK: NYC, July 2, 1927. CCNY.

PETERS, JEAN (Elizabeth): Canton, OH, Oct. 15, 1926. Ohio State U.

PETERS, MICHAEL: Brooklyn, NY, 1948.

PETTET, JOANNA: London, Nov. 16, 1944. Neighborhood Playhouse.

PFEIFFER, MICHELLE: Santa Ana, CA, 1957.

PHILLIPS, LOU DIAMOND: 1962, Phillipines, UTx.

PHILLIPS, MacKENZIE: Alexandria, VA, Nov. 10, 1959.

PHILLIPS, MICHELLE (Holly Gilliam): NJ, June 4, 1944.

PHOENIX, RAINBOW: 1973

PHOENIX, RIVER: Madras, Ore., 1970.

PICERNI, PAUL: NYC, Dec. 1, 1922. Loyola U.

PINCHOT, BRONSON: NYC May 20, 1959, Yale.

PINE, PHILLIP: Hanford, CA, July 16, 1925. Actors' Lab.

PISCOPO, JOE: Passaic, NJ. June 17, 1951.

PISIER, MARIE-FRANCE: Vietnam, May 10, 1944. U. Paris.

PITILLO, MARIA: 1965, Mahwah, NJ.

PLACE, MARY KAY: Port Arthur, TX, Sept., 1947. U. Tulsa.

PLAYTEN, ALICE: NYC, Aug. 28, 1947. NYU.

PLEASENCE, DONALD: Workshop, Eng., Oct. 5, 1919. Sheffield School.

PLESHETTE, SUZANNE: NYC, Jan. 31, 1937. Syracuse U.

PLOWRIGHT, JOAN: Scunthorpe, Brigg, Lincolnshire, Eng., Oct. 28, 1929. Old Vic.

PLUMB, EVE: Burbank, Ca, Apr. 29, 1958.

PLUMMER, AMANDA: NYC, Mar. 23, 1957. Middlebury Col.

PLUMMER, CHRISTOPHER: Toronto, Can., Dec. 13, 1927.

PODESTA, ROSSANA: Tripoli, June 20, 1934.

POITIER, SIDNEY: Miami, FL, Feb. 27, 1924.

POLITO, LINA: Naples, Italy, Aug. 11, 1954.

POLLAN, TRACY: 1962, NYC

POLLARD, MICHAEL J.: Pacific, NJ, May 30, 1939.

PORTER, ERIC: London, Apr. 8, 1928. Wimbledon Col.

POWELL, JANE (Suzanne Burce): Portland, OR, Apr. 1, 1928.

POWELL, ROBERT: Salford, Eng., June 1, 1944. Manchester U.

POWER, TARYN: Los Angeles, CA, 1954.

POWER, TYRONE IV: Los Angeles, CA, Jan. 1959.

POWERS, MALA (Mary Ellen): San Francisco, Dec. 29, 1921. UCLA.

POWERS, STEFANIE (Federkiewicz): Hollywood, CA, Oct. 12, 1942.

PRENTISS, PAULA (Paula Ragusa): San Antonio, TX, Mar. 4, 1939. Northwestern U.

PRESLE, MICHELINE (Micheline Chassagne): Paris, Aug. 22, 1922. Rouleau Drama School.

PRESNELL, HARVE: Modesto, CA, Sept. 14, 1933. USC.

PRESTON, WILLIAM: Columbia, Pa., Aug. 26, 1921. PaStateU.

PRICE, LONNY: NYC, Mar. 9, 1959, Juilliard.

PRICE, VINCENT: St. Louis, May 27, 1911. Yale.

PRIMUS, BARRY: NYC, Feb. 16, 1938. CCNY.

PRINCE (P. Rogers Nelson): Minneapolis, MN, June 7, 1958.

PRINCE, WILLIAM: Nicholas, NY, Jan. 26, 1913. Cornell U.

PRINCIPAL, VICTORIA: Fukuoka, Japan, Mar. 3, 1945. Dade Jr. Col.

PROCHNOW, JURGEN: Germany, 1941.

PROVAL, DAVID: Brooklyn, NY, 1943.

PROVINE, DOROTHY: Deadwood, SD, Jan. 20, 1937. U. Wash.

PROWSE, JULIET: Bombay, India, Sept. 25, 1936.

PRYCE, JONATHAN: Wales, UK, June 1, 1947, RADA.

PRYOR, RICHARD: Peoria, IL, Dec. 1, 1940.

PULLMAN, BILL: Delhi, NY, 1954, SUNY/Oneonta, UMass.

PURCELL, LEE: Cherry Point, NC, June 15, 1947. Stephens.

PURDOM, EDMUND: Welwyn Garden City, Eng., Dec. 19, 1924. St. Ignatius College.

PYLE, DENVER: Bethune, CO, May 11, 1920.

QUAID, DENNIS: Houston, TX, Apr. 9, 1954.

QUAID, RANDY: Houston, TX, 1950, UHouston.

QUAYLE, ANTHONY: Lancashire, Eng., Sept. 7, 1913. Old Vic School.

QUINE, RICHARD: Detroit, MI, Nov. 12, 1920.

QUINLAN, KATHLEEN: Mill Valley, CA, Nov. 19, 1954.

QUINN, AIDAN: Chicago, IL, Mar. 8, 1959.

QUINN, ANTHONY: Chihuahua, Mex., Apr. 21, 1915.

RADNER, GILDA: Detroit, MI, June 28, 1946.

RAFFERTY, FRANCES: Sioux City, IA, June 16, 1922. UCLA.

RAFFIN, DEBORAH: Los Angeles, Mar. 13, 1953. Valley Col.

RAINER, LUISE: Vienna, Aust., Jan. 12, 1910.

RALSTON, VERA: (Vera Helena Hruba) Prague, Czech., July 12, 1919.

RAMPLING, CHARLOTTE: Surmer, Eng., Feb. 5, 1946. U. Madrid.

RAMSEY, LOGAN: Long Beach, CA, Mar. 21, 1921. St. Joseph.

RANDALL, TONY (Leonard Rosenberg): Tulsa, OK, Feb. 26, 1920. Northwestern U.

RANDELL, RON: Sydney, Australia, Oct. 8, 1920. St. Mary's Col.

RASHAD, PHYLICIA (Ayers-Allen): Houston, Tx. June 17, 1948.

RASULALA, THALMUS (Jack Crowder): Miami, FL, Nov. 15, 1939. U. Redlands.

RAY, ALDO (Aldo DeRe): Pen Argyl, PA, Sept. 25, 1926. UCLA.

RAYE, MARTHA (Margie Yvonne Reed): Butte, MT, Aug. 27, 1916.

RAYMOND, GENE (Raymond Guion): NYC, Aug. 13, 1908.

REAGAN, RONALD: Tampico, IL, Feb. 6, 1911. Eureka College.

REASON, REX: Berlin, Ger., Nov. 30, 1928. Pasadena Playhouse.

REDDY, HELEN: Australia, Oct. 25, 1942.

REDFORD, ROBERT: Santa Monica, CA, Aug. 18, 1937. AADA.

REDGRAVE, CORIN: London, July 16, 1939.

REDGRAVE, LYNN: London, Mar. 8, 1943.

REDGRAVE, VANESSA: London, Jan. 30, 1937.

REDMAN, JOYCE: County Mayo, Ire., 1919. RADA.

REED, OLIVER: Wimbledon, Eng., Feb. 13, 1938.

REED, REX: Ft. Worth, TX, Oct. 2, 1939. LSU.

REEMS, HARRY (Herbert Streicher): Bronx, NY, 1947. U. Pittsburgh.

REEVE, CHRISTOPHER: NJ, Sept. 25, 1952. Cornell, Juilliard.

REEVES, KEANU: 1965.

REEVES, STEVE: Glasgow, MT, Jan. 21, 1926.

REGEHR, DUNCAN: Lethbridge, Can., 1954.

REID, ELLIOTT: NYC, Jan. 16, 1920.

REINER, CARL: NYC, Mar. 20, 1922. Georgetown.

REINER, ROB: NYC, Mar. 6, 1945. UCLA.

REINHOLD, JUDGE (Edward Ernest, Jr.): Wilmington, DE, 1957. NCSchool of Arts.

REINKING, ANN: Seattle, WA, Nov. 10, 1949.

REMAR, JAMES: Boston, Ma., Dec. 31, 1953. Neighborhood Playhouse.

REMICK, LEE: Quincy, MA. Dec. 14, 1935. Barnard College.

RETTIG, TOMMY: Jackson Heights, NY, Dec. 10, 1941.

REVILL, CLIVE: Wellington, NZ, Apr. 18, 1930.

REY, FERNANDO: La Coruna, Spain, Sept. 20, 1917.

REYNOLDS, BURT: Waycross, GA, Feb. 11, 1935. Fla. State U.

REYNOLDS, DEBBIE (Mary Frances Reynolds): El Paso, TX, Apr. 1, 1932.

REYNOLDS, MARJORIE: Buhl, ID, Aug. 12, 1921.

RHOADES, BARBARA: Poughkeepsie, NY, 1947.

RICHARDS, JEFF (Richard Mansfield Taylor): Portland, OR, Nov. 1. USC.

RICHARDSON, NATASHA: 1964, London

RICKLES, DON: NYC, May 8, 1926. AADA.

RIEGERT, PETER: NYC, Apr. 11, 1947. U Buffalo.

RIGG, DIANA: Doncaster, Eng., July 20, 1938. RADA.

RINGWALD, MOLLY: Rosewood, CA, Feb. 14, 1968.

RITTER, JOHN: Burbank, CA, Sept. 17, 1948. U.S. Cal.

RIVERS, JOAN (Molinsky): Brooklyn, NY, June 8, 1933.

ROBARDS, JASON: Chicago, July 26, 1922. AADA.

ROBERTS, ERIC: Biloxi, MS, Apr. 18, 1956. RADA.

ROBERTS, RALPH: Salisbury, NC, Aug. 17, 1922. UNC.

ROBERTS, TANYA (Leigh): NYC, 1955.

ROBERTS, TONY: NYC, Oct. 22, 1939. Northwestern U.

ROBERTSON, CLIFF: La Jolla, CA, Sept. 9, 1925. Antioch Col.

ROBERTSON, DALE: Oklahoma City, July 14, 1923.

ROBINSON, CHRIS: Nov. 5, 1938, West Palm Beach, FL. LACC.

ROBINSON, JAY: NYC, Apr. 14, 1930.

ROBINSON, ROGER: Seattle, WA, May 2, 1941. USC.

ROCHEFORT, JEAN: Paris, 1930.

ROCK-SAVAGE, STEVEN: Melville, LA, Dec. 14, 1958. LSU.

ROGERS, CHARLES "BUDDY": Olathe, KS, Aug. 13, 1904. U. Kan.

ROGERS, GINGER (Virginia Katherine McMath): Independence, MO, July 16, 1911.

ROGERS, MIMI: Coral Gables, FL, 1956

ROGERS, ROY (Leonard Slye): Cincinnati, Nov. 5, 1912.

ROGERS, WAYNE: Birmingham, AL, Apr. 7, 1933. Princeton.

ROLAND, GILBERT (Luis Antonio Damaso De Alonso): Juarez, Mex., Dec. 11, 1905.

ROLLINS, HOWARD E., JR.: 1951, Baltimore, MD.

ROMAN, RUTH: Boston, Dec. 23, 1922. Bishop Lee Dramatic School.

ROMANCE, VIVIANE (Pauline Ronacher Ortmanns): Vienna, Aust. 1912.

ROME, SIDNE: Akron, OH. Carnegie-Mellon.

ROMERO, CESAR: NYC, Feb. 15, 1907. Collegiate School.

RONSTADT, LINDA: Tucson, AZ, July 15, 1946.

ROONEY, MICKEY (Joe Yule, Jr.): Brooklyn, Sept. 23, 1920.

ROSE, REVA: Chicago, IL, July 30, 1940. Goodman.

ROSS, DIANA: Detroit, MI, Mar. 26, 1944.

ROSS, JUSTIN: Brooklyn, NY, Dec. 15, 1954.

ROSS, KATHARINE: Hollywood, Jan. 29, 1943. Santa Rosa Col.

ROSSELLINI, ISABELLA: Rome, June 18, 1952.

ROUNDTREE, RICHARD: New Rochelle, NY, Sept. 7, 1942. Southern Ill.

| Victoria Principal | Burt Reynolds | Isabella Rossellini | John Sala | Susan Sarandon | John Shea |

ROURKE, MICKEY: Miami, FL, 1950.

ROWE, NICHOLAS: London, Nov. 22, 1966. Eton.

ROWLANDS, GENA: Cambria, WI, June 19, 1934.

RUBIN, ANDREW: New Bedford, MA, June 22, 1946. AADA.

RUBINSTEIN, JOHN: Los Angeles, Ca, Dec. 8, 1946, UCLA.

RUBINSTEIN, ZELDA: Pittsburg, Pa.

RUCKER, BO: Tampa, Fl, Aug. 17, 1948.

RUDD, PAUL: Boston, MA, May 15, 1940.

RULE, JANICE: Cincinnati, OH, Aug. 15, 1931.

RUPERT, MICHAEL: Denver, CO, Oct. 23, 1951. Pasadena Playhouse.

RUSH, BARBARA: Denver, CO, Jan. 4, 1929. U. Calif.

RUSSELL, JANE: Bemidji, MI, June 21, 1921. Max Reinhardt School.

RUSSELL, JOHN: Los Angeles, Jan. 3, 1921. U. Calif.

RUSSELL, KURT: Springfield, MA, Mar. 17, 1951.

RUSSELL, THERESA: 1958, Los Angeles

RUSSO, JAMES: NYC, Apr. 23, 1953.

RUTHERFORD, ANN: Toronto, Can., Nov. 2, 1917.

RUYMEN, AYN: Brooklyn, July 18, 1947. HB Studio.

RYAN, MEG: 1962, NYC NYU

RYAN, TIM (Meineslschmidt): 1958, Staten Island, NY. Rutgers U.

SACCHI, ROBERT: Bronx, NY, 1941. NYU.

SAINT, EVA MARIE: Newark, NJ, July 4, 1924. Bowling Green State U.

ST. JACQUES, RAYMOND (James Arthur Johnson):CT.

ST. JAMES, SUSAN (Suzie Jane Miller): Los Angeles, Aug. 14, 1946. Conn. Col.

ST. JOHN, BETTA: Hawthorne, CA, Nov. 26, 1929.

ST. JOHN, JILL (Jill Oppenheim): Los Angeles, Aug. 19, 1940.

SALA, JOHN: Los Angeles, CA., Oct. 5, 1962.

SALDANA, THERESA: Brooklyn, NY, 1955.

SALINGER, MATT: New Hampshire, 1960. Princeton, Columbia.

SALMI, ALBERT: Coney Island, NY, 1925. Actors Studio.

SALT, JENNIFER: Los Angeles, Sept. 4, 1944. Sarah Lawrence Col.

SANDS, TOMMY: Chicago, Aug. 27, 1937.

SAN JUAN, OLGA: NYC, Mar. 16, 1927.

SARANDON, CHRIS: Beckley, WV, July 24, 1942. U. WVa., Catholic U.

SARANDON, SUSAN (Tomalin): NYC, Oct. 4, 1946. Catholic U.

SARGENT, RICHARD (Richard Cox): Carmel, CA, 1933. Stanford.

SARRAZIN, MICHAEL: Quebec City, Can., May 22, 1940.

SAVAGE, JOHN (Youngs): Long Island, NY, Aug. 25, 1949. AADA.

SAVALAS, TELLY (Aristotle): Garden City, NY, Jan. 21, 1925. Columbia.

SAVIOLA, CAMILLE: Bronx, NY, July 16, 1950.

SAVOY, TERESA ANN: London, July 18, 1955.

SAXON, JOHN (Carmen Orrico): Brooklyn, Aug. 5, 1935.

SCALIA, JACK: Brooklyn, NY, 1951.

SCARPELLI, GLEN: Staten Island, NY, July 1966.

SCARWID, DIANA: Savannah, GA. AADA, Pace U.

SCHEIDER, ROY: Orange, NJ, Nov. 10, 1932. Franklin-Marshall.

SCHEINE, RAYNOR: Emporia, Va., Nov. 10th. VaCommonwealthU.

SCHELL, MARIA: Vienna, Jan. 15, 1926.

SCHELL, MAXIMILIAN: Vienna, Dec. 8, 1930.

SCHLATTER, CHARLIE: 1967, NYC, Ithaca Col.

SCHNEIDER, MARIA: Paris, Mar. 27, 1952.

SCHRODER, RICKY: Staten Island, NY, Apr. 13, 1970.

SCHWARZENEGGER, ARNOLD: Austria, July 30, 1947.

SCHYGULLA, HANNA: Katlowitz, Poland. 1943.

SCOFIELD, PAUL: Hurstpierpoint, Eng., Jan. 21, 1922. London Mask Theatre School.

SCOLARI, PETER: Sept. 12, 1956. Scarsdale, NY, NYCC.

SCOTT, DEBRALEE: Elizabeth, NJ, Apr. 2.

SCOTT, GEORGE C.: Wise, VA, Oct. 18, 1927. U. Mo.

SCOTT, GORDON (Gordon M. Werschkul): Portland, OR, Aug. 3, 1927. Oregon U.

SCOTT, LIZABETH (Emma Matso): Scranton, Pa., Sept. 29, 1922.

SCOTT, MARTHA: Jamesport, MO, Sept. 22, 1914. U. Mich.

SCOTT-TAYLOR, JONATHAN: Brazil, 1962.

SEAGAL, STEVE: 1951.

SEAGULL, BARBARA HERSHEY see Hershey, Barbara

SEARS, HEATHER: London, Sept. 28, 1935.

SECOMBE, HARRY: Swansea, Wales, Sept. 8, 1921.

SEGAL, GEORGE: NYC, Feb. 13, 1934. Columbia.

SELLARS, ELIZABETH: Glasgow, Scot., May 6, 1923.

SELLECK, TOM: Detroit, MI, Jan. 29, 1945. USCal.

SELWART, TONIO: Watenberg, Ger., June 9, 1906. Munich U.

SERNAS, JACQUES: Lithuania, July 30, 1925.

SERRAULT, MICHEL: Brunoy, France, 1928, Paris Consv.

SETH, ROSHAN: New Delhi, India, 1942.

SEYLER, ATHENE (Athene Hannen): London, May 31, 1889.

SEYMOUR, ANNE: NYC, Sept. 11, 1909. American Laboratory Theatre.

SEYMOUR, JANE (Joyce Frankenberg): Hillingdon, Eng., Feb. 15, 1951.

SEYRIG, DELPHINE: Beirut, 1932.

SHANDLING, GARRY: Tucson, Az, 1950, UAz.

SHARIF, OMAR (Michel Shalhoub): Alexandria, Egypt, Apr. 10, 1932. Victoria Col.

SHARKEY, RAY: Brooklyn, NY, 1952. HB Studio.

SHATNER, WILLIAM: Montreal, Can., Mar. 22, 1931. McGill U.

SHAVER, HELEN: St. Thomas, Ontario, Can., 1951.

SHAW, SEBASTIAN: Holt, Eng., May 29, 1905. Gresham School.

SHAW, STAN: Chicago, IL, 1952.

SHEA, JOHN V.: North Conway, NH, Apr. 14, 1949. Bates, Yale.

SHEARER, MOIRA: Dunfermline, Scot., Jan. 17, 1926. London Theatre School.

SHEEDY, ALLY: NYC, June 13, 1962. USC.

SHEEN, CHARLIE (Carlos Irwin Estevez): Los Angeles, Ca., 1961.

SHEEN, MARTIN (Ramon Estevez): Dayton, OH, Aug. 3, 1940.

SHEFFIELD, JOHN: Pasadena, CA, Apr. 11, 1931. UCLA.

SHEPARD, SAM (Rogers): Ft. Sheridan, Il, Nov. 5, 1943.

SHEPHERD, CYBILL: Memphis, TN, Feb. 18, 1950. Hunter, NYU.

SHIELDS, BROOKE: NYC, May 31, 1965.

SHIRE, TALIA: Lake Success, NY, Apr. 25, 1946. Yale.

SHIRLEY, ANNE (Dawn Evelyn Paris): Apr. 17, 1918 NYC.

SHORE, DINAH (Frances Rose Shore): Winchester, TN, Mar. 1, 1917. Vanderbilt U.

SHORT, MARTIN: Toronto, Can, 1950, McMasterU.

SHOWALTER, MAX (formerly Casey Adams): Caldwell, KS, June 2, 1917. Pasadena Playhouse.

SHUE, ELIZABETH: 1964, South Orange, NJ. Harvard

SIDNEY, SYLVIA: NYC, Aug. 8, 1910. Theatre Guild School.

SILVER, RON: NYC, July 2, 1946. SUNY.

SILVERMAN, JONATHAN: Los Angeles, Ca, Aug. 5, 1966, USCal.

SIMMONS, JEAN: London, Jan. 31, 1929. Aida Foster School.

SIMON, SIMONE: Marseilles, France, Apr. 23, 1910.

SIMPSON, O. J. (Orenthal James): San Francisco, CA, July 9, 1947. UCLA.

SINATRA, FRANK: Hoboken, NJ, Dec. 12, 1915.

SINCLAIR, JOHN (Gianluigi Loffredo): Rome, Italy, 1946.

SINDEN, DONALD: Plymouth, Eng., Oct. 9, 1923. Webber-Douglas.

SINGER, LORI: NYC, May 6, 1962, Corpus Christi, TX. Juilliard.

SKALA, LILIA: Vienna. U. Dresden.

SKELTON, RED (Richard): Vincennes, IN, July 18, 1910.

SKERRITT, TOM: Detroit, MI, Aug. 25, 1933. Wayne State U.

SKYE, IONE (Leitch):1971, Hollywood, Ca.

SLATER, CHRISTIAN: Aug. 18, 1969, NYC.

SLATER, HELEN: NYC, Dec. 15, 1965.

SMIRNOFF, YAKOV (Yakov Pokhis): Odessa, USSR.

SMITH, ALEXIS: Penticton, Can., June 8, 1921. LACC.

SMITH, CHARLES MARTIN: Los Angeles, CA, 1954. CalState U.

SMITH, JACLYN: Houston, TX, Oct. 26, 1947.

SMITH, JOHN (Robert E. Van Orden): Los Angeles, Mar. 6, 1931. UCLA.

SMITH, LEWIS: Chattanooga, Tn, 1958. Actors Studio.

SMITH, LOIS: Topeka, KS, Nov. 3, 1930. U. Wash.

SMITH, MAGGIE: Ilford, Eng., Dec. 28, 1934.

SMITH, ROGER: South Gate, CA, Dec. 18, 1932. U. Ariz.

SMITHERS, WILLIAM: Richmond, VA, July 10, 1927. Catholic U.

SMITS, JIMMY: 1956, Brooklyn, NY. Cornell U.

SNODGRESS, CARRIE: Chicago, Oct. 27, 1946. UNI.

SOFONOVA, ELENA: 1956, Russia

SOLOMON, BRUCE: NYC, 1944. U. Miami, Wayne State U.

SOMERS, SUZANNE (Mahoney): San Bruno, CA, Oct. 16, 1946. Lone Mt. Col.

SOMMER, ELKE (Schletz): Berlin, Nov. 5, 1940.

SORDI, ALBERTO: Rome, Italy, June 15, 1919.

SORVINO, PAUL: NYC, 1939. AMDA.

SOTHERN, ANN (Harriet Lake): Valley City, ND, Jan. 22, 1907. Washington U.

SOUL, DAVID: Aug. 28, 1943.

SPACEK, SISSY: Quitman, TX, Dec. 25, 1949. Actors Studio.

SPANO, VINCENT: Brooklyn, NY, Oct. 18, 1962.

SPENSER, JEREMY: Ceylon, 1937.

SPINER, BRENT: Houston, Tx.

SPRINGER, GARY: NYC, July 29, 1954. Hunter Col.

SPRINGFIELD, RICK (Richard Springthorpe): Sydney, Aust. Aug. 23, 1949.

STACK, ROBERT: Los Angeles, Jan. 13, 1919. USC.

STADLEN, LEWIS J.: Brooklyn, Mar. 7, 1947. Neighborhood Playhouse.

STAFFORD, NANCY: Ft. Lauderdale, FL.

STALLONE, FRANK: NYC, July 30, 1950.

STALLONE, SYLVESTER: NYC, July 6, 1946. U. Miami.

STAMP, TERENCE: London, July 23, 1939.

STANDER, LIONEL: NYC, Jan. 11, 1908. UNC.

STANG, ARNOLD: Chelsea, MA, Sept. 28, 1925.

STANLEY, KIM (Patricia Reid): Tularosa, NM, Feb. 11, 1925. U. Tex.

STANWYCK, BARBARA (Ruby Stevens): Brooklyn, July 16, 1907.

STAPLETON, JEAN: NYC, Jan. 19, 1923.

STAPLETON, MAUREEN: Troy, NY, June 21, 1925.

STEEL, ANTHONY: London, May 21, 1920. Cambridge.

STEELE, TOMMY: London, Dec. 17, 1936.

STEENBURGEN, MARY: Newport, AR, 1953. Neighborhood Playhouse

STEIGER, ROD: Westhampton, NY, Apr. 14, 1925.

STERLING, JAN (Jane Sterling Adriance): NYC, Apr. 3, 1923. Fay Compton School.

STERLING, ROBERT (William Sterling Hart): Newcastle, PA, Nov. 13, 1917. U. Pittsburgh.

STERN, DANIEL: Bethesda, MD, 1957.

STEVENS, ANDREW: Memphis, TN, June 10, 1955.

STEVENS, CONNIE (Concetta Ann Ingolia): Brooklyn, Aug. 8, 1938. Hollywood Professional School.

STEVENS, FISHER: Chicago, IL, Nov. 27, 1963. NYU.

STEVENS, KAYE (Catherine): Pittsburgh, July 21, 1933.

STEVENS, MARK (Richard): Cleveland, OH, Dec. 13, 1920.

STEVENS, SHADOE (Terry Ingstad): 1947.

STEVENS, STELLA (Estelle Eggleston): Hot Coffee, MS, Oct. 1, 1936.

STEVENSON, PARKER: CT, June 4, 1953, Princeton.

STEWART, ALEXANDRIA: Montreal, Can., June 10, 1939. Louvre.

STEWART, ELAINE: Montclair, NJ, May 31, 1929.

STEWART, JAMES: Indiana, PA, May 20, 1908. Princeton.

STEWART, MARTHA (Martha Haworth): Bardwell, KY, Oct. 7, 1922.

STIMSON, SARA: Helotes, TX, 1973.

STING (Gordon Matthew Sumner): Wallsend, Eng., Oct. 2, 1951.

STOCKWELL, DEAN: Hollywood, Mar. 5, 1935.

STOCKWELL, JOHN: Galveston, Texas, March 25, 1961. Harvard.

STOLER, SHIRLEY: Brooklyn, NY, Mar. 30, 1929.

STOLTZ, ERIC: California, 1961, USC.

STORM, GALE (Josephine Cottle): Bloomington, TX, Apr. 5, 1922.

STRAIGHT, BEATRICE: Old Westbury, NY, Aug. 2, 1916. Dartington Hall.

STRASBERG, SUSAN: NYC, May 22, 1938.

STRASSMAN, MARCIA: New Jersey, 1949.

STRAUSS, PETER: NYC, Feb. 20, 1947.

STREEP, MERYL (Mary Louise): Summit, NJ, June 22, 1949., Vassar, Yale.

STREISAND, BARBRA: Brooklyn, Apr. 24, 1942.

STRITCH, ELAINE: Detroit, MI, Feb. 2, 1925. Drama Workshop.

STRODE, WOODY: Los Angeles, 1914.

STROUD, DON: Hawaii, 1937.

STRUTHERS, SALLY: Portland, OR, July 28, 1948. Pasadena Playhouse.

SULLIVAN, BARRY (Patrick Barry): NYC, Aug. 29, 1912. NYU.

SUMMER, DONNA (LaDonna Gaines): Boston, MA, Dec. 31, 1948.

SUTHERLAND, DONALD: St. John, New Brunswick, Can., July 17, 1934. U. Toronto.

SUTHERLAND, KIEFER: 1967, Los Angeles, Ca.

SVENSON, BO: Goteborg, Swed., Feb. 13, 1941. UCLA.

SWAYZE, PATRICK: 1952, Houston, Tx.

SWEENEY, DANIEL BERNARD: 1961, Shoreham, NY

SWINBURNE, NORA: Bath, Eng., July 24, 1902. RADA.

SWIT, LORETTA: Passaic, NJ, Nov. 4. 1937. AADA.

SYLVESTER, WILLIAM: Oakland, CA, Jan. 31, 1922. RADA.

SYMONDS, ROBERT: Bistow, AK, Dec. 1, 1926. TexU.

SYMS, SYLVIA: London, June 1, 1934. Convent School.

SZARABAJKA, KEITH: Oak Park, IL, Dec. 2, 1952, UChicago.

T, MR. (Lawrence Tero): Chicago, May 21, 1952.

TABORI, KRISTOFFER (Siegel): Los Angeles, Aug. 4, 1952.

TAKEI, GEORGE: Los Angeles, CA, Apr. 20. UCLA.

TALBOT, LYLE (Lysle Hollywood): Pittsburgh, Feb. 8, 1904.

TALBOT, NITA: NYC, Aug. 8, 1930. Irvine Studio School.

TAMBLYN, RUSS: Los Angeles, Dec. 30, 1934.

TANDY, JESSICA: London, June 7, 1909. Dame Owens' School.

TAYLOR, DON: Freeport, PA, Dec. 13, 1920. Penn State U.

TAYLOR, ELIZABETH: London, Feb. 27, 1932. Byron House School.

TAYLOR, ROD (Robert): Sydney, Aust., Jan. 11, 1929.

TAYLOR-YOUNG, LEIGH: Wash., DC, Jan. 25, 1945. Northwestern.

TEAGUE, ANTHONY SKOOTER: Jacksboro, TX, Jan. 4, 1940.

TEAGUE, MARSHALL: Newport, Tn.

TEEFY, MAUREEN: Minneapolis, MN, 1954; Juilliard.

TEMPLE, SHIRLEY: Santa Monica, CA, Apr. 23, 1927.

TERRY-THOMAS (Thomas Terry Hoar Stevens): Finchley, London, July 14, 1911. Ardingly College.

| Helen Slater | Eric Stoltz | Linda Thorson | Barry Tubb | Leslie Uggams | James Victor |

TERZIEFF, LAURENT: Paris, June 25, 1935.

TEWES, LAUREN: 1954, Pennsylvania

THACKER, RUSS: Washington, DC, June 23, 1946, Montgomery Col.

THAXTER, PHYLLIS: Portland, ME, Nov. 20, 1921. St. Genevieve.

THELEN, JODI: St. Cloud, MN., 1963.

THOMAS, DANNY (Amos Jacobs): Deerfield, MI, Jan. 6, 1914.

THOMAS, MARLO (Margaret): Detroit, Nov. 21, 1938. USC.

THOMAS, PHILIP MICHAEL: Columbus, OH, May 26, 1949. Oakwood Col.

THOMAS, RICHARD: NYC, June 13, 1951. Columbia.

THOMPSON, JACK (John Payne): Sydney, Aus., 1940. U. Brisbane.

THOMPSON, MARSHALL: Peoria, IL, Nov. 27, 1925. Occidental.

THOMPSON, REX: NYC, Dec. 14, 1942.

THOMPSON, SADA: Des Moines, IA, Sept. 27, 1929. Carnegie Tech.

THOMSON, GORDON: Ottawa, Can., 1945.

THORSON, LINDA: June 18, 1947, Toronto, Can. RADA

THULIN, INGRID: Solleftea, Sweden, Jan. 27, 1929. Royal Drama Theatre.

TICOTIN, RACHEL: Bronx, NY, 1958.

TIERNEY, GENE: Brooklyn, Nov. 20, 1920. Miss Farmer's School.

TIERNEY, LAWRENCE: Brooklyn, Mar. 15, 1919. Manhattan College.

TIFFIN, PAMELA (Wonso): Oklahoma City, Oct. 13, 1942.

TILLY, MEG: Texada, Can., 1960.

TODD, ANN: Hartford, Eng., Jan. 24, 1909.

TODD, RICHARD: Dublin, Ire., June 11, 1919. Shrewsbury School.

TOGNAZZI, UGO: Cremona, Italy, 1922.

TOLO, MARILU: Rome, Italy, 1944.

TOMEI, MARISA: Brooklyn, NY, Dec. 4, 1964, NYU.

TOMLIN, LILY: Detroit, MI, Sept. 1, 1939. Wayne State U.

TOOMEY, RÉGIS: Aug. 13, 1902, Pittsburgh, Pa.

TOPOL (Chaim Topol): Tel-Aviv, Israel, Sept. 9, 1935.

TORN, RIP: Temple, TX, Feb. 6, 1931. U. Tex.

TORRES, LIZ: NYC, 1947. NYU.

TOTTER, AUDREY: Joliet, IL, Dec. 20, 1918.

TOWSEND, ROBERT: Chicago, 1966.

TRAVERS, BILL: Newcastle-on-Tyne, Engl, Jan. 3, 1922.

TRAVIS, RICHARD (William Justice): Carlsbad, NM, Apr. 17, 1913.

TRAVOLTA, JOEY: Englewood, NJ, 1952.

TRAVOLTA, JOHN: Englewood, NJ, Feb. 18, 1954.

TREMAYNE, LES: London, Apr. 16, 1913. Northwestern, Columbia, UCLA.

TREVOR, CLAIRE (Wemlinger): NYC, March 8, 1909.

TRINTIGNANT, JEAN-LOUIS: Pont-St. Esprit, France, Dec. 11, 1930. Dullin-Balachova Drama School.

TRYON, TOM: Hartford, CT, Jan. 14, 1926. Yale.

TSOPEI, CORINNA: Athens, Greece, June 21, 1944.

TUBB, BARRY: 1963, Snyder, Tx., AmConsv.Th.

TURNER, KATHLEEN: Springfield, MO, June 19, 1954. UMd.

TURNER, LANA (Julia Jean Mildred Frances Turner): Wallace, ID, Feb. 8, 1921.

TURNER, TINA (Anna Mae Bullock) Nutbush, Tn, Nov. 26, 1938.

TURTURRO, John: Brooklyn, NY, Feb. 28, 1957, Yale.

TUSHINGHAM, RITA: Liverpool, Eng., 1940.

TUTIN, DOROTHY: London, Apr. 8, 1930.

TWIGGY (Lesley Hornby): London, Sept. 19, 1949.

TWOMEY, ANNE: Boston, Ma, June 7, 1951, Temple U.

TYLER, BEVERLY (Beverly Jean Saul): Scranton, PA, July 5, 1928.

TYRRELL, SUSAN: San Francisco, 1946.

TYSON, CATHY: Liverpool, Eng., 1966, RoyalShakeCo.

TYSON, CICELY: NYC, Dec. 19, 1933, NYU.

UGGAMS, LESLIE: NYC, May 25, 1943, Juilliard.

ULLMANN, LIV: Tokyo, Dec. 10, 1938. Webber-Douglas Acad.

UNDERWOOD, BLAIR: 1964, Tacoma, Wa. Carnegie-MellonU

USTINOV, PETER: London, Apr. 16, 1921. Westminster School.

VACCARO, BRENDA: Brooklyn, Nov. 18, 1939. Neighborhood Playhouse.

VALANDREY, CHARLOTTE: (Anne-Charlotte Pascal) Paris, 1968.

VALLI, ALIDA: Pola, Italy, May 31, 1921. Rome Academy of Drama.

VALLONE, RAF: Riogio, Italy, Feb. 17, 1916. Turin U.

VAN ARK, JOAN: June 16, 1943, NYC. Yale.

VAN CLEEF, LEE: Somerville, NJ, Jan. 9, 1925.

VAN DE VEN, MONIQUE: Holland, 1957.

VAN DEVERE, TRISH (Patricia Dressel): Englewood Cliffs, NJ, Mar. 9, 1945. Ohio Wesleyan.

VAN DOREN, MAMIE (Joan Lucile Olander): Rowena, SD, Feb. 6, 1933.

VAN DYKE, DICK: West Plains, MO, Dec. 13, 1925.

VAN FLEET, JO: Oakland, CA, Dec. 30, 1919.

VAN DAMME, JEAN CLAUDE: 1961, Belgium.

VANITY (Denise Mathews): 1963, Niagra, Ont., Can.

VAN PATTEN, DICK: NYC, Dec. 9, 1928.

VAN PATTEN, JOYCE: NYC, Mar. 9, 1934.

VAN PEEBLES, MARIO: 1958, NYC, ColumbiaU

VARSI, DIANE: Feb. 23, 1938, San Francisco, Ca.

VAUGHN, ROBERT: NYC, Nov. 22, 1932. USC.

VEGA, ISELA: Mexico, 1940.

VENNERA, CHICK: Herkimer, NY, Mar. 27, 1952. Pasadena Playhouse.

VENORA, DIANE: Hartford, Ct., 1952. Juilliard.

VENUTA, BENAY: San Francisco, Jan. 27, 1911.

VERDON, GWEN: Culver City, CA, Jan. 13, 1925.

VEREEN, BEN: Miami, FL, Oct. 10, 1946.

VICTOR, JAMES (Lincoln Rafael Peralta Diaz): Santiago, D.R., July 27, 1939. Haaren HS/NYC.

VILLECHAIZE, HERVE: Paris, Apr. 23, 1943.

VINCENT, JAN-MICHAEL: Denver, CO, July 15, 1944. Ventura.

VIOLET, ULTRA (Isabelle Collin-Dufresne): Grenoble, France.

VITALE, MILLY: Rome, Italy, July 16, 1938. Lycee Chateaubriand.

VOHS, JOAN: St. Albans, NY, July 30, 1931.

VOIGHT, JON: Yonkers, NY, Dec. 29, 1938. Catholic U.

VOLONTE, GIAN MARIA: Milan, Italy, Apr. 9, 1933.

VON DOHLEN, LENNY: Augusta, Ga., Dec. 22, 1958, UTex.

VON SYDOW, MAX: Lund, Swed., July 10, 1929. Royal Drama Theatre.

WAGNER, LINDSAY: Los Angeles, June 22, 1949.

WAGNER, ROBERT: Detroit, Feb. 10, 1930.

WAHL, KEN: Chicago, IL, 1957.

WAITE, GENEVIEVE: South Africa, 1949.

WAITS, TOM: 1949.

WALKEN, CHRISTOPHER: Astoria, NY, Mar. 31, 1943. Hofstra.

WALKER, CLINT: Hartfold, IL, May 30, 1927. USC.

WALKER, NANCY (Ann Myrtle Swoyer): Philadelphia, May 10, 1921.

WALLACH, ELI: Brooklyn, Dec. 7, 1915. CCNY, U. Tex.

WALLACH, ROBERTA: NYC, Aug. 2, 1955.

WALLIS, SHANI: London, Apr. 5, 1941.

WALSH, M. EMMET: Ogdensburg, NY, Mar. 22, 1935, Clarkson Col., AADA.

WALSTON, RAY: New Orleans, Nov. 22, 1917. Cleveland Playhouse.

WALTER, JESSICA: Brooklyn, NY, Jan. 31, 1940. Neighborhood Playhouse.

WALTERS, JULIE: 1950, London

WALTON, EMMA: London, Nov. 1962, Brown U.

WANAMAKER, SAM: Chicago, June 14, 1919. Drake.

WARD, BURT (Gervis): Los Angeles, July 6, 1945.

WARD, FRED: San Diego, Ca.

WARD, RACHEL: London, 1957.

WARD, SIMON: London, Oct. 19, 1941.

WARDEN, JACK: Newark, NJ, Sept. 18, 1920.

WARNER, DAVID: Manchester, Eng., 1941. RADA.

WARREN, JENNIFER: NYC, Aug. 12, 1941. U. Wisc.

WARREN, LESLEY ANN: NYC, Aug. 16, 1946.

WARREN, MICHAEL: South Bend, IN, Mar. 5, 1946. UCLA.

WARRICK, RUTH: St. Joseph, MO, June 29, 1915. U. Mo.

WASHBOURNE, MONA: Birmingham, Eng., Nov. 27, 1903.

WASHINGTON, DENZEL: Mt. Vernon, NY, Dec. 28, 1954. Fordham.

WASSON, CRAIG: Ontario, OR, Mar. 15, 1954. UOre.

WATERSTON, SAM: Cambridge, MA, Nov. 15, 1940. Yale.

WATLING, JACK: London, Jan. 13, 1923. Italia Conti School.

WATSON, DOUGLASS: Jackson, GA, Feb. 24, 1921. UNC.

WAYNE, DAVID (Wayne McKeehan): Travers City, MI, Jan. 30, 1914. Western Michigan State U.

WAYNE, PATRICK: Los Angeles, July 15, 1939. Loyola.

WEATHERS, CARL: New Orleans, LA, 1948. Long Beach CC.

WEAVER, DENNIS: Joplin, MO, June 4, 1924. U. Okla.

WEAVER, MARJORIE: Crossville, TN, Mar. 2, 1913. Indiana U.

WEAVER, SIGOURNEY (Susan): NYC, Oct. 8, 1949. Stanford, Yale.

WEBBER, ROBERT: Santa Ana, CA, Sept. 14, 1925. Compton Jr. Col.

WEDGEWORTH, ANN: Abilene, TX, Jan. 21, 1935. U. Tex.

WELCH, RAQUEL (Tejada): Chicago, Sept. 5, 1940.

WELD, TUESDAY (Susan): NYC, Aug. 27, 1943. Hollywood Professional School.

WELDON, JOAN: San Francisco, Aug. 5, 1933. San Francisco Conservatory.

WELLER, PETER: Stevens Point, Ws., June 24, 1947. AmThWing.

WELLES, GWEN: NYC, Mar. 4.

WESLEY, BILLY: July 1966, NYC.

WESTON, JACK (Morris Weinstein): Cleveland, OH, Aug. 21, 1915.

WHITAKER, JOHNNY: Van Nuys, CA, Dec. 13, 1959.

WHITE, BETTY: Oak Park, IL, Jan. 17, 1922.

WHITE, CAROL: London, Apr. 1, 1944.

WHITE, CHARLES: Perth Amboy, NJ, Aug. 29, 1920. Rutgers U.

WHITE, JESSE: Buffalo, NY, Jan. 3, 1919.

WHITE, VANNA: Feb. 18, 1957, North Myrtle Beach, SC

WHITMAN, STUART: San Francisco, Feb. 1, 1929. CCLA

WHITMORE, JAMES: White Plains, NY, Oct. 1, 1921. Yale.

WHITNEY, GRACE LEE: Detroit, MI, Apr. 1, 1930.

WHITTON, MARGARET: Philadelphia, PA., Nov. 30.

WIDDOES, KATHLEEN: Wilmington, DE, Mar. 21, 1939.

WIDMARK, RICHARD: Sunrise, MN, Dec. 26, 1914. Lake Forest.

WIEST, DIANNE: Kansas City, MO, Mar. 28, 1948, UMd.

WILBY, JAMES: 1958, Burma

WILCOX, COLIN: Highlands, NC, Feb. 4, 1937. U. Tenn.

WILDE, CORNEL: NYC, Oct. 13, 1915. CCNY, Columbia.

WILDER, GENE (Jerome Silberman): Milwaukee, Ws., June 11, 1935. UIowa.

WILLIAMS, BILLY DEE: NYC, Apr. 6, 1937.

WILLIAMS, CINDY: Van Nuys, CA, Aug. 22, 1947. LACC

WILLIAMS, DICK A.: Chicago, IL, Aug. 9, 1938.

WILLIAMS, ESTHER: Los Angeles, Aug. 8, 1921.

WILLIAMS, JOBETH: 1953. Houston, Tx. BrownU.

WILLIAMS, ROBIN: Chicago, IL, July 21, 1952. Juilliard.

WILLIAMS, TREAT (Richard): Rowayton, CT. Dec. 1, 1951.

WILLIAMSON, FRED: Gary, IN, Mar. 5, 1938. Northwestern.

WILLIAMSON, NICOL: Hamilton, Scot; Sept. 14, 1938.

WILLIS, BRUCE: Penns Grove, NJ, Mar. 18, 1956.

WILLISON, WALTER: Monterey Park, CA., June 24, 1947.

WILSON, DEMOND: NYC, Oct. 13, 1946. Hunter Col.

WILSON, FLIP (Clerow Wilson): Jersey City, NJ, Dec. 8, 1933.

WILSON, LAMBERT: Paris, 1959.

WILSON, NANCY: Chillicothe, OH, Feb. 20, 1937.

WILSON, SCOTT: Atlanta, GA, 1942.

WINCOTT, JEFF: 1957, Toronto, Canada.

WINDE, BEATRICE: Chicago, Jan. 6.

WINDOM, WILLIAM: NYC, Sept. 28, 1923. Williams Col.

WINDSOR, MARIE (Emily Marie Bertelson): Marysvale, UT, Dec. 11, 1924. Brigham Young U.

WINFIELD, PAUL: Los Angeles, May 22, 1940. UCLA.

WINFREY, OPRAH: Kosciusko, Ms., 1953. TnStateU.

WINGER, DEBRA: Cleveland, OH, May 17, 1955. Cal State.

WINKLER, HENRY: NYC, Oct. 30, 1945. Yale.

WINN, KITTY: Wash., D.C., 1944. Boston U.

WINTERS, JONATHAN: Dayton, OH, Nov. 11, 1925. Kenyon Col.

WINTERS, ROLAND: Boston, Nov. 22, 1904.

WINTERS, SHELLEY (Shirley Schrift): St. Louis, Aug. 18, 1922. Wayne U.

WITHERS, GOOGIE: Karachi, India, Mar. 12, 1917. Italia Conti

WITHERS, JANE: Atlanta, GA, Apr. 12, 1926.

WONG, RUSSELL: 1963, Troy, NY. Santa Monica Col.

WOODARD, ALFRE: Nov. 8 in Tulsa, Ok. Boston U.

WOODLAWN, HOLLY (Harold Ajzenberg): Juana Diaz, PR, 1947.

WOODS, JAMES: Vernal, UT, Apr. 18, 1947. MIT.

WOODWARD, EDWARD: June 1, 1930, Croyden, Surrey, Eng.

WOODWARD, JOANNE: Thomasville, GA, Feb. 27, 1930. Neighborhood Playhouse.

WOOLAND, NORMAN: Dusseldorf, Ger., Mar. 16, 1910. Edward VI School.

WOPAT, TOM: Lodi, WI, Sept. 9, 1951, UWis.

WORONOV, MARY: Brooklyn, Dec. 8, 1946. Cornell.

WORTH, IRENE: (Hattie Abrams) June 23, 1916, Neb. UCLA.

WRAY, FAY: Alberta, Can., Sept. 15, 1907.

WRIGHT, MAX: Detroit, MI, Aug. 2, 1943, WayneStateU.

WRIGHT, ROBIN: 1966, Texas.

WRIGHT, TERESA: NYC, Oct. 27, 1918.

WYATT, JANE: Campgaw, NJ, Aug. 10, 1911. Barnard College.

WYMAN, JANE (Sarah Jane Fulks): St. Joseph, MO, Jan. 4, 1914.

WYMORE, PATRICE: Miltonvale, KS, Dec. 17, 1926.

WYNN, MAY (Donna Lee Hickey): NYC, Jan. 8, 1930.

WYNTER, DANA (Dagmar): London, June 8, 1927. Rhodes U.

YORK, DICK: Fort Wayne, IN, Sept. 4, 1928. De Paul U.

YORK, MICHAEL: Fulmer, Eng., Mar. 27, 1942. Oxford.

YORK, SUSANNAH: London, Jan. 9, 1941. RADA.

YOUNG, ALAN (Angus): North Shield, Eng., Nov. 19, 1919.

YOUNG, BURT: Queens, NY, Apr. 30, 1940.

YOUNG, LORETTA (Gretchen): Salt Lake City, Jan. 6, 1912. Immaculate Heart College.

YOUNG, ROBERT: Chicago, Feb. 22, 1907.

YOUNG, SEAN: 1960, Louisville, Ky. Interlochen.

ZACHARIAS, ANN: Stockholm, Sw., 1956.

ZADORA, PIA: Hoboken, NY. 1954.

ZAPPA, DWEEZIL: 1970, Hollywood, Ca.

ZETTERLING, MAI: Sweden, May 27, 1925. Ordtuery Theatre School.

ZIMBALIST, EFREM, JR.: NYC, Nov. 30, 1918. Yale.

ZUNIGA, DAPHNE: 1963, Berkeley, Ca. UCLA

Walter Abel

Fred Astaire

Mary Astor

Ray Bolger

OBITUARIES

WALTER ABEL, 88, Minnesota-born film, stage, radio, and TV character actor, died March 26 in a nursing home in Essex, CT. Active on Broadway from 1919 to 1976, he appeared in a vast number of films, including *Out of a Clear Sky* (1918), *Liliom, The Three Musketeers, The Lady Consents, Two in the Dark, Fury, Wise Girl, Green Light, Racket Busters, Arise My Love, Miracle on Main Street, Hold Back the Dawn, Beyond the Blue Horizon, Star Spangled Rhythm, Holiday Inn, Mr. Skeffington, The Affairs of Susan, Kiss and Tell, Skylark, Follow the Boys, Duffy's Tavern, The Kid from Brooklyn, 13 Rue Madeleine, Dream Girl, So This is Love, Night People, Island in the Sky, Bernadine, Raintree County, Handle With Care, Mirage,* and *Grace Quigley* (1985). He is survived by two sons.

YVES ALLEGRET, 79, prominent French director who launched the career of actress Simone Signoret (his wife from 1944 to 49) and a leading figure of post-World War II French cinema, died of undisclosed causes Jan. 31 in Paris. He began as assistant director to his older brother, Marc Allegret, and made short subjects in the 30's, including *The Girls of France,* shown at the 1939 New York World's Fair. His films include *Le Demons de l'aube* (1946, Signoret's first major role), *Dedoc, d'Anvers (Dedee), Une si jolie petite plage (Riptide)* (considered to be his masterpiece), *Maneges (The Cheat), Les Orgueilleux (The Proud and the Beautiful), La Meilleure part, Germinal, Les Miracles n'ont lieu qu'une fois, Mam'zell Nitouche, La Jeune folle, Oasis, Mefiezvous fillettes,* and *Mords pas - on t'aime* (1976). He was to receive a career achievement French Cesar Award at the Palais des Congres March 7. Survived by his daughter with Signoret, actress Catherine Allegret.

JEAN ANOUILH, 77, Bordeaux-born screenplay writer and director and foremost French dramatist of his generation, died of a heart attack Oct. 3 at Vaudois U. Hospital Center in Lausanne, Switzerland. His screenplays include *Les Otages, Cavalcade d'Amour, Monsieur Vincent, Anna Karenina* (1947), *Caroline Cherie, La Mort de Belle, La Ronde, Time for Loving* (1971), and several of his stage successes were filmed, notably *Becket* and *Waltz of the Toreadors.* He is survived by his second wife, a son, and three daughters.

FRED ASTAIRE, 88, Nebraska-born screen, stage, radio, and TV dancer, actor, and choreographer whose incomparable elegance, charismatic personality, and creative genius made him one of our greatest screen legends, died of pneumonia in the arms of his wife, former jockey Robyn Smith, on June 22 in Los Angeles, CA. After early stage success, partnered with older sister Adele, in 11 Broadway shows, he danced with filmdom's most glamorous leading ladies, first gaining star status partnered with Ginger Rogers in *Flying Down to Rio* (1934), followed by *The Gay Divorcee, Roberta, Top Hat, Follow the Fleet, Swing Time, Shall We Dance?, Carefree, The Story of Vernon and Irene Castle,* and *The Barkleys of Broadway* (1949). His nearly 40 films also include *Dancing Lady* (his debut), *The Broadway Melody of 1940, Second Chorus, You'll Never Get Rich, Holiday Inn, You Were Never Lovelier, The Sky's the Limit, Ziegfeld Follies, Yolanda and the Thief, Blue Skies, Easter Parade, Three Little Words, Let's Dance, Royal Wedding, The Belle of New York, The Band Wagon, Daddy Long Legs, Funny Face, Silk Stockings, On the Beach, The Pleasure of His Company, Notorious Landlady, The Midas Run, The Towering Inferno, The Amazing Dobermans, The Purple Taxi, Ghost Story, Finian's Rainbow, That's Entertainment,* and *That's Entertainment Part 2* (dancing at age 68). His many honors include the Special Academy Award in 1949 for "raising the standards of all musicals," two Emmys, the 1978 Kennedy Center Honors, and The American Film Institute Life Achievement Award in 1981. He is survived by his wife, a son, a daughter, and a stepson.

MARY ASTOR, 81, Illinois-born film, stage, radio, and TV actress, 1941 Academy Award-winner for *The Great Lie,* and author of five novels, an autobiography, and a memoir, who made a successful transition from silents to sound films, and who gained further prominence in 1935 when steamy excerpts from her diary were published in retaliation for a custody suit (which she later won), died Sept. 25 of respiratory failure at the Motion Picture and Television Country House & Hospital in Woodland Hills, CA. Her more than 100 films include *The Beggar Maid* (debut), *John Smith* (1922), *Beau Brummel, Two Arabian Knights, Dressed to Kill, Success, The Bright Shawl, Hollywood, The Marriage Maker, Puritan Passions, The Rapids, Woman-Proof, The Fighting Crowd, The Fighting American, Unguarded Women, The Price of a Party, Inez from Hollywood, Oh Doctor!, Enticement, Playing With Souls, Don Q Son of Zorro, The Pace That Thrills, Scarlet Saint, High Steppers, The Wise Guy, Don Juan, Forever After, The Sea Tiger, The Rough Riders, The Sunset Derby, Rose of the Golden West, No Place to Go, Sailors' Wives, Three-Ring Marriage, Heart to Heart, Dry Martini, Romance of the Underworld, New Year's Eve, The Woman from Hell, Dodsworth, The Prisoner of Zenda, Brigham Young, The Maltese Falcon, The Palm Beach Story, Meet Me in St. Louis, Little Women, Any Number Can Play, A Kiss Before Dying, The Power and the Prize, The Devil's Hairpin, This Happy Feeling, Stranger in My Arms, Return to Peyton Place, Youngblood Hawke,* and *Hush, Hush . . . Sweet Charlotte* (1965). She is survived by a son and a daughter.

RUTH ATTAWAY, 77, Mississippi-born film, stage, radio, and TV actress, died Sept. 21 at New York Hospital of injuries resulting from a fire in her apartment. Her films include *Raintree County, The President's Lady, Porgy and Bess,* and *Being There.* A sister survives.

SHERWOOD BAILEY, 64, remembered as the red-haired, freckle-faced Spud in the *Our Gang* comedies, died of cancer in Newport Beach, CA on Aug. 6. His other films include *Too Many Parents* and *Young Tom Edison.* No reported survivors.

SPENCER GORDON BENNET, 94, New York City-born director who became Hollywood's first "Serial King," died in October in Santa Monica, CA. His films include *The Green Archer* (1925), *The House Without a Key, The Secret Code, The Masked Marvel, Code of the Pony Express, Superman* (1948), and *Perils of the Wilderness* (1956). No reported survivors.

COLIN BLAKELY, 56, Northern Ireland-born film, stage, and TV actor, died of leukemia May 7 in London. One of Britain's most popular actors, his films include *This Sporting Life, A Man for All Seasons, The Private Life of Sherlock Holmes, The Pink Panther Strikes Again, Equus, The Dogs of War, Loophole, The National Health,* and *Evil Under the Sun.* Survived by his wife and three sons.

RAY BOLGER, 83, Boston-born screen, stage, and TV actor, comedian, and dancer, forever immortalized by his portrayal of the beloved Scarecrow in MGM's 1939 classic *The Wizard of Oz,* died of cancer January 15 in Los Angeles. His other films include *The Great Ziegfeld, Rosalie, Sweethearts, Where's Charley, The Harvey Girls, April in Paris, Babes in Toyland, The Runner Stumbles,* and *That's Dancing* (1985). Among his many honors are the 1948–49 Tony Award and two Donaldson Awards, and in 1980 he was elected to the Theatre Hall of Fame. Surviving is his wife, former producer Gwen Rickard.

| Madeleine Carroll | James Coco | Calvin Culver | Viola Dana | King Donovan | Richard Egan |

WILLIAM BOWERS, 71, screenwriter who won Academy Award nominations for *The Gunfighter* (1950) and *The Sheepman* (1958), died of respiratory failure March 27 at the Motion Picture and Television Hospital in Woodland Hills, CA. His other screenplays include *Night and Day, The Web, Cry Danger, The Best Things in Life Are Free, My Man Godfrey* (1957 remake), *Alias Jesse James,* and *Support Your Local Sheriff.* No reported survivors.

CLARENCE BROWN, 97, Massachusetts-born director who won Oscar nominations for *Anna Christie, Romance, A Free Soul, The Human Comedy, National Velvet,* and *The Yearling,* died Aug. 17 of kidney failure in Santa Monica, CA. His 50 films include *The Great Redeemer* (1920), *The Last of the Mohicans, The Light in the Dark, Don't Marry for Money, The Acquittal, The Signal Tower, Butterfly, Smouldering Fires, The Goose Woman, The Eagle, Kiki, Flesh and the Devil, A Woman of Affairs, The Trail of '98, Wonder of Women, Navy Blues, Inspiration, Possessed, Letty Lynton, Sadie McKee, Chained, Emma, The Son-Daughter, Looking Forward, Night Flight, Anna Karenina, Conquest, Ah Wilderness, Wife Versus Secretary, The Gorgeous Hussy, Of Human Hearts, Idiot's Delight, The Rains Came, Edison the Man, Come Live With Me, They Met in Bombay, The White Cliffs of Dover, Song of Love, Intruder in the Dust, To Please a Lady, Angels in the Outfield, When in Rome,* and *Plymouth Adventure.* He produced *The Secret Garden* and *Never Let Me Go.* He is survived by his wife and a daughter.

KARL BRUCK, 81, Vienna-born film and TV actor best known for his role as Maestro Ernesto Faustche on CBS-TV's *The Young and the Restless* for more than a decade, died of cancer Aug. 21 at his Los Angeles home. His films include *Escape from the Planet of the Apes, The Birdman,* and *Paint Your Wagon.* A Holocaust survivor who fled Europe after losing his family, he has no reported survivors.

MADELEINE CARROLL (Marie-Madeleine Bernadette O'Carrol), England-born film, stage, radio, and TV actress who starred in Hitchcock's classics *The 39 Steps* and *Secret Agent,* died of natural causes Oct. 2 at her home outside Marabella, Spain. The blond beauty's films include *The Guns of Loos* (1928), *The First Born, What Money Can Buy, The Case Against Mrs. Ames, The General Died at Dawn, Lloyd's of London, On the Avenue, The Prisoner of Zenda, It's All Yours, Blockade, Cafe Society, Honeymoon in Bali, My Son My Son, North West Mounted Police, Virginia, One Night in Lisbon, Bahama Passage, My Favorite Blonde, White Cradle Inn, An Innocent Affair (Don't Trust Your Husband),* and *The Fan* (1949). No reported survivors.

JAMES COCO, 56, Bronx-born film, stage, and TV character actor, died Feb. 25 of a heart attack in New York. The rotund actor appeared in *Ensign Pulver* (1964 debut), *End of the Road, Tell Me That You Love Me Junie Moon, A New Leaf, Such Good Friends, Man of La Mancha, The Wild Party, Murder by Death, The Cheap Detective, Scavenger Hunt, Wholly Moses, Only When I Laugh, Hunk, That's Adequate,* and *The Chair,* and had just begun filming *Rented Lips* at the time of his death. He authored *The James Coco Diet.* No immediate survivors.

PATIENCE COLLIER (Renee Ritcher), 76, London-born screen, stage, TV and radio actress, died July 13 in London, England. Perhaps best known as the malevolent Mrs. Poulteney in *The French Lieutenant's Woman,* her other films include *The Third Secret, The Wild Affair, Baby Love, Decline and Fall . . . of a Bird Watcher, Perfect Friday, Think Dirty, House of Cards, Fiddler on the Roof, Countess Dracula,* and *The National Health, or Nurse Norton's Affair.* She also appeared in over 2,000 radio shows.

CALVIN CULVER (Casey Donovan), 43, Canandaigua, New York-born film and stage actor, died Aug. 10 of a pulmonary infection resulting from a respiratory deficiency in Iverness, FL. His films include *Casey, Boys in the Sand, The Opening of Misty Beethoven, The Back Row, Moving, The Other Side of Aspen, L.A Tool & Die, Heatstroke, Hot Shots, Sleaze, Superstars, Non-Stop, Split Image,* and *Score.* He is survived by his parents and a brother.

CATHRYN DAMON, 56, Seattle-born film, stage, and TV actress who won an Emmy for her performance as Mary Campbell on TV's *Soap,* died of cancer May 4 at Cedars-Sinai Medical Center in LA. Her films include *How to Beat the High Cost of Living* and *She's Having a Baby.* She is survived by her mother and sister.

VIOLA DANA (Virginia Flugrath), 90, Brooklyn-born screen and stage actress, died of heart failure July 3 in Woodland Hills, CA. After her 1913 stage success in *Poor Little Rich Girl* she became one of the highest-paid ingenues in more than 50 silent films, including *The Flower of No Man's Land, Aladdin's Other Lamp, Flower of the Dusk, Glass Houses, In Search of a Thrill, Kosher Kitty Kelly, Naughty Nanette, Salvation Jane, Rosie O'Grady, The Parisian Tigress, Merton of the Movies, Revelation,* and *The Show of Shows* (1929). There are no reported survivors.

HAL K. DAWSON, 90, screen, stage, and TV character actor, died Feb. 17 of a stroke in Loma Linda, CA. His films include *Another Language* (1933), *The Country Girl,* and *Airport,* and he appeared in over 100 TV shows. Survived by his wife and daughter.

PRISCILLA DEAN, silent-screen star who wanted her age kept secret, died Dec. 27 of natural causes in Leonia, NJ. Her films include *The Two-Soul Woman* (1918), *Paid in Advance, The Virgin of Stamboul, Wild Honey, Under Two Flags, Drifting, The Siren of Seville, A Cafe in Cairo, The Crimson Runner,* and *Outside the Law.* She was married to the late ace aviator Lt. Leslie Arnold, who flew around the world in 1924. She left no relatives.

HUGH DEMPSTER, 86, London-born film and stage actor, died Ap·il 30 of heart failure in Chicago. His films include *The Student's Romance, Waltz Time, Babes in Bagdad, East of Suez, The Saint, Lady Windermere's Fan, Happy Go Lovely, Anna Karenina,* and *Moulin Rouge.* Survived by his wife and brother.

JAMES DOBSON, 67, Tennessee-born screen, stage, radio, and TV actor and director, died of a heart attack Dec. 6 in Hollywood. His films include *Those Were the Days, Law and Order, The Richest Man in Town, Boomerang, The Red Badge of Courage, Flying Leathernecks, The Tanks Are Coming, For Men Only, I Dream of Jeannie, The Rose Bowl Story, Force of Arms, The Tall Stranger, Jet Attack, Armored Command, Captain Sinbad, Mutiny in Outer Space, Harlow,* and *The Undefeated.* Survived by a brother.

KING DONOVAN, 69, film, stage, and TV character actor and husband of Imogene Coca, died June 30 in Connecticut after a long illness. His films include *All the King's Men, Mystery Street, His Kind of Woman, Easy to Love, Private Hell 36, Riders to the Stars, Not as a Stranger, Shockproof, Alias Nick Beal, The Redhead and the Cowboy, The Enforcer, Angels in the Outfield, The Merry Widow, Singin' in the Rain, The Magnetic Monster, The Beast from 20,000 Fathoms, The Caddy, Broken Lance, Invasion of the Body Snatchers, The Cowboy, The Defiant Ones, The Perfect Furlough, The Hanging Tree, The Thrill of it All,* and 1982's *Nothing Lasts Forever* with Coca. He directed Jayne Mansfield in *Promises! Promises!* He is survived by his wife and three children.

Bob Fosse

Wynne Gibson

Hermione Gingold

Jackie Gleason

Joan Greenwood

Elizabeth Hartman

KEN DRAKE, 65, film, stage, and TV character actor, died Jan. 30 of a heart attack in Springville, CA. He was seen in *Twelve O'Clock High, The New Interns, Butch Cassidy and the Sundance Kid,* and *The Great Northfield Minnesota Raid.* Survived by his daughter (LA *Times* theatre writer Sylvie Drake), actress Jessica Drake; his son, stage manager Robert Drake; and his mother and brother.

RICHARD EGAN, 65, San Francisco-born rugged leading man in films, died of prostate cancer July 20 in Santa Monica, CA. His films include *The Damned Don't Cry, One Minute to Zero, Demetrius and the Gladiators, The View from Pompey's Head, Love Me Tender, The Untamed, Violent Saturday, Slaughter on 10th Avenue, The Revolt of Mamie Stover, A Summer Place, The Hunters, Pollyanna, The Destructors,* and *The Sweet Creek County War.* He is survived by his wife, four daughters, and a son.

BENSON FONG, 70, Sacramento, California-born Chinese-American character actor of film and TV, and owner of California's popular Ah Fong's restaurants, died Aug. 1 of a stroke in Los Angeles. Best known as Charlie Chan's son on screen and from TV's *Kung Fu,* his films include *Behind the Rising Sun, The Chinese Cat, Charlie Chan in the Secret Service, The Purple Heart, Thirty Seconds Over Tokyo, The Scarlet Clue, Keys of the Kingdom, China Sky, The Shanghai Cobra, First Yank in Tokyo, Red Dragon, Dark Alibi, Deception, Calcutta, Boston Blackie's Chinese Adventure, Korea Patrol, The Peking Express, His Majesty O'Keefe, Dragonfly Squadron, Conquest of Space, The Left Hand of God, Three Came to Hell, Walk Like a Dragon, Flower Drum Song, Girls! Girls! Girls!, Our Man Flint, The Love Bug, The Strongest Man in the World, Oliver's Story,* and *Jinxed.* He is survived by his wife and five children.

BOB FOSSE, 60, Chicago-born stage and screen director and choreographer who won the triple crown in 1972 with an Oscar for *Cabaret,* an Emmy for *Liza With a Z,* and two Tonys for *Pippin,* died of a heart attack in Washington, the night of the revival of his musical *Sweet Charity* at the National Theatre. One of the true geniuses of the musical theatre, Fosse began his career as a dancer and actor on Broadway and in the films *Give a Girl a Break, The Affairs of Dobie Gillis, Kiss Me Kate,* and *My Sister Eileen* (also choreographing). He choreographed *The Pajama Game* and *Damn Yankees,* and directed and choreographed *Sweet Charity, Lenny* (Oscar nomination), *All That Jazz* (four Oscars), and *Star 80* (1983). He is survived by his daughter Nicole, by his ex-wife and frequent collaborator Gwen Verdon.

WYNNE GIBSON, 82, New York-born screen, stage, radio, and TV actress, died of a stroke May 15 in Laguna Niguel, CA. Her more than 40 films include *Nothing But the Truth* (1929), *Children of Pleasure, The Fall Guy, The Gangbuster, June Moon, City Streets, Road to Reno, If I Had a Million, Ladies of the Big House, World and the Flesh, The Strange Case of Clara Deane, Lady and Gent, The Captain Hates the Sea, Racketeers in Exile, Gangs of New York, Cafe Hostess, Forgotten Girls, A Miracle on Main Street, Double Cross, The Falcon Strikes Back,* and *Mystery Broadcast* (1943). No reported survivors.

HERMIONE GINGOLD, 89, English-born stage, screen, and TV actress and comedienne best remembered as the retired courtesan in *Gigi,* in which she duetted "I Remember It Well" with Maurice Chevalier, died May 24 in New York City, where she lived. She moved from success on the London stage to Broadway and a Donaldson Award for *John Murray Anderson's Almanac* in 1954, and films including *The Music Man, Bell Book and Candle,* and *A Little Night Music.* She also wrote articles, revue sketches, the play *Abracadabra,* and her tongue-in-cheek autobiography, *The World Is Square: My Own Unaided Work.* Among her survivors are a sister and two grandchildren.

JACKIE GLEASON, 71, Brooklyn-born actor, composer, and conductor, nicknamed "The Great One" by Orson Welles, and forever immortalized by his enduring comic portrayal of Ralph Kramden on TV's *The Honeymooners,* died June 24 of cancer of the colon and liver at his home in Fort Lauderdale, FL. In a career that spanned six decades, his films include *Navy Blues, All Through The Night, Orchestra Wives, Springtime in the Rockies, The Hustler* (1961 Oscar nomination), *Requiem for a Heavyweight, Soldier in the Rain, Nothing in Common, Gigot, Papa's Delicate Condition, Skidoo, How to Commit Marriage, Don't Drink the Water, How Do I Love Thee? Mr. Billion, The Sting II, The Toy,* and the three *Smokey and the Bandit* films, in which he played Sheriff Justice. Survivors include his third wife and two daughters.

LORNE GREENE, 72, Ontario-born film, stage, radio, and TV actor best known as Ben Cartwright on TV's *Bonanza,* died Sept. 11 of adult respiratory distress syndrome in Santa Monica, CA. Along with his many TV credits, he appeared in such films as *The Silver Chalice, Tight Spot, Autumn Leaves, The Hard Man, Peyton Place, The Gift of Love, The Last of the Fast Guns, The Buccaneer, The Trap, The Errand Boy, Earthquake, Tidal Wave, Klondike Fever, Vasectomy!, A Delicate Matter,* and *Battlestar Galactica.* He is survived by his wife and three children.

JOAN GREENWOOD, 65, London-born stage, screen, and TV actress, died Feb. 28, apparently of a heart attack, in her London home. The husky-voiced actress appeared in films including *Kind Hearts and Coronets, The Man in the White Suit, The Detective, The Gentle Sex, Saraband for Dead Lovers, He Found a Star, The Water Babies, Mysterious Island, The Moon Spinners, The Amorous Prawn, A Girl in a Million, Latin Quarter, Knave of Hearts, Flesh and Blood, October Man, Stagestruck, Moonfleet, Tight Little Island,* and *Tom Jones.* She was married to the late actor Andre Morrell, and is survived by a son.

PAUL GROESSE, 81, Hungary-born art director who won three Academy Awards (in collaboration with Cedric Gibbons) for *Pride and Prejudice, The Yearling,* and *Little Women,* died of pneumonia May 4 in Woodland Hills, CA. His other films include *The Firefly, The Great Waltz, The Human Comedy, 30 Seconds Over Tokyo, King Solomon's Mines, Rhapsody,* and *The Catered Affair,* and he was also Oscar-nominated for *Madame Curie, Annie Get Your Gun, Too Young to Kiss, The Merry Widow,* and *Lili* (all with Gibbons), *The Music Man, Twilight of Honor,* and *Mister Buddwing* (the last two with George W. Davis). A past president of the Society of Motion Picture Art Directors, he is survived by his son and daughter, his wife having died two months earlier.

IRENE HANDL, 85, one of Britain's best loved screen and TV character actresses, and a novelist, died Nov. 29 in her native London. Her films include *I'm All Right Jack, On a Clear Day You Can See Forever, The Private Life of Sherlock Holmes, A Kid for Two Farthings, The Belles of St. Trinian's, Morgan—A Suitable Case for Treatment* (aka *Morgan!*), *Adventures of a Private Eye, Stand Up Virgin Soldiers, Silent Dust, One Wild Oat, Pimpernel Smith, The Girl in the News, The Last Remake of Beau Geste, Hound of The Baskervilles, Temptation Harbor, The Perfect Woman, Brothers in Law, The Key, School for Scoundrels, Doctor in Love, Two-Way Stretch, Make Mine Mink, A French Mistress, Double Bunk, A Weekend with Lulu,* and *Smashing Time.* No survivors were reported.

ELIZABETH HARTMAN, 45, Ohio-born screen and stage actress, nominated for an Academy Award for her film debut in *A Patch of Blue* (1965), died June 10 after jumping from the 5th-floor window of her Pittsburgh apartment. Her other films were *The Group, You're a Big Boy Now, The Fixer, The Beguiled, Walking Tall,* and *The Secret of NIMH* (voice characterization, 1982). She is survived by her mother, sister, and brother.

| Rita Hayworth | John Huston | Danny Kaye | Madge Kennedy | June Knight | Arthur Lake |

RITA HAYWORTH (Margarita Carmen Cansino), 68, New York City-born dancer and actress who became a screen legend, died May 14 at the New York home for her daughter, Princess Yasmin Aga Khan, after having suffered for many years from Alzheimer's disease. After a series of early films, beginning with *Dante's Inferno* in 1935, billed as Rita Cansino, the red-haired screen goddess found her greatest success in such films as *Only Angels Have Wings, Blondie on a Budget, Angels Over Broadway, Susan and God, The Strawberry Blonde, Affectionately Yours, Blood and Sand, You'll Never Get Rich, You Were Never Lovelier, My Gal Sal, Tales of Manhattan, Cover Girl, Tonight and Every Night,* her trademark vehicle *Gilda, Down to Earth, The Lady from Shanghai, The Loves of Carmen, Affair in Trinidad, Salome, Miss Sadie Thompson, Fire Down Below, Pal Joey, Separate Tables, They Came to Cordura, The Story on Page One, The Happy Thieves, Circus World, The Money Trap, The Poppy Is Also a Flower, The Rover, The Road to Salina,* and *The Wrath of God.* She is survived by two daughters, Rebecca (by Orson Welles), and Yasmin (by Aly Kahn).

JOHN HUSTON, 81, Missouri-born director, writer, and actor, two-time Oscar winner, one of the greatest filmmakers of all time and a screen legend, died in his sleep of complications from emphysema in Middletown, RI, where he was filming *Mister North,* producing and had co-written, under the direction of his son, Danny. His more than 54 films include (as director) *The Maltese Falcon, In This Our Life, Across the Pacific, Report from the Aleutians, The Battle of San Pietro, Let There Be Light, Key Largo, We Were Strangers, The Asphalt Jungle, The Red Badge of Courage, The African Queen, Moulin Rouge, Beat the Devil, Moby Dick, Heaven Knows Mr. Allison, The Barbarian and the Geisha, The Roots of Heaven, The Unforgiven, The Misfits, Freud, The Night of the Iguana, Reflections in a Golden Eye, Sinful Davey, A Walk with Love and Death, The Kremlin Letter, Fat City, The Mackintosh Man, The Man Who Would Be King, Wise Blood, Phobia, Victory, Annie, Prizzi's Honor* (winning an Oscar for his daughter, actress Anjelica Huston), and *The Dead* (1987). He directed and acted in *The Treasure of the Sierra Madre* (Best Writer and Best Director Oscars, 1948, and also winning an Oscar for his father, actor Walter Huston), *The List of Adrian Messenger, The Bible, Casino Royale, The Life and Times of Judge Roy Bean,* and *Under the Volcano* (1984), and also acted in *The Cardinal, Candy, De Sade, Myra Breckinridge, The Deserter, Man in the Wilderness, Battle for the Planet of the Apes, Chinatown, Breakout, The Wind and the Lion, The Word* (TV), *Winter Kills, Lovesick,* and *Young Giants* (1983). His many honors include the American Film Institute's Life Achievement Award in 1983. He is survived by his daughter, actress Anjelica, sons Tony and Danny, two adopted children, Pablo and Allegra, and three grandchildren.

JOYCE JAMESON, about 55, screen, stage, and TV actress who began her career in the stage revues of former husband Billy Barnes, died Jan. 16 in Burbank, CA, resulting in a coroner's investigation to determine the cause of her death. She appeared in such films as *Showboat, Tales of Terror, The Comedy of Terrors, The Balcony, Good Neighbor Sam, Boy Did I Get a Wrong Number!, The Split, Company of Killers, The Apartment, The Outlaw Josey Wales, Every Which Way But Loose, The Man Who Loved Women, Run Simon Run,* and *Death Race 2000.* She is survived by her son, musician Tyler Barnes.

LANG JEFFRIES, 55, U.S.-born film and TV actor, died Feb 12 of cancer in Huntington Beach, CA. His films include *Revolt of the Slaves* (co-starring with his then wife, Rhonda Fleming, 1961), *Don't Knock the Twist, Alone Against Rome, Sword of the Empire, The Spy Strikes Silently, The Spy with a Cold Nose, Lotus for Miss Kwan, Mark Donan—Agent Z-7, Operation Ocean, Mission Stardust, The Hotheads,* and *Requiem for a Gringo.* Survived by his wife, mother, and brother.

DANNY KAYE, 74, Brooklyn-born screen, stage, and TV actor, comedian, and conductor, immortalized on film as *Hans Christian Andersen,* died March 3 at Cedars-Sinai Medical Center in LA, of a heart attack brought on by internal bleeding and post-transfusion hepatitis. The carrot-topped actor's films include *Up in Arms* (1943 debut), *Wonder Man, The Kid from Brooklyn, The Secret Life of Walter Mitty, A Song Is Born, The Inspector General, On the Riviera, Knock on Wood* (produced by Dena Prods., the company named for his daughter, and his personal favorite), *White Christmas, The Court Jester, Merry Andrew, Me and the Colonel, On the Double, The Man from the Diners' Club, The Five Pennies,* and *The Madwoman of Chaillot.* The subject of the Emmy-nominated Edward R. Murrow documentary, *The Secret Life of Danny Kaye,* his honors include a Special Tony Award (1953), a Special Academy Award (1954), an Emmy Award (1963), the Cue Entertainer of the Year Award (1971), the Jean Hersholt Humanitarian Award (1982), and the Kennedy Center Honors (1984). He was made a Chevalier in the Legion of Honor (1986), awarded the Knight's Cross of the First Class of the Order of Danneborg by the Danish government, and was UNICEF'S ambassador-at-large for 34 years. He is survived by his wife, composer-lyricst Sylvia Fine, who collaborated on many of his, successes, and his daughter, Dena Kaye.

MADGE KENNEDY, 96, Chicago-born stage and screen actress, died June 9 of respiratory failure in Woodland Hills, CA. Twenty-five years after early Broadway and silent film stardom, she returned in such films as *The Marrying Kind, Let's Make Love, Main Street to Broadway, The Rains of Ranchipur, Lust for Life, The Catered Affair, North by Northwest, They Shoot Horses, Don't They?, The Baby Maker, The Day of the Locust,* and *Marathon Man.* She leaves no survivors.

ESMOND KNIGHT, 80, British actor whose film and stage career spanned more than 60 years, died Feb. 23 on location in Egypt with *The Balkan Trilogy.* Other films include *Anne of the Thousand Days, Robin and Marian, The Yellow Dog, The Red Shoes, Hamlet, Henry V, The Halfway House, Holiday Camp, The Arsenal Stadium Mystery, The Element of Crime, Sink the Bismarck, Waltzes from Vienna, Richard III, The Silver Fleet, End of the River,* and *Where's Jack.* Survivors were not reported.

JUNE KNIGHT, 74, screen and stage dancer and actress, died June 16 of complications from a stroke in Los Angeles, Ca. Her films include *Take a Chance, Ladies Must Love, Cross Country Cruise, Gift of Gab, Wake Up and Dream, Broadway Melody of 1935, Vacation From Love,* and *The House Across the Bay.* She retired in 1946, and is survived by husband Jack Buhler.

ARTHUR LAKE, 81, screen, TV, and radio actor forever remembered for his portrayal of Dagwood Bumstead in the *Blondie* series, died of a heart attack Jan. 9 at his home in Indian Wells, CA. In addition to other films, he appeared as Dagwood in more than two dozen films, including *Blondie Meets the Boss, Blondie on a Budget,* and *Blondie Brings Up the Baby,* as well as on the radio and TV series. He is survived by his wife, Patricia, and his son, Arthur Jr.

MERVYN LeROY, 86, San Francisco-born Oscar-winning director, producer and sportsman, died in his sleep Dec. 13 at his Beverly Hills, CA estate, after a long illness, suffering from Alzheimer's disease. He won an Honorary Oscar in 1945 for *The House I Live In,* and the Irving Thalberg memorial Award in 1975. His over 90 films as either director, director-producer, or producer include *No Place to Go* (1927 debut), *Harold Teen, Broadway Babies, Playing Around, Show Girl in Hollywood, Numbered Men, Local Boy Makes Good, Heart of New York, High Pressure, Big City Blues, Hard to Handle, Elmer the Great, The World Changes, Heat Lightning, Happiness Ahead, The King and the Chorus Girl, The Great Garrick, Mr. Dodd Takes the Air, Flying Romeos, Oh Kay, Naughty Baby, Little Johnny Jones, Too Young to*

Joseph
Levine

Mervyn
LeRoy

Liberace

Scott
McKay

Dean Paul
Martin

Lee
Marvin

Marry, Gentleman's Fate, Tonight or Never, The Great Sinner (uncredited co-director), *Little Caesar, I Am a Fugitive from a Chain Gang, They Won't Forget, Gold Diggers of 1933, Tugboat Annie, The Wizard of Oz, Babes in Arms, Mister Roberts, Waterloo Bridge, Sweet Adeline, Anthony Adverse, Waterloo Bridge, Escape, Blossoms in the Dust, Madame Curie, Thirty Seconds Over Tokyo, Little Women, No Time for Sergeants, Five Star Final, The FBI Story, In the Good Old Summertime, Wake Me When It's Over, Latin Lovers, The Green Berets* (uncredited), *Quo Vadis, The Bad Seed, Home Before Dark, A Majority of One, Gypsy,* and *Moment to Moment* (1966). He is survived by his third wife, a daughter, and his son Warner, who achieved success on Broadway and as operator of Tavern on the Green in Central Park.

JOSEPH E. LEVINE, 81, Boston-born screen and stage producer, nicknamed the "Boston Barnum," died July 31 in Greenwich, CT after a brief illness. The leading independent producer of the late 60's, he presented, produced, or distributed some 497 films, including *Godzilla, Hercules, Two Women, Divorce, Italian Style, 8½, Marriage, Italian Style, Darling, The Carpetbaggers, Harlow, The Graduate, The Producers, The Lion in Winter, Carnal Knowledge, Attila, Jack the Ripper, The Adventurers, Hercules Unchained (aka Hercules and the Queen of Lydia), Salvatore Giuliano, Boccaccio '70, Fabulous World of Jules Verne, The Wonders of Aladdin, Morgan the Pirate, The Thief of Bagdad, Boys Night Out, Sodom and Gomorrah, The Empty Canvas, Casanova '70, The Tenth Victim, Sunflower, The Sky Above, the Mud Below, Woman Times Seven, Only One New York, The Hellfire Club, Zulu, Sands of the Kalahari, Darling, The Idol, Romeo and Juliet* (ballet feature), *The Spy With a Cold Nose, Baby Love, A House Is Not a Home, The Oscar, The Caper of the Golden Bulls, Generation, Stiletto, Don't Drink the Water, C.C. and Company, Sunflower, Promise at Dawn, The Day of the Dolphin, The Night Porter, A Bridge Too Far, A Touch of Class, Magic,* and *Tattoo* to name just a few. His many awards include his favorite, the Harvard Business School Communications, Arts and Entertainment Clubs' first-ever "Man of the Year" award in 1978. He is survived by his wife, the former band singer Rosalie Harrison, a son, a daughter and two grandchildren.

LIBERACE (Wladziu Valentino Liberace), Wisconsin-born pianist whose flamboyant and extravagant stage personality earned him the title of "Mr. Showmanship" and made him a legend, died Feb. 4 at his Palm Springs, CA home of AIDS. He gained stardom and won two 1952 Emmy Awards for the NBC *Liberace Show,* and his films include *East of Java* (1949 debut), *South Sea Sinner, Footlight Varieties, Sincerely Yours, When the Boys Meet the Girls,* and *The Loved One.* His books include *Liberace Cooks! Recipes From His Seven Dining Rooms, Liberace,* and *The Things I Love.* Survivors include a sister.

JERRY LIVINGSTON, 78, Denver-born songwriter for stage, screen, and TV, died July 1 at his Beverly Hills, Ca. home. His many song hits and film scores include Oscar nominations for "Bibbidy Bobbidy Boo" from *Cinderella,* and for his scores for *Cat Ballou* and *The Hanging Tree.* Survived by his wife and a son.

CHARLES LUDLAM, 44, Northport, L.I.-born, avant-garde actor, playwright, and founder of New York's Ridiculous Theatre Company, director and producer, died of pneumonia resulting from AIDS on May 28. The winner of six Obie awards, a Drama Desk Award, and the Rosamund Gilder Award, he made his film debut in *The Big Easy.* He is survived by his mother and two brothers.

ROUBEN MAMOULIAN, 90, Russian-born distinguished, innovative stage and screen director, died Dec. 4 of natural causes in Woodland Hills, CA. His films include *Applause, City Lights, Dr. Jekyll and Mr. Hyde, Love Me Tonight, Song of Songs, Queen Christina, We Live Again, Becky Sharp, The Gay Desperado* (1936 NY Films Critics Award for Best Director), *High Wide and Handsome, Golden Boy, The Mark of Zorro, Blood and Sand, Rings on Her Fingers, Summer Holiday, The Wild Heart, Gone to Earth,* and *Silk Stockings* (1957). His Broadway successes include the landmark musicals *Oklahoma!, Carousel,* and *Porgy and Bess,* and his play *The Devil's Hornpipe* (written with Maxwell Anderson) was filmed in 1959 as *Never Steal Anything Small.* His many honors include the 1982 D. W. Griffith Award from the Directors Guild of America. He is survived by his wife, artist Azadia Newman.

DANIEL MANDELL, 92, New York City-born Academy Award-winning film editor of *Pride of the Yankees* (1942), *Best Years of Our Lives* (1946), and *The Apartment* (1960), died June 8 in Huntington Beach, CA. His other films include *These Three, Porgy and Bess, Guys and Dolls, The Fortune Cookie, Witness for the Prosecution, The Westerner, Arsenic and Old Lace, The Real Glory,* and *Hans Christian Andersen.* He is survived by his wife, a sister, and two children.

DEAN PAUL MARTIN, 35, actor, rock performer, tennis pro, Air National Guard captain, and son of Dean Martin, was killed when his fighter jet crashed March 23 on a snowy mountain near March Air Force Base, CA. He appeared in the 1979 film *Players.* He is survived by son Alex (by ex-wife Olivia Hussey), his mother and father, and six brothers and sisters.

LEE MARVIN, 63, New York City-born screen and stage actor who won a 1965 Oscar for his dual role in *Cat Ballou,* died Aug. 29 of a heart attack in the arms of his wife, at Tucson Medical Center in Arizona. His 57 films include *You're in the Navy Now* (1951 debut), *Hong Kong, We're Not Married, The Glory Brigade, The Big Heat, The Wild One, The Caine Mutiny, Bad Day at Black Rock, Pete Kelly's Blues, Shack Out on 101, Pillars of the Sky, Raintree County, The Comancheros, The Man Who Shot Liberty Valance, Donovan's Reef, Ship of Fools, The Professionals, The Dirty Dozen, Sergeant Ryker, Paint Your Wagon, Monty Walsh, Emperor of the North Pole, The Iceman Cometh, The Klansman, Shout at the Devil, Great Scout and Cathouse Thursday, The Big Red One, Death Hunt, Gorky Park,* and *Delta Force* (1986). He gained additional fame as the successful defendant in the landmark "palimony" suit brought against him by Michelle Triola Marvin in 1979. Survived by his wife, childhood sweetheart Pamela Feeley, and a son and three daughters.

DAVID MAYSLES, 54, documentary filmmaker, credited with his brother Albert as being one of the founders of cinema verite, died Jan. 3 after suffering a stroke in New York City. Frequently in collaboration with others, their films include *Salesman, Gimme Shelter, Grey Gardens, Showman, What's Happening! The Beatles in the USA, Meet Marlon Brando, A Visit with Truman Capote, Christo's Valley Curtain* (Oscar nomination), *Running Fence, Island, Vladimir Horowitz the Last Romantic,* and *Ozawa.* In addition to his brother, survivors include his wife, a son, John Philip, and a daughter, Celia.

SCOTT McKAY, 71, Iowa-born stage, screen, radio, and TV actor, and author of 13 plays, died March 16 of kidney failure in New York City. He was in such films as *Duel in the Sun, Kiss and Tell,* and *Thirty Seconds Over Tokyo.* He is survived by his wife, a sister, two sons, and three stepchildren.

EMILE G. MEYER, 76, New Orleans-born screen, stage, and TV character actor, died March 19 of Alzheimer's disease in Covington, LA. He appeared in some 200 TV shows and 53 films, including *Panic in the Streets, Shane, The Man with the Golden Arm, Sweet Smell of Success,* and *Blackboard Jungle.* He is survived by a son, three daughters, two sisters, and a brother.

POLA NEGRI (Barbara Apollonia Chalupiec), 87 or 92, Polish-born actress, the quintessential exotic green-eyed vamp of the 20's also known for her front-page romances with such stars as Valentino and Chaplin, died Aug. 1 in her sleep in San Antonio, TX, after a long illness. One of Poland's leading actress at 17, she appeared in *Slaves of Sin* (1918), *The Eyes of the Mummy, Carmen, Sumurun,* and *Madame DuBarry (Passion),* before going to Hollywood for films including *Bella Donna* (1923), *The Cheat, Men, The Spanish Dancer, Shadows of Paris, East of Suez, Forbidden Paradise, A Woman Commands* (her first talkie), *Mazurka* (German film), *Hi Diddle Diddle,* and *The Moonspinners* (1964). She became an American citizen in 1951, and there are no reported survivors.

GERALDINE PAGE, 62, Missouri-born screen, stage, and TV actress whose legendary performances include her 1985 Academy Award-winning role in *The Trip to Bountiful,* died June 13 of a heart attack, after being treated for kidney disease, at her Manhattan home. Her films also include Oscar-nominated performances in *Summer and Smoke, Hondo, Sweet Bird of Youth, You're a Big Boy Now, Pete 'N' Tillie, Interiors,* and *The Pope of Greenwich Village,* as well as *Taxi, Toys in the Attic, Dear Heart, The Happiest Millionaire, Monday's Child, Whatever Happened to Aunt Alice?, The Beguiled, J. W. Coop, Hazel's People, Day of the Locust, Nasty Habits, The Rescuers, Harry's War, Honky Tonk Freeway, I'm Dancing as Fast as I Can, The Bride, White Nights, Flanagan (Walls of Glass), My Little Girl,* and *Native Son.* She won Emmy Awards for *A Christmas Memory* (released as part of the 1969 film *Trilogy*) and *The Thanksgiving Visitor.* At the time of her death she was starring in *Blithe Spirit* on Broadway. She is survived by her husband, actor Rip Torn, and a brother, two sons, a daughter, and a grandson.

ROBERT PAIGE (David Carlyle), 77, Indianapolis-born film and TV actor who won a 1955 Emmy Award for outstanding male TV personality, died Dec. 21 of an apparent heart attack in San Clemente, CA. His some 65 films include *Cain and Mabel, Who Killed Gail Preston?, The Main Event, Highway Patrol, Parole Fixer, Women Without Names, Golden Gloves, The Monster and the Girl, San Antonio Rose, Hellzapoppin', Almost Married, Pardon My Sarong, Get Hep to Love, Cowboy in Manhattan, Frontier Bad Man, Fired Wife, Son of Dracula, Her Primitive Man, Can't Help Singing, Shady Lady, Tangier, The Red Stallion, The Flame, The Green Promise* (also co-producing), *Abbott and Costello Go to Mars, Split Second, The Marriage Go-Round,* and *Bye Bye Birdie.* He is survived by his wife, a daughter, two stepdaughters, and a brother.

DOROTHY PATRICK, 65, Manitoba-born film actress, died May 31 in LA of a heart attack. Her more than 30 films include *Boy's Ranch* (1945), *The Mighty McGurk, High Wall, New Orleans, Alias A Gentleman, Blonde Bandit, Tarnished, 711 Ocean Drive, Violent Saturday, Till the Clouds Roll By, Come to the Stable, Torch Song,* and *The View from Pompey's Head.* She is survived by two sons and a half-sister.

ROBERT PRESTON (Robert Preston Meservey), 68, Massachusetts-born screen, stage, and TV actor who became a legend for his portrayal of Prof. Harold Hill in *The Music Man* on both stage (1958 Tony Award) and screen, died March 21 in Santa Barbara, CA of lung cancer. His many films include *Union Pacific, Typhoon, Moon Over Burma, Northwest Mounted Police, New York Town, The Lady from Cheyenne, The Night of January 16th, Reap the Wild Wind, Parachute Battalion, Pacific Blackout, Wake Island, Night Plane from Chungking, This Gun for Hire, Whispering Smith, Blood on the Moon, Big City, The Lady Gambles, Tulsa, The Sundowners, My Outlaw Brother, When I Grow Up, Face to Face, Cloudburst, The Last Frontier, The Dark at the Top of the Stairs, Island of Love, How the West Was Won, All the Way Home, Junior Bonner, Child's Play, Mame, Semi-Tough, S.O.B., Victor/Victoria,* and *The Last Starfighter.* He is survived by his wife, former actress Catherine Feltus, and his father.

JOHN QUALEN, 87, Vancouver, B.C.-born veteran screen and stage actor, died of heart failure Sept. 17 in Torrance, CA. Best remembered for *The Grapes of Wrath,* his more than 120 films include *Our Daily Bread, Nothing Sacred, His Girl Friday, The Long Voyage Home, The Shepherd of the Hills, Casablanca, The High and The Mighty, The Searchers, Anatomy of a Murder, The Man Who Shot Liberty Valance, The Country Doctor, Reunion, Five of a Kind, The Farmer Takes a Wife, The Three Musketeers, The Road to Glory, Seventh Heaven, Angels Over Broadway, Jungle Book, Tortilla Flat, Arabian Nights, An American Romance, Captain Kidd, The Fugitive, The Big Steal, Hans Christian Andersen, The Student Prince, Johnny Concho, The Comancheros, The Prize, The Seven Faces of Dr. Lao, A Patch of Blue, I'll Take Sweden, The Sons of Katie Elder, A Big Hand for the Little Lady, P.J., Firecreek, Hail Hero!,* and *Frasier the Sensuous Lion* (1973). He is survived by his wife, three daughters, a brother, and a sister.

ALEJANDRO REY, 57, Argentine-born film and TV actor best known as playboy Carlos Ramirez on TV's *The Flying Nun,* died May 21 of cancer in Los Angeles, Ca. His many films include *Solomon and Sheba, Fun in Acapulco, Blindfold, Synanon, Mr. Majestyk, Breakout, The Swarm, Sunburn, Cuba, The Ninth Configuration, Moscow on the Hudson,* and *TerrorVision.* A U.S. citizen since 1964, he is survived by his son, Brando.

GRANDON RHODES, 82, film, stage, and TV actor, died June 9 in Encino, CA after a long illness. His more than 40 films include *Follow the Boys, The Imposter, Hollywood and Vine, The Magnificent Doll, It Happens Every Spring, All the King's Men, Born Yesterday, Detective Story, Human Desire, Revenge of the Creature, A Man Alone, The Earth Vs. the Flying Saucers, These Wilder Years,* and *The Bramble Bush.* There are no reported survivors.

HAYDEN RORKE, 76, Brooklyn-born screen, stage, and TV actor, died Aug. 19 of cancer in Toluca Lake, CA. Best known as Dr. Bellows on 140 episodes of TV's *I Dream of Jeannie,* his more than 50 films include *This is the Army, Father's Little Dividend, When Worlds Collide, Room for One More, An American In Paris, All That Heaven Allows, This Happy Feeling, Pillow Talk, I Aim at the Stars, Parrish, Tammy Tell Me True, Back Street, Pocketful of Miracles, Spencer's Mountain, The Thrill of It All, The Unsinkable Molly Brown, A House Is Not a Home, Youngblood Hawke,* and *The Night Walker.* He is survived by his two brothers.

WILLIAM ROSE, 68, Missouri-born screenwriter who won a 1967 Academy Award for *Guess Who's Coming to Dinner,* died Feb 10 on the isle of Jersey after a lengthy illness. Also Oscar nominated for *Genevieve, The Ladykillers, It's a Mad Mad Mad World,* and *The Russians Are Coming, the Russians Are Coming,* his films include *Once a Jolly Swagman (Maniacs on Wheels/*1948), *My Daughter Joy (Operation X), I'll Get You for This (Lucky Nick Cain), The Gift Horse (Glory at Sea), Song of Paris (Bachelor in Paris), The Maggie (High and Dry), Touch and Go (The Light Touch), Davy, The Man in the Sky (Decision Against Time), The Smallest Show on Earth, The Flim Flam Man,* and *The Secret of Santa Vittoria.* He received a 1973 Laurel Award from the Writers Guild of America. He is survived by a son.

RUSSELL ROUSE, 74, veteran film director and screenwriter who won a 1959 Academy Award for writing *Pillow Talk,* died Oct. 2 of congestive heart failure in Santa Monica, CA. His other film work included writing *D.O.A.* and directing *The Oscar* and *The Well,* for which he was also Oscar nominated. No survivors reported.

WALDO SALT, 72, screenwriter who won Academy Awards for *Midnight Cowboy* and *Coming Home* after having been blacklisted in 1951 for refusing to testify before the House Committee on Un-American Activities, died March 8 at Cedars-Sinai Hospital in LA. His films include *Shopworn Angel* (1938), *Tonight We Raid Calais, The Flame and the Arrow, Taras Bulba, Wild and Wonderful, The Gang That Couldn't Shoot Straight, Serpico,* and *The Day of the Locust.* He received a 1986 Laurel Award from the Writer's Guild. He is survived by his wife, playwright and poet Eve Merriam, and two daughters.

WILL SAMPSON, 53, Oklahoma-born American Indian film and TV actor and artist, died June 3, after undergoing a heart transplant, due to a combination of problems. After his 1975 film debut in *One Flew Over the Cuckoo's Nest,* he appeared in *The White Buffalo, Orca, Alcatraz: The Whole Shocking Story, The Outlaw Josey Wales, Buffalo Bill and the Indians, Old Fishhawk, Poltergeist II: The Other Side,* and *Firewalker.* The founder of American Indian Registry for the Performing Arts, he is survived by a son.

RANDOLPH SCOTT (George Randolph Scott), 89, Virginia-born screen star best known for his work in Westerns, and a top boxoffice star from the 1930's to 50's, died in his sleep March 2 at his Bel-Air, CA home after a long illness. He made more than 125 movies including *Sharp Shooter* (1928), *The Virginian, Hot Saturday, Supernatural, Home on the Range, Roberta, She, Follow the Fleet, The Last of the Mohicans, Go West Young Man, High Wide and Handsome, Rebecca of Sunnybrook Farm, The Texans, Jesse James, Susannah of the Mounties, Frontier Marshall, 20,000 Men a Year, Virginia City, My Favorite Wife, Western Union, To the Shores of Tripoli* (personal favorite), *The Spoilers, Pittsburgh, The Desperados, Corvette K-225, Gung Ho!, Follow the Boys, Belle of the Yukon, China Sky, Home Sweet Homicide, Trail Street, Gunfighters, Christmas Eve, Albuquerque, Canadian Pacific, The Doolins of Oklahoma, The Nevadan, Colt .45, Sugarfoot, Santa Fe, Fort Worth, Starlift, Carson City, Thunder Over the Plains, Rage at Dawn, Seven Men From Now, 7th Cavalry, The Tall T, Shoot-Out at Medicine Bend, Decision at Sundown, Buchanan Rides Alone, Ride Lonesome, Comanche Station,* and *Ride the High Country* (1962). He is survived by his wife, a son, a daughter, and a sister.

JOAN SHAWLEE, 61, New York-born film and TV actress best remembered as Sweet Sue in *Some Like It Hot,* died March 22 in her Hollywood home after a long bout with cancer. Her many films include *House of Horrors* (1946), *Lover Come Back, Inside Job, Buck Privates Come Home, I'll Be Yours, Prehistoric Women, The Marrying Kind, All Ashore, A Star Is Born, Conquest of Space, Pride of the Blue Grass, Bowery to Bagdad, A Farewell to Arms, The Apartment, Irma La Douce, Critic's Choice, The Wild Angels, Tony Rome, The St. Valentine's Day Massacre, Live a Little Love a Little, One More Train to Rob, Willard,* and *Flash and the Firecat.* TV audiences will remember her from *The Abbott and Costello Show,* and as Peaches on *The Dick Van Dyke Show.* She is survived by a daughter, a son, and two grandchildren.

DICK SHAWN (Richard Schulefand), 63 (elsewhere reported to be 57 or 58), Buffalo, NY-born screen, stage, TV, and nightclub actor and comedian, collapsed onstage in the middle of a joke about life and death, while performing at the U. of California/San Diego, April 17, and died in a hospital 45 minutes later. Best known for his performances in *The Producers* and *It's a Mad Mad Mad Mad World*, his other films include *The Opposite Sex* (1956), *Wake Me When It's Over, Wizard of Baghdad, A Very Special Favor, What Did You Do in the War Daddy?, Penelope, Way Way Out, The Goony Birds, The Solid Gold Show, Looking Up, Love at First Bite, Goodbye Cruel World* (also co-wrote), *Young Warriors, The Secret Diary of Sigmund Freud, Angel, Beer, Water, The Perils of P. K., The Check Is in the Mail, Maid to Order,* and Coppola's Michael Jackson 3-D short *Captain Eo.* He is survived by a son, three daughters, a brother, and a granddaughter.

HOWARD SHOUP, 83, film costume designer who won Oscar nominations for *The Young Philadelphians, The Rise and Fall of Legs Diamond, Claudelle Inglish, Kisses for My President,* and *Rage to Live,* died of respiratory failure at the Motion Picture and Television Country House and Hospital, apparently in May or June. No other information was reported.

MARY SPINELL, 83, character actress in some 50 films, died in NY City July 30 of natural causes. Her films include *The Godfather, The Godfather II, Next Stop Greenwich Village, Gloria, Tempest, Moscow on the Hudson,* and *The Last Horror Show* with her son, actor Joe Spinell. She is survived by three sons and two sisters.

CLINTON SUNDBERG, 81, St. Paul-born character actor in films, died of heart failure Dec. 14 in Santa Monica, CA. His many films include *Undercurrent, Love Laughs at Andy Hardy, The Mighty McGurk, The Hucksters, Good News, Easter Parade, A Date With Judy, Mr. Peabody and the Mermaid, Good Sam, The Kissing Bandit, Words and Music, Command Decision, The Barkleys of Broadway, In the Good Old Summertime, Key to the City, Father Is a Bachelor, Annie Get Your Gun, The Toast of New Orleans, Two Weeks with Love, On the Riviera, The Fat Man, As Young as You Feel, The Belle of New York, The Girl Next Door, The Caddy, Main Street to Broadway, The Birds and the Bees, Bachelor in Paradise,* and *Hotel.* There are no reported survivors.

DAVID SUSSKIND, 66, New York-born prolific producer of screen, stage, and TV, died Feb. 22 of natural causes in New York City. His films include *Edge of the City, A Raisin in the Sun, Requiem for a Heavyweight, All the Way Home, Lovers and Other Strangers, Alice Doesn't Live Here Anymore, The Pursuit of Happiness, The People Next Door, All Creatures Great and Small, Buffalo Bill and the Indians, All Things Bright and Beautiful, Loving Couples, Fort Apache The Bronx,* and *They All Laughed.* His vast TV output won more than 20 Emmys. He is survived by four children, a sister, and a brother.

KENT TAYLOR (Louis Weiss), 80, Iowa-born film and TV actor best known as TV's *Boston Blackie* of the 1950's, died in his sleep at the Motion Picture and Television Hospital in Woodland Hills, CA April 11, after a long illness. His many film credits include *Road to Reno, Merrily We Go to Hell, The Devil and the Deep, Sign of the Cross, If I Had a Million, The Story of Temple Drake, I'm No Angel, Blonde Venus, White Woman, Death Takes a Holiday, Mrs. Wiggs of the Cabbage Patch, Limehouse Blues, Ramona, Love in a Bungalow, The Gracie Allen Murder Case, Five Came Back, Mississippi Gambler, Tombstone, Gang Busters* (serial), *Alaska, House of Horrors, The Daltons Ride Again, Tangier, The Crimson Key, Playgirl, Ghost Town, Slightly Scarlet, The Phantom from 10,000 Leagues, Walk Tall, The Purple Hills, The Broken Land, The Firebrand, The Day Mars Invaded the Earth, Harbor Lights, The Crawling Hand, The Mighty Gorga, Smashing the Crime Syndicate,* and *Girls for Rent* (1974). He is survived by his wife.

VERREE TEASDALE, 80, Washington-born screen and stage actress and widow of actor Adolphe Menjou, died Feb. 17 of unreported causes. Her films include *Syncopation* (1929 debut), *The Sap from Syracuse, Skyscraper Souls, Payment Deferred, Luxury Liner, Roman Scandals, Fashions of 1934, A Modern Hero, Dr. Monica, Desirable, Madame Du Barry, A Midsummer Night's Dream, The Milky Way, First Lady* (1937), *Topper Takes a Trip, Fifth Avenue Girl, I Take This Woman, Love Thy Neighbor,* and *Come Live With Me.* No reported survivors.

ALICE TERRY (Alice Frances Taaffe), 87, Indiana-born actress best remembered as a leading lady to Valentino in *The Four Horsemen of the Apocalypse* (directed by her future husband Rex Ingram), died Dec. 22 of pneumonia in Burbank, CA, after a long illness. Her films also include *Not My Sister* (1916 debut), *Old Wives for New, Shores Acres, Hearts are Trumps, The Conquering Power, Turn to the Night. The*

Prisoner of Zenda, Where the Pavement Ends, Scaramouche, The Arab, Mare Nostrum, Lovers?, The Garden of Allah, The Great Divide, Sackcloth and Scarlet, Confessions of a Queen, Any Woman, The Magician, and she co-directed *Love in Morocco* (1933) with Ingram. She has no immediate survivors.

RAQUEL TORRES (Paula Marie Osterman), 78, Mexico-born film actress who starred in *White Shadows of the South Seas* in 1928, died of a heart attack Aug. 10 at her Malibu, CA home, after suffering a stroke. She also appeared in *The Bridge of San Luis Rey, The Desert Rider, The Sea Bat, Under a Texas Moon, Aloha, Tampico, So This is Africa!, The Woman I Stole, Duck Soup,* and *The Red Wagon,* before retiring in 1934. Survived by her sister and an adopted daughter.

PATRICK TROUGHTON, 67, London-born character actor in films and TV, best known as *Dr. Who* in the BBC-TV series in the 60's, died March 28 of a heart attack while appearing at a *Dr. Who* convention in Columbus, GA. He appeared in such films as *Hamlet* (1948), *Escape, Chance of a Lifetime, Waterfront, Treasure Island, The Black Knight, Richard III, The Curse of Frankenstein, Jason and the Argonauts, The Phantom of the Opera* (1962), *The Gorgon, The Scars of Dracula, Frankenstein and the Monster from Hell, Sinbad and the Eye of the Tiger, The Omen,* and *A Hitch in Time.* Survived by his wife, four sons, two daughters, and a stepchild.

LINO VENTURA, 68, Italian-born screen actor and one of France's most popular personalities, died Oct. 23 of a heart attack at his home in Saint-Cloud, France. His films include *Touchez pas au Grisbi* (1953 debut), *The Gorilla* series, *Montparnasse 19, Lift to the Scaffold* (aka *Frantic*), *Marie-Octobre, Razzia, Crime and Punishment, Her Crime Was Love, Dishonorable Discharge, Speaking of Murder, The Way of Youth, Le Chemin des Ecoliers, Le Deuxieme Souffle (Second Wind), Shadow Army, Classe Tous Risques (The Big Risk), L'Arme a Gauche (Guns from the Dictator), Money Money Money, The Threepenny Opera, The Valachi Papers, Three Tough Guys, The Medusa Touch, The Devil and the 10 Commandments, Le Bluff, Last Known Address, Diamond Bikini, The Contract, Butterfly on the Shoulder, Garde a Vue, Jigsaw, Sunday Lovers, Les Miserables* (1983), and *Le Septieme Cible (The Seventh Target)* (1984). He is survived by his wife, a son, and three daughters.

ANDY WARHOL, 59, Pittsburgh-born filmmaker and pop artist who once proclaimed "in the future, everyone will be famous for 15 minutes," died Feb. 22 in New York City of a heart attack that was apparently unrelated to his having gall bladder surgery two days earlier. His many films include *Sleep, Empire, Poor Little Rich Girl, My Hustler, The Chelsea Girls* (1966), "****", *Imitation of Christ, I A Man, Bike Boy, Nude Restaurant, Flesh, Lonesome Cowboys, Blue Movie, Trash, Heat, Hello Again,* and with Paul Morrissey such films as *Women in Revolt, L'Amour, Flesh for Frankenstein,* and *Blood for Dracula.* He wrote and co-produced *Bad,* and he appeared in *Driver's Seat, Imagine, Andy Warhol and His Clan, The Illiac Passion, CS Blues, Cocaine Cowboys, Blank Generation, Underground and Emigrants, Ciao Manhattan, New Cinema!, Tootsie,* and *The Look.* He is survived by two brothers.

HUGH WHEELER, 75, British-born screenwriter, playwright, librettist, and novelist, died July 26 in Pittsfield, Mass. after a long illness. His films include *Five Miles to Midnight* (1962), *Something for Everyone, Travels with My Aunt, Cabaret, A Little Night Music,* and *Nijinsky.* His novels *Black Widow, Man in the Net, The Green-Eyed Monster,* and *The Man With Two Wives* were filmed. He wrote 17 novels as Patrick Quentin, 5 as Quentin Patrick, and 8 as Jonathan Stagge, collaborating with Richard Wilson Webb, and won "Edgar" Awards from the Mystery Writers of America in 1961 and 1973. He won Tony Awards for *A Little Night Music* (1973) *Candide* (1974), and *Sweeney Todd* (1979). There are no immediate survivors.

EMLYN WILLIAMS, 81, Welsh-born actor, playwright, and director, best known for his autobiographical play and film *The Corn Is Green* and his *Night Must Fall,* died Sept. 25 in London, following recent cancer surgery. He acted in such films as *Friday the 13th* (1933, also wrote dialog), *Men of Tomorrow, Sally Bishop, Broken Blossoms* (also wrote), *I, Claudius* (documented in *The Epic That Never Was*), *The Citadel, The Stars Look Down, They Drive by Night* (1938), *Major Barbara, You Will Remember, Hatter's Castle, The Last Days of Dolwyn* (also wrote and directed), *Three Husbands, Another Man's Poison, The Magic Box, Ivanhoe, The Deep Blue Sea, I Accuse, Beyond This Place, The L-Shaped Room, Eye of the Devils,* and *The Walking Stick.* He contributed to the screenplay of *The Man Who Knew Too Much,* and his play *Someone Waiting* was filmed as *Time Without Pity* (1957). He is survived by two sons by his late wife, Irish actress Molly O'Shann.